NATIONAL GEOGRAPHIC

TRAVELER

Mexico

NATIONAL GEOGRAPHIC
TRAVELER
Mexico

Jane Onstott

Contents

How to use this guide 6–7 About the author 8
The regions 53–346 Travelwise 347–90
Index 391–97 Credits 398–99

Page 1: Wooden
mask, Tzintzuntzan
Pages 2–3: Catedral, San
Cristóbal de las Casas
Left: Cactuses, Baja
California

How to use this guide

See back flap for keys to text and map symbols.

The *National Geographic Traveler* brings you the best of Mexico in text, pictures, and maps. Divided into three main sections, the guide begins with an overview of history and culture. Following are 11 regional chapters with featured sites selected by the author for their particular interest. Each chapter opens with its own contents list.

The regions and sites within the regions are arranged geographically. Some regions are further divided into smaller areas. A map introduces each region, highlighting the featured sites. Walks and drives, plotted on their own maps, suggest routes for discovering an area. Features and sidebars give intriguing detail on history, culture, or contemporary life.

The final section, Travelwise, lists essential information for the traveler—pre-trip planning, special events, getting around, emergencies, and a language guide—plus a selection of hotels, restaurants, shops, activities, and entertainment.

To the best of our knowledge, all information is accurate as of the press date. However, it's always advisable to call ahead when possible.

Color coding

282

Each region is color coded for easy reference. Find the region you want on the map on the front flap, and look for the color flash at the top of the pages of the relevant chapter. Information in **Travelwise** is also color coded to each region.

Museo Nacional de Antropología

- 178 B2
- ✉ Paseo de la Reforma at Gandhi, Bosque de Chapultepec
- ☎ 5553-6386
- Closed Mon.
- $$
- Metro: Auditorio

Visitor information

Practical information for most sites is given in the side column (see key to symbols on back flap). The map reference gives the page number of the map and grid reference. Other details are address, telephone number, days closed, entrance charge in a range from $ (under $2) to $$$$$ (over $15), and nearest Metro station for sites in Mexico City. Other sites have information in italics and parentheses in the text.

TRAVELWISE

CHIAPAS — Color-coded region name

COMITÁN — Town name

🏨 **LOS LAGOS DE MONTEBELLO** — Hotel name & price range
$

BLVD. BELISARIO DOMINGUEZ NORTE 14 — Address, telephone & fax numbers
TEL/FAX 9/632-1092

Comitán's fanciest hotel is a lovely but slightly faded keepsake of old-fashioned propriety. — Brief description of hotel

ℹ 60 ⬛ AE, MC, V — Hotel facilities & credit card details

🍴 **EL GRECO** — Restaurant name & price range
$

CUARTA CALLE SUR OTE. 8 — Address & telephone number
TEL 9/632-5173

The set lunch of this second-story restaurant is an absolutely overwhelming array of local victuals. — Brief description of restaurant

Closed D, Sun. No credit cards — Restaurant closures & credit card details

Hotel & restaurant prices

An explanation of the price bands used in entries is given in the Hotels & Restaurants section (beginning on p. 356).

REGIONAL MAPS

Road number

Important point of interest

Important featured town

Drive start point

Airport

Point of interest

Map reference

- A locator map accompanies each regional map and shows the location of that region in the country.
- Adjacent regions are shown, each with a page reference.

WALKING TOURS

Red numbered bullets link site on map to descriptions in the text

Start point

Building outline

Point of interest not on walk route

Featured site (in bold) on walk route

Walk route

Direction of walk route

- An information box gives the starting and ending points, time and length of walk, and places not to be missed along the route.
- Where two walks are marked on the map, the second route is shown in orange.

DRIVING TOURS

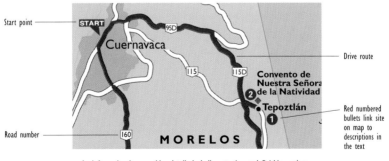

Start point

Road number

Drive route

Red numbered bullets link site on map to descriptions in the text

- An information box provides details including starting and finishing points, time and length of drive, and places not to be missed along the route, or tips on terrain.

NATIONAL GEOGRAPHIC

TRAVELER

Mexico

About the author

Jane Onstott earned a bachelor of arts degree in Spanish language and Hispanic literature from San Diego State University, with a year's study at Spain's Universidad Complutense de Madrid. Since that time she has lived and traveled extensively in Mexico and throughout Latin America. She worked as Director of Communications and Information for the Charles Darwin Research Station in the Galapagos Islands, Ecuador, and as a Spanish-language interpreter and translator in Mexico and the United States. Since 1986 Ms. Onstott has contributed to travel guides covering Mexico, Ecuador, and the United States, and to such magazines as *Brides* and *Latin Trade*. She has been a resident of San Diego County for 25 years, and has written chapters on local art, culture, and dining for the book *San Diego Best Places,* published by Sasquatch Books in 1999.

History & culture

A Mixtec priest, illustrated in the Nuttall Codex

Mexico today

IN HIS FASCINATING OPUS *THE LABYRINTH OF SOLITUDE*, NOBEL PRIZE-
winning poet and essayist Octavio Paz (1914–1998) calls his countrymen defensive,
reticent, and remote. Yet most visitors would characterize their Mexican hosts as
congenial, helpful people who love a party. This is just one example of Mexico's many
contradictions, surprises, and inconsistencies. Moved and motivated by pathos and
sentimentality, Mexicans are intense and passionate, yet hide their emotions under a
mask of serenity and indifference.

THE LAND

Mexico radiates from its physical and political
heart in the highland Valley of Mexico (Valley
of Anáhuac), into which more than one fifth
of the nation's population crowds. Built from
the remains of the ancient Aztec capital,
Tenochtitlán, in 1521, Mexico City is surrounded by some of the nation's most fertile
farmlands. While at least half of its acreage is
arid or semiarid, Mexico produces most of its
own food, especially corn, wheat, soybeans, rice,
beans, coffee, cacao, fruit, and vegetables.

This geographically diverse country is,
nonetheless, dominated by mountains.
Marching south from the U.S. border for
around 700 miles (1,120 km) are the eastern
and western ranges of the Sierra Madre (literally, "mother mountain"): the Sierra Madre
Oriental and the Sierra Madre Occidental. In
between, the Mexican Plateau cradles a series
of lesser ranges and highland valleys, and in the
north, the Chihuahua and Sonora Deserts.

Surrounded by the Pacific Ocean and the
Sea of Cortés, the Baja California peninsula is
equal parts desert and mountain, with eight
main mountain ranges, dozens of islands, and
a combined coastline of about 3,000 miles
(4,800 km). One of the world's longest and
most isolated peninsulas, it was linked top to
tip by road only in the 1970s.

A mother lode of precious minerals in the
Sierra Madre Occidental and Sierra Madre
Oriental made these rugged and frequently
inhospitable mountains among the first places
explored and settled by the Spanish, and
minerals are still an important source of
revenue. Mexico leads the world in silver
mining; copper, gold, lead, zinc, and iron are
important commodities. Especially in the
central and northwestern forests, mahogany,
walnut, rosewood, and other valuable

hardwoods are harvested, as are pines for
paper and pulp. Despite legislation in 1988 to
promote sustainable development, the practice
of cattle ranching, slash-and-burn agriculture,
and cutting of trees as a domestic fuel source
contribute to deforestation, especially in the
poorer southern region. Nature-based
tourism, although still in its infancy, may be
the solution to providing poor communities
with viable alternatives to such destructive
ecological practices.

Mountaineers are inspired by some of the
continent's tallest peaks—including Pico de
Orizaba, Iztaccíhuatl, and La Malinche—that
cluster around the 19th parallel in the Neo-
Volcanic range, at the southern edge of the
Sierra Madre Oriental. Like El Nevado de
Colima, on the Pacific coast, Popocatépetl
volcano is currently active and closed to
climbers; villages on its mountainous slopes
and in surrounding valleys have been
sporadically evacuated.

Mexico's few lowland areas include the
Yucatán Peninsula, an unusual limestone shelf
of underground rivers and cenotes (sinkholes)
jutting into the Caribbean Sea. Extending
north and west from the Yucatán along the
Gulf of Mexico is a broad expanse of steamy
tropical and semitropical lowlands laced by
rivers, swamps, and estuaries. Between that and
the narrower, longer Pacific littoral, Mexico has
5,320 miles (8,560 km) of coastline.

Along the Pacific coast and into southern
Mexico and Guatemala, the Sierra Madre del
Sur and Sierra Madre de Chiapas are two
mountain ranges whose isolation has
preserved the indigenous cultures of its
peoples, but at the cost of such basic services

**A street mural dwarfs a young girl in
Izamal, Yucatán.**

as potable water, sewage systems, schools, hospitals, and electricity.

THE PEOPLE

Few countries in the hemisphere have a greater degree of both *mestizaje* (fusion of indigenous and European blood) and indigenous identity. Nearly 30 percent of Mexicans are indigenous, while about twice that number are mestizos. (Some sources put the number of mestizos higher, with fewer indigenous people.) More than 5 million Mexicans converse primarily in an indigenous dialect, especially Mayan, Mixtec, Náhuatl, Otomí, Purépecha, and Zapotec. Although it cannot be said that whites (9 percent) make up Mexico's rich elite exclusively, it is safe to say that mestizos and Indians comprise the poor—about a quarter of the population.

In the 16th century, Spanish invaders brought draft animals and the wheel along with Renaissance-era Romanticism and

religious zeal. Dozens of independent and unique cultures were eventually conquered and catechized, although pockets of resistance held out until the 20th century. But many native peoples do retain their indigenous identities. Cultural groups such as the Lacandón and the Huichol, who fled to the dense tropical forests and inhospitable mountains, avoided significant contact with mainstream society until well into the 20th century. Even today, the Huichols living in the western Sierra

Mexico City's 120-foot-tall (36.5 m) Monumento a la Independencia, crowned by "the angel," was erected in 1910 to honor the heroes of the War of Independence.

Madre include few Catholic rituals into their spiritual belief system, retaining their traditional gods and ceremonies.

That said, most indigenous people have blended their ancient gods and customs with saints and religious rites introduced by the

Two travelers chat outside Mexico City's modernistic Hotel Camino Real, which was designed by architect Ricardo Legorreta (b. 1931) and features the works of major artists.

Spanish. Catholicism is practiced—influenced to varying degrees by indigenous dogma—by 90 percent of the population. A large number of the remaining 10 percent are evangelical Christians, whose more sober form of Christianity sometimes produces conflict with their neighbors. In highland Chiapas, traditional Tzotzil Indians have in recent decades clashed with large populations of villagers who have been converted to Protestantism or other evangelical sects. In larger, more mainstream communities, Protestants and Catholics live and work together with little contention.

Fascinating customs and cultures have attracted adventure travelers for centuries. Writer John Lloyd Stephens's (1805–1852) and artist Frederick Catherwood's (1799–1854) published accounts of buried Maya ruins intrigued the Western world in the 19th century. Since then, writers have praised and scoffed, but rarely remained indifferent to Mexico's charms and idiosyncrasies.

MODERN CHALLENGES

Born in the aftermath of the Revolution, the Institutional Revolutionary Party, or PRI (Partido Revolucionario Institucional), has been the official government party since 1929.

Polls before the 2000 elections showed that people in the most rural areas believed the PRI and the government to be synonymous, and indeed they had every reason to do so. The party won every presidential election, and most governorships, between 1929 and 1994. Beginning in 1978, opposition parties were admitted in the Lower House, or Cámara de Diputados, to promote an illusion of democratic debate, with no chance to effect real change. However, in the 1994 elections, opposition parties actually won more seats in the Lower House. In 1997, leftist candidate Cuauhtémoc Cárdenas, of the Democratic Revolutionary Party, the PRD (Partido de la Revolución Democrática), became the first elected mayor of Mexico City.

A series of significant events in the 1990s continued to mobilize the public for political change. Popular presidential candidate Luis Donaldo Colosio was assassinated in 1994. Outgoing president Carlos Salinas de Gortari—credited during his six-year tenure (1988–1994) with a host of economic advances—left behind a trail of scandal and economic chaos, including devaluation of the peso and a bank bailout costing upward of $93 billion. That same year, a guerrilla army

Heading back to Tulum, on the coast of the Yucatán Peninsula, with the early morning catch

calling itself the Zapatista Army for National Liberation, or EZLN (Ejército Zapatista de Liberación Nacional), seized control of several strategic cities in highland Chiapas. Although they quickly retreated to the forest, their Internet postings and media communiqués have drawn world attention to the plight of the nation's disenfranchised peasant populations.

The prudent economic policies of Salinas's successor, Ernesto Zedillo Ponce de León (1994–2000), helped restore the economy, but more surprising were the political reforms instigated by the Yale-educated economist. In preparation for the 2000 presidential elections, extensive reforms of electoral institutions and a large presence of foreign observers eliminated many of the usual election day "irregularities" and encouraged the electorate to participate. In addition, instead of handpicking the presumed successor, a traditional practice since the party's formation, the PRI under Zedillo held a historic nationwide primary election. The result of these groundbreaking reforms was the election of opposition party candidate Vicente Fox Quesada, of the National Action Party, or PAN (Partido de Acción Nacional), to the nation's highest office in July 2000. Accepting defeat with good grace, PRI candidate Francisco

Labastida helped to maintain calm and encouraged a peaceful transition to the historic opposition party government.

Mexico's new administration faces considerable hurdles. While trade with Canada and the United States has doubled since the North American Free Trade Agreement (NAFTA) went into effect in 1994, expanded industrialization has fouled rivers and created smog and hazardous-waste disposal problems, traffic congestion, and housing challenges, especially in the cities contiguous to the U.S. border, where industrial growth is greatest. Powerful drug cartels fight among themselves and intimidate, kill, and corrupt police and judges who refuse collusion or attempt to restrict their spheres of influence. Tensions among EZLN supporters and the military persist in Chiapas, and the demands of other small but nonetheless significant guerrilla movements in Oaxaca and Guerrero must be addressed to ensure future stability.

Despite these and other difficulties it has faced over the years, Mexico has emerged as an important player in the world economy. It is the 13th richest country, with an impressive gross domestic product, and trade agreements with Israel and Europe are in the works. Perhaps most importantly, it has avoided a

coup since 1920, longer than any other Latin American nation and, after years of political demagoguery, is enjoying ever increasing political freedoms.

FESTIVALS & FIESTAS

As a predominantly Catholic country, Mexico celebrates saints' days and other religious holidays with elaborate festivities. Mexicans are great admirers of pyrotechnics and incorporate fireworks whenever possible into their high days and holidays, creating great towers of shooting sparks and rockets that boom throughout the night. They rarely retire early on the night of a fiesta or, for that matter, on the nights preceding it.

Mexico's coastal peoples are especially known for their exuberant fiestas and love of music and dance. The country's most famous Carnaval (pre-Lenten celebration) is held in Veracruz with masked balls, lavish parades with floats and costumed participants, and

Celebrating the Festival of the Virgin of Guadalupe, Mexico City

lively all-night street parties. Those of Campeche, Mazatlán, and Cozumel are also animated, well-attended events.

Easter is a more solemn affair celebrated with much pomp and ceremony; especially moving rituals take place in Oaxaca, San Miguel de Allende, San Luis Potosí, and Taxco. Christmas represents not just a day on the liturgical calendar, but an entire season of family gatherings and special foods, processions, and music.

Celebrating the Festival of the Virgin of Guadalupe, Mexico City

For All Saints' Day and All Souls' Day, families clean and decorate their loved ones' tombs, and in some regions, hold graveside vigils and create lavish home altars in honor of their departed relatives. In Pátzcuaro, Oaxaca, Campeche, Mérida, and other cities, cultural events and public altars make the family-oriented holiday accessible to visitors. ∎

Food & drink

MEXICAN DISHES CAN BE COMPLEX BUT ARE MORE OFTEN SIMPLE AND somewhat subtle. For 5,000 years, corn has reigned as Mexico's most important food, and the plant has religious significance for the Maya, Huichol, and other indigenous groups. Mesoamericans introduced the world to squash (and delicious squash blossoms), beans, chilies, turkey, avocados, tomatoes, sweet potatoes, and chocolate. To this already varied diet the Spanish added wheat (and bread), sugar, rice, and domestic animals: beef and dairy cattle and goats.

With the goats and the dairy cows came cheese. Many varieties are made today, from tangy, crumbly *cotija* to soft, creamy *panela.* Somewhat salty *queso fresco* is crumbled over many savory dishes and served with high-sugar desserts to cut the sweet. From Oaxaca comes *quesillo,* a ball of mild but tangy string cheese. It's used to make *queso fundido,* a delicious cheese fondue served with a stack of flour tortillas and often loaded with mushrooms, chorizo sausage, or strips of mild or hot chilies.

Although tasty homemade flour tortillas typically accompany some dishes, corn tortillas are the traditional staple. Conquistador Hernán Cortés called them maize cakes: flat disks of corn milled with lime and cooked on a hot griddle. Today, neighborhood "factories" produce fresh tortillas throughout the day, although many restaurants and country women make their own. Bread rolls are served in both homes and restaurants, yet to many Mexicans, a traditional meal without tortillas is unthinkable. This said, it's true that the less affluent the family, the more tortillas (in relation to other foods) it probably consumes. For a very poor family, a meal might consist of nothing more than tortillas and salt.

A seemingly endless variety of dishes is prepared with either tortillas or *masa* (finely ground cornmeal). The latter is used to make tamales: dense, rectangular cakes wrapped in corn husks or banana leaves and then steamed. Subtly sweet, plain tamales are served as a light evening meal with coffee or hot chocolate; dessert tamales might surround sweet pineapple chunks; and savory tamales enclose pieces of meat cooked in a chili sauce.

A wide selection of savories called *botanas,* or *antojitos,* is made with tortillas or masa. Although loosely translated as "appetizers," these foods served at restaurants and from pushcarts are the dishes most foreigners are familiar with. Antojitos also include enchiladas (tortillas smothered in chili sauce) and stuffed tacos and *taquitos,* as well as *chalupas, gorditas,* and *memelas* (griddle-cooked or fried disks of masa topped with crumbled cheese, salsa, onions, and often cilantro).

If each region has its favorite antojitos, each neighborhood has its favorite *taquería.* Specializing in tacos, taquerías range from comfortable restaurants to takeout-only storefronts and bicycle-powered carts. Soft tacos consist of warm tortillas filled with grilled meats and served with a variety of condiments. In a variation, tacos (in this case often called *taquitos*) are rolled around meat or chicken, deep fried, and served with guacamole (avocado sauce) or spicy fresh salsa.

The chili pepper is the tortilla's great companion. From Yucatán's fiery habanero to the relatively mild *chile poblano,* dozens of varieties are used fresh, roasted, or dried. Drying chilies changes both their names and their flavors. For example, the blistering jalapeño when dried produces the distinctive, smoky-tasting *chile chipotle;* the light orange *chile manzano* becomes *chile cascabel.*

Every pepper has a unique flavor. Used blended or chopped, raw or cooked, chilies are combined with onion, garlic, cilantro, and tomatoes (both green and red) to make delicious salsas that accompany almost every meal. Jalapeño and serrano chilies are also served pickled (*en escabeche*), with carrots and onions.

Ground chilies were a key ingredient in *chocolate,* one of the favorite drinks of Aztec

A woman prepares fresh produce for market day in Tlacolula, outside Oaxaca city.

royalty. Today, steaming pots of this delicious hot drink are made from bars of bitter chocolate mixed with ground almonds, cinnamon, and sugar. Beaten until frothy, with water or milk, chocolate is a popular accompaniment to a plateful of *pan dulce*, or sweet bread. Coffee lovers should try wonderfully aromatic *café de olla*, boiled with cinnamon and

True tequila is produced only in Jalisco and a few other Mexican states.

piloncillo (crude brown sugar). It is definitely more satisfying than the weak *café americano* sold in U.S.-style coffee shops and diners.

Deciding if and when to purchase food from market restaurants, street stands, and itinerant vendors can be difficult. If you strictly avoid all of these, your experience of Mexico will be less than authentic, yet no one wants to risk digestive upset or more serious ailments. There's no guarantee, however, that a prosperous-looking restaurant will be more hygienic than a humble taco stand or a faded yet well-scrubbed market kitchen. If you decide to go native, head for the most popular stands and check out the vendor and his wares

for cleanliness. It's also wise to eat during peak hours, when food is still being freshly prepared and is not left sitting around. Tap water should be strictly avoided. While most vendors do use bottled water in their coffee and other water-based drinks, it's worth investigating if you are in any doubt.

Markets are a great place to mingle with the locals, and are also the place to shop for Mexico's huge variety of tropical and semitropical fruits, from which juices and their watered-down counterparts, delicious and refreshing *aguas frescas*, are made. Tourist-oriented restaurants often inexplicably offer only canned or boxed orange, grapefruit, and tomato juices instead of regional favorites such as delightful mango, papaya, guava, and watermelon.

Other popular beverages include *atole* and *horchata*. The former is a thick, filling, slightly sweet drink made of ground rice or cornmeal sweetened with sugar and served warm or at room temperature. The latter is a refreshing cool drink commonly made of filtered rice water, sugar, and cinnamon, sometimes spiked with fresh fruit and almond slivers. Unless the quality of water used is questionable, it's a shame to drink anything out of a can or bottle—with the exception of beer!

Many fine beers are brewed in Mexico. Some are regional, such as Pacífico from Mazatlán, and Montejo and León Negro from the Yucatán; others are seasonal (Noche Buena is sold only around Christmas), but most are fortunately ubiquitous. Baja California's wineries produce wine and brandies of fair to good quality. Cultivated since before the Spanish Conquest, the agave plant produces pulque, a rather gooey, fermented alcoholic beverage—definitely an acquired taste. More palatable are the distilled agave products mescal and tequila (see p. 154).

Mexico is a huge country, and the cuisine varies with the landscape and regional culture. With thousands of miles of coastline, it is known for fresh seafood, and in places such as Cabo San Lucas, at the tip of Baja, chefs have finally gone beyond simple grilling or pan-frying with garlic (*al mojo de ajo*) to add sashimi, sushi, and inspired sauces to their menus. Still, dishes such as *huauchinango a la veracruzana* remain universally popular.

Grilled whole with tomato, chili, onion, garlic, parsley, capers, and green olives, Veracruz's version of red snapper is a Mexican standard. Also popular is *ceviche*, any firm, white fish marinated in lime juice and served with fresh chopped onion, chile, tomato, and cilantro. (To make it more hygienic, many cooks briefly boil the fish before "cooking" it in lime.) Depending on the local catch, conch, octopus, or shrimp may be used as well. The lobster season is April to September, so if you see "fresh lobster" on the menu between October and March, ask where it's from.

Meat is the mainstay of the northern diet, often accompanied by *frijoles charros* (beans cooked with pork rind) and flour tortillas. As well as various types of dried, grilled, and shredded beef, northerners are fond of *cabrito,* or barbecued goat. From the north also come *huevos rancheros* (ranch-style eggs): delicious, sunny-side-up eggs served on a lightly fried corn tortilla and smothered in a mild cooked salsa. This and other breakfast favorites are often accompanied by beans and a basket of fresh tortillas.

Some of the most unusual dishes come from central and southern Mexico. Seven vastly different mole sauces are made in the state of Oaxaca alone. Among the principle ingredients of *mole verde* are pumpkin seeds (*pipián*) and chilies, which produce the green color for which it is named. Fruits and raisins make *mole mancha manteles* bright red: the name means "tablecloth-staining." The classic *mole negro* (black mole, or in Puebla, *mole poblano*) combines such diverse ingredients as stale tortillas, sesame seeds, chilies, choco-late, nuts, peppercorns, and cloves, among about a dozen others. Thought to have been invented by a Puebla nun, this convoluted recipe represents Mexican cuisine at its most complex. Cooks from Tlaxcala, Puebla, and Oaxaca compete to create the most savory adaptation.

The Yucatán Peninsula has its share of unusual and flavorful recipes, especially those from Mérida, where French, Spanish, and Lebanese immigrants have influenced dishes. Locally grown sour oranges are the key to marinated *poc chuc,* savory pork grilled with onions, tomatoes, and garlic. Venison has all but disappeared from menus, but *pollo* (chicken) and *cochinita* (pork) *pibil* are still seasoned with pungent *achiote* paste, made from the seed of the annatto tree, and cooked in a traditional pit.

Although deer have been hunted nearly to extinction, animals and plants from pre-Hispanic America are still eaten. Worms from the agave fields (*gusanos de maguey*) and

What Hernán Cortés called "maize cakes" are still eaten in many forms.

highly salted and seasoned grasshoppers (*chapulines*) from Oaxaca are fried and sold by the scoop in markets, but also appear in expensive restaurants serving nouvelle Mexican cuisine. Other delicacies include *escamoles* (ant eggs) and *huitlacoche* (black corn fungus), the latter found in crêpes and quesadillas (flour tortillas with melted cheese), as well as in more exotic recipes. With so many unusual foods to try, why settle for a ham-burger and soft drink from the inevitable chain restaurant? Right down the road, you might find freshly grilled prickly-pear cactus pads (spines removed) served with a cool glass of cantaloupe juice. ■

History of Mexico

ANCIENT PEOPLES LIVED BY THE RHYTHM OF THE SEASONS, EMPLOYING sun- and moon-based calendars much as we do today, and attuning themselves to a 52-year cycle that may have been respected as far back as the end of the Pleistocene period. Within these circles of time, great civilizations were born and buried, some living in isolation, but most trading and interacting with others from as far off as the Great Plains of the United States and the mountainous spine of Peru. No less fascinating is the history of colonial and modern Mexico, which has blended European and indigenous world views to forge one of the most important developing nations.

EARLY HUMANS

Many scholars agree that some 30,000 or even 40,000 years ago, during the late Pleistocene, humans crossed the Bering Sea from northeastern Asia to North America. Fanning across the continents, family units occupied caves and other available shelters, hunting small game and gathering food.

In the pre-Hispanic era (before the Spanish Conquest), two distinct zones composed the land we now call Mexico. Roughly north of Tampico and the tip of Baja California, extending into today's central United States, were the great, hot deserts and sweeping plains referred to as la Gran Chichimeca. Long after the arrival of European explorers, individual tribes of nomadic hunter-gatherers, collectively referred to as Chichimecas, eked out an existence in this harsh environment. In times of scarcity and drought, they were likely to rain down on the farming villages to the south in a storm of chaos and destruction.

Extending south of la Gran Chichimeca all the way to northern Honduras and El Salvador was a geographic and cultural zone now referred to as Mesoamerica. By the Archaic period (7000–1500 B.C.), many tribes had abandoned the nomadic lifestyle, establishing more sedentary villages. By about 3000 B.C., while still seasonally gathering seeds and fruit, clans had domesticated corn, which they cultivated along with squash, chili peppers, avocados, and a wide variety of other foods. By 1500 B.C., simple agricultural societies existed throughout the region.

Compelling archaeological evidence demonstrates that early Mesoamericans had contact with South American tribes. Seafaring peoples from around Ecuador and Peru brought new and improved varieties of corn, which were successfully crossed with native species. These itinerant traders also introduced fired pottery to the west coast peoples, as well as metallurgy, which was practiced only among the Purépecha (Tarascans) and the Mixtecs (based, respectively, in modern-day Michoacán and Oaxaca). Even the Purépecha language, which is unlike any in North America, has been linked linguistically to Quechua, the language of Peru.

During the early Preclassic, or Formative era (1500 B.C.–A.D. 150), certain societies became sufficiently large and differentiated by class to bring about the construction of impressive public buildings. These required an enormous commitment of man-hours, since neither beasts of burden nor the wheel were available. Among the earliest known examples of this public architecture is a massive artificial plateau, or early pyramid, built around 1350 B.C. at San Lorenzo, in Veracruz.

THE MOTHER CULTURE

The San Lorenzo pyramid was built by the Olmecs, the oldest known civilization in North America. Olmec society was stratified, with an elite class governing nonfarming classes of priests and artisans and a vast plebeian majority. Fertile tropical lowlands with extreme rainfall easily supported slash-and-burn agriculture, and the region's many rivers, lagoons, and estuaries provided an extensive transportation system.

Although there is some early evidence of Olmec culture on the southern Pacific coast, the first great centers were built along the

The smallest of such characteristic Olmec stone "portrait" heads discovered to date weighs 8 tons (8,100 kg).

Gulf, in southern Veracruz and Tabasco. For years the origins of the Olmec language eluded linguists, until clues carved in hieroglyphic writings showed it to be derivative of that of the Mixe-Zoques, whose descendants still inhabit the Pacific coast of Oaxaca and Chiapas states.

San Lorenzo was the first known Olmec city, at its apogee between about 1150 and 900 B.C. Other nearby cities later gained pre-eminence, including La Venta, Tres Zapotes, and Laguna de los Cerros. At San Lorenzo, rainwater was diverted from the pyramid by drains of basalt. Quarried in the Tuxtla Mountains near Laguna de los Cerros and at other sites, the stone was rolled, dragged, and floated to San Lorenzo in uncanny feats of engineering. Thrones, stelae, and other monumental works of artistry were created, including immense stone heads thought to honor important rulers.

Other forms of art characteristic of the Olmec are its exquisite masks and portable statuettes. Many of these pieces portray deities such as the jaguar and a half-man, half-jaguar being, which may have represented a bridge between the feline god and the ruling dynasty. Jade, greenstone, obsidian, and other materials were imported, as were agricultural products. Olmec exports, including carved symbolic ax-heads of jade and carved wooden and stone masks and figurines, have been found as far north as Tlatilco, in the Valley of Mexico, and south to the highlands of El Salvador. Although cultural borrowing among highland and Gulf coast cultures was a two-way street, the major artistic, intellectual, and political contributions came from the Olmecs.

As the Olmec culture waned in importance in the tenth century B.C., other cities and city-states emerged in Oaxaca and the highland valleys of central Mexico. Strategically perched above the confluence of three valleys in Oaxaca, Monte Albán prospered from about 500 B.C. At Cuicuilco, south of Mexico City, the round, terraced pyramid built around 400 B.C. (and engulfed by lava from the nearby Xitle volcano some 500 years later) was one of the earliest and most unusual structures of the Preclassic period.

In the Soconusco region of Chiapas, Izapa forms an important link between Olmec and

Maya cultures. This large city peaked in size and artistic achievement between about 300 and 50 B.C., when its inhabitants carved a great number of stelae in a highly narrative, pictorial style similar to those produced in early Maya art. Scattered throughout the region, these monuments demonstrate a devotion to rituals tied to astronomy, agricultural cycles, fertility, and other natural events. Significant similarities between the Maya and the Olmecs include representations of a "Long-Lipped God" (precursor to the Maya rain god Chac) and the use of Long Count (see below) date glyphs. Some experts attribute the latter to the Maya; equally reputable scholars credit the Olmec. The same debate surrounds the earliest hieroglyphic writing system.

CLASSIC CIVILIZATIONS

One of Mexico's earliest and most fascinating civilizations was that of the ancient Maya, who occupied the Yucatán Peninsula, as well as the highlands and lowlands of Chiapas and Central America. (With 3 million people, the Maya today constitute Mexico's largest indigenous population, and many still practice ancient ways.) Maya culture began to blossom just before the Christian era. Its cities produced learned mathematicians as well as artists and architects. With none of the instruments known to the modern world, the Maya achieved great accuracy in astronomy. They had a place-value system of numbers and used several different calendars, including a 365-day solar calendar and a 260-day ritual calendar. The two calendars were meshed to

Battle scenes like those in this ancient fresco at Bonampak helped disprove early theories of Maya pacifism.

produce a 52-year cycle in which each day had prophetic significance. Although other ancient civilizations used these cyclical calendars, only the Olmec and the Maya used the Long Count, a noncyclical calendar. It had a definite start date (by Western reckoning August 11, 3114 B.C.) and was used to record historical events. The Maya also used the most sophisticated system of writing in Mesoamerica: a phonetic script often employing rebuses, or written puns.

The Mayas' exquisite palaces and temples of quarried limestone were faced with brightly painted plaster. Where stone was plentiful,

elaborate pictorial and hieroglyphic messages were carved into limestone lintels and stelae. Elsewhere throughout the Maya world, modeled and carved stucco was used to glorify births, marriages, deaths, victories in battle, and other momentous events involving the royal families.

While most Preclassic Maya cities were rather isolated and autonomous, extensive communication characterized the Classic Maya civilizations. "White roads" (sacbés), elevated highways raised up to 15 feet (4.5 m) above the surrounding jungle, gleamed white in the Maya night, possibly to aid couriers who traveled between cities during the cooler hours. These roads, paved with flat stones and stucco, may have served military and religious purposes as well as facilitating commerce and transportation. Sacbés not only joined one city to another, but also were internal roadways, linking the most important buildings within a city, possibly to help transport icons from temple to temple.

Early on, the Maya established trade with Teotihuacán, in central Mexico, built by a Totonac-speaking people from the Gulf coast. Teotihuacán, in turn, traded as far north as the Oasis America tribes of northern Mexico and the southwestern United States. Like the Maya, the Teotihuacanos were mathematicians and astronomers. Hundreds of years after the demise of the great city of Teotihuacán, Aztec lords made pilgrimages to the ruins to consult with the gods and to bring home relics for their own palaces and altars. According to Aztec legends, the gods gathered there to

Teotihuacán fell into ruin around A.D. 600, when some of its most important buildings appear to have been purposefully burned or dismantled. In Oaxaca, Monte Albán was abandoned around 700, and the decline of the great Maya cities began about a hundred years later. For no obvious reason, ceremonial centers were left by their creators to crumble, often to be reused later by others as places of worship or as burial grounds.

POSTCLASSIC MESOAMERICA

While previously accepted theories held that Classic Maya cities were brought down by peasant revolts, there was actually a relatively smooth and seamless transition to the Postclassic phase between approximately A.D. 900 and 1200. The most important distinction between the Classic and Postclassic eras was the substitution of tribal councils for the kingdoms that had previously ruled. After 1200, monumental art depicting the glories of kings and queens was replaced with more utilitarian public art and architecture.

Another popular misconception regarding the Postclassic era (900–1521) in general is that it was characterized by a breakdown of society and increased warfare. Upon reexamining the evidence, however, most archaeologists agree that warfare and ritual sacrifice continued more or less apace during the period preceding the Spanish Conquest (1521). The clearest example of this is shown in the rise of the Mexica, or Aztecs (see p. 184), an extremely warlike people who sacrificed victims in truly astonishing numbers.

Ritual sacrifice took place throughout Mesoamerica. The standard practice was to rip out the victim's heart with a ceremonial flint knife. Other unfortunates were trussed and rolled down steep pyramids, shot with arrows, or slow roasted on a Divine Hearth. Prior to crop planting, children were sacrificed to appease Tláloc; their frantic cries were thought to please the rain god. In acts of self-sacrifice, nobles bled their arms, tongues, earlobes, and genitals for penitence and purification.

Later played as a spectator sport among traveling teams, pre-Hispanic ball games originated as one-on-one contests of life and death among rival lords. Important captives taken in war were subjected to a ritual ball game in

Statues of the lesser god Chac Mool, such as this one at Chichén Itzá, have been found from the Yucatán to the central plateau.

bring about the current era—the Fifth Sun—sacrificing themselves and in the process creating the sun and the moon. These celestial bodies, honored in two of the largest pyramids in the Western Hemisphere—the Pirámide del Sol and Pirámide de la Luna—would, along with all else in the world, disappear in the inevitable demise of the Fifth Sun, as the previous four worlds had been cataclysmically undone. Mesoamericans expected the world to end and begin anew with each successive era, or "sun." The epoch of the Fifth Sun was expected to be wiped out by earthquakes at the end of one of the 52-year cycles.

which death to the loser assured perpetuation of life and continued success for the winning tribe. The games, played on a rectangular court, had variations, but usually involved using the hips, legs, and arms to pass a small, solid rubber ball through a stone hoop.

Fearing the threat of sacrifice less than a tortuous death during the worst droughts,

The long and triumphant reign of Moctezuma Xocoyotzin (R.1502–1520) was ended by Hernán Cortés.

Chichimec tribes periodically migrated south. The result of one such incursion was the settlement of Tula, which lies north of the Valley of Mexico. The Chichimeca-Tolteca (more commonly called the Toltecs) soon established themselves as people of culture and learning.

For years archaeologists theorized, excavated, and debated to determine whether the Toltecs had, through trade or conquest, come to influence the important Maya site of Chichén Itzá on the Yucatán Peninsula. Conclusive evidence has shown, however, that Tula was actually a trading outpost of Chichén

Itzá, and that Maya influence traveled north to the central plateau and not vice versa. The last of the important Chichimec tribes to migrate south were the Aztecs, or Mexica, who wandered from a place they called Aztlán (meaning "place of herons") to found a city in the middle of Lake Texcoco, in the Valley of Mexico, in the late 13th century. In a few hundred years, the Aztecs rose from illiterate nomads from the north to the dominant force in Mesoamerica. With its extensive market-places, fine palaces filled with richly dressed lords and ladies, and impressive temples housing a panoply of gods, the city of Tenochtitlán astounded the invading Spaniards. Well-engineered causeways linked the island city to the mainland, and "floating" gardens surrounding the city (see p. 208) provided a ready source of food.

When future conqueror of New Spain Hernán Cortés was two years old, in 1487, some 80,000 people were sacrificed during the dedication of a new temple in Tenochtitlán. Beaten nonstop during the four-day blood-bath, snakeskin drums marked the rise and fall of flint knives as black-painted priests, their long hair matted with blood, ritually sacrificed victims to the war god Huitzilopochtli.

During the reign of Moctezuma Ilhuicamina (Moctezuma I, R.1440–1469), Flower Wars were introduced with the purpose of providing rival armies with soldiers for sacrifice. Although the Flower Wars were sham conflicts (a fact the soldiers were not privy to), most of the battles unleashed by the Aztecs were thoroughly real and rarely lost. The Aztecs controlled some 370 cities and had a standing army of 150,000 soldiers, with more in reserve.

One kingdom the Aztecs never conquered was that of the Purépecha, or Tarascans, of Michoacán in the Central Highlands. As one of the few Mesoamerican peoples to use metallurgy, the Purépecha had a definite edge on the battlefield with their bronze weapons. They also differed from other cultured Mesoamerican tribes in religion. Ignoring the rain god Tláloc and other deities so important to their neighbors, the Purépecha worshiped a family of related gods and goddesses linked to creatures of the heavens, Earth, and the underworld.

CONQUEST & EARLY COLONIZATION

Into this world of power, conflict, and beauty burst a new (and in many ways equally violent) enemy: Spain. In the name of Emperor Charles V, Hernán Cortés (1485–1547) and his troops brought the supposed salvation of Christianity and the undeniable curse of serfdom. The Europeans also introduced the wheel, firearms, and beasts of burden, and spread the concept of metallurgy.

An inspired military leader and fervent Catholic, Cortés was driven nearly as much by a love of adventure and a sincere motivation to Christianize the Indians as by a desire for gold and other treasures. Cortés was initially commissioned to explore and chart new lands to the west by the governor of Cuba. Ignoring orders to return to Cuba and relinquish his command, he and his relatively small army were soon involved in skirmishes with native peoples who had been tested and hardened by internal wars and conflicts with the Aztecs. During these early battles the Aztecs' foes and vassals were impressed with the Spaniards' horses and firearms, and other previously unknown accouterments of combat. All of this was reported to Emperor Moctezuma II (R.1502–1520), in Tenochtitlán.

The emperor had cause for concern. Ancient prophesy predicted the year 1 Reed, during which Cortés appeared from the east, as the year in which the god-king Quetzalcóatl would return to reclaim his throne, abandoned several centuries before. Wielding booming cannons and commanding strange, armored beasts (horses), Cortés was initially thought to be Quetzalcóatl, and Moctezuma sent gifts of gold, fine garments, and rich food to the Spanish bivouacked on the coast, while simultaneously begging them to return from wherever they came.

Bent on finding the source of the golden treasures and meeting the legendary Aztec leader, Cortés and his most trusted captains scuttled their ships to dispel any thoughts of retreat. They preserved sails and hardware, however, which were used to outfit boats built two years later during a four-month siege that demolished the Aztec capital at Tenochtitlán.

Details of the Spanish battles, alliances, and eventual conquest were recorded by Bernal Díaz, a soldier, who later described them in a fascinating narrative entitled *True History of the Conquest of New Spain*. One detail not overlooked by the sagacious soldier was the importance of the two translators—Jerónimo de Aguilar and la Malinche. The former was a Spanish soldier shipwrecked on a previous expedition and enslaved by the Maya. When

The indigenous culture variously impressed, astonished, and horrified the Spaniard Hernán Cortés.

returned to Cortés, he spoke Mayan and Spanish. A young girl of noble descent, la Malinche had been sold into slavery in Tabasco, and thus spoke Mayan and classical Náhuatl, the Aztec tongue.

La Malinche, baptized and renamed doña Marina by the Spaniards, proved especially helpful to them, with her well-worded translations, grasp of politics, and ability to turn potential foes into allies. Despite horses, cannons, and other military advantages, the Spanish Conquest would not have been possible without the allied strength of Aztec foes: the Tlaxcalans, Totonacs, and, as the end drew

near, some of the subject kingdoms that surrounded Tenochtitlán.

Before waging outright war on the Aztecs, a large contingency of Spanish soldiers was entertained for months in the fortified city of Tenochtitlán, almost as captive guests. Emperor Moctezuma wavered between friend and foe as an increasingly indignant retinue of nobles and priests urged him to sacrifice the Spanish to Huitzilopochtli, god of war. Soon held hostage by his guests and dismissed by his detractors, Moctezuma was killed by his own people during a battle. Afterward, Cortés, la Malinche, and some of the remaining soldiers fled the capital in a daring nighttime exodus.

The last Aztec emperor, Cuauhtémoc (*R.*1520–1521), was captured and, when he refused to reveal a cache of gold and treasure, was subsequently tortured and hanged. La Ciudad de México, or Mexico City, was raised from the rubble of Tenochtitlán using the forced labor of the conquered people. Favored by fate, his own cunning, and the bravery of his Spanish soldiers, Cortés had crushed the mighty Aztec empire just two years after landing in the New World.

In the chaotic early years of the colony, plebeians who had suffered under the Aztec regime saw one harsh reality replaced with another. And while they would avoid the dreaded sacrificial slab, they were statistically more likely to be worked to death in a mine or dispatched by smallpox, measles, or some other imported disease. Millions of Indians died in the first hundred years of Spanish

Depiction of the Cholula battle (1519), which took place before the conquest of Mexico

people, depending on Indian labor to work the mines and fields and help run their households.

The conquerors were given girls and women by the tribes they bested in battle, and by the Aztecs who initially treated them as honored guests, producing a caste called mestizos (part European, part Indian). The settlers kept concubines, or less often, took Indian women as legitimate wives.

Unlike the Aztec nobles, who accepted the offspring of their mistresses and raised them in privilege, most Spaniards refused to recognize their bastard children. Consequently, the first generations of mestizos enjoyed no legal status whatsoever. Largely spurned by both Indians and whites, a renegade class was created, with no cultural group and no place within the emerging colony.

Although Indians and mestizos generally suffered ignoble lives, indigenous lords and other lucky individuals who swore fealty to the king were named local strongmen, or caciques, and became bosses ruling over their former dominions. Both caciques and encomendados demanded large amounts of tribute from the peasants, and, whenever possible, usurped Indian lands.

To escape virtual slavery on the encomiendas (and later, on the haciendas that ruled rural Mexico until the 20th century), some Indians fled to the stark deserts or the most inhospitable mountain ranges. Many of those who remained flocked for Catholic baptism, encouraged by the appearance in 1531 of the dark-skinned Virgin of Guadalupe near a shrine to the Indian goddess Tonántzin (see p. 193).

For nearly three centuries of colonial rule, enormous mineral wealth and free or nearly free labor brought great riches to Spain. In the Sierra Madre, gold, silver, iron, zinc, and other minerals also created fabulous personal fortunes. In the wake of the miners, or sometimes leading the way, religious orders established mission churches to convert the natives to Christianity. First to arrive were the Franciscans, who set about catechizing the surrounding areas, followed shortly by the Dominicans, Augustinians, and others. The Jesuits and Franciscans braved the hinterlands of the north and (with the Dominicans) the difficult terrain of Baja California. The Jesuits were expelled from New Spain in 1767 by King

domination, possibly more than 90 percent of the indigenous population.

The New World was ruled by a viceregal system. Under the viceroy (answerable only to the king of Spain) were *audiencias* (judicial bodies) in Mexico City and Guadalajara, which controlled a hierarchy of officials, each serving at the whim of his superior. Enormous land grants *(encomiendas)* were awarded to some individuals *(encomendados)*, and despite regulations their word was virtually law. Unlike the New England settlers, who drove the indigenous people from their lands (and much later herded them into reservations), Mexico's conquerors interacted with the native

Charles III, who was convinced by rival orders that they were becoming too influential.

INDEPENDENCE

Rich in land and prosperous mines, the Catholic Church was a powerful force in colonial Mexico. Government was weak, and largely controlled by the Church and rich,

Benito Juárez spoke Zapotec before Spanish, and studied for the priesthood before switching to law.

influential families. Despite the wealth and power of some *criollos* (people of Spanish descent born in Mexico), their class did not enjoy all the privileges afforded *peninsulares,* Spaniards born in Spain. Inspired by the American Revolution and the ideals of the Enlightenment—the 18th-century movement rejecting traditional European agendas in favor of more pragmatic approaches to society's problems—dissatisfied criollos and priests bent on social reform began to plot independence in the early 19th century.

Royalist forces learned of a conspiracy in 1810, and the Independence Movement was launched a bit sooner than planned under priest Miguel Hidalgo y Costilla (1753–1811) and intellectuals from Morelia and Querétaro. Not all of Mexico was united in the cause. Isolated Yucatán, for example, had more ties to Europe than to Mexico City. And most peninsulares, having little if anything to gain from independence, remained loyal to Spain.

After initial rebel victories, the Royalists regrouped. The war dragged on with isolated insurgent attacks and little chance of a full-scale success on either side. Also called the "Plan of Three Guarantees" (which were for Mexico to remain Catholic, to be headed by a constitutional monarch, and to guarantee the same rights to those born in the New World as those born in Spain), the Plan de Iguala was signed by Agustín de Iturbide (1783–1824) and rebel leader Vicente Guerrero in 1821. Spain barely opposed losing the colony, and signed the Treaty of Córdoba that same year, through which the conditions set forth in the Plan de Iguala were implemented. According to the agreed-upon covenant, the rich resumed their lives of privilege while the poor remained their chattels. Catholicism continued as the official religion of Mexico.

What followed was a half century of reconstruction and political and economic chaos. Agustín de Iturbide reigned for less than a year as head of the new constitutional monarchy before being forced into exile. After his ousting, a succession of feeble and impoverished governments took turns over-throwing one another. Antonio López de Santa Anna (1794–1876), an energetic general from Veracruz, acted as president on multiple occasions, in between starting and stopping various rebellions throughout the nation. In the countryside, the *campesinos* were ruthlessly exploited as large landholders stole communal lands and the caciques (see p. 31) terrorized anyone who was bold enough to complain.

The weak central government invited foreign intervention. In 1838 the French blockaded the port of Veracruz during the Pastry War, a dispute over damages suffered by a baker and other French nationals during earlier riots in Mexico City. In 1846 the United States declared war on Mexico on trumped-up complaints in order to annex Texas and coveted lands to the west. Landing at Veracruz,

U.S. troops soon captured the Mexican garrison at Chapultepec Castle, Mexico City. As a result of the Mexican-American War (1846–48), the United States gained Texas, New Mexico, Arizona, and Alta California; Mexico lost half of its territory, retaining the Baja California peninsula and lands south of the Río Bravo (called the Rio Grande in the United States).

During the war, fearful whites in the isolated Yucatán Peninsula formed a Maya army, which immediately turned its weapons on the wealthy elite who had so incautiously armed it. Unsophisticated in waging war, the Maya, after launching bloody raids that struck fear into the rich Spanish landholders, succeeded in taking the most important cities and towns of the peninsula. With no desire to rule, they merely wanted revenge and the return of their ancestral lands, and after their few successes simply laid down their weapons and returned to the seasonal planting. But they had not calculated the consequences of their actions. The whites and mestizos reorganized themselves and counterattacked. About half of the Yucatán Maya population was murdered in the ensuing reprisals.

In the ensuing political chaos, Zapotec lawyer Benito Juárez (1806–1872) helped promulgate the Reform Laws, intended primarily to separate Church and state and to reduce the influence of the Church. The ensuing Reform Wars (1858–61) were eventually won by the liberals under Juárez. But empty national coffers forced him to default on international debts, giving France an excuse for invading Mexico and installing (with the approbation of the conservatives) the Austrian Maximilian of Habsburg (1832–1867) as emperor. A short-lived but symbolically important victory against the French invaders was won on May 5, 1862. Young and poorly armed, the defenders routed the French military contingent in a battle that is reenacted each year in Puebla and celebrated throughout the country.

The Second Empire, as it was called, lasted but three short years (1864–67). A just man, Maximilian angered the conservatives by refusing to retract liberal reforms. Still, a foreign king ruling Mexico suited nearly no one, and after French troops were recalled to fight Prussia, the emperor was captured and

executed in Querétaro in 1867. President-in-exile Benito Juárez returned to rule the nation for nearly five years before dying of a heart attack in 1872.

Despite his intentions, Juárez's policy of confiscating church property had a disastrous effect on indigenous people. Church lands communally worked by campesino farmers

Porfirio Díaz's dictatorial presidency spanned more than three decades.

were auctioned and snatched up by wealthy hacienda owners. Many indigenous and mestizo campesinos were then forced to work for slave wages on fields they had formerly tilled for their own families.

THE PORFIRIATO

While Juárez is nonetheless lauded as a hero, Porfirio Díaz, who came to power in 1876, is a more controversial figure. Under Díaz, economic and political stability was finally achieved. Construction of an extensive railway system moved goods for national and international consumption, mining and other industries prospered, and foreign investment boomed. A great admirer of European art and architecture, the Oaxaca-born mestizo commissioned luxurious public buildings during his 33-year presidency, which was in reality a thinly veiled dictatorship.

The Porfiriato (era of Porfirio Díaz) revived the economy, restored order out of chaos, and created public works. However, journalistic freedom and political dialogue were strongly repressed, and a national police force, *los rurales,* snuffed out any protest in the countryside. Although an emerging middle class did benefit from a form of trickle-down economics, the peasantry suffered the usual indignities: their lands were illegally confiscated and their people tied to large haciendas by debt-peonage. In a situation that was tantamount to slavery, poor peasants were paid a pittance and bound to the estate on which they worked by debts incurred from purchases such as soap, corn, and coffee from the plantation store. Subsequent generations were held responsible for their forefathers' debts, and so remained trapped by the hacienda system.

REVOLUTION & RECONSTRUCTION

Under the banner of "Effective suffrage, no reelection!", the wealthy, reserved Francisco I. Madero (1873–1913) mobilized the Mexican public against the patriarch Díaz, who was exiled to Europe in 1911. Despite early hopes for a peaceful transition to a more egalitarian system, a lack of consensus on reform agendas soon divided military leaders with wildly disparate goals. Madero's agenda was political reform. In Morelos, south of Mexico City, Emiliano Zapata (1879–1919) fervently demanded the return of stolen communal lands and other agrarian reforms to benefit dispossessed peasants.

Treachery characterized the long and bloody Revolutionary War (1911–17). As president of the republic, Madero was jailed and then assassinated by dissatisfied generals. Zapata was killed in a perfidious ambush arranged by the rival revolutionary (and landowner) Venustiano Carranza (1859–1920). Charismatic (but often unduly violent) military tactician Pancho Villa (1878–1923) was murdered in an ambush several years after the end of fighting.

The Revolution cost approximately two million lives, and many of the victims were unarmed civilians. The conflict dragged on until 1920, when the ideals of the Constitution of 1917 were adopted. The country was economically devastated by years of war. Political unrest reigned, and subsequent transfers of presidential power through nominal elections were accompanied by revolts and instability.

The Constitution promised agrarian reform, but redistribution of land was ignored until General Lázaro Cárdenas del Río (1895–1970) was elected president in 1934. Truly committed to the poor, the mestizo from Michoacán expropriated and redistributed nearly 50 million acres (20 million ha), creating 180,000 *ejidos,* or communal farms. Alarming foreign investors and governments

and conservative nationals, Cárdenas's most sweeping reforms were to nationalize the railroads and the oil companies. While encouraging unions and labor organizations, he eliminated the cronies of his predecessor, Plutarco Elías Calles, who had—as tradition dictated—chosen him as successor to the presidency.

It was Calles who enforced previously ignored articles of the new Constitution limiting the power of the Church. When the incensed clergy urged boycotts of church services, enraged Catholics began fighting detractors in grisly street battles. Even after the insurgency, later dubbed the Cristero Revolt , was put down, temples were ransacked and colonial art stolen. The Church's long-standing influence in affairs of state had ended, although most of Mexico's population remained staunchly Catholic.

Supporters of Venustiano Carranza, head of the new government in 1916, pass through the U.S. 6th Infantry's camp near San Antonio, Mexico, on their way to fight Pancho Villa.

TWENTIETH-CENTURY MEXICO

Prior to 1910, Mexico City was a quiet capital with colonial churches, surrounded by traditional indigenous villages. The Revolution's extreme unrest brought country people to the safety of the capital, where many remained. During the Second World War, Mexico was launched into the industrial era, and waves of workers relocated to the capital to fill factory jobs. President Miguel Alemán (1946–1952) encouraged development of infrastructure and attracted

foreign and national investment in industry.

Created in 1929 as the National Revolutionary Party, or PNR, the Institutional Revolutionary Party (PRI) became the official government party, adopting the tricolor of the Mexican flag and ruling with virtual impunity. Internal squabbles and an inability to capital-ize on the discontent of campesinos (poor farmers and rural dwellers) and the middle classes rendered the opposition parties totally ineffective, and enabled the PRI to maintain the status quo. From 1929 until 2000, the PRI never lost a presidential election.

World War II brought industrialization to Mexico, after which the country's economy continued to grow. But a population explosion resulted in an ever increasing number of poor, and reforms by Adolfo Ruiz Cortines (1952–1958) and others never truly eased their burden. Heavy investment in petroleum production left the economy vulnerable to

fluctuations in the world market for this commodity, and the drop in oil prices in the early 1980s led to recession and huge foreign debt. But although discontent was manifested to one degree or another under various PRI presidencies, the country's system of one-party politics was never seriously challenged.

So Mexicans were stunned, and many were jubilant, when late in the evening on July 2, 2000, former Coca-Cola executive and Guanajuato state governor Vicente Fox

Independence Day parade, San Cristóbal de las Casas

Quesada was announced as the president-elect for PAN, the National Action Party.

Political reform has come about slowly, but considering the depth of cronyism and corruption, remarkably peacefully. How the business-oriented, slightly-right-of-center PAN will fare in the 21st century is a subject of intense debate both within Mexico and around the world. ■

The arts

INFLUENCED BY ITS MULTIETHNIC ROOTS, MEXICAN CULTURE IS AS expressive and varied as the landscape. Spanish baroque architecture quickly mutated to become Mexican baroque, inspired by indigenous themes and a passion for abundance and flamboyance. Folk-dance troupes re-create pre-Hispanic dances in *belle époque* theaters, while in the craggy Sierra Madre, Yaqui men still perform the Deer Dance *(Danza del Venado)* for its original, spiritual purpose. Mestizo culture can be admired in the nation's regional dances, many of which attuned immigrants' instruments and dance steps to an entirely Mexican sensibility.

ARCHITECTURE

Before the Conquest, Mesoamerica's oldest cities and ceremonial centers were laid out much like modern towns. Temples and palaces framed a central plaza, or *zócalo*, in the heart of the town. Along one side was a church; along another the most important public buildings, including the seat of local government. Nearby plazas held open-air markets, and side roads led to businesses and residential neighborhoods. Stone, adobe, and mortar were the main building materials, supplemented by wood and natural fibers such as straw. Important buildings boasted elaborate painted murals and stone carvings; ornamentation and color were important themes.

European tastes and techniques have influenced Mexico's architecture since the 16th century, when the Spanish conquistadors employed indigenous slaves to build palaces and churches from the stones of ruined temples. European images quickly replaced those of the indigenous peoples; paintings of warriors in feathered headdresses disappeared and instead conquerors in helmets stood out on walls and in bold relief on carved stone pillars. Fragments of ancient carvings can, however, still be seen in the walls of churches and city halls from Mexico City to Mérida.

The Spaniards concentrated their construction efforts in populated areas where labor was easy to exploit. Churches and monasteries were among the earliest colonial-era structures, designed in the prevailing European styles. Many of the finest cathedrals were built over several centuries and consist of baroque, Gothic, and plateresque (richly ornamented, suggesting silverware) elements with Mexican influences. Flying buttresses, gargoyles, stained glass, and wooden ceilings carved in the Mudejar style (a blending of Spanish and Arabic artistic elements) were all used in the more ornate cathedrals. In the 17th century, facades were covered with decorative high-relief carvings and multiple religious statues characteristic of the Churrigueresque style (Spanish baroque, named after Spanish architect Benito Churriguera). Moorish-style domes were covered with tiles from Puebla in the 18th century. A flurry of construction in the neoclassical style took place in the late 18th and early 19th centuries, until the War for Independence brought a halt to building.

Some of the first colonial-era residences were monasteries and convents, with cavernous domed-ceiling rooms and elaborately tiled kitchens. European architects and engineers designed palaces for the elite, with multiple patios framed by one- or two-story wings. A similar pattern emerged at haciendas from the Yucatán to Chihuahua. Mexico's colonial-era buildings have survived earthquakes, floods, and gun battles; entire colonial cities, such as San Miguel de Allende, in Guanajuato, are now considered national historic treasures by UNESCO. Several massive monasteries have been restored in Querétaro and Oaxaca, and some of the Yucatán Peninsula's finest haciendas now house first-class hotels.

Modern Mexican architecture incorporates design elements introduced by pre-Hispanic, colonial, and Mexican builders. Office towers, government buildings, and resort hotels mimic the pyramids of Teotihuacán and Chichén Itzá; tiles such as those seen covering

A dancer at a Virgin of Guadalupe feast day celebration (December 12) sports an ornate headdress.

17th- and 18th-century buildings in Puebla appear in modern stairways, bathrooms, and kitchens. Craftsmen in Guanajuato have become famous for their *bóvedas,* domed ceilings made entirely of brick.

The first significant skyscraper in Mexico City was designed by Leonardo Zeevaert and erected in 1956 near the frothy art nouveau

Bright colors mark Ricardo Legorreta's Camino Real Hotel, Mexico City.

Palacio de Bellas Artes. The sleek glass Torre Latinoamerica is surrounded by traditional colonial structures, including the exuberantly Churrigueresque Iglesia de San Francisco (1524) and the Casa de los Azulejos, which was built in 1596 and completely covered in handpainted tiles in 1737.

Juxtapositions of old and new styles can be seen in the work of architect Pedro Ramírez Vázquez, who designed the Museo Nacional de Antropología, in Chapultepec Park. With a layout similar to that of an ancient Aztec city, stately buildings face a central patio dominated by an enormous open shelter of carved stone and aluminum. Similar use of natural

and fabricated elements are characteristic of the sleek structures of German-born Mathias Goeritz, who immigrated during the rise of Nazism and taught at both the University of Guadalajara and UNAM, the National Autonomous University, in Mexico City. But far and away the most influential architect of the 20th century was Luis Barragán (1902–1988). His use of clean lines and vivid colors in monumental structures emphasized the importance of the natural elements, including sunlight, in the overall architectural design.

Of the many architects to follow in Barragán's footsteps, one of the most prolific and highly successful is Ricardo Legorreta (1931–). Like that of his friend and predecessor Barragán, Legorreta's innovative style combines massive plain walls painted vivid colors to reflect the movement of light. Collaboration between these two greats produced the Camino Real hotel in Mexico City, with walls and niches painted hot pink, marigold yellow, and deep lavender. This achievement led to many commissions for Legorreta, who is considered one of today's top architects, and who has designed more than a hundred buildings in Mexico and abroad.

The use of brilliant color is, in fact, one of the defining elements of the Mexican aesthetic sense. Plain adobe or stucco structures are painted cobalt blue with marigold trim, lime green, canary yellow, or *rosa mexicano*—a deep pink. Advertisements, public service messages, and campaign slogans in bright colors compete for attention on the facades of homes and businesses, retaining walls, and any other available surface.

ART
Mexico's artistic heritage far predates the European invasion. In 790, Maya artists covered the walls of the Temple of the Paintings at Bonampak, in southeast Chiapas, with murals depicting fierce battles and harmonious tableaux of the royal family. Olmec sculptors carved gigantic round heads in basalt around 1150 B.C., and some of the cave paintings found in Baja California are believed to be 5,000 years old.

But the arrival of Spanish conquistadors drastically changed Mesoamerican art. The Catholic Church became the dominant force in everyday life. Saints and Virgins replaced pantheistic gods and goddesses, and Indian artists were made to paint and sculpt foreign images. European artists and artisans began arriving in New Spain soon after the conquerors, and their indigenous apprentices learned to paint biblical scenes on magnificent *retablos*, the ornate, gilded altarpieces that adorned colonial churches. Sixteenth-century religious art replaced the murals and serpentine sculptures, though Indian artists never completely ignored their origins. Angels drifting through murals sometimes show Maya, Mixtec, and Zapotec features; scrollwork incorporates ancient symbols for wind and fire. The finest Mexican painters were sent to study in Seville and Florence, and Mexican viceregal art retained a primarily Eurocentric tone.

As *criollo* and mestizo artists emerged in the 17th century, Mexican art began to take on a distinct flavor. The dark-skinned Virgin of Guadalupe, who purportedly appeared in 1531 to the Indian convert Juan Diego, was a purely Mexican creation whose image spread throughout the country. Mexicans looked back to indigenous history for inspiration, and painters began portraying scenes depicting Spanish and Aztec warriors in battle.

Mexico's first formal art school, the Real Academia de las Bellas Artes de México, was established in Mexico City in 1731, and European sculptors and painters were commissioned to instruct Mexican artists. Art was superseded by war during the early 19th century as Mexicans battled for independence, though a few of the country's most famous artists and sculptors emerged in the midst of conflict. The portraits of José María Estrada (1830–1862) and landscape paintings of José María Velasco (1840–1912) are cited in particular as evidence of an established Mexican art scene in the 1800s. Velasco is considered the master of 19th-century academic painting; he specialized in landscapes, skillfully depicting the lakes and volcanoes in the Valley of Mexico and the candelabra cactus of Oaxaca. Several of his finest works can be seen at the Museo Nacional de Arte in Mexico City (see p. 190).

The early 20th century was Mexico's belle époque—at least for the wealthy. Under the dictatorship of General Porfirio Díaz (see pp. 33–34), who idolized all things European, Mexicans schooled in European styles and fashions began to celebrate an emerging sense of identity. While still heavily influenced by European training, Mexican artists used their exposure to impressionism, symbolism, and art nouveau styles to embrace Mexican themes. Young artists focused on the iniquities

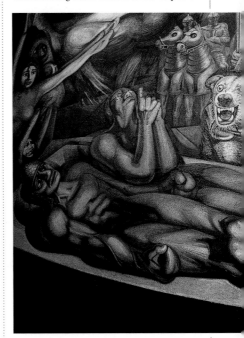

David Alfaro Siqueiros's mural "Torture of Cuauhtémoc" is on display at Mexico City's Palacio de Bellas Artes.

of the dictatorship, and demanded a revitalization of Mexican culture. Gerardo Murillo (1875–1964), one of the most influential painters and intellectuals of the era, protested the European influences in Mexico by changing his surname to Atl, which in the Náhuatl language of the Aztecs means "water." Dr. Atl's work consists mainly of landscape paintings; his view of volcanoes serves as the design for the glass and metal curtain at the Palacio de Bellas Artes (see p. 190).

Many of Mexico's most famous 20th-century artists studied under Dr. Atl, who was as much a spiritual leader as a teacher of art.

He first proposed the idea of covering public buildings with murals by Mexican artists in the early 1900s; the Revolution of 1910 put his plans on hold.

This episode in history solidified the young artists' passion for their country and their desire to create truly Mexican works of art. In 1921, Education Minister José Vasconcelos asked Atl to paint murals (now destroyed) at the Escuela Nacional Preparatoria (National Preparatory School). In 1922, Vasconcelos initiated the muralist movement, which took dominated the art scene for nearly 50 years. Atl's students, including Diego Rivera (1886–1957) and José Clemente Orozco (1883–1949), began tracing the entire history of Mexico on the walls of the country's most significant buildings, incorporating

pre-Hispanic themes, the Conquest, and the Revolution into massive storyboards.

The muralists quickly became Mexico's most famous artists, and politics their favorite theme. "We repudiate so-called easel-painting," David Alfaro Siqueiros (1896–1974) declared in 1922. "Art should no longer be the expression of individual satisfaction, which it is today, but should aim to become a fighting, educative art for all." The most famous muralists painted on canvas as well as walls, but even then they seemed captivated by the tragedies they witnessed or heard about during the Revolution. After training in Europe, painter Francisco Goita (1882–1980) joined Pancho Villa's army as an artistic chronicler of the struggle for freedom and equality. His paintings are gruesome reminders of war.

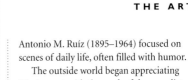

Antonio M. Ruíz (1895–1964) focused on scenes of daily life, often filled with humor.

The outside world began appreciating Mexican art with the work of the muralists, who became virtual folk heroes and spokespersons for their country. Orozco, Siquieros, and Rivera all created murals in the United States. Miguel Covarrubias (1904–1957), who contributed to some of Mexico City's most famous murals, worked as an illustrator and cartoonist for the *New Yorker* and *Vanity Fair* in the 1920s and '30s. Rufino Tamayo (1899–1991), one of a small group of painters who preferred to create modern art rather than focus on politics, spent much of his life in New York City.

Today, Mexico has a thriving art scene, as shown by the multitude of galleries and art schools in Mexico City, Oaxaca, San Miguel de Allende, and other centers. Cutting-edge art is displayed at Mexico City's Museo José Luis Cuevas, where a few Picassos and the works of other contemporary artists are displayed with Cuevas's erotic sculptures (see p. 210).

FOLK ART

Weavers, potters, woodcarvers, and glass-blowers all feel at home in Mexico, where everyday items are often simple works of art. Early Mesoamerican civilizations created decorated clay water vessels; the Mixtecs crafted fabulous jade and gold pendants and other jewelry—some of the finest in the world at their time. Indigenous artisans quickly learned European techniques after the Conquest, and a new form of folk art emerged from the blend of natural materials, native talents, and foreign influences. Today, popular art is one of Mexico's richest treasures, and craftsmen and women are among its most famous artists.

Mexican folk art is both functional and fanciful, and often reflects patterns and themes handed down for centuries. Weavers in Oaxaca incorporate the highly stylized fret designs from the ruins of Mitla in their woolen rugs. Huichol Indians in Nayarit painstakingly reproduce ancient symbols of lizards and snakes in beaded ceremonial bowls and in shoulder bags. Enterprising craftsmen and women throughout the country create inexpensive paintings in Day-Glo colors on

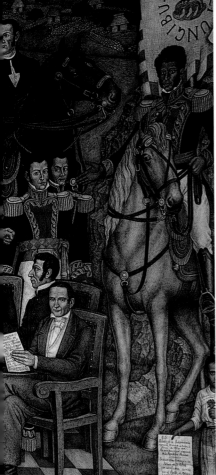

Architect Juan O'Gorman's "The Independence Mural" combines cultural commentary and superb craftsmanship.

Mexico's 20th-century artists were devoted to the concept of *mexicanidad,* the celebration of their native origins, natural surroundings, and cultural quirks. Much of their work was violent, inflammatory, and highly emotional, but even the most political artists paused from time to time to depict the beauty in their surroundings. Diego Rivera's paintings of tortillamakers and flower sellers portray Mexico's indigenous peoples with beauty and dignity. Rivera's wife, artist Frida Kahlo (1907–1954), known for her anguished self-portraits, often dressed in the gorgeous indigenous costumes of the Tehuana women of Oaxaca. The lesser-known painter paper made from the amate tree, used since pre-Hispanic times to make ledgers and important books.

Religious themes appear in all forms, from painted tin portraits of the Virgin of Guadalupe to handpainted tile groupings of the Stations of the Cross. Nativity scenes, called *nacimientos,* are created from almost

Oaxaca state is rich in crafts, including embroidered clothing, jewelry, and many styles of pottery.

any material, from fragile blown glass to woven straw. The Mexican fascination with all things macabre emerges in multiple forms, from miniature dioramas of skeletons at play to papier-mâché *judases*—garish, larger-than-life-size devils and other characters used in Semana Santa (Holy Week) processions.

Every imaginable material may become art in the hands of a Mexican artisan. In Oaxaca, a whole celebration is devoted to carved radishes. The earth itself has always been a source of inspiration; museums throughout the country are filled with clay vessels and figurines created by the Olmec, Maya, Mixtec,

and Aztec cultures. Pottery is one of Mexico's oldest art forms, and one of its most popular.

Clay is molded and fired into imaginative shapes. The Lancandón Indians in remote Chiapas model red clay into crocodiles and birds; Nahua Indians in Guerrero create water vessels with human shapes. Certain regions are known for their exquisite, fragile pieces. Mata Ortíz pottery, from the Casas Grandes region in Chihuahua, is treasured by knowledgeable collectors, as is the glossy black pottery from San Bartolo Coyotopec, Oaxaca.

The Spanish conquistadors were responsible for some of Mexico's finest ceramics. With very few exceptions, pre-Hispanic potters were unfamiliar with glazing, and the Spaniards imported artisans from their homeland to create fine majolica tiles and tableware. These artists set to work in Puebla, where they created delicate blue-and-white talavera pieces (so named because they resembled the pottery from the town of Talavera de la Reina in Spain). While native artisans added more color, classic talavera designs remained popular, and the majolica technique is still used today to create handpainted vases, dishes, jars, and tiles in the states of Puebla, Michoacán, Guanajuato, and Jalisco.

Clay is often the favored medium for musical instruments, toys, dolls, and fantastical figurines. Nearly every early civilization played clay flutes and whistles. Modern artisans let their imaginations soar, creating elaborate scenes of vividly colored miniature figures in ridiculous tableaux. Adam and Eve, the Virgin of Guadalupe, angels, devils, and regular human beings are portrayed in realistic and absurd situations. Some dioramas are as tiny as matchboxes; others as large as a young child. Some of the best painted-clay artists work in Michoacán and Puebla. Potters in Oaxaca make life-size terra-cotta dolls called *muñecas bordadas;* some in Toluca and Puebla specialize in enormous polychromed tree of life figurines stacked with tiny figures and symbols.

Playfulness exerts itself in woodcarving as well. Dragon-like *alejibres* carved from soft wood and painted in almost garish yellows and pinks started appearing in Oaxaca in the 1980s, along with more lifelike animal characters called *animalitos.* The most elaborate creations now command hundreds of dollars in upscale galleries. Primitive wooden dolls are common among most indigenous groups. The Tarahumara of the Copper Canyon fashion them wearing typical white shirts and pants, while artists in Chiapas have created an entire industry in wood dolls wearing wool cloaks and ski masks like Zapatista rebels.

Wood is frequently employed to create masks, which have been used in religious ceremonies since pre-Hispanic times. The mask makers of Guerrero, Tlaxcala, Morelia, Chiapas, and Oaxaca are especially talented and prolific. Used in folk dances and religious processions, their masks represent saints and demons, poets and politicians, animals and pink-cheeked conquistadors. Some even have realistic glass eyes that open and shut at the tug of a string.

Glass beads were the first gifts and objects of barter of the Spanish, who later introduced glass blowing to native artisans. Exceptional hand-blown glassware and miniatures are today produced in small family workshops as well as large factories, especially in the states of Puebla and Mexico, and around Guadalajara, Jalisco.

Chiapas is home to brilliantly woven and embroidered *huipiles* (blouses) covered with Maya designs. The residents of indigenous villages throughout the state shun modern fashion in favor of woolen ponchos and cotton huipiles covered with vivid embroidered designs. The intricate patterns represent Maya legends and lore. Villagers are identified by their dress, be it the distinctive blue shawls of San Juan Chamula or the beribboned hats worn for special ceremonies in Zinacantán. Villagers in some parts of Oaxaca still wear indigenous dress and create shawls, belts, huipiles, and blouses that are true works of Mexican art.

Religious themes play an important role in Mexican folk art. Many of the masks and costumes used in regional dances represent saints and sinners. Small paintings on metal, called ex-votos, are used to express gratitude for a religious figure's assistance in solving some problem. Ex-votos first appeared in the late 18th century and picture the devotee in pain or injury praying to a saint or to the

Virgin or Jesus Christ. The story of the miraculous cure or resolution to a problem is detailed in script below the scene. A chapel at the Basílica de Guadalupe in Mexico City is filled with ex-votos praising the Mexican saint.

Milagros—small tin, silver, or occasionally gold charms shaped as various body parts, houses, cows, or cars—are also used as pleas

Skeletons, like this one of papier-mâché, pervade Mexican folk art and feature widely in Day of the Dead celebrations.

for divine intercession. Penitents pin these charms to the robes of statues of favorite saints and pray for relief from pain or the miraculous appearance of a cow or a new car. In recent years, some artists have incorporated milagros into jewelry, creating silver chains draped with tiny hearts, legs, and heads.

Mexico's silver tradition began with the Mixtecs: formidable pre-Hispanic metalsmiths whose gold and silver jewelry adorned the ruling elite. During the colonial period, huge quantities of gold and silver were used in the interior decoration of Catholic churches and in religious artifacts. Silver and other precious

metals are still mined, and modern artisans take inspiration from traditions both old and new to produce jewelry and other handicrafts, mainly of silver. Much of it comes from Taxco, Guerrero—an entire city dedicated to silversmithing.

Printmaking became a popular means of expression in the late 19th century under the hand of José Guadalupe Posada (1852–1913), long considered Mexico's greatest lithographer. Posadas's engravings and etchings in metal

and wood were used to print broadsheets distributed by street vendors. His highly detailed etchings depicted crooked politicians with wickedly humorous skeletal bodies and skulls.

A whole genre of broadsheets called *calaveras* (skulls) was created for Day of the Dead celebrations. They satirized everyone and everything with mocking verse and illustrations. Originally created for the masses, Posadas's broadsheets and calaveras caught the attention of artists of the early 20th century.

Some nearly deified him as the originator of a truly Mexican art movement. His calaveras certainly provided inspiration to future artists and have become synonymous with modern Day of the Dead celebrations.

Papier-mâché is one of the most popular mediums in Mexican folk art and is used for everything from masks to the ubiquitous *piñatas*. The Linares family of Mexico City is famous for its papier-mâché skeletons, skulls, dragons, and life-size devils. Glamorous

Mariachis in Plaza de Garibaldi, Mexico City

papier-mâché dolls from Guanajuato wear exaggerated makeup and glittery jewelry.

Everything from gold to gourds is used to create art in Mexico. Collectors crave items as simple as a wooden spoon and as intricate as a beaded mask. Certain parts of the country—especially Oaxaca, Chiapas, and Michoacán—are veritable living museums with markets that feel like galleries.

MUSIC

Every Mexican is a musician in his or her soul. As the saying goes, *"También de dolor se canta cuando llorar no se puede."* ("Sorrow also sings, when it runs too deep to cry.")

The most famous and familiar tunes are the *rancheras,* typically played and sung by mariachi musicians with violins, trumpets, and a variety of guitar-like instruments. Some of these songs of lost loves and defeat date back to the Mexican Revolution, when roving musicians carried the ballads of the war-torn northern regions to Mexico City. The *charro* (Mexican cowboy) movies of the 1930s and '40s spread ranchera music throughout the country, and the composer José Alfredo Jiménez added dozens of new songs to the mariachi repertoire.

Until the rise of mariachis and rancheras, most Mexican music was regional, based on indigenous and religious traditions. The advent of radio, film, and television spread mariachi music around the country, until it became a national emblem. The popularity of regional music grew as well, and Mexicans came to appreciate the marimbas of Chiapas and the romantic boleros of composer Agustín Lara, who added the sensual rhythms of Veracruz.

Soulful, passionate ballads are at the core of most of the music played in Mexico. Singers stand out for their ability to evoke all the emotions of even the most common tunes such as "Cielito Lindo" ("Beautiful Little Sky") and "La Paloma" ("The Dove"). Lola Beltrán's passionate singing made her the long-reigning queen of rancheras from the 1950s, while María Félix carried the romantic lyrics of tropical ballads to the sands of Acapulco in the 1940s, captivating the international artsy set with the rhythms of Mexico. Today's balladeers, including Juan Gabriel, Luis Miguel, and Alejandro Fernández, rely on old favorites to enhance their modern repertoires and bring cheers from their fans.

Romance and loss still inspire Mexico's modern musicians, even the wildest members of the latest musical craze—*rock en español.* Mexico's rock 'n' rollers still love a good heartbreaker but also move forward by combining traditional instruments, electronics, and political themes. Carlos Santana,

raised near the border in Tijuana, was the first breakthrough artist to bring Mexican influences into the international mainstream. Others have risen to superstardom and garnered fanatical followings both within Mexico and beyond in the process. The pop-rock group Maná and alternative rock band Café Tacuba are well-known outside Mexico, and new sounds are emerging from a burgeoning underground music scene.

Each part of the country has a particular sound. *Norteño* bands combine accordion, bass, and guitar with polka and ranchera melodies to create a rousing country and western sound popular in the northern regions of Mexico. The lyrics often touch on themes of immigration and national politics. *Cumbia,* salsa, and marimba music, with a tropical

beat, bring dancers to their feet in Veracruz, home of the overplayed "La Bamba." The brassy *banda*, or band music, of Sinaloa has a German undertone, which was contributed by immigrants in the 1920s. Familiar and unusual sounds travel the air waves all over the country. And everywhere, people are singing.

DANCE
Dance in Mexico dates back to Indian cultures and forward beyond "La Macarena." Catholic ritual and indigenous tradition have fused to create dances such as those celebrated during the Easter season by the Yaqui and Maya of Sonora. Deer masks and flowers are elements that remain from an important pre-Hispanic ritual asking that the deer sacrifice itself for the good of the people. Today, deer-

Veracruz's famous Carnaval always features a brass band.

dancers join with others representing Jesus and the Marys to defend the Church from evil men (represented by the Pharisees) in elaborate dances that are held throughout the land.

Ballet folklórico dance groups abound in all parts of the country; some of the finest appear in the most popular tourist destinations. Young children perform in central plazas large and small, and grow up to compete for spots in professional troupes. The reigning favorite is ruled by Amalia Hernández at Mexico City's Palacio de Bellas Artes; watching the theater's Tiffany curtain rise to reveal gorgeously costumed dancers is a necessary ritual for any fan of Mexican dance.

Traditional folkloric dancing began in the 1800s, combining pre-Hispanic, Spanish, and mestizo steps and themes. Regional dances echo the music of immigrants and the rhythms of nature. In San Luis Potosí, dancers perform the *huapango,* similar to the Spanish fandango. In Veracruz, couples dance the disciplined *danzón,* which originated in Cuba. Veracruzanos are also fond of salsa, cumbia, and any dance with a tropical Caribbean beat. Even the most famous of all Mexican dances, *el jarabe tapatío* (the Mexican hat dance), originated among mestizos.

The states of Oaxaca, Michoacán, Yucatán, Jalisco, Chiapas, and Veracruz are renowned for their numerous folk dances. In Oaxaca, dancers from throughout the state perform at the annual Guelaguetza, a two-week-long celebration of ethnic heritage held in July. The costumes for dances from Oaxaca and Chiapas are among the most gorgeous imaginable and are works of art that enhance the beauty of the movements and of the wearers. The *jaranas* of Yucatán are performed every Sunday at the *zócalo* in Mérida. The Dance of the Old Men (*Danza de los Viejitos*), which originated in Michoacán, provides the humorous interlude in performances around the country. Less familiar dances are performed during religious holidays, especially around Semana Santa (Holy Week). The Cora Indians of Nayarit dance in hallucinogenic agitation for days on end, while the Tarahumara of the Copper Canyon engage in tumultuous, eerie mock battles between soldiers and the Pharisees.

Dancing is part of all celebrations, from birthday parties to formal fiestas. Mexicans of all ages show up at dance halls and clubs to waltz, dance salsa and merengue, or move to the beat of *rock en español.* Mexican discos are typically elegant places, where clients dress to impress and dance till dawn.

LITERATURE

Mexico's first books were codices, made of bark paper and animal skin and filled with paintings and symbols. The Maya were particularly prolific and created two of pre-Hispanic Mexico's most important books, along with several codices relating historical events. The *Popol Vuh,* written between 1554 and 1558, is an epic account of supernatural legend and

Many young men and women practice folk dancing, like those in this University of Guadalajara troupe.

lore, while the *Chilam Balam,* written during the 17th and 18th centuries, offers a more realistic account of astronomical observations and historic events. Numerous books in the Náhuatl and Mixtec languages have also remained intact, as have many more stone and stucco carvings relating stories of battle, birth, death, and royal succession.

Although some Spaniards worked to preserve native books and writings, others were appallingly successful in their post-Conquest campaign to destroy documents they considered works of Satan. One of the most important records of the Conquest itself

is *La Historia Verdadera de la Conquista de la Nueva España (True History of the Conquest of New Spain)* by Bernal Díaz del Castillo (ca 1492–1581), a conquistador who later in life related the events of the Conquest with startling clarity.

As might be expected, the ruling Spaniards stuck to European and religious themes in poetry, theater, and literature. The first printing press, which arrived in Mexico in 1537, was used primarily to disseminate information about science, nature, and the country's settlement. A Mexican style of literature began emerging in the 16th century, as mestizos and *criollos* began drawing on indigenous themes. The most famous writer of the colonial era was Sor Juana Inés de la Cruz (1651–1695), a nun and prolific poet. Her theme was frequently

the plight of the citizens of New Spain, who suffered under Spanish restraints as Mexico's wealth was plundered for the motherland. In one of her most famous poems she wrote:

Señora, I was born in the land of plenty…
to no other land on Earth is Mother Nature
    so generous.
Europe knows this best of all
for this many years, insatiable,
She has bled the abundant veins
of America's rich mines.

Newspapers began to appear in the early 1800s, as did the first novel expressing Mexican sentiments—*El Periquillo Sarniento (The Itching Parrot)*, by José Joaquin Fernández de Lizardi (1776–1827). The printed word was largely used to further political campaigns and social causes in the 19th century, though a few writers created novels with Mexican themes. Francisco I. Madero (who later became Mexico's president) wrote one of the first significant pieces of political nonfiction. His *The Presidential Succession of 1910* was instrumental in the downfall of Porfirio Díaz.

Of all the literature produced in the 20th century, *El Laberinto de la Soledad (The Labyrinth of Solitude),* published in 1950, stands out as the definitive portrait of the Mexican psyche. Author and Nobel laureate Octavio Paz (1914–1998) attempted to analyze and describe the character of his countrymen and capture the essence of *mexicanidad.* Though controversial, his book is considered a masterpiece, and Paz was revered as the elder statesman of Mexican writers. Carlos Fuentes, author of *La Región más Transparente (Where the Air is Clear)* and the *El Gringo Viejo (The Old Gringo),* is another modern master.

Statesman and author Carlos Fuentes

FILM

Mexico's earliest films helped popularize mariachi music and the lifestyle of the northern Mexico cowboys. Pancho Villa's exploits were a popular theme, as were the trials and tribulations of urban families. They united Mexicans unaccustomed to the music and culture of distant regions, and by the 1930s Mexican film was receiving worldwide attention.

Mexican filmmakers and actors benefited from Hollywood's fascination with Mexico's topography. Many early U.S. Westerns were filmed in northern Mexico, and Hollywood stars frequented the resorts of Acapulco in the 1940s. Dolores del Río (1905–1983), who regularly partied with the Hollywood elite on Caleta Beach, was beginning to gain fame outside Mexico when she caught the eye of the international press at the 1946 Cannes Film Festival. As the star of *María Candelaria* (1944), the hit film directed by Emilio Fernández (1904–1986), Del Río helped popularize Mexican cinema, as did Mario Moreno (1911–1993), better known as Cantinflas, "the Charlie Chaplin of Mexico," and Germán Valdés (also known as Tin Tan). Actress María Félix and actors Jorge Negrete and Pedro Infante were idolized by fans in the forties. Films including *Enamorada* (directed by Fernández) and *Distinto Amanecer* (Julio Bracho) became instant classics. Mexico's most famous director of the 1950s, Luis Buñuel (1900–1983), was a Spaniard who fled his country during the Civil War. His *Los Olvidados* (1950) is another Mexican masterpiece.

A flurry of schlock horror films drew a loyal following in the 1950s and 1960s. Many were heavy-handed remakes of Mexican originals. One of these was Jerry Warren's 1963 *Attack of the Mayan Mummy,* adapted from the 1957 Mexican film *La Momia Azteca.* The greatest cult film of all appeared in 1970, when Alejandro Jodorowsky came out with *El Topo,* a violent hodgepodge of surrealism and Western cowboy images. More serious themes emerged in the 1980s. Director Gregory Nava delved into the miseries of illegal immigration in the acclaimed 1983 film *El Norte* (1984). Roberto Rodríguez portrayed modern northern Mexico in his 1993 *El Mariachi* and again in 1995 with *Desperado,* starring Antonio Banderas.

The most famous film to come out of Mexico in the 1990s was *Like Water for Chocolate (Como Agua Para Chocolate),* the soulful interpretation of Laura Esquivel's best-selling novel directed by husband Alfonso Arau. Today, Mexican filmmakers compete for funding, awards, and attention with their peers around the world, and Mexican actors are gaining fame in their own country. ∎

An isolated, jagged finger of mountains and desert between the Pacific Ocean and the Sea of Cortés, Baja California was once Mexico's forgotten peninsula. Today it contains the country's fastest-growing tourist destination.

Baja California

Barnacle-encrusted gray whale

Baja California

THOUGH SUPERFICIALLY BARREN AND DESOLATE, THE BAJA CALIFORNIA peninsula has long entranced scientists and adventurers. The author John Steinbeck (1902–1968) explored the coast of Baja around 1940 and wrote in his *The Log from the Sea of Cortez:* "The very air here is miraculous, and outlines of reality change with the moments. A dream hangs over the entire region." A similar feeling inspires a more modern cadre of adventurers, dedicated to exploring every crevice and cove of Baja.

Long and lean, the Baja California peninsula gradually separated from the mainland five million years ago along the San Andreas Fault, bringing with it a series of mountain ranges. At its widest, it stretches just 120 miles (193 km) along the U.S. border. The bulk of Baja's tourists visit the Tijuana–Ensenada corridor or the resorts at Los Cabos, 860 miles (1,300 km) to the south. Between the two lies the Baja of myth and mystery.

At least five indigenous groups were living in Baja when Padre Juan María Salvatierra established the mission church in Loreto in 1697. As missionaries and European adventurers made their way up the peninsula, the native population was decimated by battles or disease. Only about a thousand indigenous people now live in Baja, some following their forefathers' traditions in remote communities.

Baja's two coastlines attract fishermen, surfers, divers, and sailors craving extremes. The Pacific side is renowned for its awesome waves, massive billfish, and migrating whales; the Gulf of California (also called the Sea of Cortés) is a biologist's dream. Here, thousands of species of marine creatures flourish in protected coves and open waters. Nearly every environmental group in the world has an interest in protecting the Gulf of California from commercial fishing and any development that threatens its natural balance.

Despite the harshness of Baja's terrain, its plant and animal life is surprisingly abundant and varied. Stately cardón cacti, bizarre

Baja's desert wilderness offers plenty of solitude for those seeking to get away from it all.

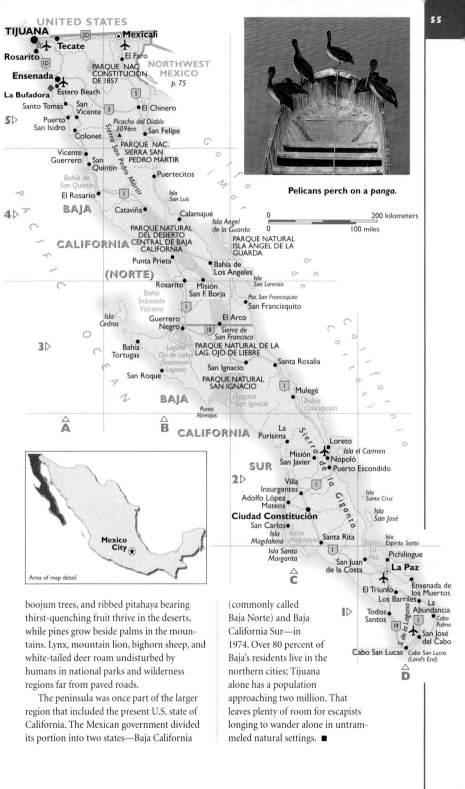

TIJUANA

Rosarito

Ensenada

La Bufadora

Santo Tomás

Puerto
San Isidro

Tecate

Mexicali

El Faro

PARQUE NAC.
CONSTITUCIÓN
DE 1857

Estero Beach

San
Vicente

Colonet

NORTHWEST
MEXICO
p. 75

El Chinero

Picacho del Diablo
3096m

San Felipe

Vicente
Guerrero

San
Quintín

PARQUE NAC.
SIERRA SAN
PEDRO MÁRTIR

Puertecitos

*Bahía de
San Quintín*

El Rosario

BAJA

Cataviña

Calamajué

Isla
San Luis

Isla Angel
de la Guarda

Punta Prieta

PARQUE NATURAL
DEL DESIERTO
CENTRAL DE BAJA
CALIFORNIA

PARQUE NATURAL
ISLA ANGEL DE LA
GUARDA

CALIFORNIA

(NORTE)

Rosarito

Misión
San F. Borja

Bahía de
Los Angeles

Isla
San Lorenzo

*Bahía
Sebastián
Vizcaíno*

Guerrero
Negro

Pta. San Francisquito

San Francisquito

Isla
Cedros

El Arco

18

Sierra de
San Francisco

Bahía
Tortugas

*Laguna
Ojo de Liebre
(Scammon's
Lagoon)*

PARQUE NATURAL DE LA
LAG. OJO DE LIEBRE

Santa Rosalía

San Roque

San Ignacio

PARQUE NATURAL
SAN IGNACIO

Mulegé

*Laguna
San Ignacio*

*Bahía
Concepción*

BAJA

Punta
Abreojos

Pelicans perch on a *panga*.

0		200 kilometers
0		100 miles

CALIFORNIA

La
Purísima

Misión
San Javier

SUR

Loreto

Isla el Carmen

Nopoló

Puerto Escondido

Villa
Insurgentes

Adolfo López
Mateos

Ciudad Constitución

San Carlos

Isla
Magdalena

*Bahía
Magdalena*

Santa Rita

Isla
Santa
Margarita

Isla
Santa Cruz

Isla
San José

Isla
Espíritu Santo

*Bahía
La
Paz*

San Juan
de la Costa

Pichilingue

La Paz

El Triunfo

Los Barriles

Todos
Santos

19

Ensenada de
los Muertos

La
Abundancia

Cabo
Pulmo

San José
del Cabo

Cabo San Lucas

*Cabo San Lucas
(Land's End)*

**Mexico
City**

Area of map detail

boojum trees, and ribbed pitahaya bearing
thirst-quenching fruit thrive in the deserts,
while pines grow beside palms in the mountains. Lynx, mountain lion, bighorn sheep, and
white-tailed deer roam undisturbed by
humans in national parks and wilderness
regions far from paved roads.

The peninsula was once part of the larger
region that included the present U.S. state of
California. The Mexican government divided
its portion into two states—Baja California

(commonly called
Baja Norte) and Baja
California Sur—in
1974. Over 80 percent of
Baja's residents live in the
northern cities; Tijuana
alone has a population
approaching two million. That
leaves plenty of room for escapists
longing to wander alone in untrammeled natural settings. ■

Tijuana to Ensenada

Tijuana
🅰 55 A5
Visitor information
✉ Av. Revolución 711 at Calle 1
☎ 66/88-05-55

TIJUANA IS MEXICO'S FOURTH-LARGEST CITY; ENSENADA IS Baja California's largest port. In between, an ever multiplying number of hotels, businesses, and oceanfront rentals has grown steadily over the past few decades, engulfing once isolated fishing villages and resort hotels alike. But tourism to this region is not new. Since the days of U.S. Prohibition, Tijuana has been attracting day- and night-trippers with its dance halls and discos, raucous bars, and bullfights. South of town, beachfront hotels between Rosarito and Ensenada have long attracted Southern Californians for weekend getaways.

TIJUANA

Like most border towns, Tijuana is somewhere between here and there. For some, it's a shopping destination or a chance to get a

Tijuana's Centro Cultural houses the wonderful Museo de las Californias.

glimpse of Mexico while vacationing in Southern California. For others it's the gateway to adventure farther south.

Whatever their goal, many tourists see only Tijuana's legendary main street—engaging, overbearing **Avenida Revolución.** The shopping opportunities actually begin at the border, forming an unending corridor of *piñatas,* ceramic Day-Glo piggy banks, and unglazed clay pots. U.S.-style restaurants such as Sanborns and Caesar's (birthplace of the Caesar salad) make the uneasy visitor feel at home among the garish shops and strip joints.

At the **Plaza Monumental de Tijuana Bullring** *(Paseo Monumental s/n at Playas de Tijuana, tel 66/86-15-10)* sequined bullfighters the equal of any in Mexico divert 1,000-pound (450 kg) bulls with a flourish of their heavy silk capes.

East of downtown looms the **Centro Cultural Tijuana** *(Paseo de los Héroes at Mina, tel 66/87-96-00, $).* Housed in its futuristic-looking, dun-colored dome is the thousand-seat **Omnimax theater** *($).* The adjacent museum has a bookstore, restaurant, and two floors featuring fine arts and anthropology exhibits. The new **Museo de las Californias** *(Tel 66/87-96-41, closed Mon., $$)* displays about 500 pieces that highlight the peninsula's history, with items from mammoth tusks and mission replicas to 20th-century housewares and farm tools.

ROSARITO

Just 18 miles (29 km) south of Tijuana lies Rosarito. Today, this fast-growing city heads its own municipality boasting 20 miles (32 km) of coastline with fine beaches. As the Convention and Visitors Bureau brochure says, "Dollars are accepted everywhere. English is universally spoken." More than 500 shops, stores, and stalls cater to visitors (especially Southern Californians), selling glazed and

Rosarito
🅰 55 A5
Visitor information
✉ Blvd. Juárez at Oceana Plaza mall
☎ 661/20396

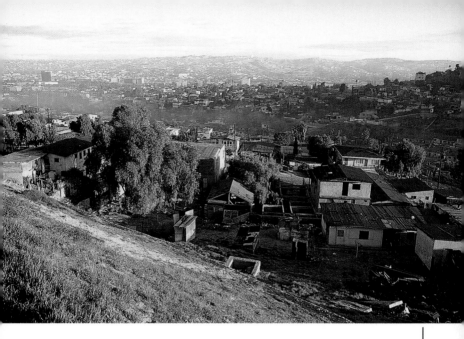

unglazed pottery, wrought-iron hardware, clunky handcarved wooden furniture, and handicrafts from throughout Mexico. Most shops are along busy **Boulevard Benito Juárez,** where you'll also find bars, hotels, and restaurants.

ENSENADA

About 18 miles (29 km) to the south of Rosarito, Ensenada hugs the northern end of long, well-protected **Bahía de Todos Santos,** discovered by Portuguese explorer Juan Cabrillo in 1542. After shipping, Ensenada's most important industries are fishing, agriculture (primarily olives and grapes), and tourism. Proximity to the U.S. border, an abundance of seafood restaurants, and plenty of watersports and fishing make this a favorite weekend getaway. And, of course, there's shopping, concentrated along busy **Avenida López Mateos,** where folk-art stores and hotels are interspersed with restaurants, bars, and cafés.

Horseback riding on Ensenada's wide beaches is popular, although the horses standing on the beach look rather miserable. Whale-watching excursions leave from the **Sportfishing Pier** *(Blvd. Costero near Av. Macheros)* from December to March. From the same pier, overnight fishing trips depart, netting bass, bonito, rockfish, and, occasionally, yellowtail. The best fishing is June through September.

South of Ensenada, a natural blowhole called **La Bufadora** shoots up jets of ocean water 80 feet (24 m) high. Below the waterspout, the rocky cove at **Punta Banda** is popular with divers, fishermen, and kayakers. Kayaks are more easily launched, however, at **Estero Beach,** an estuary halfway up the bay with boat ramps, sailboarding, and fishing.

Taste a local vintage at the **Bodega de Santo Tomás** *(Av. Miramar 666, tel 61/78-33-33),* a hundred-year-old winery with a small café, gallery, and bookstore. Tours are generally conducted Mon.–Fri. at 11 a.m., 1 p.m., and 3 p.m., Sat. and Sun. by appointment, but if possible call ahead to confirm times and to book a tour. ∎

Looking down on the border town of Tijuana, the fourth largest city in Mexico

Ensenada
🅰 55 A5
Visitor information
✉ Blvd. Costero at Blvd. J. Azueta 540 (at the northern entrance to town)
☎ 61/78-36-75

The towering peaks of Baja's Sierra de la Giganta, near Loreto

Baja Peninsula drive

Until 1974, mostly die-hard naturalists, explorers, and anglers bumped down rutted dirt and sand roads to the tip of the Baja Peninsula. Then the government paved Highway 1, opening Baja to a wider audience. Fortunately, the drive is still arduous enough to discourage crowds. The road meanders from the Pacific to the Gulf of California, passing by and through several mountain ranges. Gravel and dirt side roads lead to rocky coves, sandy beaches, and steep mountain peaks. Some off-road attractions are fairly accessible, while others require high-clearance and four-wheel-drive vehicles, and are reserved for the unique breed of adventurers who claim Baja as their own.

Angeles Verdes (Green Angels, see p. 350) patrol the highway to assist stranded travelers, and local mechanics are extraordinarily ingenious, but drivers should be prepared for heat, potholes, arroyos (watercourses), and wandering cows. Fuel up frequently, and always carry plenty of water, a jack and good spare tire, maps, and spare parts. Forget about speeding past the scenery—many of the crosses at the roadside mark the spot where incautious drivers have died. Instead, take the time to enjoy Baja's extraordinary landscape of cacti, canyons, mesas, and coves.

Hwy. 1 begins just after the San Ysidro border crossing (open 24 hours), connecting San Diego County with **Tijuana ❶** (see p. 56). Some travelers stop to shop and

sightsee in Tijuana; others head south to **Rosarito** (see pp. 56–57) and the shore break at **Cantamar.** Nearby **Puerto Nuevo** (also known as Newport)—once a clutch of friendly lobster shacks—now has three dozen restaurants specializing in lobster, refried beans, rice, and tortillas.

After the frequently congested stretch of Hwy. 1 from Tijuana to Ensenada, the true Baja experience begins. The road descends into the undulating wine country around **Santo Tomás,** then ascends a steep grade and evens out as it passes remote ranches and vineyards at **San Vicente.** Serious agriculture occupies the land around **Colonet, Camalú,** and **Vicente Guerrero.** Tomato fields run for miles, interspersed with clusters of makeshift huts that house field workers from mainland Mexico. Side roads lead from Colonet to the formidable peaks of the **Sierra San Pedro Mártir,** far out of sight to the east.

Restaurants (try the local pismo clams), grocery stores, hotels, and beaches make **San Quintín ❷,** 115 miles (185 km) south of Ensenada, a sensible place to break for lunch or the night. Asphalt and dirt streets lead to **Bahía de San Quintín** (79 miles/129 km south of Colonet), where a late 19th-century English wheat-farming venture quickly succumbed to drought. Remnants of the gristmill decorate the bar at the Old Mill Motel beside the bay, which is a popular spot for sportfishing.

Some of northern Baja's best beaches lie along the 36-mile (58 km) stretch of Hwy. 1 between San Quintín and **El Rosario,** which has grocery stores and a gas station. South of El Rosario, Hwy. 1 jogs abruptly east to enter Baja's eerie central desert. Most travelers stop to pose beside one of the many towering cardón cacti or wavy branched cirio trees. Some are tempted to camp beside the spooky, flat-topped mesas that would make ideal UFO landing strips. The mesas and low hills give way to fields of enormous boulders around **Cataviña.** A sign indicates the turnoff, 65 miles (105 km) south of Cataviña, to a rough paved road heading east to **Bahía de Los Angeles** (see p. 73). Later, other signs point to a further turnoff 32 miles (53 km) south at another **Rosarito,** where high-clearance vehicles can detour 22 miles (35 km) to **Misión San Francisco Borja** (see p. 73).

The next important stop is **Guerrero Negro,** 145 miles (234 km) south of Cataviña, at the Baja California Sur state line. Important as a supply stop but otherwise unexceptional, the bleak, windy town is headquarters for whale-watching expeditions (*Dec.–March;* see pp. 68–69). Nearby **Laguna Ojo de Liebre** (also known as Scammon's Lagoon) is a mating and birthing ground for gray whales and has a large salt-evaporation plant, which produces around a million tons of salt annually.

South of Guerrero Negro the highway cuts inland and up into the mountains for 88 miles (142 km) to **San Ignacio ❸,** a true

Sportfishing is big business up and down the length of the Baja Peninsula.

high-desert oasis (see p. 62). The highway swoops downhill, first touching the Gulf of California at **Santa Rosalía.** Short detours to the south bring you to **Caleta San Lucas,** a mangrove-lined cove with good snorkeling and fishing, and to **Bahía Santa Inés ❹,** where the long, eponymous bay provides great shelling, diving, fishing, and sailboarding.

A riverbed thick with lush palms marks the entrance to **Mulegé** (see p. 63), and it becomes increasingly difficult to keep your eyes on the road. Beautiful **Bahía de la Concepción ❺,** a narrow bay scalloped with coves containing clear, aquamarine water, appears like a glistening mirage. Take a break for a swim at **Coyote, Santispac,** or **Requesón Beaches** and join the campers and kayakers for a cool drink at one of the simple palm-thatched restaurants. The next stop along Hwy. 1 is **Loreto ❻** (see p. 63), 84 miles (136 km) south of Mulegé. **Misión San Javier** (see pp. 73–74), an hour inland up a passable dirt road, may well be Baja's most impressive historic church.

After Loreto, Hwy. 1 climbs into the rusty red **Sierra de la Giganta** in a series of switchbacks and hairpin turns to the Santo Domingo Valley, **Villa Insurgentes,** and

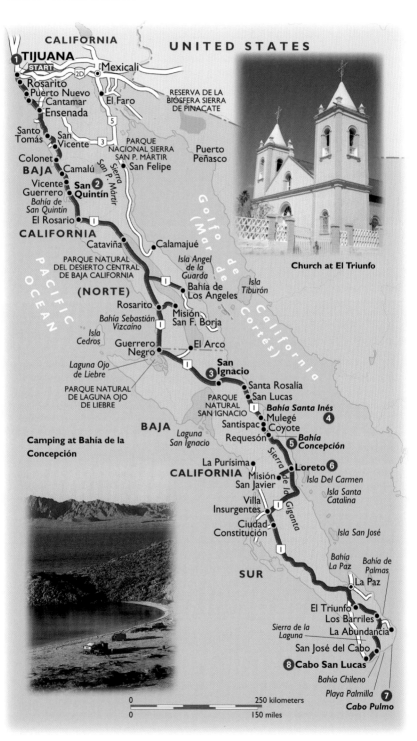

CALIFORNIA

UNITED STATES

1 **TIJUANA**
START
2D
Mexicali

Rosarito
Puerto Nuevo
Cantamar
Ensenada
El Faro

RESERVA DE LA
BIÓSFERA SIERRA
DE PINACATE

5

Santo
Tomás
San
Vicente
3

Colonet
Camalú
BAJA
Vicente
Guerrero
*Bahía de
San Quintín*
El Rosario

Sierra
San P. Mártir

PARQUE
NACIONAL SIERRA
SAN P. MÁRTIR
San Felipe

San 2 **Quintín**

Puerto
Peñasco

CALIFORNIA

Cataviña

Calamajué

PARQUE NATURAL
DEL DESIERTO CENTRAL
DE BAJA CALIFORNIA

*Isla Angel
de la
Guarda*

Isla
Tiburón

Church at El Triunfo

(NORTE)

Bahía de
Los Angeles

Rosarito

*Bahía Sebastián
Vizcaíno*
Misión
San F. Borja

*Isla
Cedros*

Guerrero
Negro
El Arco

*Laguna Ojo
de Liebre*

**San
3 Ignacio**

PARQUE NATURAL
DE LAGUNA OJO
DE LIEBRE

Santa Rosalía
San Lucas
Bahía Santa Inés 4

PARQUE
NATURAL
SAN IGNACIO

Mulegé
Coyote

BAJA

Santispac
*Laguna
San Ignacio*
Requesón
*Bahía
5 Concepción*

**Camping at Bahía de la
Concepción**

La Purísima
CALIFORNIA
Misión
San Javier

Loreto 6

Isla Del Carmen

*Isla Santa
Catalina*

Villa
Insurgentes

Isla San José

Ciudad
Constitución

Sierra de la Giganta

*Bahía
La Paz*

*Bahía de
Palmas*

SUR

La Paz

El Triunfo
Los Barriles
La Abundancia

*Sierra de la
Laguna*

San José del Cabo

8 **Cabo San Lucas**

Bahía Chileno

Playa Palmilla 7

Cabo Pulmo

PACIFIC OCEAN

Golfo de California (Mar de Cortés)

0   250 kilometers
0   150 miles

Mulegé, among Baja Sur's greenest oases, attracts many winter visitors.

Ciudad Constitución, Baja Sur's third largest town. Gas up, check the tires, and replenish your water supply here. Wheat, alfalfa, cotton, and corn farms nourished by water from deep wells are the only distractions during the next leg of the journey.

It's almost impossible to keep from speeding through the barren moonscape of dull desert during the 134 miles (216 km) between Constitución and **La Paz.** The road edges **Bahía La Paz** before entering Baja California Sur's busy state capital, a good place to pass the night (see pp. 66–67).

Passing forests of organ and cardón cacti, Hwy. 1 crosses the **Sierra de la Laguna**

- ⚑ See also area map p. 55 A5–D1
- ▶ Tijuana
- ⬌ About 1,125 miles (1,800 km)
- ⏲ 4 days to 2 weeks
- ▶ Cabo San Lucas

NOT TO BE MISSED
- San Ignacio
- Bahía de la Concepción
- Loreto
- Cabo Pulmo

range south of La Paz and travels through **El Triunfo,** a quirky old mining town. The Gulf of California beckons at **Los Barriles,** the entrance to the fast-growing **East Cape** region. Several remote fish camps and semi-luxurious hotels sit at the end of dirt roads throughout the area. Sailboarding is very popular at nearby **Bahía de Palmas,** while a detour 11 miles (17 km) south of Los Barriles accesses the East Cape beach road. The pavement ends at La Abundancia. After that, rough travel over washboard roads rewards with sugar-fine beaches dotted with strange rock formations. There's great fishing and reef diving at **Cabo Pulmo** ❼, an underwater preserve.

From Los Barriles, the road swings inland and widens into a four-lane, divided highway at the international airport serving Los Cabos. It passes **San José del Cabo** (see p. 71) and skirts the coast, passing surf spots at **Costa Azul** and **Acapulquito. Playa Palmilla** is particularly recommended for swimming, while **Bahía Chileno** and **Bahía Santa María** are perfect snorkeling and diving spots. The journey ends at **Cabo San Lucas** ❽ and Baja California's best-known rock: the natural arch at Land's End (see p. 72). ■

Local fishermen
ply the islands off
the coast of
Loreto.

San Ignacio to Loreto

AFTER CROSSING INTO BAJA SUR AT GUERRERO NEGRO,
Highway 1 heads east toward the Sea of Cortés. Ninety sun-baked
miles (145 km) later, the road meets spring-fed San Ignacio, the first
stop in a succession of historic towns. With its well-preserved mission
church poking above the date palms, San Ignacio offers a glimpse into
traditional Baja. Santa Rosalía presents a 19th-century mining town
hardly touched by modern trappings, while Mulegé and Loreto echo
mainland Mexican villages with their historic missions and plazas, and
the Gulf of California adds an element of adventure to central Baja.

San Ignacio
🗺 55 C3
**Visitor
information**
✉ Av. Hidalgo 5
☎ 115/40150

The sleepy mountain town of **San
Ignacio** greets the traveler like a
heat-induced mirage. Its Jesuit
founders planted date palms and
orange and fig trees at this desert
oasis, and Dominicans completed
the lava-stone **Iglesia de San
Ignacio de Loyola** adjacent to
the main plaza. Stop in for Sunday
Mass, or visit its small **museum**
(Closed Sun.). San Ignacio serves as
a base for whale-watching excursions to **Laguna San Ignacio**
(see p. 69), and backcountry treks
to prehistoric rock paintings (see
p. 65) in the mountains. Both can
be arranged in town or in advance.

Highway 1 first kisses the gulf
46 miles (74 km) southeast of San
Ignacio at **Santa Rosalía,** established by German copper-mining
entrepreneurs in the late 19th
century, then run by the French.
The cast-iron **Iglesia de Santa
Bárbara** *(Calle Obregón near the
plaza)* was designed by Gustave
Eiffel and shipped in pieces from
France. Arrow-straight streets lined
with wooden houses (built as
homes for miners from India and
China) give Santa Rosalía a
"company town" feel. The mine's
French managers lived on the mesa
north of town, overlooking railroad

tracks and the sea. Check out the view from the restored 19th-century **Hotel Francés** *(Av. 11 de Julio 15 at Jean M. Cousteau, Col. Mesa Francia, tel 115/22052).*

Despite its exotic origins, Santa Rosalía is rather unattractive, and most visitors move on after just a short visit. Small hotels serve travelers using the ferry between Santa Rosalía and mainland Guaymas.

Lush **Mulegé,** 38 miles (61 km) south of Santa Rosalía, attracts U.S. and Canadian snowbirds escaping the Northern winter and sports enthusiasts who revel in the town's slow pace, tourist facilities, and green river valley by the sea. Visitors trek into the surrounding mountains to see cave art at **San Borjitas, Trinidad,** or **Piedras Pintas,** or fish, kayak, snorkel, or sailboard along the rocky coast.

Mulegé is centered among orange trees and date palms; small hotels, adventure-tour companies, and restaurants cluster near the plaza. Established in 1705, damaged by a hurricane in 1770, and abandoned in 1828, the town's restored mission church **Santa Rosalía de Mulegé** lies south of the center on Calle Zaragoza. A former prison at the north end of town houses the **Museo de Mulegé** *(Closed Mon.),* with local memorabilia.

Tucked between the golden sierras and the languid Gulf of California, **Loreto** was once the religious and political center of the peninsula. Its **Misión Nuestra Señora de Loreto** *(Salvatierra, between Sears & Misioneros)* was built in 1687 and restored in the 1970s. Check out the gilded altar, a statue of the Virgin believed to perform miracles, and the museum.

Loreto was Baja's capital for a hundred years before a devastating 1829 hurricane. After that the seat of government was moved to La Paz, and Loreto drifted into obscu-

rity. In 1974 the Mexican government pegged the town as a major tourist destination and installed telephones, electricity, paved streets, and an international airport. Neighborhoods rose beside a resort hotel at **Bahía Nopoló;** an 18-hole golf course soon followed. Nearby **Puerto Escondido** got a new marina and an expanded RV park and hotel.

Today, few planes land at the airport and Loreto retains its provincial air. A handful of hotels and restaurants cater to Loreto's loyal followers and sightseers, who cherish its isolation. Rich feeding grounds around **Isla Coronado,** seahorse-shaped **Isla El Carmen,**

Loreto
⊠ 55 C2
Visitor information
✉ Palacio del Municipio, Plaza Cívica
☎ 113/50411

and tiny **Isla Danzante** lure fishermen to schools of dorado, tuna, roosterfish, and billfish, while snorkelers and divers swim with rays and tropical fish, and kayakers paddle around the islands. ∎

Our Lady of Loreto was the first California mission church, built in 1687.

Cave paintings of Baja California

Prehistoric mural paintings are found throughout central Baja California, most at an elevation of more than 1,000 feet (305 m). Some are on exposed rocks, while others crowd the walls and ceilings of caves both small and large. Red and black pigments were most commonly used, in addition to yellow, orange, pink, and white. Some images appear to have been sketched first in white chalk, charcoal, or paint. Favorite subjects were humans and deer (the latter often pierced with arrows), but artists depicted all the creatures that shared their world, including birds, reptiles, rabbits, squids, fish, turtles, whales, and manta rays.

Paintings found within each of the main mountain ranges exhibit a characteristic style. Human figures *(monos)* predominate in the Sierra de Guadalupe near San Ignacio. These are stiff, often bulb-shaped figures with vertical stripes and outstretched arms and legs. In the Sierra de San Borja, large, red figures were painted on huge granite boulders, while to the south, in the Sierra de San Juan and Sierra San Francisco, artists chose the walls and ceilings of caves up to 30 feet (9 m) high as their canvases. Figures from the San Francisco range tend to be red on one half, black on the other, with elaborate head gear.

North and south of this central region, other artistic innovations are seen. Figures in the south tend toward abstraction: Some are filled in with a checkerboard pattern. Northwest of San Borja, paintings tend to be

The walls of Cueva Pintada, Baja California Sur, are covered with depictions of fish, birds, and people (above), while the cave's overhang features huge, polychromatic designs (left).

of a more whimsical nature and employ a broader range of colors, including more pinks and yellows.

But who created these paintings, why, and when? Jesuit priests noted them in the 17th century. The priests' indigenous converts, the Cochimí, attributed the paintings to "giants from the north." Today, experts disagree as to the paintings' provenance, but radiocarbon tests from the Cueva del Ratón site in the San Francisco range date them at nearly 5,000 years old. (Previous estimates had set the newest paintings at 500 to 2,000 years old.) Scholars agree, however, that newer images are superimposed on older ones, indicating that the authors valued the act of creation more than the artistic result.

Several factors determine the quality of surviving paintings, including the rock surface's durability, location, and exposure to the elements. One of the most magnificent and often visited sites is Cueva Pintada, north of San Ignacio in the San Francisco range. Five hundred feet (150 m) of walls and ceilings are covered with paintings of men, women, birds, and sea creatures. How the artist reached the ceiling is not known, but palm trunks or the fibrous skeleton of the cardón cactus may have served as ladders or scaffolding.

UNESCO designated the Sierra de San Francisco and its cave paintings a World Heritage site in 1993, and government and private organizations are collaborating to preserve the sites, involve local communities, and make the art more accessible to visitors. Guided trips to the Sierra Santa Marta and Sierra San Francisco can be organized in San Ignacio, next door to the mission *(Tel 115/40222)*. The best (coolest) time to visit is between November and February. ∎

La Paz

DESPITE THE CITY'S FABULOUS LOCATION ON THE GULF OF California and its beautiful nearby beaches, La Paz's character is defined not by tourism but by its busy port and university. This capital city of fewer than 200,000 souls, seated at the bottom of a C-shaped bay, is sophisticated (by Baja standards), with visiting theater and symphonic groups and several worthwhile museums. It's famous for its streaky vermilion sunsets, observed equally well from a solitary, sandy beach on a turquoise inlet or an open-sided restaurant along the bayfront promenade. Nearby are excellent deep-sea fishing and the peninsula's best diving.

The Spanish briefly explored the area in the 16th century, for the most part leaving the cactus-strewn peninsula in peace until the founding of a Jesuit mission in 1720. In a sad irony, the mission was abandoned less than 30 years later, after introduced diseases such as smallpox wiped out almost all of the potential converts. Today a

The pearls

Inspired by tales of fierce, independent women to the west, Spanish conquistador Hernán Cortés led an expedition to the Baja Peninsula, which he presumed to be an island. The Spaniards named it California after an island in Garci Ordóñez de Montalvo's popular Spanish novel *Las Sergas de Esplandian (The Exploits of Esplandian)*, published in 1510. During his visit, Cortés is said to have obtained some of the area's precious white, pink, and black pearls from the island of Espíritu Santo. By the time author John Steinbeck published his allegorical novel about the misfortunes of a poor oyster-diving family, *The Pearl*, in 1947, La Paz's oysters were history, finished off by a mysterious blight. ∎

cathedral of the same name, **Nuestra Señora de la Paz,** Our Lady of Peace *(Revolución de 1910 at 5 de Mayo),* occupies the site of the original mission.

The cathedral faces **Plaza Constitución,** which along with the 3-mile (5 km) seawalk, the *malecón,* is one of La Paz's favorite meeting spots. On the opposite side of the square, the **Biblioteca de Historia de las Californias** *(Madero at 5 de Mayo, tel 112/53767)* shows paintings, old documents, and information in Spanish and English about cave paintings, missions, and other regional topics. Interesting exhibits on the region's geology, history, and folklore can be found at the **Museo de Antropología** *(Altamirano at 5 de Mayo, tel 112/20162, closed Sun., $),* although they are labeled in Spanish only.

Whale lovers should check out the **Museo de la Ballena** *(Navarro at Altamirano, $).* Whale-watching trips can be arranged December through March with the larger hotels and with tour operators in the area.

The best beaches are found to the north of town on the thumb of land that separates La Paz Bay from the Gulf of California. Simple, beachfront restaurants overlook the

La Paz
🅰 55 D1
Visitor information
✉ Tourist wharf on Paseo Alvaro Obregón at 16 de Septiembre
☎ 112/40100 or 112/40103

turquoise bay at **Playa Pichilingue,** near the docks where daily ferries depart for the mainland at Topolobampo and Mazatlán. The pretty cove at **Puerto Balandra** has no services. At the point, popular **El Tecolote** beach has rest rooms, restaurants, and watersports equipment for rent.

Boats can be rented to **Isla Espíritu Santo,** about 5 miles (8 km) offshore. One of the best dive spots at La Paz, the "Island of the Holy Spirit" offers great visibility almost year round. July through September are the best months to dive with hammerhead sharks and manta rays near **El Bajo (Marisla) Seamont,** off the island's north shore. Kayakers can explore the coves and inlets off the 14-mile-long (22.5 km) island, and off smaller **La Partida** and **Los Islotes** to the north, both of which have large sea lion colonies.

Gorgeous, more isolated beaches such as **Punta Coyote** and **San Evaristo** are accessible from La Paz via dirt roads, and **La Ventana** and **Ensenada de los Muertos** can be reached as a day-long excursion south of La Paz along Highway 286. You'll pass cactus fields and cattle ranches as you climb into the Sierra de la Laguna, soon replaced by rolling hills and farmlands around **San Juan de los Planes,** where corn, chilies, tomato, and beans are grown. Beyond this small agricultural town, dirt and gravel roads lead to excellent fishing, swimming, and boating beaches. ■

La Paz's promenade faces calm gulf waters, protected by El Mogote, a long, narrow sandbar.

Whales great & small

Whether literature, movies, television, or actual close encounters have influenced your idea of whales, it's doubtful that these beautiful creatures will leave you indifferent. Orcas, with their large, conical teeth, no-nonsense markings, and the misleading moniker "killer whale," command respect. As the largest mammal on record, the blue whale is nearly mythical—it's difficult to imagine an animal that weighs nearly two tons at birth.

Intelligent and curious, whales are mammals whose ancestors returned to the water millions of years ago, retaining the lungs developed on land but adapting well to aquatic life. Today scientists acknowledge approximately 40 different species. These include baleen whales, which feed on krill (planktonic crustaceans and larvae) and small fish strained through horny plates descending from the upper jaw; and toothed whales, which include orcas, sperm whales, porpoises, and dolphins.

There is no better destination for whale spotting than the Baja California peninsula. Of the ten (some scientists say eleven) surviving baleen whale species, eight are found in the Gulf of California—more than anywhere else on Earth. Visitors may sight the streamlined finback whale, second in size only to the blue. The humpback is often spotted breaching (hauling its gargantuan body completely out of the water) or slapping the surface with a flipper or scalloped tail. Less often seen are Bryde's, minke, sei, and northern right whales. Bottlenose dolphins bodysurf the translucent waves near the shore, while common dolphins perform astounding acrobatics that make

Above: A diving whale shows off its broad, flat fluke.
Left: A gray whale at San Ignacio Lagoon. The whales migrate to Baja from the northern Bering Sea to mate and give birth; they are generally seen January to mid-April.

them seem anything but common. Although less gregarious than the humpback, barnacle-encrusted gray whales may approach kayaks or *pangas* (skiffs), allowing thrilled observers the occasional caress.

Gray whales tarry in the protected lagoons of Baja's Pacific Coast; prime breeding grounds include Laguna Ojo de Liebre (also called Scammon's Lagoon) and Laguna San Ignacio, as well as Bahía Magdalena (Mag Bay), the latter protected from the open ocean by a 40-mile-long (64 km) barrier island. Each year an estimated 18,000 to 24,000 gray whales migrate south from summer feeding grounds in the northern Bering Sea. Of these, an unknown number complete the marathon migration to give birth or mate in the relatively warm, shallow, and inviting lagoons and estuaries off the Baja Peninsula. The journey—one of the most ambitious undertaken by any mammal—is an astonishing 5,000 miles (8,045 km). ■

How to see the whales

Many reputable tour operators lead excursions of 4 to 14 days; a good number depart from San Diego, California, just across the Mexican border. Cruises focusing on the Pacific Coast (where primarily gray whales are spotted) depart San Diego for Scammon's and San Ignacio Lagoons, and may stop en route at Todos Santos, San Martín, San Benito, or Cedros Islands. Trips to Bahía Magdalena often begin and end in La Paz, Baja California Sur. Land-based excursions charter small planes to camp at San Ignacio or other locations. Inside sheltered lagoons, passengers board pangas to get closer to the marine mammals and their babies. And while fin-back, humpback, blue, and gray whales are seen in the species-rich Gulf of California, whale-watching excursions there are less common. Recommended are: Baja Expeditions, 2625 Garnet Ave., San Diego, CA 92109 (Tel 858/581-3311 or 800/843-6967); Natural Habitat Adventures, 2945 Center Green Court, Suite H, Boulder, CO 80301 (Tel 800/543-8917); and Searcher Natural History Tours, 2838 Garrison St., San Diego, CA 92106 (Tel 619/226-2403). ■

Cabo San Lucas
📍 55 D1
Visitor information
✉ Av. Lázaro Cárdenas s/n
☎ 114/34180

Los Cabos

DRAMATIC DESERT SCENERY, BEAUTIFUL BEACHES, AND plenty of action draw visitors to the tip of Baja's narrow peninsula, where the Gulf of California's turquoise waters meet the Pacific Ocean. The deep-sea fishing is world-renowned. In the 1940s, John Wayne, Ernest Hemingway, and others would come in small private planes to hunt and fish, when Cabo San Lucas consisted of a scattering of humble homes opening onto dusty, nameless streets. Today less than three hours from several major U.S. airports, and also easily accessible from La Paz via the transpeninsular highway (completed 1974), Cabo has lost its isolation, but not its desert-by-the-sea allure.

The harbor at Cabo San Lucas

By the 1960s, a handful of comfortable, seaside hotels had sprung up among the organ cacti and spindly ocotillos. Several decades and millions of investment dollars later, **Cabo San Lucas** has grown up, although not necessarily matured: at night spots like Squid Roe and

The Giggling Marlin, the mainly American crowd tends to down lots of tequila shooters and dance on the bar. Warm weather, a relaxed atmosphere, and excellent sports facilities lure all types of travelers to the tip of one of the world's longest peninsulas.

Posh resort hotels and five 18-hole golf courses line the 23-mile (37 km) beachfront corridor north of Cabo San Lucas. (To avoid confusion, Cabo San Lucas, San José del Cabo, and the corridor in between have been dubbed "Los Cabos.") Most resorts along the corridor have their own beaches and cater to those content to stay put—not a bad idea, since cab rides

in this relatively isolated area begin at around $20. With multiple swimming pools, hot tubs, and restaurants, as well as European-style spas and gym facilities, these vacation spots offer a variety of activities to entertain their guests. If you plan to do much exploring beyond your hotel's swim-up bar, you might consider renting a car.

San José del Cabo was established by the Jesuits in the 18th century. Flowering acacia and Indian laurel trees partially shade the typical Mexican plaza, with its lacy wrought-iron bandstand and matching benches. Fronting the plaza is San José's simple yet winning church, its whitewashed

interior decorated with rather naively drawn gilded accents. Boutiques and restaurants with English-language menus surround the square and line the street into town, but these soon give way to one- and two-story houses and shops geared toward locals. While Cabo San Lucas offers proximity to the marina and boisterous nightlife, San José has a more subdued, more Mexican attitude.

San José's closest beach is **La Playita,** a long, wide stretch of sand perfect for walks or fishing from skiffs. Heading south toward San Lucas, **Costa Azul** and

San José del Cabo

✈ 55 D1

Visitor information

✉ Calle Zaragoza at Mijares

☎ 114/22960, ext. 150

Mural and artist in San José del Cabo

The arch at Land's End, seen here from Playa del Amor, is accessible only by boat.

Acapulquito Beaches are favored by surfers, while just beyond, **Playa Palmilla** (at the Hotel Palmilla) is the closest recommended swimming beach. **Chileno** and **Santa María Bays** are great for diving and snorkeling as well as swimming. The former rents dive and snorkel equipment and the latter snorkel gear and shade umbrellas. **Playa Médano,** on the bay at Cabo San Lucas, is popular for its unlimited watersports. Waverunners, jet skis, catamarans, and banana boats crowd the bay, while overhead, parasailers get a bird's-eye view of Land's End and **El Pedregal,** an exclusive community of American film stars and wealthy retirees. Underneath Cabo's trademark rock arch, **El Arco,** is **Playa del Amor,** accessible by water taxi or inexpensive glass-bottomed boat tour. More secluded beaches can be reached in ATVs or four-wheel-drive vehicles.

The bay's rocky outcrops make for good diving. At a depth of 90 feet (27 m) are the mysterious **sand falls,** a seemingly endless cascade created as the current drags fine sand over an undersea crag and into deeper water. Sportfishing, however, remains Los Cabos' most enduring draw; more marlin and swordfish are caught here than anywhere else in the world. Each October hundreds of serious anglers gather for Bisbee's Black & Blue Marlin Tournament, a three-day event with a purse exceeding $1 million. Although the best billfishing (except for marlin) is generally June through September, the fishing is excellent year-round, for wahoo, tuna, grouper, red snapper, dorado, swordfish, shark, and roosterfish, among others.

A visit to the old mission town of **Todos Santos,** 40 miles (65 km) north of Cabo San Lucas, is a chance to see something outside the tourist zone. Although there's not much to do, the town's few streets have several worthwhile restaurants and art galleries. Hikes into the as yet relatively untouched Sierra de la Laguna can be arranged through area hotels or tour operators throughout Los Cabos. ∎

The craggy peaks of the Sierra San Pedro Mártir rise above Bahía de Los Angeles.

More places to visit in Baja California

BAHÍA DE LOS ANGELES

Surrounded by the stark peaks of the eastern San Pedro Mártir mountains, "L.A. Bay" is a beautiful base for fishing, diving, kayaking, and relaxing up and down the Gulf of California, more often referred to as the Sea of Cortés. Offshore, 45-mile-long (72 km) Angel de la Guarda island serves as a barrier for the town's C-shaped bay, which is subject to 22-foot (7 m) tidal surges. To the south is a string of smaller islands, including **Isla Raza,** a sanctuary for seabirds. The town's small museum, on the west side of the plaza, displays peninsular fauna, marine life, and Indian artifacts. Rugged four-wheel-drive vehicles continue on to **Punta San Francisquito,** 81 miles (131 km) south on isolated Bahía Santa Teresa, where there are rustic cabins, a restaurant, and a fish camp.
🗺 55 B4

MISIÓN SAN FRANCISCO BORJA

This isolated mission was established by the Jesuits in 1759, farmed by the Franciscans, and completed by the Dominicans. The fine stone church—one of the most impressive in Baja, surrounded by fig, olive, and date orchards— was abandoned in 1818 after disease decimated the local Indian converts. Located 22 miles (35 km) east of Rosarito, near Guerrero Negro (not to be confused with the beach resort north of Ensenada), the active church holds Sunday services. Hire a local to guide you to the area's rock art. Only sturdy vehicles with high clearance should attempt the drive.
🗺 55 B4

MISIÓN SAN JAVIER

Considered the loveliest and best preserved of all Baja's missions, San Javicr, south of Loreto, was the second to be built on the peninsula (between 1699 and 1759). This Moorish-style church, located in a deep valley, contrasts dramatically with the simple, thatch-roofed adobe huts found in this region of the Sierra de la Giganta. Admire the stained-glass windows, the 18th-century wooden altar covered in gold leaf, and the statue of St. Francis. Although high-clearance vehicles can make the rocky, three-hour drive from Loreto in dry weather, a four-wheel-drive vehicle is best. Hire a guide in Loreto or the tiny town of San Javier to lead you to rock paintings in the region. The town swells with pilgrims around its feast day, December 3, and celebrates the onion harvest, one of its most important crops, each August 15.

⚏ 55 C2

PARQUE NACIONAL SIERRA SAN PEDRO MÁRTIR

The granite peaks, high meadows, and fragrant forests of this 49,000-acre (20,000-hectare) national park are little visited. Although roads are rough and may be closed by winter snows, they are accessible to high-clearance vehicles. Fishing, camping, and hiking are permitted. Experienced climbers tackle Picacho del Diablo (Devil's Summit)—the peninsula's highest peak, at 10,154 feet (3,100 m) above sea level. If you prefer to photograph rather than scale the rocky mountain, don't miss the terrific view of the peak from the National Autonomous University of Mexico's observatory, at the end of the park access road. Hikers should take adequate water and supplies, as

The observatory, Sierra San Pedro Mártir

well as a map and compass; the lonely national park has no facilities and few rangers.

⚏ 55 B5 ✉ Entrance 47 miles (75 km) off Highway 1 on an unpaved road. Ranger station at Corona de Abajo 💲 $

SAN FELIPE

Until 1951, San Felipe was a sleepy fishing village on the northwestern shore of the Gulf of California, but this resort town of 20,000 now counts tourism as its main source of revenue. It is also the shrimp capital of Baja California. Hugging the northern shore of a wide, relatively shallow natural bay, the relaxed desert town squats in the shadow of Punta San Felipe, a twin-peaked headland nearly 1,000 feet (305 m) high. With less than two inches (5 cm) of rain a year, vegetation is scant, and in summer temperatures may soar to 115°F (46°C). In the winter, U.S. and Canadian snowbirds fill area RV parks and cruise the beach on ATVs. South of town, shrimp boats depart from the marina that one day promises to accommodate private craft. Fresh seafood—including tender calamari or a giant *campechana*, a cocktail of shrimp, clams, and octopus—is the main draw of the many casual restaurants along the *malecón*, or seawalk. Extreme tidal fluxes here send beachcombers searching for shells along 12 miles (19 km) of wide, grainy sand beaches south of town, many nearly deserted.

⚏ 55 B5 **Visitor information** ✉ Calle Manzanillo 300 at Av. Mar de Cortés ☎ 657/71155 or 657/71865

TECATE

Set in a bowl-shaped valley at 1,690 feet (515 m), Tecate has none of the raucous flavor of most border towns. A pleasant Mexican border burg of about 50,000 people, it thrives on a combination of light industry and agriculture, with outlying fields of grain, olives, and grapes. Visitors can tour the **Tecate Brewery** by appointment (*Av. Dr. Arturo Guerra 70, tel 665/49300*) or stroll in **Parque Hidalgo** (*Av. Juárez & Calle Ortíz Rubio*).

On weekends, sporadic full- and half-day railway tours (*$$$$*) are an excellent way to see the countryside. They run between Campos, California (in the U.S.), and Tecate (sometimes Tijuana). Recent tours have taken in the vineyards of the Santo Tomás Valley. In the U.S., call 619/595-3030 for schedule information. The city hosts the Tecate–Ensenada Bike Ride each May and is known for its delicious *pan dulce* (sweet bread) and simple unglazed pots, planters, and floor tiles.

⚏ 55 A5 **Visitor information** ✉ 1305 Callejón Libertad ☎ 665/41095 ■

The geographically diverse region of northwestern Mexico has enormous tracts of high and low desert, more than 1,000 miles (1,600 km) of coast, the world's largest volcanic field, and some of the country's richest farmlands.

Northwest Mexico

Barrel cactus

A Tarahumara man celebrates Easter according to local ritual, in which Christianity is fused with ancient rites.

Northwest Mexico

HARSH YET IMPOSING, MEXICO'S VAST NORTHWEST comprises the states of Sonora, Chihuahua, Durango, and Sinaloa. Seldom visited by tourists, it offers 10,000-foot (3,050 m) peaks clothed in pine-oak forests, North America's first- and third-largest deserts, and a 1,300-mile (2,090 km) coast. Explorers head for the extensive canyon system of Sierra Tarahumara, where it's now relatively easy to organize hiking, horseback riding, or vehicular tours to spectacular waterfalls and lost Jesuit missions.

Roughly following the Gulf of California, the formidable Sierra Madre Occidental runs northwest to southeast. The range's steeper, more dramatic eastern escarpment drops down to Chihuahua's high desert, while to the west, valleys, canyons, and peaks finally give way to the foothills and then the coast. A dozen major rivers drain into the narrow, fertile coastal plain, creating prime farmlands.

In the 16th century, European and *criollo* (Mexican-born Spanish) explorers, adventurers, and Jesuit friars began to infiltrate the harsh northern areas. Along with the elements, they faced the Chichimeca: fierce northern tribes, most of whom even the Aztecs could not conquer. Over the centuries, vast numbers of indigenous peoples, and even entire tribes, succumbed to disease, slavery, deportation, and capital punishment, although sporadic rebellions and wars lasted until the 20th century.

Despite this resistance, the Jesuits founded dozens of mission villages before their expulsion in 1767, while entrepreneurs established incredible mining empires along the western flanks of the Sierra Madre Occidental. Vast ranches supplied the mines, missions, and *presidios* (military posts) with beef, creating immense individual fortunes in the process. Today, ranching is still important, as are forestry, farming, and fishing.

Great distances between sights and a limited tourist infrastructure notwithstanding, the northwest offers an awesome variety of scenery and experiences. Explore the ruins of Oasis America culture at Paquimé (see pp. 80–81) or the surreal moonscapes of silent, solitary Pinacate, with its impossibly wide craters, underground lava tubes, black cinder cones, and shifting sand dunes. Access and services for the Copper Canyon and

Sonora's low-key beach resorts are expanding, and the region's only world-class beach resort, Mazatlán, is in full swing.

In general, the best time to visit is fall, when soaring summer temperatures have abated, and rain has clothed mountainsides in green and deserts in the fragile blooms of tenacious succulents. ■

◁6

Area of map detail

UNITED STATES

Nogales
Cananea
Agua Prieta
Janos
Lucero

CIUDAD JUÁREZ
Dunas de Samalayuca
El Barreal

◁5

Paquimé
Nuevo Casas Grandes
Cumpás
Mata Ortíz
Buenaventura
El Sueco
Ojinaga

Mazocahui
Gómez Farías
El Pastor

Hermosillo
Sahuaripa
San Nicolás
PARQUE NAC. CUMBRES DE MAJALCA
Chihuahua
Presa Luis L. León
Llanos de los Caballos Mesteños

◁4

NORTHEAST MEXICO p. 103

Cascada Piedra Volada
Tonichi
Ortíz
Presa A. Obregón
Cascada de Basaseáchic
PARQUE NAC. CASCADA DE BASASEÁCHIC
Cuauhtémoc
Delicias

Guaymas

Rosario
PARQUE NAT. BARRANCA DEL COBRE
Creel
Cascada de Cusárare
Divisadero
Presa La Boquilla
Ciudad Camargo
Bolsón de Mapimi

Ciudad Obregón
Cerocahui
Urique
Batopilas
San Ignacio
La Boquilla del Conchos
Jiménez

Navojoa
Alamos
Choix
El Vergel
Hidalgo del Parral

◁3

Yávaros
El Fuerte
San Blas
Guadalupe y Calvo
Villa Ocampo
Tlahualilo de Zaragoza

Ahome
Guanacevi
Bermejillo

Los Mochis
Guasave
El Palmito
Gómez Palacio

Topolobampo
Guamuchil
Santiago Papasquiaro

Pericos
Isla Altamura
Culiacán
Lago de Santiaguillo
Cuencamé

◁2

Altata
DURANGO
Francisco I. Madero

Mazatlán
El Salto
Copala
Concordia
Rosario
PARQUE NAT. PUERTO DE LOS ANGELES
Mezquital
Durango

CHIHUAHUA

SINALOA

◁1

Teacapan
CENTRAL PACIFIC STATES
p. 137

0   200 kilometers
0   100 miles

C
D
E
F

Chihuahua

Northwest Mexico is cattle and sheep country.

BORN OF A SILVER MINE, BATHED IN THE BLAZING LIGHT of Mexico's huge northern desert, and surrounded by mountains rich in resources, Chihuahua was destined for success. Although today cattle ranching, industry, and timber have replaced mining as the mainstays of the economy, the city continues to prosper and the silver mines still produce. Elegant colonial buildings, precocious Victorian mansions, and self-confident modern sculptures make Chihuahua—despite its disappointing dearth of tiny, big-eyed, namesake dogs—a city to be admired.

Known as the Cradle of the Revolution, Chihuahua figures largely in Mexican history. Independence heroes Miguel Hidalgo y Costilla and three of his lieutenants were executed here in

1811. Now the capital of Mexico's largest state, at different times during the French Intervention and the Second Empire (see p. 33) the city served as Benito Juárez's provisional capital. And Pancho Villa—rogue, visionary, populist hero, and once governor of Chihuahua—based his División del Norte (Northern Division) army here for a number of years during the Mexican Revolution.

Today, although the city's outer limits sprawl, the historic district is attractive and diverse. Remains of an 18th-century aqueduct give portions of the city an old European air, while the decisive lines and brilliant colors of sculptures by popular modern artist Sebastián (1948–) give the city a decidedly self-confident look. His work can be seen at the new **Museo de Sebastián,** within the Casa Siglo XIX *(Calle Colón & Escudero, tel 14/10-75-06).* The **Museo Centro de Arte Contemporaneo,** closed for some time, awaits a new home at the Casa Redonda *(Av. Technologic at Escudero).*

Well-tended gardens surround the wrought-iron bandstand, imported from Paris in 1893, at **Plaza de Armas,** the city's principal square. At one end stands the Churrigueresque **Catedral Metropolitana** *(Libertad between Calle 2 & Independencia),* dedicated to St. Francis of Assisi. Indian raids

and the expulsion of the Jesuits—who began construction in 1735—delayed the cathedral's completion for nearly a hundred years. Its facade, adorned with statues of the 12 Apostles, is topped by two slender, ocher-colored towers. Inside, note the Venetian chandeliers and the monumental German organ. The late 18th-century main altar of carved limestone is almost obscured by a neoclassic altar of Carrara marble. In the back of the church, the **Museo de Arte Sacro** *(Closed Sat., Sun., $)* has 17th- and 18th-century religious objects and paintings.

North of the main square, in the **Palacio Federal** *(Tel 14/15-14-17, closed Mon., $)*, is the small cell where Padre Hidalgo was imprisoned before his death by firing squad. You can see his Bible, crucifix, and pistol. Across the street stands the stately, three-story **Palacio de Gobierno** *(Plaza Hidalgo, Aldama 911 between Guerrero & Carranza, tel 1/410-6324)*. Visit the place of his execution, surrounded by murals depicting that event and other episodes in the region's history.

South of the city center, the Revolution and the role of Chihuahua's adoptive son, General Francisco "Pancho" Villa, are detailed at the **Museo Histórico de la Revolución Mexicana** *(Calle 10ª 3014 at Méndez, tel 1/416-2958, closed Mon., $)*. The museum is located within **Quinta Luz,** a mansion named for Villa's legal wife, Luz Corral de Villa. The stately house has original furnishings, as well as photos, documents, firearms, and the black Dodge that Villa was driving when he was assassinated in 1923. A few blocks north, **Quinta Gameros** *(Paseo Bolívar 401 at Calle 4, tel 1/416-6684, closed Mon.)* is a wonderfully restored, two-story mansion. In addition to rotating fine arts exhibits and cultural events, the museum houses a permanent collection of 19th- and 20th-century European paintings, elegant art nouveau furnishings, and Paquimé pottery (see p. 80).

On Sundays, Chihuahuenses admire the restored buildings of historic **Santa Eulalia,** 15 miles (9 km) southeast of town. ∎

Ornate facade and copper-tiled roof of the cultural center at Quinta Gameros

Paquimé

PAQUIMÉ, THE MOST IMPORTANT RUINS IN NORTHERN Mexico, was built by the Oasis America cultural group, who lived in an area extending from northwest Chihuahua and northeast Sonora to the southwestern United States. In its day this commercial center imported turquoise from the north, seashells from the west coast, and copper and obsidian from the Valley of Mexico. Its inhabitants lived in rammed-earth, multiple-story houses similar to the adobes of the Pueblo Indians to the north. Unlike Anasazi-Pueblo villages, however, Paquimé had fixed, interior stairways and an elaborate system of water collection, filtration, distribution, and disposal.

Paquimé
🗺 77 D5
Visitor information
✉ ½ mile (1 km) outside Nuevo Casas Grandes
☎ 1/692-4140
💲 $

Inhabited since about A.D. 700, this site overlooking the Casas Grandes River began to blossom some time after 1150, reaching its apogee between about 1300 and 1450 before being abruptly abandoned. Some anthropologists think it was quit earlier, possibly after devastating attacks by Apaches from the north. Five-foot-thick (1.5 m) walls may have aided defense, but their main purpose was to provide insulation from the desert's intense heat and bitter cold.

If Paquimé building design was similar to that of its northern cousins, other aspects of culture show the distinct influence of central Mexico. These include the organization of artisans by neighborhood, the veneration of the god Quetzalcoatl (Feathered Serpent),

and the use of ceremonial plazas and I-shaped ball courts.

Today the site resembles an organic, crumbling earth labyrinth. Excavation and reconstruction began in 1958. For the most part, only the first-floor exterior walls and myriad room dividers survive. The **Montículo de la Cruz** is a cross-shaped, raised adobe structure roughly oriented toward the four cardinal points and surrounded by four circular platforms. It was most likely used in agricultural or celestial rituals, although its exact purpose is not known. To the south, vestiges of a second floor can be seen at the **Casa del Pozo,** along with partially reconstructed flooring, wooden columns, and beams. A stairway leads up to a section of the stone aqueduct that

Mata Ortíz pottery

Pottery produced in the small village of Juan Mata Ortíz, 12½ miles (20 km) south of Casas Grandes, is exquisite, with extremely thin walls and a soft, bright luster. The techniques originated with Juan Quezada. He spent 15 years experimenting with clay, pigments, and firing techniques before producing his first pots. In 1976, Spencer MacCallum found a

few of these unsigned pots in a secondhand shop in New Mexico and traced Quezada to his village. A quarter century later, about a sixth of the town's population makes this internationally collected pottery without the use of a potter's wheel or kiln. While the techniques used are those developed by Quezada, many artisans have devised their own motifs and designs. ■

carried water throughout the city. One such canal fed the waterwheel, powered by one of the most impressive hydraulic water systems in Mesoamerica in its day.

Beyond the **Casa de los Cráneos** (named for the skulls and human bones found here), more than 90 grave sites were found beneath the **Casa de los Muertos** (House of the Dead). Birds—probably macaws imported from the south—were kept in adobe cages in the adjacent structure, and in the **Casa del Serpiente;** their feathers were used for ceremonial purposes. South of the Casa de los Muertos is the large **Casa de las Columnas**—originally four to five stories high and today one of the few buildings with walls more than one story tall. To the west, the

undulating, stone **Montículo de la Serpiente** is thought to have been dedicated to Quetzalcoatl, revered in central Mexico since the days of Tula (see p. 232).

The well-designed, modern **Museo de las Culturas del Norte** (*Tel 1/692-4140, closed Mon.*) highlights the Oasis America culture in general and Paquimé in particular. Among the artifacts displayed are examples of the city's delicate, attractive pottery. There is also a scale model of the site, and artifacts from the mission church built near Casas Grandes in 1660.

Most people visit Paquimé as a day trip out of Nuevo Casas Grandes, 5 miles (8 km) to the north. This small agricultural town has a few comfortable, if simple, hotels and restaurants. ■

The low, T-shaped doorways of Paquimé's houses—now in ruins—helped deter invaders.

The Seri

Historically, the panthe-istic Seri revered the sun and the moon as well the marine turtle, the pelican, and other divine manifestations. However, their lack of totems and monuments led icon-bearing Jesuit priests to consider them godless and to marvel at their unwavering disinclination to convert. The Seri were one of the last indigenous cultures in North America to integrate into European-derived culture and to accept Christianity.

This dancer emulates the deer, revered by the Seri yet also hunted as prey.

They paid a high price for their resistance to mission life and Spanish rule. In 1662, a violent rebellion by a band of Seris was quelled only when every last man and woman had been slain and their children whisked off to the mission. Hanged as cattle rustlers, deported, and decimated by introduced disease, the Seri numbered a mere 150 by the early 20th century. Today, roughly 600 individuals speak the native language; most live in the towns of Punta Chueca and El Desemboque, north of Bahía Kino on Sonora's Gulf of California coastline.

Autonomous and proud, the Seri roamed the stark deserts, plains, coasts, and offshore islands long before the arrival of the Spanish. Surviving with the ebb and flow of the seasons, they foraged for food in the Desierto de Altar and fished for shellfish. Their annual marine turtle harvest provided not only a source of food but also a ceremonial link with traditional culture. A long history of storytelling in narrative song is an important part of the Seri heritage; this lyrical recital is passed from generation to generation. Songs are sung in praise of animals that provide food, or to protect them from natural phenomena, including navigating the sometimes treacherous passage to the Isla Tiburón. Deprived of their traditional turtle harvest since 1991,

when a government ban on hunting them and collecting their eggs was put in effect, the Seri struggle to maintain their cultural identity.

Despite pressure to acculturate, the Comcaac, as they call themselves, continue to sing their songs. They support themselves by fishing and by the sale of handicrafts, particularly shell jewelry, fine woven baskets of *torote* grass, and carved ironwood statues of lizards, dolphins, and other animals. Working with the Arizona-Sonora Desert Museum, in Tucson, some Seri are cataloging their extensive knowledge of medicinal plants in hopes of renewing tribal interest in their use. In preserving their traditional knowledge, they both maintain their customs and share ancestral wisdom with the outside world.

ISLA TIBURÓN

Isla Tiburón (Shark Island), ancestral homeland to the Seri, once provided them with refuge from Spanish military expeditions and aggressive cattle ranchers. Although they are now banned from living on Mexico's largest island, which has been protected as an ecological reserve since 1963, knowledgeable Seri guides accompany visitors to the biologically diverse island to camp, hike, kayak, and snorkel.

Endangered bighorn sheep roam the island's two mountain ranges, which run north to south, while peregrine falcons, owls, and frigates patrol the skies. Blue-footed boobies show off their powder-blue appendages along lovely, secluded sandy beaches, and red, black, and white mangroves shelter a wide variety of marine fauna. There is good anchorage in the south at Kun Kaak Bay.

Contact the Gobierno de la Comunidad Seri *(Kino Viejo, Sonora, tel 624/20557)* for more information. ■

The Seri continue many of their traditional ways. Left, a Seri women burns bark off sticks used in basketmaking; above, today around 600 Seri speak the native language; below, a rare face-painting ceremony.

Cerro Colorado is one of the many craters that rise above the Gran Desierto de Altar.

El Pinacate

LUNAR-LIKE AND OTHERWORLDLY, THE LANDSCAPE OF El Pinacate is as beautiful as it is barren. Huge, craggy craters rise in startling contrast to the flatness of the surrounding desert, and in the western portion of the 1.8-million-acre (728,460 ha) park winds build shifting dunes hundreds of feet high. Geologists and photographers are especially drawn to the rich textures and striking hues of this arid region. NASA was so impressed with Pinacate's extraterrestrial appearance that it sent the crew of *Apollo 14* here to practice working with new moon-landing equipment.

Reserva de la Biósfera Sierra de Pinacate

🏞 76 B6

Visitor information

✉ Highway 8 Km 52

☎ 6/215-9864

This unique ecosystem in the Gran Desierto de Altar (Mexico's Sonora Desert), designated a UNESCO Man and the Biosphere Reserve in 1993, has the largest concentration of volcanic cones and craters on Earth. Volcanic activity that began three or four million years ago created miles of jagged lava beds so unforgiving that colonial-era wayfarers called it the "Sea of Broken Glass." More than 400 cinder cones (conical mounds formed around a volcanic vent) jut in dramatic waves along the desert floor within a 30-mile-wide (48 km) field. The tallest are

raven-colored **Cerro del Pinacate** and **Cerro del Carnegie,** at 4,000 (1,219 m) and 3,700 feet (1,128 m) respectively.

Huge maars, or craters, were probably created when bubbling magma hit groundwater, initiating explosions of steam and blasting rock and lava into the air. One of the most spectacular examples of these black behemoths is **Cráter Elegante,** about 12 miles (19 km) north of the main (east) park entrance. Rising 165 feet (50 m) from the desert floor, the crater's uneven walls are the product of prevailing winds at the time of eruption. Peering over the edge of the mile-wide (1.5 km), 800-foot-deep (245 m) crater inspires nothing short of awe. In addition to the park's ten maars, underground lava tubes and other extraordinary formations provide unlimited opportunities for exploration.

Despite its bleak and desolate first impression, the reserve sustains a variety of plants and animals. Endangered desert bighorn sheep, Sonoran pronghorn antelope, and desert tortoises share the unforgiving desert with the park's namesake, the endemic pinacate beetle. Roadrunners and rattlers are abundant, and more than 550 plant species have been identified. In spring, brief rains encourage white dune evening primroses, yellow desert marigolds, and colorful skeleton weeds to bloom.

Visitors must register at the park's main entrance, 32 miles (51 km) south of the Lukeville, Arizona/Sonoyta border crossing, on Highway 8. There are no facilities at the park; bring your own water and food, and take away all trash. The best time to visit is spring, when temperatures are least extreme and wildflowers most abundant. From late April to September, daytime temperatures may soar to 120°F (49°C); nighttime temperatures in winter can dip below freezing. Sunscreen, sunglasses, water, and a hat are essential. A high-clearance vehicle is advised; four-wheel drive is recommended but not required.

Of the park's two basic campgrounds, **El Tecolote,** 5 miles (8 km) northeast of Elegante, has the best access to hiking trails and the craters. **Cono Rojo,** 14 miles (22 km) northwest of the information center, is a better bet for those wanting to hike up to the volcanic peaks. Backcountry camping is permitted with a few restrictions. ■

Cactuses

There are about 1,650 species of cactus worldwide, but Mexico has more species and more specimens than any other country. The Sonora, driest and hottest of North America's four deserts, has the greatest diversity of species. Adaptations such as a lack of leaves, shallow wide-ranging roots, and the ability to store water for more than a year allow cactuses to thrive in the uncompromising desert.

Historically, cactuses have provided food, water, building materials, and inspiration for the desert's hardy inhabitants. The Huichol (see p. 13) and other indigenous peoples employ the hallucinogenic peyote cactus to commune with God, seek visions, and heal disease. Prickly pear, saguaro, and organ cactuses provide sweet, juicy, and nutritious fruits. Barrel cactus are a source of emergency water, while other species are burned as fuel or used as living fences. ■

The fruit-bearing organ cactus provides an important food source to desert inhabitants.

Sonora's beaches

DESERT RATS, YOUNG REVELERS FROM NEARBY ARIZONA, and snowbirds (Northerners escaping the winter) have long sought out the solitary, sandy beaches along Sonora's desert coast. Excellent sportfishing, good snorkeling and diving, and proximity to the United States have been among the region's main attractions. Over the past decade, improved tourist infrastructure and the establishment of hotels, marinas, and golf courses have attracted a more demanding clientele, yet at the same time caused disenchantment among fans of the rustic and the remote.

Puerto Peñasco

🔼 76 A5

Backed by cliffs ranging from rust red to gold, simple fishing villages and unpretentious towns from Puerto Peñasco to Guaymas have long provided fresh seafood, cold beer, and a relaxing atmosphere.

Seri men making the crossing to Isla Tiburón, their ancestral homeland and now a protected ecological park

Time-shares, hotels, condos, and private residences are popping up fast, as are restaurants and services geared toward mainly U.S. and Canadian visitors. Spring and fall see fewer tourists and more competitive prices than in the peak winter months.

Just 60 miles (97 km) from the border at Lukeville, Arizona, is **Puerto Peñasco** (*Visitor information, Blvd. Juárez 320-B*),

the first seaside town on Sonora's 600-mile (965 km) coastline. Sandy beaches, rocky coves, and extreme tidal variation attract shell collectors and lovers of long walks. The town was established in the 1920s as a shrimp camp, but long before that British explorers had named the place Rocky Point, a designation still used by most English-speakers today. Overfishing in recent years has significantly reduced the shrimp harvest, once the mainstay of the economy, and tourism is now one of the most important industries. To that end the government is developing a 150-million-dollar marina with shops, restaurants, hotels, and condos.

South of Puerto Peñasco is **Bahía Kino,** named for Padre Chini (1645–1711), the Italian-born Jesuit priest and adventurer known as Padre Kino. **Kino Viejo,** a simple fishing village, hugs the bay with its fine, sandy beaches, while to the north **Kino Nuevo** is an enclave of Canadian and U.S. vacationers and retirees. Once dominated by RV parks, the 8-mile (13 km) beachfront road that constitutes the town has an increasing number of condos, time-shares, hotels, and private residences. The **Museo de los Seris** (*2½ miles/4 km down the beach road in Kino Nuevo*) highlights the Seri culture, while the Seri themselves come to town to sell grass baskets,

pottery, ironwood statuettes, and necklaces of seashells, seeds, and animal bones. Across the channel from Bahía Kino are **Isla Tiburón** (see p. 82) and tiny **Isla San Esteban,** which have been protected as an ecological reserve since 1963.

The carmine-colored peaks of the **Sierra de Bacochibampo** —including the town's symbol, craggy Tetakawi, meaning "goat teat hill"—form a magnificent backdrop for **Bahía San Carlos** *(Visitor information, Bellamar Local 2),* one of northern Mexico's fastest-growing tourist destinations. Spindly ocotillo cacti with spidery red blooms brighten the surrounding desert in the fall, while snorkelers seek out colorful fish among the rocky outcroppings separating Bahía San Carlos and **Bahía Bacochibampo.** Divers are drawn to the 5,000-foot-deep (1,500 m) **Guaymas Trench,** which attracts an estimated 700 species of marine life. Half- and full-day fishing boat trips go after yellowtail, sailfish, marlin, and grouper; closer to shore, anglers catch triggerfish and sea bass. The well-protected bay has a full-service marina, making it a magnet for yachtspeople. A few major resorts line pretty **Playa los Algodones,** on the west end of San Carlos, offering kayaking, jet skiing, and windboarding.

A mountainous peninsula separates San Carlos from more commercial **Guaymas** *(Map ref. 77 C4, visitor information, Malecón Malpica, between Calles 22 & 23, tel 6/222-1751),* about 10 miles (16 km) to the southeast. Bolstered by a significant canning industry and a PEMEX oil refinery, Guaymas is Sonora's main port. Vermilion peaks crouch above its fine natural harbor, crowded with vessels of all shapes and sizes, including oil tankers and shrimp boats. Forecasts of large-scale expansion have so far produced only a marina and a golf course, and many visitors prefer more vacation-oriented San Carlos. Those who stay in Guaymas are usually seeking a less touristy venue or are hopping aboard the twice-weekly ferry to Santa Rosalía, in Baja California Sur. ■

Sonora's beaches lure U.S. vacationers as well as Mexicans from the scorching interior.

Sierra Tarahumara
(Copper Canyon)

MEXICANS DELIGHT IN TELLING VISITORS (ESPECIALLY those from the United States) how much bigger and better is the series of canyons collectively known as the Copper Canyon (or more accurately, la Sierra Tarahumara) than the Grand Canyon, in Arizona. And it's true that these dramatic gorges are immense and impressive. Of the six major canyons composing Las Barrancas del Cobre system, four are deeper than the Grand Canyon. In addition to their natural beauty, they are dotted with Jesuit missions, abandoned mines, early 20th-century mansions, and indigenous cave dwellings.

Chihuahua
⬛ 77 E4
Visitor information
✉ Calle Libertad at Calle Trece
☎ 14/29-34-21

Los Mochis
⬛ 77 C3
Visitor information
✉ Unidad Administrativa del Gobierno del Estado, at Allende and Ordoñéz
☎ 6/815-1090 or 6/815-4970

Opposite: Dwarfed by Sierra Madre peaks, a train trundles across one of the Copper Canyon's 37 major bridges.

LA SIERRA TARAHUMARA
During 10 to 15 million years of the Tertiary era, volcanic activity and shifting tectonic plates created this mountain range, with peaks up to 12,000 feet (3,650 m). Working on surface fissures, time and the action of rain, runoff, and underwater currents carved out the series of deep canyons known collectively as Las Barrancas del Cobre. The hard igneous strata resist erosion, causing dramatic rock formations. Among the six main canyons of the Sierra Tarahumara, depth varies from 4,986 feet (1,520 m) at Barranca Oteros to 6,135 feet (1,870 m) at Barranca Urique. Barranca Sinforosa has the highest elevation, at 8,293 feet (2,528 m) above sea level; Chínipas, at 6,555 feet (1,998 m), is lowest.

Missionaries and miners were the first non-Indians to settle in the pine-scented mountains and deep, scrubby gorges of the Sierra Tarahumara, part of the Sierra Madre Occidental west of Chihuahua. In the 17th and 18th centuries, the Jesuits established simple yet beautiful churches throughout this canyon country—despite drawn-out and widespread local resistance. At the same time, a wealth of copper gave the Copper Canyon (part of Urique Canyon)

and the region its name, and large deposits of gold and silver were discovered in Batopilas.

Forced to labor in the Spaniards' mines and toil on railroads built by Americans and Mexicans, the Indians later lost access to much of their traditionally held lands. Only ten of the 50 indigenous groups living in the Sierra Tarahumara and Chihuahua Desert in the 1600s survives today.

The stalwart Tarahumara (who call themselves Rarámuri, "people who run") number 50,000 to 60,000. Living on a simple diet of corn and beans, they are as rugged as the mountains in which they live. They can run vast distances carrying heavy loads, and team races organized as social events last days. The Rarámuri women dress in a melee of flowered and polka-dotted clothing, with long, flowing skirts, ruffled blouses, and head scarves of contrasting prints. Near tourist areas, they sell sweet-smelling pine baskets, homemade dolls, and simple pottery. Most of the men have traded the traditional white cotton breechcloths (*tagoras*) and blousey shirts for Western clothing.

The Rarámuri follow traditional migratory patterns, living in caves, along cliffs, or in houses of wood and stone near the canyon's rim in

Tarahumara girls. Note the corn cobs drying in the sun on the shed roof.

Chihuahua train station

✉ Méndez at Calle 24
☎ 14/15-77-56
💲 $$$$$ (one way along the Chihuahua al Pacífico Railway)

Los Mochis train station

☎ 6/812-0853

summer months, when temperatures at the canyon bottom may reach 113°F (45°C). The rest of the year, they move to caves or small wooden houses within the canyon. Crops are generally raised 100 feet (300 m) above sea level. Corn is the staple crop, though fruits are also grown.

CHIHUAHUA AL PACÍFICO RAILWAY

Visitors first gained access to this breathtaking canyon world in 1961 with the completion of the Chihuahua al Pacífico Railway. Connecting Chihuahua with Los Mochis on Sinaloa's coast, the narrow-gauge, 415-mile (670 km) line passes 87 tunnels. Of its 37 major bridges, the longest stretches nearly a third of a mile (0.5 km) over a dizzying gorge. To pass the best canyon scenery during daylight hours, travel from west to east and sit on the right side of the train.

Sixty miles (96 km) into the journey, the train begins an impressive ascent, climbing more than 7,500 feet (2,286 m) in just over 150 miles (241 km). Along the way and at the all-too-brief station stops, you'll be rewarded with

magnificent canyon views. East of Creel, the canyons give way to alpine mountains and high valleys backed by tremendous peaks. The train begins a gradual descent through fertile farmland and high meadows to the city of Chihuahua.

To get the most out of your rail adventure, spend one or more nights along the train route. Creel has the most hotels, restaurants, and services and is the most convenient departure point for trips into the canyons. Divisadero has excellent canyon views and several hotels offering lodging. At the floor of its eponymous canyon, Batopilas is a long journey from Creel but, once reached, is another good departure point for canyon exploration.

WEST TO EAST

If you start your tour in the west, consider bypassing **Los Mochis** and spending a day in charming **El Fuerte,** 50 miles (80 km) to the east, built as a fort and later used as a major trading post for gold and silver miners. The town still functions as a commercial center for the surrounding farms and ranches. Like nearby Alamos, El Fuerte is an engaging town with cobblestone

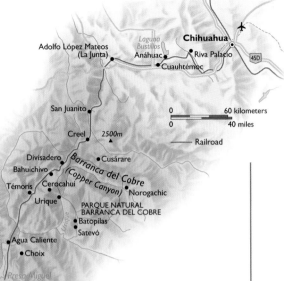

Chihuahua

Adolfo López Mateos
(La Junta)   Anáhuac   Riva Palacio
Cuauhtémoc

Laguna
Bustillos

45D

San Juanito

0   60 kilometers
0   40 miles

Creel   2500m

Railroad

Divisadero   Barranca del Cobre   Cusárare
Bahuichivo   (Copper Canyon)
Témoris   Cerocahui
Urique   Norogachic

PARQUE NATURAL
BARRANCA DEL COBRE

Batopilas
Satevó

Agua Caliente

Choix

El Fuerte   Presa Miguel
Hidalgo

San Blas

Los Mochis

Topolobampo   15D

Guasave

**Above: The
narrow-gauge
415-mile (670 km)
Chihuahua al
Pacífico Railway
was completed
in 1961.**

streets and 18th- and 19th-century
mansions near its center. Visit the
1854 **Iglesia del Sagrado
Corazón de Jesús,** the **Palacio
Municipal,** and the **Casa de la
Cultura,** all on or around the
main square, **Plaza de Armas**
(Degollado at Rosales). The area's
lakes are well known for their
plentiful largemouth bass.

Lovely **Cerocahui** is tucked in
a deep gorge at 5,000 feet (1,525 m)
and surrounded by apple orchards
(about 10 miles/16 km south of
Bahuichivo station). The gateway to
the Urique Canyon, this small
mountain town was founded by
Jesuit priests in 1680. Here, as

throughout the sierra, the
Tarahumara dance traditional
matachines during Easter week and
other holy days. Rent a horse or go
on foot to visit the **Sangre de
Cristo** gold mines (1.8 miles/3 km)
and **Wicochic Falls** (2 miles/
3.25 km), or go on a two- to three-
day trek to Batopilas (see p. 94).
Twenty-four miles (38 km) south of
Cerocahui, **Urique** affords excellent views of its namesake canyon
and refreshing walks along the river.
The abandoned mine of **Chiflón,** a
20-minute walk away, is a good
place to swim when the weather is
hot. It's best to hire a local guide
when exploring within the canyon.

There are breathtaking views of
Urique Canyon from **Divisadero,**
where many people choose to
spend the night in one of several
hotels. There is no actual town, so
each hotel provides meals. Arrange
a guided tour or horseback riding
at **Hotel Divisadero Barrancas**
(Tel 157/83060). More magnificent
canyon views are seen on a horseback ride to **Wacajipare,** a
Tarahumara village about 2½ miles

Tarahumara flora & fauna

The very highest mountains of the Sierra Tarahumara, above 8,000 feet (2,440 m), support conifer forests, with Douglas-fir and ponderosa pine. In winter these peaks may be cloaked in snow, below skies of cerulean blue. Down to 5,900 feet (1,800 m), live oak, juniper, and twisted red *madroño* (strawberry tree) mingle with the still predominant pine, notably the pinyon pine. Between 5,900 and 4,265 feet (1,800 and 1,300 m), the pine-oak forest gives way to the arid tropical deciduous thorn forest, with scrub oak, succulents, mesquite, and some species of cactus. Below 4,265 feet (1,300 m) are the tropical and subtropical riparian forests. Here you will find fan palms next to evergreens, orchids, and wild figs, and, in the humid areas, ceiba, bamboo, and river cane.

About 30 percent of Mexico's mammals can be found in the Sierra Tarahumara, many increasingly rare. At the higher elevations live black bear, mountain lion, rattlesnake, and the endangered Mexican wolf. Deer, bobcat, coyote, wild boar,

white-tail deer, and collared peccary are wide-ranging but elusive and rarely sighted. Most frequently seen are raccoon, skunk, hare, gray fox, squirrel, and bats. Coral snakes and beaded lizards, both poisonous, inhabit the arid tropical thorn forest, while near the canyon bottom live jaguar, jaguarundi, and boa constrictor. Wandering cattle, goats, and pigs upset nature's delicate balance, stripping vegetation traditionally eaten by other species. Throughout the region there are around 50 species of freshwater fish, including catfish, rainbow trout, carp, mullet, and mojarra.

Many species of birds (there are more than 360 in the region) can be seen along the canyon's rim, among them the vermilion flycatcher, black vulture, crested caracara, thick-billed parrot, zone-tailed hawk, and hairy woodpecker. At the canyon's base live the colorful violet-crowned and Lucifer hummingbirds, oriole, tanager, and the magnificent, endangered military macaw. Near rivers look for lilac-crowned parrot and elegant trogan. ∎

Above: The mission church at Satevó, on the canyon floor. Other missions can be found at San Ignacio de Arareko and Cusárare. Above, left: Mexican wolves live at the higher altitudes of the Sierra Tarahumara.

(4 km) into the gorge.

The train continues to **Creel,** about 36 miles (58 km) from Divisadero and definitely worth a visit. Fifteen years ago, there were many horses but few hotels along the packed-earth main street. Today Creel is connected by paved highway to Chihuahua (see pp. 78–79), and visitors benefit from a range of amenities, although the town retains its cowboy charm. Guides, pack animals, horses, and organized tours can be arranged.

A few miles south of Creel, **San Ignacio de Arareko** and its mission church are now accessible by paved road. Outside town, you can rent a rowboat for fishing in **Lago Arareko,** a 100-acre (40 ha) reservoir with woodland campsites and simple cabins. Primitive camp-

ing is permitted in surrounding valleys, each named for its unique rock formations: **Valle de los Hongos** (mushrooms), **Las Ranas** (frogs), **Las Chichis** (breasts), and **Bisabírachi** (penises). About 15½ miles (25 km) from Creel, **Cascada de Cusárare** waterfall can be visited on a long day or an overnight camping trip.

About 75 miles (120 km) northwest of Creel, in **Parque Nacional Basaseáchic,** are Mexico's first- and second-highest waterfalls. The 1,486-foot (453 m) **Cascada Piedra Volada** was only recently discovered (at least by outsiders), in 1995. The national park was named for **Cascada Basaseáchic,** best seen during or right after the rainy season (June–October), when the falls plunge

Creel

🏕 77 D4

Creel is the jumping-off point for a visit to the Cusárare Waterfall.

800 feet (243 m) into a rocky pool. Tiny **Batopilas** perches beside a jade-green river of the same name on the canyon's floor. Connected to the world by a paved road only for the last 20 years, the town was originally established in the early 17th century by Spaniards looking for precious metals. These they found in abundance, sometimes as polished silver rocks strewn along the riverbed. Wealth from mining paid for some of the elegant Porfiriato-era mansions that today enliven this remote town. From Batopilas, hike or ride to the abandoned, fired-brick mission at **Satevó** (4 miles/6.5 km), or take a shorter hike to abandoned **Hacienda San Miguel** or to the stone dam that still supplies the town's aqueduct. Satevó is a "dry" town, gas is expensive, and most restaurants serve just the basics. There are half a dozen simple lodgings. An alternative to the magnificent but hair-raising five-hour, 87-mile (140 km) car or bus trip from Creel is a several-day horse or mule trek from Cerocahui. ∎

The stalwart burro

Sure-footed and stoic, the burro doesn't deserve its bad rap. Aside from meaning small donkey, in Mexico the word burro is also used for an idiot, a losing horse, or a drudge. In English, the burro's ancestor, the ass, is also a stupid, stubborn, or perverse person. Despite the negative anthropomorphisms, *campesinos* from Baja to the Yucatán depend on donkeys to carry both themselves and their loads.

Especially useful in rocky, steep terrain, donkeys can carry more weight per pound than horses and survive with less water. They also eat thorny brush, making them well suited to desert and mountain environments. In folklore, the dark cross on their withers is said to be a mark of divine protection bestowed on the species in return for having delivered the Virgin Mary safely to the Holy Land from Egypt. ∎

Hidalgo del Parral

SNUGGLED IN AN ISOLATED VALLEY BETWEEN THE foothills of the Sierra Madre and the Chihuahua Desert, Hidalgo del Parral is among the country's richest mining towns. Parral (as it's usually called) produced lead, copper, and silver for more than 350 years before being exhausted in the 1980s. The city also gained fame as the place where Revolutionary hero Pancho Villa was assassinated.

Built in the Italian Renaissance style, the Casa de Alvarado still belongs to the mining family after which it is named.

During the 16th and 17th centuries, indigenous slaves worked Parral's mines, suffering enormous loss of life due to unsafe conditions and constant overwork. The miners created altars within the cramped and dangerous tunnels, frequently dedicated to their patron saint, Nuestra Señora de Fátima. Above ground, the hugely wealthy metal barons built churches and cathedrals, often encrusting columns and walls with crude or refined ore.

The **Parroquia de San José** *(Francisco Moreno at General Benítez, tel 152/20950)* is decorated with chunks of ore, and its baroque altarpiece of pink quarrystone is edged in fine gold. Constructed three centuries later, the **Templo de Nuestra Señora de**

Fátima overlooks the city near La Prieta mine. It has a plain facade and single bell tower, but its interior walls are also encrusted with silver, gold, copper, and zinc ore.

Parral's mines are played out, but centuries of wealth have left their mark, and along the city's winding, narrow streets are some lovely mansions. Silver mining peaked in the mid- to late 19th century, and many palatial homes date from that era. **Casa de Alvarado** *(Lic. Verdad & Riva Palacio)* has a brilliant neo-baroque portal and limestone facade carved with human faces and animal figures.

The small **Museo del General Francisco Villa** *(Barreda at Juárez)* has been enlarged and remodeled. ∎

Hidalgo del Parral
🅰 77 E3
Visitor information
✉ Miranda at República de Cuba
☎ 152/25282

Durango

NESTLED IN THE FERTILE GUADIANA VALLEY, NEAR THE eastern foothills of the Sierra Madre Occidental, the city of Durango is an important agricultural and industrial center. Its colonial past is visible in the well-maintained vintage buildings in the city center—a national historic monument. Friendly people, a mild climate, clean, well-signed streets, and a dearth of tourists make Durango an ideal stop for those seeking a bite of "real" Mexico off the tour-bus trail.

Durango
🅰 77 E2
Visitor information
✉ Calle Florida 1106
☎ 1/811-2139

Founded in 1563, the city began as an outpost in the wilds of Nueva Vizcaya, New Spain's huge northern province. Both the city and the surrounding region developed slowly, plagued by extreme hostilities between the Spaniards and the Tepehuán and Acaxe Indians. Durango finally flourished in the early 1900s, when the completion of a railroad to Mexico City established it as a shipping center for lumber and minerals from the productive mountains nearby.

The surrounding hills still produce substantial amounts of silver, gold, copper, and iron. One of the world's largest iron ore deposits can be found at **Cerro del Mercado,** just north of the city. Hundreds of tons of iron ore are transported from this virtual mountain of metal every day.

Durango's historic buildings cluster downtown near the main square, the **Plaza de Armas** (*Av. 20 de Noviembre at Juárez*). On Sunday afternoons the state band serenades from the bandstand, which is surrounded by gardens and fountains. The **Catedral,** with its impressive baroque facade, commands the plaza to the north. Locals tell of a young local girl who killed herself after learning of the death of her lover, a French soldier. The girl's ghost is said to hover near sunset in the west bell tower, from which she jumped. Among the cathedral's most precious icons is

Handsome colonial-era houses are sprinkled throughout the historic district. An excellent example of 18th-century Churrigueresque architecture is the **Casa del Conde de Suchil** (*5 de Febrero at Madero, closed Sat., Sun.*), originally the region's mint and now a Banamex bank. The beautiful, neo-classic **Teatro Ricardo Castro** (*Av. 20 de Noviembre at Bruno Martínez, tel 1/811-7766*) hosts opera, orchestra, and dance, and serves as a film venue.

For an overview of local culture and art, visit the **Museo de las Culturas Populares** (*Juárez 302 Norte & Gabino Barreda, closed Mon., $*), which displays a collection of folk art made by local Mennonites as well as Huichol, Acaxe, and Tepehuán Indians. Modern handiwork, including leather goods and typical wool *sarapes* (blankets), can be found at the **mercado municipal** (*Av. 20 de Noviembre at Pasteur*). The **Museo Regional de Durango** (*Victoria 100 Sur & Aquiles Serdán, tel 1/813-1094, closed Mon., $*), known locally as "El Aguacate," has paintings by colonial master Miguel Cabrera (1695–1768) as well as exhibits on regional history and archaeology. ■

its gilded *sillería* (row of choir stalls), adorned with bas-relief carvings of saints and apostles.

One block west of Plaza de Armas is the multi-arched **Palacio de Gobierno** (*5 de Febrero between Bruno Martínez & Zaragoza, tel 1/811-5600, closed Sat., Sun.*). It was built by a Spanish mining tycoon, then seized by the state after the end of colonial rule. Now government headquarters, its interior features colorful murals depicting Durango's history.

Film sets

Since the 1950s, hundreds of films have been shot on location outside Durango, most of them Westerns. Clear blue skies, a temperate climate, and the absence of power lines and other trappings of modern society make the region well-suited to the role of outdoor film set. *Romancing the Stone* (1984) was filmed here, as was *Wagons East* (1994).

About 8 miles (12 km) north of Durango, Villa del Oeste (*Tel 1/810-1212, closed Mon., $*) shimmers like a mirage on the dusty horizon. Built in the 1950s, it was for decades one of Durango's most important sets. When film production dwindled in the 1980s, locals moved in, transforming the scenario into a living, breathing Western town. Other sets to visit in the area include those at Chupaderos, Cañón de los Delgado, and Rancho La Joya (still owned by John Wayne's family). ■

Mazatlán & environs

DESPITE ITS FAMOUS PRE-LENTEN MARDI GRAS celebration, its world-class billfishing, and some of the tastiest seafood on the planet, Mazatlán is not one of Mexico's most sought-after seaside resorts. But admirers of this bayside city of nearly 700,000 couldn't care less if it's spurned by the masses. Fifteen miles (24 km) of beaches stretch north and south of downtown, and hotel and restaurant prices are about half of those in Cancún or Los Cabos.

Just 12 miles (19 km) south of the Tropic of Cancer, Mazatlán enjoys a semitropical climate. Warm year-round, it is hottest and steamiest at the height of the rainy season, in August and September, but even then the humidity doesn't compare to that of resorts farther south.

Most visitors come for the combination of sand, sun, and nighttime fun. The **Zona Dorada** (Golden Zone), north of **Punta Camarón** (Shrimp Point), has some of Mazatlán's most popular beaches. Crowded throughout this bustling hotel zone are shell and souvenir shops, sidewalk bars, and beachfront restaurants. Resort hotels rent watersports equipment, and the bay has gentle breakers. Uniformed vendors stroll the sand, selling everything from flower-shaped mangoes on a stick to Talavera pottery and hammocks. Just offshore lie three islands: **Isla de Pájaros, Isla de Venados,** and **Isla de Lobos.** Of the birds, deer, and wolves for which they are respectively named, only the first are in evidence.

The north end of the Golden Zone (sometimes referred to as "la Zona Platinum") is home to the newest resorts, including **El Cid Mega Resort,** a four-property hotel and time-share complex with a marina and 27-hole golf course. Surfers catch good waves at **Playa las Brujas** (Witch's Beach), where thatch-roofed restaurants sell fresh seafood and host live dance bands

on Sunday afternoons. Walkers and joggers tend to favor **Playa Cerritos** (Little Hills Beach) around the point north of Playa las Brujas. These and other beaches are accessible by public buses, taxis, and *pulmonías* (open-sided taxis).

South of the Zona Dorada, the city's long *malecón* (beachfront promenade) begins at **Playa Norte.** One block inland is the **Acuario Mazatlán** (*111 Av. de los Deportes, tel 69/81-78-15, $$*), where you can see 150 marine species in backlit aquariums, as well as the sea lion, bird, or dive shows. In addition to gift shops, a snack bar, a botanical garden, and a small aviary, there is an extensive children's playground.

A large statue of a naked fisherman and his female companion—known to the locals as "los Monos Bichis," or "the Naked Monkeys"—presides over the south end of the bay. Fishing boats depart from **Playa los Pinos,** where an informal fish market is held daily just after dawn. Farther south, during high tide, young men dive into the shallow water from the 45-foot (15 m) cliffs at **El Mirador.**

Walk inland to admire the streets of historic downtown, its 19th- and 20th-century homes in various states of repair and disarray. Many of the one- and two-story, brick and stucco buildings are painted in bright pastel colors with white trim, their windows and doors protected by intricate

Mazatlán
Ⓜ 77 D2
Visitor information
✉ Tiburón at Camarón Sábalo, 4th floor, Banrural building
☎ 69/16-51-60

wrought-iron grillwork. The civic and religious heart of the city is **Plaza Revolución** *(Between Calles Flores, Nelson, 21 de Marzo, & Juárez)*. Mango and watermelon vendors sit in the shade of tall coconut palms and shiny leafed Indian laurels, while in the cool, dark, subterranean diner underneath the gazebo bandstand, teenagers linger over burgers and soft drinks. On the north side of the square, two distinctive, yellow-tiled spires top the **Catedral.**

A few blocks north of the square is the bustling **Mercado Pino Suárez** *(Juárez & Aquiles Serdán),* a typical market selling clothing and souvenirs, in addition to skinned cow's heads and other victuals. Mazatlán's oldest square, **Plazuela Machado** *(Constitución between Frías & Carnaval)* is surrounded by sidewalk cafés. The plaza was a gift from Filipino-born Juan Machado, who made a fortune here in commerce and mining in the 1830s and 1840s.

Back at the beach, the road winds south past several lookout points with views of the bay and the world's second-highest lighthouse (500 feet/152 m) at **Cerro de la Cresteria,** accessed by a steep, rocky path. From here you will see **Isla de la Piedra** (Stone Island, but really a peninsula), popular with families for weekend picnics. Enjoy a walk through the simple fishing town and a meal or a cold beer at one of the many beachfront seafood shanties. Also here is Mazatlán's new 18-hole

Young men in Old Mazatlán imitate the high divers of Acapulco, who plunge into turbulent, rocky waters from the 45-foot-high (15 m) cliffs at El Mirador.

Colorful Mardi Gras decorations line Mazatlán's downtown parade route.

Carnival

Mazatlán's Carnaval, among the world's most elaborate pre-Lenten celebrations, is also a cultural and family event. The tradition began as friendly battles between 19th-century stevedores, who pelted each other with flour-filled eggshells and recited *comparsas* (rhyming verses mocking their rivals). When rhymes and eggs turned to insults and rocks, town officials replaced the free-for-all with organized parades of decorated floats, regional *tambora* bands (oompah bands with wind and percussion instruments), and a reigning queen and king.

Today, tens of thousands of revelers toss confetti instead of flour, and the rhyming tradition continues as a poetry competition. Friday night "Flower Games" consist of a ballet and orchestral and tambora music at the baseball stadium. Saturday night's "Batalla Naval" is a mock naval battle and stirring fireworks display on Olas Altas Bay. ■

Estrella del Mar golf course *(Tel 69/82-33-00).* Small boats ferry passengers *($)* over from the east side of downtown Mazatlán (save your ticket for the return trip).

Near the base of Cerro de la Crestería, Mazatlán's sportfishing fleet has a dozen boats eager to help you catch sailfish, marlin, yellowfin tuna, and sea bass. Mazatlán is one of Mexico's premier billfishing destinations—its fishing boats catch and release 12,000 fish each year. Nearby, ferry boats depart for La Paz, in Baja California.

Organized tours and independent travelers make trips daily to the former mining towns of Concordia and Copala. While neither town is terribly grand, the journey into the hills fronting the Sierra Madre Occidental is interesting. Just outside **Concordia** (30 miles/48 km from Mazatlán), chunky carved furniture and unglazed ceramic pottery are for sale. In Concordia itself, admire the baroque **Catedral de San Sebastián,** on the main plaza, and take a walk around town before continuing another 15 miles (24 km) to smaller, more isolated **Copala,** winding up into the mountains off Highway 40.

Copala's single street leads to the rustic **Catedral de San José,** where young men sell miniature churches carved from the region's thorny *pochotla* tree. Younger boys offer rides on their tiny donkeys— or a picture of themselves on the sleepy beasts. Visit the church and admire the town's colorful adobe houses dressed in peach and red-violet bougainvillea, organ cacti, and flowering flamboyant trees. Then there's nothing to do except dine in one of the town's three pleasant restaurants before heading back to civilization. Those who want to linger can find rooms to rent in two of the restaurants. ■

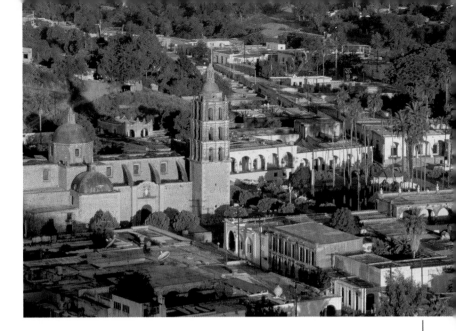
Some of the old mansions in Alamos have been converted to inviting bed-and-breakfasts.

More places to visit in Northwest Mexico

ALAMOS

Begun as a mountain mining town, Alamos was among the most lucrative in the 19th century. Yaqui Indian rebellions and the Mexican Revolution eventually put the mines out of business, and the town declined. In the 1940s, crumbling yet still elegant Andalusian-style mansions were discovered and renovated by wealthy foreigners. During high season you can take a Saturday morning **house and garden tour** (*Calle Comercio 2, $$$*). At other times, just relax and enjoy Old Mexico with a glamorous twist.

On the smart **Plaza de Armas** you'll find the modest **Museo Costumbrista de Sonora** (*Tel 642/80053, closed Mon., Tues., $*), which highlights Sonora's history, and the **Iglesia de la Purísima Concepción,** a Spanish colonial stone church with a three-tiered bell tower. Locals and tourists promenade around poplar-shaded **Parque Alameda** and shop in the surrounding stores and the municipal market.

For a good view of the town, hike or drive south on Calle Juárez up to **El Mirador** (The Lookout). If you want to go farther afield, most hotels can arrange visits to abandoned silver mines and Mayo villages (where artisans make traditional wooden masks). Little-visited but nevertheless worthwhile, **Cuchujaqui Ecological Reserve** comprises pine-oak, low deciduous, thorn, and semitropical forests and has more than 200 species of birds.
🗺 77 C3 **Visitor information** ✉ Juárez 6 ☎ 642/80450

BORDER TOWNS

Nogales and Ciudad Juárez are the largest and most touristic of northwestern Mexico's nine border crossings. Often the destination of bargain-hunting Americans, they also attract the younger crowd bent on finding fun in a Mexican bar. Whether visited as a day trip or a first stop in Mexico, the border towns offer regional cooking, souvenir shopping, and a dash of culture, as well as the usual rough-and-tumble border bar scene.

Avenida Obregón, the main sightseer's drag in **Nogales,** isn't far from the border crossing. Lively Cinco de Mayo (May 5) celebrations offer bullfights, horse races, handicraft sales, and festive parades.

Ciudad Juárez is a major border crossing. It is also Mexico's leader in *maquiladoras* (international manufacturing plants) and headquarters for a major Mexican drug cartel. Visitors passing through or on a day trip from El Paso, Texas, needn't fear the drug trade, however. On the west side of the city's **Plaza Principal** (*Av. 16 de Septiembre at Mariscal*) stands the mission church **Nuestra Señora de Guadalupe,** with its outstanding carved ceiling beams. About 30 miles (50 km) outside town, visit the **Dunas de Samalayuca,** an impressive swath of shifting sand dunes.

Nogales 🅰 77 C5 **Ciudad Juárez** 🅰 77 D6

CUAUHTÉMOC

Although established in Chihuahua state since 1921, the Mennonite communities living north and south of Cuauhtémoc still speak their Low German dialect and wear traditional farmer clothing—overalls and button-down shirts for the men, and long-sleeved dresses, kerchiefs, and broad straw hats for the women. This large Mennonite group has found peace in Mexico's northern desert, having first fled Europe in search of religious freedom, and later Canada after refusing military service during World War II.

The Mennonites' tidy looking villages, called *campos menonitas* in Spanish, are numbered, not named, and the woodframe, pitched-roof houses stand in contrast to the typical Mexican towns in the surrounding plains. Day tours out of Chihuahua take you to see their homes. Visit any day but Sunday, which is dedicated to religious services.

🅰 77 D4

ROSARIO

If you haven't had your fill of quaint, colonial, former mining towns, visit sun-baked Rosario, whose mines churned out vast quantities of gold and silver for nearly 300 years. Much of the gold seems to have ended up on the baroque altarpiece of **Iglesia de Nuestra Señora del Rosario.** Unlike many of northern Mexico's plain Jesuit mission churches, this 18th-century temple is deliciously baroque. After excessive tunneling of nearby mines caused the original church to sink, it was moved, stone by stone, to its present location on the town square. Rosario is best known among Sinaloans as the birthplace of Mexican mariachi singer and actress Lola Beltrán (1932–1996).

🅰 77 E1

HERMOSILLO

Four hours south of the U.S. border at Nogales is Hermosillo, Sonora's mid-size state capital, surrounded by golden plains and backed by jagged mountain peaks. It makes a convenient stopping place for travelers headed south. Walk around the battered yet appealing historic district, admiring the **plaza** (*Pino Suárez, P.E. Calles, Yáñez, & Monterrey*), where the neoclassic **Catedral de la Asunción** indulges a few neo-Gothic whims. The crest of the **Cerro de la Campana** affords a fine view of the city; at its base, the **Museo Regional de Sonora** (*Jesús García at Calle Esteban Sarmiento, tel 62/13-12-34, closed Mon., $*) has exhibits on Sonora's history, geology, and anthropology.

South of town, the government-run **Centro Ecológico de Sonora** (*Carretera a Guaymas Km 2.5, tel 62/50-10-34, closed Mon., Tues., $*) is a center for ecological research and preservation. A 2-mile-long (3 km) path meanders past exhibits of some 300 plant and 240 animal species, many of them endemic to the region. If you come to town in mid-July, join vintners, wine-lovers, and the general populace in an annual celebration of the grape harvest at Fiesta de la Vendimia.

🅰 77 C4 **Visitor information** ✉ Edificio Estatal, Calle Comonfort & Paseo del Canal ☎ 62/17-00-44 or 62/17-02-69

TEACAPÁN

Near Sinaloa's rural southern border, Teacapán and its environs are famous for their plums, shrimp, and mangoes. Cattle ranches and coconut plantations line the 18-mile-long (28 km) peninsula leading to the seaside community. Stop at one of the area's peaceful, white-sand beaches, including **La Tambora, Las Lupitas, Las Cabras,** and **Los Angeles.** Day tours from Mazatlán explore Teacapán's estuaries and mangroves, where you can see ducks from Canada, white and pink herons, flamingos, and many other migratory and resident bird species.

🅰 77 E1 ∎

Like the Franciscan missionaries, who produced everything they needed, people from Mexico's arid northeastern states today are hardy and self-sufficient, and are happiest when left alone by the powers-that-be in Mexico City.

Northeast Mexico

Juan Soriano sculpture in Monterrey

Northeast Mexico

AS IN NEIGHBORING TEXAS, THINGS IN NORTHERN MEXICO JUST SEEM *bigger*. Distances in the northeast are certainly vast. This factor, combined with a dearth of mineral wealth (Zacatecas excepted) and the fierceness with which the Chichimec Indians (see p. 28) defended their territory, led to minimal immigration in colonial times. Pirate raids and swampy, mosquito-ridden lagoons made the east coast undesirable as well. However, the late 20th century saw a change in the region's fortune. Monterrey's development of a major brewery, in addition to glass production, cement plants, and iron and steel foundries, has led to its emergence as the nation's leading manufacturing city.

In 1547, the discovery of a rich silver mine in Zacatecas encouraged exploration to the north. But unlike its western counterpart, the Sierra Madre Oriental contained relatively few precious metals. To encourage settlement in the mid-18th century, the Spanish Crown granted resolute individuals huge landholdings for sheep and cattle ranches. A wealth of available land and lax Mexican immigration policies led many U.S. citizens to settle the northern Mexican territories; by the time Texas declared itself independent of Mexico in 1836, the ratio of U.S. immigrants to Mexicans living there was four to one.

Below the border at the Río Bravo (known as the Rio Grande in the United States), sheep and cattle ranching continue to contribute to northern Mexico's economy and culture. Meat is the mainstay of the northern diet, often served with bread rolls or flour tortillas instead of the corn tortillas ubiquitous in central and southern Mexico. Along with *machaca* (dried, shredded beef) and barbecued kid, a favorite meal is *carne a la tampiqueña*—thin, grilled or charbroiled steak accompanied by rice, *frijoles charros* (beans cooked with pork rind and cilantro), grilled green onions, fresh salsa, and avocado.

Mexico's only gypsum dune fields are found in the Area Protegida Pozas de Cuatrociénegas.

In addition to ranching, the inhabitants of inland valleys in the Sierra Madre Oriental practice subsistence agriculture, harvesting apples, prickly pears, nuts, and pine nuts. Fishing and shrimping form the base of the coastal economy, although petroleum rules in Tampico. Meanwhile, manufacturing opportunities in border cities and in the Monterrey–Saltillo corridor continue to grow.

Outside the major population centers, northeastern Mexico's wilderness areas invite exploration by adventurous travelers. Appearing like mirages in the scrubby desert are ancient archaeological sites, small towns with gold- and silver-studded churches, and productive vineyards. Despite limited infrastructure, backpacking, canyoneering, and rock climbing are gaining popularity in the rugged and still wild mountain ranges. ■

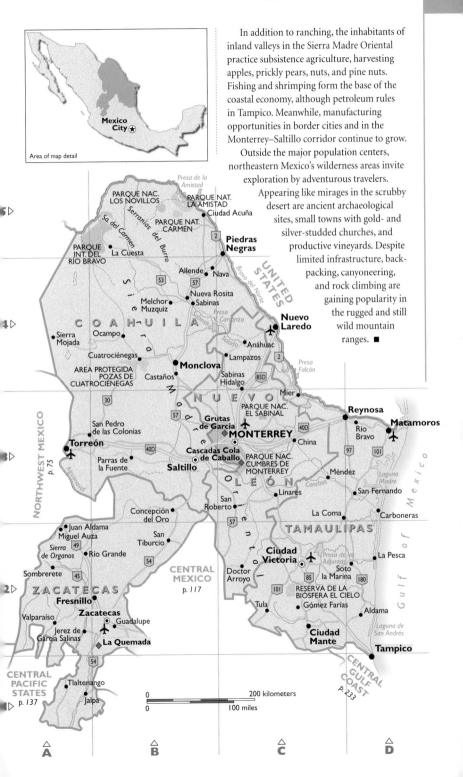

Area of map detail

Mexico City ★

Saltillo
△ 105 B3
Visitor information
✉ Blvd. Francisco Coss at Manuel Acuña, at the Old Train Station
☎ 8/412-5122

Saltillo

SALTILLO, CAPITAL OF THE STATE OF COAHUILA AND THE oldest city in northeastern Mexico, was founded by Spaniards and Portuguese in 1575 as a strategic station along the Camino Real (Royal Highway). Twenty years later, 87 converted Tlaxcala Indian families from central Mexico voluntarily resettled near the town to help Christianize and pacify anarchistic desert tribes. They brought their weaving traditions, and today the *sarape de Saltillo*, a bright-colored woolen blanket, is a universally recognized Mexican icon.

The refreshingly untouristy city of Saltillo feels both old and modern.

Although the mile-high city sprawls with suburbs and industrial complexes, its historical center is visually appealing, with buildings in a variety of architectural styles. Brick and stucco homes surround the town's open main square, **Plaza de Armas** *(Hidalgo at Juárez)*. Wrought-iron benches face inward to the stone-and-bronze central fountain and outward to the pink-stone **Palacio de**

Gobierno. Behind the state government palace is **Plaza de la Nueva Tlaxcala,** a public square whose eye-catching, classic-style statue depicts the city's founders: Spaniards, Tlaxcaltecans, and friars. Three blocks northwest, **Plaza Acuña** *(Aldama between Allende & Flores)* is surrounded by stores, cafés, and the municipal market, where you can shop for leather goods, Saltillo's colorful sarapes, and locally made pottery.

Facing Plaza de Armas is one of northern Mexico's most gorgeous churches, the baroque **Catedral de Santiago de Saltillo** *(Tel 8/414-0230)* and adjoining chapel. Built between 1745 and 1800, the base of its Churrigueresque facade is adorned with spiral Solomonic columns covered with fruit and flowers, and its magnificent wooden doors are carved with the images of St. Peter and St. Paul. Inside, note the beautiful workmanship of the carved and gilded pulpit, the two side altarpieces, and on the right front altar, the silver frontal.

On the east side of town, the **Museo del Desierto** *(Prol. Pérez Treviño 3745, Parque las Maravillas, tel 8/410-6633, $$)* is a wonderful new steel-and-glass museum covering not only desert plants, animals, geology, paleontology, and ecosystems, but also regional Indian cultures and post-Conquest history. ■

Las Pozas de Cuatrociénegas

MANY THINK OF DESERTS AS BARREN, LIFELESS EXPANSES of brown earth and tumbleweeds, but they can be places of surprising beauty, and the Chihuahua Desert has some wonderful surprises. Bubbling out of the desert at Cuatrociénegas, hundreds of mineral springs form crystalline pools, lagoons, superficial rivers, and salt marshes lined with sedges and bunchgrass. Wander the adjoining stark-white gypsum dunes on your own, or hire a guide. To see the far-flung pools, you'll need your own transportation.

Cuatrociénegas
 105 B4
Visitor information
✉ Presidente Carranza 107, Cuatrociénegas
☎ 8/696-0574

Nestled between two spurs of the Sierra Madre Oriental, the **Area Protegida Pozas de Cuatrociénegas** (Pools of the Four Marshes Protected Area) forms a rare desert wetland. These grasslands, scrub forest, gypsum dunes, and mineral springs have been protected since 1995. Hundreds of pools—from 1 to 262 feet (30 cm to 80 m) in diameter—are fed by deep subterranean aquifers. Mineral content and the presence of organic materials and algae determine each pool's clarity and color.

Because of its isolation, this unusual desert wetland has a high ratio of endemic fish and reptiles. Of the 16 known fish species, half are found nowhere else. Swimming and snorkeling, permitted in four areas within 6 to 11 miles (10 to 18 km) of the town of Cuatrociénegas, are delightful here, especially in the winter, when the water typically reaches 70–82°F (21–28°C).

Mezquites is a slow-flowing river fed by a series of springs, whose depth varies from about 6 inches to 6 feet (15 cm to 1.8 m) along the mile-long (1.5 km) stretch that is open for bathing. A natural channel connects two crystal-clear blue pools at **Becerra.** These sites ($) have *palapa* palm shades and rustic bathrooms. The greenish pool at **Playitas,** used mainly by locals and with no services, is accessed by a dirt road. The crystal-clear pool at **Shurince,** which

Snorkeling in the mineral pools at Cuatrociénegas is especially pleasant in the winter, when water temperatures reach 70–82°F (21–28°C).

shrinks dramatically in summer, is part of a larger system of interconnected rivers and a lagoon.

Exposed deposits of gypsum from pools such as Shurince are generally blown west, forming sparkling white dunes that tower several stories above the desert floor. Visit the dunes at Becerra springs ($), or hire a guide ($$$$ per group) at Cuatrociénegas's city hall (municipio). ∎

Monterrey & environs

SEATED IN A VALLEY AT 1,765 FEET (540 M) ABOVE SEA LEVEL, Monterrey is surrounded by the craggy, abrupt peaks of the Sierra Madre Oriental. Dramatic Cerro de la Silla (Saddle Hill), symbol of the city, lies to the west. A modern, independent-thinking city, Monterrey is the third-largest in Mexico (after Mexico City and Guadalajara). As a leader of industry, it enjoys the nation's highest per capita income and has one of the highest literacy rates.

Monterrey
🇲 105 C3
Visitor information
✉ 5 de Mayo 525 Oriente
☎ 8/345-6745

Opposite: With an important university and international commerce, today's Monterrey disavows its insouciant founding.

Monterrey grew slowly, hindered by fierce Chichimec Indian raids, several serious floods in the 17th and 18th centuries, and the Mexican-American War, when the city was occupied by U.S. troops. Construction of railroad lines in 1881 and tax exemptions for industry under President Porfirio Díaz attracted U.S., French, and British as well as Mexican investors. Construction of the Cervecería Cuauhtémoc brewery in 1890 led to the establishment of a glassworks and then a foundry. Today, Monterrey's economy is centered around these industries, as well as cement, bricks, steel, petrochemicals, and automotive products.

In the 1980s, 40 central city blocks separating the state and city government buildings were razed to create the 100-acre (40 ha) **Macroplaza,** or **Gran Plaza** (*Between 5 de Mayo, Av. de la Constitución, Zuazua, & Zaragoza*), a series of green spaces punctuated with fountains and statues. A great place for relaxing and people-watching, this busy, popular park is surrounded by some of Monterrey's early modern buildings, including the steel-and-glass **Condominio Acero building** and the rust red-colored **Faro del Comercio,** a 230-foot (70 m) obelisk designed by Luis Barragán (see p. 40), the father of contemporary Mexican architecture. At the north end of the Macroplaza, at 5 de Mayo, enter the **Palacio de Gobierno** to admire the building's leaded-glass windows honoring heroes of the Revolution, as well as its gleaming parquet floors, crystal chandeliers, and other lovely neoclassic elements.

Extending west from the south end of the narrow park is the **Zona Rosa,** a ten-block pedestrian zone with stores, cafés, juice bars, restaurants, and downtown's nicest hotels. At the southeast corner of the park, the adobe-colored **Museo de Arte Contemporaneo de Monterrey** (*Zuazua at Padre Raymundo Jardón, tel 8/342-4820, closed Mon., $*) sports architect Ricardo Legorreta's trademark marigold, purple, and pink accents. The contemporary art museum hosts installation art and other avante garde exhibits on the ground floor, with a permanent collection of works upstairs. Across the street, the **Catedral de Monterrey** (*Zuazua 1100 Sur, tel 8/340-3752*) has been rebuilt several times owing to fires and floods; its interior was remodeled in the 19th century in the neoclassic style. Worth noting are five murals in the apse, painted in 1942. Near the northeast end of the Macroplaza, the **Museo de Historia Mexicana** (*Dr. Coss 445 Sur, tel 8/345-9898, closed Mon., $*) provides a fascinating visual history of the nation, with artifacts, religious icons and clothing, scale models, installations, and illustrative maps. Exhibits of

Science and technology are the focus of the Science Museum at Monterrey's Centro Cultural Alfa, enjoyed by kids and adults alike.

popular art and culture fill the first-floor galleries.

Behind the cathedral, antiques shops, cafés, and bars are cropping up in the restored 19th-century homes of the **barrio antiguo,** an older neighborhood currently in vogue. Within this 15-block area of cobblestone streets and 19th- and early 20th-century houses you will find one of the city's few remaining examples of secular colonial architecture: **La Casa del Campesino** (*Abasolo between Mina & Naranjo, closed Mon.*). Built in the mid-18th century, it contains later murals describing Mexican history in its chapel. During the barrio's late-November annual festival there are film screenings, exhibitions, and musical performances.

El Obispado (*José Rafael Verger s/n, tel 8/333-9751, closed Mon., $*) is one of the few things English writer Graham Greene liked about Mexico. He called it "as beautiful as anything out of the Middle Ages." Originally the summer home of one of the last bishops of the viceregal era, this baroque structure now houses the **Museo Regional de Nuevo León.** And while Greene's epitaph seems an exaggeration, the building itself—with its sculpted facade and the Chapel to the Virgin of Guadalupe—is more interesting than the period artifacts within.

West of town, the stately, brick-and-ivy **Cervecería Cuauhtémoc** (*Av. Alfonso Reyes 220 Norte, tel 8/328-5355, closed Sun.*) offers a free guided tour of its brewery (call in advance to arrange an English-language tour) and a sample of the brew in the outdoor beer garden. The adjacent **Museo de Monterrey** arts museum is closed indefinitely, but next door, the **Salón de la Fama** still documents the history of baseball.

"*El beis*" was introduced in the late 19th century by people from the U.S working in Mexico. Before it became established as a Mexican sport, northern Mexican teams played against U.S. teams, while those in the Yucatán played against Cubans.

Southwest of the city, on the road to Parque Ecológico Chipinque (see below), the striking **Centro Cultural Alfa** (*Av. Gómez Morín 1100, tel 8/303-0002, closed Mon., $*) houses a planetarium, an Omnimax theater, and a science museum. This modern cultural complex also has a gift shop, a restaurant, and a large mural by Oaxaca artist Rufino Tamayo (see p. 202).

PARQUE NACIONAL CUMBRES DE MONTERREY

Surrounding Monterrey, 619,000-acre (250,500 ha) **Cumbres de Monterrey** actually comprises a series of parks and attractions, each with its own administration and agenda. The park's name refers to the jagged peaks that tower over Monterrey, which lies tucked under a blanket of smog in the valley below. As is the case with many Mexican national parks and reserves, only a small portion is developed for tourism, while the rest serves as a buffer to development, a refuge for wildlife, and in this instance a natural aquifer.

Southwest of Monterrey loom the steely green peaks of **Parque Ecológico Chipinque** (*Final de Av. Gómez Marín, San Pedro, tel 8/303-0000, $*), about 12 miles (20 km) from the city center. Although representing less than one percent of the area of Los Cumbres National Park, Chipinque's varied topography includes valleys, canyons, mountain peaks, and pine-oak forests. The mammals most often seen are squirrels, gray foxes, and coati.

However, white-tailed deer and black bear are also present, as are at least 120 species of migratory and resident birds. There's no camping in the park, but you can hike or mountain bike, take short guided walks from the Visitor Center (reserve several days in advance), or scale one of the park's four peaks (with park guards if you wish). The highest summit is **El Copete de las Águilas** (Eagles' Crest), at 7,410 feet (2,260 m); the most frequently climbed and the symbol of the park is **El "M"** (pronounced EH-may). Both are accessed from a mesa near the entrance to **Hotel Chipinque** (*Meseta Chipinque 1000, tel 8/378-6600*), a stone and timber lodge with a restaurant overlooking Monterrey (best at night, when the city lights twinkle) and a faux-rustic bar.

Rock climbers are attracted to the sheer, 984-foot (300 m) walls of **Cañón de la Huasteca** (*Av. Morones Prieto s/n, Santa Catarina, tel 8/337-1388, $*), about 12 miles (20 km) west of Monterrey. These canyons once provided both local Indians and Spanish settlers with a refuge from Apache raids. In the municipality of Santiago is **Cascadas Cola de Caballo** (*Carr. Cola de Caballo Km 6 off Hwy. 85, tel 8/347-1599, $*), an 82-foot (25 m) waterfall named for its resemblance to a horse's tail. A 20- to 30-minute climb from the entrance brings you to the viewpoint; a set of stone steps leads about a third of the way up near the falls, and a separate dirt path takes you to the summit. Along the last few miles before the park entrance, locals sell wicker furniture, stone carvings, and large ceramic pots.

North of the Cañón de la Huasteca, the **Grutas de García** (*Salida a García, tel 8/347-1533, $$*) is a series of 50-million-year-old caverns filled with stalactites and stalagmites. A winding, illuminated, 4-mile (2.5 km) path and wooden stairs lead through 16 monumental caves, many with 40-foot-tall (12 m) ceilings. Guided tours are given during Semana Santa (Holy Week), on the hour between 9 a.m. and 5 p.m. You can also swim in the outdoor pool or have a meal in the site restaurant. ■

Parque Nacional Cumbres de Monterrey, just outside the city, provides a quick escape for urban residents.

Zacatecas

SURROUNDED BY CRAGGY, ARID MOUNTAINS AND UNUSUAL rock formations, Zacatecas occupies a narrow canyon at 8,900 feet (2,700 m) above sea level. It is chilly during the winter months, when blustery *nortes* (brisk, often cold winds emanating from the north) negate the otherwise warm embrace of mountain chains to both the east and west. Zacatecos are known for their friendly, open demeanor with a hint of cowboy swagger. On weekend evenings, you'll meet them on lively *callejoneadas*, festive musical parties that parade through the smaller streets, often accompanied by a mescal-bearing burro.

Zacatecas
A 105 B2
Visitor information
✉ Av. Hidalgo 403
☎ 492/40393

Zacatecas gets its Náhuatl Indian name (meaning "land where zacate grass grows") from the abundant grasses that make the surrounding areas ideal ranchlands. The city grew quickly after the discovery of a rich vein of silver at **Cerro de la Bufa** (Wineskin Hill) in 1546, despite uprisings led by the Caxcanes tribe. Financed by the silver barons, the Dominicans, Jesuits, and Augustinians established headquarters here for evangelizing the wild north, leaving a legacy of grand churches and seminaries.

The facade of the **Catedral Basílica Menor** (*South side of Plaza de Armas on Av. Hidalgo, tel 492/26211*) is cited as *the* masterpiece of Mexican baroque. Exquisitely carved of pink sandstone, the church's exterior epitomizes the Churrigueresque style, with almost overpowering ornamentation covering the three-tiered main facade. The interior, sacked during the Reform and again during the Revolution, is nearly naked. On the east side of **Plaza de Armas,** Zacatecas's rather cheerless main square, stands the 18th-century **Palacio de Gobierno** (*Tel 492/39511*), with murals of local history adorning its interior.

South of the main square, the *beaux-arts* **Mercado González Ortega** (*Hidalgo & Tacuba*) was converted from a daily market to a

shopping mall with several restaurants, losing none of its splendor during the remodeling. The **Museo Zacatecano** (*Dr. Hierro 303, tel 492/26580, closed Tues., $*) contains naive religious paintings (*retablos*), Huichol art, and 16th- to 19th-century ironwork. Now an auditorium, the nearby **Iglesia de San Agustín** sports a wonderful plateresque facade.

Baroque-style **Templo de Santo Domingo** (*Genaro Codina 227 at Plaza Santo Domingo, tel 492/21083*) has a sumptuous interior, with more than half a dozen wonderful Churrigueresque altarpieces, while 18th-century paintings decorate the octagonal sacristy. Next door, you can visit the **Museo Rafael Coronel** (*Ex-Convento de San Francisco s/n, tel 492/28116, closed Wed., $*) to see Mexico's largest collection of ceremonial masks. Housed in a 16th-century monastery, this museum also exhibits puppets, pre-Hispanic ceramics, colonial jewelry, and sketches by Coronel's father-in-law, Diego Rivera.

International art dominates the extensive collection in the **Museo Pedro Coronel** (*Av. Fernando Villalpando at Plaza Santo Domingo, tel 492/28021, closed Thurs., $*), in an 18th-century fortress. Check out works by Braque, Dalí, and Chagall, as well

as African, Indian, and Asian art. The **Museo Manuel Felguérez** *(Calle Colón s/n, tel 492/43705, closed Tues., $)* presents the abstract art collection of the museum's namesake in a 19th-century setting.

Southwest of the town center are several verdant city parks, including **Parque Alameda** *(Villalpando at Av. Torreón)* and **Parque Enrique Estrada** *(González Ortega at Manuel M. Ponce)*. The latter has an excellent view of the pink-stone aqueduct that served the city until the early 20th century. West of the park is the **Museo Goitia** *(E. Estrada 102, tel 4/922-0211, closed Mon., $)*, with 19th- and 20th-century paintings by half a dozen native Zacatecos.

For a city panorama, drive or hike to **Cerro de la Bufa,** which overlooks the city to the northeast. A museum *(Closed Mon., $)*, chapel, and rotunda commemorate the one-day battle during which Pancho Villa's División del Norte ousted government forces in the Revolutionary War (see p. 34). Alternatively, take the 2,100-foot (640 m) aerial tram, or *teleférico (Tel 492/25694, $)*, from **Cerro del Grillo.** From here you can descend into **"El Edén"** mine *(Antonio Dovali off Av. Torreón, tel 492/23002, $)*, which for more than 350 years produced silver, gold, copper, zinc, and iron at the cost of many lives.

Six miles (10 km) southeast of Zacatecas is the **Templo de Guadalupe** *(Jardín Juárez Oriente s/n, tel 492/32386)*, a former Franciscan monastery housing a collection of viceregal religious art. ■

A worker cleans the almost overpowering baroque facade of the Catedral Basílica Menor.

Ciudad Victoria
🗺 105 C2
Visitor information
✉ 19 Méndez y Doblado 220-A
☎ 1/316-8352

Reserva de la Biósfera El Cielo

EL CIELO (MEANING "THE SKY") STRETCHES BETWEEN TWO spurs of the Sierra Madre Oriental in southwestern Tamaulipas. A dramatic range of elevation (7,218 feet/2,200 m) and a favorable location near the Tropic of Cancer produce vastly distinct ecosystems, including tropical, cloud, pine-oak, and evergreen forests. Designated a biosphere reserve in 1986, the park is a haven for wildlife, while its cloud forest provides a rainwater catchment for the tropical forest and commercial agriculture to the east and southeast.

El Cielo was heavily logged for 30 years from the 1930s, but the lumber companies gave up when rugged topography and a lack of

El Cielo has four distinct ecosystems: tropical rain forest, cloud forest, pine-oak forest, and evergreen forest.

infrastructure proved overwhelming. Today, rustic restaurants and lodgings are available at some of the sparsely populated area's 26 ranches and *ejidos* (community landholdings). Ecotourism, if it takes off, may prove a viable alternative to forestry and a source of much-needed income.

The reserve has a high level of biodiversity. There are six species of feline (all endangered), white-tailed deer, black bear, and more than 250 birds species. Bird-watchers need venture no farther than the tropical forests around **El Nacimiento,** about two hours from Ciudad Victoria. Pygmy owls, amethyst-throated hummingbirds, and other

beauties can be spotted near the headwaters of the **Río Frío.** You can fish, swim in a natural pool, or sample freshwater shrimp and crayfish in El Nacimiento's simple cafés.

A regular bus service is available as far as **Gómez Farías,** where you will find a humble hotel and campground, a visitor center, and a few restaurants and stores. If you have a high-clearance vehicle, continue about an hour longer to the tiny hamlet of **Alta Cima,** which hangs above a cloud-forest valley. Hire local guides *($$)* for day hikes to mountain glens and meadows, and, in season, to waterfalls and streams. You can also arrange for guides and pack animals for longer treks into the reserve. The friendly women at **Restaurant La Fe** prepare simple but filling fare and sell local handicrafts. Adjoining the restaurant are lodgings and a campground. Beyond Alta Cima, a four-wheel-drive vehicle is advisable.

At about 4,590 feet (1,400 m) above sea level, **San José** is tucked into a green valley—the transition zone between cloud and pine-oak forest. From here hike to the **Cueva del Infernillo,** a cave containing a limpid pool. Venturing still farther, you will reach the evergreen forest around **La Gloria,** with more difficult terrain and fewer services, but a more pristine wilderness. ∎

The little explored Sierra del Carmen spills over the U.S.-Mexico border into Big Bend NP.

More places to visit in Northeast Mexico

PARRAS DE LA FUENTE

One of Northeast Mexico's prettiest historic towns, Parras de la Fuente, in Coahuila state, brings a splash of green to the desert. Secular and religious buildings cluster around the center of town; of note are the **Santuario de Guadalupe** (*Viesca & Ocampo, tel 842/20548*), with its baroque and neoclassic altarpieces, and the 16th-century **Templo de San Ignacio de Loyola** (*Treviño 103 Sur, tel 842/20548*), with its small museum of old documents, books, and viceregal-era paintings.

At 4,985 feet (1,520 m), the city and surrounding countryside enjoy a pleasant climate well suited to growing figs, dates, pecans, avocados, and grapes. Here you'll find the continent's first winery, built in the late 16th century. Originally the Hacienda de San Lorenzo, and now **Casa Madero** (*Tel 8/422-0111*), it still produces wine and brandy and offers daily tours. The harvest is celebrated each August with the week-long Grape and Wine Festival (La Fiesta de la Vendimia).

🅰 105 B3 **Visitor information** ✉ Carretera Parras Paila Km 3 ☎ 8/422-0259

SIERRA DEL CARMEN & SIERRA LAS MADERAS

Rising out of the forbidding Chihuahua Desert near the Texas border are the rugged mountains of the **Sierra del Carmen,** and to the south, the **Sierra las Maderas.** Desert foothills dotted with bare rock, creosote, opuntia cacti, and pungent mesquite lead up into this virtually uninhabited mountain range. Difficult backcountry hiking accesses dry riverbeds, flower-strewn valleys, grasslands, and, finally, ponderosa woodlands, year-round streams, and peaks more than 7,000 feet (2,130 m) above sea level.

Black bear wander in the pinyon-oak forests around **Cañón de la Media Luna** (Half Moon Canyon), where the lovely manzanita bush and the madrone expose shiny white or pinkish wood underneath blistered-looking red bark. Horse trails and old logging roads lead to deep, wooded canyons, home to bobcat, white-tail and mule deer, coyote, and mountain lion. The rugged terrain and lack of infrastructure lead some explorers to book hiking tours out of Texas' Big Bend National Park, just across the border. Others make a base camp at Cañón de la

Media Luna, accessed by gravel and dirt roads and on foot from the mining village of La Cuesta de Malena, off Highway 53.
🅼 105 B5

SIERRA DE ORGANOS

Relatively unexplored and with no facilities, this region of Zacatecas is named for the resemblance of its huge igneous rocks to the branches of the organ cactus. It's a lonely, quiet place, perfect for hiking, rock climbing, and mountain biking, but remember it's a remote destination should you have an emergency. Fantastic canyon views and rock formations have induced cinematographers to film scenes for more than 50 movies here, including *Caveman,* with Ringo Starr (1981).
🅼 105 A2

SOMBRERETE

Sombrerete, in Zacatecas, was once an important producer of lead, tin, mercury,

East of Durango, strange and beautiful basalt rock formations characterize the Sierra de Organos.

silver, and gold, and the town has some impressive secular and religious buildings in baroque and neoclassic styles. Visit the 18th-century **Templo de San Francisco** and adjoining **Capilla de la Tercera Orden,** the **Capilla de Santa Veracruz** in the **Templo de la Soledad,** and the **Templo**

de Santo Domingo, whose main facade is adorned with female caryatid columns.
🅼 105 A2

TAMPICO

Tampico has merged with Ciudad Madero in the southern extreme of Tamaulipas to form one of Mexico's major seaports and its tenth-largest metropolis. Surrounded on three sides by the Gulf of Mexico, the Pánuco River, and a maze of interconnecting lagoons, this area was fought over by pirates, Spanish settlers, and indigenous tribes throughout the 16th and 17th centuries. Today, late 19th-century and early 20th-century buildings surrounding **Plaza de la Libertad** show French and English influence, while on the waterfront enormous oil refineries, storage facilities, and tankers have replaced the more picturesque structures of former years. Marimba bands entertain on Sunday afternoons in **Plaza de Armas.** In adjacent Ciudad Madero, the **Museo de la Cultura Huasteca** (*Juana Inés de la Cruz at 1 de Mayo, tel 1/210-2217, closed Sun., $)* has exhibits on regional history.
🅼 105 D1

ZONA ARQUEOLÓGICA LA QUEMADA

About 50 miles (80 km) south of Zacatecas is La Quemada, the ruins of an ancient, unknown culture or cultures, with cylindrical, circular, and rectangular ceremonial structures built of stone, rubblework, and brick. Experts believe they were created by an agricultural group, probably between A.D. 350 and 950. Among the surviving structures is the **Salón de las Columnas** (Room of the Columns), a series of six-foot-tall (1.8 m) brick columns where Huichol Indians today hold private religious ceremonies prior to the spring equinox. The purpose of the building called the **Pirámide Votativa** (Votive Pyramid) is not clear, but the ball court is similar to those used throughout Mesoamerica. Stone and clay roads radiate for over 100 miles (160 km) from the hilltop site, possibly linking northern tribes with more militant peoples to the south. A paved road reaches the site from Highway 54, south of Zacatecas.
🅼 105 B2 ☎ Tel 492/25085 🕐 Closed the three days prior to spring equinox 🅂 $ ■

B uilt by, and often of, silver and gold, the central states embrace both the mighty Sierra Madre and the Bajío lowlands. Their great legacy is baroque and neoclassic edifices and stately plazas paid for by rich mines and successful merchants.

Central Mexico

Pottery design motif

Central Mexico

"ARRIBA, ABAJO, AL CENTRO, AL DENTRO" ("UP, DOWN, TO THE MIDDLE, TO the inside") is a Spanish drinking toast, but it also describes the colonization of Central Mexico. Spurred by the discovery of huge silver deposits in Zacatecas (up), and subsequently Guanajuato (down), Spanish entrepreneurs swarmed "the middle," to extract deposits of mineral wealth from deep within the earth. Guanajuato became a great mining city, while San Luis Potosí (with a shorter-lived silver boom), Aguascalientes, and San Miguel de Allende became important agricultural centers and way stations.

4 ▷

Luis Moya

3 ▷ Rincón de Romos

45

AGUASCALIENTE

Aguascalientes

Calvillo

7C

2 ▷

△
A

Guanajuato's adobe-lined lanes are steeped in history.

Along with the entrepreneurs came the Catholic Church. In the Sierra Gorda, the Pame tribe were persuaded to give up their nomadic lifestyle and build the missions whose mixture of indigenous and classic ecclesiastic imagery is much admired today. Forty years of warfare against the Guayachicilies around San Luis Potosí, however, proved fruitless in subduing this Chichimec tribe. Peace was achieved only after Franciscan friars convinced Spain to offer palatable terms for peace, including freedom from paying tribute.

Free-thinking clergy were among the instigators of independence from Spain, an idea conceived in Central Mexico. Intellectual and well-spoken, the idiosyncratic priest Miguel Hidalgo y Costilla is considered the father of Mexican independence. Along with Captain Ignacio Allende and others, Padre Hidalgo plotted the Revolution in Querétaro (see p. 136); his famous cry for freedom was rung on the parish bell at Dolores Hidalgo. Both men were quickly captured and executed, losing their lives but unleashing a bloody war.

After independence, mining concerns continued to thrive with an enlarged European market. On the rich plains of the Bajío region, Querétaro merchants amassed great fortunes providing luxury goods and investment capital. Individual fortunes paid for incredible masterpieces of baroque religious and secular architecture, indulging every whim with imported tiles, French furnishings, and goods made locally by talented artisans.

Today the colonial cities of the Mexican heartland merge history, European and mestizo culture, and modernity. Stunning churches and palaces—some now housing hotels, restaurants, and museums—line well-tended plazas, and internationally known musicians perform at Guanajuato's Cervantes

5 ▷

NORTHEAST MEXICO
p. 103

Huertecillas

Estación
Vanegas

Estación
Catorce   Matehuala
Real
de Catorce

Santo Domingo

Herradura   Charcas

Villa de
Ramos   Venado   Entronque
El Huizache
Presa de
Guadalupe

Salinas
de Hidalgo

S A N   L U I S

P O T O S Í

49   Ahualulco   57   Cerritos
Villa Juárez

Loreto

ZACATECAS   ✈ San Luis Potosí

Tepetates   Villa   70
Zaragoza
Villa de Arriaga   Santa María   Río Verde
del Río

Ocampo   PARQUE
NACIONAL
51   EL GOGORRÓN   Balneario
de Lourdes
San Felipe   57
San Luis
de la Paz

LEÓN ✈   Dolores
Hidalgo
Templo de
San Cayetano
45D
San Francisco   ⊙ Guanajuato
del Rincón   Silao   Presa Ignacio   San Miguel
Allende   de Allende

G U A N A J U A T O   QUERÉTARO

Cuerámaro   Irapuato   Comonfort   Querétaro ⊙
Ezequiel
Salamanca   45D   Montes
90   43   Tequisquiapan
Pénjamo   Valle de   Celaya ✈   57
Santiago   51   San Juan del Río
Lerma   Laguna
Yuriria   Salvatierra   Jerécuaro   Amealco
Moroleón   Yuriria   Presa
Solís
Acámbaro

CENTRAL PACIFIC STATES
p. 137

NORTHEAST MEXICO
p. 103

Salto del Agua
El Naranjo
80
Ciudad
del Maíz

PARQUE
NACIONAL   Alaquines
EL POTOSÍ
Cárdenas

85
Tamuín   70   Ebano
Ciudad
Valles

San Ciro
de Acosta   Verde   Xilitla

Tamazunchale
Concá   Tancoyol
Jalpan   Tilaco
3191m   Landa de
Co. Pinguicas   Matamoros

San José   120
Iturbide

AROUND MEXICO CITY
p. 211

CENTRAL GULF COAST
p. 233

El Salto

Tampaón

Moctezuma

Verde

Santa María

Mexico
City

Area of map detail

0   100 kilometers
0   50 miles

B   C   D   E

Festival (see p. 122) and at San Miguel de Allende's classical and jazz events. Posh colonial-era theaters host the opera and symphony, while *callejoneadas* (roving musical parties) attract students and other less formal types. Throughout the region there are many museums, language schools, and an eclectic range of folk and fine art for sale. ∎

Guanajuato
 119 B2
Visitor information
 Plaza de la Paz 14
 473/27622

Guanajuato

UNLIKE OTHER VENERABLE CITIES, WHICH RADIATE IN A dignified grid from the main plaza, Guanajuato's long, loopy streets intersect at odd angles. Alleys lurch crookedly uphill, decorated with geranium-filled flower boxes and washing hung to dry. A turn in a cobblestone lane may lead to an ancient stairway, a dead end, or one of more than a dozen plazas surrounded by stores, open-air cafés, and rainbow-painted homes. On Fridays and Saturdays *callejoneadas*— moveable parties—snake through town, led by student musicians dressed as Spanish troubadours.

Filled with winding streets and ornate buildings, Guanajuato is one of Mexico's most beautifully preserved colonial cities.

Guanajuato, whose name is derived from a Purépecha Indian word meaning "Hill of Frogs," begins at the bottom of a gorge, sweeping up the surrounding hills in a tapestry of multicolored dwellings. Most sights are located on or just off extended Juárez and Pocitos streets, both of which change names several times as they follow the ancient riverbed. Tunnels underneath the city divert cross-town traffic, easing mid-city congestion.

Once Mexico's most significant mining town, Guanajuato, capital of its namesake state, has a wealth of magnificent churches, museums, theaters, and homes—a successful jumble of rococo, Moorish, neoclassic, baroque, and other

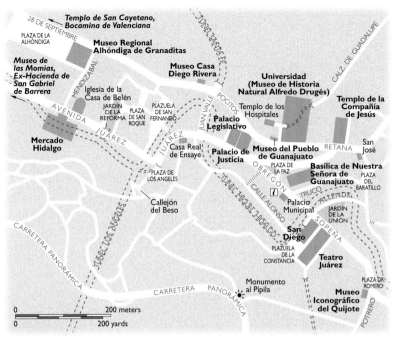

styles. An impressive example of Churrigueresque architecture is the **Templo de la Compañía de Jésus** (*Plaza de la Compañía near Hidalgo, tel 473/21827*), its fantastic pink-stone facade topped by an elegant neoclassic cupola.

The church originally pertained to the adjacent **Universidad de Guanajuato** (*Lascuráin de Retana 5, tel 473/20006*). Established in 1724 as a Jesuit college, the school is now a major university emphasizing the arts and letters. Leafy **Jardín de la Unión,** the city's social hub, occupies the former atrium of the adjacent 18th-century **Templo de San Diego Alcalá.**

Surrounding the park are restaurants, outdoor cafés, a hotel, and **Teatro Juárez** (*Calle de Sopeña s/n, at Jardín de la Unión, tel 473/ 20183, $*), whose sober neoclassic facade belies its luscious interior, with both Moorish and art nouveau elements. One long block southeast is the **Museo Iconográfico del**

Quijote (*Manuel Doblado 1, tel 473/26721, closed Mon., $*), where each of the 600 exhibits relates to Spanish author Miguel de Cervantes' Don Quixote or Sancho Panza.

Most of Guanajuato's major sights are found northwest of Jardín de la Unión; many cluster around **Plaza de la Paz** (*Calle de la Paz at Av. Juárez*). Adjacent to the neoclassic green quarrystone **Palacio Legislativo** is the beautiful **Palacio de Justicia** (Supreme Court Building), originally designed by colonial architect Eduardo Tresguerras as the home of Guanajuato's wealthiest mining baron, Count de Rul y Valenciana.

The **Museo del Pueblo de Guanajuato** (*Pocitos 7, tel 473/ 22990, closed Mon., $*) has a varied collection of secular and religious art highlighting 17th- and 18th-century sculpture, paintings, and decorated utilitarian objects. To the east, the bright yellow **Basílica Colegiata de Nuestra Señora**

de Guanajuato houses an eighth-century, polychrome statue of the Virgin on a solid silver pedestal. Thought to be Mexico's oldest Christian icon, it was the gift of King Felipe II of Spain.

Family furnishings and photos, the muralist-painter's sketches and finished canvases, and the work of contemporary artists fill the **Museo Casa Diego Rivera** *(Pocitos 47, tel 473/21197, closed Mon., $),* where Rivera was born in 1886.

Soon after its debut as a granary, the **Alhóndiga de Granaditas** was the stage for the first battle in the War of Independence, a rebel success (see p. 32). It was later captured and used as a fortress by Spanish royalists, who hung the severed heads of revolutionary leaders Hidalgo, Allende, Aldama, and Jiménez in cages from its four corners, where they remained until the end of the war. The structure now houses a museum *(Mendizabal 6, tel 473/21112, closed Mon., $),* with murals showing topical regional events as well as history, archaeology, and ethnology exhibits. Nearby is the **Mercado Hidalgo** *(Av. Juárez off Mendizabal),* a busy city market. Designed by French architect Gustave Eiffel in 1910, it is an interesting glass and cast-iron structure.

Lovers of the macabre (or the truly tacky) should visit the **Museo de las Momias** *(Explanada del Panteón, tel 473/20639, $).* Within the mummy museum are more than 100 former Guanajuato residents who have been disinterred and displayed in glass cases. A combination of dry atmosphere, unique soil composition, and their descendants' failure to pay cemetery fees permits this ultimate indignity. For a breath of fresh air, continue outside town to the **Ex-Hacienda de San Gabriel de Barrera** *(Carretera Antigua a Marfil Km 2.5, tel 473/20619, $).* Sixteen fabulous gardens, each in a different style, grace this restored hacienda, now a museum with 17th- to 19th-century European art and furnishings.

Perched above the city is the **Templo de San Cayetano,** also known as Templo la Valenciana *(Carretera Dolores Hidalgo Km 2),* built by silver baron the Count of Valenciana. The church's beautifully sculpted facade of pink quarrystone leads to an even more dazzling interior with three gilded altarpieces, respectively plateresque, Churrigueresque, and baroque. Take a tour of the adjacent **Bocamina de Valenciana** *(Carretera Dolores Hidalgo Km 5, $),* still in production. ∎

Actors perform the roles of Don Quixote and Sancho Panza at the yearly Cervantes Festival.

Festival Cervantino

Today's internationally known Cervantes Festival had its beginnings in the 1950s, when a university professor encouraged his students to perform *entremeses,* one-act Spanish playlets. The success of these informal outdoor productions led to a more organized, annual event.

Seeking to showcase artists across a wide spectrum of genres, the producers contract traditional, folkloric, and avant-garde theater and music ensembles in addition to Chinese acrobats and other world-class acts. Over the festival's 28-year history, participants have included the Royal Shakespeare Company, the New York Philharmonic Orchestra, and the Black Vampire of Argentina. Today, tens of thousands of spectators attend the two-week event, making advance hotel reservations essential. ∎

San Miguel de Allende

FEW TOWNS ARE AS SUBTLY ENCHANTING AS SAN MIGUEL. Some places dazzle, others seduce, but San Miguel de Allende most definitely bewitches. Nothing short of magic explains how somewhere so full of foreigners remains so endearingly Mexican. Awash with charming vignettes, this is a painterly town whose steep, cobblestoned streets echo the undulating lines of the surrounding hills. An energetic community of artists produces excellent folk and fine art, in addition to a jazz festival and a classical music concert series.

Originally a mule train stop along the gold and silver highway, San Miguel later prospered as a market village for surrounding haciendas. The Mexican government wisely declared it a national historic monument in 1926, preventing modern-style buildings from destroying its vintage essence. Since then, its simple but pervasive charms have been luring artists, rat-race dropouts, and students of Spanish. The **Instituto Allende** (Ancha de San Antonio 20, tel 415/ 20190) offers language courses as well as fine arts; the **Centro Cultural Nigromante** (Macías 75, tel 415/20289) teaches music, dance, painting, sculpting, and more. Both are located in gracious, two-story, balconied mansions.

Touring the town on foot is most agreeable and mildly aerobic. A good place to begin is the main square, **Plaza Allende** (Calles Correo, San Francisco, Portal Allende, & Portal Guadalupe), called "el Jardín" by most people. As you

San Miguel de Allende
🅰 119 C2
Visitor information
✉ Southeast corner of Plaza Principal, left of the cathedral
☎ 415/26565

A garlic salesman peddles his wares.

negotiate the cobblestoned streets and high sidewalks, you'll pass many churches, cozy cafés, and beautiful pastel homes—some well preserved, others deliciously decrepit. To gain entry to some of the town's mansions and lovely gardens, join a Sunday **house and garden tour** *($$$$)*, organized by the **Biblioteca Pública** *(Insurgentes 25, tel 415/20293)*. Proceeds go to local charities.

The birthplace of independence hero Ignacio Allende, at what is now the **Museo de la Casa de Ignacio Allende** *(Cuna de Allende 1, tel 415/22499, closed Mon., $)*, is worth a visit. Wonderful 19th-century architecture with baroque influences is complemented by the museum's display of colonial-era furnishings.

In San Miguel's many stores you will find outstanding utilitarian and decorative handicrafts imbuing traditional genres—including tinwork, textiles, blown glass,

papier-mâché, and jewelry—with design and technical innovations. The city itself seems to fan the artistic flame. For proof of this, look no further than the 19th-century Gothic Revival-style exterior of **La Parroquia de San Miguel Arcángel** *(south side of Plaza Allende)*, which untrained local stone cutter Cerefino Gutiérrez is supposed to have designed after looking at postcards of French Gothic cathedrals. The many-steepled church honors the town's patron saint, the Archangel Michael.

San Miguel's other five-star church is the **Oratorio de San Felipe Neri** *(Insurgentes at Llanos)*, a few blocks northeast of the main plaza. Multiple domes and towers in different styles top the pink quarrystone facade. Within, oil paintings detailing the life of Florentine saint Felipe Neri have been attributed to 18th-century Spanish master Miguel Cabrera. In the west transept, the **Santa Casa de Loreto** chapel was commissioned by the Count and Countess de la Canal, whose sculptures flank that of the Virgin Mary. The adjoining **camarín** (dressing room) is an extraordinary, eight-sided baroque alcove with three impressive altarpieces. Other worthwhile 18th-century churches are the **Templo de San Francisco** *(San Francisco at Juárez)* and, just to the east, the **Templo de Nuestra Señora de la Salud.**

For a walk outside town, bring a picnic lunch to the public cacti gardens at **El Charco del Ingenio** *(½ mile/1 km out of town, closed Nov.–March, $)*. The hot springs at **La Gruta Balneario,** 5 miles (8 km) north of town on the road to Dolores Hidalgo *(Tel 415/22530, ext. 145, closed Mon., $)*, has three interconnected mineral pools, one of them in a cave. ■

Querétaro & environs

LOCATED IN MEXICO'S FERTILE BAJÍO REGION, QUERÉTARO'S wealth of productive farmland once made it one of New Spain's most important cities. Since it was founded in 1531, the city has figured in important political dramas—from plotting independence from Spain (see p. 32) to signing the disastrous Treaty of Guadalupe Hidalgo, ceding half of the country to the United States in 1848 (see p. 33). Despite Querétaro's status as a major industrial player, its center has baroque churches, historic buildings, and museums well worth exploring.

The Templo de San Francisco (built 1540–50) overlooks Jardín Zenea, Querétaro's pleasant hub.

Plans to throw off colonial rule were nurtured in the **Casa de la Corregidora,** located on the north side of dignified **Plaza de Armas** (*Avs. Pasteur & 5 de Mayo*). In this house Doña Josefa Ortiz de Domínguez, the wife of the Spanish-appointed *corregidor* (mayor), conspired with Miguel Hidalgo, Ignacio Allende, and other intellectuals. *La corregidora* was put under house arrest and later executed. You are welcome to explore the interior courtyards of

the grand home, which now houses state government offices. On the plaza's west flank, admire the baroque facade of the 18th-century **Casa de Ecala,** built of sculpted quarrystone and effusively decorated with Talavera tiles.

The city's hub is congenial **Jardín Zenea** (*Avs. Corregidora, 16 de Septiembre, Juárez, & Madero*), a few blocks to the west, where elderly couples get up to dance when the band strikes up a melodramatic tune. Nearby, the

Querétaro
 119 C1
Visitor information
✉ Pasteur Norte 4
☎ 421/21412

dome of the 16th-century **Templo de San Francisco** is decorated with imported Spanish tiles. Within the adjoining former monastery, the **Museo Regional de Querétaro** (*Corregidora 3 Sur at Madero, tel 421/22031, closed Mon., $*) houses furnishings and paintings from the 17th to 19th centuries. A few blocks north, 19th-century **Teatro de la República** (*Juárez at Av. A. Peralta*) has seen its share of real-life drama. The formal signing of the 1917 Constitution took place here, and the predecessor of the PRI (the Institutional Ruling Party, which dominated national politics until recently.) was founded. Today, the neoclassic venue hosts plays and concerts; visitors are welcome to look inside during the day.

The severe facade of the **Iglesia**

de Santa Clara (*Madero at Allende, tel 421/21777*), built by architect Eduardo Tresguerras (1759–1833), belies an extravagant baroque interior. The same talented artist, a Bajío native, sculpted the adjoining **Fuente de Neptuno** (Neptune Fountain) in 1797. Non-guests can explore the elegant sitting room and bar of the **Casa de la Marquesa** (*Madero 41 at Allende, tel 421/21166*), noted for its Mudejar influences and extensive tilework. The **Museo de Arte de Querétaro** (*Allende at Pino Suárez, closed Mon., $*) resides in a fabulous late-baroque building, originally an Augustinian monastery. The museum's extensive collection consists primarily of 16th- to 18th-century paintings from Mexico and Europe. Note the expressions on the faces of the caryatid columns in the monumental inner courtyard.

An Eastern influence can be seen in the **Iglesia y Convento de Santa Rosa de Viterbo** (*Arteaga at Esequiel Montes, tel 421/21691*), with its Mudejar-style cupola and odd inverted flying buttresses adorned with gargoyles. Inside the church are six baroque altarpieces of gilded wood, a lovely pulpit inlaid with ivory, ebony, and silver, and an 18th-century pipe organ still used today.

After the fall of the Second Empire in 1867 (see p. 33), Maximilian of Habsburg was imprisoned in the **Convento de las Capuchinas,** a Capuchin convent, which today houses the **Museo de la Ciudad** (*Hidalgo at Guerrero, closed Mon., $*). Maximilian was later executed by firing squad on **Cerro de las Campanas** (*Morelos at Tecnológico*) on the city's west side. An **Expiatory Chapel,** built by the Austrian government in 1901, commemorates the site. Near the

Left: The extravagantly tiled flying buttresses of the 17th-century Iglesia de Santa Clara

top of the "Hill of Bells," an enormous statue of Benito Juárez presides over a wonderful view.

On the opposite side of the city, monks carry on with their devotions despite the distraction of guided visits to their early 17th-century monastery, the **Convento de la Santa Cruz** (*Independencia at Felipe Luna, Barrio de Santa Cruz, tel 421/20235, closed Mon., donation*). A miracle is said to have occurred at this spot during a battle between the Spaniards and the Otomí, the region's original inhabitants. Legend recounts that the Apostle James (Santiago, patron saint of Spain) appeared on a brilliant white horse to urge the Spaniards to victory. (The city is officially called Santiago de Querétaro.) Behind the church is the terminus of a 4,000-foot (1,200 m) aqueduct, built by the Spanish more than 250 years ago.

Less than an hour's drive southeast of Querétaro, **San Juan del Río** (*Visitor information, Av. Juárez at el Templo del Santuario*) is a prosperous market town, known for its baskets, woodcarvings, palm furniture, and semiprecious gems, especially amethysts, Mexican opals, and topaz. Although the countryside between Querétaro and San Juan is productive farm and ranchland, the connecting highway is now lined with factories, and the main reason to visit it is to purchase cut and polished gemstones.

Tequisquiapan, north of San Juan (*Visitor information, Plaza Hidalgo, Andador Independencia 1, tel 427/30295*), is smaller and more picturesque. Swimming pools with restaurants and children's games cluster outside town on the road to Ezequiel Montes, where there's also a golf course. sarapes, wicker baskets, and other local handicrafts are sold at the **Mercado de Artesanías** (*Salvador Carrizal & Ezequiel Montes*), and at stores surrounding the *zócalo*, or main square. The town hosts the yearly Fiesta del Queso y del Vino (*end of May/early June*). Inaugurated in 1976, this popular summer festival crowns a carnival queen and offers the crowds who come food and wine tastings, horse shows, bullfights, and cultural events. ■

Las Misiones de la Sierra Gorda drive

Between 1751 and 1768, five Franciscan missions were built amid the Sierra Gorda, a rugged range heading northeast of Querétaro toward Ciudad Valles, San Luis Potosí. Led by Fray Junípero Serra, Franciscan monks attempted to catechize the Pame (a Chichimec tribe) and encourage them to accept a sedentary life. The unusual mission churches exemplify Mexican baroque style and combine Christian symbols of obvious didactic intent with the sensibilities of the indigenous craftsman.

Young visitors rest on the steps outside Jalpan mission.

The drive along mountain roads is curvy yet beautifully scenic, ascending through a semi-arid landscape to mountain escarpments and valleys peppered with pines.

Lovely **Jalpan mission** ❶ *(Tel 429/ 60255)* perches on a bluff 118 miles (190 km) northeast of Querétaro on Hwy. 120. This was the first of the missions to be built (1751–58) in this isolated region. On its facade, statues of the Virgin of Guadalupe and the Virgin of Pilar symbolize the equal importance of Mexico and Spain. Near the bottom of the facade, note the double-edged symbolism of the two-headed eagle (a Habsburg icon) devouring a snake (a well-known Aztec icon). Dedicated to the Apostle James, the church has a prevalent shell motif, including a shell-inlaid entranceway.

From Jalpan head northwest on Hwy. 69 toward Río Verde. After about 20 miles (34 km) you will come to **Misión de Concá** ❷ *(Tel 01800/029-4240)*, at the entrance to town. Although both the town and adjoining mission are located in Arroyo Seco (meaning "dry riverbed") township, thermal springs abound. The striking orange-and-red-ocher facade of this church, the smallest in the Sierra Gorda, is notable for magnificent detail that mimics the

exuberant foliage of the semitropical valley in which it sits. The profuse decoration and the rather heavy-handed sculptures show the involvement of indigenous artisans. Crowning the facade is a Trinity, rarely seen in Mexico.

Return to Jalpan and continue on Hwy. 120 for about 12½ miles (20 km) to **Misión de Landa de Matamoros** ❸ *(Tel 429/25210)*, its elaborate facade resplendent with carved saints tucked within niches. The last of the mission churches to be built, Landa is also the most intact, with a church, cloister, open chapel, atrium, and four *posas*, or corner chapels.

Drive north for 6 miles (10 km). Take a right turn and follow this road for about 10 miles (16 km) to **Misión de Tilaco** ❹ *(Tel 427/33564)*. As at Jalpan, the sculptures of saints Peter and Paul flank the wide portal. Above, the images of St. Joseph and the Virgin on the second level symbolize familial devotion. Near the top of the facade, a multitude of angels flies up toward a fabulous garden.

Continue another 4 miles (6.5 km) on Hwy. 120 to the left-hand turnoff to **Misión de Tancoyol** ❺ *(Tel 427/33718)*. Drive about 10 miles (16 km) through the forested valley of Tancoyol (meaning "place of coyotes"). Dedicated to Our Lady of Light, this mission's facade is decorated with Franciscan saints and symbols, although two of the interior columns are crowned with a jaguar and a character with Indian features.

Back at Hwy. 120, you can either return to Querétaro, or make the shorter drive to Ciudad Valles, in the Huasteca region of San Luis Potosí (via Hwy. 85). The second route will take you past **Xilitla** ❻ and the fantastic open-air sculptures of Scottish eccentric Edward James (see p. 136).

All of the missions open daily at 7 a.m. and close around sunset; comfortable accommodations can be found in Jalpan and Concá. ∎

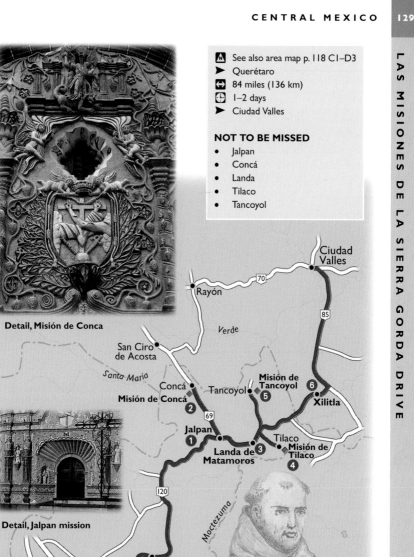

Detail, Misión de Conca

See also area map p. 118 C1–D3
➤ Querétaro
↔ 84 miles (136 km)
⏱ 1–2 days
➤ Ciudad Valles

NOT TO BE MISSED
- Jalpan
- Concá
- Landa
- Tilaco
- Tancoyol

Detail, Jalpan mission

Fray Junípero Serra

San Luis Potosí

San Luis Potosí

🗺 119 C3

Visitor information

✉ Alvaro Obregón 520, Centro

☎ 48/12-99-39

IN THE MID- AND LATE 16TH CENTURY, THE DISCOVERY OF rich veins of silver in neighboring Zacatecas and Guanajuato flamed the Spanish desire for precious metals. They struck silver at Cerro de San Pedro but established the city of Real San Luis Minas de Potosí (now San Luis Potosí) some 8 miles (5 km) away. The large mineral deposits petered out fairly quickly, but by then San Luis was firmly established as a center of ranching and commerce.

A restored historic district warms the now-industrialized state capital.

As capital of a huge region encompassing not only today's Nuevo León and Coahuila but also Texas and Louisiana, San Luis Potosí was once the most important city in northern Mexico. Although Monterrey is now the north's industrial leader, San Luis is still a vital and prosperous city, with hundreds of business enterprises.

The city maintains its sense of tradition and, in its historic center, a wealth of colonial and republican-era buildings despite being thoroughly urban. Many are neoclassic, and a number of baroque churches have been remodeled with neoclassic interiors. The busy capital was originally laid out in a grid, each of the seven neighborhoods having its own church and plaza. These areas are now fused together with skyscrapers, traffic, and all the other components of a large industrial city.

Now home to more than half a million people, San Luis is an engaging city, enjoying a mild climate with little temperature variation throughout the year. Potosinos are proud of their regional cuisine. Specialties include *enchiladas potosinas* (a cornmeal and chili mixture filled with cheese, fried, and garnished with fresh onions) and *tacos Camila* (tortillas filled with cheese, lightly fried, and buried under a medley of vegetables). The city is also known for its chocolates and for *queso de tuna*, a caramelized treat of condensed cactus juice.

Unpretentious restaurants serving the local fare are found on and around the main square, popular **Plaza de Armas,** also called Jardín Hidalgo (*between Los Bravo, Zaragoza, Othón, & 5 de Mayo*). Upscale cafés and restaurants line Avenida V. Carranza west of **Plaza de los Fundadores.** Also on this busy street is the **Casa de la Cultura** (*Av. V. Carranza 181, tel 48/13-22-47, closed Mon., $*), built in the 1920s as an elegant mansion in the English neoclassic style. The cultural center offers literary workshops, concerts, and film festivals, and doubles as a museum housing Mexican and European religious art, regional handicrafts, and pre-Hispanic artifacts.

North of Plaza de Armas, Calle Hidalgo is closed to traffic for several blocks leading to the municipal market, **Mercado Hidalgo,** making it a pleasant place to walk. South of the plaza, the neoclassic **Caja de Agua** is an unusual monument to public works. Built in 1832, this water storage tank was used by city residents until the 1900s. Water was drawn from one of eight decorated ducts around the reservoir's base. Farther south along Avenida Juárez, 18th-century **Santuario de Guadalupe** (*Calz. de Guadalupe 1005, tel 48/15-07-69*), built in the shape of the Latin cross, shows a mixture of late-baroque and neoclassic styles. Its high altar has a painting of the Virgin of Guadalupe by Jesús Corral.

On the southwest side of the city, **Parque Tangamanga** (*Diagonal Sur at Av. Himno Nacional, tel 48/ 25-14-34*) has jogging and cycling paths, lakes, mountain-bike trails, swimming pools, barbecue grills, children's play areas, a planetarium, a library, and a museum, and the city's 4,000-seat open-air theater. Also within the park is the **Museo de las Culturas Populares** (*Tel 48/17-29-76, closed Mon.*). Housed in a 19th-century hacienda, this museum of popular culture displays local folk art, musical instruments, ceremonial masks, and San Luis Potosí's famous silk *rebozos* (shawls).

About 30 miles (48 km) south of the city lies **Santa María del Río,** a town dedicated to weaving these exquisite shawls of silk (or nowadays, synthetic materials). This region is also known for its hot springs. **Balneario de Lourdes,** 12 miles (20 km) southeast of Santa María along a gravel road, has alkaline waters recommended for liver and kidney troubles, as well as a restaurant and hotel. About 38 miles (61 km) south of the capital, the **Centro Vacacional Gogorrón** has four pools of varying temperatures, and "roman baths"—private pools for up to six people. ■

The Capilla de Aranzazú, within the Museo Regional Potosino, is a chapel unique for its second-story location.

San Luis walk

San Luis Potosí was afforded city status in 1656, but many of its important buildings were constructed in the 18th and 19th centuries. Throughout the historic center are baroque, neoclassic, and Porfiriato structures, built during the presidential era of Porfirio Díaz (1877–1911), who commissioned many buildings in the European style.

Begin your walk at **Plaza de los Fundadores,** at Avs. V. Carranza and D. Carmona. At the northwest corner, visit the late 16th-century **Capilla de Loreto ①,** its facade graced with an intricate baroque portal. Inside, you will see one of Mexico's few surviving Jesuit altarpieces. Walk east on Obregón, passing the rectory of the **Universidad Autónoma,** which occupies the former Jesuit monastery.

Continue along the square's east side and turn left on Calle V. Carranza to large, open, traffic-free **Plaza de Armas ②** (*Jardín Hidalgo*), surrounded by historic buildings and shaded by flamboyant and magnolia trees. Note the sober neoclassic lines of the **Palacio de Gobierno** (*Tel 48/12-24-39*), which occupies the square's entire west flank. This state government building twice housed the interim government of Benito Juárez during the French occupation (see p. 33).

(see p. 33).

Taking a clockwise turn around the square, you will pass the oldest house in the city, the **Casa Virreina,** built in 1736 (but much

> ► Capilla de Loreto
> ↔ 0.8 mile (1.3 km)
> ⏱ 4 hours
> ► Capilla de Aranzazú

NOT TO BE MISSED
- Templo del Carmen
- Museo Nacional de la Máscara
- Templo de San Francisco
- Capilla de Aranzazú

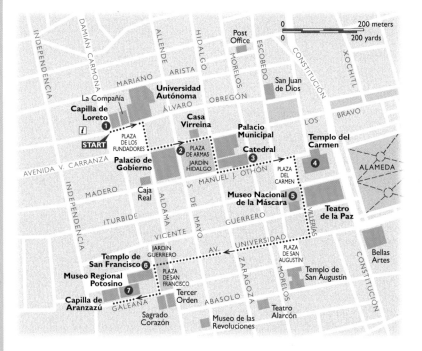

The city's limestone buildings range from pink and peach to gray and pale yellow.

remodeled). Now a restaurant, it was once the home of Mexico's only female vicereine, Francisca de la Gandara. On the northeast corner of the square is the 19th-century **Palacio Municipal** *(Tel 48/14-41-42, closed Sat., Sun.)*.

The imposing **Catedral** ❸ *(Tel 48/12-24-39)*, one of city's first baroque constructions, dominates the square's southeast corner. Note the Carrara marble statues of the apostles adorning the facade. The church has endured many remodels; inside, its neoclassic altars and Byzantine decorations were added in the 19th century.

A few blocks farther east on Calle Manuel J. Othón is the baroque **Templo del Carmen** ❹ *(Tel 48/12-28-78)*, its domes covered in multicolored tiles and its Churrigueresque facade nearly as ornate as the cathedral in Zacatecas (see p. 112). Inside, you will see the impressive side altars; the main altar, designed by architect Eduardo Tresguerras (1759–1833); and the resplendent **camarín de la Virgen,** a baroque chapel whose dazzling gold altarpiece is crowned with a giant scallop shell.

Facing lovely **Plaza del Carmen** on its southeast side is the neoclassic **Teatro de la Paz** *(Villerías 205, tel 48/12-52-09, closed Mon.)*, built during the Porfiriato era. Cross

Villerías to the French neoclassic building housing the telegraph office and the **Museo Nacional de la Máscara** ❺ *(Villerías 210, tel 48/12-30-25, closed Mon., $)*. Originally a private mansion, it now houses hundreds of ceremonial masks from throughout Mexico.

Walk south to Av. Universidad. A right turn brings you to **Plaza de San Francisco,** also known as Jardín Guerrero. Cross the long, rectangular plaza to the pink-stone **Templo de San Francisco** ❻ *(Tel 48/12-46-46)*, built in the 17th century. Note the Franciscan emblems and saints on the baroque facade. Ask permission to see the lovely Churrigueresque sacristy, with paintings by Miguel Cabrera, Antonio de Torres, and Francisco Martínez. Below the main dome, a ship-shaped crystal chandelier alludes to the evangelical travels of the order's founder, St. Francis of Assisi.

Behind the church, the former Franciscan monastery contains the **Museo Regional Potosino** ❼ *(Plaza de Aranzazú, tel 48/14-35-72, closed Mon., $)*, with pre-Hispanic artifacts and colonial-era statues and furnishings. Within the museum, the 18th-century **Capilla de Aranzazú** is a chapel unique for its second-story location and covered atrium. ∎

Silver mining, which built Real de Catorce, was never reestablished after the 1910 Revolution.

Real de Catorce

THIS NEARLY ABANDONED TOWN, ISOLATED AMID THE arid mountains and high desert of the Sierra Madre Oriental, attracts only the most curious or solitary of travelers, as well as pilgrims who come to venerate a miraculous effigy of St. Francis of Assisi. Rarely seen in town, Huichol Indians scour the surrounding hills in search of sacred peyote, a hallucinogenic plant used in mystical rituals throughout the year.

Real de Catorce
🅜 119 C4
Visitor information
✉ Calle Lanza, at Casa de la Moneda
☎ 488/23733

During its productive years between the late 18th and early 20th centuries, Real de Catorce built impressive private homes for its nearly 40,000 citizens. Many are now crumbling into ruins, while others house modest restaurants, hotels, and businesses.

It doesn't take long to complete the tourist circuit. The simple stone church, the **Parroquia de la Purísima Concepción,** is built in the traditional Latin cross format, with a single sturdy bell tower. Tucked in a side altar, its image of St. Francis of Assisi is said to have miraculous powers, attested by the hundreds of naive ex-votos (paintings giving thanks for blessings received) on display.

Thousands of pilgrims descend on the town each year to celebrate the October 4 holy day associated with the Franciscan Order's founder.

Other structures of note are the stone **palenque,** or cockfighting arena, sometimes used as an amphitheater, and the **bullring** (both from the late 18th century), as well as the dilapidated **Casa de la Moneda,** the former mint. Real de Catorce's clear, starry nights—a consequence of the town's elevation at 9,042 feet (2,756 m) above sea level—are one of its most captivating attractions. For something a little more physical than stargazing, rent a horse through one of the hotels or restaurants and make an excursion outside town. ∎

Aguascalientes

Aguascalientes
🗺 118 A3
Visitor information
✉ Palacio de Gobierno, Plaza de la Patria
☎ 4/915-1155

THE CAPITAL OF ONE OF MEXICO'S SMALLEST STATES WAS originally conceived as a defensive way station between regional silver mines and Mexico City. Farms and ranches sprang up around it to supply the mining towns, and today the city serves them as a commercial center. North of town lie its namesake hot springs and the San Marcos Winery, where the region's grapes are turned into brandy.

Aguascalientes is especially popular during its Feria Nacional de San Marcos (mid-April to early May), celebrated since the 17th century. A true "county fair," it has parades, concerts, cultural events, fireworks, bullfights, and livestock expos, with special festivities on the feast day of St. Mark, April 25. Events are held at the fairgrounds in the **Jardín San Marcos** and at **ExpoPlaza.** Pedestrian-only Calle Pani connects the two venues.

With its shade trees, fountains, and surrounding historic buildings, **Plaza de la Patria** is a welcome reminder of the city's colonial past. On the plaza is Aguascalientes' oldest church (1575), the **Basílica de Nuestra Señora de la Asunción** *(Tel 4/916-5228)*. It has endured several renovations, one resulting in its neoclassic facade of pink quarrystone. Ask to see the 18th-century paintings by Miguel Cabrera. Across the plaza, the **Palacio de Gobierno** *(Tel 4/915-1155)* contains murals by Chilean artist Oswaldo Barra Cunningham, a protégé of Diego Rivera.

East of the plaza, the **Museo de Aguascalientes** *(Zaragoza 507, tel 4/915-9043, closed Mon., $)* occupies an early 20th-century palace. See changing contemporary art and the realistic paintings of Aguascalientes native Saturnino Herrán (1887–1918). Across the street, admire the stained-glass windows of the cupola at the **Templo de San Antonio** *(Pedro Parga & Zaragoza, tel 4/915-2898)*.

With temporary exhibits and a permanent collection of young, prize-winning artists, the **Museo de Arte Contemporáneo** *(P. Verdad at Morelos, tel 4/918-6901, closed Mon., $)* is housed in an early 20th-century hacienda near the central plaza. The affiliated **Centro El Obraje** *(Juan de*

Montoro 222, tel 4/994-0074, closed Mon., $) also exhibits modern art.

Local cartoonist and engraver José Guadalupe Posada (1852–1913) created a satirical legacy of witty yet caustic political cartoons. See his work at the **Museo José Guadalupe Posada** *(Díaz de León, Jardín del Encino, tel 4/915-4556, closed Mon., $)*, a 15-minute walk south of Plaza de la Patria. ∎

Aguascalientes's state government palace (Palacio de Gobierno) typifies its counterparts throughout Mexico.

More places to visit in Central Mexico

DOLORES HIDALGO

Mexico's War of Independence officially began in this town, then known simply as Dolores. On the night of September 15, 1810, Father Miguel Hidalgo y Costilla launched the movement that resulted 11 years later in freedom from Spanish rule (see p. 32). **Casa Hidalgo** *(Morelos 1, tel 418/20171, closed Mon., $)*, the priest's former home, is now a museum with war artifacts and historic documents. Visit the baroque church, **Nuestra Señora de los Dolores,** on the main plaza, where the priest first sounded the alarm. The town's distinctive tiles can be seen adorning the better hotels and restaurants throughout Mexico; both tiles and pottery can be purchased locally. Dolores is also known for its ice cream.

🗺 119 C2 ✉ 25 miles (40 km) north of San Miguel de Allende; 30 miles (48 km) north of Guanajuato

Lovely gardens and courtyards hide behind Tamuzunchale facades.

LA HUASTECA

Encompassing parts of San Luis Potosí, Veracruz, Tamaulipas, and Hidalgo states, La Huasteca is named for the cultural group that has traditionally lived in this region of secluded valleys and wild mountains, lakes, forests, and steaming coastal plains. A good base for exploring the region is **Ciudad Valles,** San Luis Potosí's second largest city, near the state's southeast corner. Little visited by tourists, La Huasteca has a variety of natural attractions. Although adventure tourism is still in its infancy, caves await enterprising spelunkers, sheer rock walls tempt climbers, and there are many opportunities for hiking and bird-watching. Cloud-forest conditions prevail in the **Reserva de la Biósfera Abra-Tanchipa,** a 51,890-acre (21,000 ha) biosphere just north of Ciudad Valles. Abundant rainfall creates lush forests and feeds waterfalls such as **Tamul, El Salto,** and **Tamasopa,** where tropical trees sprouting wild orchids and other epiphytes surround crystal-clear pools tinged green or blue. Towns such as **Tancanhuitz** and **Tamazunchale** —with large, fairly traditional Huastec populations—can be visited on Sunday market day, to sample local delicacies, buy crafts, and perhaps listen to a *huapango,* regional music accompanied by violins, flute, *jarana* (small guitar), harp, and rhythm instruments. **Ciudad Valles** 🗺 119 D3 **Visitor information** ✉ Morelos 5, Edificio Magdalena, Ciudad Valles ☎ 1/382-4252

LAS POZAS

Near the Querétaro border and the missions of the Sierra Gorda, Las Pozas is a fantastic garden of sculptures built by surrealist poet Edward James (1907–1986). The wealthy eccentric exchanged Edwardian Britain for peyote-inspired projects in the Mexican highlands. With friend and mentor Plutarco Gastelum and a group of local artisans, the Scot occupied the last 20 years of his life creating an 80-acre (32 ha) dreamscape. About three dozen surrealist concrete structures— some 100 feet (30 m) tall—lose themselves in the equally fascinating tropical forest. At the site are a waterfall and a series of clear pools for bathing. In the nearby town of **Xilitla,** Gastelum built James an equally odd house, now a unique bed-and-breakfast. On Sundays visit Xilitla's open-air market, or take in a church service in the temple, all that remains of the 450-year-old Augustinian monastery.

🗺 119 D2 ✉ 3 miles (5 km) outside Xilitla ☎ 136/50082 💲 $ ∎

Lush and humid, the central Pacific region has a multitude of distinct destinations. There are miles of untrammeled coast, small cities full of understated charm, posh beach resorts, and some of the country's best folk art.

Central Pacific states

A close-up of Huichol Indian yarn art

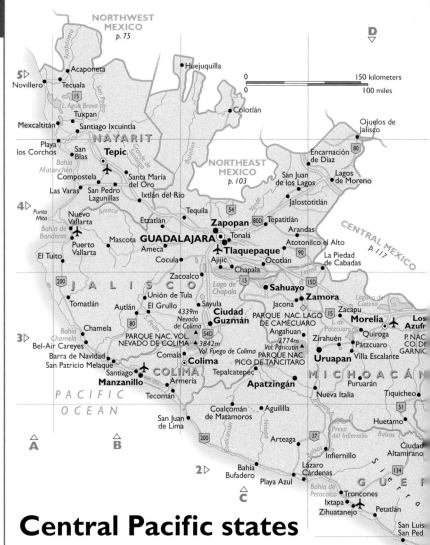

NORTHWEST
MEXICO
p. 75

D

150 kilometers
100 miles

NAYARIT

NORTHEAST
MEXICO
p. 103

CENTRAL MEXICO
p. 117

JALISCO

Lago de
Chapala

PACIFIC
OCEAN

COLIMA

MICHOACÁN

A B C

Central Pacific states

SHARING A SWATH OF COAST AND THE FOOTHILLS and mountains that rise abruptly beyond it, central Pacific Mexico has a multitude of distinctly different destinations. Manzanillo calls itself the "sailfish capital of the world," Puerto Vallarta is a fast-growing beach resort brimming with art galleries, and Michoacán's undeveloped coast is the playground of surfers and adventure-seekers. There are boutique hotels on isolated bays, lazy fishing villages on mangrove-lined lagoons, and Acapulco, with its all-night salsa clubs. Inland are straight-laced Guadalajara, land of mariachis and tequila, funky Colima, and whitewashed Taxco, looking like a misplaced Mediterranean village.

Unlike neighboring Oaxaca, few indigenous people remain in central Pacific Mexico. Most significant in number are the Nahua-speaking people of Guerrero. In Nayarit, mountain-dwelling populations of Huichols, though

small in number, maintain their cultural identity and religious practices. Shamans cure the sick and perform magic rituals, while everyday citizens are guided by an ancestral wisdom. Mirroring the Huichols' daily activities are playful, naive-looking figurines that their ancestors left in the area's unique shaft-tombs (buried at the bottom of vertical passageway) beginning around 250 B.C.

Soon after the fall of Tenochtitlán (see p. 30), the Spanish conquerors fanned out in search of further adventure, bringing to bear the usual influences, including widespread death by disease. The Indians suffered

Area of map detail

especially violent treatment at the hands of Conquistador Nuño Beltrán de Guzmán. His reign of terror stretched from Sinaloa to Guadalajara: Individuals were branded and sold as slaves, and hundreds of villages burned.

Those Indians who survived disease and injustice literally took to the hills. After de Guzmán was dispatched to a Spanish jail, Bishop Vasco de Quiroga lured the Purépecha back to their villages in today's Michoacán. He built as many hospitals as churches, and schooled indigenous artisans in useful trades.

Today, Michoacán is one of Mexico's leading producers of fine crafts, including copper cookware, wooden furniture, pottery, and elegant lacquerware. The Huichol produce fabulous yarn paintings, masks, and beaded objects for ritual use and for sale to a growing body of collectors. Throughout the region, but especially in Michoacán and Guerrero, ritual masks and elaborate costumes are used during celebrations that incorporate elements of both pre-Hispanic and Catholic ritual. ■

Silver baron don José de la Borda financed the construction of Taxco's Churrigueresque Santa Prisca church in the 1750s.

Tepic & San Blas

Tepic

M 138 B4

Visitor information

✉ Av. Mexico at Calzada del Ejército Nacional

☎ 32/14-80-71

TEPIC IS THE CAPITAL OF THE SMALL STATE OF NAYARIT, which produces much of the country's tropical fruits and most of its tobacco. In the foothills of the craggy Sierra Madre Occidental at 2,950 feet (900 m) above sea level, the small city is significantly cooler than the coast. About an hour north of Tepic is San Blas, headquarters for birders and beach bums who choose to avoid the fancy resorts. Surrounding this small fishing town are tropical forests, estuaries, and miles of sandy beaches.

TEPIC

Many Huichol men and women still wear traditional clothing.

Tepic is the traditional homeland of the Cora Indians. Along with their close relatives, the Huichol, they fled to the surrounding mountains to escape the cruel Nuño de Guzmán in the 16th century (see pp. 138–39). Today Tepic is a crossroad of agriculture and commerce, where farmers come to town to buy supplies and sell their produce. Huichol men in white cotton trousers and embroidered tunics sell their handicrafts in front of the large **catedral,** with its neo-Gothic towers. Facing the cathedral across the **plaza principal** (Av. México Norte at Lerdo Poniente) is the **Palacio del Municipio,** and surrounding the main square are restaurants and shops. Nearby, the **Museo de Cultura Popular** (Hidalgo 60 Oriente, tel 32/12-17-05, closed Sun.) displays and sells indigenous crafts, including leather, musical instruments, carved wood, and Huichol beaded objects and yarn paintings. Housed in a restored 18th-century mansion, the **Museo Regional de Antropología** (Av. México 91 Norte at Zapata, tel 32/12-19-00) displays pre-Hispanic artifacts, regional folk art, and period oil paintings.

South of the main plaza is Tepic's other most important square, **Plaza Constituyentes.** Here is the **Palacio de Gobierno** (Av. México Sur between Mina & Abasolo), a 19th-century government building with historic murals on its cupola and interior walls. About a mile (1.5 km) farther south on México Sur, Cora and Huichol Indians pray at the straw cross of the **Templo y Ex-Convento de la Cruz,** a former Franciscan mission. The adjoining monastery houses the state tourism office.

Several lovely lakes are within an hour's drive of Tepic. Off the toll road to Guadalajara, a signed road leads to **Santa María del Oro,** where horses and guides can be hired for treks into the nearby mountains. Below the village lies crystalline **Laguna Santa María del Oro,** surrounded by verdant hills. You can swim, take a picnic, or a walk around the lake, passing an abandoned gold mine and a freshwater spring. Upscale cabins are being built, but at present the only accommodations are Bungalows Koala, where kayaks can be rented. A turnoff just before Santa María leads to **Laguna de Tepeltitic.**

From Tepic, Highway 200 leads to **San Pedro Lagunillas,** another mountain lake.

SAN BLAS

An important port during the colonial era, San Blas is now a laid-back fishing town. There are no fancy hotels here, but a few good restaurants and just enough amenities to entertain a dedicated following. One drawback to a visit is the fierce mosquitoes and *jejenes* (biting gnats, or no-see-ums); bring insect repellent and cover up during the early morning and late afternoon.

San Blas's closest beach is **Playa Borrego.** You can take long walks along the often lonely beach, which terminates in an estuary after about 5 miles (8 km). This beach is infamous for its no-see-ums.

Las Islitas is a lovely stretch of beach punctuated by rocky coves. Lounge in a hammock or play a game of dominoes under a palm-thatched *ramada* (open-air eatery). Sailboats cruise the bay, which is backed by mountains. Farther round the curve of the bay toward

the small fishing village of Santa Cruz is **Los Cocos Beach,** shaded by palms.

For many the highlight of their vacation is a boat trip up **Estero San Cristóbal** to **La Tovara** freshwater spring. Herons, egrets, turtles, and other aquatic fauna haunt mazelike canals of mangroves. Rent a boat at the bridge at the entrance to San Blas or in the village of Matachén. After an hour-long ride, you'll have an hour to swim in the lovely spring. Have a drink or a bite to eat at the delightful restaurant overlooking the idyllic pool, but come early to beat the groups now bused in from Puerto Vallarta. ■

San Blas

138 B4

Visitor information

✉ Canalizo at Sinaloa, Presidencia Municipal

☎ 32/85-00-05

The ruins of the 1773 Contaduría (Counting House) lord over San Blas.

Puerto Vallarta

Puerto Vallarta
🗺 138 B4
Visitor information
✉ Juárez at Independencia, Palacio Municipal
☎ 3/222-0242

BAHÍA DE BANDERAS, ON WHICH PUERTO VALLARTA SITS, IS one of the world's biggest bays. Although it had no permanent settlements until the mid-19th century, the bay was charted and used for hundreds of years as a rest stop for pirates, priests, the military, and other sailors. Before a steamy Hollywood romance attracted the world's attention, few travelers had ever seen Puerto Vallarta, an idyllic fishing village with white-sand beaches. It's now a savvy tourist mecca with a string of high-rise hotels marching up the bay.

Puerto Vallarta shot to fame in 1963 during the filming of *Night of the Iguana*.

Puerto Vallarta became an overnight star with the highly publicized romance of Elizabeth Taylor and Richard Burton during the filming of *Night of the Iguana* here in 1963. (The film starred Burton and Ava Gardner; Taylor tagged along.) And it hasn't stopped growing or attracting vacationers since, the original fishing village having expanded to cover a 15-mile (25 km) stretch along the Bahía de Banderas.

The resort specializes in galleries and shops selling inspired fine art and excellent handicrafts, including objects made by the mountain-dwelling and spiritually attuned Huichol. Some galleries focus on the crème de la crème of folk art from the states of Oaxaca, Chiapas, and Michoacán.

The heart of the old city is **Vallarta Vieja,** where buildings are painted white by government decree. Capped in rust-colored roof tiles and draped in bright fuschia-pink bougainvillea, sunlight-dappled houses stagger up palm-covered hills. From there, the **Río Cuale** descends to divide the resort into north and south sectors. Pedestrian and automobile bridges both cross the river and access **Isla Río Cuale,** an island where restaurants, shops, and the small **Museo de Antropología** are surrounded by gardens and brushed with the best breeze in town. Below the east bridges, a sprawling

handicrafts market sells goods from throughout Mexico.

A few blocks north of the river, **Plaza Principal,** or Plaza de Armas *(Zaragoza, Morelos, Iturbide, & Juárez),* is surrounded by the city hall and the open-air **Los Arcos amphitheater,** which often hosts Sunday concerts. The seawalk, or *malecón,* stretches north from the main square, itself fronted by bars and restaurants. The malécon is a great spot at sunset, when the breeze picks up and the sun glints on a dozen entertaining bronze sculptures along its length.

New development lies north of town. First is the **Zona Hotelera,** a mass of high-rise hotels, most renting water toys along a lovely stretch of beach called **Playa de Oro.** Farther north is **Marina Vallarta,** an enclave of resort hotels and condos surrounding a 400-slip marina, a popular yacht club, and an 18-hole golf course. Fishing charters and day cruises depart from the **Maritime Terminal.** This development is a favorite among boaters, although its beaches aren't among Vallarta's prettiest.

Farther north still, **Nuevo Vallarta,** at the mouth of the Río Ameca, is actually in the state of Nayarit. Here are a yacht club, condos, and a few all-inclusive resort properties. It is a long way from the action of downtown Vallarta, but

has beautiful beaches and a more natural setting than Marina Vallarta.

Those who want to be close to the party scene congregate downtown. **Olas Altas** and **Playa de los Muertos** beaches, just south of Viejo Vallarta, are popular with tourists, locals, and vendors selling juicy mangoes, grilled fish on a stick, striped sarapes, and most everything else.

The coast highway continues south of downtown, past sandy white beaches, rocky coves, and hills sprinkled with luxury homes to **Mismaloya,** where John Huston's *Night of the Iguana* was filmed. Although an overbearing hotel and condos have spoiled its perfect setting, it's still a pretty beach with colorful fishing boats in the adjoining lagoon. Hike or drive several miles inland to **Chino's Paradise** or **El Edén,** inviting small restaurants perched above the Mismaloya River.

From Mismaloya, divers and snorkelers can hire skiffs to **Los Arcos,** a protected underwater park just offshore, or to secluded beaches farther south. Closest is jungle-lined **Boca de Tomatlán,** also accessible by car.

The beaches beyond Boca de Tomatlán are accessible only by boat. **Playa Las Animas** and **Quimixto** both have simple beachfront restaurants and good snorkeling. **Yelapa** is a Mexican Shangri-La where thatch-roofed restaurants line the beach. Tour boats descend on these lovely beaches daily, so come early or late to avoid the crowds. ■

Puerto Vallarta's emerald-green hills back up to azure mountains.

La Costa Alegre

SINCE THE EARLY 1990s, THE 280-MILE (450 KM) STRETCH OF idyllic tropical beaches between Puerto Vallarta and Manzanillo has been dubbed La Costa Alegre. Exclusive resorts have been built on a few of the loveliest beaches, and continued development is inevitable. But for the moment, Highway 200 meanders past beaches of gold or white sand lined with elegant coconut palms and backed by luxuriant green hills. Signed and unsigned roads lead to simple fishing villages, rocky coves perfect for fishing or snorkeling, and long bays with modest accommodations. Manzanillo, the Pacific's most important industrial port, manages to combine commercial fishing and shipping with tourism and excellent billfishing.

About 90 miles (145 km) south of Puerto Vallarta, **Bahía Chamela** has several lovely beaches, basic accommodations, and one intimate luxury hotel; camping is permitted. There's a village and several restaurants at **Playa Perula,** at the bay's southern end. You can fish from the rocks, sit in the shade of beachfront eateries, or rent a skiff to snorkel offshore or see the birds at nearby **Isla Pajarera,** one of half a dozen offshore islands.

Among the Costa Alegre's most exclusive resorts is **Bel-Air Careyes,** built in the 1960s, complete with tennis courts, stables, and polo field. Combining Pacific and Mediterranean styles of chic and comfort, the resort is named for the marine turtles that lay their eggs on the beaches of the delightful cove. Farther south, exquisite **Bahía Tenacatita** is slated for development, but for the moment it's a long stretch of clean white sand fringed by palms. Part of the bay is a coral-covered cove perfect for diving, swimming, and sailboarding, or you can hire a local guide for a bird-watching expedition on a nearby lagoon.

Just before the Colima state line is gorgeous **Bahía de Navidad** (Christmas Bay). At its northern end, **San Patricio Melaque** is a small but growing resort town with a good swimming beach. Crowded around the west end of its long beach is a clutch of thatch-roofed, open-air eateries—a great sunset spot. Many Guadalajara families vacation here on long weekends and holidays, including a week-long celebration for the town's patron, St. Patrick.

You can walk several miles along the sandy beach to **Barra de Navidad,** a sleepy fishing village that recently woke up to larger-scale tourism. Strung out along a sandbar extending into the bay is Barra's white beach. Thatch-roofed restaurants serve up spicy shrimp, fresh fish, and cold beers. The closest beaches are not popular with some swimmers as afternoon breezes attract windsurfers, and winter swells bring surfers. Birders haunt the mangrove lagoons, large areas of which were displaced by an exclusive golf resort and marina, the Grand Bay Hotel. The resort is across the bay on **Isla de Navidad,** or Colimilla, as it is also known.

Lagoon tours and deep-sea fishing charters are available from private operators as well as the local co-op, the **Sociedad Cooperativa de Servicios Turísticos** (*Morelos 1*). Multiple fishing tournaments are held each

Barra de Navidad
🔺 138 B3
Visitor information
✉ Jalisco 67
☎ 335/55100

The marina at Las
Hadas, Manzanillo,
attracts boaters
year-round.

year: in January, late May,
September, and November. The
town honors its patron, St.
Anthony of Padua, in the week
preceding June 13.

South of Barra de Navidad the
highway enters Colima state and
passes near, but not along, the coast
to **Bahías Manzanillo** and
Santiago. The bays are divided in
two by the Santiago peninsula, a
short spit of land on which sits **Las
Hadas** resort, opened in 1974 and
showcased in the movie *10* (1979).
The resort continues to attract the
jet set, with its brilliant white architecture, air of luxurious and exclusive comfort, and secluded location.

Unlike Ixtapa and Cancún,
Manzanillo is a real city and a
busy port. It is said that ships from
the Orient docked here two centuries before the Spanish arrived in
Mexico. Instead of a row of restaurants, hotels, and bars such as those
in Mazatlán's Golden Zone (see
p. 98), Manzanillo's attractions are
found here and there along the bay
and downtown, located at the far
eastern point of the bay. You
can learn about Mexico's western
cultures just north of downtown at
the **Museo de Arqueología**
*(Glorieta San Pedrito s/n, tel
333/22256).*

Although some of the beaches
in this industry-oriented city of
100,000 are not ideal for swimming, and the ambience is that of a
busy port, Manzanillo does have its
admirers. It is favored by Mexican
rather than foreign tourists, as well
as deep-sea anglers who come for
big game fish. ∎

Manzanillo
⚊ 138 B3
**Visitor
information**
✉ Blvd. Costera Miguel
de la Madrid 1033
☎ 333/32277

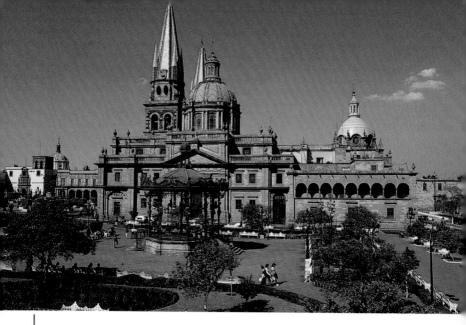

Plazas and pedestrian malls surround the cathedral in historic Guadalajara.

In & around Guadalajara

GUADALAJARA IS THE MEXICAN'S MEXICO—AN ARCHETYPE of idealized Mexican culture. It's the home town of mariachi music, the romantic ballads performed by large bands of strikingly uniformed musicians playing harps, violins, and soulful trumpets. This is the land of tequila soirees and of plantations of blue agave from which tequila is made. On Sunday afternoons, elegant equestrians known as *charros* perform stylized feats of showmanship far removed from those of any casual cowboy.

Guadalajara

138 C4

Visitor information

Morelos 102, Plaza Tapatía

3668-1600

Guadalajara (from the Arabic, meaning "river of stones") was moved several times before a final site was chosen near the west end of the 5,400-foot (1,645 m) Atemajac Valley, 300 miles (480 km) northwest of Mexico City. Several earlier settlements of the same name failed owing to drought and Indian attacks. Once established, the seat of western colonial government soon also became a capital of agriculture and ranching.

As Mexico's second-largest city, Guadalajara embraces mainstream, as well as Mexican, culture, with four 18-hole golf courses and three soccer teams, a zoo, a planetarium,

a large convention center, and a recently inaugurated horseracing track. Many visitors come to shop. Residents from surrounding haciendas and rural communities buy everything from lizard-skin boots and spurs to plows. City folk scour shops and galleries for the region's famous handicrafts: leather clothing, handblown glassware, wood-and-leather *(equipal)* furniture, handcrafted and factory tableware, and home accessories of tin, wrought iron, pewter, papier-mâché, and copper.

Many of these modern handicrafts are found in the delightful, art-driven satellite villages of

Tlaquepaque and Tonalá (see pp. 150–51), which ever expanding Guadalajara has swallowed, but not digested. In Guadalajara proper, visitors explore the *centro histórico*, a square mile surrounding the cathedral, where historic churches, museums, and shops line pedestrian malls and fountain-filled public squares.

CENTRO HISTÓRICO

Presiding over Guadalajara's historic district is the majestic **catedral** (*Av. 16 de Septiembre between Hidalgo & Morelos, tel 3614-5504*), with its yellow-tiled dome and twin spires. Earthquakes and changing fashions have led to many modifications over the years, rendering it Gothic, Moorish, baroque, and neoclassic in style. Its three naves house a dozen side altars; the sacristy is lined with colonial-era paintings.

Plazas surround the cathedral on all sides. To the west is **Plaza Guadalajara,** where free, three-hour city tours depart Saturdays at 10 a.m. (*Tel 3616-3333*) from the **Palacio Municipal,** the

municipal palace. Evening concerts are held several times a week at the art nouveau bandstand on **Plaza de Armas,** which flanks the cathedral to the south. Facing this graceful old square is the **Palacio de Gobierno** (*Moreno at Corona, tel 3668-1802, closed Sat., Sun.*), a neoclassic government edifice with Churrigueresque decorations. Murals by Jalisco native José Clemente Orozco (1883–1949) embellish the stairwell and the congressional chambers upstairs.

North of the cathedral, the **Rotunda de los Hombres Ilustres** honors Jalisco heroes—primarily writers, painters, and other artists—on a shady plaza of the same name, and horse-drawn carriages await passengers in front of the **Museo Regional de Guadalajara** (*Liceo 60, tel 3614-9957, closed Mon., $*). This comprehensive museum occupies the former baroque seminary of San José. Surrounding a typical colonial courtyard are rooms with archaeological and paleontological exhibits, including offerings from area shaft-tombs and a complete

A footbridge connects Mercado San Juan de Dios with its namesake church.

mammoth skeleton. Upstairs are colonial paintings, artifacts of West Coast cultures, and other regional history exhibits.

Downtown Guadalajara has many worthy museums. The **Casa Museo López Portillo** *(Liceo 177 at San Felipe, tel 3613-2411, closed Mon.)* is a 19th-century home with furnishings typical of an upper-class family (one of this family's sons was the former president of that name). The **Museo Clemente Orozco** *(Av. Aurelio Aceves 27, closed Sat., Sun.)* houses personal and professional artifacts of the famous muralist, as well as a huge mural, "Alegoría del Vino" ("Wine Allegory").

The **Museo de las Artes** *(López Cotilla 930, tel 3826-6114, closed Mon., $)* shows permanent

and temporary exhibits of contemporary art. Just beyond it lies the **Templo Expiatorio** *(Enrique Díaz at Ezcorza)*, a neo-Gothic church modeled on the Orvieto Cathedral in central Italy.

Behind the cathedral, **Plaza de la Liberación** is surrounded by imposing government buildings and the neoclassic **Teatro Degollado** *(Calle Belén & Av. Morelos s/n, tel 3614-4773 or 3613-1115, closed Sun.)*, inaugurated in 1866 by soprano Angela Peralta. Visit the stunning theater 10 a.m.– 1 p.m. to see the interior fresco, illustrating Dante's *Divine Comedy* among other subjects, or better yet, attend a Sunday morning **folkloric show** *($$–$$$$)* by the university dance troupe. Nearby, the **Museo de la Cera** *(Morelos 217, tel*

3614-8487, $) has 120 reasonably lifelike wax figures, including depictions of Madonna (the current one) and a complete mariachi band.

Like Monterrey's Macroplaza (see p. 108), **Plaza Tapatía** was created in the 1980s to incorporate existing churches, government buildings, shops, and public squares into a cohesive entity of green spaces, walkways, sculptures, fountains, and benches. At the east end of the 17-acre (7 ha) public square lies one of Guadalajara's landmarks, the stately **Instituto Cultural Cabañas** (Cabañas 8, tel 3668-1640, closed Mon., $), a World Heritage site where concerts, films, and performances are held. Originally an orphanage designed by Spanish architect and sculptor Manuel Tolsá, it served this role until the 1970s. Many of José Clemente Orozco's most brilliant murals adorn the walls and ceilings of this neoclassic building, which has hundreds of rooms and several dozen linked patios planted with grapefruit trees. The site museum houses more works by Orozco and hosts temporary exhibits of contemporary art.

Past the modernistic bronze sculpture depicting the Immolation of Quetzalcóatl lies the **Mercado Libertad,** also known as Mercado San Juan de Díos (Av. J. Mina at Calzada Independencia). A footbridge connects the enormous city market to the church for which it was named. Just beyond is **Plaza de los Mariachis** (Obregón at Av. J. Mina), where roving bands in matching silver-studded ensembles serenade song-starved clients at outdoor tables. The square is especially crowded at night, when some visitors might find it intimidating.

Within the city center are several churches of note. **Iglesia de Santa Mónica** (Santa Mónica 250 at San Felipe, tel 3614-6620) is considered one of Guadalajara's loveliest, its baroque facade graced with a twin portico richly decorated with Solomonic columns. South of Plaza de Armas, the **Templo de San Francisco** (Av. 16 de Septiembre 289 at Prisciliano Sánchez, tel 3614-4083) and the **Capilla de Nuestra Señora de Aranzazú** are all that remain of a 16th-century Franciscan monastery. Note the typical Mexican motif—the eagle on the prickly-pear cactus—on the facade of the former, and the gilded Churrigueresque altarpiece inside the latter.

Also south of Plaza de Armas are the **Museo de Arqueología del Occidente de México** (Calzada Independencia Sur at Av. del Campesino, tel 3619-0104, closed Mon., $), with archaeological exhibits of western cultures, and **Parque Agua Azul** (Calz. Independencia s/n, tel 3619-0328, closed Mon., $), a children's park, which also houses an orchid house, a butterfly pavilion, and an aviary. At the nearby **Lienzo Charro de Jalisco** (Dr. R. Michel 577, tel 3619-3232, $$), families congregate at Sunday noon for that most tapatío (native Guadalajaran) of traditions, the colorful charreada (rodeo; see p. 154).

ZAPOPAN

About 5 miles (8 km) northwest of central Guadalajara is Zapopan, known throughout Mexico for its diminutive statue of the Virgin of Zapopan. The 10-inch (25 cm) cornpaste statue is said to have cured epidemics and aided the Spanish in battle. After four months of travel between parish churches, the statue is brought back to Zapopan in grand style each October 12 during the Romería de la Virgen

Zapopan
138 C4
Visitor information
Av. Vallarta 6503
3110-0754

de Zapopan. Hundreds of thousands fill the streets as the Virgin's entourage heads for the baroque **basílica** *(Hidalgo at Zapata)*, begun in 1690. It's a lively party with music and folkloric dances, food vendors, mariachis, men on horseback, and kids in costume.

Next to the church is **Artesanías Huicholes,** a government-run shop selling Huichol Indian yarn paintings, beaded masks, and other handicrafts at reasonable prices. Larger than the church itself is the atrium and adjoining **Plaza de las Américas,** surrounded by the flags of North American and Latin American countries.

TLAQUEPAQUE

Once an independent village and now a suburb of Guadalajara with 300,000 inhabitants, Tlaquepaque is charming if touristy. Its inhabitants have been making pottery since the time of the Spanish incursion; in the Indian dialect, Tlaquepaque means "place on high clay hills." Traditional Tlaquepaque ceramics are fragile earthenware, although today other genres, including more durable stoneware, have been adopted.

The art of glassblowing was introduced in the 19th century, and today hundreds of shops sell miniatures and glassware in addition to pottery, textiles, silver jewelry, tin, wrought iron, high-end furniture, and household accessories. Many shops are themselves works of art, housed in gracious, restored mansions surrounding plant-filled courtyards. Most close for siesta and some all day on Sunday.

But Tlaquepaque has more to offer than just shopping. This is a fascinating place to walk: There are restaurants, lively cantinas, and several interesting churches.

Pedestrianized Calle Independencia leads to the main square, **Jardín Hidalgo,** and the 18th-century, neoclassic-Byzantine-style **Santuario de Nuestra Señora de la Soledad** *(Prisciliano Sánchez at Morelos)*. In the next block, the **Parroquia de San Pedro** *(Guillermo Prieto at Morelos)* was built by the Franciscans in 1813.

Before setting out to buy ceramics, take a look at the exhibits of traditional pottery from the Valle de Atemajac and prize-winning contemporary pieces at the **Museo Regional de la Cerámica** *(Independencia 237 at Alfareros, tel 3635-5404, closed Mon.)*, west of the main square. Across the street are a historic house and a glass-blowing factory. After a day's shopping expedition, relax at the **Parián** *(Between Independencia, Prieto, Morelos, & Madero)*, a plaza filled with lively cantinas and open-air restaurants, shops, and strolling mariachis. The town celebrates its annual Feria de San Pedro Tlaquepaque during the last week of June.

TONALÁ

Five miles (8 km) east of Tlaquepaque is Tonalá, a pre-Hispanic regional capital whose Náhuatl name means "place where the sun rises," or "place of the sun." It was also briefly the capital of Nueva Galicia before a dearth of water and other factors forced the settlers to abandon the site. Tonalá produces much of the glass and pottery sold in Tlaquepaque.

On Thursdays and Sundays vendors line the downtown streets in an informal *tianguis* (market) that has taken place since pre-Hispanic times. Throughout the week you'll find shops selling low- and high-fire ceramics, blown glass, pewter, and works of papier-mâché, tin, copper, wood, basketry, and iron. The **Casa de los Artesanos** *(Avenida de los Tonaltecas Sur 140,*

Tlaquepaque
🅰 138 C4
Visitor information
✉ Morelos 288
☎ 3635-2330

Tonalá
🅰 138 C4
Visitor information
✉ Av. Hidalgo 21
☎ 3633-0047

Opposite: Charming Tlaquepaque makes a refreshing change from congested, urban Guadalajara.

Workers harvest the *piña*, or heart, of the agave plant.

Tequila
◭ 138 C4

closed Sat., Sun.) exhibits fine handicrafts representing the work of more than 50 local artisans.

Handicrafts shops can be found up and down Avenida de los Tonaltecas and around the **plaza principal** (*Juárez, Pino Suárez, Zapata, & Madero*). Surrounding the square are the Gothic-style **Santuario del Sagrado Corazón** (*Hidalgo at Juárez*) and the **Parroquia de Santiago Apóstol** (*Pino Suárez at Juárez*), one of the oldest temples in the Atemajac Valley. Named for the town's patron saint, the Apostle James, this is the site of festivities in the days preceding July 25, when local men don masks and costumes to perform regional dances.

The **Museo Nacional de la Cerámica** (*Constitución 104 near Hidalgo, tel 3683-0494, closed Mon.*) displays ceramic pieces, both modern and ancient, from throughout Mexico. About four blocks away, the **Museo Regional de Tonalá** (*Ramón Corona 73, closed Mon., $*) has rotating fine- and folk-art exhibits in a traditional adobe, wood-beamed house.

TEQUILA

The pleasant town of Tequila, about 35 miles (56 km) northwest of Guadalajara, sits under an extinct volcano of the same name. Fields of blue agave shimmer in a spiky azure haze around the town. The heart of the agave, or maguey, is used to make tequila in its various forms. Unique not just to Mexico but to the region, true tequila can be made only in Jalisco and four other states (see p. 154).

Although the larger distilleries such as Sauza and José Cuervo give tours, it's best to arrange ahead of time; most prefer to give tours in the mornings, and not on payday. For a hassle-free excursion from Guadalajara, take the Saturday **Tequila Express,** an eight-hour train tour including lunch, mariachis, and folkloric dancers. Tickets can be purchased through Guadalajara's Chamber of Commerce (*Av. Vallarta 4095 at Niño Obrero, tel 3122-7920, $$$$$*). Six miles (10 km) south of Tequila, in **Amatitán,** the **Hacienda San José del Refugio** (*Tel 3613-9585*) is a 10,000-acre (4,000 ha)

family-run agave plantation of 8 million plants and a distillery producing Herradura tequila, which sets industry standards for efficiency and cleanliness. Tours (*$$$*) are available daily on the hour between 9 a.m. and noon (call ahead to confirm).

LAGO DE CHAPALA

About 25 miles (40 km) southeast of Guadalajara lies Mexico's largest natural freshwater lake, Lago de Chapala. Its agreeable climate, tree-lined lakefront promenades, and surrounding mountains convinced President Porfirio Díaz to establish a vacation home here. Later discovered by Canadian and U.S. expats, its three principal towns are now home to thousands of foreign residents.

Unfortunately, deforestation of the surrounding woods and resulting erosion have sullied the lake, and an explosion of water hyacinths and pollution from the Lerma River contribute to its problems. Additionally, the growth of Guadalajara and surrounding towns has caused the lake to shrink

dramatically, as this is the source of the region's drinking water.

The principal town is **Chapala,** where Mexican families stroll and shop for folk art on weekends. In the early 1920s D. H. Lawrence (1885–1930) penned his first novel, *The Plumed Serpent*, whilst staying in a house on Calle Zaragoza. Restaurants that once lined the lakeshore serve typical *charales* (fried fish) and tequila accompanied by *sangrita*, a chili, tomato, and orange juice chaser invented here.

Ajijic, about 5 miles (8 km) west of Chapala, is a growing town whose red-tiled adobe houses and narrow cobblestoned streets began attracting artists and writers in the mid-20th century. Galleries and stores sell fine art, handicrafts, and designer clothing. Week-long festivities lead up to the town's patron saint's day, St. Andrew, on November 30, with celebrations at the **Iglesia de San Andrés,** situated on the north side of the town plaza. Smaller villages surround the lake, including **San Juan Cosalá,** with a complex of thermal pools, a restaurant, and accommodations. ∎

Traditional crafts such as weaving endure around the Lago de Chapala area.

Chapala
🅜 138 C4
Visitor information
✉ Av. Madero 407
☎ 3765-3141

Tapatío traditions

Guadalajara's contradiction is that the traditions that make it unique are considered prototypically Mexican. In the nostalgic musicals of the 1940s, film stars Pedro Infante and Jorge Negrete personified the Mexican "everyman." When dressed as *charros* in fine felt hats and elegant dress they crooned songs of unrequited love, romance, and machismo. Tequila and charros, mariachis, and generous afternoon siestas are all traditions that both set Guadalajara (and the state of Jalisco) apart and generate a national persona.

A charro demonstrates his roping skills.

White tequila is unaged; *reposado* is aged for at least two months in wooden barrels; and *añejo* is aged at least a year in oak barrels.

If tequila is the unofficial national drink, *charrería* is the official national sport—so decreed by presidential edict in 1933. Charros perform feats of equestrian skill similar to those of a rodeo, but with more finesse and in fancy dress. Teams of six to eight compete in the pan-shaped ring, the *lienzo charro*, performing *suertes* (moves) that range from steer-throwing, bull-roping, and riding to changing horses at a dead run. *La escaramuza charra* is an elaborately choreographed and colorful women's event. Requiring fine mounts, expensive, brocaded outfits, and silver spurs, charrería is a sport for the wealthy.

Another seeming contradiction is that Guadalajara, long Mexico's second largest city, maintains a provincial atmosphere. The typical *tapatío* (Guadalajara native) is traditional, conservative, and Catholic, and like all Mexicans, intensely loyal to his region and family. Native tapatíos—including muralist and painter José Clemente Orozco and writers Juan Rulfo and Agustín Yáñez—are greatly esteemed and their works often quoted.

Guadalajarans are also immensely proud of the national drink, tequila. Made from blue agave, or maguey, a relative of the cactus, true tequila can be distilled only in Jalisco as well as designated areas of Nayarit, Guanajuato, Tamaulipas, and Michoacán.

The better tequilas contain 100 percent blue agave, although only 51 percent is required. The first agave-derived drink was pulque, a mild beer fermented and drunk throughout pre-Hispanic Mesoamerica. The Spaniards took the process further, distilling the fermented brew. When plants are 8 to 12 years old, the heart, or *piña*, weighing up to 120 pounds (55 kg), is extracted, shredded, and cooked for six to eight hours. The resulting *aguamiel* is fermented and twice distilled.

Mariachis add ambience to the *charreada*, as they do at weddings, parties, and sidewalk cafés. The name is thought to be a corruption of the French word *mariage,* meaning "wedding," as the five-piece bands often played at society weddings during the 19th century. Originally featuring two violins, a harp, and *jarana* and *vihuela* (types of guitar), these bands played romantic ballads popular after Mexican independence. Trumpets, now an integral and characteristic part of most mariachi bands, were added only in the 1930s.

All of these traditions can be experienced at the Encuentro Internacional del Mariachi y la Charrería, held each year at the end of August and beginning of September; and in October at the Fiestas de Octubre, a month of art, performances, and music of all kinds. ∎

Right: Stirring music (above) and feats of horsemanship (below) can be seen at Guadalajara's Encuentro Internacional del Mariachi y la Charrería, held in late summer.

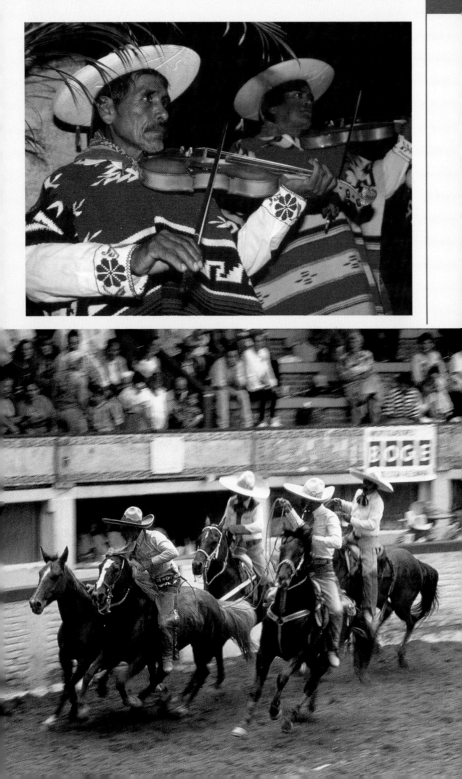

Colima & environs

FOR THOSE WEARY OF FLASHY BEACH RESORTS AND CITIES with countless colonial landmarks, Colima is a delightful retreat. The small state capital is among the safest cities of its size in Mexico, and the downtown area is alive with semitropical greenery. Colimenses take great pride in their city, and this is reflected in the cleanliness of its streets and the courtesy extended to visitors. There are interesting museums, art galleries, live music events, unusual festivals, and magic supply stores, while nearby towns provide a glimpse into the life of a gentler, even less frenetic era.

Founded by the Spanish in 1527, Colima has been repeatedly rocked by earthquakes, leaving few colonial buildings intact. However, the townspeople have taken advantage of their misfortune by transforming whole city blocks into impeccably manicured parks. No fewer than eight elegant green spaces grace the urban center, providing both a feeling of luxuriant openness and a plentiful supply of oxygen.

The city's elevation of 1,800 feet (550 m) above sea level makes it cooler and less humid than the coast, just 28 miles (45 km) away. Most days a welcome breeze blows down from the mountains backing the city, while between July and October, afternoon and early evening rain showers freshen the air. Rain or shine, from Thursday to Sunday, evening brings families and friends to the central plazas to enjoy eclectic live music ranging from mariachis and romantic ballads to modern rock.

In the heart of the city are three plazas. **Plaza Principal** (*Reforma between Madero & Hidalgo*) is dominated on the east side by the 18th-century **Catedral Santa Iglesia** (*Reforma 21, tel 3/312-0200*) and the adjacent **Palacio de Gobierno** (*Tel 3/312-0431*), whose inner courtyard is decorated with murals depicting regional history. Directly behind the

cathedral lies the **Jardín Quintero,** with **Parque Núñez,** an enormous flower garden, four blocks east at the corner of Madero and Juárez. Within walking distance of these plazas are hotels, restaurants and cafés, shops, banks, and a handful of notable museums.

The **Museo Universitario de Culturas Populares** (*Barreda & Gallardo, tel 331/26869, closed Mon.*) has exhibits of popular art, regional textiles, masks, and pre-Hispanic artifacts, including beguiling ceramic figures of short-legged, pot-bellied *tepezcuintle* dogs, once greatly esteemed (and eaten!) by local inhabitants. Its gift shop sells wonderful reproductions of pre-Hispanic pieces. Similar exhibits can be found at the smaller **Museo de Historia de Colima** (*Reforma at 16 de Septiembre, tel 331/29228, closed Mon.*). Next door, the **Sala de Exposiciones de la Universidad de Colima** (*Tel 331/29228, closed Mon.*) presents temporary exhibits of modern art. Perhaps the best permanent collection of fine art can be found in the **Pinacoteca Universidad** (*V. Guerrero 35, tel 331/22228, closed Mon.*). The work of local painters is housed in three exquisite mansions linked by courtyards filled with flower-drenched trellises.

Colima
⚑ 138 C3
Visitor information
✉ Ocampo at Hidalgo 96
☎ 3/312-8360

One block south of the *plaza principal*, the **Teatro Hidalgo** *(Hidalgo at Morelos, tel 331/30608)* stands on land given to the city by revolutionary hero Miguel Hidalgo (see p. 32), once a priest in the city. Built between 1871 and 1883, the neoclassic theater hosts concerts, plays, and the occasional opera.

Half a mile (1 km) northeast of the city center, the **Casa de la Cultura** *(Calzada Galván Norte at Ejército Nacional, tel 331/30608)* is a modern cultural complex housing a theater, a library, and a video library stocked with classic international and Mexican films. Its most important asset, however, is the **Museo de las Culturas del Occidente** *(Tel 331/23155, closed Mon.).* The Museum of Western Cultures has an excellent display of pre-Hispanic ceramic pottery, including many figures of humans, plus dogs, fish, reptiles, and other animals. One block south, **Parque Piedra Lisa** *(Calzada Galván at Aldama)* is named for its famous smooth stone, a black volcanic rock—the size of a small truck—whose top protrudes from the ground. It is smooth on one side, with steps leading up to the top on the other. Those who slide on it are said to form a lifelong connection with the city and will feel compelled to return to die in Colima.

AROUND COLIMA
North of the capital are several towns well worth visiting. **Comala** is a picture-postcard pueblo of bright white buildings with red-tile roofs 6 miles (10 km) north of

Behind these vulcanologists looms dormant Volcán de Nevado, named for its snowy peak.

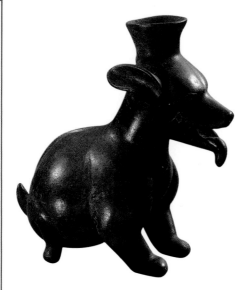

Here reproduced in red clay, *tepezcuintle* dogs were once greatly esteemed (and eaten) by locals.

Colima. Its number-one attraction is its plaza, with trees shading park benches, a bandstand, and a plain but pretty church. On weekends Colimenses gather in colonnaded restaurant-bars serving local delicacies. Favorite dishes include *sopes* (grilled rounds of *masa* smothered with spicy chicken or pork with onions). During the Fiesta de la Virgin de Guadalupe (December 1–12), vendors sell locally grown and roasted coffee and hand-carved furniture.

Five minutes outside Comala, by way of the enchanting Camino a Nogueras roadway, is **Hacienda de Nogueras** *(Closed Mon.)*, a former plantation housing a center for anthropological and cultural study. Within the complex is the **Museo Alejandro Rangel** *(Tel 331/55280)*, comprising a chapel, locally made furniture, and more of Colima's famous ceramic dogs. A small, attractive restaurant (open sporadically) offers regional specialties such as *pollo pilipan*, chicken in a pumpkin-seed and peanut sauce.

Six miles (10 km) north of Comala, indigenous traditions are maintained in **Suchitlán.** The town is famous for its carved ritual masks, used during Semana Santa (Holy Week) celebrations; these and other crafts are sold each Sunday in the Indian market. Just outside town is a small slope in the road, the **zona mágica,** said to be bewitched. On this slope, stationary vehicles and even water seem to defy gravity and run uphill. The phenomenon remains unexplained.

Fourteen miles (22 km) north of Colima is lovely **Laguna la María,**

Festivals

There are three large festivals to be enjoyed each year around Colima. The rustic Feria de San Felipe de Jesús is celebrated in the first two weeks of February in Villa de Álvarez, a community 3 miles (5 km) north of the city center. It includes horse parades, bullfights, and regional foods. Taxi drivers dressed in drag parade through town, snatching unsuspecting men from the crowds.

More commercial (and sober) is the Feria de Todos Santos (late October and early November),

which takes place on the enormous fairgrounds just east of Colima. On offer at the event are rides, food, cultural attractions, and regional handicraft exhibits.

During the Fiesta de la Virgin de Guadalupe (December 1–12) downtown Colima is lined with food stalls, live music events are offered nightly, and there are parades and clown shows. Women, children, and babies dressed in regional costume file solemnly in and out of the cathedral, paying homage to the Virgin. ■

a placid green lake surrounded by coffee groves. It offers sportfishing and rowing as well as a rustic hotel and restaurant. Many city-dwellers stop at the **Jacal de San Antonio** en route to the lake. Perched high on a cliff and with incredible views, this restaurant is open on weekends for lunch only.

Just 5 miles (8 km) beyond the lake, twin volcanoes are the main attraction at **Parque Nacional Volcán de Colima.** The park is named not for one but two imposing volcanoes just a few miles apart. **Volcán de Colima** (also called Volcán de Fuego, meaning "fire volcano") stands 12,989 feet (3,960 m) above sea level, and has erupted nine times in the last four centuries. Activity beginning in January 1999 produced shooting sparks, cascading lava, and other breathtaking pyrotechnical displays clearly visible from Colima. Such activity makes a visit to the volcano and its dormant partner, the **Volcán de Nevado** (meaning "snowy volcano"), impossible. If and when the activity subsides, check with the tourist office for maps and tours. ∎

Magic or realism?

Colima has a keen interest in mysticism and a high number of shops peddling potions and powders for performing white and black magic. This preoccupation with the spirit world reflects the locals' belief that near Colima exists a portal to another dimension, kept wide open by the active shaman community of Suchitlán (3 miles/5 km northeast of Colima). Wizards there are said to transform themselves into animals upon a large stone etched with ancient carvings of female genitalia.

Modern buildings as well as old are reputedly haunted, including a hotel, a hospital, and a café. Ghostly apparitions are taken seriously; some victims report being groped or sexually assaulted by invisible assailants. Although a belief in witches is held throughout Mexico, the exchange of paranormal experiences is a pastime particularly enjoyed by Colimenses. ∎

Colima residents enjoy the low-key restaurant-bars of nearby Comala.

Morelia

ORIGINALLY CALLED VALLADOLID AFTER THE SPANISH city, Morelia is the capital of Michoacán state, whose boundaries are roughly those of the former Purépecha (Tarascan) kingdom. Skilled artisans as well as warriors, the Purépecha were never conquered by the Aztecs, nor by the equally bellicose Chichimecs to the north. Established by Spain in 1541, the city grew slowly in the 16th and 17th centuries, and much of its architecture is subdued 18th-century plateresque. Morelia's wide avenues and expansive plazas are American rather than European in character; these, along with its many restored convents and monasteries, give the city a dignified demeanor.

Morelia

138 D3

Visitor information

✉ Nigromante 79, Palacio Clavijero

☎ 4/317-2371

Flanked by two squares, the superb three-nave sandstone **Catedral** (*Av. Madero at Juárez*), built between 1660 and 1744, blends neo-classic elements and a baroque facade whose carved columns and panels create a chiaroscuro effect. The magnificent 4,600-pipe German organ is celebrated each May during the Festival Internacional del Órgano. Locally crafted and characteristic of pre-Hispanic Purépecha art, the cathedral's 16th-century Christ in one of seven lateral chapels is made of a paste of pulverized corn stalks and orchids.

Cater-corner from the cathedral, the **Palacio de Gobierno** (*Av. Madero 63, tel 4/313-0707*) was originally a seminary where radicals José María Morelos (1765–1815) and Melchor Ocampo (1814–1861), both instruments of the independence movement (see p. 32), were schooled. Its stairwell and second floor are covered in 1970s-era murals of regional history by Michoacán artist Alfredo Zalce (1908–).

Zalce's work and that of other contemporary artists can be seen at the **Museo de Arte**

Contemporáneo *(Av. Acueducto 18, tel 4/312-5404, closed Mon.),* east of the city center. The restored Porfiriato-era house is at the edge of leafy **Bosque Cuauhtémoc.** En route to the park you'll pass the 250-arch **acueducto,** which once supplied fountains throughout the city center with drinkable water.

Bearing straight ahead instead of right past the aqueduct brings you to **Calzada Fray Antonio de San Miguel,** a two-block pedestrian mall connecting to the **Santuario de Nuestra Señora de Guadalupe.** The church's interior received a lavish redecoration in the early 20th century, with molded clay designs combining art nouveau and baroque elements.

Morelia has more than its share of religious buildings, and many today serve secular purposes. Once a Jesuit college, the **Palacio Clavijero** *(Nigromante 79, tel 4/317-2371)* now houses the tourism and other state offices and performance venues; the former church here is a beautiful public library. The **Conservatorio de las Rosas** *(Santiago Tapia 334, tel 4/312-1469, closed Sat., Sun.),* a former Dominican convent, rings with the songs of **Los Niños Cantores de Morelia,** an internationally known boy's choir. Once a Carmelite convent, the huge **Casa de la Cultura** *(Av. Morelos Norte 485, tel 4/313-1215, closed Sun.)* hosts classes and cultural events, and houses the Museo de las Máscaras, with more than 100 traditional carved wooden masks.

Showing typical Franciscan restraint, the **Templo y Ex-Convento Franciscano** *(Fray Juan de San Miguel 129 at Humboldt, tel 4/312-2486)* has a simple plateresque facade. Within the old monastery is the government-run folk-art museum and store, the **Casa de las Artesanías.**

A modern reproduction of a pre-Hispanic mask

Born and educated in the city (then called Valladolid), hero of the Independence War (see p. 32) José María Morelos y Pavón has several museums in his honor, including the **Casa Museo de Morelos** *(Av. Morelos Sur 323, tel 4/313-2651, $),* showing personal and war memorabilia. A few blocks away, an eternal flame burns in the backyard of the hero's birthplace, the **Museo Casa Natal de Morelos** *(Corregidora 113, tel 4/312-2793);* the main house contains a historical library and several Alfredo Zalce murals.

Also worth visiting is the **Mercado de Dulces,** a sweets market behind Palacio Clavijero. Here you will find *ate* (an aspic-like paste made with fruit puree and eaten with soft white cheese), crispy fried *buñuelos* sprinkled with sugar and cinnamon, sweet *empenadas,* and other local treats. The **Museo Regional Michoacano** *(Allende 305, tel 4/312-0407, closed Mon., $),* in an 18th-century palace that once belonged to Emperor Agustín de Iturbide's father-in-law, has paintings and regional artifacts. ■

Pátzcuaro & environs

DROWSING IN THE MOUNTAIN SUNSHINE AT 7,131 FEET (2,170 m) above sea level, Pátzcuaro has long been a center for indigenous culture and folk crafts. After the death of Bishop Vasco de Quiroga (see p. 139) in the mid-16th century, the region's capital was moved from Pátzcuaro to Morelia. Possibly it was the exodus of European power and authority that encouraged native traditions and folk art to flourish. Whether for its native crafts, mountain air, or the almost total lack of modern construction, this lakeside town is probably the most often visited of any in Michoacán state.

Pátzcuaro was the first capital of the Late Postclassic Purépecha kingdom (1200–1521), located in the hilly central part of today's Michoacán. On the southern shores of **Lago de Pátzcuaro,** its inhabitants fished, hunted, and gathered food, and, unlike most Mesoamericans, forged metal tools. Admired as fine craftsmen, they produced brilliant copper utensils, feather work, and *maqueado,* decorated gourds from which the Aztec nobles drank their bitter chocolate. They were excellent warriors as well, resisting absorption into the ever expanding Aztec empire.

The Purépecha were undoubtedly amazed at the total annihilation of their enemy at Tenochtitlán by the Spanish, with their Indian allies and superior weapons. King Tzimtzincha-Tangaxuan II readily accepted the terms of peace set forth by Conquistador Hernán Cortés, swearing fealty to the Spanish Crown, and accepting Christian baptism.

However, the king's fealty made little impression on the brutish conquistador Nuño Beltrán de Guzmán, who as a representative of the colonial governing body, *la real audiencia,* promptly tortured and hanged the Indian sovereign. The persecution, slavery, and torture that de Guzmán inflicted on the local Indians was so excessive—

even by 16th-century standards—that he was finally sent to a Spanish prison for the rest of his life.

After institution of a second, more benevolent audiencia, the difficult task of regaining the natives' trust was given to don Vasco de Quiroga. The Spanish judge was ordained a priest and named bishop on the same day, in 1536. By the time of his death 30 years later, "Tata Vasco" ("Grandpa Vasco") had built as many hospitals and schools as churches, and given numerous towns a craft or vocation to ensure their prosperity.

The tradition of fine craftsmanship continues to this day, and Michoacán has some of Mexico's finest decorative and utilitarian art. Traditional gourd decoration incorporated techniques introduced from Asia. Other arts include weaving, embroidery, metalsmithing, and ceramics, especially tableware.

You can purchase and watch regional crafts being made at the **Casa de los Once Patios** *(Madrigal de las Altas Torres near Lerín),* within a former convent. Another place to view regional crafts is the **Museo de Artes Populares** *(Enseñanza at Alcantarilla, tel 434/21029, closed Mon., $),* a pleasing colonial structure that once housed the Colegio de San Nicolás. At the rear is a typical Purépecha wooden dwelling.

Pátzcuaro
🗺 138 D3
Visitor information
✉ Buenavista 7
☎ 434/21214

Named for its benevolent Spanish benefactor is large **Plaza Vasco de Quiroga** *(Portales Hidalgo, Morelos, Matamoros, & Guerrero).* (Street names change at the square.) Different from most Mexican main squares, it is surrounded by houses (now hotels, restaurants, and shops) instead of municipal buildings and churches. One block away is the more intimate Plaza Gertrudis Bocanegra *(Mendoza, Libertad, Iturbe, & La Paz),* named for a heroine of the War of Independence. Facing the plaza on the north side, the **Biblioteca Gertrudis Bocanegra** *(Closed Sun.)* is an unassuming library with a fabulous and intricate mural of regional history by architect, painter, and muralist Juan O'Gorman (1905–1982).

Pátzcuaro's attraction lies more in popular culture than in ornate churches. The devout regularly visit the **Basílica de Nuestra Señora de la Salud** *(Árciga at Cerrato).* Devastated several times by fire and reassembled in a haphazard manner, it nonetheless houses a much-petitioned cornpaste Virgin of Health.

Día de los Muertos (Day of the Dead) is a living communion with deceased relatives that is celebrated throughout the region. Because of massive international interest in the festivals of neighboring Janitzio (see "The Lake Region," pp. 164–65), the Pátzcuaro tourism delegation has created a program of cultural events taking place in the week or so surrounding the celebration, October 31 to November 2.

Purépecha Indians fish in the traditional way on Lago de Pátzcuaro.

Once a year, on the Day of the Dead, family graves are cleaned and decorated with candles and flowers.

THE LAKE REGION

Many visitors are happy to stroll around Pátzcuaro and make a requisite pilgrimage to the pretty but tourist-driven island of Janitzio. But inquisitive souls should consider a trip into the rolling countryside, where many villages and small towns are known for their folk art.

Purépecha religion was based on a family of gods headed by Kurikaweri, lord of the sun and of war, and the earth goddess, Kwerawáperi. In order to convert this pantheistic people, Catholic priests introduced instructive religious plays such as the *pastorela,* a Nativity and Adoration of the Virgin. Today the lake district is known for its many colorful religious celebrations, involving masked and costumed dancers, locally made instruments, and traditional songs. Zirahuén in particular celebrates saints' days and holidays with traditional forms of music and dance.

One of the best-known and most visited islands is **Janitzio,** Lake Pátzcuaro's largest, where evocative Day of the Dead celebrations have been much publicized and massively visited by outsiders. Atop the cone-shaped island is an imposing, blocklike statue of Independence War hero José María Morelos (see p. 161), with a lookout point in one raised arm *($).* Steps from the ferry landing are lined with souvenir shops and small restaurants. Of the lake's five islands, only tiny, less touristy **Yunuén** has accommodations. Boats leave for all the islands from Pátzcuaro's wharf *(10 minutes north of town center, tel 4/342-0681, $$ round-trip).*

A 55-mile (88 km) road circumvents the lake, leaving the shore only between Ihautzio and Tzintzuntzan, two Purépecha towns that shared power with Pátzcuaro before the Spanish Conquest. Tzintzuntzan's name means "place of the hummingbirds" in Purépecha, a language related to no other in Mexico.

Both towns lie north of Pátzcuaro and on the east side of the lake. Tiny Ihuatzio is little visited except for its partially excavated Purépecha ruins. At **Tzintzuntzan,** visit the crafts market, which sells woven straw objects, simple pottery, and woodcarvings. Both the Franciscan monastery, behind the crafts market, and the **pre-Hispanic ceremonial site** *(Carr. 15 at entrance to Tzintzuntzan, $)* stand in semirestored ruin. The latter consists of a large rectangular platform supporting five *yácatas,* stepped pyramids joined to circular structures originally faced with sheets of volcanic stone. The excavated buildings have yielded burial sites, presumably of Purépecha kings. Tzintzuntzan comes alive for Easter week, Day of the Dead, and Christmas pastorelas beginning December 16.

Named for the 16th-century bishop who dedicated his later life to the native population, **Quiroga** was an important crossroad in pre-Cortesian times. Today it produces leather and painted wooden handiwork, and markets regional crafts. A candlelight procession on the first Sunday in July marks the Fiesta de la Preciosa Sangre de Cristo (Festival of Christ's Precious Blood).

Just a mile (1.5 km) beyond Quiroga, **Santa Fe de la Laguna** lives by farming, fishing, and ceramics, specializing in funerary pieces, including candelabra, urns, and vases. The free-standing cross in the atrium of the **Templo de San Nicolás** is typical to Michoacán state. The town celebrates its fiesta on September 14 with fireworks and local dances.

On the far west side of the lake, **Erongarícuaro** lies surrounded by mixed forests, and like other area towns, has chilly winters and warm, rainy summers. A U.S.-owned store makes unusual and expensive painted wooden furniture, including commissioned work.

About 10 miles (16 km) south of Pátzcuaro is **Villa Escalante** (also known as Santa Clara del Cobre), where artisans produce hand-hammered copper tableware and other decorative and utilitarian pieces. Visit the family-owned shops and factories throughout town, or the **Museo Nacional del Cobre** (*Morelos 263 at Pino Suárez, tel 4/343-0254, closed Mon., $*).

Southwest of Pátzcuaro off Highway 120, **Zirahuén** is a small town on a beautiful blue lake of the same name. Smaller and deeper than Lake Pátzcuaro, Lago Zirahuén is surrounded by pine and oak forests. Known for its music and dance, the town celebrates especially Easter week and the Day of the Holy Cross (May 3). ■

The Dance of the Little Old Men

Regional dances & masks

Indigenous cultures throughout Mexico, but especially in Tlaxcala, Guerrero, and Michoacán, celebrate feast days and festivals with regional dance. Donning masks and sometimes elaborate costumes, the townspeople replay traditional roles that survived the Conquest and, in some cases, were modified by it. Universal themes are the conquest of good over evil and the vanquishing of invaders. Wooden masks representing Spaniards, or "Moors," are painted white, bright pink, or more realistic flesh tones; they are sometimes "two-faced." Tlaxcala masks have glass eyes that open and close when a string is pulled. Animal masks may incorporate horns, whiskers, teeth, claws, and pelts to make them more realistic. Some of the country's most impressive masks are made in the village of Tocuaro, about 6 miles (10 km) west of Pátzcuaro. ■

Uruapan
⚠ 138 D3
Visitor information
✉ Juan Ayala 16
☎ 452/47199

In & around Uruapan

REGARDED BY SOME AS NEIGHBORING PÁTZCUARO'S homely sister, Uruapan is in fact an interesting colonial city in its own right. Its elevation at 2,000 feet (610 m) below Pátzcuaro gives it a subtropical climate that supports lush vegetation and year-round flowers. In the native Purépecha tongue, Uruapan means "where the flowers bloom." An enchanting national park within the city center, one of the country's largest craft fairs, and a nearby lava-covered ghost town are just three reasons to visit this untouristed market town.

The Purépecha made this region their home centuries before Father Juan de San Miguel arrived from Spain and founded the city in 1533. He built a chapel, market, and school, and founded a hospital, but also instated a feudal system that reduced the Indians to serfs. Under this Spanish *encomienda* system, Uruapan prospered as an important agricultural center. Today the city is renowned as the avocado capital of the world. This fruit can be enjoyed during the week-long Feria del Aguacate (Avocado Fair), held in early November.

The city is laid out in a grid, at the center of which is the **plaza principal.** On the north side of the plaza stands **La Huatápera** *(Jardín Morelos s/n),* the original hospital erected by Father Juan in the 16th century. Today it houses the **Museo Popular** *(Tel 452/ 43434, closed Mon., $),* displaying an impressive array of crafts from around the state of Michoacán, including a collection of the beautiful cedar lacquerware for which Uruapan is famous.

Behind La Huatápera, the city's **market** sprawls along Calle Constitución, where the locals sell produce, cheeses, and a variety of crafts, including lacquered trays, gourds, and boxes, and wooden furniture. During Semana Santa (Holy Week), the main square is

converted into a huge crafts market. During the event, beautifully carved guitars and violins from nearby Paracho are on sale at super prices.

On either side of La Huatápera, the exteriors of the **Templo de la Inmaculada** and the **Templo de San Francisco** are fine examples of plateresque architecture in local *cantera* (quarrystone). Just north of the church of San Francisco is the **Casa de la Cultura** (*García Ortiz 1, tel 4/524-7613*), a good place to learn about cultural events being held in the city.

About six long blocks west of the main plaza (a 15-minute walk), at the end of Calle Independencia, lies **Parque Nacional Eduardo Ruíz** (*Calzada Fray Juan de San Miguel s/n, tel 452/40197, $*). A model of landscape architecture, this magical park begins at the headwaters of the Río Cupatizio and follows the river for just over half a mile (1 km). Within this limited space are shady stone paths, terraced banks, bridges, waterfalls, and an explosion of flowers. A rainbow is said to form in the mist of the river every day.

Those interested in sampling the local liquor *(charanda)* can visit the **Destiladora el Tarasco** *(Carretera a Tarétan 26, closed Sun.)*. Here you will see the process by which sugarcane juice is fermented, distilled, and bottled. The Spanish-language tour ends with a free sample of the potent firewater.

More dramatic is a visit to the buried village of **San Juan Parangaricutiro,** where in 1943 the 8,400-foot (2,560 m) **Volcán Paricutín** suddenly sprang up in the middle of a farmer's field. The volcano spewed lava for eight years, and within its relatively short life it forced 4,000 people to evacuate as the lava slowly buried their homes. Today, only the upper facade of the church is visible. To get there, take a bus to **Angahuan** (northwest of Uruapan), where you can rent a horse to San Juan Parangaricutiro *($$)* or to Volcán Paricutín itself *($$$)*. Angahuan has a restaurant and rustic accommodations where you can stay if you tarry too long at San Juan Parangaricutiro, a 6-mile (10 km) round-trip hike. Sturdy shoes are recommended. ■

Only the church's upper facade protrudes above the lava that engulfed Parangaricutiro in 1943.

Ixtapa & Zihuatanejo

THEY ARE ALWAYS MENTIONED IN ALPHABETICAL ORDER, but whereas Zihuatanejo (originally Zihautlán, "Place of Women") was a pre-Hispanic settlement and an important port in the early days of the Spanish colony, modern Ixtapa was, only 30 years ago, just a coconut plantation—one of a handful of resorts developed by the Mexican government in the early 1970s. Today the two places are marketed together, pronounced in a single breath that encompasses 15 miles (24 km) of some of the Pacific coast's most scenic beaches.

After a decree in 1561 pronounced Acapulco to be New Spain's only official Pacific port, **Zihuatanejo** diminished in importance. Following centuries of obscurity, the village was connected to the outside world once again by the construction of Highway 200 in the 1960s, and visitors began to trickle in.

Today Zihua's dirt roads have been paved, and folk-art shops and international restaurants lure vacationers from the tree-shaded but sultry streets. Still a working fishing town, it has several elegant boutique hotels right on the sand. Other singular hotels are tucked up in the foothills, behind the beaches, or in the friendly downtown area. A pedestrian promenade (lit at night) connects downtown, which fronts the main beach, **Playa Principal,** to **Playa La Madera,** a pretty and easily accessible beach popular with picnicking families.

Taxis are the easiest way to reach **Playa La Ropa** (Clothing Beach). The beach's unusual name comes from a haul of silk and other exotic clothes that was washed ashore from a shipwrecked galleon.

Water taxis from the main dock in Zihuatanejo access **Playa Las Gatas,** protected from the ocean's surge by Punta El Faro headland. Named for once-prevalent nurse sharks (not cats), Las Gatas is a lovely beach that is perfect for snorkeling and swimming. Cafés serve soft drinks and *ceviche,* beer and snacks, and watersports concessions rent sailboards, wave runners, and other toys.

Located on a shallow, open bay and without the fishing fleet, the beaches at **Ixtapa** are even cleaner than those of Zihuatanejo, but are largely unprotected from the surf. The hotel zone parallels **Playa del Palmar** for several miles of wide, sandy beaches with access to all the creature comforts: shops, restaurants, bars, boutiques, and watersports rentals. An inexpensive taxi ride between the two towns takes just about 10 minutes.

More isolated beaches can be found at Ixtapa's west end, past the surf spot at **Escolleras** and the Marina Ixtapa, a 620-slip marina and yacht club on a double-pronged cove. Here also is the **Club de Golf Marina Ixtapa** *(Tel 7/553-1410).* West of the marina are several more lovely beaches. Beyond Punta Ixtapa, **Playa Quieta** is a tranquil beach with a Club Med hotel. Horses can be rented *($$$$$)* for early morning or late-afternoon jaunts on the beach at **Playa Linda** (Beautiful Beach).

From Playa Quieta pier, water taxis *($ round-trip)* access popular **Isla Ixtapa,** where you can dive or snorkel, or lounge on the beach or dine at the adjacent restaurants. On the far side of the small island, **Playa Carey** has no facilities and thus offers more solitude.

Ixtapa
🅰 138 D2
Visitor information
✉ La Puerta Mall, opposite the Hotel Presidente
☎ 7/553-1967

For those who want to do more than hang out at the beach, fishing co-ops near the pier in Zihuatanejo offer deep-sea fishing for dorado, marlin, yellowfin tuna, roosterfish, sailfish, and mackerel. Yearly tournaments in January and May are gaining popularity.

Snorkel and dive trips can be arranged through several operators, including **Zihuatanejo Scuba Center** (*Hotel Paraíso Real, tel 7/554-2147*). In addition to the Club de Golf Marina Ixtapa (see p. 168), golfers can play at the 18-hole **Club de Golf Ixtapa** (*Blvd. Ixtapa s/n, tel 7/553-1062*). Regional history and anthropology can be explored at the **Museo Arqueológico de la Costa Grande** (*Plaza Olaf Palme, tel 7/554-7552, closed Mon., $*).

About 14 miles (22.5 km) south of Zihuatanejo lies **Barra de Potosí,** a luscious beach backed by rugged mountains. Thatch-roofed restaurants on the beach provide hammocks where you can while away the day. During the dry season, boats tour the adjacent lagoon, where water fowl may be spotted. Half-day tours (*$$$$$*) are available through Ixtapa or Zihuatanejo tour operators, or you can get there by taxi or city bus. The scenery along the way is lush and beautiful.

About the same distance north of Zihuatanejo is **Troncones,** another area of beautiful beaches where mid- and high-end hotels and house rentals are cropping up, many owned by Canadian and U.S. citizens. ■

Vacationers relax under individual palm-thatch umbrellas at Isla Ixtapa.

Zihuatanejo
⊠ 138 D2
Visitor information
✉ Palacio Municipal
☎ 7/554-4455

Acapulco

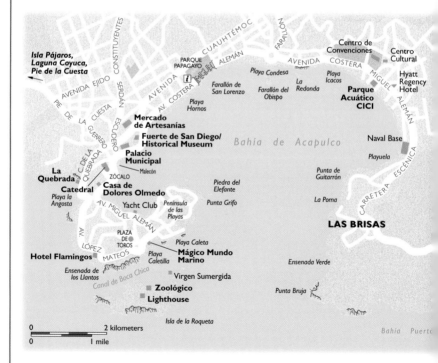

Acapulco
139 E1
Visitor information
Av. Costera Miguel Alemán 4455 (at Convention Center)
7/481-2352

DELICIOUSLY SELF-SATISFIED, THE AGED PORT CITY OF Acapulco remains a major resort destination for foreign honeymooners and Mexicans cutting loose on annual vacations. Trendy restaurants serve international and haute Mexican cuisine, while friendly seaside bistros pile on fresh shrimp and Acapulco-style *ceviche*. Still among the hippest in Mexico, the city's many discos play live and canned music until the roosters crow in the surrounding hills.

Acapulco's balmy weather ranges from hot to hotter. Summer rains (June to October) tend to exacerbate the heat instead of diminishing it. As the humidity rises, hotel prices fall, but the trade-off is high. Throughout the year, myriad species of flowering trees produce brilliant blossoms. Tropical fruits— including mango, papaya, and watermelon—appear as fresh drinks or as salads served with a squeeze of lime and a sprinkle of

powdered chili. On Thursdays, tradition calls for a late, leisurely lunch of *pozole*—hominy soup served with raw onions, avocado, and oregano.

Although jet skis, water skis, diving and snorkel equipment, and other water toys are offered by the hotels crowding Avenida Costera, this tends to be the most polluted part of the 4-mile (7 km) bay. Beaches on or near the points, such as **Playa Caleta** and **Playa**

A dazzling view of Acapulco Bay from one of the city's exclusive hilltop neighborhoods

Puerto Marqués, are the cleanest. If you're hesitant about swimming in murky waters, consider parasailing over the picturesque bay, sportfishing for sailfish or dorado, playing tennis, or golfing at one of the city's six courses.

Acapulco became absolutely hip and happening in the 1960s, when sybaritic Hollywood stars partied in private homes and exclusive restaurants above downtown, before the "scene" marched unequivocally east. Today, nostalgic Acapulqueños stop by for a cocktail at the once-glamorous **Hotel Flamingos** bar, overlooking the surf (and Acapulco's famous sunsets) around **Playitas.** The coast road winds through neighborhoods of older homes, shops, and restaurants to **La Quebrada,** where cliff divers hurtle themselves more than 15 stories into a rocky cove below. Dives (*$*) are usually performed at 1, 7:30, 8:30, 9:30, and 10:30 p.m.

The road continues to twin coves of coarse sand at **Playa Caleta** and **Playa Caletilla,** lined with informal restaurants and water equipment concessions. Separating the two beaches is **Mágico Mundo Marino** (*Tel 7/483-9344, $$*), a theme park with a sea lion show, water slides, kayak rental, and a restaurant. From Playa Caleta, a ten-minute boat ride (*daily, $$*) takes you to hilly **Isla de la Roqueta,** where glass-bottomed boats offer 45-minute cruises and animals languish in a small **zoo.** During the coolest hours of the day, climb the hill to the **lighthouse** for a view of the sweeping, palm-fringed bay.

From Playa Caleta, Avenida Costera Miguel Alemán (usually simply called "la Costera") curves past the Yacht Club to **downtown Acapulco.** Once the center of tourist attention, it is now left mostly to the locals, who hang out

200

Revolcadero, Laguna Tres Palos, Barra Vieja

chilingue Playa Puerto Marqués

Puerto Marqués

arqués

at the laid-back **zócalo.** The cathedral of **Nuestra Señora de la Soledad,** built in the 1930s, combines art deco and Moorish elements with no great success. A short cab ride from downtown takes you to **Casa de Dolores Olmedo** *(Cerro de la Pinzona s/n),* the private home of Diego Rivera's patroness, which he covered in mosaics of tile, shell, and natural stone. It may soon open to the public, but for now, you can view the wonderful exterior murals.

At the oceanfront **malecón,** or seawalk, cruise ships disgorge their passengers to haggle at the 350-stall **Mercado de Artesanías** *(Velázquez de León near 5 de Mayo),* a flea market selling T-shirts, silver jewelry, sandals, and coconut masks. "Booze cruises" *($$$$$)* offer afternoon and evening cruises with food, shows, meals, or swimming in addition to drinks.

Constructed in 1615 to protect the Manila galleons from pirates, Acapulco's **Fuerte de San Diego** was destroyed by earthquake in 1776. The fort was rebuilt of stone with a surrounding moat. The recently renovated **historical museum** *(Tel 7/482-3828, closed Mon., $)* holds permanent exhibits as well as temporary cultural expositions. Don't miss the **Museo de las Máscaras,** with 400 of Guerrero state's famous masks as well as less traditional but equally colorful woodcarvings.

Locals and visitors fill the thatch-roofed eateries lining **Playa Hornos,** or spread their picnics along the shore. Across the street, flamboyant trees and coconut palms shade children's amusement rides, snack shacks, and dusty soccer fields in the large but neglected **Parque Papagayo.** Animal shows, wave-action pools, waterslides, and swimming with dolphins lure visitors across the

street to **Parque Acuático CICI** *(Av. Costera Miguel Alemán at Cristóbal Colón, tel 7/481-0294, $$$).*

Between placid **Playa Icacos** and the Hyatt Regency hotel (which marks the end of Avenida Costera) lies a less-than-scenic proliferation of hotels, restaurants, drugstores, souvenir shops, discos, and car rentals. Jet-ski, banana-boat, and parasailing concessions line the beach, and drinks and snacks are served under palm-leaf sun shades.

The coast highway's name changes to **Carretera Escénica** as it winds east toward Acapulco's newer developments. Perched high above the ocean on either side of the highway, the exclusive private palaces and hotels of **Las Brisas** are blessed with the ocean breezes for which the suburb was named. From here there are splendid views of the bay, which positively sparkles at night. Many of the resorts on the cliff side of the highway have elevators or steep stairways to semi-private beaches.

Farther east, a number of high-rise hotels lining calm, sandy **Bahía Puerto Marqués** rent water toys, while horses wait for riders at long, wave-beaten **Playa Revolcadero.** Near the airport, you can sip a tropical drink from a seaside cabana at **Barra Vieja,** or take a boat ride around the lagoons of adjoining **Laguna Tres Palos,** a small fishing village.

Twenty-two miles (35 km) northwest of downtown, fresh-water **Laguna Coyuca** is lined with mangroves. Eat at one of the beach shacks, arrange a lagoon tour with a visit to **Isla Pájaros,** or water-ski. The long beach at nearby **Pie de la Cuesta** is a favorite for horseback riding and hammock lounging in simple thatch-roofed restaurants. Both Laguna Coyuca and Pie de la Cuesta are wonderful spots to watch the sun set. ■

Opposite: Daring cliff divers have impressed onlookers for decades—and have suffered surprisingly few mishaps.

The Iglesia de Santa Prisca rises above Taxco's center.

Taxco

DELIGHTFUL SUN-SPLASHED TAXCO WINDS UP AND DOWN narrow, cobblestone streets. U.S. expatriate William Spratling, who started Taxco's first silversmithing workshop, called it the "Florence of Mexico," but physically it's closer to a Mediterranean village. By city ordinance, its white-painted facades crowned with red-tile roofs rise no more than three stories above street level.

Most of Taxco's sights are found on or near pretty **Plaza Borda,** where patent-leather grackles voice their urgent calls from the trees. Streets radiate like spokes, surrounded by handsome two- and three-story buildings housing restaurants, silver shops, and homes. Facing the plaza are the **Museo de la Plata** (*Plaza Borda 16, tel 762/20658, $*), a small, privately owned silver museum, and the **Centro Cultural** (*Plaza Borda 14, tel 762/26617, closed Mon.*), offering art classes, cultural performances, and changing exhibits.

The original Taxco was inhabited by Thalhuica Indians, who paid tribute to their Aztec overlords in gold and silver. After the Conquest, the Spaniards established mines at the site of present-day Taxco (El Nuevo, or New Taxco), relocating workers and engineers from the old city, now known as "Taxco el Viejo." Although silver was mined for centuries and artisans in nearby Iguala were known for their goldsmithing, it was William Spratling (1900–1967) who established the first silver workshop, Las Delicias, in 1931. Today, about 80 percent of the population is involved in silversmithing, and the Ministry of Tourism estimates there are some thousand silver shops, with another thousand vendors selling at the **Saturday market** (*Av. de los Plateros s/n, near the Flecha Roja bus terminal*).

The unequivocal star of this silver city, however, is gold-drenched **Iglesia de Santa**

nailed separately to the cross. Sometimes referred to as "the Michelangelo of Mexico," Miguel Cabrera (1695–1768) executed most of the church's paintings.

As you face Santa Prisca, the city's wonderful market—a twisting warren of stalls—is a block to your right. On Thursdays, vendors here and throughout the city sell *pozole,* hominy soup served with a plate of condiments. Other regional foods include *cecina taxqueña* (thin pieces of marinated beef) and barbecued goat. Author John Dos Passos and William Spratling claimed to have invented the lime and tequila concoction "la Berta" at Berta's bar. Still going strong, the cantina claims a secret ingredient—but it's basically tequila, soda, and lime.

A portion of Spratling's collection of pre-Hispanic art is shown at the **Museo Spratling** *(Porfirio Delgado 1, tel 762/21660, closed Mon., $).* Although poorly labeled and displayed, it is worth a look. Of more interest is the nearby **Museo de Arte Virreinal** *(Juan Ruíz de Alarcón 12, tel 762/25501, closed Mon., $$),* which houses religious art and liturgical objects. The museum's prized possession is a *túmulo funerario,* a boxlike altar painted with significant scenes from the deceased's life. The beautifully restored 17th-century building has exposed ceiling beams, whitewashed walls, baked earth tiles, and great cityscapes. For an even greater view, climb the steep street behind town to the hilltop **Templo de Guadalupe,** or take the aerial tram from Los Arcos, near the visitor center on Avenida de los Plateros, to **Club de Campo Monte Taxco.** For a fee, you can play tennis or nine holes of golf here, or swim in the pool. Alternatively, sip a drink at the bar, and enjoy the view—on a clear day you can see Popocatépetl and Iztaccíhuatl. ■

Prisca *(Plaza Borda 1, tel 762/ 20183).* The pink quarrystone church is dedicated to obscure, 12th-century Roman martyr Santa Prisca. (After lions in the Roman circus refused to eat her, she was beheaded.) The ornate church was paid for entirely by mining entrepreneur don José de la Borda, who amassed (and gave away) a fortune.

The temple is said to hold 23 tons of gold leaf and, except for the lighting, almost everything is original. The manual, 256-pipe organ—which took six months to bring piece by piece by mule from Veracruz—is still played during special services. The narrow church's 12 gold and polychrome altarpieces, most of which could use a good cleaning, create a dizzying feeling of excess. Dozens of saints lean out in high relief from the exuberant main altarpiece, dedicated to the Virgin of the Immaculate Conception. The left side chapel was built for the town's indigenous population. Note the unusual crucifix, with the Christ figure's arms above the head, nails in the wrists instead of the hands, and the feet

More places to visit in the Central Pacific states

LAGOS DE MORENO
Originally a stop on the colonial silver route, Lagos de Moreno is a prosperous place, little visited by tourists. Stately churches of rose-colored limestone and a handful of colonial-era private homes surround its plazas. Located 50 miles (82 km) southeast of Aguascalientes, this small city in the central highlands of Jalisco appears to belong in a more distant era. Visit the baroque **Parroquia de la Asunción,** the parish church (*Hidalgo at the main plaza),* and the sober but elegant **Rinconada de las Capuchinas** (*Miguel Leandro Guerra at Mariano Azuela),* a former convent with a museum and cultural center.

138 D4 **Visitor information** ✉ Juárez 426 at Francisco González León ☎ 474/22466

LOS AZUFRES
About 1½ hours east of Morelia, near the city of Ciudad Hidalgo, off Highway 15, lies an area of natural hot springs called Los Azufres. Spas offer different levels of service, but most have restaurants, changing rooms, and one or more pools; some have campgrounds and offer massage or other services. For a more natural retreat with few services, head for **La Poza de los Azufres.** Located within a volcanic crater, the spring's sulfurous 104°F (40°C) waters are recommended for those with joint problems.

138 D3

PARQUE NACIONAL GRUTAS DE CACAHUAMILPA
About 19 miles (30 km) from Taxco is Mexico's largest system of underground caves. Two-hour guided tours (*Tel 762/22274, \$\$*) leave hourly 10–5, following a 1.2-mile (2 km) lighted path past intriguing stalactites, stalagmites, and rock formations. The entire system comprises about 10 miles (16 km) of tunnels and 20 caves. Minibuses leave from the Taxco bus depot; if you are traveling by car, take the marked turnoff from Highway 55.

139 E2

SANTIAGO IXCUINTLA & MEXCALTITÁN
Surrounded by ranchlands, about a half-hour's drive northeast of San Blas (see p. 141),

Santiago Ixcuintla is worth a visit for those interested in Huichol culture. Its **Centro Cultural Huichol** (*20 de Noviembre 452, tel 323/51171*) is a gallery but also a clinic, library, restaurant, and workshop for Nayarit's Huichol Indians. Masks and gourds decorated with icons, yarn "paintings," and other treasures are for sale. Ixcuintla is also the departure point for Mexcaltitán, a tranquil island fishing village on a salt-water lagoon. Although no physical evidence exists, this has been proposed as the original home of the Mexica, thought to have emigrated from a place called Aztlán to found Tenochtitlán. The **Museo Aztlán del Origen** (*closed Mon., \$*) documents the Aztec migration and exhibits indigenous art, maps, costumes, and recorded music. Colorful processions and regattas mark the feast days of town patrons St. Peter and St. Paul, June 28 and 29.

138 B5

SANTUARIO DE LA MARIPOSA MONARCA EL ROSARIO
The transvolcanic mountain range in eastern Michoacán is the winter home for one of the world's most enduring insects: the monarch butterfly. The fragile orange and black butterflies migrate up to 3,100 miles (5,000 km) from Canada and the Great Lakes, arriving at the same forests where their forebears reproduced. After resting throughout the winter, they mate. The males die; the females prepare for the long return journey beginning in early or mid-April.

    El Santuario de la Mariposa el Rosario is the better of two wintering sites open to the public. In a good year the monarchs blanket *oyamel* trees (a type of spruce) in an orange haze of several million individuals. Visit late November through March; on sunny days the insects are most active and therefore easier to see as they fly about. Park entrance is relatively inexpensive (*\$\$*), but the excursion is more interesting with a knowledgeable guide. Recommended are the state-licensed, English-speaking guides of **MMG** (*Tel 4/320-1157, Morelia),* who lead long day tours from the capital. Call for information.

139 E3 ∎

Despite its urban woes, the nation's capital has a wealth of cultural attractions and a cosmopolitan character. And its history—evident in its art, artifacts, and architecture— is one of the most fascinating in Latin America.

Mexico City

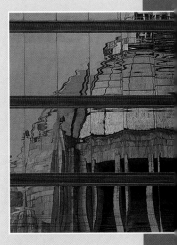

Mexico City architecture
reflects old and new.

Mexico City

MEXICO CITY TODAY IS A LOT LIKE THE LITTLE GIRL FROM THE NURSERY rhyme: When she's good, she's very, very good, but when she's bad, she's horrid. To the good, theater, dance, and musical performances—everything from marimba to Mozart—are held in dozens of theaters throughout the city, including three excellent venues on the campus of the National Autonomous University (UNAM). *Mariachi* musicians in matching, silver-studded ensembles croon romantic tunes in historic Plaza de Garibaldi. Upscale boutiques, cutting-edge art galleries, and sidewalk cafés line the main streets in Polanco, la Zona Rosa, la Condesa, Roma, and other diverse neighborhoods.

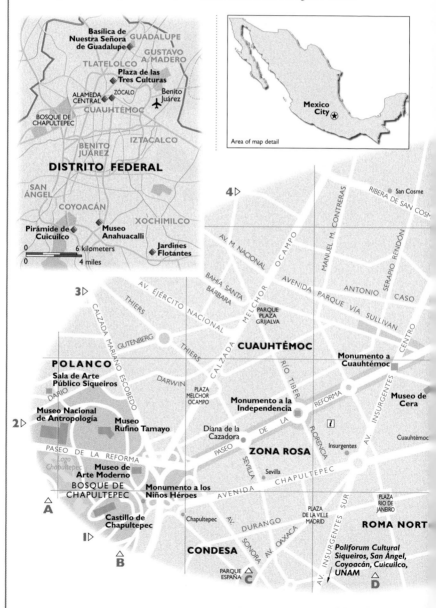

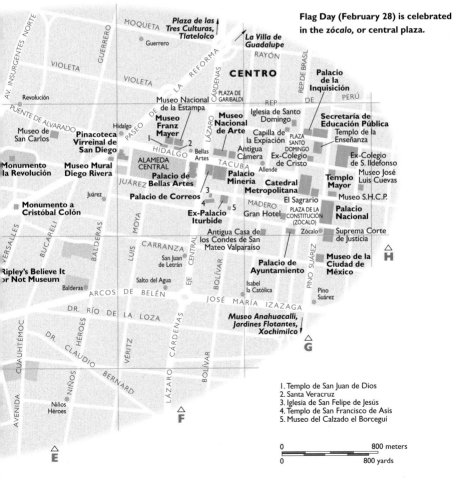

Flag Day (February 28) is celebrated in the *zócalo*, or central plaza.

AV. INSURGENTES NORTE

MOQUETA

GUERRERO

Plaza de las
Tres Culturas,
Tlatelolco

Guerrero

La Villa de
Guadalupe

RAYÓN

CENTRO

VIOLETA

VIOLETA

LA REFORMA

LA REFORMA

CÁRDENAS

PLAZA DE
GARIBALDI

REP DE BRASIL

Palacio
de la
Inquisición

Revolución

PUENTE DE ALVARADO

Hidalgo

Museo de
San Carlos

Pinacoteca
Virreinal de
San Diego

Museo Nacional
de la Estampa

Museo
Franz
Mayer

HIDALGO

Bellas
Artes

ALAMEDA
CENTRAL

Monumento
la Revolución

Museo Mural
Diego Rivera

Palacio de
Bellas Artes

JUÁREZ

Juárez

Monumento a
Cristóbal Colón

Museo
Nacional
de Arte

Iglesia de Santo
Domingo

Capilla de
la Expiación

Antigua
Cámera

TACUBA

Palacio
Minería

PLAZA
SANTO
DOMINGO

Ex-Colegio
de Cristo

Catedral
Metropolitana

El Sagrario

MADERO

Gran Hotel

PLAZA DE LA
CONSTITUCIÓN
(ZÓCALO)

Allende

REP.

DE

PERÚ

Secretaría de
Educación Pública

Templo de la
Enseñanza

Ex-Colegio
de S. Ildefonso

Museo José
Luis Cuevas

Templo
Mayor

Museo S.H.C.P.

Palacio
Nacional

Palacio de Correos

Ex-Palacio
Iturbide

Antigua Casa de
los Condes de San
Mateo Valparaiso

San Juan
de Letrán

Palacio de
Ayuntamiento

Isabel
la Católica

Zócalo

Suprema Corte
de Justicia

Museo de la
Ciudad de
México

MOYA

CARRANZA

LUIS

BALDERAS

BUCARELI

VERSALLES

Ripley's Believe It
or Not Museum

Balderas

Salto del Agua

ARCOS DE BELÉN

EJE CENTRAL

BOLÍVAR

JOSÉ MARÍA IZAZAGA

PINO SUÁREZ

Pino
Suárez

H

DR. RÍO DE LA LOZA

Museo Anahuacalli,
Jardines Flotantes,
Xochimilco

G

CUAUHTÉMOC

DR. CLAUDIO BERNARD

HÉROES

NIÑOS

VÉRITZ

LÁZARO CÁRDENAS

BOLÍVAR

AVENIDA

Niños
Héroes

F

E

1. Templo de San Juan de Dios
2. Santa Veracruz
3. Iglesia de San Felipe de Jesús
4. Templo de San Francisco de Asís
5. Museo del Calzado el Borceguí

0   800 meters
0   800 yards

Painter Frida Kahlo's childhood home is now one of the capital's 85 museums.

On the down side, about 3 million cars are crowded into the 570-square-mile (1,475 sq km) capital, spewing tons of contaminants into the air each year. At 7,400 feet (2,250 m) above sea level, the megalopolis of some 20 million people is ringed by volcanic mountains that trap the pollution. Visitors must be on the lookout for petty thieves, and if hailing a street taxi, should check the driver's posted picture ID.

Despite these considerable dangers and annoyances, el D.F. (short for Distrito Federal, or Federal District) is a fascinating mélange of the hip and the historic. Trendy restaurants in la Condesa serve carpaccio and decaf espresso, while down the street, family-run stands sell tamales and tacos. Mexico City represents the quintessence of the country's *mestizaje,* or blending of Indian and European cultures.

When the Mexica (pronounced meh-SHEE-ka) first wandered into the bowl-shaped Valle de Anáhuac (Valley of Mexico) from the north, they met people of learning: the cultured descendants of the Toltec tribe, with an accurate calendar and elaborate religious rituals (see p. 184). The Mexica, or Aztecs, founded Tenochtitlán on Lake Texcoco and, after rubbing elbows with their civilized neighbors for 200 years, amazed the Spanish conquistadors with their ingenious city of broad avenues lined with brightly painted palaces and temples. After the Conquest, the Spaniards built their new capital, Mexico City, from the ruins of Tenochtitlán and gradually filled in the lake. However, the unstable lakebed has proved a poor foundation, and today scores of 18th- and 19th-century buildings are being restored.

South and southwest of the historic center, the villages of Coyoacán and San Ángel—which predated the Spanish conquest and even the building of Tenochtitlán—have over the years retained their identities. Between the two towns are at least half a dozen captivating plazas surrounded by baroque churches, cobbled streets, and brightly painted homes with flower-filled courtyards. On weekends local artists and antiques dealers sell their wares at agreeably inexpensive prices, while an excellent assortment of the country's handicrafts are sold daily in boutiques and shops.

Xochimilco, one of the southernmost villages on former Lake Texcoco, has produced much of the region's plants and cut flowers since pre-Hispanic times. On Sundays lively groups of friends and families climb aboard *trajineras*—covered punts decorated in plastic flowers—for a leisurely cruise along Mexico City's last remaining system of canals and *chinampas,* or waterborne gardens. ■

Centro Histórico

Mexico's cherished "dark-skinned Virgin" is feted in the *zócalo*.

VICEREGAL ADMINISTRATIVE OFFICES, PROMINENT homes, cathedrals, and chapels replaced the palaces and temples of the dispossessed Mexica in the nucleus of the new city. Having weathered the centuries and survived the region's intermittent earthquakes, many still fulfill their original purpose; others house bookstores, jewelers, pawnshops, museums, and restaurants. Cosmopolitan and chaotic yet eager to please, downtown D.F. is a synthesis of ancient and modern Mexican culture—and has more churches than you could visit in a month of Sundays.

A good place to begin exploring the city is the 10-acre (4 ha) *zócalo*, or central plaza, built from the rubble of Tenochtitlán. Officially called Plaza de la Constitución, it is the world's second largest square. On the north side of the square, the **Catedral Metropolitana** *(Tel 5510-0440)*, the first cathedral in New Spain, was ordered to be built by Hernán Cortés, but later razed and replaced with the present church, finished in 1813. The dignified baroque facade is dominated by twin 18th-century bell towers.

Inside, worshipers continue to pray at the cathedral's five principal altars and 14 chapels despite the mountain of scaffolding shoring up the structure. Dusky light filters through small stained-glass windows to illuminate the dazzling **Altar de los Reyes,** a gilded wood altarpiece in Churrigueresque style, which took nearly 20 years to complete. Also Churrigueresque is the intricate facade of the adjoining mid-18th-century parish church, **El Sagrario,** covered in an army of carved saints. **La Piedra del Sol,** the 24-ton Aztec "calendar" stone now seen in the Museo Nacional de Antropología (see pp. 198–201), was discovered in El

Centro Histórico
🗺 179 G3
Visitor information
✉ Amberes 54, Zona Rosa
☎ 5525-9380
Ⓜ Metro: Insurgentes

Sagrario's courtyard. The church is closed owing to earthquake damage.

The east side of the zócalo is completely dedicated to the **Palacio Nacional** *(Tel 5228-1542)*, which displaced Aztec emperor Moctezuma's sumptuous palace. Originally the official residence of the colonial viceroys, the national palace later held the presidential offices, although Benito Juárez was the only president to use this as his official residence. Today, the palace houses various state departments, but for visitors, the draw is 18 years' worth of Diego Rivera murals highlighting Mexican history and culture. To best appreciate the unlabeled murals, hire an English-speaking guide at the foot of the stairwell. Most charge about 50 pesos. On the second floor are scenes from pre-Hispanic life at Tenochtitlán, Michoacán, Oaxaca, and Papantla. Smaller panels pay tribute to the rubber tree, corn, cacao, and the agave plant. The last mural on the second floor shows the *mestizaje* of Mexico, the blending of indigenous and Spanish blood and cultures. Cortés is shown as a hideous, syphillitic man; behind him, his mistress, La Malinche (see box, p. 207) holds a green-eyed mestizo baby.

One block south, in the **Suprema Corte de Justicia** *(Pino Suárez 2, tel 5522-1500)*, is José Clemente Orozco's mural, "La Justicia" ("Justice"), seen over the main interior staircase. On the south side of the plaza, the tiled exterior of the **Palacio del Ayuntamiento** (Municipal Palace) depicts the coats of arms of Mexico City, Coyoacán, Christopher Columbus, and Hernán Cortés. The matching structure next door was built in 1935 to accommodate growing Federal District affairs.

If you're interested in turn-of-the-20th-century architecture, don't miss the lobby of the **Gran Hotel** *(Calle 16 de Septiembre 82, tel 5510-4040)*, built as a mercantile center during the Porfirio Díaz administration. Green, faux-stone columns hide its Chicago-system foundations, a style of construction in which steel girders throughout the structure support the building's weight. The cast-iron elevators at either end of the lobby are art nouveau, and the splendid stained-glass ceiling in the lobby is representative of France's Nancy School.

Naturally, some of the city's finest architecture stems from its religious past. Built in 1588 as a Jesuit seminary, the **Ex-Colegio de San Ildefonso** *(Justo Sierra 16, tel 5702-6378, closed Mon., $)* was remodeled during the early 18th century but maintains its original baroque and neoclassic facade. Inside, dark orange walls and stone porticos surround a large central patio shaded by giant magnolias. Now owned by the National University, the museum and cultural center hosts cultural events and temporary fine arts exhibits. Don't miss the 80 or more carved cedar choir stalls, rescued from a fire at the St. Augustine monastery, in the ground floor's northwest corner. Each exquisitely rendered chair depicts a different biblical scene. Murals form another part of the museum's permanent collection. Those by José Clemente Orozco along three stories at the building's north end range from somber to cartoony. Diego Rivera's stylized "La Creación" (1922) is tucked away in the Anfiteatro Bolívar on the west side.

Nearby, the striking, ultra-baroque interior of the narrow **Templo de la Enseñanza** *(Donceles 102, tel 5702-1843, closed Mon.)* is a dazzling display of Spanish colonial wealth. Vacated during the Reform Laws, the late

By night historic downtown, dominated by the Catedral Metropolitana, regains an air of refinement.

18th-century convent church was declared a national monument in 1931 and once again functions as a place of worship.

One block north, the interior patios of the neoclassic **Secretaría de Educación Pública** *(Av. República de Argentina 28, tel 5328-1000)*, or Ministry of Education, are covered with examples of the Mexican Mural School. Diego Rivera painted nearly 200 panels between 1923 and 1928, notably "La Maestra Rural" ("The Rural Teacher") and "La Liberación del Peón" ("The Peasant's Liberation") —common themes for the socialist painter. The singular "Patriots and Parricides," by Siqueiros, decorates the stairwell near the República de Brasil street entrance.

One of Mexico's oldest squares, the **Plaza Santo Domingo** *(República de Venezuela at Brasil)* shelters the **Portal de los Evangelistas,** a colonnade where *evangelistas* (public scribes) clack away on ancient typewriters, completing job applications and "Dear John" letters for the illiterate. At the north end of the plaza,

native red *tezontle* (volcanic rock) contrasts with the white-stone Corinthian columns on the facade of the baroque **Iglesia de Santo Domingo** *(Tel 5529-3906)*. It was built in the early 18th century after floods and earthquakes ruined the first Dominican monastery in New Spain, dated 1527. Inside, note the neoclassic high altar created by Manuel de Tolsá. All that remains of the original structure is the small **Capilla de la Expiación,** or Chapel of Atonement, with its fabulous rococo altarpiece.

The Dominican-led Inquisition was aimed as much at purging political rivals from the colony as in pursuing heretics. A tribunal was established in 1521 in rented buildings surrounding the Plaza de Santo Domingo. The more permanent **Palacio de la Inquisición** *(República de Brasil 33)*, across the street, was not built for another 200 years. It was purchased in 1854 by the National University and now houses the **Museo de la Medicina** *(Tel 5529-7542, closed university holidays)*, a museum of the history of Mexican medicine. ∎

A brief history of the Mexica

The Mexica, or Aztecs, arrived in the bowl-shaped Valle de Anáhuac (Valley of Mexico) in the late 13th century. They were a poor and barbarous people—with no formal religion, calendar, or system of writing—who wandered south from a place they called Aztlán. Initially reviled and briefly enslaved by more powerful city-states in the valley, the Mexica fled in 1322 to the uninhabited wetlands at the edge of Lake Texcoco, where they founded Tenochtitlán on an island on the lake. Just 50 years later they began their rapid rise to power with a strategic marriage into the royal family of Culhuacán, their former masters.

With the ascent of Itzcóatl to the throne in 1427, there began a systematic conquest and absorption of the established lakeside cities, including Coyoacán, Xochimilco, and Atzcapotzalco—the latter providing access to important freshwater springs at Chapultepec. Through warfare, intimidation, strategic alliances, and a ruthless political agenda, the Mexica extended their domain throughout Mesoamerica. From the time their first king ascended the throne, they began to reinvent their own history and genealogy in a more favorable light, even claiming lineage back to the god-king Quetzalcóatl.

Although governed during its early years by a representative council of elders and speakers, Tenochtitlán soon developed a ruling oligarchy, the *pipiltin*. Most people lived in servitude, subject to laws governing such minutiae as what they ate, drank, and wore. Meanwhile, the extravagant lifestyle of the pipiltin necessitated a constantly expanding empire enriched by plunder and the labor and taxation of subject states. These divergent living standards are reflected in the folk belief of the time that after death nobles were regenerated as gems, beautiful birds, or fluffy white clouds, while commoners became weasels, dung beetles, and skunks.

Few peoples except the Purépecha of Michoacán and some of the fierce Chichimec tribes to the north were able to repel the Mexica war machine. The conquered paid dearly both in tribute and in victims for the sacrificial slab. The Mexica's principle god, Huitzilopochtli (Southern Hummingbird, the god of war), grew in power as the empire grew. Initially an insignificant local deity, the hummingbird demanded human sacrifice on an incredible scale, feasting on hearts and blood from captured warriors, scofflaws, and other unfortunates.

By the time a Spanish expedition under Hernán Cortés arrived on Mexico's east coast in 1519, Tenochtitlán was feared, respected, and hated almost as much by its allies as by its subject states and enemies. Only this far-flung hostility made possible one of history's most amazing conquests (see p. 29). Another important factor was timing. According to legend, Quetzalcóatl had sailed eastwards five centuries before, promising to return in the year One Reed. Cortés's arrival in that very year (a 1:52 probability) convinced the Mexica ruler, Moctezuma, of the god's return. A priest, poet, and philosopher, Moctezuma had been chosen king in 1502 based on his courage in battle, sagacity, and clarity of mind. Ironically, it was his indecision and unwillingness to acknowledge and engage the enemy that led to the downfall of the Mexica empire, and ultimately, to the conquest of Mesoamerica. ∎

Above: Human sacrifice in Mesoamerica
Right above: Moctezuma's historic first meeting with Cortés
Right below: Spanish and Aztec warriors at battle; scene from the Duran Codex

Templo Mayor

UNTIL THE SPANISH CONQUEST, THE TEMPLO MAYOR, OR great pyramid of Tenochtitlán, was the site of coronations, dedications, human sacrifice, and other important civic and religious events. Today, a partial reconstruction of the pyramid allows you to appreciate its building stages, as well as view several surviving rooms and temples. Although the ruins themselves are interesting, it's in the well-designed museum that you'll really get a feel for life in Tenochtitlán. Here, soul-stirring statues of incredible power and pathos are displayed on free-standing pedestals. Jewelry, carved shells, knives used in ritualistic self-sacrifice and human sacrifice, and many other smaller objects are arranged on beds of fine sand in attractive display cases.

Templo Mayor

🗺 179 G3

Visitor information

✉ Calle Seminario 8, northeast corner of the *zócalo*

☎ 5542-4943

🕐 Closed Mon.

💲 $$

🚇 Metro: Zócalo

Twin temples atop the Templo Mayor pyramid were dedicated to the two most important gods: the southern temple, painted red, housed the war god Huitzilopochtli; to the north was the blue shrine of Tláloc, god of rain and fertility. Still visible on the Tláloc temple are vertical black and white stripes and circles representing rain, eyes, and sky. Before it, a statue of Chac Mool, messenger to the gods, was positioned to receive the hearts of sacrificial victims.

Within the structure, thousands of priests and their acolytes lived and worshiped, accessing apartments and shrines through labyrinthine corridors of polished stone. Each ruler modified or enlarged previous structures; new walls were built out and up, and the intervening space filled with mud and rubble. At the northern extreme of the excavation, note the eagle designs in the **Eagle Warrior room,** the exclusive enclave of the respected military order.

The first four galleries are dedicated to Huitzilopochtli, with themes of war, ritualistic death, and tribute. **Gallery One** has a scale model of the Templo Mayor. In **Gallery Two** you will see votive offerings as well as objects used in sacrifice and self-sacrifice. Among these are the flint knives used to open the chest cavity of sacrificial victims, and needles of filed eagle bones with which the nobles bled their earlobes, genitals, arms, and tongues in penitence and purification rituals. **Gallery Three** houses objects traded or paid in tribute from some of the Mexica's 370 subject towns, including fine gold filigree and turquoise jewelry from Oaxaca, and carved shells from the Caribbean and Pacific coasts.

Large statues, stelae, and the life-size, ceramic standard bearers and eagle warrior statues that guarded Huitzilopochtli's temple form the core of exhibits in **Gallery Four.** Perhaps most impressive is the huge circular stone with relief carving of the moon goddess Coyolxauhqui, whose discovery by city workers in 1978 precipitated the temple's excavation. According to legend, Huitzilopochtli sprang fully armed from the womb of the earth goddess Coatlicue in order to protect her from his 400 siblings, including Coyolxauhqui. (Coatlicue had been impregnated by a feather while sweeping, and her children were outraged over her mysterious and unseemly pregnancy.) Huitzilopochtli beheaded the moon goddess, and the other antagonists fled to the sky, where they became stars. In addition to explaining the demise of the moon each month, this legend undoubtedly helped to establish the fledgling god Huitzilopóchtli during the early days of the kingdom by relating him to the long-venerated earth goddess Coatlicue.

Galleries Five to **Eight** are dedicated to Tláloc. In the first of these is a reproduction of the original wall decoration on the rain god's temple. Also exhibited are figures and images associated with Tláloc, including the frog, eaten by the Mexica as a ritualistic food. **Galleries Six** and **Seven** are dedicated respectively to the area's flora and fauna, and agriculture. The last of the main galleries appropriately describes the end of the Aztec era and the introduction of Christianity and Hispanic rule. Don't miss the last two galleries, near the exit, with fascinating exhibits regarding the cult of death. ■

VISITING THE MUSEUM

All signs are in Spanish only, but an excellent English-language audio tour (*$$*) is available. Free Spanish-language guided tours are offered Tues.–Sat.; call 5542-4943 for an English-speaking guide.

Life-size eagle warrior statues such as this one guarded Huitzilopochtli's temple.

A walk in & around historic Parque la Alameda

Originally created to be enjoyed by all classes, Alameda Park, its grassy esplanade punctuated with many trees and fountains, became a fenced and elitist park during the long reign of Porfirio Díaz. Today, as intended, it attracts all manner of people and is surrounded by historic churches, museums, and the lovely Palace of Fine Arts. East of the park, the Madero neighborhood, named for Revolution hero Francisco I. Madero (see p. 34), has seen a recent influx of government funds and extensive restoration of its historic buildings.

Begin your walk at the Sanborns flagship venue in **Casa de los Azulejos** ❶ *(Madero 4 at la Condesa, tel 5512-1331)*, one of the few nonhotel restaurants open at 7 a.m. This was a popular restaurant during the Mexican Revolution, when it hosted Pancho Villa, Emiliano Zapata, and their troops. The building's exterior is entirely covered in Puebla-style tiles; José Clemente Orozco's intriguing mural "Omnisciencia" (1925) graces the interior stairwell.

Directly across Calle Madero is the **Templo de San Francisco de Asís** *(Madero 7, tel 5518-4690)*, originally a Franciscan monastery begun in 1524 under the patronage of Hernán Cortés. Remodeled several times, the surviving Church of St. Francis of Assisi presents an excellent example of Churrigueresque design, especially in the facade and the main altar—the latter destroyed in the previous century but totally reconstructed in the 1940s. Next door is the lovely, 18th-century **Iglesia de San Felipe de Jesús** ❷, dedicated to Felipe de las Casas

Martínez (1572–1597), the first Mexican saint. Its interior is covered in large, extraordinarily beautiful paintings of saints, while the high ceiling gives the small, French neo-Gothic church the illusion of space.

One block east (toward the *zócalo*) on the same side of the street is the **Ex-Palacio de Iturbide** *(Madero 17, tel 5225-0247, closed Sat., Sun.)*, an 18th-century baroque building

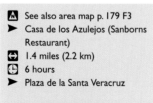

- 🅜 See also area map p. 179 F3
- ➤ Casa de los Azulejos (Sanborns Restaurant)
- ↔ 1.4 miles (2.2 km)
- ⏱ 6 hours
- ➤ Plaza de la Santa Veracruz

NOT TO BE MISSED
- Palacio de Bellas Artes
- Central Alameda
- Museo Mural Diego Rivera
- Museo Franz Mayer

A Sanborns restaurant now occupies the Casa de los Azulejos (House of Tiles).

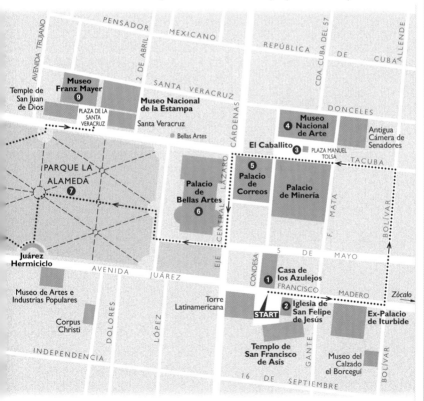

of volcanic stone. Now a Banamex bank office, it is open to the public during temporary exhibitions of its fine art collection. Emperor Agustín de Iturbide occupied the luxurious home for a few short years until his exile in 1823.

Turn left at the next corner, Bolívar, and walk two blocks to Calle Tacuba, where a number of colonial buildings, including the Biblioteca del Congreso de la Unión (*Tacuba 27*), are undergoing extensive restoration. Walk east on Tacuba to Calle Mata and the **Plaza Manuel Tolsá** ❸, named for the Spanish architect and sculptor (1757–1816) who in 1803 created the **Estatua Ecuestre de Carlos de Borbón.** The statue, which most people call **El Caballito** (referring to the mount rather than the Spanish sovereign), now stands in the

Named for its poplars, Parque la Alameda abounds in ash, pine, and jacaranda trees.

center of the plaza. Presiding over the square is the **Museo Nacional de Arte** ❹ (*Tacuba 8, tel 5512-2241, closed Mon., $*), home to a permanent collection of Mexican art with an emphasis on 19th-century paintings. The wrought-iron-and-brass staircase, baroque lamps, and painted ceiling are based on turn-of-the-20th-century European design elements.

Across the street, the **Palacio de Minería** (*Tacuba 5, tel 5521-4020, closed Sat., Sun., & university holidays*), also designed by Tolsá, is one of the city's best examples of neo-classic architecture and now houses the Engineering School of the National University (UNAM). Next door, the distinctive, plateresque-style **Palacio de Correos** ❺ (*Tacuba 1 at Eje Central, tel 5510-2999, closed Sun.*), with its facade of pinkish-yellow quarrystone, was designed by Italian architect Adamo Boari at the beginning of the 20th century. Philatelists and lovers of old books can take the staircase to the third-floor post office library. Major renovations that took place in 1999–2000 have rejuvenated its Moorish, Gothic, Venetian, and Renaissance interior design elements.

Cross busy Eje Central to examine another of Boari's creations, the exquisite **Palacio de Bellas Artes** ❻ (*Av. Juárez & Eje Central, tel 5512-1410, museum closed Mon., $$*) on the east flank of Parque la Alameda. President Porfirio Díaz commissioned the art nouveau-style, Carrara marble palace in 1904, but construction was interrupted by the Revolution. The art deco interior was completed in 1934 by Mexican architect Federico Mariscal. Murals on the second floor include "Mexico Today" (1952) and "Birth of Our Identity" (1953) by Rufino Tamayo. On the third floor are José Orozco's "La Catársis" (1935), David Siqueiros' "New Democracy" (1945), and Diego Rivera's "Man, the Controller of the Universe" (1934), a reproduction of the painting commissioned for the Rockefeller Center and destroyed the following year because of its socialist content. There's no charge to view the art on the first floor or to visit the bookstore, giftshop, or restaurant located there.

From the fine arts palace, head into **Parque la Alameda** ❼, created in the early 17th century. It was expanded in the 1900s to include the former Plaza del

Talavera tiles accent the dome of San Francisco de Asis, one of the city's earliest monasteries.

Quemadero, where the politically incorrect were burned at the stake during the Inquisition. Numerous monuments and fountains give character to the park. About halfway down Avenida Juárez you'll see the **Juárez Hemiciclo,** a monument of pale Italian marble, Doric columns, and roaring lions honoring statesman and president Benito Juárez. Across Avenida Juárez and a bit west of the monument are a visitor information booth *(Juárez 64 at Revillagigedo, tel 5518-1003)* and a 400-room hotel and convention center, currently under construction.

Cross Calle Dr. Mora at the west end of Parque la Alameda. At the rear of the Plaza de la Solidaridad, the **Museo Mural Diego Rivera** ❽ *(Plaza Solidaridad at Colón, tel 5512-0754, closed Mon.)* houses Rivera's elaborate 1947 mural "Sueño de una Tarde Dominical en la Alameda" ("Dream of a Sunday Afternoon in the Alameda"), which was moved here after the Hotel del Prado was irreparably damaged in the 1985 earthquake. A schematic identifies the historical and allegorical characters in the mural; there are portraits of Rivera, Frida Kahlo, Sor Juana de la Cruz, the Habsburg emperors, and many others. Just north of this museum, the

Pinacoteca Virreinal de San Diego *(Dr. Mora 7, tel 5510-2793, closed Mon.)* houses paintings from the Mexican colonial period, of most interest to those who like large, dark, traditional Mannerist and baroque religious paintings in elaborate gilt frames.

Reenter Parque la Alameda, walking east. At the metal-roofed bandstand, cross busy Hidalgo (at Trujano) and continue half a block east to **Plaza de la Santa Veracruz,** named for the Church of the True Holy Cross, on the east side of the square. Occupying part of the adjoining former hospital is the **Museo Nacional de la Estampa** *(Hidalgo 39, tel 5521-2244, closed Mon.),* with rotating exhibits from its permanent collection of early lithographs and linoleum prints, as well as visiting print media shows.

On the west side of the square is the baroque Templo San Juan de Dios. Next door, the **Museo Franz Mayer** ❾ *(Av. Hidalgo 45, tel 5518-2265, closed Mon.)* houses the fabulous applied arts collection of German-born financier Franz Mayer (1882–1975). The galleries surrounding a beautiful central courtyard are full of 16th- to 19th-century Mexican utilitarian and decorative art objects. A separate gallery shows European Renaissance paintings. ■

The new basilica is one of many temples honoring the Virgin at La Villa de Guadalupe.

North of Centro Histórico

NORTH OF THE HISTORIC CENTER, TWO SITES OFFER pre-Cortesian ruins, colonial churches, and a modern 20th-century cathedral. Tlatelolco is a contemporary of Tenochtitlán. Its main pyramid had adjoining temples honoring the gods Tláloc and Huitzilopochtli; they were dismantled by the Spanish to build a church to St. James the Apostle. Farther north, la Villa de Guadalupe honors the Virgin, whose miraculous appearance on Tepeyac Hill led to the conversion of tens of thousands of natives and eventually to one of Catholicism's most impassioned cults. Both are usually included on tours to Teotihuacán, an important archaeological site about an hour to the north (see pp. 228–29).

Tlatelolco
179 F4
Visitor information
✉ Av. Lázaro Cárdenas at Flores Magón
🚇 Metro: Tlatelolco

TLATELOLCO

Tlatelolco was established in 1338 by a dissident group who left Tenochtitlán to build their own city near the northernmost part of Lake Texcoco. Although allied in matters of mutual security with the Tenochcan kings, Tlatelolco refused to accept their sovereignty but was finally subjugated in 1473 by Axayácatl. An important center for merchants and traders, this city served as the Aztec's most important market—amazing Cortés's visiting troops with the variety and quality of goods for sale.

Visitors today can see the reconstructed ruins of Tlatelolco, the last stand during the siege that brought down the Aztec empire. As was customary, the **Iglesia de Santiago Tlatelolco,** completed in 1609, was built with stones from the dismantled pyramids. Indian peasant Juan Diego, who witnessed the apparition of the Virgin of Guadalupe in 1531 (see p. 193), was baptized here at the baroque font, with its shell motif characteristic of

St. James the Apostle. To the right of the church, the former Franciscan monastery was the first college to tutor Indians of noble birth, teaching history, philosophy, and Latin.

Mention Tlatelolco to most Mexico City residents, and they'll remember it as the site of a massacre of student demonstrators by government troops just before the 1968 Olympic games. Although there is no official death toll, up to several hundred young demonstrators were gunned down during a political rally. A simple monument on the north side of the temple acknowledges that tragedy.

Don't miss David Alfaro Siqueiros's mural "Cuauhtémoc Against the Myth," combining sculpture with fresco work. It is in the Tecpan building, at the far side of the quadrangle behind the church and monastery, at the site of Cuauhtémoc's former palace.

LA VILLA DE GUADALUPE

Every Mexican schoolchild knows the story of Juan Diego, to whom the Virgin of Guadalupe is said to have appeared on three occasions at Tepeyac Hill. When Bishop de Zumárraga asked the Chichimec Indian for proof of the miracle, the Virgin showered Juan Diego with roses. Returning to the bishop with his precious cargo wrapped in his cloak, Diego found that the roses had disappeared, to be replaced by the image of the Virgin.

An estimated 15 million people make the pilgrimage to Tepeyac each year, many on December 12, the Virgin's feast day. The new, round **Basílica de Nuestra Señora de Guadalupe** (*Tel 5577-6022*) was built between 1974 and 1976 to accommodate the faithful. Although unimpressive from the outside, the cavernous structure is imposing inside, with its undulating, wood-slat ceiling,

modern stained-glass windows, floor of polished Mexican onyx, and main altar of Carrara marble. The cloak of Juan Diego, with the Virgin's image clearly visible, is the basilica's most important icon, situated way up high at the back of the church behind the main altar.

An annex of the old basilica houses the **Museo de la Basílica de Guadalupe** (*Tel 5781-6810, $*), with religious paintings as well as offerings and ex-votos left over the years by the devout.

Beyond the T-shirt vendors and painted ponies for taking snapshots is the 18th-century **Capilla del Pocito** (*Tel 5577-3844*), built at the site of a miraculously appearing spring. This lovely round baroque chapel has a dome of blue and white Talavera tiles and exterior walls of tile, quarrystone, and volcanic rock. Inside, the walls of the tiny chapel are covered with little angel scenes in pastel colors. The holy well for which the temple is named is now dry. At the top of Tepeyac Hill, the **Capilla de las Rosas** denotes the spot of the Virgin's first alleged appearance. ■

Pre-Hispanic icons dominate this costume, worn in celebration of the Virgin's feast day.

La Villa de Guadalupe
🅰 179 G4
✉ Plaza de las Américas 1
🚇 Metro: La Villa

Bosque de Chapultepec, Paseo de la Reforma, & environs

BOSQUE DE CHAPULTEPEC ONCE PROVIDED DRINKING water for the Aztec nation and housed the royal hunting preserves, vacation palaces, and gardens. Today a source of much-needed oxygen, the 2,000-acre (800 ha) park has a zoo and a castle, an elegant restaurant on a swan-dotted lake, and nearly a dozen museums. Bisecting the park and connecting it to the historic center is elegant Paseo de la Reforma, one of the few contributions of the ill-fated Emperor Maximilian (see p. 33).

Bosque de Chapultepec

178 B2

Metro: Chapultepec, Auditorio, Constituyentes

The **Monumento a los Niños Héroes** marks the eastern entrance of the park *(Metro: Chapultepec)* and the spot where six young cadets leapt to their deaths rather than surrender to U.S. troops during the Mexican-American War. Here, biking and jogging trails wend their way around monuments, fountains, and most of the park's museums. Lovers embrace beneath the pines, palms, and

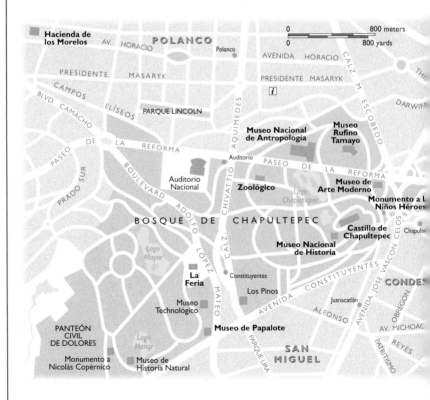

jacarandas, or converse on wooden park benches. With lots of possibilities for inexpensive family entertainment, the park becomes quite crowded on weekends, especially Sundays, the traditional day for family outings.

The two-story **Museo de Arte Moderno** *(Paseo de la Reforma at Gandhi, tel 5211-8729, closed Mon., $)* exhibits the country's most important 20th-century artists, temporary displays, and sculptures of aluminum, stone, bronze, iron, and ceramic in a rambling garden. There is a small but excellent shop and a well-stocked bookstore.

Across the street, the **Museo Rufino Tamayo** *(Paseo de la Reforma at Gandhi, tel 5286-6519, closed Mon., $, Metro: Chapultepec)* houses the international contemporary art collection of Oaxaca painter and sculptor Rufino Tamayo (1899–1991), including works by Picasso, Miró, Fernando Botero, and others. To the west lies the fabulous **Museo Nacional de Antropología** (see pp. 198–201).

Just beyond the modern art museum is the **Castillo de Chapultepec,** begun in 1785 as a retreat for Spanish viceroys but interrupted by the War of Independence. Perched on a small hill, the building was finished as a military academy and remodeled by Emperor Maximilian of Habsburg and again by president Porfirio Díaz. Since 1939, it has housed the **Museo Nacional de Historia** *(Tel 5515-6882, closed Mon., $),* whose historical displays and period furnishings are enhanced by murals by Juan O'Gorman, José Clemente Orozco, and David Alfaro Siqueiros. From the castle, walk or board the miniature tram *($)* to the free **Zoológico de Chapultepec** *(Tel 5553-6263, closed Mon., Metro: Auditorio),* with a petting zoo and pony rides. Nearly 300 species reside in the zoo's reasonably large, open-air enclosures. There are native species, including the endangered Mexican gray wolf and lynx, as well as giraffes, lions, white rhino, and American bison.

Midway through the park, west of Avenida López Mateo, are several child-friendly attractions. The **Feria de Chapultepec** *(Tel 5230-2136, closed Mon., $–$$$, Metro: Constituyentes)*—an amusement park with roller coaster, a rowing lake, a restaurant, and a coffee shop—appeals to both young and old. The interactive **Museo del Papalote** *(Av. Constituyentes*

Right: A modern sculpture and skyscraper dominate the east end of Paseo de la Reforma.

CALZ. OCAMPO

CUAUHTÉMOC

Monumento a Cristóbal Colón, Monumento de Cuauhtémoc

Monumento a la Independencia

iana de la azadora

PASEO DE LA REFORMA

ZONA ROSA

AV. SEVILLA

Sevilla

AVENIDA CHAPULTEPEC

DURANGO

Museo de Cera, Ripley's Believe It or Not Museum

PARQUE ESPAÑA

AV. NUEVO LEÓN

PARQUE SAN MARTÍN

AV. INSURGENTES

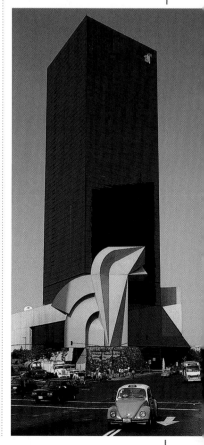

Business is conducted over coffee.

268 at Periférico, tel 5237-1700 or 5224-1260, $$, Metro: Constituyentes) offers "touch-me" exhibits for kids, including a musical staircase, a five-story maze, and a wheelchair obstacle course. There's a separate charge for viewing films in the IMAX theater. During February and March, the *Swan Lake* ballet is performed on an island on **Lago Menor;** the rest of the year resident swans abide a less theatrical existence on nearby **Lago Mayor,** interrupted only by people in rented rowboats.

Connecting the park and Avenida Juárez, **Paseo de la Reforma** was once lined with gracious mansions and flowering trees. Today, monumental sculptures decorate the major traffic circles, while busts of Mexico's heroes line both sides of the street. Closest to Parque Chapultepec is **Diana de la Cazadora** *(at Río Misisipi)*, a nude bronze statue that was clothed for 25 years from 1942 owing to a burst of civic modesty. The Roman huntress is once again

as artist Juan Fernando Olaguíbel (1896–1971) intended. A graceful, bronzed, winged figure (commonly called *el angel,* or "the angel") sparkles atop a 120-foot-tall (36.5 m) Corinthian column at the **Monumento a la Independencia** *(At Av. Florencia)*. The monument was erected in 1910 to honor the heroes of the War of Independence, whose sculptures in Italian marble are found near the base.

A classic bronze statue on a stone pedestal honors the last Mexica emperor, **Cuauhtémoc** *(At Av. Insurgentes)*. Its base is carved with scenes of the ruler's capture and subsequent torture by Spanish conquistadors. Four friars surround Christopher Columbus at the **Monumento a Cristóbal Colón** *(At Av. Morelos)*, representing the evangelization of the Americas. Just a few blocks southwest of Parque la Alameda, on Avenida Juárez, is the metal, yellow-painted sculpture "Cabeza de Caballo." The modernistic, 90-foot

(28 m) piece is the work of Chihuahua sculptor Sebastián (1948–), who studied at the San Carlos Academy.

NEIGHBORHOODS

North of Chapultepec lies **Polanco,** a mix of well-to-do houses behind high garden walls, businesses in high- and low-rise buildings, hotels, foreign embassies, and restaurants. It was developed in the 1940s when the extensive grounds of **Hacienda de los Morales** (see Restaurants, p. 369) were divided and sold. Chic cafés and restaurants become packed during peak hours, especially along the main thoroughfare, Presidente Mazaryk, and adjacent streets.

The traditional favorite for fine dining and nightlife is the **Zona Rosa,** or Pink Zone, a pie-shaped piece of real estate bordered by Avenida Insurgentes, Paseo de la Reforma, and Chapultepec. The compact neighborhood is a mélange of two-story shops, Internet cafés, and boutiques interspersed with high-rise buildings, and is easy to negotiate on foot—especially along the handful of pedestrian-only streets. For some light laughs, visit **Ripley's Believe It or Not Museum** *(Londres 4, tel 5546-3784, $)* or the adjacent **Museo de Cera** *(Tel 5547-3784, $),* where revolutionaries and rock stars are re-created as life-size wax statues.

Luring some of the shoppers and diners from the Zona Rosa are two neighborhoods to the south: **La Condesa** and **Colonia Roma.** The former is especially known for its hip and trendy restaurants, cafés, and nightspots, many in restored art deco buildings for which this part of the city is known. East of Avenida Insurgentes, the wealthy built lovely homes in Colonia Roma during the first half of the 20th century. The neighborhood declined when residents moved to more fashionable areas such as Lomas de Chapultepec, but is currently experiencing renewed gentrification. ■

Colonial and modern architecture side by side on the Paseo de la Reforma

**Museo Nacional
de Antropología**

📍 178 B2

✉ Paseo de la
Reforma at Gandhi,
Bosque de
Chapultepec

☎ 5553-6386

🕐 Closed Mon.

💲 $$

🚇 Metro: Auditorio

Museo Nacional de Antropología

THE SPACIOUS NATIONAL ANTHROPOLOGY MUSEUM HAS recently undergone a 13-million-dollar restoration, the first since it was built in 1964. This remodel improved lighting, added English-language signage for some exhibits, and provided space for 2,000 new artifacts. Touch-screen computers in most galleries provide a wealth of information, although this is given in Spanish only.

Depiction in gold of the Mixtec sun god

Chihuateotl statue, the Aztec goddess who escorted the sun midday to evening

Opposite: Finds in the Mexica room include the Aztec sun stone.

The remodel did not change the basic structure of the complex of buildings, designed and built by architect Pedro Ramírez Vázquez, and called "one of the most satisfying in modern Mexico" and "an incomparable example of institutional architecture" by author and photographer Hans Beacham in his book *The Architecture of Mexico: Yesterday and Today* (1969). Four large buildings surround a central courtyard, whose open space is nearly half covered by an enormous aluminum canopy supported by a single column faced in carved stone. From the top of the support, an unusual structural element, water splashes down to the patio floor in a refreshing juxtaposition of art, architecture, and precipitation.

In 12 huge exhibition halls surrounding the ground-floor courtyard is Mexico's finest archaeological collection, devoted exclusively to pre-Hispanic civilizations. After breezing through the first three rooms in a sort of crash course in anthropology, visit the remaining rooms in any order, as they are organized according to region. Since the collection is so large, it makes sense to concentrate on the cultures that interest you most. Choose from Preclassic (Valley of Mexico), Teotihuacán, Toltec, Mexica (Aztec), Oaxaca, Gulf Coast, Maya, Northern

Mexico, and Western Mexico. Spectacular and varied archaeological treasures along with photographs, paintings, dioramas, and reproductions of murals and temples create a satisfying portrait of pre-Conquest civilizations. The lack of complete information in English is a drawback for many (resolved to some degree by using the English-language audio tour or by hiring a guide). In most salons, informative video presentations in English and Spanish run consecutively. If you have an interest in pre-Hispanic cultures, one day will probably not be sufficient for studying all the exhibits. Consider dedicating several mornings or afternoons to the museum, visiting other attractions in Parque Chapultepec, or wandering adjacent neighborhoods when the scope and grandeur of the exhibits begin to overwhelm you.

Behind many of the galleries you'll find outdoor patios and gardens sheltering stone sculptures and stelae, reconstructions of houses, and other fascinating, alfresco, large-scale exhibits. In the Maya room, don't miss the full-size reproduction of the royal tomb from the Temple of the Inscriptions at Palenque, Chiapas, and, in the back garden, reproductions of the murals of Bonampak and a Chenes-style temple from Hochob, Campeche.

The museum has too many fabulous pieces to name, but you must not fail to see the following: Teotihuacán gallery—reproduction of Tepantitla murals; Toltec gallery—Atlante sculptures and mother-of-pearl-encrusted warrior (both from Tula); Mexica gallery— 24-ton sun stone, statue of earth goddess Coatlicue, and the pregnant monkey vessel of polished obsidian (the museum's most costly piece—once stolen but later recovered); Oaxaca gallery—jade bat god mask, Mixtec jewelry, and reproduction of Monte Albán's Tomb 104; Gulf Coast gallery—colossal stone head (Olmec), "adolescent from Tamuin" statue, associated with the corn god; Maya room— carved lintels and stelae from Yaxchilán, clay figurines from Jaina, and Chac Mool from Chichén Itzá.

The ethnology exhibits on the second floor are similarly arranged by region and cultural group. Dioramas and glass-cased exhibits show ceremonial and everyday clothing, as well as masks, pottery, baskets, musical instruments, toys, and all the accouterments of daily life among Mexico's diverse ethnic populations. ■

Macuilxochitl, the Aztec god of music and dance, represented here in a tortoiseshell motif

Above: Coatlicue, the Aztec earth goddess

Left: Maya sculpture depicting a figure emerging from a flower, found at Isla Jaina, Campeche state

Right: The Zapotec goddess of 13 snakes

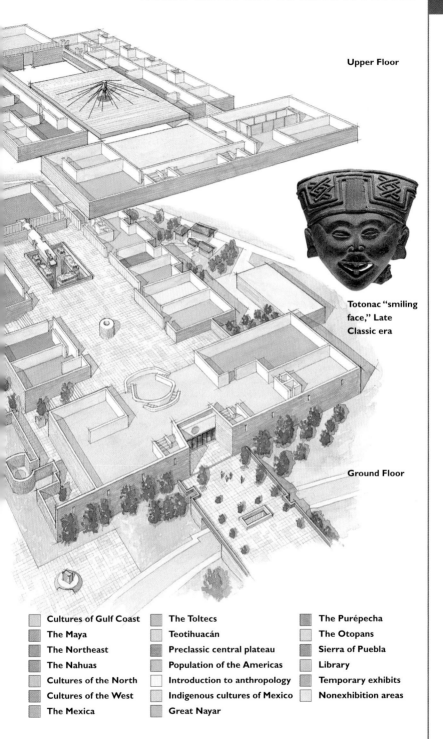

Upper Floor

Totonac "smiling face," Late Classic era

Ground Floor

Cultures of Gulf Coast	The Toltecs	The Purépecha
The Maya	Teotihuacán	The Otopans
The Northeast	Preclassic central plateau	Sierra of Puebla
The Nahuas	Population of the Americas	Library
Cultures of the North	Introduction to anthropology	Temporary exhibits
Cultures of the West	Indigenous cultures of Mexico	Nonexhibition areas
The Mexica	Great Nayar	

The Mexican mural school

Following conquest and colonization, Mexico began to adopt European values and artistic styles. This preoccupation with Old World aesthetics was redoubled during the 34-year reign of Francophile dictator Porfirio Díaz. After Mexico's chaotic Revolution focused attention on land reform and other populist issues, nostalgic Mexicans living abroad spawned an artistic and political movement venerating indigenous people and the working classes. They integrated the intellectualism of Marxism and the romanticism of the Spanish Civil War with a desperate passion for their native Mexico. Many artists participated, but the "Big Three" were Diego Rivera, David Alfaro Siqueiros, and José Clemente Orozco.

The mural movement flourished between 1920 and 1970, especially in the early days under the patronage of prominent philosopher and education minister José Vasconcelos. Although the muralists' radical political views seemingly conflicted with the agenda of the conservative, pro-business administrations of the period, the Mexican government became their patron, and huge public spaces their canvases. The murals' nationalistic content and socialistic spirit to some degree substituted for actual revolutionary measures, constituting a sort of political and artistic placebo for the masses. Working within the system, the artists spoke their piece and pursued their art, while the government seemed to support both the arts and radical politics.

Best known outside Mexico is the allegorical work of Diego Rivera (1886–1957). Showing artistic talent from an early age, he entered Mexico City's prestigious San Carlos Academy at the age of ten. After years of experimentation and travel through northern Europe, Paris, and Russia, Rivera developed an unequivocal style. Favoring a palette of deep pastels, he painted rounded, nearly neckless, brown-skinned folk wearing seamless trousers. The simple themes and engaging designs he chose were meant to inspire and educate the common people he almost religiously portrayed in his art. Both Rivera and fellow muralist David Alfaro Siqueiros (1896–1974) were members of the Mexican Communist Party. Siqueiros' work, known for its experimental and innovative technical character, is moody—often violent and chaotic—with strong, bold colors.

The murals of José Clemente Orozco (1883–1949) were influenced by his early work as a caricaturist, although in later years his simple yet stirring style became more expressionistic. The work of all three men centered on social ills and human suffering—especially that of their compatriots.

Less well known than the Big Three, architect and painter Juan O'Gorman (1905–1982), a Coyoacán native, produced realistic murals and paintings in exquisite color and detail. The work of internationally proclaimed Oaxaca impressionist muralist, painter, and sculptor Rufino Tamayo (1899–1991) was taken less seriously at the time because of its lack of direct social commentary. Fermín Revueltas, Alva de la Canal, Fernando Leal, and Miguel Covarrubias are among others who contributed to the wealth of murals in Mexico City. ∎

Viewing the murals

Below is a partial list of places in Mexico City where these masterpieces can be found.

On or near the zócalo: Ex-Colegio de San Ildefonso (see p. 182); Palacio Nacional (see p. 182); Secretaría de Educación Pública (see p. 183); Suprema Corte de Justicia (see p. 182).

La Alameda: Museo Mural Diego Rivera (see p. 191); Palacio de Bellas Artes (see p. 190).

Bosque de Chapultepec: Museo Nacional de Historia (see p. 195).

Universidad Autónoma Nacional de México (UNAM): Biblioteca Central, Estadio Olímpico, and Rectoría (see p. 207). ∎

Right: Father Hidalgo is the centerpiece of this Orozco mural depicting oppression.

San Ángel
🅰 178 D1
Visitor information
✉ Av. Revolución at Madero (Casa de la Cultura)
☎ 5616-2097
🚌 Bus: "San Ángel" bus from Insurgentes at Paseo de la Reforma

South of Centro Histórico

MEXICO CITY'S MOST IMPORTANT NORTH–SOUTH AXIS IS 18-mile-long (29 km) Avenida Insurgentes, which skirts the eastern edge of the Zona Rosa. It continues south past the 50-story World Trade Center (formerly the Hotel de México), the Plaza México (the world's largest bullring), and a stunning Diego Rivera mural decorating the curved facade of the Teatro de los Insurgentes. After a few more miles it reaches San Ángel and its neighbor, Coyoacán, two charming towns that have been absorbed by ever growing Mexico City.

SAN ÁNGEL

San Ángel is so pretty that it's been declared a national historic monument. Called Tenanitla before the Conquest, this quiet town of cobblestone streets and colonial- and Republican-era homes is anchored by two pleasing squares, **Plaza de San Jacinto** and, one block away, **Plaza del Convento.** Shoppers and vendors fill the former on Saturdays, when the overflow from the weekly crafts market, **Bazar del Sábado** *(Plaza San Jacinto 44, tel 5616-0082),* sets up camp under the pines, cedars, and yucca trees

shading the plaza. Also on Plaza de San Jacinto is the simple 17th-century church for which the square is named and the **Casa del Risco** *(Plaza San Jacinto 15, tel 5616-2711, closed Mon.)*, an 18th-century residence housing an art museum and cultural center. In the main courtyard, you can't miss the unusual fountain, encrusted with mirrors and shells, as well as European and Mexican ceramic tiles, plates, platters, and cups. Temporary exhibits fill the ground-floor halls, while on the second floor, the permanent collection consists of 15th- to 19th-century European and Mexican paintings. The adjacent library *(Closed Sun.)* has 31,000 volumes related to international law, Mexican history, and criminology.

Just across busy Avenida Revolución, it's a pleasure to prowl around the cloisters and chapels of the **Museo del Carmen** *(Av. Revolución 4, tel 5550-4896, closed Mon., $, Metro: Quevedo)*, a museum of primarily religious paintings and artifacts. The former Carmelite monastery, with its magnificent domes of Talavera tiles and exquisite gilded altarpiece in the first-floor chapel, is every bit as interesting as the museum exhibits.

Items of contemporary art from a permanent collection are shown in rotation in the modern, low-ceilinged, glass and aluminum **Museo Carrillo Gil** *(Av. Revolución 1608 at Av. Altavista, tel 5550-6284, closed Mon., $)*. In addition to paintings by the Big Three of the Mexican Mural School (see p. 202), there are oils, pen and ink, gouache, and pencil drawings by lesser-known artists.

A short uphill walk along Avenida Altavista brings you to the **Museo Casa Estudio Diego Rivera y Frida Kahlo** *(Diego Rivera 2, tel 5550-1518, closed Mon.,*

$, Metro: Quevedo), a boxlike modern house on steel stilts designed and built by architect and artist Juan O'Gorman. Frida Kahlo and her husband, Diego Rivera, occupied these two houses separated

by a catwalk. The first two-story building held Rivera's gallery and, above, his studio. Kahlo both lived and worked in the house behind. The museum has a small collection of the artists' photographs, letters, documents, and personal effects, as well as sketches and paintings by their contemporaries.

COYOACÁN
About 2 miles (3 km) from San Ángel is equally engaging Coyoacán, home to artists and journalists from Mexico and elsewhere, giving it an artistic and intellectual ambience. If you're walking, stop along the way at the **Parque de la Bombilla** *(Av. Insurgentes Sur at La Paz)*, where joggers follow meandering trails under willow, pine, ash, and avocado trees. On

Above: Shoppers browse at one of Mexico City's ubiquitous daily markets.
Above right: Frida Kahlo, who painted dozens of self-portraits, at work on "Portrait of Mrs. Jean Wight" (1931)

Coyoacán
🅰 178 D1
Visitor information
✉ Jardin Hidalgo 1
☎ 5659-2256, ext. 181

weekends kids kick balls and practice tai-chi, and peanut and cotton-candy vendors appear. During the week it's less lively, but you can have space to admire the **Monumento al General Alvaro Obregón,** dedicated to the post-Revolution-era president assassinated in 1928 during the Cristero Revolt (see p. 35). East of the Parque de la Bombilla is the pleasant **Museo Nacional de la Acuarela** (*Salvador Novo 88, tel 5554-1801, closed Mon., Metro: Quevedo*). A variety of styles of gouache and watercolors are represented here in a collection donated by watercolorist Alfredo Guati, whose work is also shown.

Calle La Paz intersects with Avenida Francisco Sosa, lined with carefully maintained homes, many of them restored colonials, as well as shops, ice-cream parlors, restaurants, and bars. This is the main street of Coyoacán, a prosperous city when the Mexica first arrived in the Valley of Mexico. It was soon swallowed and digested by the more powerful newcomers. Hernán Cortés also made his headquarters in Coyoacán after the Conquest. The brick-red structure mistakenly cited as his home, the **Palacio de Cortés** (*Jardín Hidalgo 1*), houses city government offices and a visitor information booth. Presiding over the opposite side of the square is the **Templo de San Juan Bautista** (*Jardín Hidalgo 8, tel 5554-6376*). Although constructed in the 16th century, little remains of the original building except the facade and the pilgrim's archway. Inside, its stained-glass windows portraying Franciscan saints illuminate the large, single-nave church and elaborate main altar.

Cafés, restaurants, boutiques, and bookstores surround adjacent **Jardín del Centenario** (*Carrillo Puerto & Centenario*), and, on weekends, vendors, locals, and tourists mill about. As in San Ángel, artists sell oil and acrylic paintings, framed etchings, and other works at reasonable prices.

About five blocks north of the plaza is the **Museo Frida Kahlo** (*Londres 247, tel 5554-5999, closed Mon., $, Metro: Coyoacán*). Self-taught artist Frida Kahlo (1907–1954) was born and died in this cornflower-blue house, which is decorated with items from the popular Mexican culture she embraced. She began to paint during convalescence from a bus accident suffered as a teenager, adopting a deliberately naive style full of Mexican icons and imagery. Her intensely personal canvases, generally smaller-format oil paintings, reflected her constant physical pain and the mental anguish brought on by her infertility and husband Diego Rivera's philandering. Underestimated artistically during her lifetime, this independent woman has become something of a feminist folk hero. In addition to her illustrated diary, love letters, and handpainted body cast are about a dozen of her paintings; the furnishings and decorations form a fabulous folk-art collection.

Five more blocks north and east bring you to the **Museo Leon Trotsky** (*Río Churubusco 410, tel 5554-0687, closed Mon., $, Metro: Coyoacán*). The house where the exiled Russian revolutionary lived contains his documents and personal effects. A friend of artists Kahlo and Rivera, Trotsky was assassinated (an ice pick through the brain) by Spaniard Ramón Mercader in 1940. The former Communist leader had survived at least one other attempted murder —involving machine guns this time—in which the muralist David Siqueiros, an ardent Stalinist, was allegedly involved.

A storyteller draws a crowd in Coyoacán.

Latin America's largest and oldest university, the **Universidad Autónoma Nacional de México, or UNAM** *(Av. Insurgentes Sur s/n, tel 5622-6470, Metro: Copilco or Universidad)*, was founded in 1553. Originally occupying different buildings throughout the city, the 800-acre (320 ha) campus was established in the 1950s around the El Pedregal lava fields, south of San Ángel. If you visit the university campus, don't miss Juan O'Gorman's stunning mosaics, which cover all four sides of the Biblioteca Central (Main Library). Nearby, David Alfaro Siqueiros's glass-mosaic mural, "The People for the University, The University for the People," covers the north wall of the Rectoría, or Administration Building, while other dramatic murals cover the south wall and the tower. Directly across Avenida Insurgentes Sur, Diego Rivera's high-relief, natural stone mosaic on the exterior of the **Estadio Olímpico** (Olympic Stadium) depicts ancient and modern sports. ∎

La Malinche

In a rust-red, two-story house on the southeast side of Plaza la Conchita, in Coyoacán, Hernán Cortés is said to have installed his interpreter, mistress, and the mother of his son Martín: La Malinche. Called Malintzin in Náhuatl and doña Marina by the Spaniards, the young woman was apparently sold as a slave to noblemen, who gave her, along with others, as a gift to Cortés. For the Spaniards, Malinche proved an invaluable interpreter, adviser, and even military strategist who well understood their enemy. Although her motivations and actions are not really known, this controversial and important historical figure was branded a traitor to the indigenous people. In the modern Mexican lexicon, *"un malinchista"* is a person of questionable patriotism or cultural loyalty. ∎

Decorated punts glide along the town's canals, often followed by floating food vendors and musicians.

Xochimilco

FAMOUS SINCE PRE-CORTESIAN TIMES FOR ITS FLOWERS, Xochimilco is the last place you can see the remains of the system of canals and artfully engineered garden plots that once threaded Lake Texcoco. This laid-back town (its name means "place of flowers") also has a lovely old cathedral and one of the country's best museums.

Xochimilco

⚑ 179 G2

Visitor information

✉ Calle del Pino 36, Barrio San Juan

☎ 5676-0810

About 15 miles (24 km) southeast of downtown Mexico City, Xochimilco is best known for its *trajineras* (punts) that float the canals, these days sporting mostly artificial flowers. The scene is festive on weekends, when families party and picnic as they wind down from the working week. There are several docks in the main part of town; boats departing from **Embarcadero Celada,** on the west side, tour the **Parque Natural Xochimilco** ecological reserve, created in 1993. You also can tour the reserve's botanical gardens on foot.

The tree-shaded fortified monastery of **San Bernardino de Siena** was built by Franciscans in the late 16th century. It has a plain, sweet, pink facade in the classical style and, inside, a spectacular main altarpiece. Cross the street to the **Mercado,** a great place to take photographs or just admire the local produce, cut flowers, and flowering plants on sale.

No trip would be complete without a visit to the fabulous **Museo Dolores Olmedo Patiño** (*Av. México 5843, tel 5555-1016, closed Mon., $$, tren ligero: La Noria*). Numerous drawings and paintings collected by Señora Olmedo include the work of friend and protégé Diego Rivera and colleagues. There are more than 600 pre-Hispanic pieces and a fine collection of Mexican folk art. Have a bite to eat in the glass-walled café, set amidst a garden of cacti and purple-flowered jacarandas. ∎

More places to visit in Mexico City

ANTIGUA CASA DE LOS CONDES DE SAN MATEO VALPARAÍSO
Now housing Banamex offices, this building is one of the city's best examples of 18th-century civic architecture. Note the corner tower with the image of the Virgin of Guadalupe and the family coat of arms on the building's facade. Inside is an unusual double spiral stairway, designed to be used by both servants and their masters without the two groups having to meet.
🔼 179 G3 ✉ Isabel la Católica 44 at Carranza ☎ 5225-6088 🕐 Closed Sat., Sun. 🚇 Metro: Isabel la Católica

CUICUILCO
Located within sight of Xitle volcano, which destroyed the city in about A.D. 300, the Cuicuilco archaeological site is considered the oldest in the Valley of Mexico, dating from the Preclassic era. The most important structure is a rare, circular, four-layered pyramid with an interior altar, discovered in 1922. The *in situ* museum displays photographs of the excavation and artifacts found there, including stelae and the figure of Huehueteotl-Xiuhtecuhtli, the god of fire portrayed as an old man.
🔼 178 D1 ✉ Av. Insurgentes Sur s/n at Periférico, Col. Ysidro Favela ☎ 5606-9758 💲 $ 🚇 Metro: Universidad

EX-COLEGIO DE CRISTO
This slightly scruffy, lopsided 18th-century residence has an interesting collection of caricatures, old engravings, and political cartoons depicting everyone from Fidel Castro and Bill Clinton to Pope John Paul II.
🔼 179 G3 ✉ Donceles 99 ☎ 5704-0459 💲 $ 🚇 Metro: Zócalo

MONUMENTO A LA REVOLUCIÓN
Initiated by president Porfirio Díaz to house legislative offices, this huge art deco building was finished instead as a tribute to the fallen in the Mexican Revolution, which interrupted construction. Inside is the **Museo Nacional de la Revolución,** containing documents, photos, and memorabilia from that war.
🔼 179 E3 ✉ Plaza de la República, Col. Tabacalera ☎ 5546-2115 🕐 Closed Mon. 💲 $ 🚇 Metro: Revolución

Papier-mâché folk art from the Anahuacalli Museum collection

MUSEO ANAHUACALLI
This unusual-looking museum has room to display only 2,000 of its 55,000-piece collection of pre-Hispanic art donated by Diego Rivera. Represented are cultures from Guanajuato (Rivera's home state), the Valley of Mexico, and Teotihuacán, but especially the Pacific states of Colima, Nayarit, and Jalisco. The black volcanic rock and onyx building was designed by Rivera and inspired by pre-Hispanic structures.
🔼 179 G2 ✉ Calle del Museo 150, Col. San Pablo Tepetlapa ☎ 5617-3797 🕐 Closed Mon. 💲 $ 🚇 Metro *(tren ligero):* Xochipingo

MUSEO DE LA CIUDAD DE MÉXICO
Built of red volcanic stone in the 16th century, this elegant house was redone in the baroque style several hundred years later. It is now a museum of history and culture, offering pre-Hispanic pieces, several rooms of period furnishings, and salons for temporary fine art exhibits. Note the carved wooden doors, imported from the Philippines, and on the courtyard fountain, a *nereda,* or female figure with three tails. Musical performances are held periodically.

179 G2 ✉ Pino Sears 30 ☎ 5522-3640 ◷ Closed Mon. and national holidays 💲 $ 🚇 Metro: Zócalo

MUSEO DE SAN CARLOS

Just a few blocks northeast of the Monumento a la Revolución (see p. 209) is this lovely if restrained neoclassic mansion. Diego Rivera and other greats were educated in this former academy of fine arts. Today, its important collection of 15th- to 19th-century European paintings includes Spanish Gothic panels and renaissance, Mannerist, baroque, neoclassic, romantic, and symbolist works.
179 E3 ✉ Puente del Alvarado 50, Col. Tabacalera ☎ 5566-8522 ◷ Closed Tues. 💲 $ 🚇 Metro: Revolución

MUSEO DEL CALZADO EL BORCEGUÍ

Latin America's only museum dedicated solely to shoes has 15,000 exhibits. These include historic shoes (Napoleonic- and Louis XV-era shoes, Chinese slippers, NASA moon boots); folk art representing shoes; and 175 pairs of celebrity shoes, belonging to the likes of Gregory Peck and Pierre Cardin. This fascinating museum is connected to the store of the same name, established in 1895 and specializing in comfortable and orthopedic shoes.
179 F3 ✉ Bolívar 27, 2nd floor ☎ 5512-1311 ◷ Closed Sun. 🚇 Metro: Allende

MUSEO JOSÉ LUIS CUEVAS

Painter and sculptor José Luis Cuevas's erotic etchings are rather incongruously housed in the cloister of this 16th-century former convent, a lovely building declared a national monument in 1932. Cuevas's 26-foot-tall (8 m) bronze "La Giganta" dominates the central patio, while smaller statues and paintings line the passageways. On Sundays, the museum often hosts performances of theater, dance, and music.
179 G3 ✉ Calle Academia 13 ☎ 5542-6198 ◷ Closed Mon. 💲 $ 🚇 Metro: Zócalo

MUSEO S.H.C.P.

The first-floor galleries are a bit barren and disappointing, but those on the second floor of this former archbishop's palace are more interesting. These include the "paid-in-kind" collection, acquired through the Mexican system that allows artists to pay income tax in artwork rather than pesos, as well as "hereditary estates" handed down to artists' heirs.
179 G3 ✉ Antiguo Palacio del Arzobispado, Moneda 4 ☎ 5228-1241 💲 $ 🚇 Metro: Zócalo

PLAZA DE GARIBALDI

Five blocks north of the Palacio de Bellas Artes, elegantly uniformed mariachi bands arrive each evening to vie for customers in this famous square. There's no shortage of local color, including taco vendors and pickpockets. Bars and small restaurants facing the plaza run the gamut from cantinas full of maudlin men crooning over a bottle of tequila to live-music dance clubs. It's especially spirited on November 22, the feast day of Santa Cecilia, patron saint of music, with fireworks, folk dancing, food, crafts, and, of course, mariachis.
179 F4 ✉ Av. Lazaro Cardenas at Honduras 🚇 Metro: Garibaldi

POLIFORUM CULTURAL SIQUEIROS

David Alfaro Siqueiros's "The March of Humanity" covers both exterior and interior surfaces of this 12-sided structure, built specifically for the project. On Saturday and Sunday afternoons, a Spanish-language sound-and-light show enhances the relief and sculptural elements of the unusual mural. (English-speaking groups are accommodated by appointment.) The space doubles as a venue for cultural events.
178 D1 ✉ Insurgentes Sur 701 at Filadelfia ☎ 5536-4520 💲 $ 🚇 Metro: Chilpancingo

SALA DE ARTE PÚBLICO SIQUEIROS

Just before his death, Siqueiros donated his home and its contents to the government, which now displays his finished and unfinished work, including drawings, paintings, sketches, and the mural "Maternity." A second-floor gallery exhibits changing contemporary art.
178 A2 ✉ Tres Picos 29, Col. Polanco ☎ 5545-5952 ◷ Closed Mon. 💲 $ 🚇 Metro: Auditorio ∎

With its missions and cathedrals, haciendas, archaeological ruins, and markets where Otomí and Náhuatl languages are still spoken, the small central region embodies pre-Cortesian, colonial, and post-Revolutionary Mexico.

Around Mexico City

An amazing baroque interior

Around Mexico City

WITH FEW EXCEPTIONS, THE MAJOR CITIES OF THE CENTRAL PLATEAU, surrounding the Valle de Anáhuac (Valley of Mexico), represent pre-Aztec centers. At the time of the Spanish Conquest they were held in the vicelike grip of the Triple Alliance— Tenochtitlán, Texcoco, and Tlacopan. Cuernavaca was an exclusive spa for the Aztec nobility, and it still attracts the rich and famous, who come on weekends and holidays to their second homes. Priests and nobility made pilgrimages to Teotihuacán, as we do today, to marvel at an ancient culture whose origins remain mired in mystery.

Civilization flourished in the river valleys, plains, and semitropical lowlands surrounding the crescent-shaped Valley of Mexico. So close to the defeated Tenochtitlán and the new capital, Mexico City, the central plateau was promptly carved up by the Spanish Crown. Among the cities Hernán Cortés received from King Carlos V of Spain were Toluca and Cuernavaca, today capitals of México and Morelos states. As a reward for being Spain's indispensable allies during the Aztec campaign and beyond, Tlaxcala enjoyed privileges denied the majority of the conquered peoples.

Unlike the Maya, whose great culture was nearly 500 years past its prime at the time of Spanish Conquest, and the nomadic northern tribes, indigenous culture in the central plateau was in full flower in the 16th century. Skilled indigenous artisans and European craftsmen together produced some of Mexico's most intriguing architecture. Inspired by their desire to convert the natives and glorify God, the Spanish built magnificent cathedrals and far-flung mission churches; Indian craftsmen enthusiastically embraced the baroque style. In Puebla, gilded and

Tepoztlán's isolated valley setting made it a popular retreat in the 1960s and '70s.

polychrome sculpted plasterwork combined with Talavera tiles adorn myriad churches and private palaces to create an exuberant architecture unique to the state. The monastery murals at Ixmiquilpan, Hidalgo, have unusual native imagery: jaguars, Aztec eagles clutching snakes, and violent battle scenes among native warriors.

Forming a tight circle around Mexico City, the states of Hidalgo, Tlaxcala, Puebla, Morelos, and México are today influenced by their proximity to the capital. Now highly industrialized, the state of México surrounds the Federal District on three sides and has benefited from the accessibility to banks,

transportation, and the powers-that-be. Most of the capital cities of these states are industrialized, yet preserve outstanding churches and secular colonial buildings. ■

Area of map detail

Cuernavaca
🅰 213 B2
Visitor information
✉ Av. Morelos Sur 187, Colonia Las Palmas
☎ 7/314-3872

Cuernavaca

SINCE PRE-HISPANIC TIMES CUERNAVACA (FROM THE Náhuatl name Cuauhnáhuac, meaning "wooded valley") has been much admired. Its temperate climate and generous rainfall make it well suited for growing both agricultural products and ornamental plants. Mexican nobility vacationed here, and Hernán Cortés built himself a palace. For centuries, Cuernavaca has provided a second home for Mexican and international diplomats, politicians, musicians, and other elite. In early April, the Flower Fair beckons with music and garden shows, while outside the city, rivers and more than 40 spas and water parks lure those looking to commune further with nature.

The former palace of Hernán Cortés

In spring, Cuernavaca blossoms—even if the *guayaba* trees that gave natives their nickname, *guayabos,* are now few and far between. In the large plaza, people stroll past the plain millennium clock, installed for the year 2000 but already looking half a century old. On the east side, the formidable **Palacio de Cortés** (*Av. Leyva 100, closed Mon.*) has interior murals by Diego Rivera. Inside the palace is the **Museo Cuauhnáhuac** (*Tel 7/312-8171, $*), which has displays of colonial art as well as archaeological and historical exhibits.

The **Catedral de la Asunción** (*Av. Morelos at Hidalgo*) has a huge atrium designed to hold many potential Indian converts. Its ornate altarpieces were removed in 1959 by reformist priest Sergio Méndez Arce, unveiling wall murals of Mexican San Felipe de Jesús's martyrdom in Japan. Further evidence of the "new Catholicism" is seen in its modern stained-glass windows, a resurrected Christ (instead of a crucifix), and the popular **mariachi mass,** held Sunday mornings at 11. Climb up to the high bell tower for an excellent view over the city.

Not to be missed is the **Museo Robert Brady** (*Nezahualcóyotl 4, tel 7/318-8554, closed Mon., $$*), home of the wealthy American collector and expatriate of the same name. Throughout this fabulous house are a thousand pieces of fine and folk art from Mexico and throughout the world, placed in inspired juxtaposition.

Stroll through the landscaped grounds of **Jardín Borda** (*Av. Morelos at Hidalgo, tel 7/312-9237, closed Mon.*), established by the Taxco mining tycoon José de la Borda. The mansion here later became the summer home of Emperor Maximilian. Visit the site museum (*$*), with exhibits from the French emperor's reign, or listen to music in the garden café during the evening. For more live entertainment, head for the hipper cafés and cantinas around **Plazuela del Zacate** (*Galeana at Hidalgo*). ∎

Xochicalco

Xochicalco
◮ 213 B2
✉ 24 miles (38 km)
south of Cuernavaca
via Highway 95
☎ 7/329-4415
$ $

FROM ITS PERCH ON A SERIES OF LOW TERRACED HILLS, the "Place of the House of Flowers" archaeological site covers 60 acres (25 ha), most of which are still unexcavated. The fortified city flourished between A.D. 700 and 900, and is considered by some a bridge between the Toltec civilization established in Tula in the tenth century and the Teotihuacán civilization, which disappeared abruptly around A.D. 700. The ruins weren't discovered until the Mexican Revolution, when according to legend, General Emiliano Zapata noticed bullets ricocheting off the grassy hill they were defending. Upon investigation, the "hill" turned out to be a buried pyramid.

The site spreads down from its high point at the **Plaza Ceremonial.** Facing this sacred square is Xochicalco's most important structure, the **Templo de Quetzalcóatl,** richly adorned in bas-relief carvings of the god. Within the snakes' coils is the repeated figure of a cross-legged personage resembling a Maya priest named 9 Wind, the birth date of Quetzalcóatl. Different types of calendars carved on the pyramid's walls have led to speculation that Zapotec, Maya, and Gulf Coast tribes met together at Xochicalco to discuss astronomy or to synchronize their calendars.

Below, the **Plaza de la Estela de Dos Glifos** (Two Glyph Stelae Square) was a large grassy meeting place with a stele carved with the date 10 Sugarcane 9 Reptile Eye. Still farther down the hill, the I-shaped ball court is considered to be one of the first built on the central plateau and has been influenced by Maya design.

An unusual feature at the site is the underground observatory, where twice a year (May 14–15 and July 28–29), when the sun is at its zenith, a hexagonal shaft of light appears on the floor of the cave. The light enters through a hole bored 26 feet (8 m) through solid rock. There are also the ruins of a cistern for storing water and a *temescal* steam bath.

The site museum (signed in Spanish only) contains many archaeological pieces, including a sun god statue, pottery, and examples of hieroglyphic writings. ∎

Carvings of Quetzalcóatl, the Feathered Serpent, cover this temple.

Los Conventos del Volcán drive

The Franciscan, Dominicans, and Augustinians divided up the area that now forms tiny Morelos state. Northeast of Cuernavaca lies a necklace of Dominican and Augustinian monasteries established soon after the Conquest. This route through the foothill valleys is especially dramatic in the winter months, when snowcapped Popocatépetl and slumbering Iztaccíhuatl appear, giving the route its name, "the Volcano Monasteries."

Murals are used to brighten up the facades of many modern Mexican buildings.

From Cuernavaca, drive about 16 miles (26 km) east on Hwy. 95D to Hwy. 115. Follow Hwy. 115 in the direction of Cuautla to **Tepoztlán ❶**, where you can buy handicrafts and *amate* (bark paper) at the weekend market. In 1550 Dominican friars ousted the god of pulque, Ometochtli, from his temple and used the stones to build the **Convento de Nuestra Señora de la Natividad ❷**, located on the town's main plaza. The friars weren't totally successful, as the town is known for its blending of Christian and pre-Hispanic rituals, especially during Mardi Gras and the celebration of Our Lady of the Nativity on September 7.

The church and former monastery combine Gothic and Renaissance elements in a simple style. Around the church's plateresque doorway are symbols of the Virgin: the sun, moon, and eight-pointed stars. Dominican symbols include the foliated cross, fleur-de-lis, and torch-bearing dogs. From the cloister, there are views of the seamed hills of the Sierra Tepozteca, where remnants of a pre-Hispanic pyramid, **Tepozteco,** can be reached after an hour's hike.

Continue about 20 miles (32 km) toward Cuautla to **Oaxtepec ❸,** once a retreat for the lords of Xochimilco and the Emperor Moctezuma, and now home to one of the state's largest water parks. Some historians call it "Tenochtitlán's granary," as its orchards and fields were an important source of food for the Aztec capital. Oaxtepec's 16th-century **Convento de Santo Domingo** is surrounded by ancient willows, jacarandas, and *amate* and rubber trees. Throughout the adjoining monastery you will see monochrome paintings of Dominican saints.

From Oaxtepec, head north on Hwy. 142 for about 6 miles (10 km) to **Tlayacapan ❹** ($), whose **Convento de San Juan Bautista** is characterized by its monumental simplicity. The church's pale stone-and-white-stucco facade is crowned with an *espadaña*, a row of small bells in individual arches. Within the refectory museum are a half-dozen wooden, polychrome statues, and within the private chapel there are paintings of Augustinian saints, friars, and the four Evangelists.

Drive east on Hwy. 2 for 6 miles (10 km) past basalt bluffs to the neglected **Convento de Totolapan.** This Augustinian monastery, once virtually covered in paintings, is today in bad repair. Continue on the same road, which curves south to the **Convento de Atlatlahuacan,** about 9 miles (14 km). The former Augustinian monastery is enclosed by

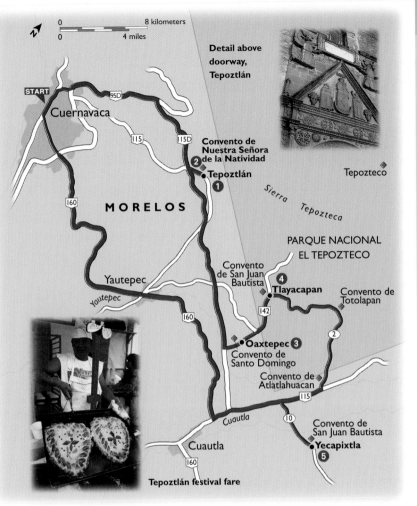

0 8 kilometers
0 4 miles

START

Cuernavaca

95D

115
115D

**Convento de
Nuestra Señora
de la Natividad**

2

●Tepoztlán
1

Detail above
doorway,
Tepoztlán

Tepozteco ◆

160

MORELOS

Sierra Tepozteca

**PARQUE NACIONAL
EL TEPOZTECO**

Yautepec

Yautepec

**Convento
de San Juan
Bautista**
4

●Tlayacapan

**Convento de
Totolapan** ◆

160

142

2

●Oaxtepec 3
**Convento de
Santo Domingo**

**Convento de
Atlatlahuacan** ◆

115

Cuautla

10

**Convento de
San Juan Bautista**

●Yecapixtla
5

Cuautla

160

Tepoztlán festival fare

---

a huge, crenelated atrium; the cloister contains earth-tone portrayals of early saints. Dedicated to St. Matthew, the church has a blue nave full of saints and folk altars tucked in candlelit niches.

Continue south on Hwy. 2, turning right onto Hwy. 115 toward Cuautla, and left after about 3½ miles (6 km) onto Hwy. 10 to **Yecapixtla 5,** which is surrounded by fields of sugarcane and corn. A slave market during pre-Hispanic times, this town later became a regional Augustinian priory. At the back of the fortlike, single-story **Convento de San Juan Bautista** stands Cortés's Palace, where the conqueror sometimes stayed. The church's simple renaissance facade has a rose window and a plateresque portal. Inside, note the

◪ See also area map p. 213 B2
▶ Cuernavaca
⟷ 80 miles (128 km)
🕒 One day
▶ Cuernavaca

NOT TO BE MISSED
- Tepoztlán
- Tlayacapan
- Yecapixtla

Augustinian insignia of the ornate Isabelline pulpit. Head back to Hwy. 115, continue south, and then turn west on Hwy. 160 to return the 39 miles (62 km) to Cuernavaca. ■

Cholula

🔺 213 C2

Visitor information

✉ Calle 4 Poniente 103

☎ 22/47-31-16

In & around Cholula

CHOLULA IS THOUGHT TO HAVE BEEN ESTABLISHED BY supporters of Quetzalcóatl fleeing religious persecution in Tula; its name means "place of flight." The god-king Quetzalcóatl may have stopped here as well, leaving a cult of devoted followers before sailing east on a raft of snakes, or rising phoenix-like from a self-immolation, according to different legends. Today home to the 60-year-old Universidad de las Américas, Cholula and surrounding villages have some of Mexico's most stunning churches. Forced to abandon the Quetzalcóatl cult by the Spanish, indigenous artisans built inspired churches. Combining pre-Hispanic and European motifs and techniques, they created an eloquent, irrepressible baroque.

Talavera tiles cover the facade of the church at Acatepec.

At the dawn of the 16th century, Cholula was a powerful city and an important commercial center under the dominion of the Aztecs. Despite the advice of his Tlaxcala Indian guides, Hernán Cortés stopped here for ten days during his initial march to Tenochtitlán. Upon learning of a plan to slaughter and sacrifice his troops, he ordered a massacre of soldiers and citizens after delivering a speech discouraging idolatry and human sacrifice. The Cholulans' resounding defeat reinforced Cortés's image as an all-seeing superior being.

Within two years the Aztec capital had been conquered, and the Spaniards set about reinventing Cholula, replacing Quetzalcóatl's temples with Christian churches. Abandoned since late Postclassic times, Mesoamerica's largest pyramid, the **Gran Pirámide de Tepanapa** (*Av. Morelos at Calle 6 Norte, $*), was probably just too big to dismantle. The huge structure of sun-dried adobe bricks was constructed in distinct phases over a 1,000-year period (roughly 300 B.C. to A.D. 700).

Unlike other archaeological sites, Tepanapa is accessed exclusively through a 5-mile (8 km) honeycomb of tunnels. Enter on your own, or hire a guide (*$$–$$$*) at the entrance. A small site museum displays period pottery and a cutaway model showing the different layers of the pyramid. Perched on top of the 230-foot (70 m) structure is the **Iglesia de Nuestra Señora de los Remedios.** The late 16th-century church affords a superb view of the city and, on clear days, of Popocatépetl and Iztaccíhuatl volcanoes.

Brightly painted restaurants and shops surround Cholula's large **zócalo,** or main square (*Blvd. Miguel Alemán at Morelos*), some tucked into the arcade on the west side. On the east side lies the entrance to the **Convento San Gabriel** (*Calle 2 Norte s/n*), built by the Franciscans on the site of a pre-Hispanic temple. Inside the monastery is the fascinating **Capilla Real**—modeled after the great mosque of Córdoba, Spain—a maze of columns and colonnades topped by 49 domes. It is currently closed owing to earthquake damage.

Just a few miles south of Cholula are two famous "Indian baroque" churches, unique for their blend of European and native elements. Said to have been designed and executed entirely by native people, the church at **Santa María Tonantzintla** is one of the hemisphere's most astonishing

artistic accomplishments. Every inch of the interior is covered in polychrome and gilded, sculpted plaster ornamentation: cherubs (some with Indian faces), flowers, fruit, vines, saints, rosettes, and scrolls. On columns on either side of the main altar, look for mirrors representing respectively wisdom, morality, truth, and humanity.

Less than a mile (1.5 km) farther south is the astonishing **San Francisco Acatepec** church, its fabulous tiled facade a breathtaking barrage of bright yellow, blue-and-white flowered, green, and unglazed brick-red tiles.

Another happy marriage of Old and New World cultures can be found in the town of **Chipilo,** a few miles beyond Acatepec. Many

of the townspeople whose great-great-grandparents emigrated from Venice have retained some of their Italian recipes and traditions, including making homemade sausages and dairy products. Today the town is known for its rustic handmade furniture.

Less than 10 miles (16 km) northwest of Cholula, **Huejotzingo** is home to an ancient **Convento Franciscano** *(Closed Mon., $)* built between 1529 and 1570. See the cloister, kitchen, and charming chapel, and in the adjoining church admire the beautiful plateresque altar. Huejotzingo is known for its wool *sarapes* (blankets), sold at the outdoor Saturday market, and for its boisterous carnival celebrations. ∎

Nuestra Señora de los Remedios church sits upon the Gran Pirámide de Tepanapa, the focal point of the Cholula archaeological site, with Popocatépetl volcano rising beyond.

Popocatépetl & Iztaccíhuatl

Less than 50 miles (80 km) southeast of Mexico City tower active Popocatépetl and its slumbering companion, Iztaccíhuatl. At 17,802 feet (5,426 m) and 17,343 feet (5,286 m) respectively, these geologic giants are the second- and third-highest mountains in Mexico, outpeaked only by Pico de Orizaba, in Veracruz (see p. 244). Popocatépetl has erupted at least 36 times, the last major event being in A.D. 820. It has been the subject of legends and the object of worship since Quetzalcóatl reigned, but it is its recent activity that concerns geologists and the villagers living nearby.

Although Popo and Izta (as they are affectionately called) are both classified as stratovolcanoes, Izta has long been dormant and has no crater. Popo, on the other hand, began to rumble and quake in 1993, with belches and explosions of gas, ash, and rocks. The next year, 25,000 people were evacuated from vulnerable villages when ash and red-hot rocks began to rain down its snowy slopes.

According to legend, Popoca was a poor but valiant youth in love with Mixtli, the lovely daughter of Tizoc, lord of Mexico. Popoca went to battle in hopes of gaining the rank of Caballero Aguila, or Eagle Warrior, thus meriting marriage to the princess. Imagining her beloved's death and her own marriage to the most ambitious and cruel of her suitors, Mixtli killed herself. Returning triumphant from battle and finding his lover dead, Popoca laid the princess's body atop a high mountain, hoping the snow would revive her. He remained by her side with his smoldering torch, and so the pair gave shape to Popocatépetl (Smoking Mountain) and Iztaccíhuatl (Sleeping Woman).

More than just a fairy tale, Popocatépetl and Iztaccíhuatl figure in modern-day religious ritual. Many villagers consider them to be living beings—simultaneously mountains, humans, and gods. They refer to the pair as "don Gregorio and doña Rosita," who bring rain and fertility to their fields. For the corn-planting season, local rainmakers conduct prayers at sacred sites on both volcanoes, one within a mile (1.6 km) of Popo's crater.

However, Popo is now closed to mountaineers. Still open is the technically more challenging Iztaccíhuatl. Both are accessible from Paso de Cortés, 10½ miles (17 km) off Highway 115. The pass is named for the Spanish conquistador, who is said to have first glimpsed the city of Tenochtitlán from here. ■

**Above: Beyond a farmer's cornfields loom Popocatépetl (left) and Iztaccíhuatl.
Right: More than 20 million people live within 50 miles (80 km) of active Popo.**

Puebla

THE CITY OF PUEBLA WAS ESTABLISHED IN 1531 IN A GREEN valley surrounded by three of Mexico's tallest volcanoes—Pico de Orizaba, Popocatépetl, and Iztaccíhuatl. Located within the geologically active "Ring of Fire," the region is periodically rocked by earthquakes; a 1999 quake damaged some of Puebla's precious historic buildings and gorgeous churches, now being restored.

Puebla
🗺 213 C2
Visitor information
✉ 5ta Calle Oriente 3
☎ 2/246-2044

Although established as a center of agriculture and trade, Puebla soon diversified to manufacture textiles, glass, and ceramics. To the Moorish-inspired motifs in blue and white imported from Talavera, Spain, indigenous and mestizo craftsmen added earthy reds, oranges, and greens, creating a unique ceramic tradition. Tiles, used in conjunction with effusively carved plasterwork (often painted and gilded) and other baroque ornamentation, created a unique architectural style seen throughout the capital and surrounding towns.

It's not just the architecture of Puebla that overwhelms the senses. Poblano chefs use the huge variety of chilies grown in the region to create many distinctive recipes.

Traditionally prepared around Independence Day, *chiles en nogada* are hot peppers stuffed with a sweet meat mixture, smothered in walnut cream sauce, and garnished with pomegranate seeds. Prepared using bitter chocolate, nuts, sesame seeds, and chilies, *mole poblano* is a complex sauce served over turkey, chicken, or pork.

The sunny yellow kitchen where mole was allegedly first concocted can be found in the **Convento de Santa Rosa,** a nunnery confiscated during the Reform and now housing the **Museo de Arte Popular Poblano** (*Calle 14 Poniente 305 at 3 Norte, tel 2/232-9240, closed Mon., $*). The museum showcases folk crafts from throughout the state, including masks and inlaid furniture. **The Museo de Arte Religioso** (18 Poniente 103, tel 2/232-0178, closed Mon., $,) is another convent-cum-art museum. In addition to paintings and other more traditional exhibits, look for an unusual display: the preserved heart of the convent's founder.

Surrounding the shady **Plaza Principal** (Av. A. Camacho between 2 Sur & 16 de Septiembre) are many impressive buildings, including the French neoclassic-style **Palacio Municipal** (Portal Hidalgo 14, tel 2/246-1899). At the plaza's northeast corner, the red-brick, sculpted-plaster, and tile facade of the **Casa de los Muñecos** is as fascinating as the colonial paintings within the **Museo Universitario** (2 Norte 2, tel 2/246-2899, closed Mon., $).

Opposite is the impressive **Catedral de la Inmaculada Concepción** (16 de Septiembre at 3 Oriente, tel 2/232-2316), with its severe twin towers and massive interior containing five naves and 14 side chapels. The main altar, by colonial master Manuel Tolsá, is of gold, marble, and smoky onyx.

Behind the cathedral, the **Casa de la Cultura** (5 Oriente 5, tel 2/246-3186, $) comprises a theater, art galleries, and a concert hall. Situated inside the House of Culture is the **Biblioteca Palafoxiana,** named for the Bishop Palafox, who donated his large personal library. The collection now numbers more than 40,000 tomes. Another local philanthropist donated the pre-Colombian artifacts, European and American colonial art, and 20th-century Mexican art found at the **Museo Amparo** (Calle 2 Sur 708 at Av. 9 Oriente, tel 2/246-4210, $).

North of the cathedral, the **Iglesia de Santo Domingo** (5 de Mayo at 4 Poniente, tel 2/242-3643) houses the city's most ornate

Brickwork as well as decorative tiles embellish Puebla facades.

chapel. Dedicated to Our Lady of the Rosary, the **Capilla del Rosario** is a mind-bending baroque surfeit of decorated gilt plasterwork. A few doors down, the **Museo Bello y Zetina** (5 de Mayo 409 at 6 Oriente, tel 2/232-4720, closed Mon.), the lavishly decorated former home of one of Puebla's wealthy families, is a good example of secular opulence.

The 18th-century **Casa del Alfeñique** (4 Oriente 416 at 6 Norte, tel 2/241-4296, closed Mon., $)—named for the similarity of its ornately carved plaster facade to a popular sugar candy of the same name—houses a museum of colonial and pre-Hispanic artifacts. In the same neighborhood, crafts stalls sell alfeñique and other typical candies, in addition to factory-made Talavera pottery, at **El Parián** (2 Oriente & 6 Norte), on the old **Plaza San Roque.** You can buy local artwork from workshops at the **Barrio del Artista** (6 Oriente & 6 Norte) and **Callejón de los Sapos** (Calle 4 Sur near Av. 7 Oriente), two lively shopping districts. ■

Tlaxcala & Cacaxtla

Tlaxcala

▲ 213 C2

Visitor information

✉ Av. Juárez 18 at Lardizábal

☎ 2/465-0900

MOST PEOPLE VISIT TLAXCALA TO SEE THE FABULOUS PRE-Hispanic murals at Cacaxtla. But murals aside, Tlaxcala is a lively and historic town. Surrounding the fountain-filled plaza, patio restaurants serve regional specialties under the arched colonnade. Shops sell folk art, including carved wooden canes, striped sarapes, and colorful carnival masks used throughout the region. Proud of both its Spanish and indigenous ancestry, the town's motto is "Heritage of Two Cultures."

Tlaxcala's colorful parish church of San José

Both the tiny state and its capital city are named for the Tlaxcaltecans, whose hatred for the Aztecs made them Hernán Cortés's trusted Indian allies. Relatively well treated for their loyalty, the Tlaxcaltecans voluntarily resettled in places as far-flung as Santa Fe, New Mexico, and San Cristóbal de las Casas, Chiapas, to aid converting reluctant indigenous groups.

Tlaxcala boasts the first permanent church in New Spain. The Franciscan monastery **Ex-convento de la Asunción,** at Plaza Xicotencatl, was built from the stones of a pyramid to the rain god Tláloc. The sacristy holds the baptismal font where the four lords of Tlaxcala were baptized before Cortés marched on Tenochtitlán; the cloister now houses the **Museo**

Regional de Tlaxcala *(Tel 2/462-0262, closed Mon., $),* with pre-Hispanic and colonial artifacts and paintings.

Many of the 16th-century buildings surrounding **Plaza de la Constitución** preserve the lower portions of their original facades, giving the square a historic uniformity. On the northwest corner, the **Parroquia de San José** *(Tel 2/462-1106)* has been decorated in brick and Talavera tiles after several remodels. The brick and rococo plaster **Palacio de Gobierno** *(Tel 2/465-0900)* graces the plaza's north side. Throughout the state government building's interior, complex murals describe the city's indigenous roots and historical events. The **Museo de Artes y Tradiciones Populares** *(Emilio*

Sánchez Piedras 1, tel 2/462-2337, closed Mon., $) shows samples of pulque (fermented cactus liquor) and regional weaving and masks, and has demonstrations of how they are made.

On the east side of town, the 18th-century **Basílica de Nuestra Señora de Ocotlán** (*Pocito de Aqua Santa, Carr. a Santa Ana Chiautempan, tel 2/462-1073*) was built at the site of several miraculous appearances of the Virgin Mary within a pine forest (*ocotlán*). The baroque sanctuary's highly ornate portal and twin bell towers are elaborately carved in white plaster, but even more stunning is the elaborate interior, which took indigenous artist Francisco Tlayotehuanitzin more than 20 years to complete. The octagonal **Camarín de la Virgen** (Virgin's Dressing Room) is completely engulfed in gilded and polychrome angels, saints, flowers, and garlands. At nearby **Capilla del Pocito de Agua Santa** (Chapel of the Holy Spring), pilgrims purchase red-clay vessels for carrying off some of the site's sacred water.

The ruins of a fortified city at **Cacaxtla,** 12 miles (19 km) southwest of Tlaxcala (*Tel 2/416-0000, $*), contain what are arguably Mexico's most important pre-Hispanic murals, discovered only in 1975. Natural pigments mixed with nopal cactus gel were used to paint vivid scenes in blue, red, yellow, black, and white. A combination of Classic lowland Maya painting style and non-Maya hieroglyphics led scholars to believe the murals were painted by Gulf Coast émigrés, the Olmeca-Xicalanca. This group of warrior-merchants flourished between the mid-seventh and tenth centuries, concurring with the demise of nearby Teotihuacán.

A huge structure the size of four football fields contains at least eight layers of construction. Throughout the enormous building, adobe walls, corridors, and open courtyards were covered in stucco and decorated with complex murals. The largest scene, about two thirds intact, depicts warriors dressed as jaguars, apparently in the act of sacrificing rival bird-warriors. Less bellicose murals show images related to trade and fertility.

Most tours to Cacaxtla stop at **Xochitécatl,** a mile (1.6 km) north of Cacaxtla (*Free with Cacaxtla admission*), where pepper trees sprout on an unusual spiral pyramid of compacted sand covered in stone. Related to fertility, this structure may have been dedicated to the wind god Ehécatl. Both Cacaxtla and Xochitécatl have site museums. ■

Among the best preserved Mesoamerican murals are those at Cacaxtla. This detail shows a nearly life-size "bird-man."

Pachuca & around

THE SILVER AND GOLD MINES IN PACHUCA AND THE surrounding hills, worked since before the Spanish Conquest, have played out and been resuscitated or relocated several times. Yet mining still contributes significantly to the economy, augmented by the manufacture of textiles, cement, and other products. Streets and alleys wind up and down the hilly city, meeting at small plazas that are fronted by contemporary and neoclassic buildings. Like a microcosm of Mexico's heartland, tiny Hidalgo state—in which Pachuca lies—is a patchwork of pulque haciendas, arid plains, working and depleted mines, and 16th-century monasteries.

The old city of Pachuca radiates from the severe, rather formal **Plaza de la Independencia** *(Matamoros at Allende).* Dominating the square is the neo-classic **Reloj Monumental,** an imposing clock tower with an eight-bell carillon. Built just prior to the Revolution, its marble statues represent Liberty, the Constitution, Reform, and Independence.

Southeast of the main plaza, the fortress-style **Templo y Ex-Convento de San Francisco** *(Arista and Casasola, tel 7/715-2965)* began life as a Franciscan church and monastery but has seen many uses over its more than 400-year history, including as stables and a jail. Today it houses the **Centro Cultural de Hidalgo;** the atrium and orchard have been converted to pretty plazas and gardens.

Within the former monastery is the **Teatro de la Ciudad,** built by the Spanish inventor of the "patio system" for amalgamizing silver using quicksilver. Free museums include the small **Museo Regional de Historia** *(Tel 7/714-3989, closed Mon.)* and, on the top floor, the **Museo de la Fotografía** *(Tel 7/714-3653, closed Mon.),* with changing exhibits of historic photos from the adjoining **Fototeca Nacional.** The National Photographic Archives offers a reproduction service of its 900,000 images, many from the Mexican Revolution.

Pachuca is located at the northern extreme of the Valley of Mexico, just 56 miles (90 km) northeast of Mexico City. Beyond rises the Sierra Madre Oriental, and en route lies **Mineral Real del Monte,** 7 miles (11 km) northeast on Highway 105, a charming old mining town that has seen ups and downs over the centuries. After a violent miner's strike, the mine was sold to an English consortium, which went bankrupt 25 years later. During its brief tenure, the British firm used miners from Cornwall—who brought their traditional meat pies, or pasties (called *pastes* in Mexico), and soccer. They also built English-style cottages, all still very much in evidence. The tombstones of the English buried in the town graveyard face Britain.

A few miles beyond and off Highway 105 lies **Huasca,** a charming town of cobblestone streets and bright white buildings, known for its pottery. A smaller road leads from Mineral Real del Monte to the mining town of **Real del Chico** and the adjacent **Parque Nacional El Chico** *(Tel 7/715-0994),* with well-marked hiking and mountain-bike trails through pine, oak, and juniper

Pachuca
- 213 B3
Visitor information
- ✉ Av. Revolución 1300, Col. Periodistas
- ☎ 7/718-4489 or 7/718-4390

forest. On weekends city-dwellers flee to the 6,670-acre (2,700 ha) park to fish several lakes, rock climb, or simply enjoy the mountain air. There are restaurants, and camping is permitted. In June 2000 a luxurious hotel was inaugurated within the park.

About a half-hour away, **Actopan,** 23 miles (37 km) north of Pachuca on Highway 85, celebrates its weekly market each Thursday. Right in the center of town, the **Templo y Convento San Nicolás** *($)*, begun by the Augustinians in 1548, is one of Mexico's most admired buildings. Note the well-proportioned plateresque facade and the barrel vaulting above the **capilla abierta** (open chapel), with its trompe l'oeil coffered ceiling.

Most remarkable, however, are the murals. Many are renditions of illustrations from medieval books vividly painted in blue, brown, ocher, and red. The Apocalypse scenes in the open chapel are among the finest in Mexico. Painted over in layers of whitewash after the Council of Trent—a church edict set forth in the 16th century banning profanity, nudity, and apocalyptic themes in sacred art—they have only recently been uncovered.

Throughout Hidalgo state are over a dozen important former monasteries, built in the 1600s near the largest Náhua and Otomí centers. The Franciscans produced more modest houses of worship in the west, while the Augustinians took the east and built more slowly and lavishly. (See pp. 216–17.) ■

Sunlight warms the pinnacles of El Chico National Park.

Teotihuacán

🅰 213 B3

✉ 30 miles (48 km) northeast of Mexico City

☎ 595/60052

Teotihuacán

RISING ABOVE A GOLD, GRASSY PLAIN TO THE NORTHEAST of Mexico City are the ruins of the first true metropolis in the Western Hemisphere. It outlived its contemporary, imperial Rome, and was the greatest city in the Americas until the Mexica (Aztecs) built Tenochtitlán nearly 700 years later. The Mexica elite made frequent pilgrimages to the ruins of Teotihuacán and gave the city its Náhuatl name, meaning "where men become gods."

Scholars today know very little about the people who constructed this magnificent city, or why they abandoned it just a few centuries after it reached its Golden Age, roughly A.D. 200 to 500. Theories include overpopulation, rampant disease, internal power struggles, and rebellion of the masses. Systematic burning of ceremonial buildings points to the purposeful destruction of the city.

At the height of its power, however, fine palaces and temples adorned with bas-relief sculptures and brilliant murals lined **Avenida de los Muertos** (Avenue of the Dead), a broad, straight avenue paved with volcanic stone, set with dazzling mica, and aligned with both the stars and terrestrial landmarks. Its leaders excelled in architecture and astronomy, and had a well-developed religious system. An extensive commercial network extending to the Petén region of Guatemala was probably initiated around the first century A.D.

Today, many of the ceremonial buildings lining Avenue of the Dead have been partially reconstructed, although without their colorful stucco facades. At its southern end stands **La Ciudadela,** the compound of plazas and temples that formed Teotihuacán's administrative and ceremonial center and also the principal secular royal palace for many generations of unknown kings. La Ciudadela is dominated by the **Templo de Quetzalcóatl.**

This temple honored the Plumed Serpent, worshiped as the god of war, water, the dawn, and agriculture. Although the building's lower level was originally entirely covered in fanged serpent sculptures, those on three sides were pulled down not long after its inauguration. The intact west wall is hugely impressive, with rows of stone serpent heads interspersed with images of Tláloc and feathered shells.

At the far extreme of the 2½-mile (4 km) avenue is the **Pirámide de la Luna** (Pyramid of the Moon), a royal funerary monument with tombs dating back to the first century A.D.; the oldest of these may be that of the founder of the royal dynasty. Just over a hundred tall, narrow steps lead to the summit, where you will be rewarded with a view of the arrow-straight Avenue of the Dead, sacred **Cerro Gordo** (Fat Hill) to the north, and lonely plains dotted with prickly-pear cacti and pepper trees. The pyramid has six layers of construction; in contrast, the main structures of the Pyramid of the Sun and the Pyramid of Quetzalcóatl were built mostly during a single phase.

Smaller, related structures are symmetrically arranged on both sides of the Avenue of the Dead; the most impressive is the **Palacio de Quetzalpapálotl.** Within the building's rooms, open patios, and antechambers are some well-preserved murals. Square stone pillars in the interior patio are

An archaeologist cleans a mural at an apartment in the Teotihuacán barrio of La Ventilla.

decorated with low-relief sculptures of the building's namesake, the Feathered Butterfly, while the temple below it is adorned with a fascinating sequence of quetzals (looking more like parrots), sea shells, and split-tongued Tláloc masks.

Across the avenue, the **Pirámide del Sol** (Pyramid of the Sun), the third largest pyramid in the world, squats like an immense behemoth. Although its base is nearly as broad as that of the Great Pyramid at Giza, at 213 feet (65 m) tall it is less than half the height of the Egyptian pyramid. Underneath the tremendous structure winds a honeycomb of tunnels and caves, which the Aztecs considered the birthplace of the world. Although the four-level, 244-step pyramid has more than twice as many steps as the Pyramid of the Moon, it is slightly easier to climb as the steps are shorter. Thousands of people converge on the structure near dawn each spring equinox hoping to receive a supercharge of celestial energy.

In addition to its ceremonial and commercial functions,

8-square-mile (20 sq km) Teotihuacán was, at its apogee, home to approximately 175,000 people. Neighborhoods of one-story dwellings had shared patios and kitchens, with private apartments for each family. East of the Pyramid of the Sun, several restored apartment complexes with vivid if fractured murals can be visited. The most impressive are those at **Tepantitla,** whose mural depicting the rain god Tláloc in his paradise is re-created at the Museo Nacional de Antropología, in Mexico City (see pp. 198–201).

To get the most out of your visit, spend the preceding night at the Hotel Villas Arqueológicas Teotihuacán (book in advance; see p. 371) within the archaeological zone itself and take advantage of the site's 7 a.m. opening time. Otherwise, take a day trip from Mexico City by limo, bus, or licensed taxi. Near the Ciudadela entrance are a restaurant, a bar, and a warren of souvenir stalls, while the site museum and botanical gardens are located near the Pyramid of the Sun. ■

While Europe stumbled through the Dark Ages, Teotihuacán's culture shone like a beacon around Mesoamerica.

Tepotzotlán

THE CHURCH AND FORMER SEMINARY AT TEPOTZOTLÁN, two masterpieces of Mexican baroque overachievement, are reason enough to visit this town, but also housed within the lavish complex is perhaps the country's finest colonial art museum. Tepotzotlán itself, with a population of 50,000 and less than an hour's drive north of Mexico City, is a breath of fresh air after the congested capital.

Tepotzotlán
🗺 213 B3
Visitor information
✉ Plaza Hidalgo 99
☎ 5/876-2771

The first evangelists to arrive here were Franciscans, soon replaced by the Jesuits at the end of the 16th century. A generous bequest allowed the order to build the **Seminario de San Martín,** a seminary for young indigenous noblemen, the **San Francisco Javier** novitiate, and a language school to teach priests Náhuatl, Otomí, and Mazahua.

Carvings of saints, angels, and floral and shell motifs cover San Francisco Javier's limestone facade.

The lovely **Iglesia de San Francisco Javier** we see today is the result of an intensive (and expensive) remodel of the facade, belfry, and altarpieces almost immediately after the church was completed. Imagine the distress of the priest and generations of indigenous craftsmen who had constructed the magnificent edifice

when the Jesuits were suddenly expelled from New Spain in 1767, just after its completion.

Not even the complex Churrigueresque facade of the church prepares you for its excessive, impressive interior. Within the church one gilded, intricately carved altarpiece leads to the next; there are five on each side in addition to the ebullient main altar dedicated to St. Francis Xavier.

To the right of the nave are three fascinating rooms. The **Casa de Loreto** is a re-creation of the home of the Virgin Mary, said to have been miraculously transported to Loreto, Italy, after the Muslims invaded the Holy Land. The **Relicario de San José,** richly decorated in paintings and gold, houses Jesuit relics. Last is the octagonal **Camarín de la Virgen,** the dazzling "dressing room" of carved plaster reserved for the statue of Our Lady of Loreto.

In the adjoining edifice, the **Museo Nacional del Virreinato** *(Tel 5/876-0332, closed Mon., $)* has a fantastic collection of three centuries of colonial and folk art: paintings, jewelry, ecclesiastic accouterments, porcelain, ivory statuettes, and other treasures. Don't miss the **Capilla Domestic,** a chapel covered floor to ceiling in gold leaf and carved polychrome stucco. More museum exhibits are located on the second story; on the lower level are the kitchen, pantry and cold room, temporary exhibits, and the gift shop. ■

The ruined city of Malinalco was hewn from the living rock.

More places to visit around Mexico City

AUGUSTINIAN MONASTERIES

Two groups of Augustinian monasteries are found in eastern Hidalgo: one in the north, in the rugged Sierra Alta, the other on the dry plains called El Mesquital. Padres set out to convert the Otomí in the sierra in 1537, establishing **Atotonilco el Grande** (today in poor condition) and **Molango,** a rustic mission with a breathtaking valley view. The best of the group is **Metztitlán.** One of Mexico's finest fortress monasteries, it has the region's only surviving original high altarpiece. There is a wonderful view of the subtropical river valley from the terraced atrium, said to be built on an ancient temple to the moon. The town's name means "moon in the middle."

The plains group consists of **Actopan** (see p. 227), **Epazoyucan,** and **Ixmiquilpan.** Built on a hill associated with the rain god, Tláloc, Epazoyucan is best known for its magnificent 16th-century frescoes. Ixmiquilpan's murals are unique for their many vivid battle scenes and unrestrained indigenous imagery and iconography.

Just outside the ruins at Teotihuacán is **Acolman** (*Tel 595/71644*), built from the stones of a temple to Quetzalcóatl and noted for its fine plateresque facade.

MALINALCO

Subjugated by the Mexica, or Aztecs, just 50 years before the Spanish Conquest, Malinalco (*Closed Mon., $*) is a ceremonial center carved into living rock. Its **main temple** is entered through the zoomorphic "mouth" of a large fanged serpent. Within is a circular room decorated with relief sculptures of eagle and jaguar motifs; it is believed to have been dedicated to warriors of those cults. It's a long walk up 400 steps to reach the few restored buildings, but you're rewarded with a wonderful view over the valley. The site is about a mile (1.5 km) from Malinalco, whose name means "place of grass blossoms." This pretty village is a popular weekend escape from Mexico City; its **Augustinian monastery** (*Closed Mon., $*) has many fine frescoes in its cloister.

🅰 213 B2

TOLUCA

Toluca is Mexico's highest capital city, at 8,760 feet (2,670 m) above sea level. The city fell to the Aztecs in 1472 and was later presented to Hernán Cortés by King Carlos V. Today, it's a sprawling center of industry, and although its famous **Friday market** (which functions daily) has been relocated near the bus station, there are many museums and things to see centrally. Around the main square are buildings of native volcanic rock, arcaded shops and restaurants, and the **Cosmovitral Jardín Botánico** (*Lerdo de Tejada, Degollado, & Ignacio Rayón, closed Mon., $*), a botanical garden decorated in stained-glass panels. The **Museo José María Velasco** (*Av. Lerdo de Tejada 400, tel 7/213-2814, closed Mon.*) and the adjacent **Museo Felipe Gutiérrez** show the work of these 19th-century painters. The **Centro Cultural Mexiquense** has a library, a bookstore, a gift shop, a restaurant, and museums of anthropology, modern art, and México state's varied folk art.

Metepec, on the outskirts of Toluca, is famous for its pottery, especially the elaborate

Sweets for sale at the Toluca market

"trees of life," portraying the fall from grace and decorated with Adam and Eve, angels, devils, and saints.
🅰 213 A2 **Visitor information** ✉ Urawa 100 at Paseo Tollocan ☎ 7/219-5190

TULA

Founded by the Spanish around a Franciscan monastery in the early 16th century, Tula was in a previous incarnation the pre-Hispanic capital of the Toltec culture, also called Tollan. Descendants of Chichimeca "barbarians" from the north established Tollan as the center of an important alliance of city-states. King Topoilzin, later associated with the god Quetzalcóatl (who abhorred human sacrifice), was forced to flee around A.D. 987 by enemies devoted to the fierce god Tezcatlipoca, or Smoking Mirror. Under the rule of the latter faction, Tula became a powerful city. It was once thought to have influenced or invaded Chichén Itzá because Chac Mool statues have been found there and because of the similarity of the sites' architectural styles and artifacts (see pp. 338–41). However, Tula is now considered to have been a link along an Itzá trade route stretching north to Paquimé. At its height between A.D. 900 and 1150, it was destroyed by invaders from the north—most likely by the Chichimec tribes from which it was descended.

The archaeological site is perched on a promontory about a mile (1.5 km) outside of Tula. The excavated portion of the city—one of the largest in Early Postclassic Mesoamerica, covering 5.4 square miles (14 sq km)—consists of several ball courts, pyramids, and temples. The most important building excavated so far is **Pirámide B.** Its temple roof was supported by four tall pillars in the form of Toltec warriors, called Atlantes. (One of the four on site is a replica; the original is at the Museo Nacional de Antropología in Mexico City, see pp. 198–201) Bas-relief sculptures on the outer walls depict coyotes, jaguars, eagles devouring hearts, and composite creatures thought to represent Quetzalcóatl. At the site museum note the statue of Chac Mool, the reclining messenger god brought north from the Yucatán Peninsula.
🅰 213 B3 ☎ 7/732-0705

VALLE DEL BRAVO

About 90 miles (145 km) west of Mexico City, Valle del Bravo is a whitewashed, red-roofed town with popular restaurants and galleries surrounding the main plaza. The town, overlooking **Laguna Avandaro,** an artificial lake with watersports, is visited by wealthy *defeños* (Mexico City residents) escaping the capital on weekends and vacations.
🅰 213 A2 ■

Not even the tropical heat can dampen the spirit of Mexico's Central Gulf coast inhabitants, whose ancestors conceived Mesoamerica's first true civilization. And the irrepressible jungle still smothers hundreds of archaeological sites.

Central Gulf coast

Jade figurines, found at La Venta, near Villahermosa

Central Gulf coast

RAIN FORESTS, RIVERS, AND RUINS ATTRACT ADVENTUROUS TRAVELERS TO Tabasco and Veracruz, which form a thin curve of land cupping the Gulf of Mexico. Geographically impressive, the Central Gulf coast contains vast lowland plains and, in odd juxtaposition, the country's highest volcanic peak: snowcapped Pico de Orizaba. Its people are as exuberant as its landscape, famed for their spicy cooking, lively dances, and sentimental songs.

More than 40 rivers etch the landscape of Veracruz, creating endless marshy swamps, which frustrated the Spanish conquistadors in the 16th century. The state's coastal plains stretch 424 miles (684 km) along the oil-rich Bay of Campeche, although its beaches are not conducive to swimming and sunbathing. Waterfalls streak the Tuxtla Mountains in the north, where the Tempoal, Tamesí, and Panuco Rivers meet, while the Tonalá River creates a natural border between Veracruz and Tabasco to the south. In both states, corn, cacao, tobacco, vanilla, and coffee plantations cover valleys and plateaus in a lush green checkerboard that sometimes smothers the ruins of ancient civilizations.

Though its hot, humid, and often bug-ridden terrain is far from welcoming, the gulf coast has a rich pre-Hispanic history. Mesoamerica's first

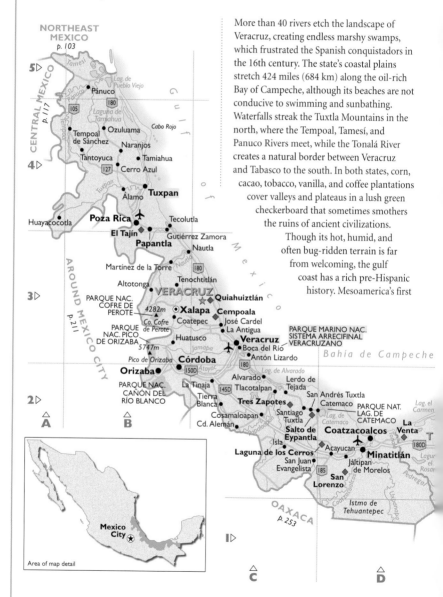

El Puerto de Veracruz bustles with commerce, the navy, and tourism.

known civilization, the Olmecs, flourished in this region between 1200 and 400 B.C. Many remote Olmec sites have been uncovered in Tabasco and Veracruz, but visitors needn't traverse the wilderness to explore ancient cultures. Villahermosa, in Tabasco, has two fine museums showcasing stelae, altars, and sculptures from Mesoamerica's Mother Culture, including giant stone heads and delicately incised ceremonial masks and ax-heads of fine jade.

In Veracruz, the country's second most important archaeology museum displays Olmec artifacts along with those of the Huastec and Totonac cultural groups, whose descendants still live throughout the state. El Tajín, in northern Veracruz, is one of Mexico's most intriguing archaeological sites, depicting what scholars call the "Classic Veracruz" style of art and architecture.

History buffs follow the Ruta de Cortés, an amazing journey of conquest that began with the Spaniard's arrival on the gulf coast in 1519 and ended two years later with the fall of Tenochtitlán. Adventure travelers struggle up steep trails to the summit of Pico de Orizaba, raft the Antigua and Filobobos Rivers, and explore the jungles around Lake Catemaco, while culture buffs are content to wander the port city of Veracruz, haunting the dungeons of San Juan de Ulúa, dancing in the lively Plaza de Armas, or feasting on seafood spiced with chilies and garlic. ■

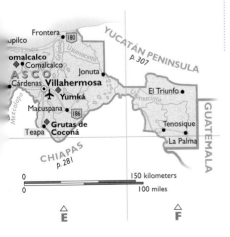

El Tajín

🅰 234 B4

Visitor information

✉ 10 miles (16 km) southwest of Papantla

☎ 28/41-85-00

💲 $

El Tajín

SURROUNDED BY EMERALD-GREEN HILLS, EL TAJÍN MUST have been resplendent at the height of its influence, when stuccoed pyramids painted bright blue and red surrounded the city's great plazas. Although abandoned for around 800 years, the uniformity and density of its construction, the fascinating bas-relief carvings, and the tropical setting still make this a breathtaking site, worth the effort to find.

The ball game served as a ceremonial staging ground of good versus evil, light versus darkness, in order to assure the continued prosperity of the initiating tribe, and the 17 ball courts unearthed thus far at El Tajín are ample proof of the importance of sacrifice and

Small plaster figurines may have originally occupied the 365 niches of El Tajín's most outstanding pyramid.

auto-sacrifice (such as bloodletting) in this society.

Archaeologists aren't sure who built this ceremonial and residential city, which was established during the Early Classic period but reached its height toward the end of the Late Classic (A.D. 600–900). A uniformity of design and the repetition of the step-and-fret pattern characterize its architecture. Pyramids were built in the *talud y tablero* style found at Teotihuacán

(see pp. 228–29); in fact, a marked reciprocal influence is seen in these contemporary cities. This distinctive style consists of slanted walls *(taludes)* capped with overhanging vertical panels *(tableros)*. By about A.D. 1200 the site was abandoned, having been burned in an attack—possibly by Chichimecs (see p. 28) to the north.

The site was named by the Totonacs of northern Veracruz, who believe that the 12 ancient ones, or Tajín, live here and cause rain. The jungle-clad city was not discovered until the late 18th century. A major restoration project began in 1992; to date about 30 (one-fifth) of the structures have been restored.

Near the entrance, the **Grupo Plaza del Arroyo** is made up of four stepped pyramids surrounding a large plaza. Beyond are four ball courts consisting of opposing walls on either side of a rectangular court. Although many of El Tajín's ball courts have bas-relief carvings, the most intricate and well-preserved panels are found at the **Juego de Pelota Sur**. Scenes show the god of death witnessing men preparing for war (the ball game), and the final outcome: a ritualistic death to the loser. Central panels on the east and west sides show the god of rain piercing his penis in a ritual self-sacrifice to produce the intoxicating drink pulque.

Just to the north, a large number of buildings are clustered

around the magnificent **Pirámide de los Nichos,** named for its 365 deeply recessed niches, one for each day of the solar calendar. This relatively stocky structure has a single steep stairway on the east side. Hidden within is a duplicate structure, although without the niches. The step-and-fret pattern at the top is repeated on many other structures, including **Edificios 5** and **12,** to the right and left, respectively.

Farther north, the buildings in the group called **Tajín Chico** were most likely the residences of elite citizens. Note the Maya arch on the south side of **Edificio A** and the remnants of murals on **Edificio C,** shaded by a palm-thatch roof. Edificio de las Columnas has carved columns with narrative scenes of rituals practiced by the ruling elite. Three of the columns from the "Building of the Columns" can be found in the modern site museum. Items typical of Classic Veracruz civilization, which predominated along the gulf coast plain, include finely carved ritual objects associated with the ball game: yokes (u-shaped stones, probably replicas of players' belts); *palmas* (objects that hung from the belt); and *hachas,* possibly used as scoring devices.

Adjacent to the museum, gift shop, and restaurant, the **Voladores de Papantla** perform a strange flying ritual for the benefit of visitors. Dressed in elaborate costumes—decorated with sequins, beads, and fringe, and with headdresses encrusted with mirrors and plastic flowers— five Totonac men climb to the top of a hundred-foot (30 m) pole. Inspired by the music of flute and drum performed by their leader, the other four men dive backwards, tied by a rope at the waist that is fastened at its other end to a frame at the top of the pole. With arms outstetched, each "flyer" completes precisely 13 revolutions before landing on the ground. The number of revolutions totals 52, the number of years in an important Mesoamerican religious cycle. The group usually performs at the request of a tour guide, or when enough people congregate. ■

Local men perform a ritualistic flying dance near Papantla's cathedral.

Xalapa

🔺 234 B3

Visitor information

✉ Enrique 14 (Palacio Municipal), north side of Parque Juárez

☎ 28/12-85-00, ext. 130

Xalapa & environs

XALAPA (ALSO SPELLED JALAPA) DESERVES ITS SOBRIQUET, the "Athens of Veracruz," for its culture if not its climate. At 4,680 feet (1,427 m) above sea level, Veracruz's hilly capital city has a bizarre climate of rain, sun, and fog. Once an important stagecoach stop between Mexico City and the port of Veracruz, modern Xalapa is one of the republic's most exciting capitals. This university town offers art cafés, theater, dance troupes, a fine symphony orchestra, and a world-class anthropology museum. Set on a series of verdant terraces, it is filled with pretty parks and lakes, and the surrounding countryside is famous for its coffee beans and exotic flowers.

Xalapa's heart is **Parque Juárez** *(Enrique between Revolución & Clavijero),* a well-groomed garden overlooking the city and the countryside beyond. On clear mornings, there is a breathtaking view of snowcapped Pico de Orizaba, a dormant volcano and Mexico's highest mountain at 18,850 feet/5,747 m (see p. 244). Within the urban park, **El Agora** houses an art gallery, theater, and cinema; it's also the place to find out about the city's many cultural performances, including state orchestra and ballet folkloric shows. Across Calle Revolución, the 18th-century **catedral** is remarkable for its unusual sloping nave.

For most, the highlight of a stay in Xalapa is a visit to the **Museo de Antropología** *(Av. Xalapa s/n, tel 28/15-09-20, $).* This modern masterpiece, imitating the city's terraced cityscape, consists of nine staggered platforms surrounded by gardens. The collection is dedicated to Veracruz's three most influential indigenous cultures: the Huastec, Totonac, and Olmec—the latter considered the mother of Mesoamerican culture.

Among the thousands of exhibits are massive stone heads carved by the Olmecs, a bone-filled burial ground, carved jaguars, were-jaguars (half-man, half-beast), murals, jade masks, and ritually deformed skulls. An enormous model re-creates the ruins of El Tajín (see pp. 236–37).

Five blocks southeast of Parque Juárez, large, circular **Parque los Berros** is named for the watercress that once grew here. This favorite gathering place of Xalapeños (people from Xalapa) for nearly two centuries is a quiet retreat from the bustling city's noisy traffic, and has served as backdrop for the novels of local author Sergio Galindo. Two blocks south, **La Zona de los Lagos** is Xalapa's most popular spot for a Sunday outing; paths meander around a series of lakes surrounded by a wooded canyon. Overlooking the lake at the western entrance to the park is the handsome, 19th-century **Centro Cultural de los Lagos** *(Paseo de los Lagos, tel 28/12-12-99),* showing changing exhibits of arts and crafts.

Venture outside the city to admire the lush countryside. (If you

visit between November and March, bring a thick sweater and a raincoat—the light but constant rain known as *chipi-chipi* can be chilling.) The **Jardín Botánico Francisco Javier Clavijero** *(Antigua Carretera a Coatepec Km 2.5, tel 28/42-18-27)* is a beautiful botanical garden displaying more than 1,500 varieties of flora found throughout Veracruz state. It features a small arboretum, a large pond with aquatic plants, and a winding, shady path through a riot of greenery.

About 7 miles (12 km) farther south is rural **Coatepec**, famous for its orchids and coffee beans. Visit the **Museo Invernadero María Cristina** *(Miguel Rebolledo 4, tel 28/16-03-79),* a greenhouse blooming with orchids. Not far from the city center, hike or take a horseback ride in the 32-acre (13 ha) **Agualegre** *(Río La Marina s/n),* a water park with multiple swimming pools and a water slide for the kids.

Eleven miles (19 km) southwest of Xalapa is the **Cascada de Texolo**, a 132-foot (40 m) waterfall that featured in the movie *Romancing the Stone* (1984). To get there, take a taxi to the small town of Xico and then walk about 2 miles (3 km). A set meal is served daily at the site restaurant overlooking the impressive gorge.

Six miles (10 km) east of Xalapa lies **Hacienda Lencero** *(Carretera a Veracruz Km 10, tel 28/12-85-00, closed Mon., $),* a 16th-century estate-turned-inn once owned by a Spanish conquistador named Lencero, and later by General Antonio López de Santa Anna (see p. 32). Now a museum of 19th-century furnishings, it has a pretty chapel and extensive gardens surrounded by oaks and other cool-climate trees, plus a small, spring-fed lake. ∎

Veracruz's oldest city, Xalapa, has an interesting mix of colonial and modern buildings.

Veracruz

Puerto de Veracruz is colorful—literally as well as figuratively.

VIBRANT AND VIVACIOUS VERACRUZ IS A BUSY PORT WITH a lively attitude, and visitors are either charmed or repelled by the city's extremes. The climate is hot and sultry, the beaches less than appealing, and the downtown a crowded, cacophonous urban jungle. But those who love Veracruz do so with a passion echoing that of sentimental Jarochos, as city-dwellers are called. They're entranced with the rhythm of marimbas, the scent of salt air, and the whirl of heel-stomping fandango dancers in the main plaza.

Veracruz

◭ 234 C3

Visitor information

✉ Zaragoza at Independencia, Palacio Municipal

☎ 2/841-8500, ext. 4110

Prisoners at the forbidding, historic **Fuerte de San Juan de Ulúa** (*Av. San Juan de Ulúa s/n, closed Mon., $*) had a less favorable view of the city. Constructed between 1535 and 1692, the gray-stone fortress served as a defense against pirates and the French and United States naval invasions of Mexico. But the fort is more famous as a brutal dungeon where disease, famine, and flooding awaited those who crossed the dreaded Puente de los Suspiros (Bridge of Sighs) into Ulúa's dank cells. For over three centuries religious and political prisoners were tortured here. In 1915, Venustiano Carranza claimed Ulúa as a presidential residence—surely a deterrent to anyone seeking that office. The complex is now a museum well worth touring with a knowledgeable guide.

Shipyards and commercial docks line the waterfront east of Ulúa to the pleasant **Paseo del Malecón,** a seaside walkway reminiscent of the *malecón* in Havana. Visiting Cubans feel very much at home in Veracruz, where the *danzón,* a highly disciplined dance that originated in Cuba, is embraced with extraordinary fervor. In the evenings, both professionals and amateurs dance at the city's main square, **Plaza de Armas** (*Avs. Independencia, Zamora, Lerdo, & Zaragoza*).

The crowded plaza, shaded by laurels, is a natural meeting place for city-dwellers. Musicians and dancers often perform on the plaza's center stage; visitors are encouraged to join in the staccato steps of the *jarocho fandango* and the stylized, waltzlike moves of the danzón. Fronting the plaza are the 17th-century **Palacio Municipal** and the 18th-century **Catedral de Nuestra Señora de la Asunción,** topped with a tiled dome. Travelers immune to the noise of the never-ending street scene may want to take a room at one of several colonial-style hotels facing the plaza.

Marimba musicians in crisp, white, pleated shirts play at **Los Portales,** a block-long colonial-era building at the south side of the plaza. The colonnade shades café tables where elderly gentlemen sip cups of *lechero,* a frothy mix of coffee and steamed milk. At the wildly popular **Café del Portal** (*Av. Independencia at Zamora, tel 2/931-2759*) customers clink their spoons against tall glasses to beckon waiters bearing kettles of hot coffee and milk. This coffee house was once home to the most famous café of all—the **Gran Café de la Parroquia.** After a family feud (conducted with typical jarocho ferocity), la Parroquia moved near the malecón. Visit both places and clink your spoon to order a lechero and *bambas* (local sweet rolls).

Several museums highlight the city's tumultuous history. The **Museo de la Ciudad** (*Zaragoza 397 at Esteban Morales, tel 2/931-8410, closed Mon.*) devotes considerable space to Carnaval, celebrated with wild abandon since the mid-19th century. **Baluarte de Santiago** (*Francisco de Canal at Farías, tel 2/931-1059, closed Mon., $*) is the last remaining section of a series of stone walls and forts that

once encircled the city. The **Casita Blanca Museo de Agustín Lara** (*Blvd. Ruíz Cortines s/n, Boca del Río, tel 2/937-0209, closed Mon., $*) honors one of Mexico's most famous musicians and the composer of sensual boleros, including "María Bonita" and "Veracruz," which are played over the museum's sound system.

The city's beaches are generally bleak, with brown sand and murky waters. The best are located south of town at **Playa Mocambo** and **Boca del Río.** Those interested in local sea life might want to avoid swimming altogether in favor of a visit to the **Acuario Veracruz** (*Blvd. Manuel Ávila Camacho at Av. Xicoténcatl, tel 2/932-7984, $*), containing a replica of a tropical forest. A series of galleries displays different marine domains. The doughnut-shaped Main Gallery houses gulf coast species, while in the Freshwater Gallery are specimens from Mexico's lakes, lagoons, rivers, and estuaries. In the Reef Exhibit, seahorses and sea stars, eels, and octopuses cruise outcrops of slow-growing coral. ∎

Young and old participate in Veracruz's spirited pre-Lenten Carnaval, the biggest and best in Mexico.

Drive: Arrival of the conquerors

Searching for a route to the East in the early 16th century, Spanish fleets from Cuba encountered instead a fascinating new land. Gifts of gold from friendly Indians were enough to incite future expeditions, and in 1519, 34-year-old Hernán Cortés led a third, historic voyage. Now wary, the Indians came prepared for battle, but the Spaniards' horses and superior weapons made up for their small numbers. Soon joining the Spanish ranks were a shipwrecked Spaniard and an Indian noblewoman who had been sold into slavery by her mother. Speaking Spanish, Mayan, and Náhuatl between them, this pair of interpreters was instrumental in the Spanish success.

Begin the drive in **Quiahuiztlán ❶**, 43 miles (70 km) north of Veracruz. Strategically placed atop Cerro de Bernal and terraced for defensive purposes, it was nonetheless invaded by the Toltecs and then the Aztecs. Quiahuiztlán's Totonac king was the first to make an alliance with Cortés. Today, much of the ruined city remains unexcavated. Most impressive for visitors are a great number of tombs, built in the style of miniature Aztec temples, which have yielded ceramic vessels decorated with geometric and animal motifs. On a clear day, you can see the cove where the Spanish ships anchored.

Head south along Hwy. 180 about 17 miles (27 km) to the ruins of **Cempoala ❷**, a prosperous city that amazed the Spaniards with its gleaming plaster palaces surrounded by gardens and orchards. Anxious to shrug off the yoke of their recently acquired Aztec overlords, this Totonac kingdom also allied with the Spaniards, providing porters and soldiers. The aid of Quiahuiztlán, Cempoala, and the 20-odd related "Hill Tribes" was crucial to Cortés's success in battle. The most important excavated structures include the **Templo Mayor,** constructed of river stones, and the **Templo de las Chimeneas**.

Continue south on Hwy. 180 to **La Antigua ❸**. Landing on the beach on Good Friday, Cortés named the place La Villa Rica de la Vera Cruz (Rich Villa of the True Cross) in honor of the Catholic holiday. Shelters were built and a contingency of soldiers maintained while others marched inland to Tenochtitlán. During the early years of the Conquest, supplies and booty were shipped in and out of the port, providing a vital link to Spain and the Caribbean islands.

When Veracruz was moved to its present location around 1600, this city became "la antigua Veracruz" ("the former Veracruz"), and later simply La Antigua. Visit **La Ermita del Rosario** (Av. Independencia s/n), Mexico's first Catholic chapel, and the **Casa de Cortés,** the ruined Spanish headquarters, draped in vines and sprouting fig trees.

Keep south on the coast highway to the port city of **Veracruz** (see pp. 240–41). After seeing the city, continue to **Boca del Río ❹**, another stop along the conquerors' route. Thirty years ago it was just a simple fishing village at the mouth of the Jamapa River; today it is a busy resort. On weekends, Veracruz families spend long lunches at the lively riverside restaurants, serenaded by local musicians. (The restaurants are open, although less lively, throughout the week.) During June's regional livestock exposition, Boca del Río hosts cock fights, horse races, and other equestrian events.

About 41 miles (66 km) south of Boca del Río is **Alvarado ❺**. Surrounded by water, it faces the sea and is bordered by the huge Laguna de Alvarado, which is fed by several important rivers. This attractive fishing town is known for its lively fandango music, and the celebrations held each Sunday during May for the Fiesta de la Cruz de Mayo. ∎

🅜 See also area map p. 234 C3–C2
▶ Quiahuiztlán
↔ 75 miles (120 km)
🕓 A full day (plus time in Veracruz)
▶ Alvarado

NOT TO BE MISSED
- La Antigua
- Veracruz, Boca del Río
- Alvarado

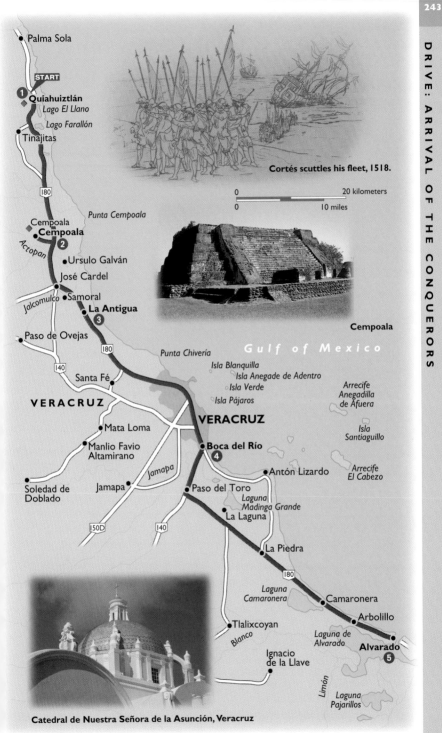

Palma Sola

START

1 Quiahuiztlán
Lago El Llano

Lago Farallón

Tinajitas

180

Punta Cempoala

Cempoala
Cempoala
2

Actopan

Ursulo Galván

José Cardel

Jalcomulco Samoral

La Antigua
3

Paso de Ovejas

180

Punta Chivería

140

Santa Fé

VERACRUZ

Mata Loma

Manlio Favio
Altamirano

Jamapa

Soledad de
Doblado

Jamapa

150D   140

Cortés scuttles his fleet, 1518.

0   20 kilometers
0   10 miles

Cempoala

Gulf of Mexico

Isla Blanquilla
Isla Anegade de Adentro
Isla Verde

Isla Pájaros

Arrecife
Anegadilla
de Afuera

Isla
Santiaguillo

VERACRUZ

Boca del Río
4

Antón Lizardo

Arrecife
El Cabezo

Paso del Toro

Laguna
Madinga Grande

La Laguna

La Piedra

180

Laguna
Camaronera

Camaronera

Arbolillo

Tlalixcoyan

Blanco

Laguna de
Alvarado

Alvarado
5

Ignacio
de la Llave

Limón

Laguna
Pajarillos

Catedral de Nuestra Señora de la Asunción, Veracruz

Córdoba & environs

BOTH CÓRDOBA AND ORIZABA WERE FOUNDED TO protect colonial trade caravans along the Mexico City–Puebla–Veracruz road. They are located in the foothills of the Sierra Madre Oriental, and so are much cooler than the steamy coast and warmer than Xalapa. Geared toward industry and commerce, these two prosperous cities are separated by the luxuriant Metlac River ravine, with miles of hiking trails. From here, intrepid (and experienced) trekkers can assault Mexico's highest peak, Pico de Orizaba, which looms above the luxuriant landscape to the northwest.

For hundreds of years Córdoba thrived on wealth from vast sugarcane plantations maintained by legions of black slaves. Today the city is relatively large and modern. Historic buildings surround pretty

Symmetrical, snowcapped Citlaltépetl, also called Pico de Orizaba, is the third highest peak in North America.

Parque 21 de Mayo, where the Iglesia de la Inmaculada Concepción has a priceless gold altarpiece.

The city's most popular attraction is the **Portal de Zevallos,** a lovely arcade where people meet over locally grown coffee or refreshing mint juleps. A few miles west, **Fortín de las Flores** is famous for its greenhouses and private gardens, best visited during the Fiestas de Mayo, when nursery

tours can be taken. In the 20th century, coffee replaced cane as the area's leading export, but the local method of preparing the beans (fermenting instead of roasting) is seriously polluting the area's rivers.

Though it has a brewery, and cement and textile factories, small, industrial **Orizaba** is nonetheless a pleasant city, retaining some colonial and neoclassic architecture. Facing the main square is the old town hall, an iron building in the art nouveau style purchased from Belgium and reassembled here in 1894. The "new" **Palacio Municipal** (Av. Colón Poniente 230), an attractive neo-Gothic building, has a large mural by José Clemente Orozco.

Housed in a 19th-century baroque oratory, the **Museo de Arte del Estado** (Av. Oriente 4 between Calle Sur 23 & Calle Sur 25, tel 2/724-3200, closed Mon., $) shows primarily 18th-century oil paintings. The new **Museo de Arqueología** (Calle Sur 9 at Calle Oriente 4, tel 2/725-4622, closed Sun.) has 400 pre-Hispanic artifacts and a historical archive.

Dominating all other peaks in Mexico is dormant **Pico de Orizaba,** at 18,855 feet (5,747 m). Its Náhuatl name, Citlaltépetl, means "star mountain." Amateurs can hike the trails along the lower slopes, but only experienced hikers should attempt the summit. ■

Tlacotalpan

ON THE BANKS OF THE WIDE RÍO PAPALOAPAN IS Tlacotalpan, named a World Heritage site for its beautiful location and well-maintained pre-Revolution buildings. When Mexico was a colony of Spain, this important port and shipyard received schooners and side-wheel steamships that imported European goods and exported tobacco, exotic woods, cotton, and sugarcane.

The town declined in importance with the completion of competing railroad lines and the advent of the Revolution. However, it maintains an air of seductiveness lost in more modern cities. Lining the streets are imposing mansions with ancient red-tile roofs, their Arabesque-style portals brightly painted in Kelly green and cobalt blue, coral, and sunshine yellow, with accents in contrasting colors. Open doorways offer a glimpse of cool patios and ornate front rooms, while the colonnades provide welcome shade.

Visit the **plaza principal,** with its lacy, Mudejar-style bandstand, and the parish church, the **Parroquia de San Cristóbal,** which has beautiful altarpieces of carved wood. The **Museo**

Jarocho Salvador Ferrando *(Manuel M. Alegre 6, closed Mon., $)* exhibits the paintings of the local artist, as well as furnishings and artifacts from the 19th century.

Tlacotalpan vigorously celebrates its patron saint, the Virgen de la Candelaria, from January 31 to February 9. The first three days see musical parades on horseback and El Encuentro de Jaraneros (Meeting of the Revelers), when young and old perform the physically challenging regional dance, the *jarana,* accompanied by harp and guitar. On February 1 there is bull-running and more dancing, while on the saint's feast day, February 2, her icon is serenaded by mariachis during a festive river parade of boats. ■

Tlacotalpan
🄰 234 C2
Visitor information
✉ Palacio Municipal, Plaza Zaragoza
☎ 288/42050

Los Tuxtlas & Catemaco

THE LOS TUXTLAS MOUNTAIN RANGE RISES ABRUPTLY from sea level to about 5,000 feet (1,500 m). One of seven broad geographic zones composing Veracruz state, it is an area of great natural beauty and contains a range of ecosystems, including the continent's northernmost tropical rain forest. However, expanding cattle ranches and farms have dramatically reduced the forests. Tobacco is an important crop, and San Andrés Tuxtla is a cigar-manufacturing center as well as the seat of regional government. Los Tuxtlas' quarries provided the Olmecs the enormous stones from which they carved their famous basalt heads. Today, the region's most visitor-oriented town is Catemaco, in a forested lakeshore setting.

Below: The Olmec Laguna de los Cerros site, at the eastern edge of the Tuxtla Mountains and now smothered in vegetation, allowed easy access to basalt.

Santiago Tuxtla, 140 miles (225 km) south of Veracruz, is a commercial hub for the area. While not particularly geared to tourists, it's a pleasant, traditional foothill town with some impressive and photogenic old mansions. In the main square, **Parque Juárez,** is the **Cabeza de Cobata,** the largest of the colossal Olmec heads found so far and the only one with its eyes closed. The **Museo Regional Tuxteco** *(Parque Juárez, tel 294/70196, $)* exhibits other Olmec artifacts, including some from the **Tres Zapotes** site, 8 miles (13 km) away. One of Mesoamerica's oldest cities, Tres Zapotes was where the first giant Olmec stone head was discovered, in a farmer's field in 1860. Lively equestrian events, some dating back to medieval Spain, are held during July festivities honoring the city's patron saint, the Apostle James.

San Andrés Tuxtla, 9 miles (14.5 km) to the east, took Santiago's place as regional capital in the 19th century. Today it is primarily known as a cigarmaking center with a colorful spring celebration, the Feria de la Primavera, held in May. About 7½ miles (12 km) outside town off the road to Catemaco is **Salto de Eypantla,** a wide, roaring waterfall. At the

parking lot, little kids offer to guard your car while their older brothers lead you down the sometimes slippery slope to a viewing area and a jumble of open-air kitchens. More remote, and not so easy to find, are **Poza de la Reina,** an idyllic natural pool, and **Cola del Caballo,** a waterfall resembling a horse's tail. Both are located in the hills above the northeast shore of **Laguna de Catemaco.**

About 7 miles (11 km) east of San Andrés, **Catemaco** hugs the west shore of Mexico's third-largest natural lake. The languid town has quite a reputation among Mexicans and foreign visitors for its large number of *brujos* (witches) and *curanderos* (healers). Touts whistle at prospective customers as they drive into town, hoping to direct incoming traffic to their patrons' place of business. People throughout Mexico—including the middle and upper classes—consult purveyors of the magic arts to cure ills from lumbago to broken hearts and *mal de ojo,* the evil eye. Catemaco's notoriety in a country full of such practitioners is due in part to its annual witches' convention, to which the public is not invited.

Perhaps the presence of so many shamans attracted the movie moguls to film *Medicine Man*

(1992) here, with Sean Connery. Some of the location work was done at **Proyecto Ecológico Nanciyaga** (*Tel 294/30199*), a privately owned, 100-acre (40 ha) nature preserve on the north shore. You can visit it as part of a short lake tour arranged in Catemaco, but it's much more fun to rent one of the minuscule wooden cabins and spend the night. *Temazcal* sweat-lodge ceremonies can be arranged in advance. For no extra charge, you can take a mud bath and, after baking in the sun, rinse off in a crystalline spring. Kayaks and rowboats are available for cruising the lake. Adjacent to Nanciyaga, **La Jungla** campground, as its name implies, is also set in the tropical jungle. These and other natural areas surrounding the lake hide a large number of resident and migratory bird species. ∎

Above: The sun sets on Lake Catemaco.

Villahermosa

WITH ITS WILTING TROPICAL HEAT DEFLECTED OFF A cityscape of modern cement, glass, and concrete structures, there's physically not much to recommend Villahermosa, Tabasco's capital. However, those who spend a day or two here usually develop an odd affection for this business-oriented city whose economy is based on petroleum and commerce. There are seafood restaurants, several excellent anthropology museums, and a pedestrian-only zone with a good mix of hotels, cafés, and small museums. And like their neighbors the Veracruzanos, the Tabascans are animated, flirtatious, and friendly.

Founded during Cortés's 1519 exploration, the regional capital was first located at Santa María de la Victoria, named for a minor victory that bore an important result. Defeating a contingency of Tabascan Indians in a skirmish, the Spaniards received a gift of 20 slave women, including La Malinche, who became their invaluable interpreter (see box on p. 207).

Situated on the wide, navigable Grijalva River, the city evolved as a distribution center for rubber, cacao, dyewood, coffee, and bananas. It was later relocated to its present, more easily defended, site and renamed Villahermosa.

Modern Villahermosa sprawls along both banks, and unlike many other Mexican cities, few of the most visited sites are clustered around the main square. Taxis are the easiest way to negotiate the city.

Just a block away from the river, **Parque Benito Juárez** *(between Calles Guerrero & Independencia at Martínez Escobar)*, the city's pleasant if unexciting main plaza, is surrounded by the white neoclassic **Palacio de Gobierno** and at the other extreme, the odd-looking **Templo de la Concepción,** a mid-20th-century church with Gothic-style elements.

Behind the state government building, north of the main plaza, lies a pedestrian-friendly zone called the **Zona Luz** or La Zona Remodelada. About eight blocks of urban blight were bulldozed in the 1970s to create a brick-paved zone of art galleries, shops, cafés, and ice-cream stands. Several free museums are worth visiting if you're in the area, including the **Casa Museo Carlos Pellicer** *(Saenz 203, tel 9/312-0157, closed Mon.),* with personal effects of the late Tabascan poet and cultural activist, and the **Museo de Cultura Popular** *(Zaragoza 810, tel 9/312-1117, closed Mon.).* More interesting is the **Museo de Historia de Tabasco** *(Juárez at 27 de Febrero, closed Mon.),* a museum of the state's history within the **Casa de Azulejos,** an early 20th-century building featuring a tiled facade and eclectic architectural elements.

Southwest of the historic center you will find **CICOM,** a large complex with a popular restaurant, museum, public library, and important theater. The latter, modern **Teatro Esperanza Iris,** was inaugurated in 1981 and named for a well-known Villahermosa singer and actress. The theater hosts the National Ballet as well as concerts, folkloric shows, and other performances.

The important **Museo Regional de Antropología Carlos Pellicer Cámara** *(Carlos Pellicer 511, tel 9/312-9521,*

Villahermosa
🅰 235 E2
Visitor information
✉ Paseo Tabasco 1504
☎ 9/316-3633

closed Mon., $$) is within the same complex. The anthropology museum gives great attention to the Olmec civilization, which thrived in the Middle Preclassic period (approximately 1200–400 B.C.). On the first floor are galleries for temporary exhibitions and a room for the monumental-size pieces of Maya and Olmec origin. The second floor contains exclusively Olmec and Maya displays, two important cultures that shared a common border around the Tabasco lowlands. Exhibits from these cultures include ceramic and carved stone pieces, such as small jade figurines of mythical were-jaguars—half-human, half-jaguar babies with cleft heads.

The museum tour is best started on the third floor, where maps show the distribution and evolution of civilization throughout Mesoamerica. There are Preclassic pieces from the central plateau and funerary masks, jewelry, and ceramics from Classic-era Teotihuacán. Totonac and Huastec cultures are represented with anthropomorphic and zoomorphic figurines, "smiling face" figures, and wheeled toys. Typical of Classic Veracruz civilization are the axes, yokes, and *palmas*, ritual artifacts inscribed with bas-reliefs that are related to the ball game.

On the west side of town, the **Tabasco 2000** complex has a cultural center, a major shopping mall, a convention center, and a planetarium. Also within this vast complex are the City Hall, or Palacio Municipal, and the

Basalt stone heads like this one are now considered monumental portrait-sculptures of Olmec leaders.

Serpentine and colored clay blocks form an unusual jaguar mask mosaic, now on display at La Venta Museum.

luxurious Camino Real Hotel. The tourist information center is located nearby.

At the south end of the serpentine **Laguna de las Ilusiones** is the al fresco **Parque Museo La Venta** *(Av. Ruíz Cortines at Laguna de las Ilusiones, tel 93/15-22-28, $$)*, where more than 30 large Olmec sculptures are set amid lush tropical foliage. Located on a 2-square-mile (5 sq km) island within a coastal swamp near the Tonalá River, **La Venta,** 43 miles (70 km) to the west, rose in importance with the decline of the San Lorenzo settlement, where more colossal heads have been found than anywhere else. San Lorenzo was violently overthrown, and its monuments defaced, around 1200 B.C., after which La Venta apparently reigned as the center of Olmec influence. Now thought to have been a residential as well as ceremonial city, La Venta produced a cone-shaped clay pyramid 110 feet (33 m) tall, the largest of its period in Mexico. Found at the site were a group of 16 small jade figures and an unusual mosaic of serpentine blocks and

ground and colored clays that formed a geometric jaguar mask—now on display at La Venta Museum. When petroleum was first exploited at La Venta, many of these priceless treasures were transferred to this specially designed museum in Villahermosa. (Other artifacts can be found in the Xalapa and Mexico City anthropology museums.)

Free Spanish-language tours are available, or take a self-guided tour (exhibits are labeled in English and Spanish). There's also a small zoo *(closed Mon.)*, with spider monkeys, reptiles, and some of the region's larger mammals. A winding path continues past Olmec "altars" (now thought to be thrones), stelae, and jaguar-boys. The huge basalt heads with characteristic full lips and wide noses, wearing what look like football helmets, are considered monumental portrait-sculptures of Olmec leaders.

Ten miles (16 km) east of Villahermosa at Dos Montes is **Yumká** *(Tel 93/56-01-15, $$)*, a 250-acre (100 ha) park. Two-hour guided tours cover the state's three primary ecological zones: savanna, tropical forest, and lagoons. Visitors can walk through a section of tropical rain forest and across a hanging bridge, and can take a short tram ride through the savanna, ending at a children's playground, restaurant, and gift shop. There is a small additional charge for a boat trip through the lagoon. ∎

Adventure tourism

For those seeking an active holiday, Mexico does not disappoint. There are plenty of adventure sports opportunities on offer in out-of-the-way places throughout the country.

Mountain climbers will be inspired by Mexico's "Ring of Fire" volcanic belt, which offers some of the most impressive peaks in the hemisphere, including Pico de Orizaba, the country's highest at 18,855 feet (5,747 m). Iztaccíhuatl provides a challenging yet non-technical climb along many routes, while La Malinche, at 14,636 feet (4,461 m), provides first-timers with a one-day, warm-up ascent.

In Querétaro, rock climbers can scale one of the Americas's largest monoliths, Peñón de Bernal, by different routes of various levels of difficulty. At 8,284 feet (2,525 m) above sea level, the summit perches atop a 157-foot-high (48 m) arête. More accessible are the boxy limestone canyons of Cañón de la Huasteca, between Monterrey and Saltillo in Cumbres de Monterrey National Park. Characterizing the arid, rugged terrain are such sheer cliffs as the 1,000-foot-high (300 m) Torre Diablos and 1,640-foot (500 m) Pico de Independencia. **Aventurismo Guías Profesionales** *(Blvd. Antonio Cárdenas 2431-2, Fracc. Miravalle, Saltillo, Coah., tel/fax 8/417-2469)* leads three-day treks in the area for experienced swimmers and rock climbers. Adventurers hike, swim, rappel, and make jumps into the Matacanes and Hidrofóbia Rivers, accessing little-visited caves and subterranean rivers on long, somewhat strenuous day hikes.

For exuberant, semitropical vegetation visit La Huasteca region, comprising parts of San Luis Potosí, Hidalgo, Tamaulipas, and Veracruz states. This is a land laced with waterfalls, which form grottos and crystalline turquoise pools edged in lacy ferns. Adventure outfitters such as **Eccosports** *(Cerrada de Félix Cuevas 224-B Col. Del Valle, 03100 México D.F., tel 5559-3560, e-mail info@eccosports.com.mx)* offer trips combining rock climbing and rappelling with spelunking and rafting.

With its abundant rainfall, lush vegetation, and more than 40 rivers, Veracruz is Mexico's premier rafting destination. One of the most thrilling excursions is a kayak or raft descent of Río Pescados, between Xalapa and Veracruz. Winding through deep canyons dressed in lush semitropical vegetation, the river encompasses 35 class III and IV rapids during a wet, three-hour whitewater trip. The Antigua River (part of the same system) offers class III and IV rapids during the wet season only, roughly July–November. And a few hours north of Xalapa, the Río Filobobos (Class II and III) provides access to the ruins of El Cuajilote and Vega de la Pena (A.D. 200–900), recently discovered within the tropical forest. **Veraventuras** *(Santos Degollado 81, Int. 8, 91000 Xalapa, Veracruz, tel 2/818-9579, fax 2/818-9680, www.dpc.com.mx/veraventuras)* leads trips throughout the state. ∎

More places to visit in the Central Gulf coast

COMALCALCO

The ruined city of Comalcalco lies about 35 miles (56 km) northwest of Villahermosa. Its name means "place of baked clay, or bricks." A lack of suitable local stone meant the builders had to make their temples and pyramids of oven-baked bricks of sand, crushed shells, and clay. Occupied since the first century A.D., this Chontal Maya city (the westernmost of any known Maya site) saw the height of its civilization in the Late Classic period, as did Palenque (see pp. 290–93) and Yaxchilán (see pp. 302–303). Almost two dozen of its nearly 300 structures have been restored, including a ball court, palaces, and temples.
🅰 235 E2 🅢 $

COSTA ESMERALDA

This 13-mile (21 km) stretch of coastline between **Nautla** and **Tecolutla** consists of flat, often lonely sand beaches, bathed by the Gulf's murky waters, lined with palms and interspersed with estuaries. Tecolutla is more geared to visitors, with moderately priced hotels and restaurants serving fresh sea bass, oysters, and *huachinango* (red snapper).
🅰 234 B3

IN SITU MUSEUMS

Although the best places in the region to see Olmec artifacts are the museums at Villahermosa and Xalapa, several *in situ* museums provide an excuse to see the places where some of these magnificent artifacts were found. Ten of the colossal heads excavated so far were found at **San Lorenzo,** which flourished between about 1200 and 900 B.C. There's little visible at the site itself, but the pole-and-thatch huts seen en route, past pasturelands and cane fields, are almost identical to those used by the Olmecs. It's a rough road and should be attempted only with high-clearance vehicles. Nearby, you can tour the museums at **El Azuzal,** where three fabulous figures excavated in 1987 are still on site, sheltered by a simple thatch hut. Two human figures, sitting cross-legged and wearing chest ornaments and strange flowing headdresses, sit one behind the other before a jaguar statue.
🅰 234 D2

PARQUE MARINO NACIONAL SISTEMA ARRECIFINAL VERACRUZANO

Nearly 130,000 acres (52,600 ha) of offshore reefs are protected in this national marine park. Just off the port of Veracruz and surrounding the Isla Verde and Isla de Sacrificios are a series of reefs where a number of shipwrecks make for interesting diving, to about 120 feet (36 m). The marine park extends south to Punta Antón Lizardo, where slightly deeper reefs can be explored. Several Veracruz operators offer dive cruises.
🅰 234 C3 **Dorado Divers** ✉ Blvd. Avila Camacho 865, Veracruz ☎ 2/931-4305 **Tridente** ✉ Blvd. Avila Camacho 165, Veracruz ☎ 2/931-7921

TEAPA

Surrounded by tropical vegetation and backed by blue mountains, Teapa is the municipal seat of the county of the same name, about 32 miles (52 km) from Villahermosa, Tabasco. In town is a picturesque square and several 18th-century Jesuit and Franciscan churches. You can take a drive out to the sulfurous **El Azufre Spa** (with restaurant and simple lodgings) or walk about a mile (1.5 km) to the **Grutas de Coconá.** These subterranean limestone caves have interesting rock formations (bring a flashlight).
🅰 235 E2

TUXPAN

Tuxpan, a port city 7 miles (11 km) in from the sea on a river of the same name, has sandy beaches and luxuriant river scenery. Archaeological finds show this site to have been continuously occupied between the Preclassic and Postclassic periods (see pp. 25–28). Locally excavated artifacts preserved in the **Museo de Arqueología** include pieces found at the ancient Huastec city of Tabuco, across the river. Known for their outgoing personalities, the townspeople celebrate "spring carnival" in May, and, in preparation for the feast day of the patron saint, the Virgin of the Assumption (August 15), a country fair.
🅰 234 B4 **Visitor information** ✉ Av. Juárez 20 ☎ 7/834-0177 ■

From Tehuantepec to Tuxtepec, Oaxaca's ethnic groups give the region a distinctly indigenous and idiosyncratic flavor. Many still rely on *curanderos* (healers) and the intervention of saints to cure ills of the flesh and of the spirit.

Oaxaca

Bright wooden devils for sale

Oaxaca

THE STATE OF OAXACA FORMS THE ELBOW OF A GEOGRAPHIC ARM extending south and east to embrace the indigenous heart of Mexico. This is a mountainous land caught in the clutch of the eastern and western Sierra Madre. Dozens of fractured ranges lead to isolated high valleys draped with mist, where tiny hamlets are accessible only on foot or by burro. Farmers goad ox teams up impossible angles to plow their fields, relying on summer storms to water their one or two yearly corn crops. To encourage rain they may pray to ancient gods as well as Catholic saints; despite a deep devotion to the Virgin, many Oaxaqueños observe pre-Christian rituals and believe in the existence of *nahuales,* wizards able to take on different shapes.

Oaxaca counts 570 municipalities, more than any other state. Physical isolation contributes to traditionalism; each village does things its own way. Trique women in mountain villages weave cherry-colored *huipiles* (loose, calf-length dresses) with bright bands of color; near the border with Guerrero, Amuzgo women create brocaded designs for their fine cotton huipiles. During *las velas,* traditional neighborhood parties in the Isthmus of Tehuantepec, Zapotec women proudly don fancy stiff lace headdresses and petticoats,

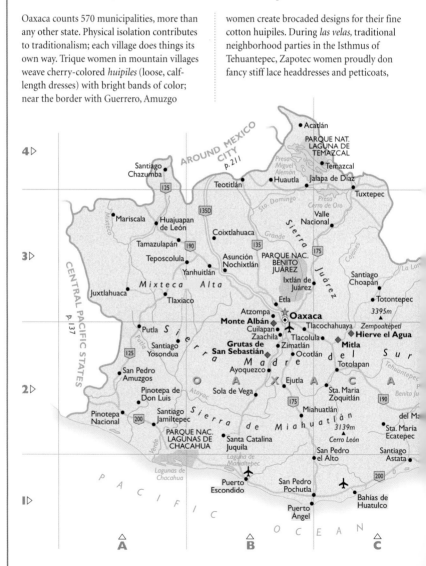

flowing skirts, and short, brightly embroidered velveteen huipiles.

Of the state's 15 major ethnic groups, the Zapotecs and Mixtecs are the largest, occupying both coastal and mountain regions. Their ancestors built the large ceremonial centers whose ruins dot the central valleys today. Grandest of all, Monte Albán was a contemporary of Teotihuacán, in Central Mexico, reaching its peak of civilization during the Classic period. Its stone-lined ball courts and well-proportioned pyramids overlook Oaxaca, the capital city, which stretches out in the valley below.

The city of Oaxaca is a delightful base for exploring the region. People crowd the *zócalo,* or main plaza, sipping coffee in the outdoor cafés that surround the forest-green bandstand, where lively marimba bands play. The historic center is peppered with carefully restored architectural treasures, including the sumptuous Santo Domingo church and former monastery, the latter home to Oaxaca's wonderful regional museum. Excursions to magnificent churches and monasteries surrounding the city reveal the extraordinary wealth and aesthetic sensibilities of the Dominican Order in the 16th and 17th centuries.

Oaxaca's 320-mile (515 km) Pacific coast is another important tourist destination. Hotels are popping up along the nine beautiful bays of Bahías de Huatulco, one of the smallest of Mexico's planned seaside resorts. Puerto Escondido, a world-famous surf spot, has natural beauty and casual restaurants and hotels. Outside the tourist destinations, fishing villages and inland towns lure adventurous travelers with annual religious festivals and unusual folk art, including masks, pottery, and textiles. ■

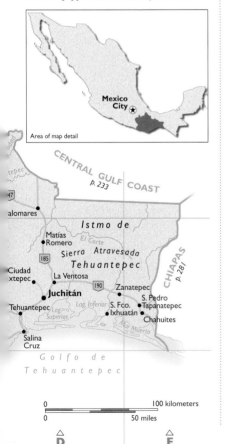

Area of map detail

CENTRAL GULF COAST
p. 233

Istmo de
Tehuantepec

Matías Romero
El Corte
Sierra Atravesada

Ciudad xtepec
La Ventosa
CHIAPAS
p. 281

Juchitán
Zanatepec
S. Pedro
Tehuantepec
S. Fco. Tapanatepec
Lag. Inferior
Superior
Ixhuatán
Chahuites
Mar Muerto

Salina Cruz

Golfo de Tehuantepec

alomares

tepec
47

0   100 kilometers
0   50 miles

D   E

Chilies are a staple food and a source of Vitamin C.

Oaxaca

IT'S SAID THAT IF YOU SAMPLE *CHAPULINES*, A HIGHLY seasoned local delicacy, you're sure to return one day to Oaxaca. But more of a draw (and less of an acquired taste) than its famous fried grasshoppers is the colonial heart and multiethnic soul of the capital city itself. Baroque churches of locally mined stone glow in the semitropical sunshine; at an elevation of 5,085 feet (1,550 m), Oaxaca enjoys warm weather most of the year, rarely getting too hot or cold. On wrought-iron benches in the main square and adjacent Alameda, people chat, read newspapers, and enjoy the sunshine filtering through the trees, while the state orchestra performs in the shadow of the 16th-century cathedral on lazy Sunday afternoons.

Oaxaca

 254 B3

Visitor information

✉ Independencia 607 at García Vigil

☎ 9/516-4828

Only the state of Michoacán gives Oaxaca serious competition in the variety and quality of its folk art. Towns and villages surrounding the capital produce an astonishing variety of items. The Zapotec towns of Teotitlán del Valle and less famous Santa Ana del Valle have been making hand-loomed wool *tapetes* (rugs) for centuries. Other crafts—including smoky black pottery from San Bartolo Coyotepec and carved wood figures from Arrazola—are more recent innovations. These and many more fine handicrafts are sold in upscale shops on and around Calle Alcalá, a pedestrian-only street north of the *zócalo*. If you enjoy bartering and have the time, check the fixed prices in the shops first, and then hit **Abastos** or **Benito Juárez markets,** where handicrafts are sold along with everything from vice grips to love potions that double as floor polish. Better yet, head into the surrounding countryside, to the towns where the items are produced, for some serious bargains and a glimpse of rural life.

While folk art is an important element of Oaxacan culture, the city also has an impressive fine arts and cultural scene. Upcoming and established artists treat regional themes and imagery in contemporary compositions; quite a few excellent galleries are housed in one- and two-story buildings of green, gold, or rose quarrystone. The city hosts an annual international film festival, and free art films are shown weekend nights at **Cinema El Pochote** *(Av. García Vigil 817, tel 9/514-1194)*.

Excellent museums also demonstrate the city's commitment to arts and culture. The **Museo de Arte Prehispánico Rufino Tamayo** *(Av. Morelos 503, tel 9/516-4750, closed Tues., $)* displays the private collection of Oaxacan abstract painter, muralist, and sculptor Rufino Tamayo (1899–1991), donated to the state in 1975. About 2,000 pieces representative of pre-Cortesian Mexico are displayed in a restored colonial home in the heart of downtown. The **Museo de Arte Contemporáneo de Oaxaca,** or **MACO** *(Alcalá 202, tel 9/514-2818, closed Tues., $)*, is housed in an even more imposing, two-story colonial residence. On the second floor, the permanent collection includes the work of the late Oaxacan naive painter Rodolfo Morales, and of graphic artist Francisco Toledo. Temporary exhibits on the first and second levels show a variety of media.

If the city's 27 historic churches are considered works of art, one of the most cherished is the **Basílica de Nuestra Señora de la Soledad** *(Av. Independencia 107 at Galeana, tel 9/516-7566)*, built in the late 17th century to honor Oaxaca's patron saint, Our Lady of Solitude. Oaxacans petition the Virgin for favors, making special pilgrimages culminating on

December 18, her feast day. Visit the museum to see gifts left by devotees—from plastic flowers and severed braids to naive ex-votos (pictorial expressions of thanks) painted on wood or tin. The basilica is on the site of a garrison maintained by the Aztecs, who controlled the region in the 15th century.

During this period of Aztec domination, artisans from Tenochtitlán were installed in several neighborhoods, or barrios, each dedicated to a particular craft. Just north of downtown, Xochimilco's centuries-old weaving traditions are still practiced today. Listen for the clacking of enormous looms on Calle Boloños Cacho, east of the pretty parish church, to find weaving workshops where you can purchase custom-made cloth. East of **Parque El Llano** (a city park officially named Parque Juárez), the barrio of Jalatlaco was once a leather-working town. Although few today practice the craft, the quiet cobblestone streets and brightly painted homes and neighborhood restaurants provide a window into Oaxaca's past. ■

Oaxaca's tranquility and year-round mild climate make it a pleasure to visit.

A walk around historic Oaxaca

Oaxaca has a multitude of interesting and historic sites radiating from its shady main plaza, a tranquil, traffic-free place marking the end of this walking tour. On pedestrian-only Calle Alcalá, shops and restaurants occupy pastel-tinted, two-story buildings erected soon after the city was founded by the Spanish in the 16th century.

The shady and traffic-free zócalo is a peaceful place to sit or stroll.

Begin your walk at the **Arcos de Xochimilco ❶,** south of Calzada Héroes de Chapultepec on García Vigil. The arches of this 18th-century stone aqueduct shrink as the 985-foot (300 m) structure stretches south toward downtown. Individual arches now provide access to modest apartment dwellings. Walk several blocks south along García Vigil to the **Iglesia del Carmen Alto ❷,** where the aqueduct's waters were originally stored. The church hosts a lively fair for the feast day of the Virgin of Carmen (July 16), which initiates the Guelaguetza, an annual festival of dance and music with its roots in pre-Hispanic tradition. Just beyond and across the street from the Church of Carmen Alto is the **Museo Casa de Benito Juárez ❸** (*García Vigil 609, tel 9/516-1860, closed Mon., $*), the historic house where Oaxaca's revered statesman lived as a youth in the early 19th century.

Turn left and cross Plazuela del Carmen to Oaxaca's pedestrian-friendly Calle Alcalá and the **Templo y Ex-Convento de Santo Domingo ❹,** home to the **Museo Regional de Oaxaca** (*Alcalá at Constitución, tel 9/516-2991, closed Mon., $*). Continue east along Plazuela A. Gurrión and Calle Constitución to Calle Reforma. Half a block north on Reforma, stop in at the **Museo de Filatelia de Oaxaca** (*Reforma 505, tel 9/516-8028, closed Mon.*), an 18th-century building handsomely restored in 1998. The café on the open-air back patio of this stamp museum serves light meals.

Return south along Calle Reforma to the **Ex-Convento de Santa Catalina** (now the Hotel Camino Real), home to the nuns of the Immaculate Conception until the Reform Laws of 1859. Keep south along Reforma, turning right on Morelos and left onto 5 de Mayo. One block south, the *belle époque* **Teatro Macedonio Alcalá** is a venue for city theater and dance.

Keep south along 5 de Mayo and turn right on Colón. Two blocks west (Colón becomes Las Casas), enter the **Mercado Benito Juárez ❺,** established in 1892. Here you will find locally made blocks of chocolate (for delicious, cinnamon-laced hot cocoa), string cheese (*queso oaxaqueños*), and piles of fresh vegetables and exotic fruits as well as some clothing and souvenirs. Continue to the **Iglesia San Juan de Díos ❻** (*Aldama at 20 de Noviembre*). Although architecturally unimpressive, Oaxaca's first church is dear to its people. The original adobe-and-thatch temple was christened in 1526; the present structure replaced it in the mid-17th century.

A few steps to the east, the **Mercado 20 de Noviembre** was originally a hospital for the adjoining convent. Today it's jammed with informal eateries serving chicken soup, beef stew, and other simple fare. Women sell sweet and savory breads from bins and large wicker baskets at the front of the market.

Exit the market and walk north along Miguel Cabrera to the attractive main plaza, the *zócalo* (officially called Plaza de la Independencia). At the back of the neoclassic **Palacio de Gobierno ❼,** on the south side of the square, a colorful, two-story mural

Outshone by its brightly painted neighbor, a building's facade receives attention.

summarizes Oaxaca history, with the spotlight on native son Benito Juárez. Cross the square to the 16th-century **Catedral** ❽, on the adjoining plaza, La Alameda. Dedicated to the Assumption of the Virgin Mary, the cathedral has been damaged three times by earthquakes, the most significant in 1714. Its 17th-century pipe organ was completely refurbished in 1991.

The **zócalo** is without a doubt the finest place in the city to rest and refresh yourself. Choose a bench under the Indian laurel trees, or order a meal or a drink at one of the many cafés under the plaza's shady porticos. ■

► Arcos de Xochimilco
⟷ 1.6 miles (2.5 km)
⏱ 4 to 5 hours
► Zócalo

NOT TO BE MISSED

- Templo y Ex-Convento de Santo Domingo
- Museo Regional de Oaxaca
- Mercado Benito Juárez
- Catedral
- Zócalo

Oaxaca's Dominican monasteries

THE SPIRITUAL CONQUEST OF NEW SPAIN WAS LAUNCHED after the Spanish army under Hernán Cortés literally flattened Tenochtitlán (the site of present-day Mexico City). Franciscan friars were the first ecclesiastics to arrive, establishing themselves throughout populous Central Mexico. A few years later, the Dominicans headed south of Mexico City.

Oaxaca
🅜 254 B3
Visitor information
✉ Independencia 607 at García Vigil
☎ 9/516-4828

Frequently criticized for the exorbitant sums spent on their temples, the zealous Dominicans imported skilled designers from Europe. Working with equally talented local craftsmen, priest-architects blended renaissance motifs with Gothic and Mudejar elements of the Spanish plateresque school. Even the thick buttressed walls and stocky towers—intended to help withstand the area's earthquakes—don't detract from the rich embellishment and the high quality of locally quarried stone. The Dominican preoccupation with aesthetics is evident in the unique architectural design, elaborate altarpieces, and fine paintings in a chain of

monasteries stretching from Puebla to Guatemala, many of them in Oaxaca state.

Churches were vandalized after the Reform Laws of 1859 expelled the religious orders. The **Iglesia y Ex-Convento de Santo Domingo,** one of the first and most intoxicating of Oaxaca's church-monasteries, suffered considerable damage during a stint as an army barracks. Today it has been scrupulously refurbished at great expense. The church's narrow *retablo* facade, elaborately carved in four tiers and flanked by two majestic bell towers, is in transitional Renaissance style, with traces of baroque. Inside, bright white

stucco honeycombed in gold and polychrome relief extends to vaults, domes, and niches. In fact, every inch of the dazzling interior is covered in high-spirited, Puebla-style decoration. The genealogy of the order's founder, Santo Domingo de Guzmán (ca 1170–1221), spreads seductively if naively in a grapevine motif across the underchoir at the temple's entrance. On the right side of the church, the abundance of scrolls, angels, and arabesques decorating the **Capilla del Rosario** (Rosary Chapel) nearly drowns the saints and apostles portrayed.

The two-story, white limestone cloister of the adjoining monastery is home to the **Museo Regional de Oaxaca** *(Alcalá at Constitución, tel 9/516-2991, closed Mon., $)*. The first floor houses temporary exhibits, an excellent gift

At Oaxaca's Santo Domingo de Guzmán church, bright white stucco, honeycombed in gold and polychrome relief, extends to vaults, domes, and niches.

20th-century artists & *el tequio*

A Zapotec word translated as "the burden," *el tequio* refers to a person's obligation to contribute to his community, a custom practiced since the days of Monte Albán. Francisco Toledo, a highly successful contemporary painter and graphic artist from Juchitán, in the Isthmus of Tehuantepec, takes this obligation seriously. He has funded or contributed his seemingly limitless energy toward many cultural endeavors in Oaxaca, among them the creation of the Instituto de Artes Gráficos, a wonderful graphics art library and museum, a Braille library, Mexico's first stamp museum, and a papermaking workshop in Vistahermosa, Etla (north of Oaxaca). Fellow artist Rudolfo Morales, who died in 2001, was equally active. Between the two, they formed "los Amigos de Monte Albán," a nonprofit organization working to preserve Monte Albán, and dedicated a good deal of time and money toward the restoration of Oaxaca's priceless Dominican monasteries. ■

shop, and the **Biblioteca Francisco de Burgos,** a library with more than 20,000 historical tomes. Walk up the double baroque staircase to the second floor, its doorways and ceiling richly decorated in the lavish Puebla style. Ten former monastic cells now exhibit artifacts representative of regional culture from prehistoric to post-Revolutionary times; an additional 14 galleries are organized by theme,

The cloister at the Ex-Convento de Santo Domingo now houses the Museo Regional de Oaxaca.

cistern

wash house

kitchen garden

novices' latrine

novitiate

main stairway

The narrow, four-tiered facade of Oaxaca's Santo Domingo is in transitional Renaissance style, with traces of baroque.

chapter house

including ceramics, music, and medicine. Gallery 3 houses the invaluable treasures excavated from the tombs at the Zapotec site of Monte Albán (see pp. 264–65), including gold, silver, shell, and jade jewelry. Free tours of the **botanical gardens** are usually given in the early afternoon (arrange English-language tours in advance).

Other important monasteries in the Valley of Oaxaca include **Cuilapan,** which is on the road to **Zaachila** (see p. 271);

Tlacochahuaya, with an outstanding 1620 pipe organ (see p. 266); and the Iglesia del Santo Cristo at **Tlacolula de Matamoros** (see p. 268). In the Mixteca Alta region north of Oaxaca, **Yanhuitlán** was recently restored using many original construction techniques. Of note are its elegant plateresque "door within a door" on the north portal and the stunning main altarpiece containing important 16th-century paintings. Farther on are **Coixtlahuaca,** once the site of a temple to the god Quetzalcóatl; and **Teposcolula,** whose open chapel is said to be the loveliest in Oaxaca. ■

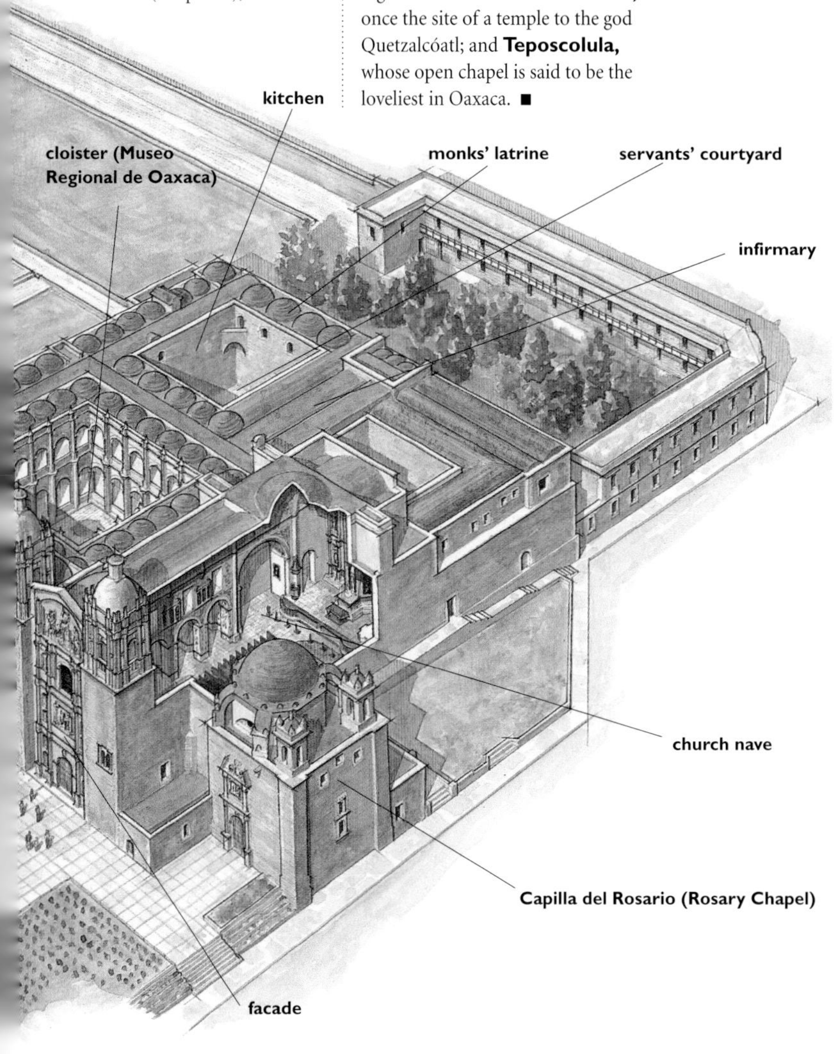

kitchen

cloister (Museo Regional de Oaxaca)

monks' latrine

servants' courtyard

infirmary

church nave

Capilla del Rosario (Rosary Chapel)

facade

Monte Albán

A MILLENNIUM BEFORE THE ARRIVAL OF THE SPANIARDS IN 1521, the Zapotec city now known as Monte Albán was flourishing. Sweet-smelling copal incense wafted from gracefully designed, precisely aligned temples. Architects contrived cisterns to collect rainwater and built a specialized irrigation system. Trade flourished; busy open-air markets sold local goods and imported jade beads, stone implements, metal, minerals, and pigments. Archaeological evidence suggests that trade routes extended as far away as Teotihuacán, north of present-day Mexico City.

Animals were domesticated, deer and other beasts and birds were hunted in the surrounding valleys, and hillsides were terraced and planted with crops and fruit trees. Society was stratified, with warlords, warriors, priests, and bureaucrats among the upper class. Artisans and craftspeople lived and worked in separate districts, according to their craft. There was no central ruler; control was probably shared among families with a common ancestor. As in colonial Oaxaca centuries later, the wealthiest and most influential families lived closest to the central plazas.

Although the Zapotecs were the principal architects of this remarkable city, the original inhabitants may have been Mixe-Zoques from the isthmus, or even relatives of the Olmecs of Veracruz. The Zapotecs (or one of their predecessors) first inhabited the site about 500 B.C., and for reasons unknown abandoned it after around 12 centuries of continuous settlement.

A hundred or more years later, the Mixtecs made the site into an elaborate cemetery. The dead were buried in rectangular and cross-shaped tombs decorated with glyphs, murals, or sculptures, and accompanied by offerings made of ceramic, shell, or precious metals. More than 220 burial sites have been discovered and explored. The

most fabulous, **Tumba 7,** yielded more than 500 pieces of gold, amber, and turquoise jewelry, as well as other exquisite articles of jade, silver, crystal, and finely sculpted bone. Most of the artifacts are on display at the Museo Regional de Oaxaca (see p. 258).

Today, several of these tombs are open to visitors, including **Tumba 104,** located on the northwest perimeter of the site. Note the god of corn, Pitao Cozobi, embedded at the top of the facade. Inside are multicolored frescoes showing important people in ceremonial dress. The carved slab in the antechamber originally sealed the tomb.

Aside from the tombs at the north end of the artificial mesa, the place to explore is the **Gran Plaza,** once the heart of the city. At either extreme are the **Platforma Norte** and the **Platforma Sur,** each with stone steps flanked by wide balustrades. Buildings were generally made of irregularly shaped stones cemented with mud, and then covered with facing stones and layers of stucco; newer buildings were superimposed on older ones. **Estructura I,** in the center of the Great Plaza, is a typical Zapotec construction. Single or double scapulary panels at the top of buildings (the latter evident on **Edificio H**) symbolized the sky, or the jaguar's jaw.

Monte Albán

🔺 254 B2

✉ 6 miles (10 km) southwest of Oaxaca

☎ 9/516-1215

💲 $

The earliest inhabitants built structures of monolithic block walls, some plain, others with elaborate bas-relief sculptures. One of the best-known examples of the latter is the **Galería de los Danzantes,** on the west side of the plaza. It is engraved with large nude male figures depicting slain enemies and the rulers of defeated towns. Their names and those of their towns are inscribed on or alongside their mutilated corpses in Zapotec hieroglyphics. **Estructuras K, L,** and **IV Sur** were among the first constructed. In **Estructura H,** the tomb of five young men yielded one of the greatest Zapotec works of art—a jade mask of the bat god. The skeletons were also adorned with breastplates, necklaces, earflares, pearls, and

shells, now in the Museo Nacional de Antropología (see pp. 198–201).

At the plaza's northeast corner, the *juego de pelota,* or ball court, is representative of those in the region. This I-shaped court is flanked on both sides by sloping, stepped walls, and, unlike those in Central Mexico and the Yucatán, shows no evidence of ball hoops.

There's a well-stocked gift shop and bookstore, and a restaurant with an excellent view of the valley. Buses depart on the half-hour from the **Hotel Ribera del Angel** *(Calle Mina 518, five blocks southwest of the zócalo, tel 9/516-6666, $$).* There's a surcharge for staying beyond three hours, but this small amount is worthwhile for those who want to examine the site and museum thoroughly. ■

Monte Albán, perched on a hill overlooking three valleys, was among the most advanced cities of its time.

Mitla drive

East of Oaxaca along Hwy. 190 lie four archaeological sites, several 17th-century Dominican monasteries, the world's fattest tree, and Zapotec towns backed by the sun-baked Oaxaca hills. Smoky blue mountains form a persistent backdrop, seemingly rising from the stubby cornfields along either side of the highway.

About 8 miles (13 km) southeast of Oaxaca, the pride of tiny **Santa María el Tule ①** is its 2,000-year-old *ahuehuete*, or Montezuma cypress tree. Wider than it is tall, the gnarled tree towers above the 17th-century church at its side. Local imagination has found figures in the bark and limbs of the 138-foot-wide (42 m) tree as incongruous as the derrière of Mexican actress and violinist Olga Breesky, the face of Jesus, and a turkey. Behind the church, open-air kitchens serve up local specialties.

Four miles (6.5 km) farther along the highway, turn right toward **Tlacochahuaya ②**, a small Zapotec village with a picturesque plaza and adobe houses surrounded by stone hills and cornfields. Completed in the early 17th century, the town's Dominican church and monastery perch on the base of the pre-Hispanic temple mound that provided building materials. Covering the interior walls and vaulted ceiling are stylized vignettes of cherubs and flowers rendered in red, gold, blue, and green by indigenous artists. Don't miss the pipe organ, built in 1620, in the choir loft.

Return to the highway and after about a mile (1.5 km), turn right onto a dirt road to **Dainzú** *(Tel 9/516-0123, $)*. Evidence suggests that this terraced Zapotec city was a contemporary of Monte Albán, and was inhabited some time after 300 B.C. Look for bas-relief carvings of ball players with jaguar faces along the lower section of **Edificio A,** the remains of a step-platform structure.

Another mile (1.5 km) farther along the highway is the turnoff to prosperous **Teotitlán del Valle ③,** famous for its hand-loomed Zapotec rugs. Purists prefer undyed wool or natural dyes such as the increasingly rare cochineal, a cactus parasite, but most rugs these days are made of wool or synthetic fibers tinted with commercially produced dyes. Some people make a pilgrimage to Teotitlán simply to lunch at **Tlamanalli** *(Av. Juárez 39, tel 9/524-4006, closed Mon. & dinner, $$$),* a Zapotec restaurant of some renown.

☒ See also area map p. 254
   B3–C2
► Oaxaca
↔ 35 miles (56 km)
⊕ All day
► Mitla

NOT TO BE MISSED
- Santa María el Tule
- Tlacochahuaya
- Tlacolula
- Mitla

START

Oaxaca

Monte
Albán

Cuilapan
de Guerrero

San Agustín
de la Juntas

Atoyac

San Bar
Coyote

131

Mural detail from Tlacochahuaya's church

Above: The 2,000-year-old *ahuehuete* tree at Santa María el Tule

Benito Juárez

0   8 kilometers
0   4 miles

Tutla

1 Santa María
el Tule

Teotitlán
del Valle
3

190

Tlacochahuaya

Abasolo

2

Dainzú

Geometric design, Mitla

OAXACA

Santa Ana
del Valle

Villa Díaz Ordaz

Guelávia
Lambityeco

Tlacolula de Matamoros
4 5

Teitipac

Yagul

Villa de
Mitla

6 7
Mitla

190

Matatlán

View over Yagul

Continue along Hwy. 190 about 5 miles (8 km) to the ruins of **Lambityeco** *(Closed Mon.)*, an important salt-mining center abandoned about A.D. 750 in favor of Yagul, to the southeast. The interior panels of the altar in the **Casa del Coqui** (Estructura 195) are decorated with figures and symbols of the city's leading lords and ladies. Note the two identical masked figures of Cocijo, god of rain, thunder, and lightning on **Estructura 190;** each holds a water vessel in the right hand and a lightning bolt in the left.

Back on the highway, continue just a mile (1.5 km) to **Tlacolula de Matamoros ❹,** where women in distinctive flowered headscarves and plaid skirts preside over the busy Sunday market. A smaller market is held throughout the week. Within the **Iglesia del Santo Cristo,** the town's 17th-century

A young rug seller

Dominican church is the **Capilla del Rosario ❺,** or Rosary Chapel, a stunning example of gilded plasterwork and polychrome relief. Note the fine detail on the wrought iron of the choir grille and pulpit.

Continue southeast along the highway a few miles to **Yagul** *(Tel 9/516-4828, closed Mon., $)*, a fortified Zapotec city built on a hilltop for defense. The discovery of more than 30 tombs confirms that this was a residential area; inhabitants were customarily buried underneath the doorway of their homes. The **Palacio de los Seis Patios** may have served as a principal residence.

After another 3 miles (5 km), a short detour off Hwy. 190 takes you to the impressive ruins of **Mitla ❻** *(Tel 9/568-0316),* whose name comes from the Náhuatl word *mictlán,* meaning "land of the dead." The Zapotecs shifted their base of operations to this ceremonial city—and to other centers such as Zaachila, Cuilapan, and Lambityeco—about the time Monte Albán was abandoned (A.D. 700–800). They called the city Lyobaa, meaning "place of rest" or "burial place," and built tombs both above and below ground. As at Monte Albán, Mitla was taken over by the Mixtecs after it was abandoned by the Zapotecs around the 11th century. It was still in use when the Spanish arrived.

The site consists of five groups of buildings once guarded by a fortress on a nearby hill. Of the two that have been excavated, the more exceptional is the **Grupo de las Columnas,** where long masonry halls surround a central plaza. In the first complex, the **Templo de las Columnas** is named for the six enormous pillars that originally supported wooden beams and a large, flat roof. From this structure, enter the **Patio de las Grecas ❼,** named for the intricate step and fret stone mosaics that adorn its walls. Mitla's almost uniformly geometric decoration reflects the Mixtec influence. As in the Puuc region of the Yucatán, the area's fine limestone made possible such artistic achievement. Unlike those found throughout Mesoamerica at the time, the Mixtec designs lack beasts, gods, and human figures. The narrow rooms surrounding the patio were most likely tombs, and the site itself home to the High Priest of the Zapotec nation and his retinue as well as visiting royalty and soldiers.

The **Grupo de la Iglesia** is what remains of a similar structure disassembled to build the 16th-century **Iglesia de San Pablo Apostol,** named for Mitla's patron saint, the Apostle Paul. Some evidence of this shared heritage can be seen on the stones forming the church's exterior walls. Behind the church, several small structures with decorated lintels and patios are all that remain of the original building. English-language signs explain the Zapotec and Mixtec artifacts displayed at the **Museo de Mitla de Arte Zapoteca** *(Av. Juárez 2, tel 9/568-0316, $).* ∎

Hierve el Agua

ALTHOUGH HIERVE EL AGUA'S NAME MEANS "THE WATER boils," the site's two jade-green pools and the spring that feeds them are cool; the name refers to the way the mineral spring bubbles from the rock. Once diverted by local Indians for crop irrigation, the spring has more recently been channeled to form two inviting swimming pools. The overflow of highly mineralized spring water dripping over the adjacent cliffs produces a series of petrified waterfalls and more than one postcard-perfect picture.

On weekends, extended families stake out prime spots under the few shade trees close to the pools—especially in hot weather. Weekdays, particularly during the cooler months, it's not unusual to find yourself alone in the dry, scrubby landscape, where a looping trail leads into the canyon for excellent views of the site's unique mineral formations. At the few humble farms nearby, teams of cream-colored oxen plow cornfields surrounded by agave plants from which homemade mescal is made.

The site has a parking lot, restrooms, changing facilities, and tiny, palm-thatched picnic tables. Midway between the parking lot and the pools, local women sell *tlayudas* (large, slightly leathery tortillas with meat or beans), bowls of beans, and other simple fare.

This is a convivial scene, but to spend the night after the crowds have headed home is a wonderful experience. A half-dozen clean cabins—a few with equipped kitchens, the others with private bathrooms—provide comfortable if spartan accommodations (reserve in advance through the Oaxaca tourist office). There are no stores, so bring provisions and make an evening meal to enjoy under the stars. In the morning, you'll usually have the pools to yourself before the first bus arrives at around 10:30. ■

The refreshing mineral springs at Hierve el Agua are especially popular on weekends during hot weather.

Hierve el Agua

🅰 254 C2

✉ 50 miles (80 km) from Oaxaca off Hwy. 190, 3 miles (5 km) past San Lorenzo Albarradas

☎ 01-956/20922 (cell phone)

Towns around Oaxaca

SURROUNDING THE CAPITAL, TOWNS LARGE AND SMALL
produce the folk art that fills the shops in downtown Oaxaca. Some
are prosperous, such as Teotitlán del Valle (see p. 266), whose internationally known weavers have built imposing two-story homes.
Others remain poor, with packed dirt streets and fields of corn and
alfalfa surrounded by rolling, fawn-colored hills. Zapotec is still spoken in many homes where traditional arts—especially weaving,
ceramics, and carving—continue to be practiced.

Oaxaca
254 B3
**Visitor
information**
✉ Independencia 607
   at García Vigil
☎ 9/516-4828

Although the Spanish conquerors
introduced new methods of
production, the local people have
maintained many of their ancestors'
forms and techniques. The Spaniards
also restricted metalsmiths to working with nonprecious metals, and
craftsmen today produce beautiful
work in stamped and molded tin.
Symbols such as crosses and saints
are juxtaposed with scorpions,
birds, frogs, and other traditional
icons that emerge from primitive
backstrap looms.

   Due west of Oaxaca, dusty
Atzompa squats in the shadow of
Monte Albán. It is famous for its
green-glazed tableware and unique,

unglazed *muñecas bordadas*
(embroidered dolls) designed by
the late Teodora Blanca: 2–3-foot
(0.75–1 m) female figures studded
with elephant heads, lizards, and
other zoomorphic figures. Artisans
along the town's streets will show
you their wares if available, but
most of the finest work is found at
Oaxaca's Abastos market or the
FONART store (see Shopping,
p. 384). The scene is quite different
in **Arrazola,** where family workshops double as showrooms for
colorful *alebrijes,* carved and
painted wooden creatures ranging
from miniatures to monsters over
several feet long.

San Martín Tilcajete, like Arrazola, produces fantastic painted wood figures. Some artisans specialize in devils, others in barroom drunks; the majority make fanciful animals as well. **La Unión Tejalapan** produces wonderfully naive wooden statuettes, including endearing crèches and funky farm animals. Rarely visited by tourists, the town is spread over a series of dry rolling hills, and most artisans sell to shops in Oaxaca.

South of Oaxaca along Highway 175 are several historic towns, including **San Bartolo Coyotepec** (7½ miles/12 km from Oaxaca), famous for its black pottery. Overnight firing of the unglazed pottery in pit kilns produces lustrous patinas from gunmetal gray to sooty black. Shop at the town's co-op, across from the pretty parish church, or wander through town and check the individual artisans' showrooms. Another 7½ miles (12 km) south brings you to **Santo Tomás Jalietza,** where the town's open-air cooperative sells belts, table runners, and other goods made on traditional backstrap looms. The same distance again brings you to **Ocotlán,** known for its fine machetes and knives, the latter sometimes carved with picaresque sayings. The restored Dominican monastery and church on the town plaza are well worth exploring.

Wooden carts driven by oxen or horses trundle along the road leading into **Zaachila,** surrounded by the rolling hills of the Zimatlán valley. Early Thursday mornings, locals arrive at the **animal market** on the outskirts of town to barter for shrieking piglets, big-eyed baby burros, and other farm animals. In the town center, the traditional market remains in full swing until mid-afternoon. Visit one of the two pre-Hispanic tombs excavated so far, as well as the appealing 18th-century church dedicated to the Virgin of Juquila. ■

Loading straw in Asunción's fields, near Ocotlán

Market towns

These market towns serve local communities, not tourists, but they offer a chance to visit rural Oaxaca and purchase local produce and typical folk art.

Monday Miahuatlán, 62 miles (100 km) south of Oaxaca on Hwy. 175.

Tuesday Ayoquezco, 93 miles (150 km) south of Oaxaca on Hwy. 131; Zimatlán, 15½ miles (25 km) south of Oaxaca off Hwy. 131.

Wednesday San Pedro y San Pablo Etla, 12 miles (19 km) north of Oaxaca off Hwy. 190.

Thursday Zaachila, 9½ miles (15 km) south of Oaxaca on Hwy. 175 West.

Friday Ocotlán 20½ miles (33 km) south of Oaxaca on Hwy. 175 East.

Saturday Mercado de Abastos, Oaxaca (see p. 256).

Sunday Tlacolula (see p. 268), east of Oaxaca on Hwy. 190. ■

Oaxaca's spectacular festivals

Even the humblest village celebrates its patron saint, sometimes spending the greater part of the annual budget on week-long festivities. Local men lead parades with dissonant yet triumphant trumpets, tubas, and drums; close behind, young beauty queens ride on allegorical floats atop pickup trucks. Shrieking with delight, crowds scatter before *los toros,* reed towers spitting dangerous firecrackers and wielded by zealous young men. Most impressive of all, everyone joins the party.

Radish sculptures made for La Noche de Rábanos (December 23)

Great-grandmas and tiny tots may nod off, but everyone remains until the chill air and the exuberant drunks finally urge families home.

Throughout the state, pre-Cortesian beliefs overlap iconoclastic Christianity to produce rituals as intoxicating as a shot of pure cane liquor. This is literally the case in the eccentric Paso y Credo, a solemn religious procession in which the men of Pinotepa de Don Luis (see p. 274) march from dusk to dawn around the town, taking a ritualistic sip of liquor about every third step. In an Easter-week celebration, the town's men and boys, their bodies painted white with purple icons and slogans, fight a mock battle representing their ancestors' attack on invading Spaniards.

Other traditions, including the Día de los Muertos (Day of the Dead, or All Souls' Day), demonstrate not a clash, but a blending of New and Old World traditions. Near the end of October, villagers and city-dwellers throughout the region begin rejuvenating family graves: weeding, cleaning headstones, painting crosses and crypts. From the evening preceding All Saints' Day (November 1), families begin to entice deceased children—*los angelitos,* or little angels—to the graveside with candles, favorite foods, and (in true Mexican style) loud rockets. As throughout Mexico, Oaxacans relieve gloominess with exuberant partying, and piety is tempered with *picardía,* a mischievous irreverence. Altars—some humble, others lavish—are arranged with traditional sugar-candy skulls embellished with Day-Glo colors, along with yellow-orange *cempasúchil* (marigolds), peanuts, and *pan de muerto* (sweet bread decorated with skulls). These rituals continue through All Souls' Day (November 2) to honor deceased adults.

Even unequivocally Christian celebrations have a unique Oaxaca flavor. On Viernes Santo (Good Friday), purple-robed penitents in long, pointed hoods perform a solemn procession through town in El Desfile del Silencio, the Silent Procession. On a more lighthearted occasion, mongrels wearing glasses, cats in glossy capes, birds in beribboned cages, and box turtles in the grubby hands of young owners crowd the courtyard at La Merced church on August 31 for the Blessing of the Animals.

The Christmas season brings nonstop celebrations, including *las calendas,* in which celebrants dance from church to church holding baskets of offerings on their heads. One of Oaxaca's most unusual traditions is La Noche de Rábanos (Radish Night), held December 23. To compete in this classic secular Yule tradition, growers fashion sophisticated tableaux out of carved radishes, toothpicks, and moss.

For more Oaxaca festivals, see "Entertainment & Activities," p. 389. ∎

Right, above: Masked revelers enjoy the Carnaval at Tlaxiaco.
Right, below: Zapotec women from the Isthmus of Tehuantepec in party mood

Oaxaca's coast

OAXACA'S COAST ARCS EAST TO WEST, FROM THE BORDER with Guerrero to Chiapas, as if tracing a line along the bottom half of a shallow bowl. Zapotecs and, to a lesser extent, Mixtecs are found up and down the coast; Zoques and Mixes make their home around the isthmus. Chatinos moved into the area around Laguna de Chacahua when the Mixtecs retreated at the arrival of the Spaniards; Zapotec lords fled to the Isthmus of Tehuantepec when the Mixtecs overran the last Zapotec kingdom, Zaachila, in the 14th century. Cultures blend, but in many cases, indigenous peoples speak their own languages and continue many of their great-grandparents' traditions.

Pinotepa Nacional
🅜 254 A2

Parque Nacional Lagunas de Chacahua
🅜 254 A1

Opposite: One of the state's many beautiful beaches; this one is near Puerto Ángel.

PINOTEPA NACIONAL

The inhabitants of Pinotepa Nacional and the surrounding municipality are characterized as strong, proud, and independent. Most are the descendants of Chatinos, Mixtecs, and blacks—the latter slaves who were shipwrecked and escaped during the early days of the colony. About an hour from the coast, Pinotepa Nacional is not a stop on the tourist trail, but it's an important commercial center. Until well into the 20th century, Pinotepa women wore nothing above the waist except a plain white cotton shawl. Many today still wear striking straight wrap skirts of red, purple, and lilac stripes whose pattern varies subtly from one village to the next.

The predominantly Mixtec men throughout the municipality perform elaborate dances at Carnaval, Easter, and major feast days, using masks and story lines passed down over generations. Working around scripts whose meanings have faded with time, dancers don masks of rabbits, dogs, and two-faced Spaniards. **Pinotepa de Don Luis,** 15 miles (24 km) northeast of Pinotepa Nacional, vigorously celebrates both Carnaval and Semana Santa (Holy Week), the former climaxing on the Sunday before Ash Wednesday. There are no tourist accommodations outside

Pinotepa Nacional. Visitors may be asked to contribute toward the musicians' refreshments. Be respectful and ask permission before taking photos. Pinotepa Nacional itself has significant Easter celebrations, especially Good Friday and Easter Sunday, celebrated with fireworks, dances, and processions.

PARQUE NACIONAL LAGUNAS DE CHACAHUA

Bird-watchers should check out the coastal lagoons and mangrove swamps of 35,000-acre (14,164 ha) Parque Nacional Lagunas de Chacahua, about halfway between Pinotepa Nacional and Puerto Escondido. Boat tours are especially rewarding during the winter months, when migrating birds arrive. The park entrance is about 17 miles (27 km) along a fairly good dirt road off Highway 200. It's more convenient to book a tour in Puerto Escondido; **Turismo Rodimar** (Av. Pérez Gasga 905, tel 9/582-0737, $$$$$) offers dependable day trips that include time for a simple lunch at Cerro Hermoso beach. The same operator runs daily tours to **Laguna de Manialtepec,** a 10-mile-long (16 km) mangrove lagoon less than 10 miles (16 km) from Puerto Escondido. In the rainy summer season the Manialtepec River forms

A Chacahua restaurant owner shares a laugh with her customers.

an estuary, which birds—including anhinga, parrots, jacanas, and heron—find especially attractive. During the winter you will see the migratory species.

PUERTO ESCONDIDO

Coastal tourism doesn't gain a foothold until Puerto Escondido, now connected directly to Oaxaca City by Highway 131 as well as via Pochutla (Highway 175). Surfers were the first to discover this small town, whose name means "hidden port." Until a paved road was completed in the 1970s, they bumped for miles down a bad dirt road to attack some of the world's best waves. Today they can fly in on major airlines for the surf competitions held each August and mid-November, the latter coinciding with the town's *fiesta,* a lively week of cultural events, sportfishing championships, and a beauty pageant. A major festival honoring la Virgen de la Soledad culminates on December 18, when local fishermen take their patron saint on an ocean-going procession that sets out from the main beach.

Puerto Escondido

⚠ 254 B1

Visitor information

✉ Blvd. Benito Juárez s/n at Fracc. Bacocho

☎ 9/582-0175

Puerto Escondido is one of those towns that somehow maintains its identity while catering nonstop to outsiders. The main tourist drag, a four-block-long pedestrian promenade nicknamed **el adoquinado** (the paved road), slows down conspicuously only during the hottest hours at midday and sudden downpours. Otherwise, it's pretty much an endless parade. But the mix of foreign and national visitors is nice, the prices are reasonable, and seafood is served from open-air eateries right on the sand. Gangs of barefoot kids play on the palm-studded beach or hawk homemade key chains and seashell trinkets, and by noon the fishermen are disgorging their catch at **Playa Marinero,** the town's most central beach. Some boats transport sunbathers to nearby **Puerto Angelito** and **Playa Carrizalillo,** two secluded coves (also accessible on foot or by taxi) where simple seafood shanties serve up fried fish, *ceviche,* beers, and sodas. At the west end of the city, a few private condos and three- and four-star hotels perch on tawny cliffs overlooking **Playa Bacocho,** where a strong undertow discourages swimmers.

East of the main beach, surfers talk shop in palm-thatched, second-story restaurants as they scan **Playa Zicatela** for swells. Sipping a sunset cocktail at one of the many restaurants and bars facing Zicatela Beach, or from the wide green lawn at Hotel Posada Real, at Playa Bacocho, is highly recommended.

For a pre-Hispanic experience, visit one of two *temazcalli:* tiny, traditional-style sweat lodges built of native rock. Throwing aromatic water on hot coals, which are replenished from the outside by a trap door, produces cleansing steam. **Villas Temazcalli** (*Av. Infranganti 28 at Calle Temazcalli, tel 958/ 21023, $$$*) offers massage and both personal and ceremonial steam baths on a cliff above Zicatela beach. After you emerge—purified, relaxed, and exfoliated—you can sip a cup of tea and gaze at the ocean below. **Hotel Aldea del Bazar** (*Av. Benito Juárez s/n, Playa Bacocho, tel 958/20508*), at Playa Bacocho, also has a temazcalli.

PUERTO ÁNGEL

Once the state's most important port, Puerto Ángel, 51 miles (83 km) southeast of Puerto Escondido, is a sleepy town with a small navy base. Rocky headlands rise on either side of the secluded bay, and basic hotels, restaurants, and homes straggle up the hills and canyons. In 1997 Hurricane Pauline dealt this small community—along with others throughout Oaxaca and Guerrero states—a very nasty smack. Palm-thatched roofs were blown off, homes flooded, and possessions swept away in rivers of mud. But private donations of food, water, and clothing brought relief, and later, self-determined communities cleaned up the mess

and affixed new roofs (some people opted for sturdier but less aesthetic tin roofs), and Puerto Ángel was soon back on track.

There's not much to do except watch the fishermen haul in their catch and explore the area's beaches. If you want to swim close to town, the cleanest beach is **Playa Panteón,** on the west side of the bay; otherwise, hire a fisherman to take you to **Playa la Boquilla,** a quiet beach on a pleasant cove a few minutes away. The most famous beach in the area is **Playa Zipolite,** about 4 miles (6 km) away, where topless sunbathing is accepted. Here and in adjacent **San Agustanillo,** industrious locals have set up informal thatch-roofed restaurants and basic lodgings along the wide, palm-studded, sandy beaches, while the kids peddle *pescadillas* (grilled fish in a flour tortilla), and sodas and beers in buckets of rapidly melting ice. San Agustanillo is popular with bodysurfers, although dangerous riptides make swimming risky.

For an educational outing visit **El Centro Mexicano de la Tortuga** (*Domicilio Conocido, closed Mon., $*), in nearby Mazunte. Take the obligatory guided tour to see the turtles in large tanks and learn about the conservation of Mexico's seven marine turtle species and several freshwater species. Involving local people in the project provides them with economical alternatives to poaching endangered turtles and their eggs. Until recently, selling turtle meat, oil, and eggs was a viable business venture.

BAHÍAS DE HUATULCO

There's no doubt that Huatulco, about 31 miles (50 km) northeast of Puerto Ángel, has abundant natural beauty and charm. Nine lovely bays with dozens of pellucid lagoons crowd its 21-mile (35 km)

Puerto Ángel

▲ 254 B1

Bahías de Huatulco

254 C1

Visitor information

✉ Plaza San Miguel, Blvd. Santa Cruz at Calle Monte Albán, Bahía Tangolunda

☎ 958/71541

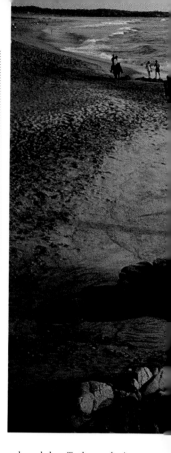

coastline. Clear water and plenty of rocky coves make for great snorkeling, and swimming is pleasant year-round. There's no shortage of sunshine or palm trees, and the rugged mountains of the Sierra de Miahuatlán looming just beyond the beach only make the scene more intimate.

Huatulco's coastline first attracted the attention of FONATUR, the Mexican tourism development board, in the 1960s. Construction began in the 1980s, and since then, the once innocent Mixtec fishing village has received a significant makeover. Buildings here are limited to six stories, 70 percent of the development's land has been set aside as an ecological reserve, and mid-range and economical hotels are to be built along with the exclusive five-star resorts. The plan is to attract two million visitors (who will generate one quarter of the state's income) by the year 2010, so if you prefer a bit of solitude with your sunshine, get there quick.

Scenic **Bahía Tangolunda** was the first bay developed and has reached its maximum density of six resorts. Located here are the Sheraton and Maeva hotels, the area's only 18-hole golf course (*Tel 958/10037*), and Mexico's largest Club Med. Concessions rent sailboards, catamarans, and other water toys. You can get PADI dive certification, rent diving gear, or book a snorkel tour through **Action Sports Marina** (*Tel 958/10055*). **Playa Consuelo** and **Playa el Arrocito** are small beaches on Tangolunda accessible only by boat.

Bahía Santa Cruz has also been developed, with hotels, shops, and several plazas surrounded by cafés. At the southern end of the bay, the underwater preserve at **Playa La Entrega** attracts divers and snorkelers. To the north, tiny **Playa Yerbabuena**, accessible only by boat, is a good place to get away from it all. Sportfishing or bay tours can be arranged at the **Marina Santa Cruz,** through La Sociedad Cooperativa Tangolunda (*Tel 958/70081*), or in Tangolunda Bay through **Cantera Tours** at the Sheraton Hotel (*Tel 958/10030*). **Bahía Chahué,** the largest of the bays, now accommodates private yachts in its 160-slip marina and has several new hotels and shops, and a beach club.

About a mile (1.5 km) inland from Bahía Chahué, **Crucecita** is a pleasing, custom-built town with restaurants, a lively night scene, and budget and mid-range hotels within a few blocks of the main square. Other services include banks, a post

office, and a market, where the locals shop. While it's easiest to get to Crucecita (or from one bay to another) by taxi, inexpensive city buses also make the circuit every 15 minutes or so.

A popular day trip into the lush coastal mountains is a tour of one of the **coffee plantations** established by European immigrants in the 19th century. Tour operators can also arrange day trips to the Centro Mexicano de la Tortuga at Mazunte, Bahía Manialtepec, and Lagunas de Chacahua.

ISTMO DE TEHUANTEPEC
Of the three principal cities in the Isthmus of Tehuantepec, only commerce-oriented **Salina Cruz** is on the water, and touristic accommodations throughout the region are rustic. Neither **Juchitán** nor **Tehuantepec** is terribly scenic—they are sweltering hot and often dusty. Those who visit are inexorably drawn by strength of the culture and the lively, witty people who live here, most descendants of Zapotecs. Travelers often stop off here en route to Chiapas, or to experience *las velas,* exuberant celebrations held throughout region between April and September—mainly in May. Town life centers around the main plaza and the market, the latter presided over by women in short *huipiles* (boxy blouses) and billowing, ankle-length skirts. In Juchitán, visit **La Casa de la Cultura** (*Jose F. Gómez, one block from the plaza*), which displays 20th-century art and archaeological pieces. ∎

Puerto Escondido boasts a string of beaches to suit everyone.

Istmo de Tehuantepec
255 D2

More places to visit in Oaxaca

GRUTAS DE SAN SEBASTIÁN

An interesting excursion from Oaxaca is a trip to the eerie, unlit, underground caves at San Sebastián. Local youths guide you through the 1,300-foot-long (400 m) cave, which has five chambers measuring 65–230 feet (20–70 m) in height. Bring a strong flashlight, and comfortable walking shoes for exploring the cave and the gentle hills of the surrounding countryside. This is a Tourist Yu'u Destination (see below).

🅰 254 B2 **Visitor information** See Oaxaca, p. 256

SAN PEDRO AMUSGOS TO LA MIXTECA ALTA

A few shops selling the finely embroidered *huipiles* (boxy blouses) for which the Amuzgo women are known cluster along Highway 125 as it passes **San Pedro Amusgos,** 32 miles

Tourist Yu'u cabins allow you to overnight at such beauty spots as Hierve el Agua.

(51 km) north of Pinotepa Nacional (see p. 274). The town celebrates its namesake saint, St. Peter, on June 29 with costumes and a colorful procession, and the Fiesta de la Virgen del Rosario on the first Sunday in October. The two-lane highway winds through the Mixteca Alta region on its way to the capital, passing faded but engaging **Tlaxiaco,**

once a strategic Aztec garrison and the site of one of Oaxaca's first Dominican monasteries.

🅰 254 A2–A3 **Visitor information** See Oaxaca, p. 256

SHRINE OF THE VIRGIN OF JUQUILA

Every year hundreds of thousands make a pilgrimage to pray at the shrine of la Virgen Morena de Juquila (the dark-skinned Virgin of Juquila). Some come part or all of the way on foot to show their devotion. The object of adoration is a diminutive statue to which great miracles have been attributed. According to legend, when a fire destroyed much of the village, including the house where the icon was kept, the statue was unharmed, its skin darkened. **Santa Catalina Juquila,** a simple town surrounded by mountains, has a fresh, cool climate and plenty of no-frills hotels to accommodate the pilgrims. On the days preceding the saint's day, December 8, there are religious and cultural festivities, including a dawn rosary, processions, and later food, music, dance, and, of course, fireworks.

🅰 254 B2 **Visitor information** See Oaxaca, p. 256

TOURIST YU'U DESTINATIONS

One of the most comfortable ways to overnight in rural Oaxaca is by staying at Tourist Yu'u cabins. The state government paid for the construction of clusters of cabins in areas of scenic beauty or cultural interest outside the capital. Basic yet clean and comfortable cabins sleeping up to eight people have bunk beds, tables and chairs, toilets, and showers; many have kitchens with stove, refrigerator, and some utensils. This is a real example of environmental tourism and allows you to spend one or more nights in places of natural beauty such as Hierve el Agua (see p. 269) and San Lorenzo. In most cases, cabins are located at the edge of or outside town. Don't expect professional hoteliers or an abundance of restaurants; instead, bring a sense of adventure and some snacks and provisions. Reservations should be made through the state tourism board in the city of Oaxaca.
Visitor information See Oaxaca, p. 256 ∎

Isolated, culturally rich Chiapas offers jungle-draped pyramids and breathtaking scenery. Adopting Christianity early on, the Maya have maintained their own spiritual beliefs, resulting in one of Mexico's most synergistic versions of Catholicism.

Chiapas

Flower motif on the church at San Juan Chamula

Chiapas

TO SPEAK OF CHIAPAS IS TO SPEAK OF THE MAYA, THE LARGEST NATIVE American group north of Peru. About a quarter of Chiapas's people speak an indigenous tongue, and the highland Maya alone have four distinct languages. Owing in large part to centuries of governmental neglect, indigenous communities carry on a traditional way of life. Councils of elders administer rural highland communities, and weavers incorporate thousand-year-old designs in their complicated brocaded *huipiles*. Corn is both literally and figuratively the staff of life; planting and harvesting the grain, and cooking daily tortillas, are activities bound by ritual and blessed with devotion.

The early 16th-century Spanish conquest of Chiapas was particularly swift and brutal. Discouraged by the lack of gold and other riches, the conquerors established San Juan Chamula as a slave market and inflicted other atrocities. Distance from the regulatory *audiencia* (see p. 31) in Mexico City meant little or no meddling in their affairs. Even by the standards of the day, treatment of the Indians was harsh, and Bishop Bartolomé de las Casas eventually persuaded the Spanish Crown to revoke many of the Spanish-held land holdings.

Unlike the Aztecs, the Maya at the time of the Conquest were far removed from their Golden Age (A.D. 250–900), when great cities such as Palenque and Yaxchilán flourished. Among the most advanced civilizations of the world at that time, the Classic Maya achieved great heights in mathematics, astronomy, architecture, and the arts.

Today, Chiapas is one of Mexico's most rural states, its economy based on fishing, forestry, and agriculture. Coffee, cotton, bananas, and cacao are among its most important exports, and subsistence agriculture

Tzotzil men from San Juan Chamula; most locals still dress traditionally.

is widely practiced. Mostly mountainous, Chiapas shares a fringe of tropical lowlands with neighboring Tabasco, Campeche, and Guatemala. The state capital and transportation hub, Tuxtla Gutiérrez, lies on a central plain surrounded by plateaus. Little visited by foreign tourists, the Pacific coast is a series of estuaries and fishing villages accessed almost exclusively by rural roads.

Abundant rain produces waterfalls, lakes, and the *selva lacandona,* one of North America's last remaining rain forests. This endangered land is home to the small Lacandón tribe (for which it is named), who fled Spanish encroachment in their Yucatán homeland. Until a few generations ago, this forest-dwelling people worshiped at the jungle-shrouded ruins of Bonampak. Today, this and other archaeological sites, only

partially rescued from the surrounding jungle, are among the state's most powerful tourist magnets. Its other big draw is San Cristóbal de las Casas, a colonial city whose abundance of traditional culture and indigenous handicrafts attracts droves of visitors despite the area's well-publicized political problems. ■

Mexico City

Area of map detail

Tuxtla Gutiérrez

⚑ 283 B3

Visitor information

✉ Blvd. Belisario Domínguez 950, Edificio Plaza de las Instituciones

☎ 9/612-4535 or 9/612-5509

Tuxtla Gutiérrez & environs

TUXTLA MEANS "PLACE OF MANY RABBITS" IN NÁHUATL, and Gutiérrez refers to Joaquín Miguel Gutiérrez, who championed Chiapas's union with Mexico in 1824. This large, hot metropolis replaced San Cristóbal de las Casas as the state capital in 1892 after San Cristóbal sided with the Royalists during the War of Independence. Tuxtla is an important commercial and distribution center for coffee, tobacco, and other locally produced products.

Tuxlta's main thoroughfare is Avenida Central, which divides the sprawling main square, **Plaza Cívica.** Surrounding this central plaza are the post office, modern **Catedral San Marcos,** and

Women from Chiapa de Corzo demonstrate a complicated lacquerware technique.

several government offices. More attractive is **Parque de la Marimba** (*Av. Central at Calle 8 Poniente*), a shady square where couples dance to live marimba music each evening. If you're not a dancer, look for a coveted folding chair and enjoy the band.

Northeast of the city center, at **Parque Madero,** those who read Spanish can learn about regional archaeology and colonial history in the **Museo Regional de Chiapas** (*Calzada de los Hombres Ilustres, tel 9/613-4479, closed Mon., $*). Also in the park, the **jardín botánico** has labeled tropical plants while the **Centro de Convivencia Infantil** offers miniature golf and other kids' amusements.

Although it is actually a government-run folk-art shop,

the **Casa de las Artesanías** (*Blvd. Belisario Domínguez 2035, tel 9/612-2275, closed Sun.*), northeast of the zócalo, seems more like a handicrafts museum with an ethnographic museum at the rear.

The capital's principal attraction is the peaceful, well laid-out **Zoológico Miguel Álvarez del Toro** (*Calzada Cerro Hueco s/n, tel 9/612-3754, closed Mon., $*), about 5 miles (8 km) southeast of downtown. The zoo gives a great overview not just of Chiapas's native animals, which are the only species represented, but also of its plant life. Iguanas, chachalacas (pheasant-like birds), and other harmless creatures roam free, while the more dangerous beasts are kept in expansive enclosures that imitate as much as possible their own habitats. A small museum, store, and restaurant complete the complex.

About half an hour east of Tuxtla Gutiérrez is **Chiapa de Corzo,** a take-off point for boat trips along Cañón del Sumidero (see opposite), but an interesting town in its own right. At the time of the Spanish invasion, the bellicose Chiapaneco tribe dominated the region, having established themselves around 1300. They fought with Maya towns for control of local salt mines and cacao fields, and generally made life so unpleasant that the Maya allied themselves with the Spaniards.

As soon as the Spaniards had dispatched the Chiapanecos for whom

Some people hire a taxi in Tuxtla Gutiérrez for a tour along the rim of Cañón del Sumidero. You can find a restaurant at one of the five lookout points, La Atalaya.

the state is named, they enslaved their former Maya allies. A Spanish settlement established in Chiapa de Corzo in 1528 was soon abandoned for the fresher, mosquito-free climate at what is now San Cristóbal de las Casas.

It's impossible to get lost in Chiapa de Corzo. The main square is crowned by **La Pila,** an octagonal fountain (1562) said to have been inspired by the diadem of Spain's Queen Isabella. Adjacent to the 16th-century **Ex-convento de Santo Domingo,** one block south of the plaza, the **Museo de la Laca** (*Closed Mon.*) shows lacquered gourds made in the town, as well as other lacquered objects from around the world.

One street from Chiapa de Corzo's main plaza, motorboats

depart for tours of the impressive **Cañón del Sumidero.** This steep-walled canyon was created millions of years ago by the wild **Río Grijalva,** which was tamed by the construction in 1981 of the **Chicoasen Dam.** Rocky red walls rise as high as 3,280 feet (1,000 m) above the brownish-green river.

Although the canyon is striking, the two- to three-hour boat trips (*$$*) that are run from Chiapa de Corzo, or from Cahuaré (6 miles/ 10 km east of Tuxtla Gutiérrez), can be disappointing. The roar of the boat engine generally precludes commentary, and although egrets, kingfishers, crocodiles, and other animals are present, they aren't often sighted as the boat speeds along. It's an interesting excursion, but don't expect a guided nature tour. ■

San Cristóbal de las Casas

SURROUNDED BY MAGNIFICENT PINE-COVERED PEAKS, San Cristóbal accepts its beauty with the naiveté of a child. Simple homes in a range of bright colors line cobblestone streets, and even the hordes of foreign backpackers don't diminish the city's cozy, exotic appeal. At 6,890 feet (2,100 m) above sea level, the chilly evenings are perfumed with the smoke from wood-burning stoves and stone fire-places. The climate is conducive to warm sweaters and jeans, not the bare-as-you-dare ensembles of sweltering Tuxtla Gutiérrez. Visitors en route to Palenque and the lakes at Montebello find themselves postponing travel plans and dreaming of long-term residency.

After an intense but fruitless resistance by the Chiapaneco Indians, the city of Villareal de Chiapa de los Españoles was established in 1528 by Spaniard Diego de Mazariego. It was later renamed San Cristóbal de las Casas in honor of its patron, St. Christopher, and its protector, Dominican monk Bartolomé de las Casas (1474–1566). As the first bishop of Chiapas, de las Casas fought to improve the lives of indigenous men, women, and children under the devastating *encomienda* system, which was tantamount to slavery (see p. 31).

The Spaniards organized the new town in barrios, each with its own church, patron saint, and industry. Today, tradition-minded townspeople still retain neighborhood loyalties, visiting **La Merced** for sweets and wax religious figures, and **Guadalupe** for handmade wooden toys, candles, and leather. The best fireworks are still said to be found in **Santa Lucía.** These neighborhoods are just a few blocks west, east, and southeast of the *zócalo,* respectively.

The **zócalo,** officially Plaza 31 de Marzo, is the physical and social nucleus of the city. It is surrounded by arcaded stores and restored older houses—now banks, bars, hotels, and restaurants. On the west flank is the courtly neoclassic **Palacio**

del Municipio, while to the north stands the **Catedral** *(Tel 9/678-6570),* built in the 16th century and later remodeled inside and out in the baroque style. Its unusual facade, with stylized floral details, makes a striking background for photos.

Two churches perched above the city provide good views and an energizing, if short, uphill walk. The **Templo de Guadalupe** *(End of Real de Guadalupe)* is on the west side. The **Templo de San Cristóbal** *(Hermanos Domínguez at Ignacio Allende)* is higher up and has a better view, but opens only on Sundays and for the feast of the town's patron, St. Christopher.

Solomonic columns and other baroque elements fancify the intricate but soiled facade of the **Templo y Ex-Convento de Santo Domingo** *(20 de Noviembre at Comitán, tel 9/678-6570).* Inside, note the graceful, gilded wood altarpieces and outstanding carved pulpit. Filling the church's extensive atrium is an open-air market of regional crafts. Within the adjacent former monastery, **Sna Jolobil** *(Tel 9/678-2646, closed Sun.)* sells intricate pieces of brocade and other exquisite hand-loomed textiles. This indigenous-run co-op has rescued the dying weaving art in several highland villages. Next door,

San Cristóbal de las Casas

ⓜ 283 B3

Visitor information

✉ Av. Miguel Hidalgo 2

☎ 9/678-6570

the **Museo de los Altos de Chiapas** (*Tel 9/678-1609, closed Mon., $*) has Spanish-language exhibits describing the area's history and culture.

More interesting is a visit to the living, labyrinthine **mercado municipal** (*Av. General Utrilla at Nicaragua*), just a few blocks north. The daily market is especially vivid on Saturdays, when Tzeltal and Tzotzil men and women arrive dressed traditionally in brilliant garments, the women's long braids woven with jewel-toned ribbons.

If you want to learn more about native weaving and culture, visit the **Museo Sergio Castro e Hijos** (*Guadalupe Victoria 61, tel 9/678-4289, donation*). Art historian Sergio Castro gives nightly lectures and slide shows about local weaving and shows his considerable collection. He speaks Spanish, French, Italian, and English, so call when you hit town to schedule a visit on the appropriate night.

Another home-turned-museum is **Na Bolom** (*Av. Vicente Guerrero 33, tel 9/678-1418, closed Mon., $*). Longtime Chiapas residents Swiss photojournalist Trudy Blom and her husband, Danish archaeologist Franz Blom (both deceased), for decades welcomed students, researchers, and Lacandón Indians into their home. Their legacy is a unique guesthouse, restaurant, botanical garden, and research library. Informative English-language guided house tours are given in the afternoon (Spanish-language tours take place in the morning). ∎

The colors of the cathedral's facade—red, yellow, white, and black—represent the four directions in the Maya world view. The cross also has pre-Hispanic connotations.

Maya villages around San Cristóbal

RELIGION, SPIRITUALITY, FAMILY, DUTY, AND SOCIAL hierarchy are important to the Maya of Chiapas, and are the threads from which everyday life is woven. Ceremony and custom pervade daily ritual. Society is hierarchical, and village elders still wear the impressive and unusual symbols of their office during ceremonies. Even the elaborate designs woven painstakingly into textiles have significance for both weaver and wearer. Culturally and sometimes physically isolated from mainstream Mexico, the Tzotzil and Tzeltal villages around San Cristóbal maintain ancient traditions as they deal with armed conflict and the interference of well-meaning outsiders.

The Chamula are a large and relatively prosperous group of Tzotzil-speaking people with their municipal seat in **San Juan Chamula,** about 7 miles (11 km) from San Cristóbal. Most women and girls in San Juan wear distinctive, hairy, black-wool wrap skirts held in place by wide cotton belts, and short-sleeved, blue or white blouses lined with decorative trim. Traditional menswear is white cotton trousers and shirt, with a fleecy wool cloak for warmth.

The physical and spiritual center of this traditional town is its enchanting church, dedicated to St. John the Baptist, the Chamulans' most important manifestation of God. The beauty of the church's facade would move all but the most hopeless philistine. An arched

doorway—decorated with rows of stylized flowers in sea green, vivid violet, hot pink, gold, and blues—contrasts soulfully with the simple lines of the bright white facade.

The church offers no formal services and has no pews. Seated on the floor amid fragrant pine needles and powerful copal incense, worshipers chant prayers while lighting rows of tiny candles of different colors. Lining the walls are Catholic saints dressed in clothing respectfully woven by the local women. Taking photographs or video recordings inside the church is both strictly forbidden and severely punished with fines and/or jail sentences.

Visitors to town must register at the tourist office, pay a small fee to visit the church, and get a short but stern admonition about church protocol. Visit San Juan Chamula on Sunday if possible, when the church square is filled with vendors, or during a holiday celebration.

About 5 miles (8 km) away, **Zinacantán** is a dusty town whose Tzotzil inhabitants are known for their flowers. Lilies, chrysanthemums, gladioli, and roses grow in their fields and gladden their altars. They can be purchased at the town's small Sunday market,

Left: Carnival celebration in Tenejapa

San Cristóbal de las Casas
◭ 283 B3
Visitor information
✉ Av. Miguel Hidalgo 2
☎ 9/678-6570

although many growers sell them wholesale in the steamy lowlands. Embroidered flowers adorn the women's bright white *huipiles* (blouses) and the thinly striped pink shirts of the men.

Sights in Zinacantán include the **Iglesia de San Lorenzo** *(Isabel la Católica at 5 de Febrero, $)* and the adjacent **Museo Sna Tsotz Levetik,** a traditional building with utilitarian and decorative items.

A half-day guided tour *($$$)* is an excellent way to visit Zinacantán and San Juan Chamula and can be arranged through Na Bolom (see p. 287) or area tour operators. Guides usually visit specific families and arrange weaving demonstrations; they know what can and can't be photographed and have interesting anecdotes. Except for children begging, the indigenous people in Chiapas do not appreciate being photographed. Area tour operators also offer horseback riding tours to San Juan Chamula *($$$).*

A dramatic ride through the mountains due north of San Cristóbal brings you to **San Pedro Chenalhó,** set in a pretty river valley. As the center for negotiations between government and Zapatista factions, this usually relaxed Tzotzil town has become increasingly suspicious of outsiders. The Sunday market day is still a celebrated rural ritual, however, and reason enough to visit without fear.

Equally rewarding in terms of mountain scenery is a drive to the Tzeltal village of **Tenejapa,** set in a pretty river valley 17 miles (27 km) northeast of San Cristóbal. ■

A colorful Sunday market occupies the plaza in front of San Juan Chamula's church.

Palenque

MORE THAN JUST AN AWESOME ARCHAEOLOGICAL SITE, Palenque has one of the region's last remaining patches of evergreen tropical forest. Epiphyte-draped trees surround graceful pyramids topped with delicate temples, glowing the color of rich cream in the tropical sun. Small rivers crisscross the site, and a series of cascades fills the Queen's Bath, where today's plebeian visitors may now bathe. Trails through unexcavated portions of the 4,400-acre (1,780 ha) reserve lead to parties of squawking parrots and shrieking howler monkeys, where silent Jesus Christ lizards and snakes slink under damp fallen leaves.

Its intense wild setting as well as its harmonious, graceful architecture make Palenque magic. Corbeled vaults permit larger doorways and give the buildings a light, refined appearance enhanced by delicate roofcombs, mansard roofs, and T-shaped windows evocative of the wind god, Ik. Of all the Maya sites, it is among the most elegant, mysterious, and accessible.

Accessibility was the key to Palenque's initial success. Built on a natural terrace overlooking the floodplain of the Río Usumacinta, the city served as the center of trade between the Petén region, the highlands of Chiapas, and the Grijalva Valley. Knowledge and ideas as well as trade goods flowed along the wide Usumacinta, especially during the Late Classic era (A.D. 600–800), when Palenque flourished. Under leaders such as Pakal the Great and his oldest son and successor, Chan Bahlum, Palenque joined Calakmul, Tikal, and Copán as one of the most influential kingdoms of the lowland Maya.

Large panels throughout the city were commissioned to illustrate the royal dynasty and its accomplishments. A dearth of suitable stone in the region explains the use of exquisite bas-relief carvings, in limestone and stucco, in lieu of the stelae favored elsewhere in the Maya world. Many of the carvings were ordered by Chan Bahlum, who traced his lineage back 11 generations, beginning with a mythic ruler nicknamed "Lady Beastie."

Among the most stellar examples are the three elaborate stucco panels within the **Templo de las Inscripciones,** containing about 620 glyphs. Royalty in elaborate feathered headdresses stand on monster masks; each holds a representation of the god K'awil, one of three gods worshiped as mythic ancestors. Access to the temple is now severely limited; get permission to join a 15-minute tour (at 4 p.m.) at the INAH office at the site entrance first thing in the morning.

The monumental structure was commissioned by Chan Bahlum's father, Pakal the Great (or Kan-Hanab-Pakal II), as his royal tomb. Unveiled by Mexican archaeologist Alberto Ruz Lhuillier in 1952 after four seasons of excavation, this is to date Mexico's most elaborate burial site. Sixty-six narrow steps lead deep within the pyramid to the crypt, where portraits of prior sovereigns decorate the walls in stucco relief.

Still bearing traces of red paint, the sarcophagus's 5-ton lid of intricately carved limestone depicts Pakal's descent into the underworld. Near the top, a bird symbolic of the

Palenque
🅰 283 C4
Visitor information
✉ Av. Juárez at Abasolo
☎ 934/50356

heavens perches on the sacred ceiba tree. The crypt's contents, including Pakal's remains and rings, necklaces, ear spools, and a funerary mask in a mosaic of jade, with eyes of obsidian and shell, are displayed at Mexico City's Museo Nacional de Antropología (see pp. 198–201).

Across the Río Otolum, the **Grupo de la Cruz** (Cross Group) is currently under excavation. In 1998, finds in Temple 19 revealed a previously unknown ruler, Uc-Pakal-Kinich, as well as possible liaisons with rulers at Copán, in present-day Honduras. Surrounding a large plaza, the group takes its name from crosslike images found in the **Templo de la Cruz Foliada.**

Within its sunken courtyard, several sets of carvings depict

captured enemy rulers in various poses of submission and mutilation. Depicting not a cross but a holy ceiba tree decorated with corn stalks, the stone panel shows ruler Chan Balum's ascent to power. At the north end of the plaza, five tiers lead to the large **Templo de la Cruz,** which also displays the World Tree motif. Its roofcomb, one of the highest in Palenque, is in excellent condition. Here, panels depicting the royal ancestors emphasize their role as mediators between heaven and Earth. On the west side of the plaza, themes of war and sacrifice dominate the well-preserved **Templo del Sol,** where the face of the jaguar-man god peers from a Maya war shield.

Back across the river, the **Palacio** served the royal family as

Mist envelops the Temple of the Inscriptions. The nine tiers of the 65-foot (20 m) stepped pyramid on which it rests most likely correspond to the nine levels of the Maya underworld.

both ceremonial and living quarters. The complex of vaulted galleries and rooms surrounding interior courtyards was built and added to over many centuries.

On the west steps, glyphs heralding the birth of Pakal the Great are among the site's earliest, while its unusual, four-tiered tower (possibly an observatory) was built just before the city's disintegration.

Northeast of the Palace, divergent paths enter the jungle shade, a welcome respite from the intense tropical sun. After crossing **Río Murciélagos** (Bat River), a right-hand path leads to **Grupo C,** a half-dozen small temples surrounding a central plaza. The left-hand path leads to **Grupo Murciélagos** (Bat Group), a residential complex

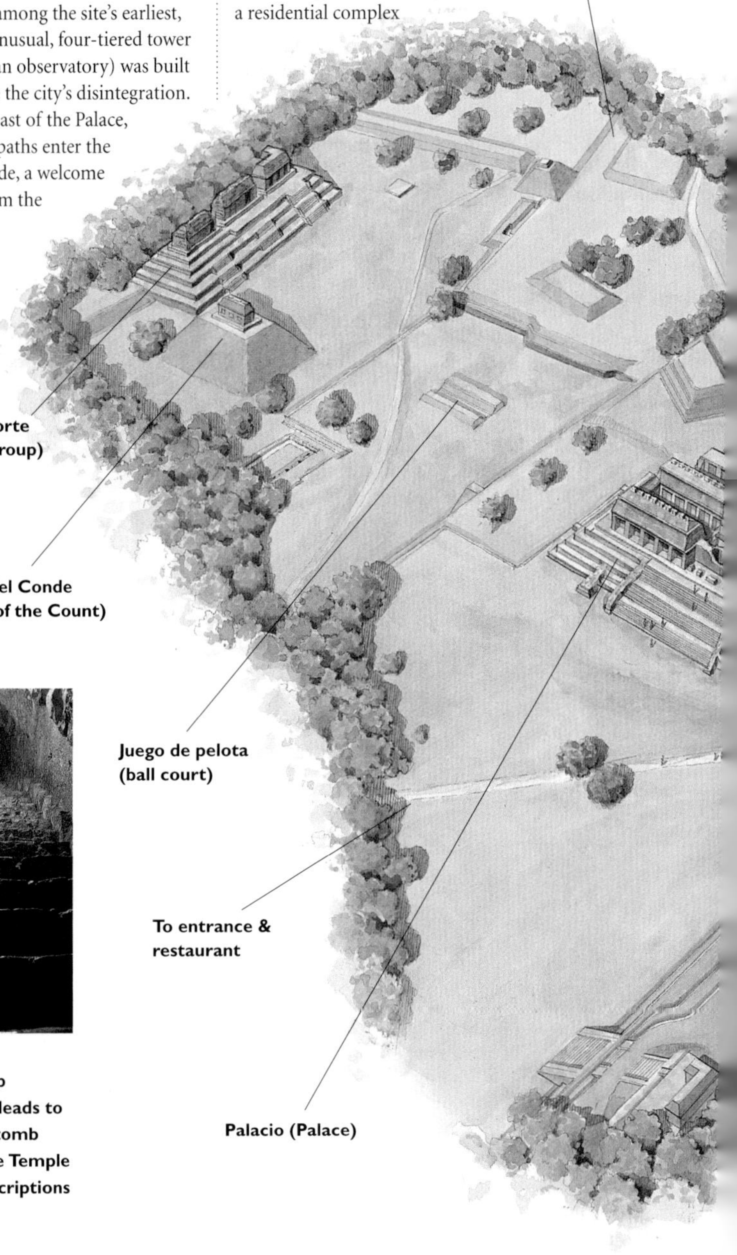

To Grupo C, Grupo Murciélagos (Bat Group), & Baño de la Reina (Queen's Bath)

Grupo Norte (North Group)

Templo del Conde (Temple of the Count)

Juego de pelota (ball court)

To entrance & restaurant

Palacio (Palace)

This steep staircase leads to a buried tomb within the Temple of the Inscriptions

for Maya nobles, and to a series of cascades forming the **Baño de la Reina** (Queen's Bath), a swimming hole today enjoyed by both visitors and locals.

East of the Río Otolum, the four-tiered **Templo del Conde** (Temple of the Count) was named for the 19th-century German eccentric who set up housekeeping here. Nearby is a compact **juego de pelota** (ball court), as well as the **Grupo Norte**, whose plazas and temples were among the last constructed before the city's demise.

A hat, sunscreen, and water will help mitigate the strong sun and steamy heat. Retreat to the restaurant for a meal or cool drink during the hottest hours of the day, or to the air-conditioned **site museum** (*Closed Mon.*), where your ticket stub gains entrance at no additional cost. Excellent exhibits are labeled in English, Spanish, and Tzotzil. Among the museum's collection is the **Palace Tablet,** an intricate stone relief detailing the lineage of Palenque's rulers. Shuttles (*$*) link the ruins and Avenida Juárez, in Palenque town. ■

Panels throughout the city are inscribed with glyphs illustrating the royal family and its accomplishments.

Templo de la Cruz Foliada (Temple of the Foliated Cross)

Templo de la Cruz (Temple of the Cross)

Templo del Sol (Temple of the Sun)

Río Otolum

Templo de las Inscripciones (Temple of the Inscriptions)

Large stone tablets dot the 4,400-acre (1,780 ha) site.

Drive: Palenque to Parque Nacional Lagunas de Montebello

This route follows the Pan-American Highway (Highway 199) between Chiapas's most famous ruins, Palenque, and Parque Nacional Lagunas de Montebello. The highway climbs out of the tropical jungle to rolling hills and lush temperate valleys around Ocosingo before continuing steeply to the evergreen mountains around San Cristóbal de las Casas. From this endearing colonial city, the route descends slightly in elevation to end at the Guatemalan border. On the way you'll visit major and minor ruins, foamy white waterfalls forming crystalline blue pools, indigenous villages, and prosperous mestizo towns and cities.

An aerial view of the ruins of Toniná

Recommended places to overnight en route are Palenque; rustic Rancho Esmeraldas, outside Ocosingo; San Cristóbal de las Casas; and either Comitán de Domínguez or the elegant Parador Santa María, near Chinkultic and the Lagunas de Montebello.

After visiting the ruins at **Palenque ❶** (see pp. 290–93) drive south along Hwy. 199 for about 14 miles (22 km) to see the 130-foot (40 m) waterfall at **Misol-Ha** *($)*, most impressive when swollen with late-summer and fall rains. Swim in the pool at the base of the waterfall, or explore the cave behind the falls, which leads to a subterranean pool. The site has restrooms, basic camping facilities, and simple restaurants.

About 25 miles (40 km) to the south, follow a dirt road for several miles to the extraordinary falls of **Agua Azul ❷** *($)*. Surrounded by exuberant tropical vegetation,

the river plunges into a rocky gorge, forming hundreds of frothy white falls and, during the dry season, crystal-clear pools that give the site its name: "blue water." Near the parking lot are two main viewpoints plus lots of small restaurants and souvenir stands. Hike down the canyon to bathe in a series of interconnected pools or up past the campground for a different view.

Continuing south, the highway curves and climbs past lovely vistas of patchwork fields and farms, abandoning the sometimes oppressive lowlands for the refreshing climate around the Ocosingo Valley, with mixed broadleaf vegetation and many species of birds. Little visited by tourists, **Ocosingo** is a pleasant, fairly prosperous mestizo town.

A detour of about 6 miles (10 km) southeast of Ocosingo on a paved road brings you to the important but little-known ruins at **Toniná ❸** *($)*, which flourished at the beginning of the tenth century, around the time Palenque was being abandoned. Here, one of the tallest pyramids of the Maya world rises 230 feet (70 m) above the Grand Plaza, commanding an awesome view of the valley and the mountains to the south. Most likely the city's Mayan name, meaning "big house of stones," refers to this massive pyramid.

Construction of this structure took place over more than a thousand years. Successive generations built new palaces and temples; to date, four of the former and ten of the latter have been identified throughout the seven-level pyramid. In 1992, the remarkably well-preserved Mural of the Four Suns was discovered on the sixth level. The 13-foot-long (4 m) stucco painting represents a Maya codex

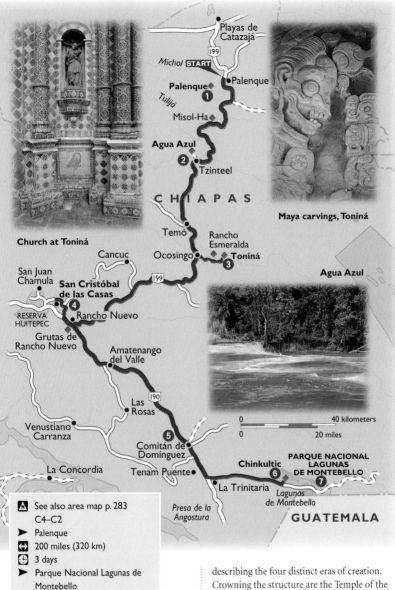

Maya carvings, Toniná

Church at Toniná

Agua Azul

0   40 kilometers
0   20 miles

See also area map p. 283
C4–C2
► Palenque
⟷ 200 miles (320 km)
⏱ 3 days
► Parque Nacional Lagunas de
   Montebello

NOT TO BE MISSED

- Palenque
- Agua Azul
- Toniná
- San Cristóbal de las Casas
- Parque Nacional Lagunas de
  Montebello

describing the four distinct eras of creation.
Crowning the structure are the Temple of the
Prisoners and the Temple of the Smoky
Mirror. Near the base of the pyramid on the
right side lies the sarcophagus of one of the
city's last rulers, Tzotz-Choj.

Just before the ruins at Toniná, a long dirt
road leads to **Rancho Esmeralda** (see
Hotels, pp. 375–76). By advance arrangement
with this guesthouse and working macadamia-
nut farm, you can take a four-hour horseback

riding tour of the luxuriant Ocosingo Valley, or an air excursion via small plane over the same area or to Laguna Miramar (see p. 305) or the ruins at Yaxchilán and Bonampak (see pp. 302–304).

Return to Hwy. 199, and continue west for 70 miles (112 km) along this and Hwy. 190, passing cattle ranches, small farms, and coffee plantations, to **San Cristóbal de las Casas ❹** (see pp. 286–87). After visiting this engaging city, return to Hwy. 190 (the Pan-American Highway) and head southeast toward the Guatemalan border.

Turn right about 8 miles (13 km) after San Cristóbal on a signed dirt road to the **Grutas de Rancho Nuevo** (*Closed in inclement weather, $*). This maze of caves, studded with limestone stalagmites and dripping stalactites, was discovered in the early 1960s and has only recently been explored. New walkways and improved illumination allow visitors solo access to a tunnel nearly 1,640 feet (500 m) long. You can also hire a horse and guide to explore the surrounding pine forest. Restrooms, shade *palapas*, and a simple restaurant are other recent additions.

Continue along the Pan-American Highway; after about 10 miles (16 km), look for a right-hand road leading to the Tzeltal village of **Amatenango del Valle.** You'll spot the entrance to this unsigned pottery-making town by the characteristic unglazed, burnished clay pots and animal figures in front of homes along the highway. The decorative and utilitarian vessels are fired in the traditional way, under an open-air wood fire. Since Amatenango's women spend their time building pots instead of weaving, they buy the cloth for their *huipiles* (blouses) and embroider them with simple designs in red and yellow.

Continue south another 25 miles (40 km) to **Comitán de Domínguez ❺** (*Visitor information, Calle Central Benito Juárez 6, Plaza Principal*), a wonderful small city currently being restored to its colonial splendor with federal grant money. Built by the Spanish as a commercial and transportation hub, the city today serves the same function for Tzeltal Indians and mestizos in outlying ranches.

For crystalline water, visit Agua Azul in the dry season.

If you're interested in Mexican history or simply like republican-era edifices and antiques, it's worth a look at the **Casa-Museo Dr. Belisario Domínguez** (*Av. Belisario Domínguez Sur 35, tel 9/632-0013, closed Mon., $*). The medical doctor and Chiapas senator was a Revolution hero whose frank and unflattering assessment of the Huerta administration led to his assassination in 1913. Dr. Domínguez was born in this gracious house in 1863; preserved here are his instruments, pharmaceuticals, and other medical paraphernalia as well as photographs, documents, and letters dating from the Mexican Revolution.

Other sights of interest in Comitán are the **Catedral Santo Domingo de Guzmán** (*Av. Castellanos at Calle Central*), the **Iglesia San Caralampio** (*Primera Calle Norte Oriente at Cuarta Av. Oriente Norte*), and the **Museo de Arte Hermila Castellanos** (*Belisario Domínguez 51, tel 9/632-2082*), with excellent contemporary Mexican art.

Beyond Comitán, it's less than 10 miles (16 km) to **Tenam Puente** (*$*), a large but unremarkable archaeological site. Built on a strategic hilltop location, this religious center and residential area flourished during the Classic and Early Postclassic periods, after the Maya had abandoned cities such as Palenque.

Continue along the Pan-American Highway, detouring after 10 miles (16 km) onto the road marked "Lagunas de Montebello." Not far down the road, a left-hand dirt road leads to **Chinkultic ❻** (*$*), a Maya city abandoned just a few hundred years after reaching its apogee during the Late Classic period (A.D. 600–900). Not many structures have been restored on this site, but there's an incredible view from the top of the main pyramid—a rather steep climb from the park entrance. Swim in the **cenote azul** (the sinkhole is a bit hard to find; ask the park guard), or visit the ball court, less impressive since its bas-relief sculpture was moved to the Museo Nacional de Antropología in Mexico City (see pp. 198–201).

The last stop of the journey is **Parque Nacional Lagunas de Montebello ❼** (see pp. 298–99), where more than a dozen lakes of various hues can easily be seen from different viewpoints. ∎

**Parque Nacional
Lagunas de
Montebello**
🅰 283 C2
**Visitor
information**
✉ Palacio del
Municipio, Comitán
☎ 9/632-4047

Parque Nacional
Lagunas de Montebello

LAKES OF DIFFERENT HUES ARE SPRINKLED THROUGHOUT this national park like a handful of translucent marbles flung down by a tempestuous giant. The presence of different kinds and levels of oxides causes the lakes to take on different shades, especially noticeable when the sun is shining brightly. Some glow a deep green, others are emerald, steel gray, greenish-blue, violet, or pale blue. Lagunas de Montebello, Chiapas's only national park, comprises 14,880 acres (6,022 ha) of temperate forest along Mexico's southern border with Guatemala.

**One of the park's
50-plus lakes, near
the Guatemalan
border**

Because of weeds growing on the lake bottom and occasional drownings over a period of many years, locals do not recommend swimming in the majority of these lovely lakes. (Bear in mind that

Mexicans are generally not avid swimmers.) However, even they deem a few lakes safe, and others can be toured on log rafts, rowboats, and pedalboats. The most accessible lakes have nearby parking lots and food and soda stands attended by local women eager to prepare you a simple meal or, at the very least, sell you a bag of chips and a drink.

Young local men wait at the park entrance, ready to hop in your car and give you a lake tour for an appropriate tip. Just beyond the entrance gate, the paved road forks. The left-hand road leads to the **Lagunas Coloradas** (Colored Lakes), appropriately named for the variety of colors you'll see. From

the parking lot at **Laguna Encantada** (Enchanted Lake), half a dozen lakes can be appreciated as a slice of water in the distance.

At the far end of the road, hike around large **Laguna Bosque Azul,** take an inexpensive rowboat tour, or rent a pedalboat. Boys offer hour-long horseback excursions in the forest, where you can see native birds, a small cave, and two sink-holes. There is a parking lot and simple restaurant.

To visit the southern lakes, return to the park entrance and take the right fork toward Tziscao, about 7½ miles (12 km) distant. First you will come to large **Laguna de Montebello** (a ten-minute walk down a dirt road), which is recom-mended for swimming. Park right at the broad lakeshore, where locals rent out their horses and sell snacks.

Continue toward Tziscao. A signed road leads to a cluster of five lovely lakes, **Cinco Lagos,** which can be viewed from the lookout point. (This group is about a 30-minute walk from the main road.) Farther along the paved road, deep-blue **Lago Pojoj** lies down a steep road. The last of the park's major lakes is **Tziscao,** named for the community along its eastern shore. The **Tziscao Lodge** is at the time of writing still being remodeled, but a new tourist facility has restrooms, a restaurant, and shaded tables. You can swim at the sandy beach or take a rowboat trip around the lake. Motor boats are not permitted on Montebello's lakes.

The lake district is about 30 miles (48 km) southeast of Comitán, where you can pick up a map at the tourist office. The best way to tour the park is by car. If you choose to take a bus or taxi, these can easily be found in Comitán. Buses access both Laguna Bosque Azul and Tziscao, and you can alight at any point in between. ■

The Maya calendar

The Maya and the Aztecs shared the same 260-day ceremonial calendar (*Tzolkin* in Mayan or *Tonalamatl* in Náhuatl), a ritualistic almanac used for astrological prophecies as well as decision-making in daily affairs. Each day was ruled by several lords whose personalities influenced the day, much as the sun, moon, and planets affect daily life according to astrologers. In one of the most significant coincidences in the history of human conflict, Spanish conquistador Hernán Cortés appeared in the very year (1 Reed) of Toltec god-king Quetzalcóatl's prophesied return to power. Convinced of the fulfillment of holy prophecy, the Emperor Moctezuma barely rebelled against his fate (see p. 29).

The Tzolkin, or sacred calendar, was a cyclical calendar of 260 days. As with our days of the week, its 20 named days followed each other in endless succession. Combined with each day was a number from 1 to 13, for a total of 260 days, such as 2 Ahau or 8 Eb. Each day was ruled by the lord of its name and of its number. The number 13 was lucky, so both the 13th day and days paired with the number 13 were often auspicious.

In addition to this sacred calendar, mathematicians devised a 365-day solar calendar, which they knew to be only an approximation of the Earth's solar orbit. This calendar, called the Haab, consisted of 18 periods of 20 days each (totaling 360), plus five unlucky days at the end of the period, called *Uayeb*. The days between the end of one "year" and the beginning of the next were, according to Maya astronomers and priests, extremely unstable and dangerous, as they pertained to neither one year nor the other. The two calendars were then meshed, like two cogs of unequal size, to form the Calendar Round, which permitted a deeper level of both practical and spiritual interpretation. Crops were planted, battles waged, and rulers crowned on the most auspicious dates. The cycle repeated every 52 years.

As these cyclical calendars eventually repeated themselves, they were not useful in recording the date of historical events. For this reason the Maya invented the Long Count, a calendar based on multiples of 20. The most basic unit was a day (called a *kin*, or sun), followed by a *uinal* (20 days), a *tun* (360 days), and so on. Think of it as expressing a date this way: "It happened 5 centuries, 8 decades, 3 years, 2 weeks, and 4 days ago."

Throughout the Classic era, dates carved on thousands of stelae throughout the Maya world precisely recorded birth, death, marriage, ascension to power, and decisive battles, providing today's scientists with many clues about ancient Maya history. According to this manner of reckoning, Creation occurred in the year 0.0.0.0.0., which Maya expert Sir Eric Thompson (1898–1975) interpreted as August 11, 3114 B.C. Most scholars still agree. Its ceremonial date is 4 Ahau 8 Cumku.

Fascinated by mathematics as both a scientific tool and an art, the ancient Maya played endlessly with numbers, had a place-value system of counting, and invented the concept of zero (perhaps adapting an earlier Olmec idea). Using simple observation and their advanced mathematical knowledge, they calculated the orbit of Venus and other planets nearly as precisely as astronomers do today. ∎

The monkey glyph signals "day"; in its hand, the god's head represents six; the skull below stands for ten. The whole thus means 16 days.

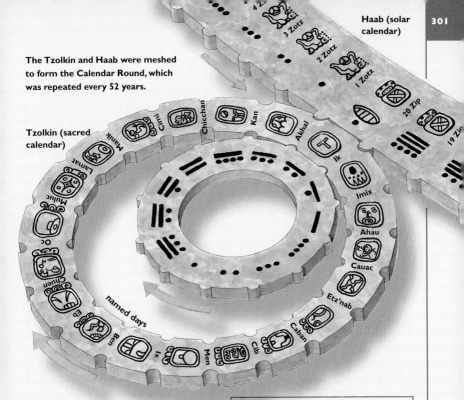

Haab (solar calendar)

The Tzolkin and Haab were meshed to form the Calendar Round, which was repeated every 52 years.

Tzolkin (sacred calendar)

named days

The unlucky five-day Uayeb comes at the end of the Haab.

Month glyphs of the Haab

Pop
Uo
Zip
Zotz

Zec
Xul
Yaxkin
Mol

Ch'en
Yax
Zac
Ceh

Mac
Kankin
Muan
Pax

Kayab
Cumku
Uayeb

The numbers

•	• •	• • •	• • • •
1	2	3	4
___	•	• •	• • • •
5	6	7	8
• • • •		•	• •
9	10	11	12
• • •	• • • •		•
13	14	15	16
• •	• • •	• • • •	
17	18	19	0

The Maya system of counting was based on 20 "digits," literally ten fingers and ten toes. The numbers 0–19 could be written either with head glyphs or using a place-value system based on five. A dot represented 1; a bar, 5; and a seashell or similar glyph, the placeholder 0. These numbers could be written horizontally or vertically. For example, the number 20 would be

Yaxchilán & Bonampak

BOTH YAXCHILÁN AND BONAMPAK FLOURISHED IN THE
Late Classic era, united by royal marriage, at times divided by warfare.
As it did for other Maya centers in eastern Chiapas, the luxuriant
Lacandón rain forest, or *selva lacandona,* supplied their needs, while
the wide Usumacinta River and its many tributaries facilitated transportation. Today, these and other protected enclaves form a tiny
buffer against deforestation in the threatened Lacandón rain forest
and an untouristy destination for lovers of Maya lore.

Yaxchilán
 283 D3

Their jungle location is part of the
allure of these two remote archaeological sites. Towering mahogany
trees host vines and blossoming
epiphytes, creating a home for colorful toucans, parrots, flycatchers,
orioles, and tanagers. Vampire bats

**The small
Lacandón tribe
fled to the rain
forest during the
Spanish colonial
period to escape
persecution.**

hang in the damp chambers of
ruined limestone palaces, cen-
tipedes creep along moist green
walls, mosquitoes suck your blood.
Although Yaxchilán is more extensive, and its setting more lush, both
sites have a wonderful, wild, "lost in
the jungle" feel.

About 118 miles (190 km)
southeast of Palenque, **Yaxchilán**

was built on a terrace at a large bend
in the Usumacinta River. Howler
monkeys roar from the tops of
enormous ceiba trees, held sacred
by the Maya as the Tree of Life. The
humid tropical air seems to have
eased the rigid poses of temples,
palaces, and stelae, which blend with
—but don't completely succumb
to—the pervasive rain forest.

Enter the site through Building
19, or **el Laberinto** (the
Labyrinth), named for its maze of
small rooms. The upper story consists of a central hall annexed by a
series of rooms; narrow stairways
lead to subterranean chambers. The
facade, originally covered in molded
and painted stucco, gives way to
remnants of roof combs above a
wide cornice. This and other vine-
draped, gray-green buildings that
inspired the name "Place of Green
Stones" face the broad, grassy **Gran
Plaza.** Among these are a steam
room (**Edificio 14**) and an I-shaped
juego de pelota, or ball court.

Graceful roof combs and upper
facades with remnants of beautifully
worked figures in stucco and stone
are among Yaxchilán's most impressive elements. The large number
of intricately carved lintels and
stelae tell tales of conquest and ceremonial life: Epigraphers have identified glyphs symbolizing ascension to
power, birth dates, and marriage.
Among the most impressive lintels
are those found on Buildings 12, 16,
and 22. Stele 11, moved to the Gran

Plaza from several miles away, is the site's pièce de résistance. The larger figure represents Yaxchilán's most important ruler: Pájaro Jaguar, or Bird Jaguar.

South of the Gran Plaza, stairs lead up to the **Gran Acrópolis,** which commands a fantastic view of the site. Here you will find the well-preserved **Edificio 33,** with its headless sculpture of Pájaro Jaguar, to whom the building is dedicated. The temple's elaborate roof combs are intact, but its fabulous lintel is now at the British Museum in London. Short walks through the jungle bring you to the **Acrópolis Sur** (where **Edificio 40** has traces of original murals) and the **Acrópolis Pequeña,** with excellent bas-relief lintels in **Edificios 42** and **44.**

A less important center under the jurisdiction of Yaxchilán, **Bonampak,** to the south, was established around the year A.D. 600 near the Lacanjá River, a tributary of the Usumacinta. The first outsiders to visit were two Americans working for the United Fruit Company, who in 1946 convinced a Lacandón Indian to reveal the site of devotional rituals.

The highlight of a visit to Bonampak is the murals of the **Templo de las Pinturas** (Temple of the Paintings). Although the re-creation at Mexico City's Museo Nacional de Antropología (see pp. 198–201) shows the murals with their original, brilliant colors and bold outlines, the fading scenes viewed *in situ* still convey a wondrous force. In the first room, the royal family exults in its heir apparent, while musicians entertain. Above the doorway, the lord of Bonampak, Chaan Muan, is resplendent in embroidered loincloth, jaguar-skin skirt, jade collar, and headdress of quetzal feathers.

Violent battle scenes dominate the second room. A captive kneels in supplication before Chaan Muan, while others are tortured and humiliated. A prisoner of rank slumps in exhaustion on the temple steps. In the third chamber, victory is celebrated with elaborate ritual. Elite women perform a bloodletting of the tongue, while lords in grand costume execute a graceful dance.

Carved lintels, stelae, and vine-draped buildings characterize Yaxchilán.

Bonampak
🔺 283 D3
Visitor information
☎ 934/50356
(Palenque)

Bonampak's powerful murals date from the end of the eighth century A.D.

These murals rank among the finest of Classic Maya art. Attention was paid to expression, foreshortening makes perspective realistic, and each panel is a harmonious triumph of composition. The murals, dated 790, seem to be the last work done at the site. Chaan Muan and his bride from Yaxchilán, Lady Rabbit, may have been the last rulers at Bonampak. No evidence has been found that the baby boy so proudly presented in the temple paintings was ever crowned.

Other temples and palaces on the Gran Plaza and adjoining **Acrópolis** can be explored with the help of a Lacandón Indian guide. Park entrance is free but each visitor must pay for the services of a member of the Lacandón community, who accompanies groups or individuals *($$$)*. Some guides merely take you along without commentary; others relate tales and legends of their forefathers—sometimes strangely interwoven with Bible stories introduced by missionaries during the past century.

Long overland day tours from Palenque visit both sites; a one-hour boat trip from Frontera Corozal (where comfortable tourist accommodations are available) completes the journey to Yaxchilán. Tours in small aircraft can be arranged from Ocosingo, Comitán, and Palenque; most spend one hour at Bonampak and three hours at Yaxchilán. Three- or four-day tours include a visit to Tikal, in the Petén region of Guatemala just across the Usumacinta River.

Some tours tout a long hike to the ruins of Bonampak, which sounds more exciting and adventurous than it really is. Most of the walk is down the recently paved road, and many hikers complain of sore feet, sunstroke, boredom, or exhaustion. In whatever fashion you arrive, bring mosquito repellent, water, sunscreen, and a wide-brimmed hat, as well as a passport or international identification and tourist card, without which you may not pass military checkpoints. Deadly and territorial fer-de-lance and other poisonous snakes are found here, so watch where you put your hands and feet. ■

Dugout canoes provide convenient transportation in the ever shrinking rain forest.

More places to visit in Chiapas

RESERVA DE LA BIÓSFERA EL TRIUNFO

Located in the Sierra Madre de Chiapas, El Triunfo Biosphere Reserve was established in 1990. Most of its 494,000 acres (200,000 ha) constitute a buffer zone; approximately one fifth of this region of mountains, valleys, and plains has been designated federal land. Pine, mixed, and low tropical forests are home to several species of endangered cats; rare quetzal birds hide in the cloud forest. Permission to enter the reserve must be obtained a week in advance, and visits are advisable only during the dry season *(mid-November–mid-May).* The park entrance is about 115 miles (184 km) south of Tuxtla Gutiérrez via Angel Albino Corzo. The only accommodations are a rustic lodge, though camping is permitted.
🗺 283 B2 **Visitor information** ✉ Argentina 389 at Colombia, Tuxtla Gutiérrez
☎ 9/614-0378

RESERVA DE LA BIÓSFERA MONTES AZULES

Together with Calakmul Biosphere Reserve and the Petén region of Guatemala, Montes Azules represents the largest remaining virgin rain forest north of the Amazon Basin. The 818,000-acre (331,000 ha) reserve, whose name means "blue mountains," changes significantly in elevation, from near sea level at the Lacantún River, in the south, to around 5,250 feet (1,600 m) in the more mountainous west. The varied topography produces swamps, lakes, rivers, evergreen and tropical rain forest, palm forest, and pine and oak forest. Of the 3,000 plant species, there are 320 species of orchids alone. The best months to visit are January through September.

Services within the park are limited. The town of Emiliano Zapata is working to establish ecotourism and offers lodgings in communal cottages. Guided camping trips of four days or more take you to **Laguna Miramar,** the largest lake in the Lacandón rain forest, with excellent hiking, snorkeling, and canoeing. Trips can be arranged through the **Dana Association,** San Cristóbal *(Tel/fax 9/678-0468).* It is possible to get to Lake Miramar by road (about five hours from Ocosingo) or by small plane, a thrilling 30-minute ride via **Servicios Aereos San Cristóbal** out of Comitán *(Tel 9/632-4662)* or Ocosingo *(Tel 9/673-0188).*

Near the park's southern border is **Ara Macao** *(Reforma Agraria, tel 015/2015928),* a government-funded, community-run ecotourism lodge. The comfortable, simple cabins are located on the right bank of the Lacantún River, where you can swim, fish, or explore in a dugout canoe. Local guides lead hikes into the surrounding forest, where there are harpy eagles, hawks, yellow-throated toucans, and the endangered red macaw for which the reserve is named. Its about five hours south of Palenque along federal and state highways to the town of Reforma Agraria; small planes can be chartered in Ocosingo or Comitán.

▲ 283 D3

RESERVA HUITEPEC

On the eastern slope of 8,860-foot (2,700 m) Volcán Huitepec, one of the highest mountains in the Chiapas range, is Huitepec *(Closed Mon., $)*, a 335-acre (135 ha) nature reserve.

Oak forest prevails at the lower elevations; higher up are cloud forests cloaked in epiphytes and ferns. Many of the 300-plus plant species have been used for generations by local Maya for medicinal and religious purposes. Trekkers may see foxes, armadillos, flying squirrels, and raccoons, but more easily spotted are some of the reserve's 60 resident bird species. You can wander the forest trails on your own any day of the week or arrange a Tuesday, Thursday, or Saturday guided visit through **Pronatura,** based in San Cristóbal de las Casas *(María Adelina Flores 21, tel 9/678-5000).*

▲ 283 B3

TAPACHULA

Most people visit Tapachula as the gateway to Guatemala, but this is a friendly city with several interesting sights in the surrounding countryside. Maya stelae and artifacts can be seen at the **Museo Regional del Soconusco** *(Palacio Municipal, west of main plaza, tel 9/626-4173),* or you can see them *in situ* at the **Izapa** *(Carr. A Talisman s/n, $),* a spread-out archaeological site about 15 minutes outside town. About half a mile (1 km) from the entrance is **Grupo F,** the best restored, with altars and ball court in addition to pyramids and stelae. Northeast of Tapachula and a stone's throw from Guatemala, the town of **Unión Juárez** makes an excellent base for mountain excursions. Bring your bathing suit and take an agreeable alpine walk to the **Cascadas de Muxbal,** where a waterfall tumbling into a narrow gorge forms a pretty pool. Mountaineers can make an overnight assault on 13,400-foot (4,085 m) **Volcán Tacaná.** About 7 miles (11 km) outside town, the working coffee plantation of **Santo Domingo** *(Tel 9/621-2063, $)* was built by early 20th-century German immigrants using imported materials. The chalet-like structure has recently been restored and has a coffee museum and a restaurant serving regional food.

▲ 283 C1 **Visitor information** ✉ 4ta Av. Norte 16 at Calle 1 Poniente, Edificio Genopa ☎ 9/625-5409 ■

A keel-billed toucan peers from its nest in the rain forest of Montes Azules.

Two-lane highways connect the Yucatán Peninsula's diverse attractions—including lovely beaches and intriguing Maya ruins—like the path on a child's board game. With little exception, the peninsula is as flat as a tortilla.

Yucatán Peninsula

A street scene in convivial Campeche

Warm water and the Palancar reef bring cruise ships and solo travelers to Cozumel island.

Yucatán Peninsula

ALONG THE LENGTH OF QUINTANA ROO'S CARIBBEAN COAST, LOVERS HIDE out on sugar-sand beaches, birders stalk their prey among the mangroves, and cruise ships put in at palm-studded harbors used by the Maya a thousand years ago. Throughout the Yucatán Peninsula, rural towns doze in the shadow of whitewashed 16th-century monasteries. Each of the peninsula's three states—Quintana Roo, Campeche, and Yucatán—has scores of archaeological sites shrouded in jungle. Visitors can go deep-sea and fly fishing, snorkel along the world's second largest reef, and dive in underground rivers or in one of thousands of sinkholes. No place in Mexico has so much variety in so compact an area.

The Yucatán Peninsula is a land without lakes or rivers, yet is covered in tropical forests. Rainwater filters through the porous subterranean limestone shelf to create an extensive underground river system. Sinkholes (*cenotes* in Spanish, *dzonot* in Maya) form when this thin layer of limestone collapses, revealing deep green pools or shallow turquoise lagoons. More than 2,000 have been discovered in the state of Yucatán alone.

Water was sacred to the ancient Maya, who worshiped the rain god Chac. Respected mathematicians, astronomers, and architects, the Maya built fabulous cities during the Classic era (A.D. 250–900). Cosmology, history, celestial events, and community achievements were recorded in the *Chilam Balam*—a living document added to until the 19th century. The Maya also covered stelae and

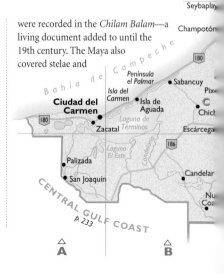

p. 233

other stone monuments in phonetic hieroglyphs. Luckily, many survived to be examined, but most of the Maya books were burned by Franciscan monks.

The Yucatán is an amalgam of distinct cultures. It is mainly Maya and Spanish, but waves of Lebanese, French, and other immigrants came as well. Its unique cuisine combines the region's famous citrus fruits, honey, and fiery habanero chilies with saffron, annatto, capers, prunes, and other unusual flavors.

Festivals reflect the diversity too. Hanal Pixan (All Souls' Day) is celebrated in Mérida, Campeche, and throughout the countryside by preparing regional foods and altars for the dead. Campeche and Cozumel are known for their pre-Lenten carnivals, and upstart Cancún has its jazz festival. ■

Mexico City

Area of map detail

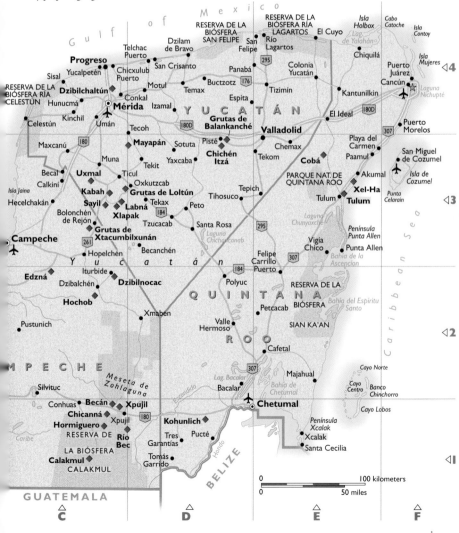

The continued growth of Cancún and other resorts on the Quintana Roo coast is inevitable.

Quintana Roo

Quintana Roo became a state in 1974, shortly after the Mexican government baptized Cancún. It didn't take long for both entities to swell beyond all expectations. The state contains wildly popular vacation destinations, significant Maya ruins, and a coastline that exceeds all superlatives.

The semitropical climate is perfect most times of year, though hurricanes do blow through between September and November. The crystalline Caribbean washes white-sand beaches from Cancún to Chetumal, on the border with Belize. Scrubby jungle just dense enough to evoke mystery covers most of the limestone terrain. Subterranean rivers flow through caves and into cenotes, enormous wells of cool, deep-blue water. Tropical fish swim lazily in underwater reserves, while sea turtles lumber ashore on summer nights to lay their eggs. All living creatures seem to enjoy their time in Quintana Roo.

Cancún attracts most of the state's visitors. Travelers with adventure in mind come to sample the resort's luxuries, then rush toward more challenging experiences. They explore the Riviera Maya—the latest marketing moniker for the coastline between Cancún and Tulum. Success has led to a frenzy of development in this area, and old-timers bemoan what they call its "Cancúnization."

The second longest chain of coral reefs in the world runs between Quintana Roo's mainland coast and the islands of Cozumel and Isla Mujeres. Sections of the reefs are littered with wrecked galleons from the 19th century and earlier, when English pirates crashed on the coral here. The coral they destroyed has grown back; the same can't be said for that crushed by modern cruise ships. Cozumel has become a major cruise port, much to the dismay of marine biologists and scuba divers.

Quintana Roo is suffering growing pains. Those who care about its natural resources are often pitted against those who see dollar signs wherever they look. Fortunately, some of the region's most precious attributes have been preserved in nature parks or enhanced in tasteful resorts. However, continued growth is inevitable, so you'd better get there soon. ■

Cancún

CANCÚN IS THE NOUVEAU RICHE OF THE RESORT WORLD. However, although it may lack culture, it is undeniably rich in real estate. The aquamarine sea laps the shores of the offshore island's northern coast and inland lagoons, while slapping a bit more energetically against the beautiful, white-sand beaches along the east-facing Caribbean. Sultry days drift into warm evenings, when welcome breezes ruffle tall coconut palms. Designed in 1970 and developed jointly by government agencies and private investors, Cancún now draws 2.5 million visitors a year.

Cancún
🗺 309 F4
Visitor information
✉ Av. Tulum 26
☎ 9/884-8073

Having been conceived and born of practicality rather than passion, Cancún lacks the flirtatious verve of resorts such as Acapulco and Puerto Vallarta, both of which grew rapidly but naturally out of existing villages. But for those with cash to spend, it can still be a wonderful playground. The all-inclusive resorts provide a wide variety of activities for those whose idea of vacation heaven is a palm-shaded lounge chair or parasailing above their very own beach.

Most of the larger beachfront hotels rent aquatic equipment, including boogie boards, snorkeling gear, sailboards, yachts, and personal watercraft, and many offer fishing, diving, and skin-diving tours, party boats, and other such waterborne activities.

Like other resort destinations, Cancún has large shopping malls and boutiques, although fewer open-air markets. Discos rock well into the morning, and restaurants offer international, regional, Mexican, and California cuisine. The ¼-mile-wide (0.5 km) island has two 18-hole golf courses at present. One is at the **Hilton Cancún Beach & Golf Resort** (*Tel 98/81-80-16*), and a second, the 72-par **Pok-Ta-Pok** course (*Blvd. Kukulcán Km 7.5, tel 98/83-12-77*), is in the middle of Nichupté Lagoon.

Perhaps more exciting for culture lovers are the dozens of well-restored Maya ruins found throughout the peninsula. Tulum (see p. 320) and Chichén Itzá (see

pp. 338–41) are two and three hours' drive, respectively, from Cancún. Rent a car or take a tour to visit these impressive ruins, or to snorkel in sinkholes, dive the peninsula's underground rivers, or visit historic cities such as Valladolid or Mérida in Yucatán state. Cancún is a convenient base for day trips south along the coast and a good point of departure for tours throughout the region. ∎

Its beaches are still Cancún's most impressive asset.

Playa del Carmen is hipper, and less expensive, than neighboring Cancún.

Riviera Maya drive

You could easily drive from Cancún to Tulum in three hours, but it's better to linger for a couple of days. Dubbed the "Riviera Maya," the coast along Highway 307 is full of diversions. Divers head for spooky cenotes (sinkholes) and caves or sunlit coves teeming with tropical fish; beach bums choose between bikini and beer hangouts or secluded stretches of untrammeled sand; sightseers climb pyramids; shoppers browse through folk-art boutiques; and everyone eats at least one meal of fresh fish a day.

Not long ago Hwy. 307 had only two lanes. Pickups and buses lumbered along at a leisurely pace, sharing the asphalt with villagers lopping off roadside branches with machetes for fuel. A few signs pointed the way to campgrounds and small hotels on white-sand beaches. The highway is now four lanes wide, and hulking motor coaches whiz past idle wanderers in VW bugs. Bold entryways announce the presence of theme parks; more modest signs lead the way to special haunts.

Puerto Morelos ❶, 22 miles (36 km) south of Cancún, has so far not undergone large-scale development. It remains a sandy village with a plain plaza near the waterfront; its greatest attraction is the coral reef just a short distance offshore. A small number of hotels, restaurants, and tour operators cater to divers and tourists seeking a laid-back

Mexican town with few frills and a great attitude. Vehicles bound for Cozumel line up by the ferry dock south of town.

The rich and famous hide out at the coast's most exclusive hotel, on **Punta Maroma,**

▲ See also area map p. 309 F4–E3
► Cancún
◆ 80 miles (130 km)
◕ 3 hours to 3 days
► Tulum

NOT TO BE MISSED
- Tres Ríos
- Playa del Carmen
- Xcaret
- Paamul
- Tulum

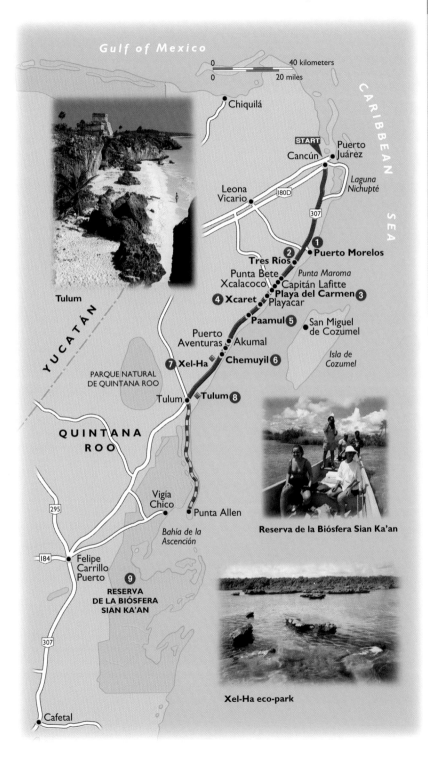

Gulf of Mexico

0   40 kilometers
0   20 miles

CARIBBEAN SEA

Chiquilá

START
Puerto Juárez
Cancún

Laguna Nichupté

Leona Vicario   180D

307

1 ● Puerto Morelos

2 Tres Ríos
Punta Maroma
Punta Bete
Xcalacoco   Capitán Lafitte
4 Xcaret   **Playa del Carmen 3**
Playacar

Paamul 5   San Miguel de Cozumel

Puerto Aventuras   Akumal
7 Xel-Ha   Chemuyil **6**   Isla de Cozumel

YUCATÁN

PARQUE NATURAL DE QUINTANA ROO

Tulum   **Tulum 8**

QUINTANA ROO

Vigía Chico
295   Punta Allen

Bahía de la Ascención

Reserva de la Biósfera Sian Ka'an

184   Felipe Carrillo Puerto

9
RESERVA DE LA BIÓSFERA SIAN KA'AN

307

Cafetal

Tulum

Xel-Ha eco-park

while adventurers turn off at **Tres Ríos** ❷ (*Tel 9/887-4977, $$$$*), a natural park. Three rivers feed into the sea at this 370-acre (150 ha) property. You can swim, snorkel, and canoe on the rivers and in the sea, and ride horses and bikes along jungle trails by the white beach. Several dirt roads lead to **Punta Bete,** 14 miles (22 km) south of Puerto Morelos, beloved by escapists of moderate means. Some head to **La Posada del Capitán Lafitte,** one of the first clusters of cabanas on the

Once a hidden cove, Xcaret is now one of the peninsula's hottest attractions.

coast. Others camp out at **Xcalacoco,** where the same families have been serving grilled fish to guests and campers for 20 years. Here day-trippers will find restaurants, a dive shop, and a congenial gathering of sunworshipers.

Playa del Carmen ❸, 6 miles (10 km) south of Punta Bete, has long been the main stop between Cancún and Tulum. In the past two decades, it has grown from a small town without telephones into a city of about 50,000 inhabitants. Banks, supermarkets, auto supply stores, and budget hotels are jumbled together along Av. Juárez, the main entrance to town from Hwy. 307. A steady stream of trucks and taxis continues to the pier, where ferries depart for Cozumel. International restaurants, excellent folk-art shops, and quirky small hotels line Av. 5 and the beach north of town. You can arrange diving, boating, and

archaeological tours, or just kick back, drowse in a hammock, and become part of the scene. The south side of town gives way to **Playacar,** an ambitious development with an 18-hole golf course and several hotels spread about manicured lawns dotted with small Maya ruins.

Travelers with time constraints are delighted to immerse themselves in man-made natural-effect settings at **Xcaret** ❹ (*Tel 9/871-4000, $$$$$*), five minutes south of Playa del Carmen. Spend a full day to get the most out of the steep admission; some activities and rental gear cost extra. You can visit the aviary, museum, botanical garden, and butterfly pavilion, float down an underground river with natural skylights, snorkel in the saltwater lagoon, hike through caves, ride horses, swim with dolphins (expensive and involved), eat at one of five restaurants, and nap on the sand. Stick around for the evening show, a long but captivating blend of Maya stories and Mexican folkloric dances.

The marine lagoon at Xel-Ha

Once you've passed Xcaret the traffic thins out around **Paamul** ⑤, the antithesis of a theme park. Turtles and humans like to burrow into this little haven, the former digging nests in the sand, the latter booking a few nights in a modest hotel. The water is calm, snorkeling and diving are satisfactory, and the restaurant serves homemade tacos and fresh fish.

Those who yearn for deluxe amenities head for **Puerto Aventuras,** a planned resort with hotels, condos, a 250-slip marina, and a nine-hole golf course. Stop by the **Museo Pablo Bush Romero,** named for the region's most famous scuba diver. Exhibits cover early scuba gear, the reefs, and booty from shipwrecks. Divers tend to congregate at nearby **Akumal,** where Romero was head-quartered in the 1920s. Hotel cabanas and private homes line the cove here.

Years ago a battered billboard announced the entrance to **Chemuyil** ⑥, "The Most Beautiful Beach in the World," 2½ miles (4 km) past Akumal. The perfect curve of sparkling sand and tranquil sea is still gorgeous, and campers string their hammocks from arcing palms. **Xel-Ha** ⑦ (Tel 9/884-9422, $$$$), the coast's first eco-park, has been revived by the Xcaret team. Mature tropical trees shade path-ways leading to an aquamarine cove dotted with the tips of snorkels. Tulum bus tours often stop here—at times humans seem to outnumber fish. Come early to appreciate it.

The Riviera Maya route ends at **Tulum** ⑧ (see p. 320). Its ruins are famous, but the town remains a quiet settlement. Gas stations, hotels, restaurants, and markets serve those passing through on Hwy. 307, and a narrow road by the sea passes small hotels and campgrounds. This road ends at the **Reserva de la Biósfera Sian Ka'an** ⑨ (see pp. 320–21), a fitting reminder of the Quintana Roo coast as it used to be. ∎

Islands & diving

THE WORLD'S SECOND LONGEST CHAIN OF CORAL REEFS lies just beneath the Caribbean's crystalline surface and stretches from the northern tip of the Yucatán Peninsula to Belize. Oceanographer Jacques Cousteau filmed the reefs in the 1960s; dive organizations now call the chain one of the top three dive spots in the world. Divers can access the reefs from Isla Mujeres, Cancún, and the Quintana Roo coast, but their mecca is Isla de Cozumel.

Cozumel
⚐ 309 F3
**Visitor
information**
✉ 5ta Av. Sur
☎ 9/872-7563

**Cozumel
Association of
Dive Operators**
☎ 9/872-5955, fax
9/872-5966

Isla Mujeres
⚐ 309 F4
**Visitor
information**
☎ 9/877-0307

Opposite: A diver
explores Tankah
Cenote, one of
thousands of
sinkholes in the
Yucatán.

Maya women once traveled from the mainland to **Cozumel** to honor Ixchel, the goddess of fertility. Today's pilgrims arrive in planes or ferries from Playa del Carmen, 12 miles (19 km) west, to worship the reefs. Underwater visibility of 80 to 100 feet (23 to 30 m), water temperatures hovering around 80°F (26°C), a 67,133-acre (27,170 ha) marine reserve, and dozens of competent dive operators all enhance Cozumel's reputation.

Divers float with slow currents along gardens of white, lavender, and pink corals and sponges beside electric-blue angelfish, hot-pink wrasse, yellow butterflyfish, and red grouper, while snorkelers witness similar sights at **Laguna Chankanaab** (*Tel 9/872-2940, $$$*), where shallow reefs are home to more than 60 species of fish.

Cozumel has many attractions on land as well. Island life is centered around the town of **San Miguel,** where streets are lined with high-quality shops and restaurants. The island's oldest hotel, La Playa, houses the excellent **Museo de la Isla Cozumel** (*Tel 9/872-1434, $*), with exhibits on the reefs and local history. The island's longest road curves along the southern tip to the wild windward side where waves and winds batter limestone coves. Turn-offs lead to the solitary lighthouse on **Punta Celarain** and a parade of *palapa* (palm-thatch) restaurants at **Playa San Francisco.** Sea turtles nest

on windward beaches in summer; biologists usually set up camp at **Punta Morena** to protect the turtles' eggs from poachers.

Inland are the ruins of **San Gervasio** (*Carretera Transversal, $*). This ceremonial center was occupied from A.D. 300 to 1500 and may have contained more than 300 buildings. About a dozen have been restored, including a temple honoring the goddess Ixchel.

Maya women were also drawn to **Isla Mujeres,** where a few scattered ruins honor Ixchel. Divers and escapists favor this 5-mile-long (8 km) limestone shelf just 8 miles (11 km) northeast of Cancún for its laid-back attitude. Even the sharks take it easy. Black-tip and nurse sharks often doze in 80-foot-deep (24 m) underwater caves. Experts believe a lack of carbon dioxide and overabundance of oxygen from underwater springs puts the sharks into this somnolent state. They don't even move when divers glide by, though there's always the chance of encountering a well-rested shark ready for lunch.

Scattered reefs along the island provide more typical underwater sights; **Mexico Divers** (*Av. Gustavo Rueda Medina at Madero, tel 9/877-0131*) offers trips to the shark caves and **Manchones Reef.** Snorkelers head for **El Garrafón** (*Carretera Garrafón*), an underwater reserve restored in 1999 by the same people who created Xcaret (see p. 314). The waters off

century. It was built by a Spanish pirate, Fermín Mundaca de Marechaja, who fell in love with an island woman. A similarly destitute **Maya ruin** sits at the southern tip of the island by an old lighthouse.

manta ray

Tour agencies on Isla Mujeres offer bird-watching and snorkeling trips to **Isla Contoy,** 19 miles (30 km) north. Undeveloped and protected as a national wildlife park, the small island is home to around a hundred species of birds, including pelicans, cormorants, and flamingos. Visitors are not allowed to spend the night on the island; dedicated bird-watchers should hire a boat captain to take them to Contoy at dawn, when the birds are most active. ■

lookdown

Isla's main beach, **Playa Norte,** are more suitable for swimming than snorkeling, and there are several palapa bars, restaurants, and small hotels here. The town consists of a few streets with more restaurants, hotels, and shops; bare feet and bathing suits are perfectly acceptable in almost all establishments.

Hacienda Mundaca, south of town and now a ruin covered with vines, dates back to the 19th

Above left: Blue damsels on the reef off Cozumel Below: El Garrafón reef, Isla Mujeres

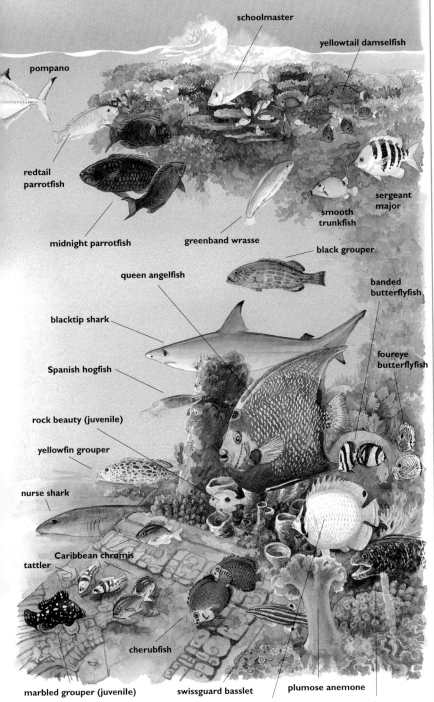

schoolmaster

yellowtail damselfish

pompano

redtail parrotfish

sergeant major

midnight parrotfish

smooth trunkfish

greenband wrasse

black grouper

queen angelfish

banded butterflyfish

blacktip shark

foureye butterflyfish

Spanish hogfish

rock beauty (juvenile)

yellowfin grouper

nurse shark

Caribbean chromis

tattler

cherubfish

marbled grouper (juvenile)

swissguard basslet

plumose anemone

spotfin butterflyfish

spotted moray

Tulum & Si'an Kaan

AN ALABASTER LIMESTONE CASTLE SITS ATOP A GRASSY bluff overlooking the Caribbean Sea at Tulum. Six hundred years ago, Maya sailors relied on beams of light from the castle's windows as they made their way to shore through treacherous reefs. The first Spanish explorers, on the other hand, crashed on the coral; those who survived made their way through a 3,000-foot-long (915 m) wall protecting the small community from invasion by land or sea.

Tulum
- 309 E3
- ☎ 9/883-3671
- $ $

Reserva de la Biósfera Sian Ka'an
- 309 E2

Amigos de Sian Ka'an (Cancún)
- ☎ 9/848-2136

Detail of the Descending God at Tulum

Tulum may well be the most popular archaeological site on the Maya circuit; it's certainly the most accessible. Busloads of tourists arrive every morning from Cancún, just 80 miles (130 km) to the north. For a while, it appeared that Tulum would be loved to death. But the government stepped in just in time, in 1993 building a visitor center away from the site. Visitors walk or take a jitney bus to the ruins and must follow prescribed paths when inspecting the 60 or so buildings. You can no longer climb to the top of **El Castillo,** which rises 40 feet (12 m) above a lawn dotted with restored temples and walls, and only those with the most vivid imaginations can picture the city in its prime.

Between A.D. 1100 and the Spanish Conquest, Tulum was a prosperous trading center, possibly ruled by a wealthy merchant class. Its citizens worshiped the **Descending God,** whose portrait can still be seen above the doorway of the temple of the same name. This upside-down god may represent the Bee God, an important deity in a region known for its fine honey. Paintings in the **Templo de los Frescos,** now shaded with thatched roofs and roped off, depict Maya gods and goddesses.

The Spanish explorers who survived shipwreck on the reefs below Tulum in 1511 found a busy commercial center whose buildings were decorated with bright red,

blue, yellow, and white paint. Two of the sailors stayed at Tulum. One, Gonzalo Guerrero, married a Maya woman and fathered the first mestizo children on the peninsula. He helped the Maya fight off Spanish invaders in 1517, but by the end of the century Tulum was a ghost town.

Though Tulum was the only major site right by the sea, the Maya lived and worked all along the Quintana Roo coast. Engineers built an elaborate system of canals dotted with shrines in the mangrove lagoons just south of Tulum. Their work is protected in the 1.3 million-acre (516,110 ha) **Reserva de la Biósfera Sian Ka'an,** 2 miles (3 km) south of Tulum, the last remaining expanse of undeveloped land on the Caribbean coast.

Sian Ka'an encompasses 62 miles (100 km) of beach, two bays, fresh and saltwater lagoons, and the Punta Allen Peninsula. Declared a World Heritage site by UNESCO in 1987, it is home to several thousand residents, most of Maya ancestry. The majority live around the community of Punta Allen at the tip of the 22-mile-long (35 km) peninsula and make their living from lobster fishing. Sustainable fishing is allowed in Sian Ka'an; there are even a couple of fishing lodges open to the public.

A dirt road runs the length of the peninsula, passing a ranger station at the park entrance and continuing on past idyllic beaches,

over small bridges, and through dense, low jungle. The drive can easily take three hours; bring plenty of fresh water, snacks, and a spare tire. A couple of small hotels and restaurants in Punta Allen fulfill basic needs.

Bird-watchers and archaeology buffs are better off joining a boat tour with **Amigos de Sian Ka'an** *(Tel 9/887-1970)* in Cancún,

a private nonprofit organization that works closely with park officials. More than 350 species of birds have been spotted in the lagoons; fish include snook, tarpon, and bonefish. The shallow boats glide at a leisurely pace past herons' nests, swimming turtles, and solitary Maya ruins, as guides describe the origins of Sian Ka'an, which means "birth of the sky" in Mayan. ∎

Tulum was a thriving commercial city when the first Spaniards arrived.

More places to visit in Quintana Roo

CHETUMAL

Few visitors make it as far as Chetumal, the capital of Quintana Roo. The peaceful city faces Chetumal Bay, where manatees hide in secret coves and herons fly along the shore. Hotels and restaurants are geared toward business travelers and those crossing into Belize.
309 D1   **Visitor information**   ✉ Av. 5, one block from the beach   ☎ 9/832-5073

COBÁ

Less famous than the seaside ruins at Tulum, Cobá rises from dense jungle about half an hour's drive from the coast. The archaeological site covers 81 square miles (210 sq km) and may have been the largest city on the peninsula. Only five percent of the structures have

Climbing the steep sides of Cobá's tallest pyramid, Nohuch Mul

been restored, and visitors often wander in total solitude through steamy heat to climb the majestic pyramid of **Nohuch Mul.** The climb up its 120 steps is exhausting but rewarding. The frequent squawks of wild parrots and the rare rustling of the branches by playful squirrel monkeys break the absolute silence as you stand high above the treetops. Remains of a ball court, small pyramids, and temples lie at the end of barely cleared trails. Many ornate stelae, carved with life-size depictions of both kings and queens and lengthy hieroglyphic texts, stand amid the vegetation. Present-day Maya still burn candles and incense and worship before two or three

of these stelae. Carry plenty of water and a map obtained from the rangers at the entrance.
309 E3   ✉ Carretera a Cobá, 30 miles (48 km) west of Tulum

KOHUNLICH

Amazing stucco masks with bulging eyes and protruding tongues decorate the main pyramid at Kohunlich. This little-visited Maya site may contain over 200 structures, but to date only five have been restored. The most impressive is the **Pirámide de los Mascarones,** where six-foot-tall (2 m) bas-relief masks in stucco dating from the Early Classic era (ca A.D. 300–450) are said to portray the sun god. The site is usually deserted, and there are no facilities. Bring plenty of water.
309 D1   ✉ 42 miles (67 km) west of Chetumal on Hwy. 186   🅂 $

LAGUNA BACALAR

Fed by freshwater and saltwater streams and springs, Laguna Bacalar, 25 miles (40 km) north of Chetumal, is Mexico's second-largest lake, often called the "Lake of Seven Colors" for its varying shades of green and blue water. The shores are lined with vacation homes, *balnearios* (bathing resorts), restaurants, and a few hotels. It's a good base for those wishing to explore remote Maya ruins in the interior.
309 D2

XCALAK

Divers and escapists imagine they're headed to heaven when they enter the **Península Xcalak.** The 40-mile-long (64 km) peninsula is the last undeveloped haven on the coast (except for Sian Ka'an). Rumors of impending development abound, but for now a 30-mile-long (48 km) paved and dirt road runs south from Majahual to the tiny fishing-oriented community of Xcalak. Reefs line the coast just offshore, but the pièce de résistance is **Banco Chinchorro,** a 24-mile-long (38 km) reef littered with shipwrecks. Boat captains in Xcalak and at the hotels transport divers to Chinchorro when the seas are calm. **Costa de Cocos** (*Tel 983/80478*), an idyllic hotel with cabanas on the sand, has a full dive shop.
309 E1 ■

The temples at Hochob have elements of both Río Bec- and Chenes-style architecture.

Campeche

Maya ruins, well signed in English and Spanish, dot the state of Campeche, many with recently installed visitor centers or small bookstores. Calakmul lies buried deep within Mexico's largest remaining rain forest, but Edzná, the best known and most visited pre-Hispanic site, is less than an hour's drive from the visitor-friendly capital city, Campeche. Dozens of other archaeological sites throughout the small state are easily reached along flat, two-lane roads with minimal traffic. Campeche, with its wonderfully restored colonial buildings, makes an excellent base for area excursions.

Campeche may be the country's most languorous capital city. Traffic trundles along slowly within the compact historic district, once enclosed by a hexagonal wall to protect its citizens from pirate attacks. Today, pedestrians stroll the recently refurbished *malecón*, while businessmen discuss oil prices over long lunches at their favorite restaurants. Seafood is the specialty here, and fleets to the south fish for octopus, bay shrimp, and pompano. *Pan de cazón* is not, as its name implies, a bread-based dish, but a filling casserole of shredded thresher shark, tortillas, black beans, and tomato sauce.

Campeche's west-facing beaches along the eponymous bay don't attract many foreign tourists, but wading birds fish in the shallow, warm waters off soft-sand, grass-strewn beaches at pretty Seybaplaya, and small cities such as Champotón attract hunters and sports fishers. Highway 186 heads inland from service-oriented Escárcega to access the ruins at Xpujil, Becán, and Chicanná before continuing east to the Yucatán coast. The most adventurous travelers will want to explore the wild and varied jungles of Calakmul Biosphere Reserve, where hundreds of Maya ruins lie unexcavated.

A newish road heading north from Xpujil makes it possible to continue to the Chenes-style ruins around Hopelchén, passing en route some of the Maya dwellings still used in the countryside. Round or oval houses of thick adobe walls and high thatch roofs, usually painted white but occasionally plain adobe or a startling sky blue, provide the tradition-minded Maya inhabitants with a cool respite from the impressive peninsular heat. ■

Campeche

THE UNIQUE AND RELATIVELY ISOLATED CITY OF Campeche exudes an aura of swashbuckling romance. Once completely walled to fend off marauding pirates, it retains a quiet, 17th-century elegance unmatched by other colonial cities. There are several interesting museums to explore, but by far the most spectacular attraction is the city itself. An ongoing renovation of downtown facades is transforming Campeche into a living museum of colonial and republican-era architecture. Since 1987, hundreds of structures have been restored in delicious tones of pale yellow, earthen brown, celery and dill green, deep gold, and ocher red.

Campeche
🅜 309 C3
Visitor information
✉ Av. Ruíz Cortines s/n, Plaza Moch-Couloh
☎ 9/811-9255

Founded in 1540 by Francisco de Montejo (see p. 333), Campeche gained importance as a port through which gold and silver passed en route to Spain. This wealth did not escape the notice of pirates, who for nearly two centuries besieged the city, sometimes inflicting wholescale massacres. Houses were burned, citizens robbed, women raped; in short, the city was continually sacked.

It was not until 1686 that the Spanish Crown finally took adequate preventive measures. The city was entirely walled, and after twin forts were erected, the pirate attacks finally ceased.

Today, the old city, **Viejo Campeche,** is a compact zone measuring five blocks by nine. Although the walls that once coddled the city in a hexagonal cocoon have largely been destroyed, the seven bastions, or *baluartes,* are mostly intact, and those that were demolished have been rebuilt. The two original entrances that once allowed the only access to the city still stand.

The land gate, **Puerta de Tierra** *(Calle 18 opposite Calle 59),* provides a dramatic background for a two-hour sound and light show *($$)* featuring dancers and musicians. The schedule varies depending on the season, but there are performances most weekend evenings, and sometimes during the week in high season. The sea gate, **Puerta del Mar** *(Calle 8 at Calle 59)*, is now just a large commemorative arch two blocks from the seawall.

Within the compact city center, the neoclassic **Catedral de la Concepción** *(Calle 55 at Calle 10, tel 9/811-9255)* incorporates renaissance elements. At the far right end of the large single nave stands a brilliant Holy Sepulcher of carved ebony covered in silver angels. Built between 1650 and 1850, the cathedral stands on the north side of the **plaza principal.**

Unlike the main squares in other Mexican cities, Campeche's tranquil park hardly ever seems busy—the majority of townsfolk are found strolling the seaside walkway, the *malecón,* in the evening. The plaza livens up on Sunday evenings, however, when the symphony orchestra plays in the central bandstand.

Wandering around the city is one of the most pleasant things to do in Campeche. Guided evening walking tours depart daily at 6 p.m. from the municipal tourist office on the west side of the cathedral *(Tel 9/811-3989)*. For those who prefer to ride, daily tram tours *($)* also depart from the main plaza at 9:30 a.m., 6 p.m., and 8 p.m.

You will have to venture outside the historic center to visit the **mercado municipal** *(Av. Circuito Baluartes between Calles 51 & 55)*. Except for fine "Panama-style" hats and some woven goods, Campeche is not known for its crafts, but souvenirs and T-shirts, as well as locally grown produce and other everyday items, can be found.

Located in strategic defensive positions at both ends of the city are Campeche's two historic forts. The completion of imposing **Fuerte San Miguel** *(Av. Escénica s/n)* in 1771 finally put an end to pirate raids. At the south end of the city, this hilltop fort now contains the city's best museum, the **Museo de la Cultura Maya** *(Tel 9/811-9255, closed Mon, $)*. Housed here are pre-Hispanic artifacts from throughout the state, including quite a few of Jaina island's statuettes portraying people of various stations and professions (see p. 331), and half a dozen spectacular jade funerary masks discovered at Calakmul (see pp. 329).

Northeast of the city center, at **Fuerte San José** *(Av. Francisco Morazan s/n)*, is the **Museo de Armas y Barcos** *(Tel 9/816-6593, closed Mon., $)*. The Museum of Arms and Boats displays 18th-century weapons, religious art, manuscripts, and model ships. Both forts provide great views.

Several of the bastions that once punctuated the city's hexagonal walls also house small museums. At **Baluarte San Carlos** *(Calle 8 at Calle 65, closed Mon.)*, a simple exhibit consists of a model of the city as it looked during the 18th century and a few other artifacts; you can also visit the dungeon. **Baluarte de la Soledad** *(Calle 8 at Calle 57)*, on the south side of the main plaza, houses a collection of carved Maya stelae in the **Museo de las Estelas** *(Tel 9/816-0507, closed Mon., $)*. The exhibit would be much more interesting, however, with some sort of explanation. **Baluarte de Santiago** *(Calle 8 at Calle 49, closed Sat., Sun.)* was the last bulwark completed, at the turn of the 18th century. Within its thick walls, completely rebuilt in the mid-1950s, is a small botanical garden. ∎

One of two hilltop fortifications that protected the port from pirates

Edzná
🔺 309 C2
✉ 28 miles (45 km) southeast of Campeche
💲 $

Edzná

EDZNÁ WAS INHABITED BY 400 B.C. AND SERVED AS A regional capital between A.D. 400 and 1000, but its greatest period of influence and monument building corresponds to the Late Classic era (A.D. 600–900). Although not abruptly abandoned as other Mesoamerican cities, its population dwindled slowly after A.D. 1000, finally disappearing at the end of the Postclassic period around 1450. Its appeal lies in the symmetry and monumental character of its structures and in the well-designed layout of the city center.

Located at a crossroads and trade route between the northern Yucatán Peninsula, the southern lowlands, and Ah Kin Pech (today's Campeche city), Edzná shows the influence of several architectural styles. Classic-era carved stelae, many still on site,

The Templo de los Cinco Pisos, the site's largest structure, was originally faced with stucco and paint.

are common to the southern lowlands, as are roofcombs and corbeled arch roofs. The most telling element of the Puuc style is the complex and symbolic stone mosaics adorning the temple facades.

Unique to Edzná, however, was its vast system of irrigation, constructed between 200 B.C. and A.D. 100 without beasts of burden, metal tools, or the wheel. During the rainy season, when the wide river valley often flooded, water was

collected and redirected to a multitude of reservoirs via canals.

The buildings excavated to date cluster in the vicinity of the main plaza, **Plaza Principal,** and the adjacent **Gran Acrópolis.** South of the former are the well-restored **juego de pelota** (ball court) and the **Templo Sur.** The temple surmounting this five-level structure appears to be of a different style and was probably added during the Late Classic period.

The site's largest and most impressive building is the **Templo de los Cinco Pisos** (Five-story Temple), located on the Great Acropolis. Sanctuaries on each level are accessed via a tall central staircase; the tiny temple at the top is crowned by the remnants of a roofcomb. A recently discovered solar phenomenon occurs each year at the planting season (May 1–3) and again at harvest (August 7–9). Because of the tilt of the Earth, the sun enters the normally dark interior to illuminate the face of the sun god, Kinich-Ahau, on a stele within.

Some of the site's oldest structures have been found on the **Pequeña Acrópolis,** south of the Great Acropolis. Each of the four buildings seated on this raised base face one of the cardinal directions. West of this acropolis is the **Templo de los Mascarones,** with its modeled plaster masks of the rising and setting sun god on the east and west flanks, respectively. ■

Reserva de la
Biósfera Calakmul

Reserva de la
Biósfera
Calakmul
309 C1

THE CALAKMUL BIOSPHERE RESERVE IS MEXICO'S LARGEST remaining tropical forest. This slightly elevated spine on the flat back of the Yucatán Peninsula forms an ecological link between the tropical rain forests of Guatemala's Petén region and the drier, shorter forests to the north. Within the reserve and easily reached by highway are the Maya ruins of Xpujil, Chicanná, and Becán. Meanwhile, Hormiguero, Calakmul, and Río Bec require a bit more effort to reach, but reward the traveler with a true "lost in the jungle" feeling.

Covering more than 1.7 million acres (723,185 ha), Calakmul provides a refuge for nearly a hundred species of mammals, including some of Mexico's endangered felines, such as the puma and jaguar. There are 235 known bird species, including toucans, parrots, macaws, and peninsula natives such as the ocellated turkey.

Despite its protected status, the biosphere is threatened by forestry and colonization. Immigrants from Tabasco, Veracruz, and Chiapas have settled here in various waves since the 1950s, bringing slash-and-burn agriculture, ranching, and hunting. About 4,000 people live within the park boundaries. The nonprofit Pronatura Península de Yucatán, directly involved in park management, works with communities in reforestation and in developing sustainable industries such as pig farming and honey production.

When the municipality of Calakmul was formed in 1996, the town of **Xpujil** became its seat of government. Highway 186 bisects the park at this tiny town, which has a few restaurants and basic hotels, a regional bus service, and a phone and fax service. The two-lane highway stretches east and west, connecting Chetumal, the capital of Quintana Roo, with Escárcega—a major crossroads and regional supply center for Campeche state. Heading north from Xpujil, a paved road leads to Hopelchén, the Chenes region, and Yucatán state.

Visitors can book tours out of Campeche or hire a guide through the Chicanná Ecovillage Resort (see p. 380), near Xpujil. All of the archaeological sites are open daily 8–5 and charge admission Monday to Saturday ($).

As they are within a few miles of each other and just off the highway, Chicanná, Becán, and Xpujil can be explored in a day. These sites combine elements of the Chenes architectural style (most notably

The endangered jaguar, one of the mammal species that has its home in Calakmul

their zoomorphic "mask" doorways), prevalent in northern Campeche, with the Río Bec style, typified by twin lateral towers topped by false temples, rounded corners, and false stairways.

Chicanná is a small site whose Mayan name means "house of the

snake's mouth." Occupied during the Late Preclassic period, it reached its peak during the Late Classic, when it may have served as an elite community dependent on nearby Becán.

Brown-and-white pea birds shriek as you cut through a small forest of sapodilla trees to Chicanná's main plaza, around which several ruined buildings are grouped. Typical of the site's Chenes-style structures, the facade of **Estructura II** forms an enormous mask representing the creator god Itzamná. The principal doorway represents the god's open mouth; above it, carved stones depict fangs, nose, and crossed eyes. Along the sides of the building, vertical rows of stone-mosaic Chac masks were once covered in stucco

and bright red pigment. These elements and themes are repeated on many of the site's structures.

Becán, less than a mile (1.5 km) away, served as the capital of the Río Bec area. A long moat built during the earliest days of settlement enclosed the site's largest and tallest buildings and various plazas, an inner city reserved for the elite.

Coiled in front of **Estructura III** are the remains of a round altar representing the feathered serpent god, Kukulcán (called Quetzalcóatl by the Toltecs and others to the north). A dank, dark, bat-lined tunnel penetrates **Estructura VIII,** leading from the building's base on the south side to the east side at the second level. From the top of this pyramid you can see the Temple of the Three Towers at Xpujil, about 5 miles (8 km) to the northeast.

Named for a plant that grows abundantly in the area, **Xpujil** (Cat's Tail), like Chicanná and Becán, flourished in the Late Classic era and combines Chenes and Río Bec architectural styles. Built-in benches such as those found in **Estructuras III** and **IV** suggest the buildings were living quarters.

About 14 miles (23 km) southwest of Xpujil, **Hormiguero** (Ant Hill) was named for the looters' tunnels that researchers found snaking through the site in 1933. Three distinct groups of buildings (North, Central, and South) are surrounded by clusters of dwellings. The Río Bec style predominates, typified by the side towers with rounded corners and false stairways of **Estructura II,** in the South Group. The tropical forests surrounding the ruins are interrupted by pastures, savannas, and marshes. Half-day excursions can be arranged in Xpujil.

Río Bec refers to a group of at least 18 ceremonial structures so spread out that archaeologists are

**Left: Structure III, in Calakmul
Above: Becán was once the capital of the Río Bec area, but like other sites nearby remains largely unrestored.**

unsure if they belonged to a single community. Hire a guide in Xpujil to take you on a hiking tour to this site on the Bec River.

One of the least-studied of the important Maya ruins, **Calakmul** is located deep within the reserve, 37 miles (60 km) off Highway 186. Although a road from the highway was paved in 1993, it can be difficult to negotiate during the rainy season, when four-wheel-drive vehicles are recommended.

Discovered in 1931 by U.S. botanist Cyrus Lundell, this extensive city—built on a floodplain and once near a large freshwater lake—is related stylistically to the nearby Petén region of Guatemala. Calakmul was continuously inhabited for more than 1,500 years, from the Middle Preclassic era (500–300 B.C.) to the Late Postclassic period (A.D. 1200–1521).

The site apparently had several periods of growth and success. For 500 years it was the capital of a kingdom called **Cabeza del Serpiente** (Serpent's Head), uniting such lowland cities as Dos Pilas, Naranjo, and Caracol. After the death of its leader Jaguar Claw and a significant defeat to Tikal in Guatemala, Calakmul appears to have strengthened relations with its northern neighbors of the Río Bec area, and buildings such as **Estructura V** show the influence of the Río Bec style. During this time a great number of stelae were carved and erected. The city declined in importance, and after A.D. 1000 was used almost exclusively as a ceremonial center. ■

Hopelchén, Hochob, & Dzibilnocac

DIRECTLY EAST OF CAMPECHE CITY IS HOPELCHÉN, A small but important town that makes an interesting stop off the tourist trail. Mennonites from surrounding farms come here to sell their homemade cheese and to purchase supplies. Although their young people sometimes rebel, they generally wear traditional farmer clothing and still speak the Low German dialect of their ancestors. South of town are Hochob and Dzibilnocac, two small archaeological sites demonstrating the Chenes-style architecture of the region.

Hopelchén
309 C3

Hochob
309 C2

Dzibilnocac
309 C2

Due north of Xpujil is **Hochob,** 9 miles (14 km) from Dzibalchén off the Dzibalchén–Chencho road. To date, three plazas and four buildings have been excavated, seated on an artificially leveled hill. The giant mask facades of the **Palacio del Este** (East Palace) and **Palacio Principal** (Main Palace), both on Plaza I, provide examples of one of the most important elements of Chenes architecture. The former building has a zoomorphic figure; the latter, the sun god Itzamná, whose squinting eyes appear above the doorway. Chac masks adorn the edges of the Main Palace, and the remains of roofcombs can be seen.

Behind the palace, several cavities in the ground are all that remain of an ancient irrigation system. The false stairways and towers crowned by false temples on **Estructura III,** also on the first plaza, are typical of Río Bec style.

North of Dzibalchén along a paved secondary road, the little-excavated ruins at **Dzibilnocac** are found in the town of Iturbide. Although platforms, pyramid bases, palaces, and vaulted chambers are strewn throughout the site, only one building has been excavated. Combining various architectural elements, the three-story **Templo Palacio** (Estructura I) has the false stairways and temple-topped towers characteristic of the Río Bec style. Well-preserved Chac masks adorn the top temple. The site was a mid-sized ceremonial center between about A.D. 250 and 900, but was inhabited as early as 500 B.C. ∎

A young man from Becal deftly weaves a straw hat.

More places to visit in Campeche

NORTHERN CAMPECHE

Between Campeche city and Yucatán state, Highway 180 passes a series of small towns, each with at least one sight of interest. Sixteenth-century **Hecelchakán,** 37 miles (60 km) north of Campeche, is admired among Campechanos for its *cochinita pibil* (baked pork seasoned with achiote), sold at informal eateries in the main square. **Isla Jaina** (just offshore) is not open to the public, but its famous statuettes can be seen in Hecelchakán's **Museo Arqueológico del Camino Real** *(Closed Mon.).* About 15 miles (24 km) beyond, it's worth stopping in **Calkiní** to see the cloistered **Clarisa convent church,** with its beautiful carved pulpit and main altarpiece.

Just before the Yucatán border is **Becal,** the birthplace of the famous *jipis,* straw hats varying from very fine, expensive "Panama hats" (a misnomer that annoys Campechanos no end) to colorful, floppy, coarse models to use at the beach. The hats are produced in cellars beneath residents' homes, where humidity keeps the palm fiber supple.
▲ 309 C3

CAMPECHE'S COAST

Although Campeche is not known for its beaches, a drive down the coast holds a few pleasant surprises. One of the prettiest stretches of beach is found around **Seybaplaya,** an unpretentious fishing town about 20 miles (32 km) south of Campeche. The narrow beach, lined with brightly painted skiffs, heads north about a mile (1.5 km) to **Payucán,** where herons, pelicans, and sandpipers stalk their prey in shallow waters streaked turquoise, gray-green, and blue. Another hour or so south is **Champotón,** the largest town between Campeche and the unattractive, business-oriented oil town of **Isla del Carmen,** farther south. It was in the bay at Champotón, now named **Bahía de la Mala Pelea** (Bay of the Evil Fight) that the Maya soundly defeated the Spaniards for the first time. The unremarkable yet pleasant coastal city of Champotón is a takeoff point for local hunting and fishing expeditions.
▲ 308 B2

GRUTAS DE XTACUMBILXUNÁN

Near the Yucatán border, the Caves of Xtacumbilxunán are a series of underground limestone chambers with interesting formations. The ancient Maya held these and other caves sacred as a link between this world and the next. If you're driving north from Hopelchén, it is worth the short detour off Highway 261 to visit the caves. It's best to book a tour out of Campeche, as the cave watchman/guide sometimes goes on a walkabout, and it's not recommended to enter the system alone.
▲ 309 C3 ∎

Yucatán

At the top of the peninsula, pie-shaped Yucatán is the flattest state, with the poorest soil and the least rainfall. Here the tropical forest is low, dense, and scrubby. Hot year round, it is particularly sultry during the rainy months of late summer and fall, when biting bugs are at their worst. December through February is the coolest time of year, when locals dress up in sweaters, while visitors in shorts and cotton shirts still break a sweat.

While its beaches are not the white-sand and turquoise-water variety of the Riviera Maya, an isolated coastline offers cheaper prices and an opportunity for discovery. Celestún and Río Lagartos lure bird-watchers, and nearby Isla Holbox is an island haven for escapist fishermen. Coastal infrastructure is limited but growing; accommodations are generally basic. The 48-mile (80 km) stretch along the northern Yucatán coast between Progreso and Dzilám de Bravo is being developed as la Nueva Yucatán. The state's days of innocence and isolation may be numbered, and it remains to be seen how its development will progress.

Yucatán's main draw, however, is its Maya ruins. Despite the pressure of busloads of visitors, Chichén Itzá remains among Mexico's top archaeological sites. Strategically placed throughout the large site are Mesoamerica's largest ball court, a sacrificial sinkhole, and stepped pyramids covered in bas-relief carvings.

Yucatán's other antique jewel, Uxmal, is one of a half-dozen excavated sites forming the Puuc Route, a loop of archaeological sites south of Mérida. In the same area of low, rolling hills are unassuming towns with lonesome Franciscan convents, orange-scented markets, and loads of appeal for the inquisitive traveler.

Once dedicated to corn and cattle, and later to sugarcane and then sisal fiber, the peninsula's haciendas were sold and subdivided during post-revolutionary land reforms. Today, many have been transformed into luxurious, rural hotels and restaurants. ■

Chichén Itzá is one of the Yucatán's most studied and fascinating sites.

Mérida

Fruit vendor

THERE IS LITTLE IN MÉRIDA TO REMIND YOU OF ITS PAST AS one of the most important ceremonial cities in the Postclassic Maya world: T'ho (meaning "fifth place"). Some vestiges remain of its days of wealth and European elegance, when *henequen* (sisal) profits paid for elegant Italian furnishings and foreign vacations. Isolated geographically and culturally from the rest of Mexico, Mérida's elite tended to look outside for cultural inspiration. Forged by indigenous labor under the brutal hacienda system, tempered with Maya resilience and sense of self, and enriched by the contributions of immigrants, Mérida is mestizo, but different from anywhere else in Mexico.

Unlike Tenochtitlán, which was felled in a four-month siege (see p. 30), T'ho resisted the invaders for 15 years. The resolute Maya first battled Francisco Montejo (el Adelantado) and later his son, Montejo el Mozo, who finally prevailed in 1542.

Today, Mérida is a city of almost a million people. Hotels are clustered in historic downtown, with the fanciest high rises along **Prolongación de Paseo Montejo.** Restaurants range from air-conditioned bistros with French menus to fan-cooled terraces and outdoor cafés. Carriages drawn by bedraggled-looking horses compete with cars, cabs, and diesel-belching buses on the streets downtown. Restored churches and theaters are scattered among modern one- and two-story structures in deep pastel colors—some charming, others crumbling.

Many second- and third-generation buildings surround the city's cultural and civic heart, the **zócalo,** or Plaza Mayor *(between Calles 60 & 62, 61 & 63).* Now a bank, the **Casa de Montejo** *(Calle 63, south side of the plaza)* is one of the city's finest examples of secular plateresque architecture, although only the facade is original. Note the Montejo family crest above the grilled balcony.

Across the plaza to the east, the original church has been incorporated into the **Catedral San Idelfonso** *(Calle 60 at 61),* begun in 1561 and added to over the centuries. Inside, 12 massive columns support the ribbed vaults over the

Mérida
🄰 309 C4
Visitor information
✉ Teatro Peon Contreras, Calle 60 between Calles 57 & 59
☎ 9/924-9290

nave of the Spanish Romanesque interior. Left of the main altar, the **Cristo de las Ampollas** (Christ of the Blisters) is a replica of the original statue, said to have survived an all-night fire with only discoloration and blisters.

Next door, the **Museo de Arte Contemporáneo** *(Calle 60 between Calles 63 & 61-A, tel 9/928-3258, closed Tues., $)* was originally the bishop's residence and now houses temporary exhibits on its second floor. There's a good view of the cathedral from the neo-classic **Palacio del Gobierno** (Government Palace), on the northeast corner of the plaza. Inside, 27 murals painted between 1971 and 1978 depict the disquieting history of regional conquest.

Some Mexican cities are lonely on Sundays, their streets empty except for visitors in search of a meal. Not so Mérida, where everyone seems to stroll the city center, showing off their best clothes. The zócalo and adjoining plazas, mercifully closed to traffic, become venues for free folkloric dance performances, crafts and antiques bazaars, and impromptu street theater. Get a schedule of events at the tourist office, located in a corner of the Italianate **Teatro Peon Contreras** *(Calles 59 & 60)*. If you're in the neighborhood any day before 1 p.m., stop in to admire the theater's frescoes and the early 20th-century marble staircase, restored in the early 1980s. Better still, catch one of the twice-monthly performances of the folkloric ballet. Across the street, outdoor cafés make tiny but convivial **Parque Hidalgo** a perfect people-watching spot.

Mérida's sultry tropical climate can be oppressive. The town snaps out of its heat-induced torpor after sundown, when evening breezes ruffle the palms in **Parque Santa Lucía** *(Calles 60 & 55)*. On

The fancy version of the Yucatecan *huipil* is the *terno*, shown here.

Thursday evenings at 9 p.m., musicians play while young men and women perform regional dances. On Saturdays after 8 p.m., tourists and locals gather for **Noche Mexicana** *(Paseo de Montejo & Calle 47)*, an outdoor festival of music, dance, and local crafts. Just up the street is the **Palacio Cantón**—an apricot-and-cream mansion of Carrara marble, Doric and Ionic columns, and Italianate *beaux-arts* details—housing the **Museo de Antropología e Historia** *(Calle 43 & Paseo de Montejo, tel 9/923-0557, closed Mon., $)*. Although the Museum of Anthropology and History has only a limited number of artifacts, it's worth the admission price to see the early 20th-century mansion.

Charming as Mérida is, its buses and cars pollute more than they should. The wooded areas, boating lake, children's playgrounds, and small zoo at **Parque Centenario** *(Av. Itzaes between Calles 59 & 65)*, at the city's western boundary, provide a refreshing escape from urban overload. The **Ermita de Santa Isabel** *(Calles 66 & 77, church closed weekdays)* is another peaceful refuge, with a pre-Hispanic altar and other Maya artifacts in the well-tended botanical gardens. Also known as Our Lady of the Successful Journey, the peaceful church was once a stopping place for travelers en route to Campeche.

At its founding, Mérida's core was reserved for the elite, surrounded by Indian towns and later mixed and mestizo neighborhoods. Each enclave was a world within itself, its social and religious life centered around the parish church. Although swallowed by the city in the 20th century, these barrios still have active churches and lively markets, and make an interesting detour from the main tourist routes.

Visit **Barrio de Santiago,** in the northeast sector, on Tuesday evenings, when 1940s-era bands play in the park facing the **Templo de Santiago Apostle** *(Calles 59 & 70)*. Closest to the main plaza is **Barrio San Juan,** with a 16th-century church *(Calles 69 & 62)* dedicated to St. John. About eight blocks southwest of the main square, the **Barrio de San Cristóbal** welcomed Lebanese and Italian immigrants in the 19th century. Its church *(Calles 50 & 69)* has a sober yet impressive interior decorated with images of the Virgin of Guadalupe (see p. 193).

Northwest of the city center, **La Mejorada** was once separated from San Cristóbal by a hill, demolished during the War of Independence. The former Franciscan monastery *(Calles 59 & 50)* now houses a school of architecture and the **Museo de Arte Popular** *(Closed Mon.)*, which displays folk art collected from the Yucatán and throughout the rest of Mexico.

Mérida makes a logical base for trips throughout the region, as it has a central location and good services. There are intimate bed-and-breakfasts and five-star high rises with full amenities, and excellent restaurants serving Yucatecan, Mexican, Lebanese, French, Italian, and international cuisine. There are plenty of shops, too. Choose from the region's Panama-style straw hats, wonderful hammocks, filigree jewelry, tropical clothing, or the locally made anise and honey liqueur, Xtabentun. ∎

Mérida's cathedral—begun in 1561, making it the oldest in mainland America—has a sober, restrained Renaissance facade.

Progreso
🗺 309 C4
Visitor
information
✉ Calle 80 No. 176 at
   Calle 37
☎ 9/935-0104

Coast & coastal reserves

WHILE QUINTANA ROO ATTRACTS SYBARITES AND SCUBA divers, Yucatán's coast draws slightly more introverted types, such as fishermen and birders. The ever increasing popularity of the Riviera Maya may have encouraged the Yucatán's development of a 24-mile (39 km) corridor between Telchac Puerto and Dzilám de Bravo, called "la Nueva Yucatán," although investors aren't rushing to the scene. Away from the crowds, natural reserves at Celestún, El Palmar, and Río Lagartos create a safe haven for domestic and migratory bird species, endangered marine tortoises, and other animal and plant species. And between these two extremes, Maya and mestizo villages languish under the tropical sun.

Like Río Lagartos, Celestún attracts both birds and birders.

With just under 50,000 inhabitants, **Progreso** is a vacation village for Meridians during the hottest summer months. Some travelers find it an interesting port city with a wide, long, sandy beach and water; to others, it's a tumble of cement and stucco buildings without much charm. Calle 19 hugs the coast, lined with seafood restaurants, hotels, and simple cafés. Progreso's original stone pier has been expanded (twice) and the harbor dredged in an effort to lure cruise ships and large commercial vessels.

After strolling on the beach or the long pier, where fishermen throw out their lines in early morning and evening, tour the 130-foot-tall (40 m) lighthouse, originally lit with kerosene (its electric beacon now shines far out to sea). **Yucalpetén,** about 4 miles (6 km) to the west, attracts many international commercial vessels into its protected harbor; a new marina for yachts is under construction. An aged but picturesque fishing fleet brings home catches of grouper, snapper, and sea bass.

The only significant stretch of beach road in the state is the 50 miles (80 km) between Progreso and Dzilám de Bravo, to the east. A two-lane highway passes salt flats used since pre-Hispanic times, and grassy dunes line the beach, accessed by sandy roads leading off from the highway. Meridians take weekend getaways in tranquil **Chicxulub Puerto,** a fishing village just east of Progreso. Straddling the coast here is the 112-mile-wide (180 km) Chicxulub

Crater, created by a meteorite about 65 million years ago and discovered in the 1940s by petroleum geologists. Its impact is thought to have created the peninsula's sinkholes. Other small fishing villages dot the coast, including **San Crisanto** and **Telchac Puerto.**

West of Mérida, **Sisal** was once the state's first important port but lost out to deeper Progreso in the latter part of the 19th century. Although it is a pleasant fishing village today with a nice beach, tourists are often drawn instead to neighboring **Celestún,** 60 miles (90 km) west of Mérida. From here small boats cruise the estuary and mangrove forests of the **Reserva de la Biósfera Celestún** in search of waterfowl, migratory shorebirds, and especially coral-colored flamingo colonies tens of thousands strong. At the edge of the estuary sits Celestún, a quiet town geared for day-trippers from Mérida and backpackers used to rustic accommodations. Three-hour birding tours (most flamingos are sighted between September and March) include a visit to a freshwater spring (ask for time to swim) and to a forest of petrified trees. Nearby **El Palmar,** a little-known haven for spider monkeys and other animals and plants, is also beginning to attract nature lovers.

Directly north of Valladolid on the north-central coast is **Reserva de la Biósfera Río Lagartos,** another wildlife sanctuary. Its long, highly saline estuary attracts white ibis, great white herons, snowy egrets, and flamingos. You can arrange three-hour bird-watching tours (*$$$ per boat*) in Valladolid, Mérida, at park headquarters (at the entrance to town) or at Restaurant Isla Contoy (*Tel 9/853-2668*). Pelicans roost in the mangroves, and herons stalk fish among their roots. You'll see the flamingo feeding grounds, although the nesting sites are off-limits.

Also great for fishing and relaxing is **Isla Holbox** (Mayan for "dark hole"), just over the Quintana Roo state line. There are five ferry crossings per day *($)*; at other times private skiffs *($$$$)* make the trip. Hotel Delfín arranges fly fishing for snook, tarpin, and bonefish, and ocean fishing for grouper and pampano *(Both $$$$$)*. The season is April–July, although ocean fishing continues year round. The hotel also rents out horses and sea kayaks. ■

As yet undeveloped, the state of Yucatán has miles of solitary beaches.

Chichén Itzá

Chichén Itzá

🗺 309 D3

✉ Highway 180,
72 miles (116 km)
east of Mérida

☎ 9/851-0124

Chichén Itzá

THE MOST ARCHITECTURALLY INTRIGUING AND MAJESTIC
Maya site on the Yucatán Peninsula is Chichén Itzá. Its earliest structures, including an ornate circular observatory, date to the Classic
era (A.D. 250–900) and echo the native Maya architectural details of
the Puuc region west of Mérida. Its famed Castillo was constructed
during the Terminal Classic or Early Postclassic period (A.D. 900–
1200). Scholars once thought this evidence of a Toltec invasion, but
most now agree that the worldly Itzá—successful merchants, who
traveled long distances, often by canoe—in fact influenced the Toltecs
at Tula as they traded with far-flung empires.

Above: Like the Europeans of the day, Mesoamericans sometimes displayed the severed heads of their enemies. Depicted here is a stone representation of this practice, called a *tzompantli*. Opposite: In the middleground is Caracol and, far beyond, the temple to Kukulkán, the feathered serpent.

Unlike the more romantic, vine-
shrouded sites of Palenque and
Uxmal, Chichén Itzá has an almost
militaristic appearance. Murals and
stelae (carved stone pillars) depict
warriors, battles, and human
sacrifice, belying the long-held
image of the Maya as a pacifist
people. Over 30 meticulously
reconstructed buildings rise above
flat, grassy fields, while hundreds of
other structures lie crumbling in
scrubby jungle. The site sprawls
over more than 3½ square miles
(9 sq km) and was once divided by
the highway between Cancún and
Mérida. Today, it is separated into
two distinct areas called the Grupo
Sur and the Grupo Norte.

Chichén's oldest structures are
located in the **Grupo Sur,** an area
first settled by the Maya around

A.D. 400. It was already deserted
when the Itzá peoples from the
south arrived in the eighth century
and began constructing a major
city. Also known as the Chontal
Maya or Putún, the Itzá were a
seafaring people from what is now
Tabasco state. The fact that they
were considered interlopers or at
least outsiders is evidenced by the
fact that their name in Mayan
means "those who speak our
language badly."

The buildings once thought to
have been Toltec-inspired dominate
the **Grupo Norte,** where
pyramids and temples were constructed atop existing structures
around the tenth century. Over
35,000 people lived in the area in
the 11th century, when Chichén
Itzá was a major religious and
commercial center. But by 1250,
the site was again deserted.

Archaeologists long believed the
Toltec of Tula, 600 miles (965 km)
to the west, conquered the Maya
of Chichén Itzá in the Early
Postclassic period (around A.D. 900)
and imposed their beliefs and
symbols upon their subjects.
However, it is now generally
accepted that the reverse is true.
Chichén Itzá actually influenced
Tula, an important link along one
of their extensive trade routes.
Turquoise found in Chichén Itzá

was traded from the Oasis America people of today's southern Arizona, and gold was imported from as far south as Costa Rica.

The confusion springs from the similarity of carvings, architectural styles, and symbols found at both Chichén Itzá's Grupo Norte and Tula, or Tollan. One of the most significant similarities is the presence of the feathered serpent god, called Kukulcán by the Maya and Quetzalcóatl by the Toltec and other groups. The serpent is particularly important at the **Castillo,** also called Pirámide de Kukulcán, Chichén Itza's most famous structure. Built atop an earlier temple, the pyramidal building has four stairways with a total of 365 steps, corresponding with the number of days in the solar calendar. A square temple at the top is believed to honor Kukulcán.

Thousands of onlookers are drawn to Castillo during the spring and fall equinoxes (March 21 and September 21). On these days, the sunlight hits the pyramid in such a way as to create a snake-shaped shadow wriggling down the steps to meet a serpent's head carved at the base. The phenomenon gives testimony to the Maya's incredible skill at mathematics and astronomy.

Chichén Itzá holds many examples of human sacrifice. Near the Castillo is the **Tzompantli,** a platform lined with stone carvings of human skulls. (A similar wall can be found at Tula.) Adjacent to this structure is the **juego de pelota,** or ball court. The traditional ball game had a religious and political significance unknown to most people today. It was a one-on-one game playing a victorious ruler against his defeated enemy—the loser would be sacrificed by being rolled down from the top of the pyramid, his arms and legs bound

tightly behind him, to smash on the ground below. The fight was fixed, of course, so that the conquering ruler could defeat the captive—a symbolic defeat of evil and darkness by light and life, and a reenactment of the creation of the world. In order to ensure his success, the conquering ruler would starve the other player for several weeks before the game and, if he still had too much spirit, break one of his arms or legs before the match. Evidence of this ritual ball game is seen in Mixtec hieroglyphics, Maya codices, and oral reports from eyewitnesses during the early years of the Spanish Conquest.

A dirt trail leads from the ball court to the **Cenote de los Sacrificios,** a deep natural well into which sacrificial victims were tossed. Mexican diver Pablo Bush Romero first investigated the well; Jacques Cousteau followed. Both found human skeletons and jade and gold figurines in the murky depths, further demonstrating the Maya belief in human sacrifice.

Back at Castillo, rows of carved stone pillars called the **Mil Columnas** front the **Templo de los Guerreros** (Temple of the Warriors), where a few bits of murals decorate the walls. More murals of a battle scene line a wall at the nearby **Templo de los Jaguares.** Several statues of the lesser god Chac Mool are scattered around the site; one of the largest sits by this cluster of ruins. The reclining figure holds a flat plate on which human hearts were presented to the gods.

More mysterious and ornate than the newer section, the Grupo Sur is dominated by the **Caracol** (also known as the Observatorio), named for its snail-like shape. Most likely used as an observatory, the Caracol has two levels of stairways and terraces leading to a circular

tower with windows facing the four cardinal directions. The Maya were keen astronomers, and studied the cycles of the moon and stars to calculate the passage of time. Their knowledge was particularly important in Yucatán, where crops had to be planted to benefit from the area's limited rainfall.

The Puuc style of architecture is most evident at the **Casa de las Monjas,** whose name, "the Nunnery," was given by the Spanish. Elaborate friezes front the crumbling staircase and window frames at the top of the long structure. Beside the Nunnery, **la Iglesia** (meaning "the Church," another Spanish reference) is also elaborately decorated with ornate carvings of animals and latticework designs. A somewhat overgrown trail leads from the Nunnery to **Chichén Viejo** (Old Chichén), where the Itzás let loose their imaginations on structures covered with masks of Chac, bas-reliefs of jaguars and gods, and delicate latticework designs. Some structures are barely visible beneath the ever encroaching jungle brush and vines.

Anyone even remotely fascinated by the Maya should spend at least one night by the ruins. There are several moderately priced hotels and restaurants in the nearby town of **Piste,** but it's worth the splurge to stay closer to the site. Archaeologists who worked here in the early 20th century stayed in cabins at the Hacienda Chichén; both it and the Hotel Mayaland are found by a back entrance to the ruins. ∎

Chac Mool was an intermediary between man and god. Note the plate for receiving sacrifice.

Uxmal & La Ruta Puuc

ONLY IN A LAND AS FLAT AS THE YUCATÁN WOULD SUCH A subtly undulating region be called "hill country." The Mayan word *puuc* describes not only this region, but the Late Classic cities that flourished here and the architectural style that defines them. With few cenotes, or sinkholes, the land could sustain these settlements only after northward-migrating people devised *chultunes* (water tanks), in which to store water for the dry months. They later created hydraulic systems as well. Between A.D. 200 and 1000, more than a hundred settlements prospered throughout the small region in south-central Yucatán and northeast Campeche.

With the demise of the Classic southern lowlands cities such as Tikal, the Puuc flourished between A.D. 800 and 1000 in what Mayanists call the Terminal Classic period. This was a period of intense and uncharacteristic political cooperation among cities, many of which were connected by *sacbés,* or white roads. In classic Mesoamerican fashion, the great religious centers were abandoned after reaching their height of civilization. Theories include over-population, depletion of resources, disease, and increased warfare, but the real reason remains a mystery.

Puuc-style architecture is admired for being among the most harmonious and well-proportioned of the Maya world. It is noted for its stone-mosaic facades, veneer masonry, small relief columns, and hook-nosed Chac masks on the facades and corners of buildings. In a land of uncertain rainfall and no surface rivers, the rain god Chac was an important deity. Walls are often smooth below, while the upper facades are decorated with elaborate geometric shapes. The "false arch," a Maya innovation, reached its most refined at the Palace of the Governor, at Uxmal.

Walled **Uxmal,** 48 miles (78 km) south of Mérida on Highway 261, was a favorite of 19th-century explorer John Lloyd Stephens (see p. 14), who visited several times with traveling companion and artist Frederick Catherwood. Capital of the Puuc region, Uxmal (meaning "thrice built") was founded around A.D. 800 and reached its peak of civilization under Lord Chac, who reigned between about A.D. 900 and 950. Its name refers to three distinct phases of construction. Considered the most lovely of the Puuc cities, it has been extensively restored but, compared to other major sites in Mexico, little studied.

Rising 140 feet (42 m) above the surrounding forest, the **Casa del Adivino** (Pyramid of the Magician) affords a great view of the site and surrounding low forest. The pyramid is also called "House of the Dwarf;" according to legend, it was built in one night by a dwarf hatched from a tiny egg. The tall structure's unusual elliptical base, rounded corners, and harmonious design make it one of the most admired buildings in Mexico—of any age. Steep staircases on either side lead to the temple at its crown, decorated with icons of the planet Venus, the sun, flowers, and serpents. This and other buildings are dramatically lit during nightly narrated sound-and-light shows in English and Spanish.

Uxmal
▲ 309 C3

Just beyond, the **Casa de las Monjas** (The Nunnery) is a quadrangle of four large, low palaces surrounding an open courtyard. Like those at many archaeological sites, the building was named by the Spaniards, who thought its 74 vaulted chambers resembled monastic cells. Covering the palace's upper interior facades are intricate carvings of Chac masks and serpents interspersed with latticework designs. Also within the central group are the **juego de pelota,** or ball court, and the simple **Casa de las Tortugas,** named for the turtles decorating the cornice (much blurred by the passage of time).

Cited as one of the most beautiful representations of Puuc-style architecture, the magnificent **Palacio del Gobernador** was built around A.D. 900 on a stepped platform. It seems to have served as both the residence and the administrative center of the ruling elite. The palace's horizontal plane is, on the east face, interrupted by perhaps the most refined false arches in the Maya world. Its frieze is covered in an intricate geometric mosaic composed of tens of thousands of carefully cut stones forming Chac masks.

The excellent travertine limestone found in the region was largely responsible for the success of Puuc-style carvings at Uxmal, epitomized in the Governor's Palace. This fine-grained limestone, ranging in color from yellow to red, can be cut into thin plates and polished to a high luster. Only around Mitla, in Oaxaca state, is such a high grade of stone found, and the Mixtecs of Mitla also produced intricate and exacting mosaics.

Just about 10 miles (16 km) to the southeast, **Kabah** was connected by a sacbé (which divides the site) to Uxmal. To the east are the greatest number of restored structures, including the impressive **Palacio de los Mascarones** (Palace of the Masks), elaborately decorated with six tiers of Chac masks, each an inlaid stone mosaic. Walk around to the back of the building to see the giant warrior sculptures wearing loincloths and beaded necklaces.

The name Uxmal (meaning "thrice built") refers to the site's three separate phases of construction.

Ticul, known for its pottery, is an unpretentious base for touring the region.

snakes. One of the best surviving examples of its type, the arch may have served commemorative purposes, or perhaps it was placed at the end of a sacbé.

The highway now loops north toward the caves of Loltún (see p. 346) to the **Ruta de los Conventos,** a series of monasteries built from the beginning of the 16th century for the catechism of the native population. While the churches and adjoining convents have lost much of their glamour, this route returns to Mérida passing typical Maya and mestizo towns. To visit the churches, arrive in the morning or late afternoon, as many are closed between noon and 4 p.m. En route, visit the wholesale market at **Oxcutzcab,** famous for its sweet oranges *(chinas).*

A 6-mile (10 km) detour off the Convent Route brings you to **Mayapan,** a late-blooming Maya city that gained importance around the time of Chichén Itzá's demise; some scholars believe Chichén was conquered by Mayapan. Mayapan lacked the excellent craftsmanship and site design of other Puuc cities, and had few important temples and no ball court. The 5-mile-long (8 km) wall, averaging nearly 20 feet (6 m) thick, suggests a fortified city. Its main temple, dedicated to Kukulkán, is a poorly constructed imitation of the Castillo, at Chichén Itzá (see p. 340). Mayapan appears to have been sacked and burned around 1440. With its demise, the Puuc alliance was disbanded and fighting broke out among the region's cities. Soon after, the Spanish conquerors arrived.

Nearby **Sayil** (meaning "home of leaf-cutter ants") is one of the oldest Puuc cities. The most important structure at this site is the three-story **Gran Palacio,** considered along with the palace of Uxmal to embody classic Puuc architecture. Containing more than 90 rooms, it must have housed the city's ruling elite. **Xlapax,** just a few miles away, is a small site and not much reconstructed. As with Sayil, its palace is decorated with masks of the rain god.

Labná (Old House) is about the same distance farther on. Although inhabited as early as the first century A.D., its most noteworthy construction is the Late Classic ceremonial arch, inscribed on the west facade with representations of thatch houses and stylized

The Ruta Puuc can be visited as a rushed day trip out of Mérida or Ticul, or as a more leisurely two-day visit. The latter has the added advantage of an overnight stay at one of several pretty hotels right at the ruins of Uxmal or in Ticul. ■

Take a dip in the magical underground pool of Cenote Dzitnup, near Valladolid.

More places to visit in Yucatán

DZIBILCHALTÚN

Dzibilchaltún, meaning "the place where there is writing on stones," lies 9 miles (15 km) north of Mérida and was one of the peninsula's most important and extensive cities, covering about 6 square miles (16 sq km). Continuously inhabited from at least 800 B.C. until the arrival of the Spanish, the large site flourished during the Late Classic period and has more than 8,000 structures (mostly unexcavated). Salt from local mines was traded throughout the peninsula. At least a dozen wide *sacbés* (white roads) connected the buildings throughout the extensive city.

The site has an excellent museum, the **Museo de los Maya,** with colonial art as well as pre-Hispanic artifacts, botanical gardens, and picnic grounds. You can swim in lovely open-air **Cenote Xlacah,** from which human bones and objects of bone, stone, ceramics, and wood have been extracted. Most of the excavated buildings surround the sinkhole, including the **Templo de los Siete Muñecos.** Its name derives from the seven clay figurines, now on display in the museum, that were excavated from beneath the temple.

🔼 309 C4 💲 $

GRUTAS DE BALANKANCHÉ

Just a few miles northeast of Chichén Itzá, the Caves of Balankanché were used by the pre-Hispanic Maya for sacred ceremonies. The outer caves were long known to locals, and a sealed chamber with ancient artifacts was discovered in 1959. The pottery shows it was used for religious ceremonies during thousands of years by Preclassic, Classic, and Postclassic civilizations. In the Terminal Classic period, the Maya rain god, Chac, was replaced with Tláloc, worshiped throughout Central Mexico. Many representations of Xipe Totec, god of spring and regeneration, have also been found.

Guided tours lead through passages to caves with impressive limestone formations of stalactites, stalagmites, and ancient ceramic artifacts. Tours leave hourly until 4 p.m., and a sound-and-light show recounts Maya history. Cave tours in English are scheduled at 11 a.m., 1 p.m., and 3 p.m.
🅰 309 D3 💲 Tours $$

GRUTAS DE LOLTÚN

Eleven miles (17 km) northeast of Labná along the Ruta Puuc are the Grutas de Loltún, one of the peninsula's most extensive cave systems. The caves were first inhabited by nomadic

Izamal was a pilgrimage site in the pre-Conquest era.

hunter-gatherers between 9000 and 3000 B.C., who left evidence of their presence in the form of stone tools. Much later, in the Classic period, the caves were used as a source of water by local inhabitants. Water vessels in both the Mayapan and Chichén Itzá Postclassic ceramic styles have been excavated. The Maya revered five physical features: trees, rocks, mountains,

mountain passes, and earth openings— cenotes and caves, which were considered holy because they presented a transition between the physical and spirit worlds.

Beginning at 9:30 a.m. and leaving approximately every 1½ hours, guided tours lead through a series of passageways to chambers of various sizes, some with prehistoric paintings or fantastic montages of stalactites and stalagmites.
🅰 309 C3 💲 $$

IZAMAL

Izamal has been an important religious center for millennia. The bustling small town's star attraction is the **Convento de San Antonio de Padua,** built from the stones of a pyramid to the god of the heavens, Itzamná, on which it sits. Its huge atrium was filled with hundreds of thousands of the faithful during a highly publicized visit by Pope John Paul II in 1993. Pony traps can be rented on the square for a tour of town, including a stop at the **Pirámide Kinich Kakmó,** all that remains of this once royal Maya city. The huge structure is currently under excavation. On Sundays a round-trip train excursion *($$$$$)* from Mérida includes lunch, a folkloric show, and a horse-drawn carriage tour as well as the train ride. You can purchase tickets through any travel agency, and board the train at 8 a.m. at the Mérida station *(Calle 55 at Calle 48, tel 9/927-7701).*
🅰 309 D4

VALLADOLID

Although it is the Yucatán's second-largest city, Valladolid has the feel of a small town. In 1847 this colonial-era agricultural center was the scene of the War of the Castes, during which the repressed Maya massacred large numbers of Spanish residents. Worth visiting are the **catedral,** on the *plaza principal,* and the large, 16th-century **Ex-Convento San Bernardino,** three blocks southwest. Outside town, you can visit holy **Cenote Dzitnup,** where light filters through a tiny hole in the ceiling to illuminate the green-blue underground spring. Valladolid also makes an alternative base for visiting the ruins of Chichén Itzá or the north coast.
🅰 309 E3 ■

Travelwise

The Virgin of Guadalupe

TRAVELWISE INFORMATION
PLANNING YOUR TRIP

WHEN TO GO

When you visit depends on what you want to do and see, budget constraints, and your tolerance for wet, hot, or humid weather. Mexico is a large and geographically diverse country, its microclimates dictated by altitude and latitude. June through October is the wettest time, and if you don't mind late-afternoon showers—which in Mexico City clear the air—consider booking your vacation during this low season to avoid the crowds and get cheaper hotel and air rates. Rain may put a damper on beach vacations, however, and late September and October are hurricane season along the Gulf and south/central Pacific coasts (and, less frequently, in Baja). Baja California and the northern deserts are extremely hot in the summer, although diehard fishermen brave the heat for the excellent fishing. Highland cities are hottest March through May, just before the rainy season, while the tropical regions of southern Mexico are hot year round but even hotter, muggier, and more bug-ridden during the rainy season. If you want to avoid both the rainy season and the high season, chose late spring (after Easter) or late fall.

High season is late November (Thanksgiving) to Holy Week (Semana Santa), with especially high hotel rates during Christmas, New Year, and Easter. Mexicans as well as foreigners frequently travel during these holidays, and reservations should be made well in advance.

Those interested in Mexican culture might want to plan their vacation around the country's many colorful fiestas, including the weeks preceding Christmas, Easter, Day of the Dead, pre-Lenten Carnaval, and many

others. See "Festivals & Fiestas" (pp. 16–17), regional chapters, and "Entertainment & Activities" (pp. 386–89) for specific suggestions. In Mexico, a city or village's saint's day is always cause for celebration. For example, places named San Juan will celebrate on the feast day of St. John, June 24; San Miguel de Allende celebrates its patron, the Archangel Michael, the days preceding September 29. Check with the government tourist office (see individual entries) for more information about specific local festivals.

WHAT TO TAKE

Although Mexicans today are less formal than before, city-dwellers are fashionable and businesspeople dress for success. Except on the more casual coast, Mexican women rarely wear shorts, and men are not seen shirtless except on the beach. Bring lightweight, comfortable clothing for tropical climes, plus a sweater or light jacket. Women should also bring slacks and at least one dressy outfit, men a light sports jacket. Much of Mexico consists of mountains and high plateaus, and while hot during the day can get chilly at night. Comfortable walking shoes are essential for archaeological sites, cobblestone streets, and long walks. A lightweight, long-sleeved shirt prevents mosquito bites, as does an insect repellent containing deet.

As well as the usual—documents and money—take sunscreen, sunglasses, and a hat as the sun is fierce. A small English–Spanish phrasebook is useful. Campers or trekkers should include iodine tablets and filters to purify water if bottled water is unavailable.

ENTRY FORMALITIES

A visa is not necessary for entry into Mexico for citizens of the

United States, Canada, the U.K., Ireland, Australia, New Zealand, and much of Western Europe. You will need a tourist card (*tarjeta de turista*), which can be obtained at embassies, travel agencies, and border crossings; they are also distributed during international flights. Travelers must provide proof of citizenship. For U.S. and Canadian citizens a certified birth certificate (not a copy) is sufficient, along with photo identification; but if you have a passport, bring it. Minors also need a certified birth certificate or passport and a notarized letter of permission from one or both guardians not accompanying the child. U.S. and Canadian citizens can stay up to 180 days with a tourist card.

DRUGS, NARCOTICS, & WEAPONS
To avoid problems, prescription drugs should be brought in their original containers. Drugs such as marijuana and cocaine are illegal, and penalties for drug offenses are strict.

Bringing weapons or ammunition to Mexico is illegal; importing either of these carries huge fines and the possibility of a jail term. Hunters must obtain permits and ID cards to import and transport firearms temporarily; it's best to make arrangements through an authorized wildlife outfitter club, such as a hunting lodge.

PETS
U.S. visitors may bring a dog (or cat) if they provide a pet health certificate signed not more than 72 hours before, and a certificate showing that the animal has been vaccinated against rabies and other contagious diseases.

VACCINATIONS & DISEASE
No inoculations are required for Mexico, but a current tetanus booster is recommended, as is a hepatitis A and/or B inoculation. For travel to rural lowland

areas, consider an antimalarial drug or protect yourself against insect bites with a good insect repellent and adequate clothing/ mosquito nets. The Center for Disease Control has a website (www.cdc.gov/travel/camerica.htm) with information about local conditions and health-related issues.

HOW TO GET TO MEXICO

BY AIR

Major airlines serving Mexico from the United States and Canada include:
Mexicana, tel 800/531-7921; Aeroméxico, tel 800/237-6639; American, tel 800/443-7300; Continental, tel 800/231-0856; and United, tel 800/241-6522.

Mexico City's Benito Juárez Airport is the connecting hub for flights throughout central and southern Mexico. If your destination is an international airport, your luggage need not pass customs in Mexico City. Confirm arriving and departing flights within 72 hours of flying. In Mexico City, use only official yellow airport taxis, which you prepay within the terminal.

BY BOAT

Many companies offer cruises to Mexico. Ports of call include Cabo San Lucas, Mazatlán, Puerto Vallarta, Manzanillo, Zihuatanejo/Ixtapa, and Acapulco on the west coast. Caribbean cruises berth at Cozumel, Cancún, and Playa del Carmen.

BY BUS

From the United States, Greyhound Lines (Tel 800/231-2222) can book travel to most of the major cities in Mexico through agreements with Mexican bus lines.

BY CAR

If you drive into Mexico, buy Mexican auto insurance. Policies issued in the United States do not cover liability within Mexico. Some cover damages, but be sure to check. One-stop insurance offices abound near the busiest border crossings and will issue policies by the day, week, or year. Some also help prepare paperwork for a Temporary Car Importation Permit, which is required when driving beyond the border zone (less than 16 miles/25 km into Mexico, Baja California and Baja California Sur exempt). These can be submitted or filled out at the Mexican customs office, at the border. The fee is about $15; use a major credit card and you'll avoid paying a cash bond (tedious, time-consuming, and costing up to $800) based on the value of the car. If you do not return the vehicle prior to the specified date (up to 180 days) you will suffer large, variable fines and possible impounding of the vehicle. The permit allows multiple reentries during the specified time period. Keep several copies of your permit in different places, as leaving the country without it is problematic.

Also required is proof of ownership of the vehicle, the original vehicle registration or car rental agreement, proof of Mexican insurance, and a valid driver's license (from your country of origin). If you do not own the car outright, you must provide a notarized letter from the bank or finance company giving permission to drive the car into Mexico.

Foreign license plates attract unwanted attention from police officers who often want cash in lieu of writing a ticket for a real or imaginary traffic violation. The officer may simply let you go on your way, take a *mordida* (literally "bite," meaning bribe), or accompany you to the police station. Be aware that a trip to the police station will be time consuming, probably cost as much as the previously mentioned "fine," and has the potential of involving you in even greater difficulties.

TRAVELING AROUND MEXICO

BY AIR

Mexicana de Aviación and its subsidiary, Aerocaribe (in the U.S., tel 800/531-7921; toll-free in Mexico, tel 01-800/502-2000; Mexico City, tel 5448-0990) and Aeroméxico and Aeromar (in the U.S., tel 800/237-6639; toll-free in Mexico, tel 01-800/021-4010; Mexico City, tel 5133-4010) are the primary Mexican airlines, with connections between most airports. Smaller airlines such as Aero California (in the U.S., tel 800-237-6225; in Mexico City, tel 5207-1392) fly to selected destinations such as Guadalajara, Hermosillo, La Paz, Los Cabos, and Mexico City.

BY BUS

Buses are ubiquitous in Mexico; where there is a road, you'll find a bus to rumble down it. For longer trips, always book first class (*primera*) or deluxe. First-class buses have air-conditioning and bathrooms and often show a video en route.

The larger towns have modern bus stations, known as the *central camionera* or *central de autobuses*, where tickets can usually be purchased in advance. Only second-class buses may be available to rural areas or tiny hamlets. Some are air conditioned, but most are not, and they stop whenever a passenger wants to board or descend, lengthening travel time.

It's a good idea to bring snacks, bottled water, and toilet paper. Some long-distance buses stop at restaurants. Check with the tourist information office to make sure the route is safe before booking overnight trips, which are discouraged by the U.S. State Department and other foreign government agencies. Robberies, while not exactly frequent, do occur on the most touristed routes, where robbers can be assured of dozens of cameras and other expensive gear. Intercity buses are cheap and frequent, but unpleasantly crowded during rush hours.

BY CAR

Roads vary greatly in Mexico, with the expensive *cuota,* or toll road, being the best maintained (and safest). The *libre,* or free roads, are usually fine, although in rainy climates potholes can be a problem. Use extra caution when driving in the countryside, as farm animals may wander onto the road. Don't drive at night, and ask about the condition of roads and the possibility of robberies in each region before you set out. In general, observe speed limits and parking regulations, and watch for speed bumps as you enter and leave towns.

Remember that posted speed limits and distances are in kilometers. The usual speed limit on highways is 100 kph (60 mph); within towns it is 30–40 kph (19–25 mph). Many road signs use symbols, not words, but a few important translations are as follows: *Circulación,* with an arrow, means one-way traffic (very common in towns); *No rebasar* or *No rebase* means no passing; and *Ceda el paso* means yield right of way. On highways, Mexican drivers often use their left-turn signals to indicate that the car behind is free to pass.

BREAKDOWNS

The government-sponsored Angeles Verdes patrol vans have aided stranded travelers since the 1960s. True to their name, the Green Angels (Tel 01-800/903-9200) are real roadside angels in an emergency, and will change flat tires, provide basic parts and towing services, and suggest competent nearby

mechanics. You must pay for parts, gasoline, or other expenses, but service is free (tip them as appropriate).

All gas stations are franchises of the government-owned oil company, PEMEX, and sell three types of fuel: Nova (leaded), Magna Sin (unleaded), and Premium (super unleaded). As a rule of thumb, fill your tank when it's half full or as often as possible when traveling to a remote area. Many stations are not open at night. It's customary to tip the attendant a few pesos (also to make sure he resets the counter to zero before fueling).

RENTAL CARS

Rental cars are expensive in Mexico, special deals are few and far between, and drop-off rates are high. Smaller, locally owned companies are sometimes cheaper than international companies such as Hertz, National, and Budget, but their cars may be not be well maintained. Rental companies require you to leave a signed credit-card voucher as a guarantee. Ask whether IVA (value-added tax) is included in the quoted price, what insurance is provided, and what the deductible is.

For day trips, consider hiring a taxi instead of renting a car. Ask the hotel manager or tourist office for a recommendation, or negotiate with a cabby you find helpful and friendly. The price will be about the same (less if you are a good bargainer) as renting a car, and you won't have to worry about driving in unfamiliar areas or parking. Often you'll also get an informal Spanish lesson or an English-speaking "tour guide" who is happy to tell you all about his native city.

BY FERRY

Auto and passenger ferries connect Baja California Sur and mainland Mexico. Travelers

intending to ferry their vehicles from Baja to Sonora or Sinaloa must obtain a Temporary Car Importation Permit (see "How to get to Mexico by car," p. 349), at the international border. The Santa Rosalía ferry (Tel 115/20013) serves Guaymas, Sonora (Tel 6/222-3390), twice weekly. The cost for the seven-hour crossing ranges from about $13 to $50 (depending on accommodations) for passengers; about $130 for vehicles (substantially more for trailers and motorhomes). Several ferries per week connect La Paz (ferry landing at Pichilingue, 10 miles/16 km to the north; ticket office in La Paz at 5 de Mayo 502, tel 112/53833) to Topolobampo, Sinaloa (Tel 686/20141). Travel time and prices are the same as for Santa Rosalía. Prices for the daily, ten-hour La Paz–Mazatlán ferry are about half as much again as for Topolobampo or Guaymas. Reservations are essential, especially during holidays; make them well in advance and reconfirm ten days to two weeks before departure. For current information and reservations online, log on to www.ferrysematur.com.mx; within Mexico, call 01-800/696-9600.

On the Caribbean coast, frequent passenger ferries (Tel 9/872-1508) and hydrofoils (Tel 9/872-0588) connect Playa del Carmen to Cozumel, just offshore; vehicular ferries depart from nearby Puerto Morelos (Tel 9/872-1722). Passenger ferries and hydrofoils are more frequent, inexpensive, comfortable, and hassle-free than the car ferry; you can rent a car, moped, or electric golf cart in Cozumel. Daily passenger ferries connect Puerto Juárez (Tel 9/877-0065), just north of Cancún, to Isla Mujeres.

BY TRAIN

Trains are poorly maintained and schedules are not kept; bus travel can be more than twice as speedy and is certainly more comfortable. Other than the exceptional train ride through the Copper Canyon on the Chihuahua al Pacífico Railway (see pp. 88–94), train travel is not recommended.

TRAVELING IN MEXICO CITY

BY CAR

Even if you have driven your own car to Mexico, park it when you get to Mexico City and take radio cabs or public transportation; the quagmire of this city's streets is best left to the locals. If you must drive, be aware that a city ordinance to reduce smog dictates which days of the week cars may circulate; this is based on the last number of the car's license plate. Foreigners as well as locals are subject to substantial fines for infractions. For information, check at a gas station, in the newspaper, or with hotel personnel.

BY BUS

Mexico City is well served by a comprehensive yet inexpensive bus service. Routes may or may not be posted at bus stops and may be available at tourist offices. One of the routes most used by tourists connects Chapultepec Park to the Zócalo via Paseo de la Reforma, Avenida Juárez, and Calle Madero. If possible avoid traveling during rush hours, as buses at that time are packed to bursting and traffic can be maddeningly slow. If you must ride on a crowded bus, follow the safety advice given in the Metro section below.

For destinations outside Mexico City, there are four major terminals. Check with the concierge or tourist office before making a long trip to the wrong bus station. Generally, Terminal del Norte (Tel 5689-

9745) serves points north; TAPO (Tel 5762-5977), points to the east; Terminal Sur, also known as Tasqueña (Tel 5762-5414), points to the south; and Terminal Poniente (Tel 5271-4519), points to the west.

BY METRO

The subway system in Mexico City is extensive and inexpensive. Beyond the city center, *el tren ligero* is a sometimes aboveground line reaching into suburbs such as Xochimilco. Metro maps are available at most stations and at tourist offices. Most lines operate from 5 or 6 a.m. to midnight. Weekday rush hours are 6–10 a.m. and 5–8 p.m.; during these hours separate cars are available for women and children to prevent them being squashed against men. While subways can be extremely crowded, negotiating the system can save you from traffic jams on the congested city streets above. Beware of pickpockets and mashers. Hold purses, cameras, and backpacks tightly, and carry currency in a money belt or hidden front pocket.

BY TAXI

Mexico City taxis have received a lot of bad press in the last couple of years, and with good reason. Robbing passengers at gunpoint was the *crime du jour* in 1997. Using radio cabs instead of roving cabs reduces risk (Tel 5271-9146, 5271-9058, or 5272-6125, or ask your concierge for a recommendation). Also, check that the driver's face matches his picture ID, which must be prominently displayed, and that the license plate number listed there is the same as the one on the car.

Taxis are often unmetered and it's best to establish a fare ahead of time. Tipping the driver is not customary. Outside Mexico City, few cab-related robberies have been reported.

BY TRAM

In Coyoacán a narrated tram ride takes tourists on a 50-minute tour *(daily 10–5, $$)* of the neighborhood's main sights.

PRACTICAL ADVICE

COMMUNICATIONS

MAIL
Although your mail will eventually get to its intended destination, service from Mexico takes from three days to a month to reach the United States. Courier service is available in most cities, but don't count on overnight service; be sure to ask how long the delivery will take. MexiPost is the government-run competition for private couriers such as DHL and FedEx. Some rural Mexicans still rely on the telegraph service, found at (or next door to) post offices, which are generally open Mon.–Fri. 9–6, Sat. 9–noon.

TELEPHONE, FAX, E-MAIL, & ADDRESSES
To call or fax Mexico from the United States or Canada, dial 011-52 and then the area code followed by the number. For long-distance calls within Mexico, dial 01, area code, and number. For toll-free calls within Mexico, dial 01-800 and the number.

Mexican area codes are in a state of transition; the system is confusing at best. Mexico City, Guadalajara, and Monterrey have absorbed their one-digit area codes to become eight-digit numbers. (If you dial just the seven-digit number, you'll get a busy signal. When dialing these cities long distance within Mexico, dial 01 and the eight-digit number.) Most other cities have switched from the old three-digit area code (called LADA) with five-digit number to a one-digit code with seven-digit phone number. Some places still have two-digit area codes and six-digit numbers, or the old-fashioned three-digit area codes and five-digit numbers. If a five-digit local number doesn't work, try adding the last one or two numbers of the area code, or call the operator.

Making international calls from Mexico is expensive. Some public phones are owned by private companies that charge exorbitant rates; if in doubt, dial 0 and ask the operator for international rates before placing a call. (If he or she refuses to tell you, by all means hang up and use a standard public phone.) Most hotels, especially chains that cater to business travelers, add a high service charge for international calls, and not all have direct-dial phones or Internet modems. Local phone calls are more reasonably priced. Many pharmacies and newsstands sell prepaid LADATEL phonecards (20, 50, or 100 pesos) for use with public phones; there are few remaining coin-operated phones. LADATEL phonecards work for quick calls outside Mexico (but time runs out quickly; make sure to use the 100-peso card). For international calls, dial 00 plus the country code (1 for Canada and the United States; 44 for the United Kingdom).

Most towns have at least one private fax service, which may charge by the minute or by the page. Cities small and large have cybercafés where you can connect to the Internet. Many offices do not have fiberoptic lines, and connections tend to be slow; try to visit during off-peak hours for a faster connection. Internet cafés generally charge a reasonable $2–4 per hour.

While most street addresses in Mexico have both street name and number, some properties in small towns—or on large boulevards—are labeled simply by street name and "s/n":

shorthand for *sin número,* meaning "without number." Whenever possible, a cross street or other reference is added. Properties along highways *(carreteras)* are often addressed simply by their distance in kilometers along the highway in question—for example, "Carr. Transpeninsular Km 19.5." In the case of streets, with the exception of those that are numbered, the designation "Calle" rarely appears in front of the name on maps or in written addresses.

FURTHER READING
Websites & links
The Mexican government tourism website is www.mexico-travel.com. *Mexico Connect* is a monthly e-zine and excellent index of sites related to living, working, and traveling in Mexico: www.mexconnect.com. *Mexico Online* has travel information and breaking news stories: www.mexonline.com. Ecotourism, environmental news, and excellent links concerning the Americas can be found at www.planeta.com.

Reading list
Arts and Crafts of Mexico, Chloë Sayer. Chronicle Books, San Francisco, 1990.
Distant Neighbors, Alan Riding. Vintage Books, New York, 1985.
The Hungry Traveler, Marita Adair. Andrews McMeel Publishing, Kansas City, 1997.
The Labyrinth of Solitude: Life and Thought in Mexico, Octavio Paz. Grove Press, Inc., New York, 1961.
The Mexicans: A Portrait of a People, Patrick Oster. Harper & Row, Publishers, Inc., New York, 1990.
Mexico: From the Olmecs to the Aztecs, Michael D. Coe. Thames & Hudson Ltd., London, 1994.
The People's Guide to Mexico, Carl Franz and Lorena Havens. John Muir Publications, Santa Fe, NM, 1995.
The Reader's Companion to Mexico, Ed. Alan Ryan. Harcourt Brace & Company, Orlando, FL, 1995.

Travelers' Tales Mexico, Ed. James O'Reilly and Larry Habegger. Travelers' Tales, Inc., San Francisco, 1994.
True History of the Conquest of New Spain, Bernal Díaz. Penguin Books, London, 1963.
Viva Mexico!, Antonio Haas. M.T.Train/Scala Books, New York, 1998.

CONVERSIONS

In general, the metric system is used. Temperatures are in centigrade, distances in kilometers, and so on.

ELECTRICITY

Mexico's electrical system operates on 110 volts AC, with outlets taking two-flat-pin rectangular plugs. Bring adapters for any appliances with three-prong plugs, and a power-surge protector for laptop computers. If a power outage or brownout occurs while you are using your computer, shut it down immediately.

ETIQUETTE & LOCAL CUSTOMS

Mexicans are very polite and very friendly, but not overly casual with strangers. Use the formal address *usted* instead of the informal *tú* when addressing people you don't know, especially in the smaller towns, away from tourist enclaves, and with elders.

When asking directions, be aware that many Mexicans find it embarrassing or impolite to decline to help, even when unsure of the address you are seeking. As they may inadvertently send you in the wrong direction to save face, ask directions often and request landmarks. Also, they rarely give specific street names, although with prompting these may be provided.

It is considered disrespectful to enter churches in skimpy

clothing, and to sightsee during church services.

LANGUAGE STUDY

Spanish-language courses are offered by private institutes and those attached to universities throughout Mexico. Some are intensive courses focusing on grammar; others offer cultural classes (for example regional cooking, handcrafts, or archaeology) or *intercambios*, casual one-on-one conversations with a compatible Mexican who wants to practice his or her English and help you with Spanish. Programs generally run from two to four weeks (or more), and students can stay with families or arrange to rent apartments or hotel rooms. Some families rent out rooms to several English-speaking students at a time. Those committed to immersing themselves in the Spanish language should ask for a family that hosts only one student at a time. You can get information, listings, and links to language schools throughout Mexico on www.worldwide.edu.

LIQUOR LAWS

The legal drinking age is 18 years, although identification is rarely checked. The sale of alcohol is prohibited on election days.

MEDIA

NEWSPAPERS & MAGAZINES
Most Mexican reporters rely on stipends from the people or government offices they cover, making impartiality impossible. The newspaper most openly critical of the government is *Reforma;* that and the left-leaning *La Jornada* are the largest circulating nationals. For those who do not read Spanish, larger cities carry the English-language daily *The News,* while towns with many English-speaking residents publish their own small weekly or monthly papers. In hotels, airports, and newsstands in larger

cities, foreign periodicals such as *Time, Newsweek,* and *U.S. News and World Report* are sold. The Sanborns chain of restaurant/bookstores is a great source of magazines, books, and periodicals about Mexican culture.

TELEVISION & RADIO
Many more Mexicans get their information from radio and television than from newspapers. In addition to two government-run television channels, there are a half-dozen private networks. The largest (and most influential), Televisa, has a line-up of Mexico's universally popular evening soap operas. Cable television is becoming available throughout the country; hotels geared to foreign tourists usually have satellite or cable TV.

MONEY MATTERS

The *nuevo peso* was introduced in 1993, when 1,000 "old" pesos became the equivalent of one "new peso." Now that the old coins and bills have been taken out of circulation, the term peso is used once again. Bills come in denominations of 20, 50, 100, 200, and 500 pesos. Always keep a supply of coins and smaller-denomination bills, especially in non-touristy areas, as change can be hard to come by. U.S. dollars are accepted in border cities and at major resorts, although you almost always get a better deal using pesos. Always keep a supply of small bills for tipping.

Canadians and other foreign travelers will avoid headaches by bringing traveler's checks and cash in U.S. dollars. You can change money at a bank, but a *casa de cambio,* dedicated exclusively to this activity, is usually faster, has longer, more convenient hours, and offers the same or only slightly lower rate. Check exchange rates online at www.oanda.com.

Automatic Teller Machines (ATMs, or *cajeros automáticos*) can be found throughout

Mexico, but make sure you have a backup of cash or traveler's checks so you won't be stranded if an ATM is broken or out of money. With ATMs you get an excellent exchange rate, but service charges are $2–12, depending on individual bank policies. Avoid using ATMs at night or in isolated locations. Credit cards also give a good exchange rate. MasterCard, Visa, and, to a lesser extent, American Express are the most commonly accepted, although mainly at larger, tourist-oriented hotels and restaurants.

The value-added tax, called IVA, is charged by some stores but ignored by others; most will add IVA if you ask for a receipt.

NATIONAL HOLIDAYS

Banks, state offices, and many other businesses close on the following holidays. Check ahead before arriving at museums or other tourist destinations. (See also "Festivals & Fiestas", pp. 16–17, and "Entertainment & Activities," pp. 386–89.)
Jan. 1 New Year's Day (Año Nuevo)
Feb. 5 Constitution Day (Proclamación de la Constitución)
March 21 Benito Juárez Day (Natalicio de Benito Juárez)
May 1 Labor Day (Día del Trabajo)
Sept. 16 Independence Day (Día de la Independencia)
Nov. 20 Revolution Day (Aniversario de la Revolución Mexicana)
Dec. 25 Christmas Day (Navidad)

OPENING TIMES

It is difficult to generalize about opening hours in Mexico, as they vary from region to region. In industrialized areas, government and business offices usually adhere to a 9–5 schedule (but some close at 3 p.m.). In hot climates, however, they may close for two to four hours in the middle of the day, reopening from 4 or 5 until 8 (others do not reopen in the afternoon). Although open until 3 or 5 p.m., banks often exchange money only in the morning. Theaters and museums normally close on Mondays, and the latter, along with archaeological sites, are frequently free on Sundays. Standard store hours are 9 until 7 or 8, with a possible siesta break in between. Remember, especially in tropical climates, to assume there will be a siesta break between approximately 2 and 4 or 5 p.m. This even applies to churches.

PHOTOGRAPHY

Black-and-white and slide films are hard to come by, so bring your own. When purchasing film, check the expiration date. Processing is inconsistent, so it's best to take your exposed film home to develop. Think twice about photographing people in regional costume; either be very discreet or ask permission.

PLACES OF WORSHIP

About 90 percent of Mexicans are Catholics; in the most historic cities and towns it seems there is a church on every corner. Remember that while these churches may seem like fabulous museums, they remain places of worship. Short shorts and skimpy tops are frowned upon (or forbidden), and men should remove their hats.

Tourist offices and hotels can provide a list of the most interesting churches in town, some of which offer mariachi or guitar mass or English-language services. Most cities and towns also have at least one Protestant (often Evangelical) church.

SAFETY

Common sense is your most valuable weapon against crime while traveling in Mexico. Be cautious, but not paranoid.

Street crime was uncommon until 1994, when the peso devaluation resulted in increased poverty and hence crime. Leave expensive jewelry at home, and don't flash wads of money or fancy cameras. Most hotels have room safes or a safe in the lobby—use them. Hold onto handbags and daypacks tightly; beware of criminals who might cut the pack open with a razor.

Mexico City unfortunately requires extra caution. Use hotel taxis. When out for a day of sightseeing and in need of a cab, ask the restaurant or shop to call a taxi for you, carry the number of a reliable radio-dispatch company, or as a last option, search for a taxi stand (sitio de taxis). (See also "Traveling in Mexico City by Taxi," p. 351.) For current safety information, contact the U.S. State Department's website at www.travel.state.gov/mexico.html.

The police in Mexico are underpaid, and graft and corruption are commonplace throughout both government and commercial bureaucracies. Although efforts are being made to eliminate la mordida ("the bite"), this form of small-time bribery continues (see "How to get to Mexico by Car," p. 349).

If you are a victim of a minor crime, consider that the criminal justice system is woefully ineffective, and decide according to your loss (and the hassle involved) the benefit of reporting it to the police. By all means, if you are the victim of a serious or violent crime, report it to your embassy or nearest consular office at once.

TIME DIFFERENCES

Most of Mexico is on Central Standard Time (CST), one hour less than Eastern Standard Time (EST). Baja California Sur, Sonora, Sinaloa, and Nayarit are on Mountain Standard Time (EST minus two hours); Baja California (Norte) is the only state on Pacific Standard Time (EST minus three hours). Daylight saving time was adopted in 1996.

TIPPING

Most Mexicans tip little if anything in the more humble places, but it's nice to leave ten percent anyway. Fifteen percent is customary for good service in tourist-oriented restaurants; always make sure the service is not included on the bill. Cab drivers are not tipped unless they wait while you shop or sightsee, which obviously requires additional payment. Hotel maids are usually given $1 per day, bellboys $1 per bag. Group tour guides should receive at least $1 per person per half-day; private guides may be tipped 5–10 percent of the tour's price. Gas station and washroom attendants should be given a small gratuity as well.

TOILETS

There is much variation in the toilets you will find in Mexico—some good, some very bad, and many without toilet seats or toilet paper. Try to use the rest room at your hotel or in restaurants, cafés, and bars when you stop for refreshments.

Except in tourist-oriented hotels and restaurants, don't throw toilet paper in the toilet, but in the basket provided. As unappealing as this seems to some, it can avoid serious plumbing problems for the proprietor and a nasty overflow for you.

TRAVELERS WITH DISABILITIES

Mexico has few accommodations for travelers with disabilities, including ramps and wide doorways, although some progress is being made. The newer hotels are usually the best bet, but advance planning is advised. The Society for the Advancement of Travel for the Handicapped (SATH), 347 Fifth Ave., Suite 610, New York, NY 10016; tel 212/447-7284, has a website at www.sath.org with general information and links to other sites.

VISITOR INFORMATION & USEFUL PHONE NUMBERS/WEBSITES

English-speaking operators working for the Ministry of Tourism can provide information about weather, holidays, safety, entry requirements, and other aspects of visiting Mexico, and can recommend hotels and restaurants. From the United States or Canada, dial 800/446-3942. Within Mexico, for general information, legal aid, or other assistance dial 01-800/90392, or in Mexico City, 5250-0151 or 5250-0123. Website: www.mexico-travel.com.

The U.S. Embassy in Mexico offers assistance to crime victims; dial 5209-9100 (24 hours a day). Visitors of other nationalities should call their embassies in the event of an emergency (see below).

Consumer Protection in Mexico City, tel 5568-8722.

Mexican Red Cross, tel 5557-5757; for an ambulance, tel 5395-1111, ext. 173 or 124.

The following numbers work throughout Mexico, although not in all towns. For telephone information, call 040; for the police, 060.

EMERGENCIES

EMBASSIES & CONSULATES

The foreign embassies are all based in Mexico City; although many other cities in Mexico have consular offices.

UNITED STATES EMBASSY
Paseo de la Reforma 305, Colonia Cuauhtémoc, 06500, México, D.F., tel 5209-9100, www.usembassy-mexico.gov.

CANADIAN EMBASSY
Schiller 529, Colonia Rincón del Bosque, 11560 Polanco, México, D.F., tel 5724-7900, www.canada.org.mx.

BRITISH EMBASSY
Río Lerma 71, Col. Cuauhtémoc, 06500 México, D.F., tel 5207-2089.

HEALTH

The most prevalent health problem experienced by travelers in Mexico is intestinal. Gastrointestinal upset may be caused simply by drinking water with a different composition from what you are used to. More serious problems result from drinking unclean water or eating improperly prepared fruit or vegetables. The most common disorder is diarrhea (often called *turista,* or Moctezuma's revenge). Although caution is certainly advised, to stop eating at humble establishments makes for a limiting cultural experience, and fancy resorts are in any case not immune to contagion.

As a general rule, drink bottled beverages, including water, and only ice made from purified water. Eat peeled fruit and vegetables, and avoid raw fish or shellfish. If you do contract turista, drink plenty of clean water and rest for a couple days until the symptoms subside. Beware of over-medicating on antidiarrhea remedies. In worst case scenarios, unclean water can lead to salmonella, hepatitis, or other more serious diseases. If you have a fever or continued severe diarrhea or headaches, seek the advice of a physician.

Air pollution in Mexico City and Guadalajara is severe (especially December–May) and can cause health problems for small children, the elderly, or those with respiratory problems. High altitude can exacerbate the problem (Mexico City sits at 7,400 feet/2,250 m above sea level and is ringed by mountains that trap the smog). To acclimatize, avoid strenuous activity, alcohol, and high-fat foods for one or two days.

Local pharmacies dispense advice as well as over-the-counter remedies; many can direct you to a doctor. The management at your hotel is also a good source for finding a health-care provider. The American Society of Medical Advice to Travelers can be reached in the United States at 716/754-4883, and in Canada at 416/652-0137.

WHAT TO DO IN A CAR ACCIDENT

Unfortunately, Mexican law prescribes that all parties involved in a vehicular accident resulting in physical harm or material damages be jailed until guilt can be established. For this reason, Mexicans involved in accidents often flee the scene. Obtaining Mexican auto insurance is essential, as it limits liability and, most importantly, it can keep you out of jail (see also "How to get to Mexico by Car," p. 349). Insurers commonly offer day, six-month, and one-year policies for either liability (including medical liability and coverage for passengers, legal aid, bail bond, and towing) or full coverage (above-mentioned services plus theft and collision/property damage).

Oscar Padilla's Mexican insurance (in the U.S., tel 800/258-8600, or try the website www.mexicaninsurance.com) has a convenient program allowing those who drive into Mexico frequently to keep an open insurance account that can be reactivated just prior to a trip by phone or Internet.

HOTELS & RESTAURANTS

While Mexico has some lovely small hotels and plenty of large resorts and business hotels, it doesn't have as many different types of accommodations as some countries. But the major resort destinations and business-oriented cities are represented by world-wide hotel chains, as well as a few Mexican-owned chains. Independently owned hotels run the range of prices, from downright cheap to absolutely upscale. In between are plenty of charming small hotels with prices much more economical than those in the United States, Canada, and Western Europe. The cities most popular with travelers have the greatest range of options.

Restaurants run the gamut from chains such as Sanborns—where kids and other creatures of habit will be comfortable in the plush upholstered booths, with familiar-looking menus—to market stalls and the elegant eateries in exclusive hotels.

ACCOMMODATIONS

Hostels are rare in Mexico, but don't despair: inexpensive lodgings are plentiful. Rural areas not usually frequented by tourists may have no formal lodgings; if in doubt ask at the city hall *(municipio)*. In states such as Oaxaca and Chiapas, the government has organized communities in areas of great natural beauty or cultural attractions to provide inexpensive lodgings. Financed by the government, these community-run lodgings are an excellent way to visit otherwise inaccessible parts of the country. Information can be obtained at state or municipal tourist offices, which may also make the reservations via shortwave radio or cell phone. Some of these communities are too small or remote to have standard phone lines.

Campgrounds such as those found in the United States and Canada are few, although RV parks are more plentiful, especially in the Baja Peninsula and the northern Pacific coast, where snowbirds flock. Camping is usually permitted on public property such as beaches; ask permission to camp on *ejido* (communally owned) lands or private property. B&Bs and guesthouses are also unusual; most are owned and run by foreigners. But connoisseurs of small, intimate hotels will not be disappointed. Cities such as San Cristóbal de las Casas, Oaxaca, and San Miguel de Allende have some one-of-a-

kind small hotels. And although many rent for hundreds of dollars a night, others—equally charming but with fewer amenities—can be had for less than $50.

Resort hotels charge resort prices: You'll pay as much for a Sheraton or Westin hotel in Mexico as in First World countries. Also, prices are usually quoted in dollars, so you'll see no savings as the peso fluctuates. Although you'll pay more at these internationally geared, often high-rise, hotels, you'll almost always get English-speaking staff, concierge service, swimming pools, smoothly running elevators, in-room safes and minibars, cable or satellite TV, and so on. Most beach resorts have at least a few all-inclusive hotels.

Hotels in business-oriented cities such as Mexico City, Guadalajara, Aguascalientes, and Monterrey may offer secretarial services, business centers, meeting rooms, computer modems, and direct-dial phones. The latter two are not as common as you might think, so if these features are important to you, ask before reserving a room. Many business-oriented hotels offer discounts on weekends (sometimes 50 percent or more) or incentives such as buffet breakfasts. Be sure to inquire about different packages, promotions, and discounts.

Rooms should be reserved well in advance at certain times. Beach resorts such as Cabo San

Lucas and Cancún fill up during holidays (Easter, July and August, and the Christmas season), while hotels in towns with popular celebrations might be booked a year in advance: for example, Taxco's Easter week, Veracruz during Carnaval, or the Christmas season in Oaxaca.

Taxes vary by state. Most charge 15 percent tax, which may be augmented by a 2 percent hotel tax. Others have a 12 percent tax. Many of the more humble establishments either don't charge tax or have included it in the price; make sure you ask in order to compare prices accurately. Unless otherwise stated, the hotels listed have private bathrooms and are open year round. Toll-free numbers listed are for making reservations from the United States and Canada. In very small towns, *"domicilio conocido"* means "known address," and indicates there are no street names but anyone can point out the establishment.

CREDIT CARDS
AE American Express, DC Diners Club, MC Mastercard, V Visa.

PRICES

HOTELS
An indication of the cost of a double room in high season, excluding tax, is given by $ signs.

$$$$$	Over $250
$$$$	$150–$250
$$$	$100–$150
$$	$50–$100
$	Under $50

RESTAURANTS
An indication of the cost of a three-course lunch or dinner without drinks, tax, or tip is given by $ signs.

$$$$$	Over $45
$$$$	$30–$45
$$$	$20–$30
$$	$10–$20
$	Under $10

RESTAURANTS

The midday meal is generally eaten between 2 and 5 p.m., although tourists, some office workers, and farmers eat before then. The set meal (called *"el menu del día"* in nicer restaurants and *"comida corrida"* in more humble eateries) is usually a bargain, but often unavailable before 1:30 or 2 p.m. This generally consists of soup, a rice or pasta plate, and an entrée, followed by dessert and coffee or tea. A beverage may also be included; *agua de sabor* is commonly served. These fruit juice and water drinks range from lemonade to watermelon water.

   Antojitos roughly translates as appetizers, but they can be filling regional specialties such as *memelas*, tacos, or enchiladas (see p. 18). Dinner is traditionally a very light meal, and although restaurants in tourist areas provide full fare, it's generally much more expensive than a lavish midday meal. In smaller or less touristy towns, and even some of the larger but less cosmopolitan cities, restaurants may close by 7 or 8 p.m. (Note: restaurants listed as "lunch only" are generally open between 1 and 6 p.m.)

   While hotel dining rooms and cafés tend to stay open from morning to late at night, some eateries open for lunch and dinner only. They may close between 5 and 6 or 7 p.m., when the dinner hour begins, and some cafés don't open before 9 or 10 a.m. If you want an early breakfast, check opening hours the day before. Check your bill before tipping, as service may be included. Closings for holidays may vary, so it is advisable to phone and reserve a table.

L = lunch
D = dinner

In the following selection, towns are arranged alphabetically under each region heading. Hotels are listed under each location by price, then in alphabetical order, followed by restaurants also by price and alphabetical order.

CATAVIÑA

🏨 LA PINTA CATAVIÑA
🍴 $$
HWY. 1, KM 173, IN CATAVIÑA
TEL 800/336-5454
FAX 858/454-2703 (BOOKING AGENT IN CA)
This wonderful hotel and restaurant abuts an oasis of palms; prehistoric cave paintings can be seen nearby. There's a spring-fed courtyard swimming pool, and the brick-domed restaurant serves delicious seafood and international dishes.
🛏 27 P 🚭 🏊
 🔲 MC, V

ENSENADA

🏨 ESTERO BEACH RESORT
$$
HWY. 1, 6 MILES (10 KM) SOUTH OF CENTRAL ENSENADA, 22800
TEL 61/76-62-30
FAX 61/76-69-25
An easygoing low-rise resort, "the Estuary" has many amenities—including driving range, boat launch, watercraft rental, and playground—to keep kids and adults happy. Kitchenettes and private patios invite long-term stays. RV hookups, camping.
🛏 104 🔲 P 🚭 🏊
 🔲 MC, V

🍴 LA EMBOTELLADORA VIEJA
$$
AV. MIRAMAR 666 AT CALLE 7
TEL 61/74-08-07
An extensive wine list includes vintages bottled in the adjacent winery, plus French and Californian wines. Tucked in *la bodega*, or wine cellar, it has loads of charm as well as delicious Mediterranean and Mexican cuisine. Distinguished Restaurants of North America (DiRoNa) award winner.

🕐 Closed Tues. 🔲 AE, MC, V

LA PAZ

🏨 LA CONCHA RESORT
🍴 $$$
CARRETERA A PICHILINGUE KM 5, 23010
TEL 112/16161, 800/999-2252
FAX 112/16218
www.laconcha.com
This often recommended resort of stylish, modern Mediterranean design sits right on the sands of beautiful Pichilingue Beach. Smallish, dark rooms overlook the lovely grounds or the Gulf of California. The beach club has an excellent dive shop, watersports equipment rentals, and full-time divemaster. Wonderful international, Mexican, and seafood dishes are served in the poolside restaurant.
🛏 151 P 🚭 ❄️ 🏊
 🔲 All major cards

🏨 CROWNE PLAZA
🍴 RESORT
$$$
MARINA NORTE FIDEPAZ, LOTE A, 23090
TEL 112/40830, 800/227-6963
FAX 112/40837
www.crowneplaza.com
E-MAIL crownelapaz@baja.net.mx
One of La Paz's most elegant, all-suites properties overlooks the Gulf of California and the public marina about 3½ miles (5.5 km) from downtown. Amenities include swim-up bar, spa, waterskiing, squash, and tennis. The **Real Hacienda** restaurant serves international and Mexican specialties.
🛏 54 P 🚭 ❄️ 🏋
 🔲 AE

LORETO

🏨 VILLAS DE LORETO
$$
SOUTH OF TOWN AT ANTONIO MIJARES, 23880
TEL/FAX 113/50586
Rooms with hot showers,

(sidebar) HOTELS & RESTAURANTS

comfy beds, and refrigerators overlook the pool and beach at this out-of-the-way inn. RV and tent camping sites are available; smoking is not permitted. Kayaking and fishing can be arranged at additional cost. Continental breakfast (included in room price) is the only meal served.
🛏10 ◻ ◻ ≋
🏨 MC, V

LOS CABOS

🏨 CASA DEL MAR
🍴 $$$$$
CARRETERRA TRANS-
PENINSULAR KM 19.5, 23400
TEL 114/40030, 800/221-8808
FAX 114/40034
E-MAIL casamar@cabonet.net.mx
A romantic beach getaway and spa with lovely grounds, several pools and flower gardens, a dusky-cool library/reading room, and lots of services. Hacienda-style rooms in a pleasing palette of golds, rosy pinks, and Mediterranean blues have furnished porches and Jacuzzi tubs overlooking the sea. The classy restaurant, also overlooking the water, serves excellent regional cuisine.
🛏55 Ⓟ ◻ ◻ ≋
🏨 AE, MC, V

🏨 PALMILLA
$$$$$
CARR. TRANSPENINSULAR
KM 7.5, 23400
TEL 114/45000, 800/637-2226
FAX 114/45100
E-MAIL palmilla@ourclub.com
White arches draped with scarlet bougainvillea add a touch of Old Mexico to one of Baja's most romantic hotels—complete with a wedding chapel. The room decor is understated and the service superb. One of Los Cabos's original properties, it has a dependable sportfishing fleet and a 27-hole championship golf course.
🛏115 Ⓟ ◻ ≋
🏨 AE, MC, V

🏨 LAS VENTANAS AL PARAÍSO
Movie stars and moguls hide out at this exclusive, expensive resort along the Los Cabos Corridor. Fireplaces, telescopes, private terraces, and fabulous custom furnishings make guests want to stay put in their rooms. Excellent restaurants, a three-level pool, and hammocks under the palms draw them out.
$$$$$
CARRETERRA TRANS-
PENINSULAR KM 19.5, 23400
TEL 114/40300, 888/525-0483
FAX 114/40301
🛏60 Ⓟ ◻ ≋ 🐾
🏨 AE, MC, V

🏨 MELIÁ SAN LUCAS
$$$$
PLAYA EL MÉDANO S/N, CABO SAN LUCAS
TEL 114/34444, 800/336-3542
FAX 114/30420
Close to the the bay, beach, marina, and Cabo San Lucas's shops, restaurants, and bars, this popular chain hotel has a large pool area often packed with partying vacationers.
🛏150 ⇄ ◻ ◻ ≋
🏨 AE, MC, V

🏨 LA PLAYITA
$$
LA PLAYITA BEACH
SAN JOSÉ DEL CABO, 23400
TEL/FAX 114/24166
E-MAIL laplayita@hotmail.com
Fishermen swap tales around the pool of this clean, casual, no-frills hotel on a long, lonely beach. There's no restaurant, but the one next door will cook your catch. Three suites have kitchenettes. Road impassable in rainy season.
🛏26 Ⓟ ◻ ≋ 🏨 AE, MC, V

🍴 CASA NATALIA
$$$$
BLVD. MIJARES 4, SAN JOSÉ DEL CABO, 23400
TEL 114/25100, 888/277-3814

FAX 114/25110
Located within an intimate boutique hotel, this excellent restaurant combines modern and traditional decor. Nouvelle Mexican and international cuisine are served indoors or on the palm-shaded patio; try the pasta with goat cheese in mescal sauce.
🕐 Closed L except for guests ◻ 🏨 AE, MC, V

MULEGÉ

🏨 SERENIDAD
$$$
HWY. 1, 2 MILES (3 KM) SOUTH OF MULEGÉ, 23900
TEL 115/30530
FAX 115/30311
www.hotel-serenidad.com
E-MAIL serenidad@mulege.com.mx
During Baja's broiling summer (when the billfish really bite), the lovely pool and gardens here offer a respite from the heat. Simple yet serene (as its name implies), this property has its own airstrip and RV park. Three well-equipped bungalows with living room and fireplace for rent by day or month. Breakfast included.
🛏50 Ⓟ 🕐 Closed Sept.
◻ ◻ ≋ 🏨 MC, V

TECATE

🏨 RANCHO LA PUERTA SPA
Since 1940, the Szekely family (and today, more than 250 employees) has been offering guests an ever increasing array of spa treatments and activities: hot riverstone massage, European facials, yoga, meditation, hiking, and loofah-salt glows, to name a few. Stays at the 3,000-acre (1,210 ha) ranch are Saturday to Saturday; first-floor, hacienda-style bungalows decorated with fine Mexican handcrafts are set among luxurious pools, spas, and gardens. Healthful, delicious, vegetarian-oriented meals and round-trip transportation from

the nearby airport at San Diego, California, are included. Reservations required.

$$$$$

HWY. 2, 3 MILES (5 KM) WEST OF TECATE, 21275

TEL 665/41155, 800/443-7565

FAX 665/41108

www.rancholapuerta.com

🛈 80 ⬛ 🏊 🅜MC, V

TIJUANA

🏨 CAMINO REAL

$$$$

PASEO DE LOS HÉROES 10305, 22320

TEL 66/33-40-00

FAX 66/33-40-01

No longer associated with the Camino Real chain, this high rise retains its fashionable and rather conservative air. The business-oriented property is near the Tijuana Cultural Center and downtown.

🛈 250 🅿 ⬍ ⬛ ⬛ 🏊 🍴 🅜All major cards

🍴 CIEN AÑOS

$$$

AV. JOSÉ MARÍA VELASCO 1407

TEL 66/34-30-39

Nouveau Mexican cuisine is elegantly presented in this gracious restaurant near the cultural center. Steaks are a specialty, as is *pollo cien años*—chicken and potatoes in a spicy, smoky chili sauce. For dessert, try the guava cheesecake or flan with burnt goat-milk topping. No shorts.

🅿 🕐 Closed Sun. after 8 p.m. ⬛ 🅜All major cards

🍴 LA ESPECIAL

$$

AV. REVOLUCIÓN 718, BETWEEN CALLES 3 AND 4 (PASAJE EL GÓMEZ)

TEL 66/85-66-54

Centrally located along the tourist zone on Avenida Revolución, this festive and relaxed restaurant has catered to both locals and tourists since 1952. Bilingual waiters bring on charcoal-grilled

meats and Mexican favorites.

⬛ ⬛ 🅜MC, V

TODOS SANTOS

🍴 CAFÉ SANTA FE

$$$

CENTENARIO 4

TEL 1/145-0340

The outdoor garden tables of this Italian café are often filled with diners from Los Cabos and La Paz. It's popular for its organic salad greens, homemade pastas, and imported wines.

🕐 Closed Tues., Sept., Oct. 🅜MC, V

NORTHWEST MEXICO

ALAMOS

🏨 HACIENDA DE LOS SANTOS

$$$

MOLINA 8, 85763

TEL 642/80222

FAX 642/80367

This antique-studded property has a billiards room, a theater, and its own 19th-century cantina. Individually decorated rooms have wood-burning fireplaces; beds are crisp with fine linens; and the adjacent spa has a full-time masseur and trainer. Children and smoking are not allowed.

🛈 21 🅿 🕐 Closed June ⬛ 🏊 🅜MC, V

CHIHUAHUA

🏨 HOLIDAY INN HOTEL & SUITES

$$$

ESCUDERO 702, FRACC. SAN FELIPE, 31240

TEL 800/465-4329

FAX 14/14-33-13

www.holiday-inn.com/chihuahuamex

E-MAIL holidayc@chih1.telmex.net.mx

Continental breakfast is included in the price of this pretty, all-suites hotel with full kitchens, located in a residential neighborhood near

the city center. The bright white, two-story hotel has a sauna and access to golf and tennis facilities nearby.

🛈 74 🅿 ⬛ ⬛ 🏊 🍴 🅜All major cards

🏨 PALACIO DEL SOL

$$$

INDEPENDENCIA 116, 31000

TEL 14/16-60-00, 800/852-4049

FAX 14/15-49-47

www.com.nex.palaciodelsol

E-MAIL palacio@infosel.net.mx

Located in the heart of the historic district, this high-rise hotel, although rather impersonal, has several lively bars and restaurants, a car-rental agency, and many other services.

🛈 183 🅿 ⬍ ⬛ ⬛ 🍴 🅜AE, MC, V

🍴 LA CASA DE LOS MILAGROS

$$

VICTORIA 812, NEAR OCAMPO

TEL 14/37-06-93

Sit indoors or out on the courtyard patio of this restored adobe hacienda. Popular with locals and visitors, it offers light Mexican meals, a festive ambience, and live folk music Thurs.–Sun. after 9 p.m.

🕐 Closed L ⬛ 🅜AE, MC, V

DURANGO

🏨 HOTEL GOBERNADOR 🍴

$$

20 DE NOVIEMBRE OTE. 257

TEL 1/813-1919

FAX 1/811-1422

This is Durango's nicest hotel, originally a jail but now a comfortable accommodation with central heating, direct-dial phones, satellite TV, and a great pool. Popular with the town's upper crust,

Restaurante La Hacienda serves regional specialties such as *caldillo durangeño*—beef soup with potatoes.

🛈 100 🅿 ⬛ ⬛ 🏊 🅜AE, MC, V

EL FUERTE

🏨 HOTEL POSADA DEL HIDALGO

$$$

HIDALGO 101, JUST OFF
THE PLAZA
TEL/FAX 689/31194
This late 19th-century
hacienda, built by Alamos's
mayor, has spacious rooms in
the original building with
imported ceiling beams and
antique or rustic furniture
(no TV); the newer building
faces a lavish garden patio.
Weekend discotheque; bass
fishing arranged.
[i] 51 P 🛇 🖼 🏊
🆔 All major cards

HIDALGO DEL PARRAL

🏨 HOTEL ACOSTA

$$$

AGUSTÍN BARBACHANO 3
TEL/FAX 1/522-0657
Parral has only simple hotels;
one of the nicer ones is this
three-story, family-run
establishment overlooking the
main plaza. The Acosta has no
restaurant, but it offers a great
view of the cathedral from its
rooftop terrace.
[i] 26 🖼 🆔 No credit
cards

MAZATLÁN

🏨 HACIENDA LAS 🍴 MORAS

$$$$$

CARR. A LA NORIA KM 9
TEL/FAX 69/16-50-45
Visitors come to spend the
night at this lovingly
refurbished former mescal
plantation; locals come to dine
on Mexican specialties and
drink excellent margaritas.
Either way you can swim in
the large outdoor pool, ride
horses in the surrounding
hills, or admire the peacocks
and the gracious grounds.
Call for reservations and for
route directions.
[i] 11 P 🛇 🖼 🏊
🆔 AE, MC, V

🏨 PUEBLO BONITO 🍴 $$$

CAMARON SABALO 2121,
ZONA DORADA, 82110
TEL/FAX 69/14-37-00,
800/990-8250
Flamingos pose on the palm-
studded grounds of this
low-rise, all-suites beachfront
hotel. Rooms have equipped
kitchens and furnished
outdoor patios. Live music
and twinkling candlelight
complement Italian and
Continental cuisine at
Angelo's Restaurant.
[i] 246 P 🖼 🛇 🏊
🖼 🆔 AE, MC, V

🏨 PLAYA MAZATLÁN

$$

RODOLFO T. LOAIZA 202,
ZONA DORADA, 82110
TEL 69/89-05-55, 800/762-5816
FAX 69/14-03-66
Mazatlán's original resort
hotel is one of the few to
resist the timeshare snare.
Nicest of the clean-smelling
rooms with tiled floors and
private terraces are those
overlooking the beach.
[i] 425 P 🖼 🛇 🏊2
🖼 🆔 MC, V

🍴 EL CUCHUPETAS

$$

REFORMA 301 AT JESUS
CARRANZA, VILLA UNIÓN
TEL 69/67-04-60
En route to the airport, Isla de
Piedra, and excursions into the
interior, El Cuchupetas offers
fresh, authentic seafood specialties. The simple restaurant
has flowered oilcloth table-
coverings, cement and tile
floors, old-time Mazatlán
photos, and bilingual menus.
Try a *campechana* (octopus,
clam, and shrimp cocktail).
P 🆔 No credit cards

🍴 MARISMEÑO

$$

OLAS ALTAS 1224 AT
CONSTITUCIÓN, CENTRO
TEL 69/12-26-12
Fresh seafood from the
owner's father's fleet is
delightfully prepared. After a

free appetizer and a delicious
margarita, try the chef's
signature dish: catch of the
day sautéed with shrimp and
potatoes. End with the
excellent custard flan.
🛇 🆔 AE, MC, V

PUERTO PEÑASCO

🏨 PLAYA BONITA HOTEL 🍴 $$

PASEO BALBOA 100
TEL 6/383-2586
FAX 6/383-5566
Some of the simple but neat
rooms have balconies with
views of Playa Hermosa
beach; all have satellite TV. The
outdoor patio at **Puesta del
Sol Restaurant** is a local
favorite, with a good breakfast
buffet Saturdays and Sundays.
The attached RV park has
laundry, hookups, recreation
rooms, and a grocery store.
[i] 122 P 🖼 🛇 🏊
🆔 MC, V

SAN CARLOS

🏨 CLUB MEDITERANÉE SONORA BAY

$$$$

PLAYA LOS ALGODONES, 85400

TEL 6/227-0007
FAX 6/227-0002
The desert meets the sea at this gorgeous, 43-acre (17.5 ha), pueblo-style complex, with Club Med's endless activities, including scuba diving. Rooms are plain but serviceable. Meals and some activities are included.
[i] 375 [P] [+] Closed Oct.–March or April [S]
[≈] [♥] [◈] AE, MC, V

SIERRA TARAHUMARA (COPPER CANYON)

⌂ MIRADOR
$$$$$
ESTACIÓN POSADA BARRANCA
TEL 681/87046, 800/896-8196
FAX 681/20046
www.mexicoscoppercanyon.com
This log-cabin lodge has a gorgeous canyon view, and arranges horse and walking tours. Rooms have heating, fireplaces, and balconies, but no phone or TV. Meals, served family-style, are included in the price.
[i] 70 [◈] AE, MC, V

⌂ MISIÓN
$$$$
11 MILES (18 KM) FROM BAHUICHIVO TRAIN STATION, CEROCAHUI
TEL 68/18-70-46, 800/896-8196
FAX 68/12-00-46
This isolated lodge, a good base for exploring the Urique Canyon, books on the American Plan. A large fireplace warms the lobby bar; simply furnished rooms are surrounded by small gardens and a vineyard. Generator electricity is available at intervals.
[i] 38 [◈] AE, MC, V

⌂ BEST WESTERN LODGE AT CREEL
$$
LÓPEZ MATEOS 61, 33200, CREEL
TEL 1/456-0071, 800/528-1234 (IN THE U.S.), 01-800/90475 (IN MEXICO)
FAX 1/456-0082

Comfortable cabins in the center of town, with wood-burning stoves, bathtubs, and small porches. Breakfast is included in the price; area excursions are arranged.
[i] 27 [S] [≈] [◈] AE, MC, V

⌂ REAL DE MINAS
$
DONATO GUERRA AT PABLO OCHOA, BATOPILAS, URIQUE CANYON
NO PHONE
The former manager of fabulous Riverside Lodge (now closed), borrowed management and decorating ideas for his own tiny and tasteful guest lodge in one of Batopilas's restored 19th-century mansions. Unfortunately, with no phone, it's first come, first served.
[i] 7 [◈] No credit cards

NORTHEAST MEXICO

MONTERREY

⌂🍴 RADISSON GRAN ANCIRA PLAZA
$$$$
AV. MELCHOR OCAMPO 443 OESTE, 64000
TEL 8/345-7575, 800/333-3333
FAX 8/344-5226
Located in the heart of downtown's pedestrian area and near the Macroplaza, this turn-of-the-20th-century hotel has been designated a World Heritage site. The open restaurant sits in the impossibly elegant lobby, with its sweeping marble staircase and cathedral ceiling.
[i] 241 [P] [⇄] [S] [S]
[≈] [♥] [◈] AE, MC, V

⌂ SHERATON AMBASSADOR
$$$$
HIDALGO 310 ORIENTE AT E. CARRANZA, 64000
TEL 8/340-7000, 800/325-3535
FAX 8/345-1984
www.sheraton.com
A lobby with lots of dark wood is enhanced by the

stained-glass ceiling and elegant furnishings in comfortable groupings. Geared toward business travelers, the modern hotel has secretarial services and in-room modems; ask about deals for executive floors and suites. Tennis and racquetball.
[i] 240 [⇄] [S] [S] [≈]
[♥] [◈] All major cards

🍴 LUISIANA
$$$
AV. HIDALGO 530 ORIENTE
TEL 8/343-1561
Friendly in a clubby, everyone-knows-you sort of way, this downtown restaurant is elegantly decorated and rather dark. It's popular for its typical northern meats—including charbroiled steak and barbecued goat—and other Mexican dishes.
[S] [◈] All major cards

PARQUE NACIONAL CUMBRES DE MONTERREY

⌂ HOTEL CHIPINQUE
$$
MESETA CHIPINQUE 1000, GARZA GARCIA, 66297
TEL 8/378-6600, 888/237-3316
FAX 8/378-6759
Perched above Monterrey in the park for which it is named, this comfortable lodge suits those who like to hike, bike, play tennis, or swim. At night there's a view of the twinkling cityscape from the restaurant-bar.
[i] 72 [P] [S] [S] [≈]
[♥] [◈] AE, MC, V

SALTILLO

⌂🍴 CAMINO REAL SALTILLO
$$$
BLVD. LOS FUNDADORES 2000, 25015
TEL 8/430-0000, 800/722-6466
FAX 8/438-0009
Popular despite its lack of executive services, this business hotel is east of historic downtown. Locals

love **La Buenavista** restaurant—gleaming with polished wood and a stained-glass skylight—for the fine cuts of beef and regional and international food, as well as Sunday brunch at the adjacent **la Huerta** restaurant.
🛈 140 🅿 🚫 🚫 ≋ 🏠 MC, V

🏨 LA CANASTA
$$
BLVD. V. CARRANZA 2485
TEL 8/415-8840
Tile floors, a low wood-beamed ceiling, roaring fireplaces in each large room, and a mix of antique and modern furnishings make La Canasta a Saltillo tradition for long business lunches. The menu features many *antojitos* (appetizers) and other Mexican dishes.
🅿 🚫 🚫 🏠 All major cards

TAMPICO

🏨 CAMINO REAL MOTOR HOTEL
$$
AV. HIDALGO 2000, 89140
TEL 1/213-8811
FAX 1/213-9226
Not part of the Camino Real chain, this pretty, low-rise hotel outside Tampico still delights with its tropical landscaping and amenities such as mini-bars and direct-dial phones. The travel agency on site books area fishing trips.
🛈 103 🅿 🚫 ≋ 🏠 All major cards

ZACATECAS

🏨 QUINTA REAL 🍴 ZACATECAS
$$$$
AV. RAYÓN 434, 98000
TEL 492/29104, 800/457-4000
FAX 492/28440
This glamorous, wonderfully odd hotel was built in a converted 19th-century bullring. Nonetheless, rooms are airy and comfortable with balconies and either bathtubs

or spas. The bar occupies the former bullpens; the elegant restaurant, serving international and regional cuisine, offers fantastic nighttime views of the 18th-century aqueduct.
🛈 47 🅿 ⚋ 🚫 🚫 🏠 AE, MC, V

🏨 HOSTAL DEL VASCO
$$
AV. ALAMEDA AT VELAZCO 1
TEL/FAX 492/20428
Bright flowers fill the central courtyard of this converted *casona*, or colonial mansion, three blocks from the cathedral. Some rooms have kitchenettes, but no utensils; street-facing balconies have no tables or chairs.
🛈 18 ⚋ ≋ ≋ 🏠 AE, MC, V

🍴 LA CUIJA
$$
TACUBA LOCAL 5 (GONZÁLEZ ORTEGA MARKET, BOTTOM LEVEL)
TEL 492/28275
A bit of everything is served in this simulated wine cellar: regional specialties include *pachole* (ground beef and pork in special sauce), the Zacatecas classic, *asado de boda*, grilled meats, and seafood. Music is played Wednesday to Sunday during late-afternoon lunch (2–5 p.m.) and again after 9 p.m.
🅿 🚫 🏠 AE, MC, V

CENTRAL MEXICO

AGUASCALIENTES

🏨 HOTEL QUINTA REAL 🍴 AGUASCALIENTES
$$$$
AV. AGUASCALIENTES SUR 601, 20270
TEL 4/978-5818, 800/457-4000
FAX 4/978-5616
www.quintareal.com
Everything about this gorgeous hotel whispers luxury, style, and tradition. Antique and modern pieces

mix well in pleasing public spaces of quarrystone and gleaming marble. Luxurious rooms with full amenities overlook the colonial-style courtyard, a bar with fireplace, and a formal dining room serving regional, national, and international cuisine.
🛈 85 🅿 🚫 ≋ 🏠 AE, MC, V

GUANAJUATO

🏨 LA CASA DE LOS ESPÍRITUS ALEGRES
$$$$
EX-HACIENDA DE TRINIDAD 1, MARFIL
TEL/FAX 473/31013
E-MAIL casaspirit@aol.com
Awash in folk art and antiques, the 16th-century "House of the Happy Spirits" B&B, several miles outside Guanajuato, has individually (and brightly) decorated rooms, some with fireplaces. Generous breakfasts are served on a covered courtyard.
🛈 8 🅿 🚫 No credit cards

🏨 QUINTA LAS ACACIAS
$$$$
PASEO DE LA PRESA 168, 36000
TEL/FAX 473/11517, 888/497-4129

www.int.com.mx/acacias
This new, centrally located, 19th-century, European-style B&B has few rooms but many pretty public spaces, including a library, bar, terraces shaded by greenery, and a spa with city view. Rooms have satellite TV, hairdryers, and cordless phones. Complete breakfast is included, and snacks and small meals are available throughout the day.
🛈 9 🅿 🏠 AE, MC, V

🏨 EX-HACIENDA DEL ANTIGUO CAMINO
$$
CAMINO ANTIGUO 12, MARFIL
TEL 473/31853
FAX 473/31853
E-MAIL antica@redes.int.com.mx
Located near the gardens of San Gabriel de la Barrera, this

gracious former hacienda offers simple charm and modern comforts. The two-story construction combining brick, stone, and whitewashed stucco has rough red floor tiles, gleaming wooden doors, and wrought-iron railings. The price of the airy, clean rooms includes breakfast.

☐ 7 No credit cards

POSADA SANTA FE
$$

JARDÍN UNIÓN 12, 36000
TEL 473/20084
FAX 473/24653

Somewhat dark corridors and rooms and heavy furnishings are offset by modest prices and an unbeatable location on the city's liveliest square. The outdoor café-restaurant is a prime people-watching spot.

☐ 45 AE, MC, V

LA HACIENDA DE MARFIL
$$

ARCOS DE GUADALUPE 3, MARFIL
TEL 473/31148

A wonderful ambience pervades this small restaurant, in a restored Mexican colonial building about 15 minutes outside Guanajuato. Sample delightful French dishes such as rabbit stew in red wine with mushrooms, or beef fillet in tamarind sauce.

☐ Open 1:30–6 p.m. Closed Mon. AE, MC, V

TRUCO 7
$

TRUCO 7
TEL 473/28374

Friendly and down-to-earth describes El Truco, which hums with conversation. The service and food—steaks, sandwiches, enchiladas, and other typical Mexican fare—are good and the colorful posters, paintings, and other bric-a-brac make for a lively atmosphere.

No credit cards

QUERÉTARO

LA CASA DE LA MARQUESA
$$$$

MADERO 41, 76000
TEL 421/20092
FAX 421/20098

Tasteful and classy but not snooty, this hotel in historic downtown is housed in a restored 1756 mansion. Suites are furnished in exquisite antiques, handpainted tiles, and plush local rugs. The formal restaurant is offputting to some, but the nouveau Mexican and upscale international dishes lure others to the elegant tables.

☐ 25 AE, MC, V

HOLIDAY INN QUERÉTARO
$$$

AV. 5 DE FEBRERO 110, 76010
TEL 421/60202, 800/465-4329
FAX 421/68902
www.holidayinn.com.mx

On Highway 57 near both downtown and the industrial zone, this ample three-story property has modern motel-like rooms with climate control, satellite TV, hairdryers, and other amenities. The large rectangular pool is great for swimming laps.

☐ 171 AE, MC, V

MESÓN DE SANTA ROSA
$$

PASTEUR SUR 17, 76000
TEL 421/42623
FAX 421/25522
E-MAIL starosa@ciateq.mx

Colonial-style furnishings reproduce those of the original, 18th-century inn. The central location and moderate price lure repeat customers. One of the three interior patios serves as an al fresco restaurant, dishing up Mexican favorites with a modern flair, such as roast kid in pepper and pulque sauce.

☐ 21 AE, MC, V

EL ARCÁNGEL
$$

GUERRERO NORTE 1
TEL 421/26542

This warm mansion-turned-restaurant has lace curtains and small square café tables inside or under a covered patio. Order traditional favorites such as squash blossom soup, chicken tacos, or chilies stuffed with cheese and cuitlacoche, a corn-fungus delicacy.

MC, V

SAN LUIS POTOSÍ

WESTIN SAN LUIS POTOSÍ
$$$

REAL DE LOMAS 1000, 78216
TEL 4/825-0125, 800/937-8461
FAX 4/825-0200
www.westin.com
E-MAIL westinslp@infosel.net.mx

Located in a residential neighborhood near the historic center, this low rise resembles a palatial hacienda. Inside, however, it is thoroughly modern and equipped with many amenities and business services.

☐ 123 AE, MC, V

PANORAMA
$

CARRANZA 315, 78000
TEL 4/812-1777
FAX 4/812-4591

Businessmen and budget travelers have remained loyal over the years to this older but still respectable property near la Plaza los Fundadores. Enjoy the view from the rooftop bar-restaurant.

☐ 120 AE, MC

POSADA DEL VIRREY
$$$

JARDÍN HIDALGO 3
TEL 4/812-3750

Piano music entertains during lunch and dinner at the converted home of Mexico's first vicereine. Facing Parque Hidalgo, this popular eatery serves regional specialties on a delightful covered courtyard. ⬨ AE, MC, V

🍴 LA PARROQUIA
$

CARRANZA 303
TEL 4/812-6681
What this downtown institution lacks in decoration it makes up for in popularity. Old gents linger for hours over coffee, while bargain-hunters hunker down over mildly priced and tasty lunch specials. It opens early and closes late.
🕐   ⬨ No credit cards

SAN MIGUEL DE ALLENDE

🏨 CASA DE SIERRA NEVADA
$$$$

HOSPICIO 35, 37700
TEL 415/20415, 800/223-6510
FAX 415/22337
Several ancient haciendas have been converted as installations for this luxurious hotel. Guest rooms are superbly and individually decorated, with lace curtains, antique dressers, and lots of locally made art and handcrafts. No children under 16.
ⓘ 24   🅿   🏊   ⬨ AE, MC, V

🏨 LA PUERTECITA
🍴 BOUTIQUE HOTEL
$$$$

SANTO DOMINGO 75, 37740
TEL 415/25011
FAX 415/25505
www.lapuertecita.com
Overlooking San Miguel from the residential neighborhood about 20 minutes' walk from town, "the Little Door" has pretty gardens with outdoor sculptures and tiled fountains. Comfortable rooms and suites have colonial-style furnishings; cut flowers adorn the lobby, library, and other public spaces. Mexican specialties are served in the chic but rustic dining room and on the garden terrace.

ⓘ 34   🅿   🕐   🏊   ⬨ AE, MC, V

🏨 VILLA JACARANDA
🍴 $$$

ALDAMA 53, 37700
TEL 415/21015
FAX 415/20883
www.villajacaranda.com
This unpretentious but very comfortable small hotel is a short walk from downtown. Rooms are decorated with hand-woven bedspreads, and have tiled baths and cable TV. In the evening, watch a movie (cocktail in hand) in the video salon, or dine in the restaurant or outdoor terrace. The chef's fabulous international cuisine has made this a repeated recipient of the Distinguished Restaurants of North America (DiRoNa) award.
ⓘ 15   🅿   ⬨ AE, MC, V

TEQUISQUIAPAN

🏨 HOTEL DEL PARQUE
$$

CDA. CAMELINAS 1
TEL 427/32939
FAX 427/30938
This small, ten-year-old, well-maintained hotel overlooks the languid, flower-filled main plaza in tranquil Tequisquiapan, which celebrates its cheese and wine fair each June.
ⓘ 21   🅿   🏊   ⬨ AE, MC, V

CENTRAL PACIFIC STATES

ACAPULCO

SOMETHING SPECIAL

🏨 QUINTA REAL

Each of the suites in this refined yet accessible hotel has a wonderful ocean view, satellite TV, mini-bar, and other comforts; some have private pools and dining areas. The cream-colored furnishings and decor are "rustic Mexican" yet comfortable. The new property perches on the bluffs with a

fabulous view of Acapulco Bay. Take a path or elevator to access the swimming pools and beach below. An on-site spa provides massage and various treatments.
$$$$

PASEO DE LA QUINTA 6, FRACC. REAL DIAMANTE, 39907
TEL 7/469-1500, 800/457-4000
FAX 7/469-1516
www.quintareal.com
ⓘ 74   🅿   ⬍   🕐   🕐   🏊   ⬨ AE, MC, V

🏨 ELCANO
🍴 $$$

AV. COSTERA MIGUEL ALEMAN 75, 39690
TEL 7/484-1950, 800/972-2162
FAX 7/484-2230
A clean, white and cerulean blue theme pervades the smallish, comfortable rooms, breezy public areas, and outdoor **Bambuco** restaurant, which serves regional favorites with modern touches such as fat shrimp tacos or red snapper grilled with asparagus, shrimp, and clams.
ⓘ 180   🅿   🕐   🏊   🍸   ⬨ AE, MC, V

BOCA CHICA
$$
PLAYA CALETA S/N, 39390
TEL 7/483-6388, 800/346-3942
FAX 7/483-9513
Guests return not for the plain but adequate rooms, but for the unpretentious, intimate location. Far from the madding crowd, the three-story property perches between Caleta Beach on one side and a beautiful rocky cove, great for snorkeling, on the other. The sushi bar is a bonus.
🛏 52 🅿 🅰 🌊 🅰AE, MC, V

MADEIRAS
$$$$
CARR. ESCÉNICA 33, FRACC. EL GUITARRÓN
TEL 7/446-5636
Sublime international food in a romantic setting with candlelight and quiet music, and open to the breeze overlooking Acapulco Bay. The set menu offers choices of soup or salad, appetizer (such as octopus in vinaigrette), main course, and dessert.
🅿 🕐 Closed L 🅰MC, V

EL OLVIDO
$$$$
PLAZA MARBELLA, AV. COSTERA M. ALEMAN S/N
TEL 7/481-0214
Modern and elegant El Olvido serves innovative haute-Mexican and international dishes. Sample the spinach salad with warm goat cheese, creamy Roquefort cheese soup, and steaks, seafoods, and pastas. For dessert, indulge in crème brûlée or tiramisu. Request a seat on the open patio facing the sea.
🕐 Closed L 🅿 🅰 🅰All major cards

EL AMIGO MIGUEL
$$
BENITO JUÁREZ 31
TEL 7/483-6981
Right on the sand, this long-time local favorite is served by an energetic young staff. Seafood dishes are traditional

and tasty, with no surprises. The bustling two-story downtown location serves equally delicious food.
🅰AE, MC, V

LA TORTUGA
$
LOMAS DEL MAR 5-A
TEL 7/484-6985
Low-cost lunch specials, combo plates large enough for two, and excellent *tortas* (breadroll sandwiches) are served in an informal outdoor downtown garden one block off Avenida Costera.
🅰No credit cards

COLIMA

AMÉRICA
$
MORELOS 162, 28000
TEL/FAX 331/27488
Half a block west of Parque Núñez, this modern and somewhat impersonal business hotel offers a gleaming interior, and a steam room—for men only.
🛏 75 🅿 🅰 🅰 🅰AE, MC, V

CEBALLOS
$
PORTAL MEDELLÍN 12, 28000
TEL 331/24444
FAX 331/20645
Built in the 1880s, this lovingly refurbished edifice has been home to three state governors. The elegantly appointed, spacious rooms have high ceilings; some have small balconies.
🛏 63 🅿 🅰 🅰MC, V

EL CHARCO DE LA HIGUERA
$$
JARDÍN DE SAN JOSÉ S/N, BETWEEN 5 DE MAYO AND TORRES QUINTERO
TEL 331/30192
A five-minute walk west of downtown, this peaceful outdoor restaurant has a varied menu, offering *tortas* (breadroll sandwiches), chicken, grilled meats, and

pozole (hominy soup). Guitar music most weekend evenings.
🅰MC, V

LOS NARANJO
$$
BARREDA 34
TEL 331/20029
Traditional-minded Colimenses head for this fan-cooled restaurant near quiet Jardín Quintero. The menu features a long list of traditional Mexican appetizers and many meat dishes, including the *filete especial* for two—steak grilled with green onions, jalapeño peppers, and bacon, served with beans and tortillas.
🅰No credit cards

COSTA ALEGRE

LAS ALAMANDAS
$$$$$
DOMICILIO CONOCIDO, NORTH OF SAN PATRICIO MELAQUE
TEL 3/285-5500 OR 888/882-9616
FAX 3/285-5027
www.las-alamandas.com
E-MAIL info@las-alamandas.com
An exclusive resort far from civilization, Las Alamandas offers guests golf, fishing, croquet, and the luxury of impeccable service and style. Drop-ins are not accepted; call in advance for reservations and directions.
🛏 8 suites, 4 villas 🌊 🏋 🅰AE, MC, V

GRAND BAY
$$$$$
ISLA NAVIDAD, BARRA DE NAVIDAD
TEL 335/55050, 888-472-6229
FAX 335/56071
www.grandbay.com
This exclusive, gated country club has recently transformed laid-back Barra de Navidad. Backed by emerald hills and fronting the ocean and lagoon, the elegant, multi-level Mediterranean-style Grand Bay, set amid lovely grounds and gardens, has a 27-hole

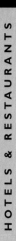

HOTELS & RESTAURANTS

golf course, tennis courts, and watersports.

 167 ⬆ ◫ ◫ ≋
🍸 ⬥ AE, MC, V

🏨 EL TAMARINDO
$$$$$
MELAQUE–PUERTO VALLARTA
HWY. KM 7.5, CIHUATLÁN
TEL 3/351-5032
FAX 3/351-5070
Open yet exclusive, this resort's wonderfully decorated villas with private plunge pool and outdoor living areas front pretty beaches and an 18-hole golf course.
ⓘ 28 villas 🅿 ≋ 🍸
⬥ All major cards

GUADALAJARA

🏨 QUINTA REAL
🍴 GUADALAJARA
$$$$
AV. MÉXICO 2727, 44680
TEL 3615-0000, 800/457-4000
FAX 3630-1797
www.quintareal.com
Just 15 years old, this luxurious property looks colonial, but has modern conveniences. All of the suites have fireplaces, bathtubs, comfortable furnishings, and locally made handcrafts. Dine on the terrace or indoors on world-class haute cuisine that uses fresh ingredients.
ⓘ 76 ⬆ ◫ ◫ ≋
⬥ All major cards

🏨 DE MENDOZA
$$
V. CARRANZA 16, 44100
TEL 3613-4646, 800/876-5278
FAX 3613-7310
A great location, reasonable rates, terrace swimming pool, and a beautiful lobby enliven this five-story hotel near la Plaza Tapatío. Great city views from the bar, and dancing on weekends.
ⓘ 110 🅿 ⬆ ◫ ◫
≋ ⬥ AE, MC, V

🏨 FRANCÉS
$
MAESTRANZA 35, 44100
TEL 3613-1190

FAX 3658-2831
Guadalajara's oldest hotel has a privileged location in the heart of the city's historic downtown. Admire the stained-glass cathedral ceiling from the intimate lobby bar. Rooms vary in size and decoration.
ⓘ 60 🅿 ⬥ AE, MC, V

🍴 LA DESTILERÍA
$$
NELSON 2916 AT AV. MEXICO
TEL 3640-3440
This vast redbrick dining room is decorated with tequila-making accouterments, and the staff dresses the part of tequila-laborers. Chefs dish up Mexican fare, while bartenders dispense almost a hundred types of tequila.
🅿 🕐 Closed Sun. D ◫
⬥ AE, MC, V

🍴 EL SACROMONTE
$$
PEDRO MORENO 1398
TEL 3825-5447
Treat all of your senses at Sacromonte, which is particularly known for its excellent service. Icons and candlelit altars provide nighttime ambience in the romantic garden. There are delicious soups (try the blue cheese) and elaborate main dishes, such as duck with deep-fried rose petals.
🕐 Closed Sun. ⬥ MC, V

IXTAPA/ZIHUATANEJO

🏨 LA CASA QUE CANTA
$$$$$
CAMINO ESCÉNICO, PLAYA LA ROPA, ZIHUATANEJO 40880
TEL 7/554-6529, 800/525-4800
FAX 7/554-7900
Attention to every detail in decor and service makes the Casa que Canta one of Mexico's top hotels. Spacious rooms with ocean views and unusual handpainted furnishings occupy several earth-toned buildings sprinkled on hillside terraces. The beach is a short walk away.

ⓘ 24 🅿 🕐 Closed Aug.
⬆ ◫ ≋ 🍸 ⬥ All major cards

🏨 WESTIN BRISAS
🍴 IXTAPA
$$$$
PLAYA VISTAHERMOSA S/N, IXTAPA 40880
TEL 7/553-2121, 800/228-3000
FAX 7/553-1031
Architect Ricardo Legoretta's clean, dramatic design and color scheme set this resort apart from the competition. Descending from the lobby toward a sandy cove, rooms have large, partially shaded patios with hammocks; the junglelike grounds are equally exquisite. Of the hotel's six restaurants, the romantic **Portofino** serves regional Italian specialties (dinner only).
ⓘ 428 🅿 ⬆ ◫ ◫
≋ 🍸 ⬥ All major cards

🍴 BECCOFINO
$$
PLAZA MARINA IXTAPA, VÍA BLVD IXTAPA S/N, IXTAPA
TEL 7/553-1770
FAX 7/553-2109
Angelo Pavia, an Italian native, brings his talents to this marina restaurant specializing in northern Italian food. The wine selection includes Mexican, Italian, French, Spanish, and Chilean vintages. Reserve a table on the lovely deck overlooking the water.
⬥ AE, MC, V

🍴 LA SIRENA GORDA
$
PASEO DEL PESCADOR 90, ZIHUATANEJO
TEL 7/557-2687
A short walk from the town pier, "The Fat Mermaid" is a popular and unpretentious thatch-roofed café serving traditional seafood cocktails, ten kinds of seafood tacos (including "surf and turf"), soups, and more filling entrees. Breakfast is recommended.
🕐 Closed Wed. ⬥ No credit cards

MANZANILLO

🏨 LAS HADAS
🍽 $$$$$
AV. DE LOS RISCOS AT VISTA
HERMOSA, 28200
TEL 333/40000, 800/722-6466
FAX 333/10121
Famous for its capricious
white Moorish architecture,
featured in the movie *10*
(1979), Las Hadas needs a
facelift. There's an 18-hole golf
course, tennis, and marina. Its
most romantic restaurant,
Legazpi, boasts four-star
service and excellent food.
🛏 220 🅿 🔄 🚭 🅰
🏊 🏋 🅰 All major cards

🍽 TOSCANA
$$$
CARR. COSTERA 3177
TEL 333/32515
The great food and a long-
standing reputation encourage
locals and tourists to revisit
this French/Italian restaurant.
The jumbo shrimp wrapped
in bacon is delightful.
🕐 Closed L 🅰 MC, V

MORELIA

🏨 VILLA MONTANA
$$$
PATZIMBA 201, 58090
TEL 4/314-0231, 800/525-4800
FAX 4/315-1423
At night, Morelia twinkles in
the distance from the terrace
bar of this lovely oasis of calm
sophistication. Beautifully
decorated cottages dot the
terraced property; landscaped
gardens are peppered with
fountains and sculptures. Small
pets are allowed, but not small
children.
🛏 36 🅿 🏊 🅰 AE,
MC, V

🏨 HOTEL VIRREY DE
🍽 MENDOZA
$$
AV. MADERO PONIENTE 310,
58000
TEL 4/312-4940, 01-800/450-2000
FAX 4/312-6719
www.hotelmex.com/hotelvirrey
Right on the *zócalo*, this
converted mansion retains its
colonial ambience with crystal
chandeliers, gleaming wood,
and antique furnishings.
Rooms and suites are equally
distinctive; the restaurant is
worth a visit for both the
sumptuous decoration and
the regional specialties.
🛏 55 🅿 🔄 🚭 🅰 AE,
MC, V

🍽 FONDA LAS
MERCEDES
$$
LEÓN GUZMÁN 47, 58000
TEL 4/312-6113
In the heart of town, this
delightful eatery is upscale but
cozy, with tables throughout
the covered patio of the
restored colonial building.
Innovative international and
regional dishes include steaks
and *pollo Azteca*—baked
mushroom-stuffed chicken.
🕐 Closed Sun. D 🅰 AE,
MC, V

PÁTZCUARO

🏨 MANSIÓN DE ITURBE
🍽 $$
PORTAL MORELOS 59, 61600
TEL 434/20368
FAX 434/23628
Odd but endearing, this
creaky, high-ceilinged hotel
dominates the Plaza de
Quiroga. Although dark and
old, the restored 17th-century
building is well maintained.
Breakfast is included, and **El
Gaucho** restaurant features
Argentine-style steaks and
live music.
🛏 14 🅰 MC, V

🏨 CABAÑAS ISLA
YUNUÉN
$
DOMICILIO CONOCIDO, ISLA
YUNUÉN
TEL 434/24473
To visit languid Yunuén Island,
on Lake Janitzio, take a ferry
boat from the Pátzcuaro dock
and rent a cozy log cabin by
the night or as a four-day
package. The comfortable
cabins (with poorly equipped
kitchenettes) accommodate
two, four, or sixteen people.
Breakfast included; lunch and
dinner also available.
🛏 6 cabins 🚭 No credit
cards

🏨 POSADA DE LA
BASÍLICA
$
ARCIGA 6, 61600
TEL 434/21108
FAX 434/20659
Rooms in this colonial hotel
are simple yet serviceable,
and the fireplaces are
welcome on chilly evenings.
🛏 12 🅿 🅰 MC, V

🍽 EL PRIMER PISO
$$$
PLAZA VASCO DE QUIROGA 29
TEL 434/20122
This second-floor restaurant
at the plaza serves
international dishes. Try the
pepper stuffed with shrimp,
brie cheese, and fine herbs,
and for dessert, baked fruit in
puff pastry drizzled with rum.
🕐 Closed Tues. 🅰 AE

PUERTO VALLARTA

🏨 CAMINO REAL
PUERTO VALLARTA
$$$$
PLAYA LAS ESTACAS, CARR.
BARRA NAVIDAD S/N, 48300
TEL 3/221-5000, 800/722-6466
FAX 3/221-6000
Gleaming marble and bright
colors prevail in this secluded
property with a beautiful,
sheltered sandy beach where
watersports equipment can
be rented. Some rooms have
balconies; those on the upper
floors also have spas.
🛏 337 🅿 🔄 🚭 🅰
🏊 🏋 🅰 All major cards

🏨 QUINTA MARÍA
CORTÉZ
$$$–$$$$
132 CALLE SAGITARIO,
CONCHAS CHINAS, 48300
TEL 3/221-5317, 888/640-8100
FAX 3/221-5327
www.quinta-maria.com
E-MAIL qmc@travel-zone.com

🚭 Nonsmoking 🅰 Air-conditioning 🏊 Indoor/🏊 Outdoor swimming pool 🏋 Health club 🅰 Credit cards   **KEY**

Suites and small apartments in this seven-level inn are eclectically decorated and overlook a small cove south of Puerto Vallarta proper. Each unit is different and wonderful—with terraces, dining rooms, kitchens, living space, and more. There is a minimum stay of three nights.
🛏 8 units 🏊 💳 AE, MC, V

🍴 TRÍO
$$$$
GUERRERO 264
TEL 3/222-2196
Tasty, innovative Mediterranean dishes with a Mexican flourish have made this restaurant a favorite with the locals. Dishes include rack of lamb served with mint sauce and ravioli, or red snapper with ratatouille and tiny roast potatoes. The garden patio and rooftop terrace are popular in the less humid season.
🕐 Closed L 💳 💳 AE, MC, V

🍴 CHICO'S PARADISE
$
CARR. A MANZANILLO KM 20
TEL 3/222-0747
This idyllic palm-roof restaurant has a great view of the Horcones River (ideal for swimming), a classic waterfall, and the surrounding jungle. Two can share a *mariscada* platter, with fresh lobster, shrimp, red snapper, and octopus.
💳 No credit cards

SAN BLAS

🏨 GARZA CANELA
🍴 **$$**
PAREDES 106 SUR
TEL 328/50112
FAX 328/50308
Run by four sisters, this pretty two-story hotel and its restaurant, **El Delfín,** is a ten-minute walk from the beach and has a pleasant garden.
🛏 45 P 💳 🏊 💳 AE, MC, V

🍴 WALAWALA
$
JUÁREZ, NEAR BATALLÓN
NO PHONE
Centrally located and with excellent service, this simple restaurant features health-conscious international and Mexican dishes such as boneless chicken breast with a mushroom sauce, rice, and veggies. They also occasionally feature live music ranging from bluegrass to blues.
🕐 Closed Sun. 💳 No credit cards

TAXCO

🏨 POSADA DE LA MISIÓN
$$$
CERRO DE LA MISIÓN 32, 40230
TEL 762/20063
FAX 762/22198
This colonial-style hotel at the outskirts of town has an open chapel and a pool surrounded by a small garden. Room rates include a buffet breakfast and dinner with a choice of appetizer, main dish, and dessert.
🛏 125 P 🏊 💳 All major cards

🏨 POSADA DE SAN JAVIER
$
ESTACAS 32
TEL 762/23177
FAX 762/22351
Rooms and small suites stagger up and down the hill below Taxco's main street, many on plant-filled stone patios. Mango and orange trees shade the grassy pool area, perfect for lounging.
🛏 26 P 🏊 💳 No credit cards

TEPIC

🏨 FREY JUNÍPERO SERRA
$
LERDO 23 PONIENTE AT MÉXICO, 63000
TEL 32/12-25-25
FAX 32/12-20-51
Right on the main square, this budget-priced hotel has

well-maintained rooms with satellite TV. Ask for a room on the top floor, which will have a great nighttime view of the church tower, or for one with a bathtub.
P 🛗 💳 💳 AE, MC, V

TLAQUEPAQUE

🏨 LA VILLA DEL ENSUEÑO
$$
FLORIDA 305, 45500
TEL 3/635-8792, 800/220-8689
FAX 3/659-6152
www.mexonline.com/ensueno.htm
This bed-and-breakfast inn has a gracious staff overseeing pretty garden patios with fountains and statues. There is no restaurant, but a Continental breakfast is included in the price, and the bar serves drinks in the garden.
🛏 10 P 💳 🏊 💳 AE, MC, V

🍴 EL ADOBE
$$
INDEPENDENCIA 95
TEL 3/657-2792
Enjoy Mexican food with a modern presentation—*chiles relleno* or shrimp *quesadillas*—

before or after you shop for *equipale* chairs trimmed in tin, freeform sculptures, or other marvelous handcrafts in the adjoining store. Musicians perform daily 2–6 p.m.

🕐 Closed D 🔇 MC, V

URUAPAN

🏨 HOTEL MANSIÓN DEL 🍴 CUPATITZIO
$$
CALZADA DE LA RODILLA DEL DIABLO 20, LA QUINTA, 60030
TEL 452/32100
FAX 452/46772
At the edge of Parque Nacional Eduardo Ruiz, this old hotel has the feel of a gracious hacienda, with fine views of the park. Fresh flowers enliven the restaurant, which serves mainly regional and Mexican cuisine.

🛏 57 🅿 ➤ 📺 🔇 AE, MC, V

MEXICO CITY

🏨 FOUR SEASONS 🍴 HOTEL
$$$$$
PASEO DE LA REFORMA 500, COLONIA JUÁREZ, 06600
TEL 5230-1818, 800/332-3442
FAX 5230-1808
www.fourseasons.com
Luxurious rooms feature the world's most heavenly feather beds. In the rooms and public spaces the ambience is sophisticated and understated luxury. There's top-notch service, and the delightful **El Restaurant** features a range of fine tequilas and scrumptious haute Mexican and international dishes.

🛏 240 🚇 Sevilla 🅿 🔇 ➤ 📺 🔇 All major cards

🏨 NIKKO MEXICO 🍴 $$$$$
CAMPOS ELISEOS 204, COLONIA POLANCO, 11560
TEL 5280-1111, 800/645-5687
FAX 5280-9191

This classy, 42-story, Japanese-owned hotel, just a short walk from the Museum of Anthropology, serves high tea weekdays, has elegant shops, and has four restaurants serving Japanese, French, and international food. Its business center is open 24 hours.

🛏 744 🚇 Auditorio 🅿 🔇 ➤ 🔇 ➤ 📺 🔇 All major cards

🏨 CAMINO REAL 🍴 MEXICO
$$$
MARIANO ESCOBEDO 700, COL. NUEVA ANZURES, 11590
TEL 5263-8888
FAX 5250-6897 OR 5250-6723
Designed by renowned architect Ricardo Legorreta, Mexico City's modernistic low-rise near Chapultepec Park has colorful marigold and hot pink accents and artwork by major artists such as Rufino Tamayo. French restaurant **Fouquet's de Paris** is recommended, and the lively cantina specializes in fine tequilas and hosts trios.

🛏 713 🚇 Chapultepec 🅿 🔇 ➤ 🔇 ➤ 📺 🔇 All major cards

🏨 DE CORTÉS BEST 🍴 WESTERN
$$
HIDALGO 85, COL. GUERRERO, 06300
TEL 5518-2184 OR 5521-0234, 800/528-1234
FAX 5512-1863
Lack of business services make this hotel best suited to vacationers rather than business travelers. The 18th-century former hospice's charming atmosphere and central location make up for the rather plain rooms.

🛏 29 🚇 Hidalgo 🅿 🔇 🔇 All major cards

🏨 CATEDRAL
$
DONCELES 95, CENTRO, 06000
TEL 5518-5232
FAX 5512-4344
www.hotelcatedral.com.mx

E-MAIL hcatedra@mpsnet.com.mx
An excellent-value hotel just behind the *zócalo* and the cathedral. Bright, clean rooms have modems and plenty of hot water; there's a travel agency, efficient staff, an adequate restaurant, and a less appealing bar.

🛏 116 🚇 Zócalo 🔇 🔇 🔇 AE, MC, V

🍴 LES MOUSTACHES
$$$$$
RÍO SENA 88, COLONIA CUAUHTÉMOC
TEL 5533-3390
Winner of the American Academy of Hospitality Science's Diamond Award for service, culinary creativity, and hygiene, Les Moustaches serves French cuisine in an elegant atmosphere. Jacket and tie required; reservations recommended.

🚇 Cuauhtémoc 🅿
🕐 Closed Sun. 🔇
🔇 MC, V

🍴 LA HACIENDA DE LOS MORALES
$$$$
VÁZQUEZ DE MELLA 525, COL. POLANCO
TEL 5281-4554
Wealthy *defeños* (people from Mexico City) and business executives dine in elegance at this restored 16th-century hacienda on the outskirts of the Polanco neighborhood. Mexican and international fare.

🚇 Polanco (plus a short taxi ride) 🔇 All major cards

🍴 SAN ÁNGEL INN
$$$$
CALLE DIEGO RIVERA 50 AT ALTAVISTA, SAN ÁNGEL
TEL 5616-2222
Reservations are recommended at this deliciously restored former Carmelite monastery, with a menu of award-winning international dishes (steak tartare, pepper-crusted steak) and live music at lunch. A

HOTELS & RESTAURANTS

roaring fire warms the clubby bar. Dress code.
AE, MC, V

🍴 LA CASA DE LAS SIRENAS
$$$
GUATEMALA 32, CENTRO, 06000
TEL 5704-3225
An intimate spot for Mexican food. The snug downstairs cantina is popular for both breakfast and a late-night drink; the second-story patio has the better view, and is more romantic.
Zócalo Closed Sun. D
AE, MC, V

🍴 CICERO CENTENARIO
$$$
REPÚBLICA DE CUBA 79, CENTRO, 06000
TEL 5521-7866
Savor a delicious margarita (choose from 200 tequilas) and regional dishes in a lovely restored colonial mansion.
Zócalo Closed Sun. D
MC, V

🍴 CAFÉ DE TACUBA
$$
TACUBA 28
TEL 5512-8482
The third-generation owners have served tacos, fried chicken, and their famous enchiladas in this popular, festive eatery since 1912; the matronly waitresses know their clientele. The restored mansion is filled with antiques, paintings, handpainted tiles, and bric-a-brac.
Allende Closed Sun. D All major cards

🍴 FONDA EL REFUGIO
$$
LIVERPOOL 166 AT AMBERES, ZONA ROSA, 06600
TEL 5525-8128
Old family recipes and an excellent location in the Zona Rosa have made this delightful restored mansion a Mexico City fixture for more than 40 years.
Insurgentes P
Closed Sun. D MC, V

🍴 FONDA LA GARUFA
$$
MICHOACÁN 93, COLONIA LA CONDESA
TEL 5286-8295
A trendy restaurant serving Argentine-style steaks as well as inspired salads and pastas. In true Condesa-neighborhood style, there are tables both indoors and out along the sidewalk.
Chilpancingo
MC, V

🍴 SPEZIA
$$
AMSTERDAM 241, COLONIA LA CONDESA
TEL 5564-1367
This Polish restaurant, featuring delightful roast duck, borscht, and grilled trout, is currently very popular with locals. The courtyard and indoor setting are elegant, but diners' dress is studied casual.
Chilpancingo P
Closed Sun. D AE, MC, V

🍴 VILLA MARÍA
$$
HOMERO 704, COLONIA POLANCO
TEL 5203-0306
Enjoy a frozen margarita spiked with tamarind juice, or just savor the rather chic, lively, crowded-but-not-noisy ambience and the tacos and other typical Mexican favorites. Romantic music 3–5 p.m., jarocho music (from Veracruz) 8–10 p.m., and mariachis late on weekends.
Polanco (plus a short taxi ride) Closed Sun. D
AE, MC, V

🍴 CAFÉ LA GLORIA
$–$$
VICENTE SUÁREZ 41, COL. CONDESA
TEL 5511-4180
This hip, casual sidewalk bistro in the Condesa neighborhood serves yummy yet inexpensive international dishes such as fresh grilled tuna with ginger butter. Also wonderful desserts

with espresso, capuccino, or American-style coffee.
Chilpancingo MC, V

AROUND MEXICO CITY

CHOLULA

🏨 VILLAS ARQUEOLÓGICAS
$$
CALLE 2 PONIENTE 601, 72760
TEL 800/258-2633
FAX 2/247-1508
In Mexico, Club Med properties are found not just at the sea but at a half-dozen archaeological sites. In the shadow of massive Tepanapa pyramid, this one has smallish but cozy rooms and well-maintained grounds.
40 P MC, V

🍴 LA LUNITA
$$
AV. MORELOS AT CALLE 6 NORTE
TEL 2/247-0011
Directly across from the great pryamid, this restaurant offers freshwater crayfish (acamaya) in spicy chipotle sauce and other seafood. Drink specials include sangria and Cholula en llamas (literally, "Cholula in flames")—cider with brandy.
MC, V

CUERNAVACA

🏨 LAS MAÑANITAS 🍴
$$$
RICARDO LINARES 107, 62550
TEL 7/314-1466
FAX 7/318-1372
Beloved for its award-winning restaurant and as a soothing retreat from city stress, this restored hacienda is set on immaculate grounds with ponds and fountains. Airy suites have antique furnishings, Mexican folk art, and huge tiled bathrooms; request one with a fireplace or large terrace. Innovative regional cuisine is served overlooking the garden courtyard.
22 P AE

🏨 LAS ESTACAS
$$
RAYÓN 30, CUERNAVACA
CENTRO, TLALTIZAPÁN (1 HR.
OUTSIDE CUERNAVACA)
TEL 7/312-4412
FAX 7/312-7610
Throngs of royal palms and
semitropical vegetation shade
this luscious property
surrounding the crystal-clear
Estacas River, used as a
location for shooting Tarzan
TV shows. The many facilities
are open to day-trippers
($$$), but its nicer to
overnight in the dormitory-
style hostel, two-story hotel,
campgrounds, or RV park.
Reservations and
transportation in Cuernavaca,
one hour away.
🅿 🏊 🚫 No credit cards

🍴 MARCO POLO
$
HIDALGO 30
TEL 7/318-4032
The northern Italian owner
of this popular upstairs
eatery overlooking the
cathedral provides appetizing,
inexpensive gnocci, lasagna,
and pizzas. It's crowded in
the evening, when locals
gather here.
🚫 MC

PUEBLA

🏨 CAMINO REAL
🍴 PUEBLA
$$$$
CALLE 7 PONIENTE 105, 72000
TEL 2/229-0909, 800/722-6466
FAX 2/232-9251
One of Mexico's earliest
monasteries has been
meticulously restored—right
down to the frescoes and
fountains—as a gorgeous,
centrally located inn. The very
refined **El Convento**
restaurant is the place in
Cuernavaca for delicious
international fare (dinner only).
Make a reservation, dress up,
and prepare to splurge.
ℹ 83 🅿 🚭 ❄ 🏊
🚫 All major cards

🏨 MESÓN SACRISTÍA DE
🍴 LA COMPAÑÍA
$$
CALLE 6 SUR 304 AT CALLEJÓN
DE LOS SAPOS, 72000
TEL 2/242-3554
FAX 2/232-4513
E-MAIL sacristi@hermes.uninet.
net.mx
Throughout this two-story
boutique hotel antique
furnishings and decorative
elements are punctuated with
more modern regional folk
art. Rooms are snug rustic
chic, the bar has live music
nightly, and the restaurant
serves delicious regional
specialties: stuffed chilies, cream
of bean soup, and, of course,
Puebla's traditional *mole
poblano* (a blend of chocolate,
nuts, chilies, and more).
ℹ 9 🅿 🕐 Restaurant
closed Sun. D 🚫 AE, MC, V

🍴 FONDA DE SANTA
CLARA
$
AV. 3 PONIENTE 307
TEL 2/242-2659
A welcoming staff
complements the generous
helpings of delicious regional
food at this picturesque,
centrally located inn. Select
from a range of scrumptious
appetizers; for a main dish try
the *tinga* (shredded chicken in
tomato sauce); then treat
yourself to a pastry dessert.
🚫 MC, V

SAN JUAN
TEOTIHUACÁN

🏨 VILLAS
ARQUEOLÓGICAS
TEOTIHUACÁN
$$
SAN JUAN TEOTIHUACÁN,
55800
TEL 595/60909, 800/258-2633
Perfectly situated at the edge
of the archaeological zone,
this low-slung, comfortable
hotel has small rooms typical
of Club Med Arqueológico
properties, plus a tennis court.
ℹ 40 🅿 ❄ 🏊 🚫 AE,
MC, V

TLAXCALA

🏨 POSADA SAN
FRANCISCO
$$
PLAZA DE LA CONSTITUCIÓN
17, 90000
TEL 2/462-6022
FAX 2/462-6818
The recently constructed
guest rooms lack the quaint
colonial atmosphere of the
original mansion, restored to
house the bar, lobby, and
restaurant. The location in
historic downtown, billiards
room, tennis court, and large
pool are pluses.
ℹ 68 🅿 ❄ 🏊 🚫 AE,
MC, V

🍴 ASADOR DEL VECINO
$$
CALLE DEL VECINO 5
NO PHONE
The "Neighbor's Grill" is a
large garden restaurant
specializing in Argentine-style
beef as well as typical regional
dishes. A sample plate would
have meat, fresh white cheese,
local sausages, and cactus
pads—all grilled.
🅿 🕐 Closed D 🚫 No
credit cards

🍴 LA CACEROLA
$$
INDEPENDENCIA 9-A
TEL 2/466-1235
Sophisticated versions of
regional cuisine are served in
the two small dining rooms of
this family-style restored
historic property on Plaza
Xicotencatl. Specialties include
myriad stuffed chilies: try a
chile relleno en salsa de pulque
(mild chili in pulque sauce).
🕐 Closed Sun. D 🚫 No
credit cards

TOLUCA

🏨 QUINTA DEL REY
$$$
PASEO TOLOCAN ORIENTE
KM 5, 52140
TEL 7/211-8777
FAX 7/216-7233
Located outside Toluca on the

HOTELS & RESTAURANTS

highway to Mexico, this six-year-old, three-story, all-suites property is done up in rustic colonial style.
[i] 66 [P] [S] [≈] [▼]
🏊 All major cards

CENTRAL GULF COAST

CATEMACO

🏨 LA FINCA
$$
CARR. COSTERA 180 KM 147
TEL/FAX 294/30322
Birders love this three-story lakeshore hotel as it is surrounded by greenery. Each room has a balcony, and the pool has a slide and spa.
[i] 51 [P] [S] [≈]
🏊 MC, V

🏨 NANCIYAGA
$
CARR. CATEMACO–COYAME KM 7 (EAST OF HWY. 180)
TEL 294/30199
For a peaceful and very rustic retreat, overnight at this New Age ecological park. Herons wade and crocs snap just outside the microscopic lakeside cabins, lit at night by hurricane lamps. Wander the jungle, row or kayak on the lake, then have body mud treatment and rinse off in the mineral spring.
[i] 10 cabins [🕐] Closed Wed. Sept.–Oct. 🏊 No credit cards

🍴 7 BRUJAS
$
MALECÓN CON MARIA ANDREA
TEL 294/30157
Despite Catemaco's reputation for sorcery, few of its restaurants are able to conjure up cooking that goes beyond acceptable. The food here is unexceptional, but the small second-story balcony of the "Seven Witches" enjoys a lakeshore breeze.
[🕐] Closed Mon. 🏊 No credit cards

COATEPEC

🏨 POSADA COATEPEC
$$
HIDALGO 9, COATEPEC 91500
TEL 28/16-05-44
FAX 28/16-00-40
www.posadacoatepec.com.mx
This former coffee villa now houses spacious, well-decorated suites with fine wood accents and satellite TV; antiques grace the lovely bar and lobby. Coffee plantation tours can be arranged.
[i] 23 [P] [≈] 🏊 AE, MC, V

VERACRUZ

🏨 FIESTA AMERICANA
$$$$
BLVD. MANUEL AVILA CAMACHO S/N, BOCA DEL RÍO, 94299
TEL 2/989-8989, 800/343-7821
FAX 2/989-8907
www.fiestaamericana.com
This seaside hotel is a favorite with business travelers as well as families; the extensive business services attract the former and the kids' activities the latter. Large, airy rooms have full amenities and luxurious bathrooms. On-site massage and multiple hot tubs are bonuses.
[i] 233 [P] [S] [S] [S] [≈] 🏊 All major cards

🏨 HOTEL MOCAMBO
$$$$
CALZADA RUÍZ CORTINES 4000, BOCA DEL RÍO, 94299
TEL 2/922-0200
FAX 2/922-0212
www.hotelmocambo.com.mx
E-MAIL hmocambo@ infosel.net.mx
Fabulous and exclusive in the 1930s, this oasis of tropical calm later faded, but never lost its charm. The art deco architecture is now "retro," the palm-studded beach still beckons, and expanded facilities include sauna, spa, and massage.
[i] 90 [P] [S] [▼] 🏊 All major cards

🍴 VILLA MARINA
$$$
BLVD. AVILA CAMACHO S/N, NEAR DESEMBOCADURAS DE HORACIO DIAZ
TEL 2/935-1034
Open 1 p.m. to 1 a.m., Villa Marina has a great seascape through its large plate-glass windows, and serves steaks, regional dishes, and international favorites. The specialty, fresh seafood, is cooked in many styles; waiters will help translate the Spanish-language menu.
[S] 🏊 MC, V

🍴 CAFÉ DE LA PARROQUIA
$–$$
CALLE 16 DE SEPTIEMBRE AT MALECÓN
TEL 2/932-1855
A clink of your coffee glass brings waiters with refills of steaming java and hot milk in this legendary Veracruz coffeehouse near the port. It's open early, but, as everything is a la carte, breakfast is no bargain.
🏊 No credit cards

VILLAHERMOSA

🏨 HYATT REGENCY
🍴 VILLAHERMOSA
$$$
AV. JUÁREZ 106, ZONA
HOTELERA, 86050
TEL 93/15-12-34, 800/228-9000
FAX 93/15-58-08
www.hyatt.com
Comfort and class describe
this nine-story business-
oriented property. Soberly
elegant rooms have the usual
five-star amenities; public
areas include several bars
and lounges. **La Ceiba**
restaurant focuses on Mexican
specialties (a different region
is featured each month), and
has an awesome Sunday
breakfast buffet.
🛈 207 🅿 🔁 🚭 🏊
🚭 All major cards

🏨 CENCALI
$$
JUÁREZ AT PASEO TABASCO
S/N, 86040
TEL 93/15-19-99
FAX 93/15-66-00
www.cencali.com.mx
Two-story Cencali (Náhuatl
for "house on the edge of the
lake") indeed abuts las
Ilusiones Lake; its grounds are
extensive and tropical, with
wandering flamingos. Small
rooms have bathtubs, and a
breakfast buffet is included in
the price. La Venta museum is
quite close.
🛈 120 🅿 🚭 🏊
🚭 AE, MC, V

🍴 LOS TULIPANES
$$
CARLOS PELLICER 511
TEL 93/12-92-09
Try some of Tabasco's unusual
dishes at "the Tulips,"
conveniently next to the
CICOM (Center for
Investigation of Olmec and
Maya Cultures) and
overlooking the Grijalva River.
There's a daily breakfast
buffet, after which regional
cuisine (try the ugly pelela-
garto fish, a large appetizer
plate) is served a la carte. The

same owners serve lunch and
dinner aboard the floating
restaurant/bar *Capitán Buelo*
(Closed Mon.).
🅿 🚭 🚭 AE, MC, V

🍴 CAFÉ DEL PORTAL
$–$$
INDEPENDENCIA 301
TEL 93/12-50-67
Marimbas play during the
breakfast buffet and again late
evening at this plaza
restaurant serving regional
specialties.
🚭 🚭 MC, V

XALAPA

🏨 HOWARD JOHNSON
LAS CONVENCIONES
XALAPA
$
AV. 20 DE NOVIEMBRE
ORIENTE 455, 91040
TEL/FAX 28/12-19-25, 800/446-
4656
www.hojo.com
Three blocks from the city
center, this dependable six-
story hotel has such perks as
free local calls and rooms with
fireplaces. It won the chain's
gold medal award, given for
cleanliness during surprise
inspections.
🛈 120 🅿 🔁 🏊 🚭 All
major cards

🏨 MESÓN DE ALFÉREZ
$
ZARAGOZA AT SEBASTIÁN
CAMACHO 2, 91000
TEL/FAX 28/18-63-51
Diluted washes of bright
Mexican colors warm the
walls of this restored historic
home just behind the
government palace. Original
materials were preserved
whenever possible during the
restoration. Some rooms have
loft bedrooms.
🛈 20 🅿 🚭 AE, MC, V

🍴 LA ESTANCIA DE
TECAJETES
$$
AVILA CAMACHO 90, LOCAL
12, PLAZA TECAJETES
TEL 28/18-07-32

With a fine view of the leafy
park for which it is named, this
downtown restaurant puts its
own spin on regional dishes,
such as chicken breast stuffed
with creamed spinach in
mushroom sauce. There's a
pianist daily until noon, and
music of one genre or
another is played most nights
after 9:30.
🅿 🕐 Closed Sun. D
🚭 AE, MC, V

🍴 LA CASA DE MAMÁ
$
AVILA CAMACHO 113
TEL 28/17-31-44
Decorated in dark tones with
antique furniture, this popular
restaurant has an impressive
international menu including
filet mignon and pork loin in
Roquefort sauce. Request a
table at the back, away from
noisy traffic.
🚭 AE, MC, V

OAXACA

BAHÍAS DE HUATULCO

🏨 QUINTA REAL
🍴 HUATULCO
$$$$
PASEO BENITO JUÁREZ 2,
BAHÍA TANGOLUNDA, 70989
TEL 9/581-0428, 800/457-4000
FAX 9/581-0429
www.quintareal.com
Characteristic of the chain,
this intimate property
embodies elegance and
comfort. Three levels of
suites, designed in understated
luxury with cream-colored
appointments, have great bay
views with all the amenities;
some have plunge pools, and
there's a shuttle to the beach
club with restaurant and pool.
Splurge for a special dinner at
Las Cúpulas Restaurant,
serving inspired international
cuisine in an elegant setting
overlooking the sea.
🛈 28 🅿 🚭 🚭 🏊
🚭 AE, MC, V

🏨 CLUB MEDITERANÉE HUATULCO
$$$
BLVD. JUÁREZ, BAHÍA
TANGOLUNDA, 70989
TEL 9/581-0033, 800/258-2633
FAX 9/581-0156
This family-oriented beachfront offers everything from kayaking to karaoke. Meals, evening entertainment, fitness classes, and gratuities are all included.
🛏 483 ⏻ Closed April–late Nov. 🅿 🏊 🎾 AE, MC, V

🏨 MISIÓN DE LOS ARCOS
$
GARDENIA 902, CRUCECITA
TEL/FAX 9/587-0165
E-MAIL losarcos@huatulco.net.mx
This intimate Mediterranean-style hotel is in Crucecita, but vans shuttle to its Santa Cruz Bay beach club. Choose fan or air-conditioning; many rooms have balconies. The Internet café serves coffee and desserts.
🛏 13 🅿 🏊 🎾 AE, MC, V

🍴 RESTAURANT DE DOÑA CELIA (AVALOS)
$–$$
PLAYA SANTA CRUZ (SOUTH OF PASEO MITLA), BAHÍA SANTA CRUZ
TEL 9/587-0128
At this Huatulco original, you can almost wriggle your toes in the sand as you order a delicious breakfast, lunch, or dinner. Outdoor tables under palm-thatch roofs are blessed by a lovely bay breeze.
No credit cards

OAXACA

🏨 CAMINO REAL OAXACA
$$$$
CALLE 5 DE MAYO 300, 68000
TEL 9/516-0611, 800/722-6466
FAX 9/516-0732
www.caminoreal.com
A converted 16th-century convent on a quiet street in historic downtown, this beautiful property is long on charm but a bit short on five-star amenities—at least for the price. Diners in the colonnaded corridor surrounding a central patio are serenaded by a trio of musicians.
🛏 90 🅿 🏊 🏊 🏊 All major cards

🏨 HOTEL VICTORIA
$$$
LOMAS DEL FORTIN 1, 68070
TEL 9/515-2633
FAX 9/515-2411
Oaxaca glitters dramatically at night from the gardens and terrace bar of this comfortable hotel above town. Art by local painters of some renown is for sale. Prices for comfortable rooms vary according to size and location. Shuttles to downtown.
🛏 150 🅿 🏊 🏊 🏊 AE, MC, V

🏨 SUITES DEL CENTRO
$$
AV. HIDALGO 306 NEAR MIER Y TERÁN
TEL 9/516-8282 OR 9/516-8383
FAX 9/516-1549
This classic downtown mansion, with great views from the rooftop terrace, has recently been restored with Talavera tiles and other authentic touches. Rent a suite with a living room and fully equipped kitchen at a bargain price. For about $30 more, you can add a second bedroom.
🛏 27 🏊 AE, MC, V

🏨 CAZOMALLI
$
EL SALTO 104 AT ALDAMA, JALATLACO, 68080
TEL 9/513-8605
FAX 9/513-3513
E-MAIL cazomalli@infosel.net.mx
A friendly hotel run by the Pérez Flores family in quiet Jalatlaco neighborhood. Cazomalli's simple but pleasant rooms surround a central courtyard. Internet service, rooftop spa, and no kids under 12.
🛏 15 🏊 AE, MC, V

🍴 EL ASADOR VASCO
$$–$$$
PORTAL DE FLORES 10
TEL 9/514-4755
Ask for a terrace table at this award-winning, second-story, long-time favorite overlooking Oaxaca's busy main plaza. In addition to scrumptious Basque specials are Mexican standards such as the *huachinango veracruzano*, red snapper in tomato sauce with green olives.
All major cards

🍴 EL NARANJO
$$
TRUJANO 203
TEL 9/514-1878
A few blocks from the *zócalo*, this courtyard restaurant has an inspired collection of recipes from throughout Mexico. After an appetizer of marinated goat cheese, try the cold tomato soup with garlic and olive oil, an organic salad, stuffed chilies, or one of the state's seven signature *mole* dishes.
AE, MC, V

🍴 TERRA NOVA
$–$$
PORTAL JUÁREZ 116, SOUTHEAST CORNER OF ZÓCALO
TEL 9/514-0533
Like the other cafés surrounding the plaza, Terra Nova is filled day and night with people-watchers. It has reasonably quick service, satisfying food, electric guitar most evenings, and an affiliated venue upstairs for indoor dining.
MC, V

🍴 LA ESCONDIDA
$
CARR. YATARENI KM 7, OFF HWY. TO MITLA
TEL 9/517-6665
Locals flock on weekends and holidays to this smorgasbord

of regional cuisine. It's even full midweek, when business-people and tourists come to this outdoor venue 15 minutes from downtown Oaxaca.
 Closed D   P   No credit cards

🍴 LA OLLA
$
REFORMA 402
TEL 9/516-6668
Very clean and dependable, the centrally located La Olla creates healthful regional, vegetarian, and international dishes. Food is made to order, and a bit slow, but local artwork entertains.
🕐 Closed Sun.   MC, V

PUERTO ÁNGEL

🏨🍴 LA BUENA VISTA
$
CALLE BUENA COMPAÑÍA, NEAR SECTOR MILITAR NAVAL
TEL/FAX 9/584-3104
Accommodations in sleepy Puerto Ángel are basic, but the "Good View" hotel has screened windows and ceiling fans. At the top of the property, enjoy the breeze as you sample fresh shrimp, fish, or chicken or vegetarian tamales in the open dining room.
ℹ 21   No credit cards

PUERTO ESCONDIDO

🏨🍴 HOTEL FLOR DE MARÍA
$$
ENTRANCE PLAYA MARINERO S/N
TEL/FAX 9/582-0536
It's a short walk to the beach from this two-story property owned by friendly Canadian (via Italy) expats. The bright rooms have handpainted flowers but no TV or phone. The rooftop terrace has hammocks, a small pool, and, in high season, a bar; at night, candles glow in the open-sided restaurant, which features Mexican and Italian specials and sublime desserts.
ℹ 24   AE, MC, V

🏨 HOTEL ARCO IRIS
$
CALLE DEL MORRO S/N, ZICATELA BEACH, 71980
TEL 9/582-1494
FAX 9/582-0432
It's the sum of its parts that makes this bungalow-style hotel worthwhile. Plain rooms have personal patios, tropical landscaping surrounds the pool, and the rooftop video bar and restaurant overlook the town's surfing beach.
ℹ 26   MC, V

🍴 CAFECITO
$
CALLE DEL MORRO S/N
TEL 9/582-0516
Packed with surfers and savvy tourists, this outdoor restaurant on Zicatela Beach serves homemade pastries and a variety of ample breakfast plates. Later on, choose from sandwiches, burgers, and fish fillets with rice and veggies.
No credit cards

TEOTITLÁN DEL VALLE

🍴 TLAMANALLI
$$
AV. JUÁREZ 39
TEL 9/524-4006
Located in the rugmaking town of Teotitlán del Valle, this unpretentiuos, lunch-only, Zapotec restaurant has been featured in *The New York Times* and *Gourmet* magazine. The Mendoza sisters cook squash blossom soup, chicken tamales, turkey in *mole* sauce, and a few pre-Hispanic favorites.
🕐 Closed D, Mon., Eastertime   No credit cards

CHIAPAS

COMITÁN

🏨 LOS LAGOS DE MONTEBELLO
$
BLVD. BELISARIO DOMINGUEZ NORTE 14
TEL/FAX 9/632-1092

Comitán's fanciest hotel is a lovely but slightly faded keepsake of old-fashioned propriety. Everything is spacious, from the ample rooms with high ceilings, to the outdoor pool and the central patio shaded by gnarled Indian laurels and tulip trees.
ℹ 60   AE, MC, V

🍴 EL GRECO
$
CUARTA CALLE SUR ORIENTE 8
TEL 9/632-5173
Although its name means "the Greek," the food here is typical *chiapaneco* (Chiapan). The set lunch of this second-story restaurant, four blocks southeast of the main plaza, is an absolutely overwhelming array of local victuals: everything from tripe to tostadas.
🕐 Closed D, Sun.   No credit cards

LAGUNAS DE MONTEBELLO

🏨🍴 MUSEO PARADOR SANTA MARÍA
$$
CARR. A LAGUNAS DE MONTEBELLO KM 22
TEL/FAX 9/632-5116
This Independence-era hacienda—about a 20-minute drive from the lakes—stands by its simple but delicious regional recipes, such as barbecued chicken with rice and *lingua pebre* (beef tongue with fried tomatoes and sherry). Six fabulous rooms are decorated with period antiques from different eras.
ℹ 6   P   MC, V

OCOSINGO

🏨 RANCHO ESMERALDA
$
CARR. A TONINÁ KM 8 (DIRT ROAD 1 MILE/1.5 KM)
FAX 9/673-0711
E-MAIL ranchoes@mundomaya.com.mx
Cabins at this rustic, rural, 26-acre (10.5 ha) guesthouse are lit by lamps; guests share

the 6-foot (2 m) clawfoot bathtub and outhouses. Filling breakfasts and dinners are served at this working macadamia-nut farm a short hike from the ruins at Toniná.
🛈 7 cabins 🅿 🚫 No credit cards

PALENQUE

🏨 CALINDA INN NUTUTÚN
$
CARR. PALENQUE–OCOSINGO KM 3.5, 29960
TEL 9/345-0100, 800/462-2434
FAX 9/345-0629
Space for camping and a children's playground surround a quick-moving, elbow-shaped river that runs right through the wooded grounds of this hotel, about ten minutes outside Palenque proper. The ample but plain rooms have cable TV.
🛈 60 🅿 🚫 ⛄ 🌊 🚫 All major cards

🏨 MAYA TULIPANES
$
CAÑADA 6, 29960
TEL 9/345-0258
FAX 9/345-1004
Simply furnished rooms have remote-control cable TV and screened windows, the grounds are pleasant, and the management is friendly. La Cañada is a quiet neighborhood close to downtown Palenque and roadside restaurants.
🛈 48 🅿 ⛄ 🌊 🚫 AE, MC, V

🍴 MAYA
$
HIDALGO AT INDEPENDENCIA, CENTRO
TEL 9/345-0042
Legions of loyal fans frequent this plain but popular restaurant in Palenque town's main square. Seafood and regional fare are served under cooling fans; a newer and more charming location in the La Cañada neighborhood (Calle Merle Green s/n, tel

9/345-0216) serves many of the same dependable dishes.
🚫 No credit cards

SAN CRISTÓBAL DE LAS CASAS

🏨 FLAMBOYANT ESPAÑOL
$
PRIMERO DE MARZO 15, 29200
TEL 9/678-0726
FAX 9/615-0087
A restored Porfiriato mansion whose interior walls are washed in warm hues with blue accents, this centrally located hotel is soothing rather than flamboyant, as its name implies. Saints in niches surround the green central patio. The pretty rooms have heaters and reading lamps, and some of the tiled bathrooms have tubs.
🛈 100 🅿 🚫 AE, MC, V

🏨 NA BOLOM
🍴 $
AV. VICENTE GUERRERO 33, 29200
TEL./FAX 9/678-1418
www.ecosur.mx/nabolom
Rooms in this historic house have fireplaces and are decorated with indigenous artifacts. Book well in advance. Meals are served family-style in the large dining room, and it's a treat to mingle with visiting artists and archaeologists around a shared table. The regional and international recipes are as down-home and wholesome as the setting. Dinner reservations are required for non-guests.
🛈 12 cabins 🚫 MC, V

🍴 LA CASA DEL PAN
$
AV. BELISARIO DOMINGUEZ
TEL 9/678-0468
Start your day with excellent hot coffee and homemade pastries, then return later for healthy vegetarian meals on the bustling inner patio of this old home. You can buy cookies, cakes, and muffins for

PRICES

HOTELS
An indication of the cost of a double room in high season, excluding tax, is given by $ signs.
$$$$$	Over $250
$$$$	$150– $250
$$$	$100–$150
$$	$50–$100
$	Under $50

RESTAURANTS
An indication of the cost of a three-course lunch or dinner without drinks, tax, or tip is given by $ signs.
$$$$$	Over $45
$$$$	$30–$45
$$$	$20–$30
$$	$10–$20
$	Under $10

munching throughout the day. Live music weekend evenings.
🕐 Closed Mon. 🚫 No credit cards

🍴 EMILIANO'S MUSTACHE
AV. CRESCENCIO ROSAS 7
TEL 9/678-7246
$
Mexican ballads blare throughout this noisy but fun restaurant decorated with Revolutionary War memorabilia. Open from late breakfast through late night (2 a.m.), it fills with locals during the evening, when delicious tacos are the most popular menu item.
🚫 No credit cards

TUXTLA GUTIERREZ

🏨 CAMINO REAL
🍴 $$$
BLVD. DR. BELISARIO DOMÍNGUEZ 1195, 29060
TEL 9/617-7777, 800/722-6466
FAX 9/617-7779
Not surprisingly, Tuxtla's nicest hotel belongs to the classy Camino Real chain. It's a sleek, modern structure which integrates pool, green spaces,

open bars and lounge areas in a pleasing way. Both the ritzy **Montebello Restaurant** (which opens at 2 p.m.) and the less formal but exceptional Azulejos are well worth a visit. The latter has a heavenly daily breakfast buffet, with many items cooked to order by a platoon of smiling chefs.

🛈 210 ⬛ 🎿 ⬛ All major cards

YUCATÁN PENINSULA

CAMPECHE

🏨 HOTEL DEL MAR
$$
AV. RUÍZ CORTINES 51, 24000
TEL 9/816-2233
FAX 9/811-1618
Despite its plain appearance and somewhat bland personality, this low-rise hotel is still popular with businesspeople. The furniture, mattresses, and carpeting of this former Ramada Inn have been replaced, the pool has been enlarged, and other needed improvements made.

🛈 146 🅿 ⬛ ⬛ 🎿 ⬛ All major cards

🏨 HOTEL DEL PASEO
$
CALLE 8 NO. 215
TEL 9/811-0084
FAX 9/811-0097
This bright, clean, low-rise hotel under an acrylic dome is situated about a ten-minute walk from the cathedral. Rooms have simple modern furnishings and cable TV. There is also a car-rental agency and underground parking.

🛈 48 🅿 ⬛ ⬛ AE, MC, V

🍴 LA PIGUA
$$
AV. MIGUEL ALEMÁN 197-A
TEL 9/811-3365
A seaside theme prevails at this longstanding favorite near the north end of town. Waiters bring the day's catch in a net for your inspection.

Somewhat formal but not ostentatious.
⊕ Closed D ⬛ ⬛ MC, V

🍴 LA MALINCHE
$
CALLE 10 NO. 396
TEL 9/811-3205
A relaxing evening venue, this lively, white-stucco restaurant has a Western mood and serves drinks, appetizers, and Mexican standards. Sample the mushrooms marinated in garlic oil, tacos, ribs, or grilled steaks or cactus pads.
⊕ Closed L ⬛ No credit cards

CANCÚN

🏨 HILTON CANCÚN BEACH & GOLF RESORT
$$$$$
BLVD. KUKULCÁN KM 17, ZONA HOTELERA, 77500
TEL 9/881-8000
FAX 9/881-8080
Formerly the Caesar Park, this high rise has a friendly, professional staff, tennis, an 18-hole golf course, and seven outdoor pools, one with a swim-up bar. In 1999 it won its fourth *Meetings and Conventions* magazine's Gold Key Award for best meeting places.

🛈 426 🅿 ⬛ ⬛ ⬛ 🎿 ⬛ AE, MC, V

🏨 LE MERIDIÉN CANCÚN
🍴 **$$$$$**
BLVD. KUKULCÁN KM 14, ZONA HOTELERA, 77500
TEL 9/881-2200, 800/225-5843
FAX 9/881-2201
Public areas and rooms are elegant and restrained, yet the comprehensive European-style spa, opened in 1999, is warm and inviting. Cuisine from southern France is the specialty at the **Côté Sud** restaurant overlooking the beach.

🎿 ⊕ Closed L 🛈 213 🅿 ⬛ ⬛ ⬛ 🎿 ⬛ All major cards

🏨 BACCARA
$$$$
BLVD. KUKULCÁN KM 11.5, ZONA HOTELERA, 77500
TEL 9/883-2077, 888/497-4325
FAX 9/883-2173
Bright one-, two-, and three-bedroom suites on the beach combine Mexican hacienda-style architecture and furnishings with modern touches. Each suite has a fully equipped kitchen, dining room, and patio with spa. Buffet breakfast is included.

🛈 23 🅿 ⬛ 🎿 ⬛ AE, MC, V

🏨 EL REY DEL CARIBE
$$
AV. UXMAL AT NADER, DOWNTOWN, 77500
TEL 9/884-2028
FAX 9/884-9857
Rooms with equipped kitchenettes crouch among the overgrown gardens surrounding a smallish pool and solar-heated spa. No restaurant.

🛈 24 🅿 ⬛ 🎿 ⬛ MC, V

🍴 LA HABICHUELA
$$$$
CALLE MARGARITAS 25, DOWNTOWN
TEL 9/884-3158
Maya statues, candlelit patios, and splashing fountains create a romantic ambience at this downtown favorite, where couples feast on nouvelle Mexican-Caribbean cuisine such as *cocobichuela*, a curried blend of lobster and shrimp.
⬛ ⬛ AE, MC, V

🍴 LA CASA DE LAS MARGARITAS
$$$
BLVD. KUKULCÁN KM 12, LA ISLA SHOPPING VILLAGE, ZONA HOTELERA
TEL 9/883-3222
A covered courtyard and second-floor balconies with perky hacienda-style decor. Live music and well-seasoned Mexican dishes. Open daily after 5 p.m

HOTELS & RESTAURANTS

HOTELS & RESTAURANTS

P ⊕ Closed L ☒
AE, MC, V

🍴 CASA ROLANDI
$$
PLAZA CARACOL, BLVD.
KUKULCÁN KM 8.5, ZONA
HOTELERA
TEL 9/883-2557
This is another in a small
series of inspired restaurants
serving Italian Lake District
cuisine in an elegant yet
unpretentious setting.
Recommended are the
homemade pastas and
carpaccio. Covered patio, bar.
☒ AE, MC, V

🍴 LA PLACITA
$$
AV. YAXCHILÁN 12, NEAR
HACIENDA
TEL 9/884-0407
Dine on the outdoor patio
or in the cool indoor
restaurant, choosing from
steak and chicken, delicious
tacos, quesadillas, and other
traditional offerings.
P ☒ AE, MC, V

CHICHÉN ITZÁ

🏨 HOTEL MAYALAND
$$$
CARR. MÉRIDA–PUERTO
JUÁREZ KM 120
TEL 9/851-0077, 800/235-4079
FAX 9/851-0129
Old and new wings set in
gardens are found throughout
the 100-acre (40 ha) site, but
the prettiest and most
secluded rooms are the
thatch-roofed, whitewashed
bungalows, which have two
hammocks on each veranda.
Ⓘ 95 P ☒ ☒ ☒ DC,
MC, V

🏨 HACIENDA CHICHÉN
$$
CARR. MÉRIDA–PUERTO
JUÁREZ KM 120
TEL 9/851-0045, 800/624-8451
FAX 9/924-8844 (IN MÉRIDA)
The cottages are rustic
country elegant, with
handwoven bedspreads,
wrought-iron bedsteads, and

dehumidifiers, but no phones
or TV. The ancient chapel is
popular with brides, and the
colossal pool beckons even
when flecked with leaves from
the trees that tower overhead.
Ⓘ 25 P ☒ ☒ ☒ All
major cards

COBÁ

🏨 VILLAS
🍴 ARQUEOLÓGICAS
COBÁ
$$
NEAR ENTRANCE TO RUINS
TEL 9/874-2087, 800/258-2633
Run by Club Med, this simple
inn is the fanciest place in
Cobá. The rooms are a bit
stark, but the open restaurant
surrounds a cool swimming
pool shaded by deep pink
bougainvillea. The hotel has an
excellent library and gift shop.
P ☒ ☒ MC, V

COZUMEL

🏨 PRESIDENTE INTER-
🍴 CONTINENTAL
COZUMEL
Vivid magenta and cobalt
furnishings set against white
walls enhance the tropical feel of
the Presidente's rooms; the suites
face perfect white beaches.
Tropical fish swim close to shore
in a crystalline cove beneath **El
Caribeño** restaurant, where
guests linger over fresh
honeydew juice and seafood
salads. The fancier El Arrecife
restaurant pampers diners with
live Spanish guitar music and
sublime Continental cuisine.
Some guests never leave the
grounds.
$$$$$
CARR. A CHANKANAAB KM 6
TEL 9/872-0322, 800/327-0200
FAX 9/872-1360
www.interconti.com
Ⓘ 253 ⊟ ☒ ☒ ☒
▼ ☒ AE, MC, V

🏨 CONDUMEL
$$
COSTERA NORTE, NORTH OF
BLVD. AEROPUERTO
TEL 9/872-0892
Hammocks hang beside the
living-room doors that open
onto a limestone terrace
above blue water at this small
condo complex owned by
one of the island's top dive-
shop operators. Full kitchens,
huge marble bathtubs, and
plush mattresses cover all
that is needed for a low-key
vacation.
Ⓘ 10 ☒ MC, V

🍴 LA CHOZA
$$
R. SALAS 198 Y AV. 10 NORTE
TEL 9/872-0958
Authentic Yucatecan cuisine,
served on Mexican crockery
under a palm-thatch roof
fulfills all dreams of a classic
tropical island meal. Superb
seafood, stuffed *chile rellenos*,
savory marinated pork
cochinita pibil, and fragrant
cinnamon-laced coffee all
tempt the senses.
☒ AE, V

HOTELS & RESTAURANTS

COCOS COZUMEL

$

AV. 5 SUR 180

TEL 9/872-0241

You could eat breakfast here every day of your stay and still not sample the entire menu of eggs with chilies and cheese, egg tacos, hashbrowns, and enormous fruit-laced muffins. The used-book exchange is a plus.

🕐 Closed D 🔘 MC, V

ISLA MUJERES

VILLA ROLANDI GOURMET AND BEACH CLUB

$$$$$

FRACC. LAGUNA MAR KM 7

TEL 9/877-0700

FAX 9/877-0100

www.rolandi.com

E-MAIL rolandi@rolandi.com

Rates at this luxurious all-suites property on a sandy cove include transportation from Cancún, continental breakfast, and lunch or dinner. Suites are fresh and modern, with natural materials and bright colors; all have wide balconies overlooking the beach with umbrella tables and spas. Open to the sea breeze, the restaurant has a varied menu of Italian dishes such as penne scallops with ginger and champagne, and arugula and watercress salad, to name just two.

ⓘ 20 🔘 🔘 🔘
🔘 MC, V

CABAÑAS MARÍA DEL MAR

$$

AV. LAZO 1

TEL 9/877-0179, 800/223-5695

There are three types of lodging here: all have refrigerators, ceiling fans, and air-conditioning. The "tower" rooms are oldest; "castle" rooms are newer, with balconies; and the one-story cabanas have hammocks overlooking the pool or garden. Beautiful Playa Norte is a few steps away.

ⓘ 73 🅿️ 🔘 🔘 🔘 No credit cards

MÉRIDA

HACIENDA KATANCHEL

A former sisal plantation is now home to Yucatán's most elegant hacienda hotel. Guests slumber in seductive suites with private wading pools and verandas, and dine on superb Yucatecan cuisine prepared with organic vegetables and fruits. European tapestries decorate the Gran Salón beside the billiard parlor; bromeliads and orchids thrive beside the main pool. Tours to nearby ruins and colonial towns can be arranged.

$$$$$

HWY. 180, 16 MILES (26 KM) EAST OF MÉRIDA

TEL 9/923-4020, 888/882-9470

ⓘ 40 🔘 🔘 🔘

FIESTA AMERICANA MÉRIDA

$$$

COLÓN 451 AT PASEO MONTEJO, 97000

TEL 9/920-2194, 800/343-7821

FAX 9/920-2198

Probably Merida's prettiest high-rise hotel, the Fiesta Americana Mérida, in the high-rent district on Paseo Montejo, has an elegant lobby and airy adjoining lounges. The pretty rooms have safe-deposit boxes, bathtubs, cable TV, and other amenities.

ⓘ 350 🅿️ 🔘 🔘 🔘
🔘 🎾 🔘 AE, MC, V

CASA DEL BALAM

$$

CALLE 60 NO. 488, 97000

TEL 9/924-8844, 800/624-8451

FAX 9/924-5011

Neither too big nor too small, this centrally located hotel is one of Mérida's oldest, but recent renovations have brightened both rooms and public spaces, including the

games room and restaurant. Facilities include travel services, car rental, and a shop.

ⓘ 51 🅿️ 🔘 🔘 🔘
🔘 AE, MC, V

ALBERTO'S CONTINENTAL PATIO

$$

CALLE 64 NO. 482 AT CALLE 57

TEL 9/928-5367

Merida's most delicious food—including wonderful vegetarian and Lebanese favorites (hummus, tzatziki, and tabbouleh) and Mexican dishes—is served in the cool, antiques-laden restaurant or on the garden patio, which is beautifully set under giant trees and a starry night sky.

🔘 🔘 AE, MC, V

EL PÓRTICO DEL PEREGRINO

$$

CALLE 57 NO. 501, BETWEEN CALLES 60 AND 62

TEL 9/928-6163

Excellent service, a charming outdoor patio filled with potted plants and trailing vines, and delicious Yucatecan, Middle Eastern, and international food make this restaurant a longtime favorite of residents as well as tourists.

🔘 🔘 🔘 AE, MC, V

PLAYA DEL CARMEN

PELÍCANO INN

$$

CALLE 8 S/N

TEL 9/873-0997

Several sand-colored buildings front Playa's most popular beach just one block from the restaurants and shops. The rooms have tiled floors, cool mint-green and blue fabrics, and blond wood furnishings; the beach restaurant is a popular hangout.

🔘 AE, MC, V

MÁSCARAS

$–$$

AV. JUÁREZ S/N

TEL 9/873-1053

The sidewalk tables facing the

HOTELS & RESTAURANTS

plaza and pier are the most sought-after seats in town; thin-crust pizzas, garlicky calamari, and imported wines are all stand outs. Check out the mask collection.
🕐 Closed L 🐾 MC, V

RIVIERA MAYA

🏨 PUNTA MAROMA
$$$$$
HWY. 307 KM 51
TEL 987/28200
www.maroma.net
Set amid a 200-acre (80 ha) jungle preserve, Maroma offers privacy, luxury, and decadent pampering. The spa has a New Age bent (crystals and yoga), the restaurant serves sublime French-Caribbean cuisine, and the rooms are artistic and architectural wonders.
🅿 🛗 🏊 🐾 AE, MC, V

🏨 KAILUUM II
$
HWY. 307 KM 45
TEL 987/30214, 800/538-6802
www. mexicoholiday.com
Camp in comfort in a tent under a *palapa* furnished with cushy beds, or swing in a hammock under the stars. There's hot water but no electricity, and meals are served family-style in the sand-floor dining room. Facilities are shared with the adjacent Posada del Capitán Lafitte, which has cabanas with ceiling fans, an indoor restaurant, a pool, and a dive shop.
🕐 Closed Sept., Oct. 🏊 🐾 AE, MC, V

TICUL

🏨 PLAZA
$
CALLE 23 NO. 202 BETWEEN CALLES 26 AND 26-A
TEL 997/20484
A simple but clean, new hotel across from the town square, with a choice of fan or air-conditioning.
🛏 24 🅿 🛗 🐾 V

🍴 LOS DELFINES
$$
CALLE 27 NO. 216, BETWEEN CALLES 28 AND 30
TEL 997/20401
This large, open-sided, thatch-roofed restaurant specializes in seafood (with many styles and sizes of cocktails and *ceviche*), but also serves regional cuisine. Open daily 11–6, it has a full bar and a pool that patrons may use.
🕐 Closed D 🐾 No credit cards

TULUM

🏨 CABAÑAS ANA Y JOSÉ
$
CARR. RUINAS–BOCA PAILA KM 7
TEL 9/887-5470
FAX 9/887-5469
www.anayjose.com
E-MAIL anayjose@cancun.com.mx
After more than a decade, this simple cabana-style hotel remains one of the best hideaways on the coast. The restaurant is excellent and the rooms are simple yet comfortable. Some don't face the sea, however.
🛏 15 🅿 🏊 🐾 MC, V

UXMAL

🏨 HACIENDA UXMAL
$$$
BESIDE UXMAL RUINS
TEL 800/235-4079
Handpainted floor tiles, intricate wrought-iron railings, and archways framing views of jungle gardens enhance the gracious Maya hospitality at this well-established hotel a short walk from the ruins. Amenities include a restaurant, bar, and satellite TV.
🛏 82 🛗 🏊 🐾 MC, V

🏨 VILLAS ARQUEOLOGICAS UXMAL
$$
CARR. UXMAL KM 76
TEL 9/976-2018, 800/258-2633
FAX 9/928-0644
A friendly, intimate place near

the archaeological site. Rooms are comfortable but less important than the grounds and public spaces, which include a tennis court, pool table, library, and gift shop. The restaurant, emphasizing French and Continental cuisine, offers a reasonably priced daily special with appetizer, soup, entrée, dessert, and coffee.
🛏 43 🅿 🛗 🏊 🐾 AE, MC, V

VALLADOLID

🏨🍴 EL MESÓN DEL MARQUES
$
CALLE 39 NO. 203, 97780
TEL 9/856-2073
FAX 9/856-2280
Right on the main plaza, this converted hacienda in historic, unpretentious Valladolid has comfortable junior suites with bathtubs. Tour groups flock to the garden patio restaurant for the lovely setting and tasty regional cuisine.
🛏 80 🅿 🏊 🐾 No credit cards

XPUJIL

🏨 CHICANNÁ ECOVILLAGE RESORT
$$
CARR. ESCÁRCEGA–CHETUMAL KM 144
TEL 9/816-2233
FAX 9/811-1618
Comfortable thatch-roofed bungalows painted pastel hues, and each with a patio, wooden tables, and leather chairs, overlook well-tended flower gardens here. The lodge communicates with civilization via radio (phone and fax lines are in Campeche city), but has direct TV in its library.
🛏 150 🅿 🏊 🐾 AE, MC, V

SHOPPING IN MEXICO

Shopping opportunities and items to buy vary greatly by region. Oaxaca and Chiapas, which have large indigenous populations, produce lovely textiles and simple but excellent pottery, among other items. From the Yucatán come colorful and comfortable string hammocks, fine Panama hats, bright embroidered blouses, and items made of cane and straw.

Mexican handicrafts are by no means the sole domain of the indigenous artisan. Boutiques and factory outlets in Guadalajara, Michoacán, and Guanajuato use modern techniques (such as lead-free glazes) in combination with traditional forms and patterns to produce high-quality tableware and a wide variety of household accessories.

Leather goods can be purchased in northern Mexico, which is cattle country, and in Central Mexico. Leather jackets, belts, briefcases, boots, and shoes are a bargain. Be sure the shoes and boots are comfortable, as Mexican footwear tends not to be as good quality as that made in Italy or Spain.

Areas to shop vary as well. Larger, more cosmopolitan cities such as Mexico City, Monterrey, and Guadalajara have shopping centers that offer a great variety. The Sanborns chain of stores sells gifts, music, perfumes and accessories, chocolates and pastries, and books and magazines. Cities known for their handicrafts generally have one or two streets lined with stores and boutiques. Virtually every city, town, and village has either a daily or weekly market; large cities have both. Inquire at the tourist office or hotel which is the most colorful *mercado* (also called *tianguis*) and which is the best for local handicrafts or whatever you are seeking.

You may also visit outlying towns on market day. Market shopping often means you are buying from the producer or his family, and it is a fun way to see the countryside and support local craftsmen and women. If possible, try to scout out a few

midtown shops first, to be aware of prices and quality before hitting village markets. Bartering is expected in marketplaces, although some vendors quote actual prices and discourage bargaining. Most, however, will start high, especially with tourists, coming down to half to three quarters of the asking price. It helps to know the value of the item you want to buy. In most cases, a few dollars difference means a lot more to the seller than it does to you.

Markets and small shops generally don't charge tax, and most don't accept credit cards. Outside the tourist areas, some are wary even of traveler's checks. If you're buying large quantities of merchandise, ask for a receipt to avoid problems with customs in your home country. The larger stores and chains do charge tax, which ranges from 12 to 15 percent from state to state. Some stores will ship items you buy there as well as items purchased elsewhere. It is illegal to export archaeological artifacts from Mexico; in any case, most if not all pieces offered for sale at archaeological sites are fakes.

The stores, malls, and markets listed below are among the best-known and most established.

BAJA CALIFORNIA

Baja has few native handicrafts. Shops in tourist enclaves— primarily Tijuana, Rosarito, Ensenada, and Los Cabos— import folk art and ceramics from mainland Mexico for sale. The wineries in the north produce decent wines and brandies.

SHOPPING AREAS
Avenida Revolución, between 2nd and 9th Streets, and down Calle 1 to the U.S. border, Tijuana, B.C. A mixed bag of garish statuettes, bright piñatas, leather wallets and purses, silver, onyx chessboards, and more.

HANDICRAFTS
Artesanías la Antigua California, Av. Obregón 220, La Paz, B.C.S., tel 1/125-5230. A medley of handicrafts from throughout the country.
Cartes, at Plaza Bonita, Cabo San Lucas, B.C.S., tel 1/143-1770. A good selection of hand-crafted accessories, along with larger home furnishings.
Tolán, Av. Revolución 1471, Tijuana, B.C., tel 6/688-3637. Pricey collection of good-quality folk art from throughout Mexico.

MALLS
Plaza Bonita, on the waterfront at Blvd. Marina, Cabo San Lucas, B.C.S. A handful of the nicest gift and curio shops in town.

MARKETS
Mercado Hidalgo, Avs. Sánchez Taboada and Independencia, Tijuana, B.C. Typical Mexican market a stone's throw from the U.S. border.

NORTHWEST MEXICO

HANDICRAFTS
Casa de las Artesanías de Chihuahua, Av. Juárez 705, Chihuahua, Chih., tel 1/437-1292. Carries regional crafts including Tarahumara dolls, drums, clay pots, and pine-needle baskets.
Casa de las Artesanías de Chihuahua, west side of main square, Creel, Chih. tel 1/456-0080. A subsidiary of the above store; it also sells regional crafts.
El Nicho Curios, Calle Comercio 4, Alamos, Son. Treasures ranging from Mexican ex-votos to old jewelry and regional pottery.
Gallery Michael, Camarón Sábalo 19, Mazatlán, Sin., tel

6/916-7816. A floor-to-ceiling collection of well-chosen Mexican crafts in a cool, classy shop.

Lourdes Gift Shop, Blvd. Beltrones, Posada de San Carlos, San Carlos, Son., tel 6/226-0022. Sells jewelry, clothing, and handicrafts from around Mexico.

MARKETS
Mercado de Artesanías, Victoria 506 and Aldama, Chihuahua, Chih. A block-wide store with jewelry, candy, T-shirts, and regional crafts.
Mercado Central, between Juárez and Serdán, Mazatlán, Sin. This huge market sells produce and other food, along with handicrafts at bargain prices.
Mercado Municipal, between Avs. 20 de Noviembre and 5 de Febrero and Calles Patoni and Pasteur, Durango, Dgo. *The* place to shop for *sarapes,* leather, and regional sweets.

NORTHEAST MEXICO

Stores in the northeast sell such utilitarian products as cowboy boots, saddles, silver belt buckles, leather jackets, fine straw hats, and Saltillo's *sarapes* (bright striped blankets). Industrial Monterrey has modern shopping malls.

HANDICRAFTS
Centro Platero Zacatecas, Fracc. Guadalupe Bernárdez, Zacatecas, Zac., tel 4/923-1007. An outlet on the outskirts of town selling silver jewelry made in its factory in Guadalupe.
El Sarape de Saltillo, Hidalgo Sur 305, Saltillo, Coah., tel 8/412-4889. Lots of the popular bright sarapes, as well as ponchos, rugs, leather, silver, copper, and pottery.
Kristaluxus, José María Vigil 400, Colonia del Norte, Saltillo, Coah., tel 8/351-6396. Leaded glassware from this world-renowned crystal manufacturer can be purchased at outlet prices.

LEATHER
Botas Recio, Allende Norte 701, Saltillo, Coah., tel 8/412-

1237. Men's shoes, belts, boots, and wallets of exotic leather (such as iguana, sea snake, ostrich, and shark); felt and fine straw hats.

MALLS & DEPARTMENT STORES
Plaza Fiesta San Agustín, Av. Real de San Agustín at Lázaro Cárdenas, Monterrey, N.L. Monterrey's largest mall, with a Sanborns restaurant/bookstore and a theater.

CENTRAL MEXICO

The central states have a tradition of fine craftsmanship. In Guanajuato state, Dolores Hidalgo is known for its handpainted ceramics and tiles; Guanajuato for its glassware; and San Miguel de Allende for its high-quality folk art in many media. In San Luis Potosí, buy finely woven silk shawls (rebozos).

HANDICRAFTS
Artes de Mexico, Calzada Aurora 47 exit, Dolores Hidalgo, San Miguel de Allende, Gto., tel 4/152-0764. This factory outlet specializes in stamped tin, but also sells other housewares.
Casa del Conde, Carr. Guanajuato–Dolores Hidalgo Km 5, La Valenciana, Guanajuato, Gto., tel 4/732-2550. A factory producing custom-made housewares of tin, copper, and German silver using old-fashioned techniques.
Casa María Luisa, Canal 40, San Miguel de Allende, Gto., tel 4/152-0130. A huge assortment of folk art, carved furniture, and household accessories.
Casa Querétana de Artesanías, Andador Libertad 52, Querétaro, Qto., tel 4/214-1235. A wide variety of ceramics, liquors and regional candies, textiles, carved figures of stone and wood, religious statues, and wool rugs.
Tonatiu Metzli, Calle Juárez 7, San Miguel de Allende, Gto., tel 4/152-0869. Specializes in ritual masks, Huichol art, and

pre-Hispanic pieces (replicas and originals).
Veryka, Calle Zacateros 6-A, San Miguel de Allende, Gto., tel 4/152-2114. Shop for Oaxacan ceramics, textiles from Guerrero, and other folk art from around the country.

JEWELRY
Joyería David, Calle Zacateros 53, San Miguel de Allende, Gto., tel 4/152-0056. Silver and gold jewelry is made on the premises.
Lapidario de Querétaro, Corregidora 149 Norte, Querétaro, Qto., tel 4/212-0030. Watch craftsmen create gold and silver jewelry using locally mined opals, amethysts, and topaz.

CENTRAL PACIFIC STATES

A wide variety of textiles and ceramics are produced in Michoacán and Guerrero. Jalisco, too, has some fine folk art, and Puerto Vallarta has a large number of shops selling fine art and handicrafts. Silver jewelry is found literally by the ton in Taxco, Guerrero.

SHOPPING AREAS
Mercado de Artesanías Turístico, Calle 5 de Mayo, Zihuantanejo, Gro. A string of stands selling souvenirs, including ceramics and silver jewelry.
Plaza Los Patios, Blvd. Ixtapa s/n, Ixtapa, Gro. Probably the best of Ixtapa's small commercial centers, with several worthwhile folk-art shops.
Saturday market, Av. De los Plateros s/n, near the Flecha Roja bus terminal. Look for the .925 stamp indicating sterling silver.

FINE ART
Sergio Bustamante, Av. Juárez 275, Puerto Vallarta, Jal., tel 3/222-1129. The oldest of Vallarta's galleries, selling Bustamante's whimsical ceramic and bronze suns and moons, papier-mâché and wood figures, and oil paintings.

HANDICRAFTS

Agustín Parra Diseño Barroco, Independencia 158, Tlaquepaque, Jal., tel 3/657-8530. Thirty years' experience building baroque and other period furniture, accessories, frames, and other objects.

Arnoldo, Palma 1, Taxco, Gro., tel 7/622-1272. Ritual and decorative stone and wooden masks, crosses, and crucifixes.

Artesanías de Jalisco, Calzadas Independencia Sur and González Gallo, Guadalajara, Jal., tel 3619-4664. Lots of locally made ceramics and blown glass.

Casa de las Artesanías, Ex-Convento de San Francisco, Fray Juan de San Miguel at Humboldt, Morelia, Mich. Two floors of regional artifacts, each stall selling the craft made in its village.

Casa de los Artesanos, Av. de los Tonaltecas Sur 140, Tonalá, Jal., tel 3/683-0590. Specializes in ceramics, wood, papier-mâché, blown glass, and wrought iron by local artisans.

Casa de los Once Patios, Pátzcuaro, Mich., see p. 162.

Coco Cabana, Agustín Ramírez 1, Playa Principal, Zihuatanejo, Gro., tel 7/554-2518. A good selection of regional and national handicrafts.

Galería José Bernabe, Hidalgo 83, Tonalá, Jal., tel 3/683-0040. Don José and family continue the 200-year-old technique of *petatillo* (low-fire black and white) ceramics and modern, lead-free, high-fire dishes and crockery.

Galería Olinalá, Lázaro Cárdenas 274, Puerto Vallarta, Jal., tel 3/222-4995. Ceremonial masks and small gift items from Jalisco and Michoacán.

Plaza de Artesanías, Juárez 145, Tlaquepaque, Jal. A cluster of shops selling regional folk art, blown glass, and pottery.

MALLS & DEPARTMENT STORES

La Gran Plaza, Av. Vallarta 3959, Guadalajara, Jal., tel 3122-3004. A modern complex west of town, with a Sanborns shop/restaurant, cinema, and many stores and restaurants.

Plaza Bahía, Costera M. Alemán 125, Acapulco, Gro., tel 7/485-6939. A large, air-conditioned mall with bowling alley, multiplex theater, go-carts, and shops.

Plaza del Sol, Avs. López Mateos Sur and Mariano Otero, Zapopan, Jal., tel 3121-5950. This huge mall has green spaces, a multiplex theater, and a Sanborns in addition to many boutiques and shops.

MARKETS

Mercado Central, Diego Hurtado de Mendoza and Constituyentes, Acapulco, Gro. A bustling, typical market in downtown Acapulco.

Mercado de Dulces, Av. Madero at Gómez Farías, Morelia, Mich. Stalls selling typical sweets of the region.

Mercado Libertad, Calzada Independencia Sur at Dionisio Rodríguez, Guadalajara, Jal. This enormous city market has souvenirs and handicrafts but mainly day-to-day necessities.

Mercado de Tetitlán, off Plaza Borda, Taxco, Gro., tel 7/622-0132. A fascinating, multilevel warren of stalls selling mostly to locals.

MEXICO CITY

Fine art galleries are found throughout the city; look in the monthly booklet *Concierge* or Thursday's *Tiempo Libre* section of *La Jornada* newspaper for show listings. Shopping is particularly pleasant in plein-air weekend markets in Coyoacán and San Ángel. Take extra precautions against pickpockets and muggers in Mexico City; carry no more cash than is needed and leave valuable jewelry and cameras at your hotel. Some advise against taking ATM cards and credit cards, although this hampers unrestrained shopping.

SHOPPING AREAS

Bazar Sábado, Plaza San Jacinto 11, San Ángel, open Sat.

only, tel 5616-0082. Exceptional handicrafts at fair prices within the two-story mansion and outside in the adjacent plaza.

Mercado de Artesanías Insurgentes, Londrés at Amberes, Zona Rosa, tel 5525-6498. A maze of handicrafts in 225 stalls.

Zona Rosa, bounded by Reforma, Niza, Av. Chapultepec, and Florencia. This compact neighborhood has many shops selling jewelry, leather, antiques, and fine art.

FINE ART & ANTIQUES

Bazar de Antiguedades, Plaza del Ángel, Hamburgo at Estocolmo, Zona Rosa, tel 5687-2090. An upscale antiques mall with more than 30 shops; about 100 dealers sell at the outdoor weekend flea market.

Jardín del Arte, Plaza Sullivan, Calle Sullivan near Reforma and Insurgentes. Each Saturday more than 100 artists exhibit and sell their paintings and sculptures in this city park.

HANDICRAFTS

Artesanías La Carreta, Insurgentes Sur 2105, San Ángel, tel 5616-2627. An astonishing collection of quality handicrafts from throughout Mexico.

Centro Artesanal La Ciudadela, Plaza de la Ciudadela at Balderas, tel 5510-1828. More than 300 shops selling crafts from all over Mexico.

FONART, Av. Juárez 89, tel 5521-0171. Folk art and hand-crafted furnishings; stock and selection can be variable.

JEWELRY

Los Castillo, Amberes 41, Zona Rosa, tel 5511-8396. Known for its unique "married metals"—a melding of silver, copper, and brass—based on traditional designs.

Tane, Amberes 70, Zona Rosa, tel 5511-9429. Bold designs in silver jewelry and flatware, with branches in many of the city's top hotels.

MALLS & DEPARTMENT STORES

Liverpool, V. Carranza 22 at 20 de Noviembre, tel 5522-8520. The closest of this department store chain to the city center.
Sanborns, Madero 4, Col. Madero, tel 5512-1331. This coffee shop/store sells English-language periodicals and books as well as perfumes, fresh pastries, chocolates, and gifts. (There are many others throughout the city.)

MARKETS

La Lagunilla, Libertad between República de Chile and Allende. Attracts antiques hunters and coin collectors (including pickpockets). Sunday outdoor flea market.
Mercado Xochimilco, Guerrero between Morelos and 16 de Septiembre, Xochimilco. A pleasant covered market (best on weekends) that is less hectic than those downtown.

AROUND MEXICO CITY

SHOPPING AREAS

La Calle de los Dulces, Puebla, Pue. Shops sell freshly made *camote* (sweet-potato candy) and other regional treats.

HANDICRAFTS

Artesanías Paulina, Av. Revolución 22, Tepoztlán, Mor., tel 7/395-2293. Regional crafts include rain sticks, ritual masks used in Carnaval celebrations, painted and carved wood, and ceramics.
Mercado de Artesanías El Parián, 2 Oriente at 6 Norte, Puebla, Pue. Souvenirs, sweets, textiles, and inexpensive ceramics are sold at a covered outdoor market.
Mercado de Artesanías, *plaza principal,* Tepoztlán, Mor. Local handicrafts and those from central and southern Mexico are sold at a Wednesday and Sunday market in the main square.
Mi Mexico Lindo, Portal Hidalgo 7, on Plaza Constitución, Tlaxcala, Tlax., tel 2/466-0606.

Tlaxcala's best selection of regional handicrafts; they sometimes have masks from nearby Tlatempan.
Quetzal, Av. Morelos 4, Cholula, Pue., tel 2/247-4794. Right on the *zócalo,* with a good selection of folk art from around Mexico.
Tianguis Sabado y Domingo, Plaza Xicotencatl, Morelos at Independencia, Tlaxcala, Tlax. Weekend folk-art market with typical carved wood, embroidered blouses, masks, and peach and pear liqueurs.

MARKETS

Mercado Cozme del Razo, Hidalgo at Calle 5 Norte, Cholula, Pue. Typical daily market selling handicrafts, fruits, vegetables, and clothing.

CENTRAL GULF COAST

While neither Veracruz nor Tabasco is known for its handicrafts, both have modern, air-conditioned shopping centers in their capital cities. The region's few typical souvenirs—including items made of vegetable fiber, woven straw fans, and carved gourds—are sold mainly in hotel and museum gift shops.

SHOPPING AREAS

Zona Luz, between Calle 27 de Febrero, Zaragoza, 5 de Mayo and Madero, Villahermosa, Tab. There's nothing special to buy, but the pleasant pedestrian-only zone has pharmacies, ice-cream stores, and clothing boutiques.

MALLS & DEPARTMENT STORES

Plaza Acuario, Blvd. Ávila Camacho s/n, Payon de Hornos, Veracruz, Ver., tel 2/932-8311. Air-conditioned and near the sea, this mall has boutiques and banks but no cinema.
Tabasco 2000, Municipio Libre 7 at Prolongación Paseo Tabasco, Villahermosa, Tab. A cool, marble-lined commercial and shopping center with hotels and restaurants.

OAXACA

This state has a wealth of valuable folk art, and the city of Oaxaca boasts many worthy artists and excellent galleries.

SHOPPING AREAS

(See also box on p. 271.)

Calle Alcalá, between Avs. Independencia and Constitución, Oaxaca. A pedestrian street with many fine shops.

FINE ARTS

Arte de Oaxaca, Av. Murguía 105, Oaxaca, tel 9/514-0910. Displays paintings by the late Rodolfo Morales, and others.
La Mano Mágica, M. Alcalá 203, Oaxaca, tel 9/516-4275. Wool rugs from Teotitlán del Valle, oil paintings, and high-end crafts.
Quetzalli, Constitución 104, Oaxaca, tel 9/514-2606. Excellent contemporary paintings by burgeoning and established artists. There's a café/bar in front.

HANDICRAFTS

ARIPO, Calle Garcia Vigil 809, Oaxaca, tel 9/514-4030. Large inventory of Oaxacan crafts, including black pottery from Coyotepec, leather, straw, textiles, and clothing.
Artesanías Chimalli, García Vigil 513-A, Oaxaca, tel 9/514-2101. A small shop with friendly service and quality handicrafts; offers shipping.
Corazón del Pueblo, Alcalá 307, Oaxaca, tel 9/516-4275. A great selection of furnishings and folk art in two stories.
FONART, Crespo 114 at Morelos, Oaxaca, tel 9/516-5764. Folk art and ceramic plates, bowls, and vases from throughout Mexico (except Oaxaca).
MARO, Av. 5 de Mayo 204, Oaxaca, tel 9/516-0670. Woman's co-op selling regional clothing, herbed mescal, and custom-made textiles.
Mercado de Artesanías, Calle J.P. Garcia near Zaragoza,

Oaxaca. Textiles and clothing exclusively are sold here, including embroidered blouses, shawls, and clothing from Tehuantepec.

MARKETS
Mercado de Abastos, Periférico between Trujano and Minas, Oaxaca. The state's largest market is a labyrinth of stalls selling cooked food, cut flowers, and just about everything else.
Mercado Benito Juárez and Mercado 20 de Noviembre, Oaxaca, see p. 258.

CHIAPAS

The Maya have a long tradition of weaving and brocade, kept alive in some towns by local women's co-ops. You'll also find wool clothing, fabrics, wooden dolls, and lots of other intriguing items, many from Guatemala.

SHOPPING AREAS
Amatenango del Valle, 18 miles (29 km) south of San Cristóbal de las Casas. Many of the humble homes in this town sell lovely unglazed pots and pottery birds.
Av. Juárez, downtown Palenque. Hammocks and souvenirs, mostly from highland Chiapas, are sold in the shops lining Palenque's main street.

BOOKS, MAGAZINES & CARDS
La Pared, Av. Miguel Hidalgo 2, San Cristóbal de las Casas, tel 9/678-6367. Mostly used books, in both Spanish and English; also a small display of fine gifts.
Taller Leñateros, Flavio A. Paniagua 54, San Cristóbal de las Casas, tel 9/678-5174. Produces handmade stationery, business cards, and books from 100 percent natural and recycled materials.

HANDICRAFTS
Galería del Ambar, Crescencio Rosas 4A, San Cristóbal de las Casas, tel 9/678-7925. Silver jewelry

incorporating Chiapas's amber; custom-made gold jewelry.
Instituto de las Artesanías, Blvd. Belisario Domínguez 2035, Tuxtla Gutiérrez, tel 9/613-5313. Doubling as a crafts store, this museum sells lacquerware, textiles, *sarapes,* and other local folk art.
J'pas Joloviletik, Utrilla 43, San Cristóbal de las Casas. Another great co-op with local woven, embroidered, and brocaded textiles and clothing.
Sna Jolobil, Ex-Convento de Santo Domingo, 20 de Noviembre s/n, San Cristóbal de las Casas, tel 9/678-7178. A women's co-op showcasing Maya weaving.

MARKETS
Mercado Municipal, Av. General Utrilla at Nicaragua, San Cristóbal de las Casas. A wonderful warren of candles, copal incense, produce, and hot food; the best market day is Saturday.

YUCATAN PENINSULA

Despite its large Maya population, the Yucatán Peninsula in general has a surprising dearth of folk art (especially in Campeche state), and much is imported from other regions. Still, dedicated shoppers will find high-quality hammocks, fine Panama-style hats, embroidered *huipiles* (sacklike, lightweight women's garments), dresses, blouses, and pleated *guayabera* shirts in sherbet colors for men. The best shopping is in Mérida and Cancún.

BOOKS, MAGAZINES & CARDS
Dante's, Calle 17 No. 138-B at Prolongación Paseo de Montejo, Mérida, Yuc., tel 9/927-7441. A good selection of books, some in English, and a popular coffee shop.
Fama, Av. Tulúm 105, Cancún, Q.R., tel 9/884-6586. Books on the Yucatán Peninsula; a large selection of English-language magazines.

HANDICRAFTS
Arte Maya, Calle 23 No. 301, Ticul, Yuc., tel 9/972-1095. Expensive, museum-quality replicas of Maya archaeological pieces as well as smaller, charming, less costly pieces.
El Aguacate, Calle 62 between 61 and 59, Mérida, Yuc., tel 9/923-1838. Silk, nylon, and cotton hammocks in many hues and sizes.
El Becaleño, Calle 65 No. 483 between Calles 56A and 58, Mérida, Yuc., tel 9/985-0581. Off-the-rack or custom-made Panama-style hats produced in Becal, Campeche.
La Sirena, Av. Morelos Lote 11, Isla Mujeres, Q.R., tel 9/877-0223. Great selection of folk art from throughout Mexico.
Los Cinco Soles, Av. Rafael Melgar Norte 27, Cozumel, Q.R., tel 9/872-0132. Fine gifts and folk art from different areas of Mexico.

JEWELRY
Joyería Palancar, Av. Rafael Melgar Norte 15, Cozumel, Q.R., tel 9/872-1468. Fine silver and gold jewelry.
Van Cleef & Arpels, Avs. Juárez and Morelos, Isla Mujeres, Q.R., Tel 9/877-0299. Expensive but worthy jewelry.

MALLS & DEPARTMENT STORES
La Isla Shopping Village, Blvd. Kukulcán Km 12.5, Cancún, Q.R., tel 9/883-5025. A new mall with marina, watersports, water taxi, and 200-plus shops and restaurants.
Plaza Kukulcán, Blvd. Kukulcán Km 13, Cancún, Q.R. Mall with 350 shops; restaurants, bars, bowling, and a theater.

MARKETS
Mercado Municipal Lucas de Galvez, Calles 56 and 56A at Calle 67, Mérida, Yuc. On the second floor of the lively municipal market, guayaberas, women's clothing, and a few other textiles, hammocks, and crafts are sold.

ENTERTAINMENT & ACTIVITIES

One of the Mexico's most fascinating types of entertainment is its colorful festivals. Religious holidays are generally lively affairs with food, dancing, and fireworks. Some are specific to a region or village, others are celebrated throughout the country (see pp. 16–17). Mexicans are dedicated sports fans. Bullfights are popular, and most large cities have at least one bullring; the fights are generally scheduled to coincide with major holidayas or festivals. *Charreadas* (Mexican rodeos) are a specialty of the northern states, Baja California, and Guadalajara (see p. 154), while *fútbol* (soccer) and baseball have a nationwide following.

Following is a listing of Mexico's most important festivals, cultural centers, and activities, by region. The popularity of nightclubs and bars waxes and wanes; those mentioned here are only the most interesting or historically important. Check with your hotel concierge or tourist information staff, or the local newspaper listings, for other evening entertainment.

BAJA CALIFORNIA

BARS
Hussong's Cantina, Av. Ruiz 113, Ensenada, B.C., tel 6/178-3210. Popular for over a century.

WINERIES
Bodegas de Santo Tomás, Av. Miramar at Calle 7, Ensenada, B.C., tel 6/178-2509. Hour-long winery tours weekdays; weekends by appointment.

BULLFIGHTS
El Toreo, Blvd. Agua Caliente s/n, 2 miles (3 km) east of downtown, Tijuana, B.C., tel 6/686-1510. The season runs from April through Oct.
Plaza Monumental, Av. del Pacífico 4, Fracc. Playas de Tijuana, Tijuana, B.C., tel 6/680-1808. The season runs from May through Sept.

CHARREADAS
Held most weekends May–Sept. Venues vary; call Tijuana Tourism Office, tel 6/681-9492.

CULTURAL CENTERS
Centro Cívico, Social y Cultural, Blvd. Costero at Av. Club Rotario, Ensenada, B.C., tel 6/177-0594. Once a casino, now a cultural center with gallery, museum, and gardens.
Centro Cultural Tijuana, Paseo de los Heroes and Av. Independencia, Tijuana, B.C., tel 6/684-1111. History, anthropology, and art museums, Omnimax theater, gift shop, and restaurant.

FESTIVALS
Bisbee's Black and Blue Marlin Tournament, Los Cabos, B.C.S. Three days in Oct., with a million-dollar purse.
Fiesta de la Vendemia, Ensenada, B.C., tel 6/178-3675. Wine tastings and cultural events hosted each Aug. by local vintners.
Fiesta de San Javier, Misión San Javier, B.C.S., Dec. 3.
SCORE Baja 1000-Mile Off-Road Race, Nov. Infamous race either from Ensenada to La Paz or an Ensenada loop.
Tecate–Ensenada Fun Bicycle Ride, June.

SPORTFISHING
World-class fishing in Bahía de Los Angeles, Los Cabos, the East Cape, La Paz, Loreto, Mulegé, and San Felipe. On the Pacific, you can fish in Ensenada and San Quintín Bay.

WATERSPORTS
With 2,000 miles (3,200 km) of coast, Baja is perfect for water adventures. The sheltered Gulf of California (Sea of Cortés) is preferred for **kayaking,** especially around Bahía de Concepción, Loreto, the East Cape, La Paz, Cabo San Lucas, and many offshore islands. Favorite Pacific coast **sailboarding** sites include Punta San Carlos, Punta Abreojos, and the bays of San Quintín, Magdalena, Santa Rosaliita, and Almejas; on the gulf, try Bahía de Los Angeles, Punta Chivato, Loreto, and the East Cape.

Diving and **snorkeling** are popular off Cabo Pulmo and the sand falls at Cabo San Lucas.
Surfing is popular but rentals are rare. Surf conditions are available through the Baja Safari Travel Club (Tel 888/411-2252). Northern Baja's best surfing is during the winter.

WHALE WATCHING
The season is from Jan. through mid-April (see pp. 68–69).

NORTHWEST MEXICO

CULTURAL CENTERS & THEATERS
Centro Cultural de Chihuahua, Ocampo at Aldama, Chihuahua, Chih., tel 1/416-1230. Music, dance, and art exhibits throughout the year.
Teatro Angela Peralta, Carnaval 47, Mazatlán, Sin. Hosts folkloric dances Dec.–April and cultural events year round.

FESTIVALS
Navy Day, Puerto Peñasco (Rocky Point) and Guaymas, Son., June 1. Boat parades, mock naval battles, fireworks, and beauty contests.
La Feria de la Fundación de Durango and la Feria Agrícola, Durango, Dur., tel 1/812-1121, two weeks in mid-July. Consecutive fairs celebrate the city's founding and agriculture and ranching. Music, folk dances, cockfights, horse races, and charreadas.
Fiesta de la Fundación del Pueblo, El Fuerte, Sin. Moveable feast honoring the town's founding, Nov. or early Dec. Carnival rides, foot races, and folk dancing.

ISLAND TOURS
Ecogrupos de México, Guaymas, Son., tel 6/221-0194. Offers week-long tours of islands in the Sea of Cortés.

PARQUE PINACATE TOURS
Ajo Stage Lines, 1041 Solana St., tel 520/387-6559 or 800/942-1981, fax 520/387-5419 (Ajo, Arizona), www.ajostageline.com. Day trips and overnight custom campouts Nov.–April out of Ajo, Arizona.

SPORTFISHING
Cortez Explorer, Marina San Carlos, Son., tel 6/226-0858. Sportfishing charters to the Guaymas Trench, offshore. **Mazatlán,** Sin. Sportfishing fleets line the harbor south of town; all have similar prices for day charters.

NORTHEAST MEXICO

BREWERY TOURS
Cervecería Cuauhtémoc, Av. Alfonso Reyes 2202 Norte, Monterrey, N.L., tel 8/328-5355. Guests sample Carta Blanca beer after a free guided brewery tour.

CULTURAL CENTERS & THEATERS
Centro Cultural Teatro Garcia Carrillo, Allende at Aldama, Saltillo, Coah. Porfiriato structure hosting concerts and cultural expositions.
Teatro Calderón, Av. Hidalgo 501 (at Plaza Goitia), Zacatecas, Zac., tel 4/922-8620. Late 19th-century opera house hosting cultural events.
Teatro de la Ciudad de Monterrey, Zuazua at Matamoros, Monterrey, N.L., tel 8/343-8974. Monterrey's large, modern theater in the heart of downtown.

FESTIVALS
Feria Estatal, Zacatecas, Zac., first two weeks of Sept. Agriculture and livestock exhibitions; cultural events.
La Morisma, Zacatecas, Zac.,

Aug. Festival includes a three-day reenactment of a battle between Moors and Christians, plays, and indigenous dancing.

FISHING
Abundant freshwater fishing (bass, catfish) in Caballero, Méndez, Vicente Guerrero, and other lakes, and surfcasting along the many coastal lagoons.

CENTRAL MEXICO

CULTURAL CENTERS & THEATERS
Centro Cultural El Nigromante (or Bellas Artes), Hernandez Macias 75, San Miguel de Allende, Gto., tel 4/152-0289. Former convent offering arts and crafts classes and cultural events.
Instituto Allende, Ancha de San Antonio 20, San Miguel de Allende, Gto., tel 4/152-0190. Cultural center with galleries, library, and theater; offers Spanish-language and art classes.
Teatro de la Paz, Segunda de Villerías, Jardín del Carmen, San Luis Potosí, S.L.P., tel 48/12-26-98. An elegant neoclassic theater in the city center.
Teatro Juárez, Calle de Sopena, at Jardín Unión, Guanajuato, Gto., tel 4/732-0397. Symphony, opera, and other performances at a lovely Porfiriato-era theater.

FESTIVALS
Feria del Queso y del Vino, Tequisquiapan, Qto., tel 4/212-1412. Two-week wine and cheese festival with outdoor theater, folk dancing, concerts, and bullfights.
Feria de San Marcos, Aguascalientes, Ags., tel 4/915-1155, second Saturday of April to first Sunday of May. Mexico's largest and oldest state fair, with cultural events, cockfights, dances, bullfights, and fireworks.
Festival Cervantino, Guanajuato, Gto., tel 4/732-7622, Sept. International cultural event with world-class performers of all genres.

Festival Internacional de Jazz, San Miguel de Allende, Gto., late Nov. A four-day international jazz event.
Fiesta de San Miguel, San Miguel de Allende, Gto., tel 4/152-6565. Traditional dancing, bullfights, fireworks, and concerts culminating at dawn on Sept. 29.

SPELUNKING
Sotano de las Golondrinas, outside the town of Tancanhuitz, east of San Luis Potosí (164 miles/264 km from Ciudad Valle), S.L.P. One of the world's best spelunking caverns.

CENTRAL PACIFIC STATES

BUTTERFLY MIGRATION
Millions of monarchs winter in Michoacán forest sanctuaries; see p. 176.

CULTURAL CENTERS
Instituto Cultural Cabañas, Guadalajara, Jal., see p. 148.

DANCING & SHOWS
Ballet Folklórico, Teatro Degollado, Calle Degollado between Morelos and Hidalgo, Guadalajara, Jal., tel 3614-4773. University of Guadalajara troupe performs regional dances Sundays at 10 a.m.
Centro Internacional Acapulco, Convention Center, Costera Alemán 4455, Acapulco, Gro., tel 7/484-7152. Twice-weekly dinner or drinks shows with Mexican dances and Veracruz's Papantla Flyers. The philharmonic plays several evenings a month.
Charreadas, Lienzo Charro de Jalisco, Av. Dr. R. Michel 577, Guadalajara, Jal., tel 3619-0315. Mariachi music and superior horsemanship can be enjoyed on Sundays at noon.
Espectáculo de la Quebrada, Plazoleta de la Quebrada, Acapulco, Gro., tel 7/483-1400. Cliff divers perform throughout the day, and at night to a dinner, dancing, and music spectacle from La Perla Restaurant at El Mirador Plaza las Glorias Hotel.

ENTERTAINMENT & ACTIVITIES

La Plaza de los Mariachis, Calz. Independencia Sur between Obregón and Mina, Guadalajara, Jal. Mariachis play all night, but some visitors feel safer in the afternoon and early evening. **Salon Q,** Av. Costera Alemán 3117, Col. Costa Azul, Acapulco, Gro., tel 7/454-3252. Dancing to live salsa and tropical music nightly after 10 p.m.

FESTIVALS
Día de Nuestro Señor de Xalpa, Taxco, Gro., March 6. Regional dances highlight this local religious celebration.
Encuentro Internacional del Mariachi y la Charrería, Guadalajara, Jal., end Aug./ beginning Sept. A week of *charro* events and mariachi music.
Feria de la Guitarra, Paracho, Mich., tel 4/317-2371, Aug. Craftsmen display and sell their handcrafted guitars and other stringed instruments.
Feria de Michoacán, Morelia, Mich., first weeks of May. Typical state fair, with rides, expos, and cultural and music events.
Festival Internacional del Organo, Morelia, Mich., tel 4/317-2371, May. International pipe-organ festival held for more than 30 years at the cathedral.
Fiestas de Mayo, Puerto Vallarta, Jal., May. A month of revelry, with art exhibits, music, fireworks, and general merrymaking.
Fiestas de Octubre, Guadalajara, Jal., tel 3650-2222, throughout Oct. Mariachis and charreadas, opera, symphony, and arts exhibits.
Fiesta de San Ysidro, Tepic, Nay., several weeks culminating on May 15. Agricultural fair during which seeds and animals are blessed.

MEXICO CITY

Tiempo Libre, published in Spanish on Thursdays in the Spanish-language newspaper *Reforma,* lists cultural events and gallery shows, as does the Friday edition of the English-language

daily, *The News. Concierge* is a free monthly publication describing cultural events, galleries, and activities throughout Mexico City.

BARS
L'Opera, Cinco de Mayo 10 at Mata, tel 5512-8959. Historic cantina with period décor, still popular for food and drink.

BULLFIGHTS
Plaza Mexico, Rodin 241 at Holbein, Col. Napoles, tel 5563-3961. Fights takes place Thursday and Sunday at 4:30 p.m. for much of the year in the world's largest bullring. Contact Ticketmaster (Tel 5325-9000) or your hotel concierge.

CULTURAL CENTERS & THEATERS
Auditorio Nacional, Paseo de la Reforma 50, Parque de Chapultepec, tel 5280-9250. An enormous venue, near Polanco and Chapultepec Park, holding mostly music and theater events.
Casa del Lago Mayor, Primera Sección, Parque Chapultepec, tel 5553-6318. A lakeshore venue hosting art exhibitions and cultural programs throughout the year.
Palacio de Bellas Artes, Av. Juárez and Eje Central, Alameda Park, tel 5521-9251. Two-hour folkloric ballets on Wednesday and Sunday evenings and Sunday mornings. The latter includes a light show highlighting the Tiffany curtain. Regular symphony, opera, and other performances.
Sala Nezahualcoyotl, Insurgentes Sur 3000, Ciudad Universitaria, tel 5622-7128. Has excellent acoustics for all types of music and theatrical events.

FESTIVALS
Blessing of the Animals, Cathedral, Jan. 17. Pets and working animals are ceremonially blessed.
Fiesta de la Virgen de Guadalupe, Basílica de la Villa de Guadalupe, Dec. 12. Hundreds of thousands of pilgrims honor the nation's patron saint.

AROUND MEXICO CITY

CULTURAL CENTERS
Centro Cultural de Hidalgo, Arista at Casasola, Pachuca, Hgo., tel 7/111-4150. Fortress-style edifice housing the City Theater and school of art, museums, gardens, and plazas.

ENTERTAINMENT
Free outdoor band concerts Sunday afternoons, Jardín Juárez, Cuernavaca, Mor.

Flower Fair, Cuernavaca, Mor., April. Gardening exhibits and competitions; entertainment.

FESTIVALS
Cinco de Mayo, Puebla, Pue., May 5. Colorful festivities mark this victorious battle against French invaders.
Festival de Nopales, Tlaxcalancingo, Pue., April. Just outside Puebla, the picturesque town of Tlaxcalancingo celebrates the prickly-pear cactus with a food fair.
Fiesta de la Asunción, Huamantla, Tlax., Aug. 14. Pamplona-style bull-running through the streets for La Noche que Nadie Duerme (The Night when No One Sleeps).
Fiesta de Hidalgo, Pachucha, Hgo., first two weeks of Oct. Hidalgo state fair.
Fiesta de Tepoztlán, Tepoztlán, Mor., early Sept. Celebration of the Nativity of the Virgin and of the Aztec god Tepoztecatl, patron of the fermented drink pulque.

SPAS & WATER PARKS
Morelos state is known for its thermal springs around which water parks and resort spas have grown; contact Cuernavaca tourist board (Tel 7/314-3872) for more details.

CENTRAL GULF COAST

CULTURE
Folkloric ballet and state orchestral performances are

held at El Teatro del Estado, Ignacio de la Llave at Ávila Camacho, Xalapa, Ver., tel 28/17-31-10.

FESTIVALS
Carnaval, Veracruz, Ver., week before Lent, moveable feast. Parades and nonstop partying begin with the ceremonial Burning of Bad Humor and climaxes on Shrove Tuesday (Mardi Gras).
Día de la Candelaria, Tlacotalpán, Ver., early Feb. A colorful Candlemas festival with bulls running through the streets and riverboat processions.
Fiesta de Corpus Cristi, Papantla, Ver., 8 weeks 4 days after Easter. Fireworks, parades, cockfights; traditional dances and performances by los Voladores de Papantla.
Fiesta de Santiago Apostle, Santiago Tuxtla, Ver., July 25. Native dances and fiesta in celebration of patron St. James the Apostle.

BOAT TOURS
Santa Cruz Bay, Bahías de Huatulco. Visit the nine bays, disembarking at one or more to enjoy the beautiful beaches.

FESTIVALS
Bendición de los Animales, Oaxaca, Aug. 31. Blessing of household pets and farm animals at La Merced church.
Fiesta de las Velas, Isthmus of Tehuantepec, May through Sept. Ancient celebrations honoring individual towns' patron saints with lively neighborhood parties. Contact Oaxaca city tourist board for dates.
Guelaguetza, Cerro del Fortín, Oaxaca, generally first two Mondays after July 16. Traditional folk dancing from Oaxaca's seven regions at a hilltop amphitheater.
La Noche del Rábano, *zócalo,* Oaxaca, Dec. 23. Contestants make intricate tableaux of carved radishes.

FOLK DANCING/DINNER SHOWS
Hotel Camino Real, Oaxaca. Folkloric shows in one of the former convent's covered stone patios.

CHIAPAS

CULTURAL CENTERS & THEATERS
Teatro Hermanos Domínguez, Diagonal Hermanos Paniagua s/n, San Cristóbal de las Casas, tel 9/678-3637. Theater hosting music and dance performances.

FESTIVALS
Fiestas de Enero, during two weeks of mid-Jan. Chiapa de Corzo has outrageous masked parades as well as dances, street festivities, and mock naval battles with fireworks.

Celebrations in Zinacantán include la Fiesta de San Sebastian, Jan. 20–22, every Friday during Lent, Easter, and Carnaval.

Celebrations in honor of la Virgin of Guadalupe the days preceding Dec. 12 in Tuxtla Gutiérrez and San Cristóbal de las Casas.

San Juan Chamula has colorful fiestas for Carnaval, Easter, and la Fiesta de San Juan (June 22–24).

TOURS
Visit indigenous villages outside San Cristóbal de las Casas on guided horse tours through area tour operators.

Hiking, canoeing, and other activities at Laguna Miramar, within the Lacandón rain forest, on three- to seven-day camping trips through DANA, tel/fax 9/678-0468.

YUCATAN PENINSULA

CULTURAL CENTERS
Casa de la Cultura, Prol. Av. Yaxchilán SM 21, Cancún, Q.R.,

tel 9/884-8364. Sponsors theater, music, conferences, and other activities.
Teatro Peón Contreras, Calle 60 between Calles 57 and 59, Mérida, Yuc., tel 9/924-9290. This lovely theater hosts music and dance performances, including bi-weekly folkloric dance shows.

DIVING/SCUBA
Aqua World, Blvd. Kukulcán Km 15.3, Cancún, Q.R., tel 9/885-2288. Full-service aquatic center; game fishing, diving, party boats.
Cozumel Association of Dive Operators, Cozumel, Q.R., tel 9/872-5955. Recommends dive and snorkel guides and operators.

ENTERTAINMENT
Noche Mexicana, Paseo Montejo at Calle 47, Mérida, Yuc., Sat. 7:30–11 p.m. Weekly street party with locals and tourists, including folk dancing, music, crafts, and food.
Sound and light shows, after dark at Chichén Itzá and Uxmal, Yuc.; also la Puerta de Tierra, Campeche, Camp.

FESTIVALS
Fieastas del Equinoxio, Templo de Kukulkán, Chichén Itzá, Yuc., first days of spring and fall. At both the spring and fall equinoxes, a serpent-like shadow descends the pyramid to align with the stone snake's head at the bottom.
Festival de Jazz, Cancún, Q.R., late May. A week of jazz performances in various venues.
Hanal Pixan, Mérida, Yuc., the days preceding Nov. 2. Traditional food and altars from around the state for Day of the Dead celebrations.
Otoño Cultural, Mérida, Yuc., last week of Oct. through first two weeks of Nov. Autumn Cultural Festival with classical music, dance, and art exhibitions.

LANGUAGE GUIDE

GENERAL
yes; *sí*
no; *no*
please; *por favor*
thank you; *gracias*
you're welcome; *de nada*
hello, hi; *hola*
goodbye; *adiós, hasta luego*
good day; *buenos días*
good afternoon; *buenas tardes*
good evening/goodnight; *buenas noches*
OK; *está bien/de acuerdo*
today; *hoy*
yesterday; *ayer*
tomorrow; *mañana*
Do you speak English?; *¿Habla usted inglés?*
I am from the U.S.; *Soy norteamericano/a*
I don't understand; *No entiendo*
Please speak more slowly; *Hable más despacio, por favor*
What is its/your name?; *¿Cómo se llama?*
My name is…; *Yo me llamo…*
Let's go; *Vamos*
At what time?; *¿A qué horas?*

HELP
I need a doctor/dentist; *Necesito un médico/dentista*
Can you help me?; *¿Me puede ayudar?*
Where is a hospital/clinic?; *¿Dónde hay un hospital/una clínica?*
Help!; *¡Socorro!*

SHOPPING
I'd like…; *Quisiera…*
How much is it?; *¿Cuánto es?*
That's very expensive; *Es muy caro*
Do you take credit cards?; *¿Acepta tarjetas de crédito?*
size; *el talle*
receipt; *el recibo/la nota*
bakery; *la panadería*
bookstore; *la librería*
market; *el mercado/tianguis*
pharmacy; *la farmacia*
shopping mall; *el centro comercial*
supermarket; *el supermercado*

SIGHTSEEING
visitor information; *información turística*
open; *abierto/a*
closed; *cerrado/a*
church; *la iglesia*
cathedral; *la catedral*
country estate; *la hacienda*
museum; *el museo*
tour; *el tour*
town; *el pueblo*
city; *la ciudad*

IN THE HOTEL
Do you have…?; *¿Hay…?*
single room; *una habitación sencilla*
double room; *una habitación doble*
with/without; *con/sin*
bathroom/view; *baño/vista*

IN THE RESTAURANT
menu; *el menú/la carta*
breakfast; *el desayuno*
lunch (main meal); *la comida*
dinner; *la cena*
check; *la cuenta*
takeout; *para llevar*
fixed-price meal; *el menú del día*
a la carte; *a la carta*
vegetarian food; *comida vegetariana*

MENU READER

See also "Food & drink," pp. 18–21.

appetizer; *el antojito*
bread; *el pan*
soup (broth); *la sopa*
soup (cream); *la crema*
salad; *la ensalada*
main course; *el plato principal*
vegetable; *verdura/vegetal*
rice; *(sopa de) arroz*
bean soup; *sopa de frijol*
refried beans; *frijoles refritos*
dessert; *el postre*
spicy; *picante*
beer; *la cerveza*
coffee; *el café*
American-style coffee; *café americano*
Mexican-stye (sweet) coffee; *café de olla*
decaffeinated coffee; *descafeinado*
tea; *el té*
milk; *la leche*
mineral water; *el agua mineral*
ice; *el hielo*
purified water; *el agua purificada*
soft drink; *refresco*
lemonade/orangeade; *limonada/naranjada*
wine; *vino*
apéritif; *aperitivo*
Cheers!; *¡Salud!*
meat; *la carne*
beef; *la carne de res*
pork; *el puerco*
goat; *la cabra/el chivo*
turkey; *el guajolote/pavo*
chicken; *el pollo*
fish; *el pescado*
lobster; *langosta*
octopus; *pulpo*
shrimp; *camarón*
squid; *calamar*

ILLUSTRATIONS CREDITS

Abbreviations for terms appearing below: (t) top; (b) bottom; (l) left; (r) right

Cover: (tl), Gettyone/Stone. (tr), Larry Dunmire. (bl), Images Colour Library. (br), Images Colour Library. Spine: Larry Dunmire.

1, Suzanne Murphy-Larronde; 2/3, National Geographic Society/Tomasz Tomaszewski; 4, Robert Holmes; 9, Mireille Vautier; 11, Suzanne Murphy-Larronde; 12/13, Streano/Havens/Trip & Art Directors Photo Library; 14, Suzanne Murphy-Larronde; 15, National Geographic Society/Tomasz Tomaszewski; 16/17, National Geographic Society/Stuart Franklin; 19, Brian McGilloway/Robert Holmes; 20, Rick Strange/AA Photo Library; 21, Nik Wheeler/Corbis UK Ltd.; 23, Suzanne Murphy-Larronde; 24/25, Gianni Dagli Orti/Corbis UK Ltd.; 26/27, Robert Frerck/Gettyone/Stone; 28, AKG - London; 29, Bridgeman Art Library/London; 30/31, Bridgeman Art Library/London; 32, AKG - London; 33, Mireille Vautier; 34/35, Hulton Getty; 36/37, National Geographic Society/Tomasz Tomaszewski; 39, Isabella Tree/Hutchison Library; 40, Viesti Collection/Trip & Art Directors Photo Library; 41, Tony Morrison/South American Pictures; 42/43, Robert Frerck/Robert Harding Picture Library; 44, Dave G. Houser/Corbis UK Ltd.; 45, Charles & Josette Lenars/Corbis UK Ltd.; 46/47, National Geographic Society/Stuart Franklin; 48/49, Jamie Carstairs; 50/1, Danny Lehman/Corbis UK Ltd.; 52, Sergio Dorantes/Corbis UK Ltd.; 53, James Davis Worldwide; 54, Tom Bean/Gettyone/Stone; 55, David Sanger; 56, Mireille Vautier; 57, Edward Parker/Hutchison Library; 58, Robert Holmes/AA Photo Library; 59, Stuart Wasserman; 60t, James Davis Worldwide; 60b, Lee Foster; 61, Robert Holmes; 62, Robert Holmes/Corbis UK Ltd.; 63, Robert Holmes; 64, David Muench/Corbis UK Ltd.; 65, Robert Frerck/Robert Harding Picture Library; 66/67, Nik Wheeler; 68, Streano/Havens/Trip & Art Directors Photo Library; 69, Stuart Westmorland/Corbis UK Ltd.; 70/71, David Sanger; 71, David Sanger; 72, David Sanger; 73, Robert Holmes/AA Photo Library; 74, Robert Holmes/Corbis UK Ltd.; 75, Mireille Vautier; 76, Robert Cundy/Robert Harding Picture Library; 78, Robert Francis/South American Pictures; 79, Nik Wheeler; 80, Eleanor S. Morris; 81, Markham Johnson/Robert Holmes; 82, VISOR S.A; 83tl, Patricio Robles Gil/Agrupación Sierra Madre; 83tr, Patricio Robles Gil/Agrupación Sierra Madre; 83b, Dirk Weisheit/DDB Stock Photo; 84, National Geographic Society/Joanna Pinneo; 85, Lee Foster; 86, Patricio Robles Gil/Agrupación Sierra Madre; 87, Markham Johnson/Robert Holmes; 89, National Geographic Society/Phil Schermeister 90, National Geographic Society/Joe McNally; 91, Markham Johnson/Robert Holmes; map by National Geographic Maps; 92, Wendy Shattil and Bob Rozinski/Oxford Scientific Films; 92/93, John Elk III/Elk Photo; 94t, Robert Aberman; 94b, Robert Frerck/ Odyssey/ Chicago/Robert Harding Picture Library; 95, Ernesto Rios/VISOR S.A; 96/97, Robert Frerck/

Gettyone/Stone; 98/99, Larry Dunmire; 100, Jan Butchofsky-Houser/Corbis UK Ltd.; 101, Kevin Schafer/Corbis UK Ltd.; 103, Robert and Linda Mitchell; 104, National Geographic Society/George Grall; 106, Rick Strange/AA Photo Library; 107, National Geographic Society/George Grall; 109, Adalberto Rios/VISOR S.A; 110, Alex Webb/Magnum Photos; 111, Patricio Robles Gil/Agrupación Sierra Madre; 113, Robert Francis/South American Pictures; 114, Scott Walker; 115, Patricio Robles Gil/Agrupación Sierra Madre; 116, Robert Frerck/ Odyssey/ Chicago/Robert Harding Picture Library; 117, Suzanne Murphy-Larronde; 118, Isabella Tree/Hutchison Library; 120/121, National Geographic Society/David Alan Harvey; 122, Eleanor S. Morris; 123, David Sanger; 124, Suzanne Murphy-Larronde; 125, Danny Lehman/Corbis UK Ltd.; 126, Iain Pearson/South American Pictures; 128, VISOR S.A; 129t, Iain Pearson/South American Pictures; 129c, Clotilde Lechuga/VISOR S.A; 129b, Corbis UK Ltd.; 130, Mireille Vautier; 131, Rick Strange/AA Photo Library; 133, Adalberto Rios/VISOR S.A; 134, Stuart Wasserman; 135, Peter Wilson/AA Photo Library; 136, John Bartholomew/Corbis UK Ltd.; 137, Diana Dicker; 139, Brian McGilloway/Robert Holmes; 140, Danny Lehman/Corbis UK Ltd.; 141, National Geographic Society/Maggie Steber; 142, Danny Lehman/Corbis UK Ltd.; 143, James Davis Worldwide; 144/145, Larry Dunmire; 146, Adina Tovy Amsel/Eye Ubiquitous; 148/149, Rick Strange/AA Photo Library; 151, Suzanne Murphy-Larronde; 152, Suzanne Murphy-Larronde; 153, Rick Strange/AA Photo Library; 154, Stuart Wasserman; 155t, Charles & Josette Lenars/Corbis UK Ltd.; 155b, Suzanne Murphy-Larronde; 156/157, Roger Ressmeyer/Corbis UK Ltd.; 158, Adalberto Rios/Mireille Vautier; 159, Robert and Linda Mitchell; 160, Rick Strange/AA Photo Library; 161, Suzanne Murphy-Larronde; 162/163, National Geographic Society/David Alan Harvey; 164, Isabella Tree/Hutchison Library; 165, Tony Morrison/South American Pictures; 166/167, Robert Frerck/Gettyone/Stone; 168/169, Larry Dunmire; 171, Kelly-Mooney Photography/Corbis UK Ltd.; 173, Philip Enticknap/Travel Library; 174/175, National Geographic Society/Sisse Brimberg; 177, David Sanger; 179, Chris Sharp/South American Pictures; 180, Picturesque Inc./Trip & Art Directors Photo Library; 181, Mireille Vautier; 182/183, Robert Frerck/Gettyone/Stone; 184, Bridgeman Art Library/London; 185t, Bridgeman Art Library/London; 185b, Bridgeman Art Library/London; 186, Nik Wheeler; 187, Peter Wilson; 189, Rick Strange/AA Photo Library; 190, Guy Marks/Travel Ink; 191, Macduff Everton/Corbis UK Ltd.; 192, David Sanger; 193, Mireille Vautier; 195, Peter Wilson; 196, Carlos Reyes-Manzo/Andes Press Agency; 197, Rick Strange/AA Photo Library; 198t, Michel Zabé; 198b, Carlos Reyes-Manzo/Andes Press Agency; 199, Robert Aberman; 200t, Carlos Reyes-Manzo/Andes Press Agency; 200c, Carlos Reyes-Manzo/Andes Press Agency; 200bl, Michel Zabé; 200br, Carlos Reyes-Manzo/Andes Press Agency; 201, Michel Zabé; 203, Kelly-Mooney Photography/Corbis UK Ltd.; 204/205, Carlos Reyes-Manzo/Andes Press Agency; 205, Bettmann/Corbis UK Ltd.; 207, M Barlow/Trip & Art Directors Photo Library; 208, Nik Wheeler; 209, Rick

Strange/AA Photo Library; 211, Robert Frerck/Gettyone/Stone; 212, Clotilde Lechuga/VISOR S.A; 214, Tony Morrison/South American Pictures; 215, Rick Strange/AA Photo Library; 216, Suzanne Murphy-Larronde; 217tr, VISOR S.A; 217bl, Ask Images/Trip & Art Directors Photo Library; 218, Tony Morrison/South American Pictures; 219, National Geographic Society/Sisse Brimberg; 220, Robert Cundy/Robert Harding Picture Library; 221, J Greenberg/Trip & Art Directors Photo Library; 222, Nik Wheeler/Corbis UK Ltd.; 223, Stuart Wasserman; 224, Iain Pearson/South American Pictures; 225, AKG - London; 226/227, Jonathan Blair/Corbis UK Ltd.; 228, National Geographic Society/Kenneth Garrett; 229, National Geographic Society/Kenneth Garrett; 230, Rick Strange/AA Photo Library; 231, VISOR S.A; 232, VISOR S.A; 233, National Geographic Society/National Museum of Anthropology, Mexico City; 235, Rick Strange/AA Photo Library; 236, Diana Dicker; 237, Diana Dicker; 238/239, Chris Sharp/South American Pictures; 240, National Geographic Society/Stuart Franklin; 241, Jamie Carstairs; 243t, Museo de America, Madrid, Spain/Bridgeman Art Library/London; 243c, Rick Strange/AA Photo Library; 243b, Dave G. Houser/Corbis UK Ltd.; 244, Edward Parker/Hutchison Library; 245, Mireille Vautier; 246/247, National Geographic Society/Kenneth Garrett; 247, Jamie Carstairs; 248/249, John Elk III/Elk Photo; 250, National Geographic Society/Kenneth Garrett; 253, Suzanne Murphy-Larronde; 255, Kelly-Mooney Photography/Corbis UK Ltd.; 256, Jill Ranford/Ffotograff; 257, R Powers/Trip & Art Directors Photo Library; 258, Cri Rodriguez/VISOR S.A; 259, Isabella Tree/Hutchison Library; 260/261, Robert Frerck/Gettyone/Stone; 262t, Macduff Everton/Corbis UK Ltd.; 262b, Mireille Vautier; 264/265 Michael Macintyre/Hutchison Library; 266, Macduff Everton/Corbis UK Ltd.; 267tl, Edward Parker/Hutchison Library; 267c, Lee Foster; 267b, Steve Watkins/AA Photo Library; 268, Dave G. Houser/Corbis UK Ltd.; 269, Isabella Tree/Hutchison Library; 270, Mireille Vautier; 271, Mireille Vautier; 272, Mireille Vautier; 273t, David Alan Harvey/Magnum Photos; 273b, National Geographic Society/David Alan Harvey; 275, Suzanne Murphy-Larronde; 276, David Alan Harvey/Magnum Photos; 278/279, National Geographic Society/David Alan Harvey; 280, Isabella Tree/Hutchison Library; 281, Jeremy Horner/Hutchison Library; 282, Mireille Vautier; 284, D. Done Bryant/DDB Stock Photo; 285, Rick Strange/AA Photo Library; 286/287, H Elton/Axiom; 288, Mireille Vautier; 289, Robert Frerck/Robert Harding Picture Library; 290/291, National Geographic/Images Colour Library; 292, Clotilde Lechuga/VISOR S.A; 293t, D. Donne Bryant/DDB Stock Photo; 293b, Ken McLaren/Trip & Art Directors Photo Library; 294, Danny Lehman/Corbis UK Ltd.; 295tl, Richard Glover/Corbis UK Ltd.; 295tr, Iain Pearson/South American Pictures; 295b, E. Hawkins/Eye Ubiquitous; 296, Isabella Tree/Hutchison Library; 298/299, James D. Nations/DDB Stock Photo; 300, National Geographic Society/Otis Imboden; 302, Mireille Vautier; 303, Fabienne Fossez/Ffotograff; 304, Charles & Josette Lenars/Corbis UK Ltd.; 305, Robert Leon; 306, Patricio Robles Gil/Agrupación Sierra Madre; 307,

Adalberto Rios Szalay/VISOR S.A; 308, Larry Dunmire/Travel Library; 310, Larry Dunmire; 311, Peter Wilson; 312, Peter Wilson; 313t, Peter Wilson; 313c, Larry Dunmire; 313b, T Bognar/Trip & Art Directors Photo Library; 314, Alison Wright/Corbis UK Ltd.; 314/315, Rick Strange/AA Travel Library; 317, DDB Stock Photo; 318t, Caroline Garside/Trip & Art Directors Photo Library; 318b, World Pictures Ltd; 320, Jenny Pate/Hutchison Library; 321, Chris Caldicott/Axiom; 322, Picturesque Inc/Trip & Art Directors Photo Library; 323, Robert Frerck/Gettyone/Stone; 324, John Elk III/Elk Photo; 325, Mireille Vautier; 326, Ask Images/Trip & Art Directors Photo Library; 327, Erwin and Peggy Bauer/Bruce Coleman; 328, James D. Nations/DDB Stock Photo; 328/329, Robert and Linda Mitchell; 330, Richard Bailey/Corbis UK Ltd.; 331, Mireille Vautier; 332, Richard A Cooke III/Gettyone/Stone; 333, Suzanne Murphy-Larronde; 334, Chris Sharp/South American Pictures; 335, Larry Dunmire; 336, Eleanor S. Morris; 337, Macduff Everton/Corbis UK Ltd.; 338, EJB Hawkins LMPA/Eye Ubiquitous; 339, Larry Dunmire; 340/341, Mireille Vautier; 342/343, Mireille Vautier; 344, Suzanne Murphy-Larronde; 345, Peter Wilson; 346, Mireille Vautier; 347, Sergio Dorantes/Corbis UK Ltd.

Published by the National Geographic Society

John M. Fahey, Jr., *President and Chief Executive Officer*

Gilbert M. Grosvenor, *Chairman of the Board*

Nina D. Hoffman, *Executive Vice President, President, Books and School Publishing*

Elizabeth L. Newhouse, *Director of Travel Publishing*

Barbara A. Noe, *Senior Editor and Project Manager*

Cinda Rose, *Art Director*

Carl Mehler, *Director of Maps*

Joseph F. Ochlak, *Map Coordinator*

Gary Colbert, *Production Director*

Richard S. Wain, *Production Project Manager*

A. R. Williams, *Editorial Consultant*

Lawrence Porges, *Editorial Coordinator*

Edited and designed by AA Publishing (a trading name of Automobile Association Developments Limited, whose registered office is Norfolk House, Priestley Road, Basingstoke, Hampshire, England RG24 9NY. Registered number: 1878835).

Virginia Langer, *Project Manager*

David Austin, *Senior Art Editor*

Susi Bailey, *Editor*

Jo Tapper, *Designer*

Inna Nogeste, *Senior Cartographic Editor*

Cartography by AA Cartographic Production

Richard Firth, *Production Director*

Steve Gilchrist, *Prepress Production Controller*

Picture Research by Zooid Pictures Ltd.

Drive maps drawn by Chris Orr Associates, Southampton, England

Cutaway illustrations drawn by Maltings Partnership, Derby, England

Coral reef illustration by Ann Winterbotham

Library of Congress Cataloging-in-Publication Data

Onstott, Jane.
       The National Geographic Traveler : Mexico / Jane Onstott.
      p. cm.
        Includes index.
        ISBN 0-7922-7897-6
         1. Mexico--Guidebooks. 2. Mexico--Description and travel. 3. Mexico--Tours I. Title.

        F1209 .067 2001
        917.204'836--dc21

                    2001042784

Printed and bound by R.R. Donnelley & Sons, Willard, Ohio.
Color separations by Leo Reprographic Ltd., Hong Kong
Cover separations by L.C. Repro, Aldermaston, U.K.
Cover printed by Miken Inc., Cheektowaga, New York.

Visit the society's Web site at http://www.nationalgeographic.com

NATIONAL GEOGRAPHIC
TRAVELER

A Century of Travel Expertise in Every Guide

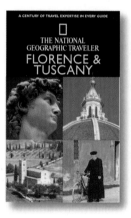

- **Arizona** ISBN: 0-7922-7899-2
- **Australia** ISBN: 0-7922-7431-8
- **Boston & Environs** ISBN: 0-7922-7926-3
- **California** ISBN: 0-7922-7564-0
- **Canada** ISBN: 0-7922-7427-X
- **The Caribbean** ISBN: 0-7922-7434-2
- **China** ISBN: 0-7922-7921-2
- **Costa Rica** ISBN: 0-7922-7946-8
- **Egypt** ISBN: 0-7922-7896-8
- **Florence & Tuscany** ISBN: 0-7922-7924-7
- **Florida** ISBN: 0-7922-7432-6
- **France** ISBN: 0-7922-7426-1
- **Great Britain** ISBN: 0-7922-7425-3
- **Greece** ISBN: 0-7922-7923-9
- **Hawaii** ISBN: 0-7922-7944-1
- **India** ISBN: 0-7922-7898-4
- **Italy** ISBN: 0-7922-7562-4
- **Japan** ISBN: 0-7922-7563-2
- **London** ISBN: 0-7922-7428-8
- **Los Angeles** ISBN: 0-7922-7947-6
- **Mexico** ISBN: 0-7922-7897-6
- **Miami and the Keys** ISBN: 0-7922-7433-4
- **New Orleans** ISBN: 0-7922-7948-4
- **New York** ISBN: 0-7922-7430-X
- **Paris** ISBN: 0-7922-7429-6
- **Rome** ISBN: 0-7922-7566-7
- **San Francisco** ISBN: 0-7922-7565-9
- **Spain** ISBN: 0-7922-7922-0
- **Sydney** ISBN: 0-7922-7435-0
- **Thailand** ISBN: 0-7922-7943-3
- **Venice** ISBN: 0-7922-7917-4

AVAILABLE WHEREVER BOOKS ARE SOLD